Studies in I
Volume 5

Inconsistency Robustness

Volume 41
Symbolic Logic from Leibniz to Husserl
Abel Lassalle Casanave, ed.

Volume 42
Meta-argumentation. An Approach to Logic and Argumentation Theory
Maurice A. Finocchiaro

Volume 43
Logic, Truth and Inquiry
Mark Weinstein

Volume 44
Meta-logical Investigations in Argumentation Networks
Dov M. Gabbay

Volume 45
Errors of Reasoning. Naturalizing the Logic of Inference
John Woods

Volume 46
Questions, Inferences, and Scenarios
Andrzej Wiśniewski

Volume 47
Logic Across the University: Foundations and Applications. Proceedings of the Tsinghua Logic Conference, Beijing, 2013
Johan van Benthem and Fenrong Liu, eds.

Volume 48
Trends in Belief Revision and Argumentation Dynamics
Eduardo L. Fermé, Dov M. Gabbay, and Guillermo R. Simari

Volume 49
Introduction to Propositional Satisfiability
Victor Marek

Volume 50
Intuitionistic Set Theory
John L. Bell

Volume 51
Metalogical Contributions to the Nonmonotonic Theory of Abstract Argumentation
Ringo Baumann

Volume 52
Inconsistency Robustness
Carl Hewitt and John Woods assisted by Jane Spurr, eds.

Studies in Logic Series Editor
Dov Gabbay   dov.gabbay@kcl.ac.uk

Inconsistency Robustness

Edited by
Carl Hewitt
and
John Woods
assisted by
Jane Spurr

© Individual author and College Publications 2015.
All rights reserved.

ISBN 978-1-84890-159-9

College Publications
Scientific Director: Dov Gabbay
Managing Director: Jane Spurr

http://www.collegepublications.co.uk

Original cover design by Orchid Creative   www.orchidcreative.co.uk
Printed by Lightning Source, Milton Keynes, UK

All rights reserved. No part of this publication may be reproduced, stored in a retrieval system or transmitted in any form, or by any means, electronic, mechanical, photocopying, recording or otherwise without prior permission, in writing, from the publisher.

By this it appears how necessary it is for nay man that aspires to true knowledge to examine the definitions of former authors; and either to correct them, where they are negligently set down, or to make them himself. For the errors of definitions multiply themselves, according as the reckoning proceeds, and lead men into absurdities, which at last they see, but cannot avoid, without reckoning anew from the beginning; in which lies the foundation of their errors...
- **Thomas Hobbes**

You cannot be confident about applying your calculus until you know that there are no hidden contradictions in it.
- **Alan Turing**

Indeed, even at this stage, I predict a time when there will be mathematical investigations of calculi containing contradictions, and people will actually be proud of having emancipated themselves from consistency.
- **Ludwig Wittgenstein**

the first task is to find a system [for inconsistency robust inference] ... which:
1. when applied to inconsistent [information] would not always entail overcompleteness [*i.e.*, infer every proposition]
2. would be rich enough for practical inference
3. would have an intuitive justification
- **Stanisław Jaśkowski**

The problem is that today some knowledge still feels too dangerous because our times are not so different to Cantor or Boltzmann or Gödel's time. We too feel things we thought were solid being challenged; feel our certainties slipping away. And so, as then, we still desperately want to cling to a belief in certainty. It makes us feel safe. ...

Are we grown up enough to live with uncertainties or will we repeat the mistakes of the twentieth century and pledge blind allegiance to another certainty?
- **David Malone**

Contents

Detailed Table of Contents ix

Preface
  Carl Hewitt xix

Part 1. Mathematical Foundations 1

1. Formalizing common sense reasoning for scalable inconsistency-robust information coordination using Direct Logic Reasoning and the Actor Model.
   Carl Hewitt 3
2. Inconsistency robustness in foundations: Mathematics self proves its own consistency and other matters.
   Carl Hewitt 104
3. Inconsistency: Its present impacts and future prospects.
   John Woods 158
4. Two sources of explosion.
   Eric Kao 195

Part 2. Software Foundations 203

1. Actor Model of computation: Scalable robust information systems.
   Carl Hewitt 205
2. Inconsistency robustness for logic programs.
   Carl Hewitt 280
3. ActorScript extension of C#, C++, Java, Objective C, JavaScript, and SystemVerilog using iAdaptive concurrency for antiCloud privacy and security.
   Carl Hewitt 336

Part 3. Applications 427

1. Some types of inconsistency in legal reasoning.
   Anne Gardner 429
2. Rules versus standards: Competing notions of inconsistency: Robustness in the Supreme Court and Federal Circuit.
   Stefania Fusco and David Olson 447
3. Politics and pragmatism in scientific ontology construction.
   Mike Travers 460
4. Modelling ungrammaticality in a precise grammar of English.
   Dan Flickinger 487
5. The singularity is here.
   Fanya S. Montalvo 490
6. Biological responses to chemical exposure: Case studies in how to manage ostensible inconsistencies using the Claim Framework.
   Catherine Blake 497
7. From inter-annotation to intra-publication inconsistency.
   Alaa Abi Haidar, Mihnea Tufi, and Jean-Gabriel Ganascia 512

Index 521

Detailed Table of Contents

Preface
Carl Hewitt... *xix*
    Videos   xix
    Overview   xx
    Part 1. Mathematical Foundations   xx
    Part 2. Software Foundations   xxxiii
    Part 3. Applications   xlii
    Illustrative Issues   xliii
    Panel Discussions   l
    Inconsistency Robustness in Cyberspace Security and Privacy   l
    Inconsistency Robustness in Medical Informatics   lxii
    Inconsistency Robustness in Foundations of Mathematics   lxiv
    Acknowledgment   lxv
    Symposia Particulars   lxv
    iRobust Scientific Society   lxvii
    End notes   lxviii

Part 1.   Mathematical Foundations   1

1. *Formalizing common sense reasoning for scalable inconsistency-robust information coordination using Direct Logic Reasoning and the Actor Model.*
Carl Hewitt.. *3*
    Abstract   3
    Introduction   5
    Interaction *creates* Reality   5
    Pervasive Inconsistency is the Norm in Large Software Systems   7
    Inconsistency Robustness   9
    Inconsistency robustness facilitates formalization   11
    Contradictions can facilitate Argumentation   12
    Inconsistent probabilities   13
    Circular information   15
    Limitations of First-order Logic   16
    Inconsistency In Garbage Out Redux (IGOR)   16
    Inexpressibility   17
    Excluded Middle   17
    Direct Logic   18
    In the argumentation lies the knowledge   20
    Direct Argumentation   20
    Theory Dependence   20
    Information Invariance   21
    Semantics of Direct Logic   21

Inference in Argumentation	22
Mathematics Self Proves that it is Open	23
Contributions of Direct Logic	24
Actor Model of Computation	24
What is Computation?	25
Configurations versus Global States	26
Actors generalize Turing Machines	27
Reception order indeterminacy	29
Actor Physics	30
Computational Representation Theorem	31
Computation is not subsumed by logical deduction	32
Bounded Nondeterminism of Direct Logic	33
Computational Undecidability	34
Classical mathematics self proves its own consistency (contra Gödel et. al.)	34
Completeness versus Inferential Undecidability	36
Information Coordination	37
Opposition of Philosophers	37
Scalable Information Coordination	38
Work to be done	39
Invariance	39
Consistency	39
Inconsistency Robustness	39
Argumentation	40
Inferential Explosion	40
Robustness, Soundness, and Coherence	40
Evolution of Mathematics	40
Conclusion	41
Acknowledgements	42
Bibliography	44
Appendix 1: Details of Direct Logic	67
Notation of Direct Logic	67
Inconsistency Robust Implication	72
Substitution of Equivalent Propositions	74
Propositional Equivalences	74
Conjunction, i.e., comma	75
Disjunction	75
Inconsistency Robust Inference	75
Soundness	76
Inconsistency Robust Proof by Contradiction	76
Quantifiers	76
Appendix 2. Foundation of classical mathematics beyond logicism	76
Consistency has been the bedrock of classical mathematics	77
Inheritance from classical mathematics	77

Nondeterministic Execution	78
Foundations with both Types and Sets	78
XML	79
Natural Numbers, Real Numbers, and their Sets are Unique up to Isomorphism	80
Appendix 3. Historical Development of Inferenital Undecidability ("Incompleteness")	82
Truth versus Argumentation	82
Turing versus Gödel	83
Contra Gödel et. al	84
How the self-proof of consistency of mathematics was overlooked and then discovered	84
Inconsistency-robust logic programs	85
Forward chaining	85
Backward chaining	86
Subarguments	86
End Notes	87

2. *Inconsistency robustness in foundations: Mathematics self proves its own consistency and other matters.*

Carl Hewitt *104*

Abstract	104
Mathematical Foundation for Computer Science	106
Mathematics self proves its own consistency	106
Monster-Barring	108
Wittgenstein: "self-referential" propositions lead to inconsistency in mathematics	109
contra Gödel et. al	110
Classical Direct Logic	112
Mathematics self proves that it is open	116
Completeness of inference versus inferential undecidability of closed mathematical theories	116
Overview	118
Conclusion	119
Acknowledgments	122
Bibliography	123
Appendix 1. Notation of Classical Direct Logic	129
Foundations with both types and sets	131
Natural Numbers, Real Numbers, and their Sets are Unique up to Isomorphism	133
Appendix 2. Historical Background	135
Gödel was certain	135
Limitations of first-order logic	136
Provability Logic	141

      Inadequacies of Tarskian Set Models   143
      Church's Paradox   143
      Curry and Löb Paradoxes   144
      Berry's Paradox   145
      Sociology of Foundations   146
  Appendix 3. Classical Natural Deduction   148
  End Notes   149

3. *Inconsistency: Its present impacts and future prospects.*
John Woods *158*
  Abstract   158
  Classical Environments   159
  Conceptual Fields   161
  Ambiguation   168
  Damage Control   169
  Expulsion and Preclusion   170
  Self-Cancellation   172
  Hostile Containment   173
  (Somewhat) Welcoming Hostile Containment   176
  Abandonment   178
  Even More Welcoming Containment   180
  Empirical Considerations   184
  Inconsistency Robustness   187
  Future Prospects   191
  Appendix on Carnap's Nihilism   192
  Appendix on Paraconsistency   193

4. *Two sources of explosion.*
Eric Kao *195*
  Abstract   195
  Introduction   195
  Boolean Inconsistency Robust Direct Logic   196
  Law of excluded middle   197
  Proof by self-refutation   199
  Discussion   200
  Conclusion   201
  Acknowledgments   201
  References   201

Part 2. Software Foundations — 203

1. *Actor Model of computation: Scalable robust information systems.*
   Carl Hewitt 205

Introduction	205
Message-passing using types is the foundation of system communication	206
Direct communication and asynchrony	208
Indeterminacy and Quasi-commutativity	209
Locality and Security	209
Robustness in Runtime Failures	210
Scalability and Modularity	210
Scalable information coordination	211
Connections	212
Information Coordination Principles	212
Interaction creates Reality	213
Organizational Programming using iOrgs	213
Actor Addresses and Implementations	215
Computational Representation Theorem	217
Extension versus Specialization	218
Language constructs versus Library APIs	218
Reasoning about Actor Systems	218
Other models of concurrency	219
Futures	220
Future work	221
Conclusion	221
Acknowledgements	223
Bibliography	225
Appendix 1. Historical background	236
Concurrency versus Turing's Model	236
Lambda-calculus	236
Petri nets	238
Simula	238
Planner	240
Smalltalk-72	240
Actors	241
Indeterminacy in Concurrent Computation	243
Nondeterminism is a special case of Indeterminism.	245
Computation is not subsumed by logical deduction	245
Actor Model versus Classical Objects	247
Hairy Control Structure	247
Early Actor Programming languages	250
Garbage Collection	250
Cosmic Cube	250
Communicating Sequential Processes	251

Smalltalk-80	253
π-Calculus Actors	254
J–Machine	255
Fog Cutter Actors	257
Erlang Actors	259
Squeak	259
Orleans Actors	259
JavaScript Actors	262
Capability Actor Systems	264
Was the Actor model premature?	268
End Notes	270

2. *Inconsistency robustness for logic programs.*
Carl Hewitt *280*

Abstract	270
Uniform Proof Procedures based on Resolution	282
Procedural Embedding redux	286
Planner	286
Control Structure Controversies	290
Control structures are patterns of passing messages	291
Edinburgh Logic for Computable Functions	292
Procedural Embedding versus Procedural Interpretation of Logic-clause Syntax	292
Scientific Community Model	298
Is Computation Subsumed by Deduction?	300
The Japanese 5th Generation Project (ICOT)	306
What is a Logic Program?	310
Logic Programs versus "Logic Programming"	312
Overview	313
Conclusion	314
Acknowledgements	315
Bibliography	315
Appendix. Inconsistency Robust Logic Programs	323
Notation of Direct Logic	323
Forward Chaining	328
Backward Chaining	329
SubArguments	329
Inconsistency-Robust Propositional Equivalences	330
End Notes	331

3. ActorScript extension of C#, C++, Java, Objective C, JavaScript, and SystemVerilog using iAdaptive concurrency for antiCloud privacy and security.
Carl Hewitt *336*

Introduction	338
ActorScript	338
Notation	340
Expressions	340
Types	340
Definitions, i.e., ≡	340
Interfaces for procedures, i.e., **Interface having** [ ]↦	341
Procedures, i.e., **Actor implements** [ ]→ , ¶ and §	342
Sending messages to procedures, i.e., ▪[ ]	342
Patterns	343
Cases, i.e., ◆ ⁏ ☑ ⁏ ⁇	343
Binding locals, i.e., **Let** ← ₒ	344
General message-passing interfaces	345
Actors that change, i.e., **Actor** and ≔	345
Antecedents, Preparations, and Concurrency, i.e., ☐ and ●	347
Implementing multiple interfaces, i.e., ⊡ and **also implements**	348
Swiss cheese	350
Coordinating Activities	352
Conclusion	356
Acknowledgements	356
Bibliography	357
Appendix 1. Extreme ActorScript	364
Parameterized Types, i.e., ◁ , ▷	364
Type Discrimination, i.e., **Discrimination**, Δ, and ∇	364
Structures, i.e., **Structure**	365
Structures with named fields, i.e., ᛗ and ⦂ᛗ	366
Processing Exceptions, *i.e.*, **Try catch**◆ ⁏ ☑ ⁏ ⁇ and **Try cleanup**	366
Runtime requirements, *i.e.*, Precondition ; **and** postcondition	366
Polymorphism	367
Arguments with named fields, i.e., ᛗ and ⦂ᛗ	368
Lists, i.e., [ ] using spreading, i.e., [∨]	369
Sets, i.e., { } using spreading, i.e., { ∨ }	370
Multisets, i.e., ⦃ ⦄ using spreading, i.e., ⦃ ∨ ⦄	370
Maps, i.e., Map{ }	371
Futures, i.e., **Future** and ↓	372
In-line Recursion (e.g., looping) , i.e. ▪[← , ←] ≜	374
Strings	375
General Messaging, i.e., ▪ and ⊡	376
Language extension, i.e., ⦅ ⦆	377
Atomic Operations, i.e. **Atomic compare update then else**	378

Enumerations, i.e., **Enumeration** ⊥ using Qualifiers, i.e., ▢	379
Native types, e.g., JavaScript, JSON, Java, and XML	380
One-way messaging, e.g., ⊖, ⇐, and ↠	382
Arrays	383
Appendix 2: Meta-circular definition of ActorScript	386
The Message eval	386
The interface Type implements ⊒	386
Future, ↓, and ⓘ	386
The Message match	387
Message sending	389
List Expressions and Patterns	390
Exceptions	391
Continuations using perform	391
Atomic compare and update	392
Cases	393
Holes in the cheese	395
A Simple Implementation of **Actor**	397
An implementation of cheese that never holds a lock	399
Appendix 3. Inconsistency Robust Logic Programs	402
Forward chaining	402
Backward chaining	402
SubArguments	403
Aggregation using Ground-Complete Predicates	403
Appendix 4. ActorScript Symbols with Readings. IDE ASCII, and Unicode code points	405
Appendix 5. Grammar Precedence	407
Appendix 6. Type Discrimination	408
End Notes	409

Part 3. Applications 427

1. *Some types of inconsistency in legal reasoning.*
Anne Gardner 429

Introduction	429
Inconsistent findings of fact: The legal background	430
Handling inconsistent findings	432
Inconsistent statutes	435
The conflicting statutes	436
Resolution through an older rule	437
Resolution through a later enactment	438
Inconsistent options	438
Consistency of approach	443
Consistency of results	442
Consistency within an opinion	443

Conclusion	445
References	446

2. *Rules versus standards: Competing notions of inconsistency: Robustness in the Supreme Court and Federal Circuit.*
Stefania Fusco and David Olson... *447*
Inconsistency robustness in court systems	447
Position Statement	452
Endnotes	458

3. *Politics and pragmatism in scientific ontology construction.*
Mike Travers *460*
Ontologies have politics	460
The defense of "marriage"	460
What constitutes a disease?	461
Contested representations in biology	462
Example: mitochondria	463
Example: genes and pathways	464
Alignment, social construction, power	465
The sociology of ontologies	466
Example: representing cellular space	466
Conceptualism, realism, pragmatism	469
The poverty of realism	469
Complexity and barrier to entry	471
Mental illness and realism	472
Pragmatism	473
Representation from the bottom up	475
Latour: circulating reference	475
Convergence and objectivity	477
Computational alternatives	477
A Platform for Knowledge	478
Where's the semantic web?	478
Prototype-based representation	479
Discourse, argumentation, provenance	480
Version control and agile software techniques	480
Wikipedia and socially-constructed knowledge bases	480
Conclusion: knowledge systems and open science	481
References	482

4. *Sentence Composition in EPGY's Language Arts and Writing Course*
Dan Flickinger *487*
English: Education Program for Gifted Youth	488
Evaluation of student answers	489
References	489

5. *The singularity is here.*
   Fanya S. Montalvo *490*
   - Intention 490
   - Kurzweil's singularity 490
   - Organizational complexity 491
   - Another kind of singularity 492
   - Possible solutions 492
   - Conclusion 495
   - Acknowledgements 496
   - Bibliography 496

6. *Biological responses to chemical exposure: Case studies in how to manage ostensible inconsistencies using the Claim Framework.*
   Catherine Blake *497*
   - Introduction 497
   - Related work 499
   - Scientific sub-languages 499
   - Scientific rhetoric 500
   - Biomedical text mining 500
   - Automating the claim framework 500
   - Case studies 501
     - Toxicology 501
     - Medicine 504
     - Epidemiology 506
   - Closing comments 507
   - References 508

7. *From inter-annotation to intra-publication inconsistency.*
   Alaa Abi Haidar, Mihnea Tufi, and Jean-Gabriel Ganascia *512*
   - Abstract 512
   - Introduction 512
   - Background 513
   - Results and discussion 514
   - Evaluating inter annotator agreement 515
   - Conclusion 518
   - Acknowledgements 518
   - Bibliography 518

Index **521**

Preface[1]

Carl Hewitt

Inconsistency[i] robustness is information system performance[2] in the face of continual, pervasive inconsistencies.[ii] Inconsistency robustness is both an observed phenomenon and a desired feature.

This volume has revised versions of refereed articles from the 2011 and 2014 International Symposia on Inconsistency Robustness conducted under the auspices of the International Society for Inconsistency Robustness.[3] The articles are broadly based on theory and practice, addressing fundamental issues in inconsistency robustness.

The field of Inconsistency Robustness aims to provide practical, rigorous foundations for computer information systems having pervasively inconsistent information in a variety of fields *e.g.,* computer science and engineering, health, management, law, *etc.*

Videos
The following online videos give an overview of Inconsistency Robustness:
- **Introduction to Inconsistency Robustness**
  https://www.youtube.com/watch?v=_R65RrishcY
- **Actors for CyberThings.** Erlang Solutions SF 2015 Keynote
  https://www.youtube.com/watch?v=DNbJY333vUs
- **Future of Software IP** http://www.youtube.com/watch?v=GuksQ4pFvWA
  Slides for this video:
  https://drive.google.com/file/d/0B79uetkQ_hCKWlM4MGNZZnBOX2c/view?usp=sharing
- **The Actor Model (everything you wanted to know, but were afraid to ask)**[4]
  http://channel9.msdn.com/Shows/Going+Deep/Hewitt-Meijer-and-Szyperski-The-Actor-Model-everything-you-wanted-to-know-but-were-afraid-to-ask

---

[i] An inference system is *inconsistent* when it is possible to derive both a proposition and its negation.
   A *contradiction* is manifest when both a proposition and its negation are asserted even if by different parties, *e.g.*, New York Times said *"Snowden is a whistleblower."*, but NSA said *"Snowden is not a whistleblower."*
[ii] a shift from the previously dominant paradigms of inconsistency denial and inconsistency elimination, *i.e.*, to sweep inconsistencies under the rug.

Overview

The following is an overview of the articles in this volume, divided into the following parts:
1. Mathematical Foundations
2. Software Foundations
3. Applications

Each of the above parts is discussed below (there is an index of the entire volume at the end).

Part 1. Mathematical Foundations

Inconsistency Robustness aspires to be a rigorous scientific field. Consequently, it must have mathematical foundations.

Article 1-1. *Formalizing common sense reasoning for scalable inconsistency-robust information coordination using Direct Logic Reasoning and the Actor Model* [i]

This article lays out the case for Inconsistency Robustness and presents Inconsistency Robust Direct Logic as a rigorous formalism for logical inference.[5]

Inconsistency Robustness builds on the following principles:
- We know only a little, but it affects us *enormously*.[ii]
- At any point in time, much is wrong[iii] with the consensus of top scientists but it is not known how or which parts.
- Science is never certain; it is continually (re-)made.

Software engineers for large software systems often have good arguments for some proposition and also good arguments for its negation. So what do large software manufacturers do? If the problem is serious, they bring it before stakeholders to try and sort it out. In many particularly difficult cases the resulting decision has been to simply live with the problem for an indefinite period.

---

[i] authored by Carl Hewitt
[ii] for better or worse
[iii] *e.g.*, misleading, inconsistent, wrong-headed, ambiguous, contra best-practices, *etc.*

Consequently, large software systems are shipped to customers with thousands of known inconsistencies of varying severity where
- Even relatively simple subsystems can be subtly inconsistent
- There is no practical way to test for inconsistency.
- Even though a system is inconsistent, it is not meaningless.

People use common sense in their interactions with large information systems. This common sense needs to be formalized so that it can be used by computer systems.[i] Unfortunately, previous formalizations have been inadequate. For example, Classical Logic[ii] is not safe for use with pervasively inconsistent information because it makes invalid inferences.[iii] Is it possible to improve on Classical Logic?

According to Feferman:[6]
> *So far as I know, it has not been determined whether such* [inconsistency robust] *logics account for "sustained ordinary reasoning", not only in everyday discourse but also in mathematics and the sciences.*

This article argues that Direct Logic is an improvement over Classical Logic with respect to Feferman's desideratum above for today's information systems that are perpetually, pervasively inconsistent. Information technology needs an all-embracing system of inconsistency-robust reasoning to support practical information coordination. Having such a system is important in computer science because computers must be able to carry out all inferences (including inferences about their own inference processes) without relying on humans.

Direct Logic is put forward as an improvement over Classical Logic with respect to Feferman's desideratum above using the following:[iv]
- **Inconsistency Robust Direct Logic** for pervasively inconsistent theories of practice, *e.g.*, theories for climate modeling and for modeling the human brain
- **Classical Direct Logic** for use of consistent mathematical theories in inconsistency robust theories

---

[i] Eventually, computer systems need to be able to address issues like the following:
- What will be the effects of increasing greenhouse gasses?
- What is the future of mass cyber surveillance?
- What can done about the increasing prevalence of metabolic syndrome?

[ii] the standard that is universally taught

[iii] See "Limitations of first-order logic" in article 1-2 of this volume

[iv] Of course, Direct Logic must preserve as much previous learning as possible.

It is important to distinguish Inconsistency Robust Direct Logic from Classical Direct Logic:
- Classical Direct Logic is a classical mathematical foundation for Computer Science. Consequently (like all classical mathematical systems), it *must* (unfortunately) have IGOR[i], *i.e.*, the rule that from a contradiction, every proposition can be inferred.[7] However, because Classical Direct Logic is consistent, IGOR does not actually apply to Direct Logic as a whole.
- Because of pervasively inconsistent information, Inconsistency Robust Direct Logic[ii] theories must *not* have IGOR.

Because it is so fundamental to inference, some version of proof by contradiction is required for Inconsistency Robust Direct Logic. An important innovation of Inconsistency Robust Direct Logic is that it has **Inconsistency Robust Proof by Contradiction**[8] which requires that a contradiction must be *implied*[9] by a hypothesis to be refuted rather than merely *inferred*.[10] As opposed to Classical Direct Logic, implication[iii] in Inconsistency Robust Direct Logic is a *much* stronger relationship than inference. Consequently, Classical Proof by Contradiction[11] is stronger than Inconsistency Robust Proof by Contradiction. Nevertheless, Inconsistency Robust Proof by Contradiction is extremely useful for more *safely*[12] reasoning about inconsistent information.

A fundamental goal of Inconsistency Robustness is to effectively reason about large amounts of information at high degrees of abstraction:

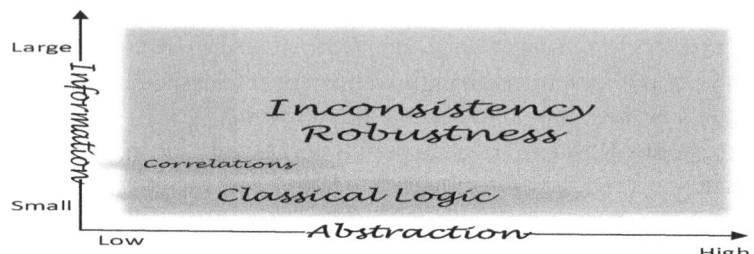

---

[i] **IGOR** is an acronym for Inconsistency in Garbage Out Redux. IGOR was expressed in Latin as *Ex contradictione quod libet* (from a contradiction, every proposition can be inferred) which harks back to Aristotle. (See "Damage-control" and following sections in article 1-3 of this volume for detailed discussion.). It is important to note that because of IGOR, inconsistencies can produce invalid inferences from inconsistent information using Classical Logic even though a contradiction is not explicitly manifest, *e.g.*, using resolution theorem proving. (See "Uniform Proof Procedures based on Resolution" in article 2-2 of this volume.)

[ii] described in article 1-1 of this volume

[iii] See "Inconsistency Robust Implication" in article 1-1 in this volume for an axiomatization of implication in Inconsistency Robust Direct Logic

Classical logic can be safely used only for theories for which there is strong evidence of consistency.

The semantics of Direct Logic is based on **argumentation**.[i] According to Minsky: *You don't understand anything until you learn it more than one way.*[13]

Inconsistency robustness differs from previous paradigms based on belief revision, probability, and uncertainty as follows:
- Belief revision: Large information systems are continually, pervasively inconsistent and there is no way to revise them to attain consistency.
- Probability and fuzzy logic: In large information systems, there are typically several ways to calculate probability. Often the result is that the probability is both close to 0% and close to 100%![ii]
- Uncertainty: Resolving uncertainty to determine truth is not a realistic goal in large information systems. There are always arguments for and against contradictory propositions.

Inconsistency Robust Direct logic facilitates common sense reasoning by formalizing inconsistency robust inference.[iii]

According to Chang,
> *Active realism* [is] *a commitment to seek out contact with reality and learn from it as much as possible (consciously, systematically and precisely).*[14]
> ...
> *But will that not interfere with the pursuit of the one truth about nature? I maintain that we need to come away from such an inoperable notion of truth. When we come to consider what "truth" means in practice, the concept splinters into several different ones, including one that is internal to a given system and nearly synonymous with "success". Realism should be a commitment to promote realistic ways of learning from reality, not a vain and hubristic attempt to prove that we are in possession of the unique truth about nature.*

---

[i] in contrast with what Chang called "*Truth Realism: the belief that accepted scientific theories possess truth, at least approximately or partially.*" [Hasok Chang. *From Incommensurability to Pluralism* Symposium on Occasion of the Farewell of Paul Hoyningen-Huene from Hannover: Science - Big Questions Revisited. July 18. 2014]

[ii] See "Inconsistent Probabilities" in article 1-1 of this volume.

[iii] According to [Minsky 1974]:
   The consistency that [classical] *logic absolutely demands is not otherwise usually available – and probably not even desirable! – because consistent systems are likely to be too "weak".*

Why keep multiple systems of knowledge alive? The immediate reason for this is the sense that we are not likely to arrive at the one perfect theory or viewpoint that will satisfy all our needs. ... If we are not likely to find the one perfect system, it makes sense to keep multiple ones, which will each have different strengths. Different benefits, practical and intellectual, will spring from different systems of knowledge. It is also important to note that the co-existence of multiple systems can facilitate productive interactions between them through integration, co-optation and competition. ....

It is important to distinguish pluralism[i] from relativism. Relativism involves an idle permissiveness and renunciation of judgment. Pluralism does not renounce judgment, yet maintains that it is better to foster a multitude of worthwhile systems, rather than only one. Pluralism as I conceive it ... is about knowledge-building, not just knowledge-evaluation.[15]

In today's information environment, each system of practice is itself pervasively inconsistent and is inconsistent with other practices. In this way, Inconsistency Robustness *generates* pluralism.

A number of philosophers oppose the results in this article:
- Some would like to stick with just Classical Logic and not consider inconsistency robustness.[16]
- Some would like to stick with the first-order theories and not consider direct inference.[ii]
- Some would like to stick with just Logic Programs (*e.g.* nondeterministic Turing Machines, λ-calculus, *etc.*) and not consider concurrency.

And some would like to have nothing to do with any of the above![17] However, the results in this paper (and the driving technological and economic forces behind them) tend to push towards inconsistency robustness, direct inference, and concurrency.

---

[i] *"a commitment to maintain multiple[e systems of knowledge in each field of inquiry"* [Hasok Chang. *Scientific Pluralism and the Mission of History and Philosophy of Science Inaugural Lecture.* Cambridge University. October 25, 2012]

[ii] Inference is direct when it does not involve unnecessary circumlocutions, *e.g.*, coding sentences as Gödel numbers.

Philosophers are now challenged as to whether they agree that
- **Inconsistency is the norm.**
- **Direct inference is the norm.**
- **Logic Program are *not* computationally universal.**

Our everyday life is becoming increasingly dependent on large software systems. And these systems are becoming increasingly permeated with inconsistency and concurrency. **As these pervasively inconsistent information systems become a major part of the environment in which we live, it becomes an issue of common sense to use them effectively. We will need sophisticated software systems that formalize this common sense to help people understand and apply the principles and practices suggested in this volume.**

Creating this software is not a trivial undertaking!

Article 1-2. *Inconsistency Robustness in Foundations*[i]

This article lays out the case for Inconsistency Robustness in Foundations and presents Classical Direct Logic for the mathematical foundations of Computer Science.

In order for Classical Direct Logic to be a useful mathematical foundation for Computer Science, it must satisfy potentially conflicting goals:
- **Expressive**: for communication with computer systems[18]
- **Powerful**: so that arguments are short
- **Consistent**: to prevent security holes

The recently discovered very simple proof of the theorem that Mathematics is consistent is given below.[ii]

---

1) $\neg$Consistent   // hypothesis to derive a contradiction **just in this subargument**

2) $\exists[\Psi\text{:Proposition}] \rightarrow \vdash(\Psi \wedge \neg\Psi)$ // definition of inconsistency using 1)

3) $\vdash(\Psi_0 \wedge \neg\Psi_0)$ // rule of Existential Elimination using 2)

4) $\Psi_0 \wedge \neg\Psi_0$ // rule of Soundness using 3)

$\vdash$ Consistent   // rule of Proof by Contradiction using 1) and 4)

Natural Deduction[19] Proof of Consistency of Mathematics

---

[i] authored by Carl Hewitt

[ii] Many of today's most prominent philosophers and logicians have cast doubt on the correctness of the proof.

Please note the following points:
- The above argument formally mathematically proves that mathematics is consistent and that **it is not a premise of the theorem that mathematics is consistent**.
- Classical Mathematics was designed for consistent axioms and consequently the rules of Classical Mathematics can be used to prove consistency regardless of other axioms.[20]
- **The self-proof of consistency (above) shows that the current common understanding that Gödel proved "Mathematics cannot prove its own consistency, if it is consistent" is inaccurate.**[21]

Wittgenstein long ago showed that contradiction in mathematics results from the kind of "self-referential"[22] sentence that Gödel used in his argument that Mathematics cannot prove its own consistency. However, using a typed notation for mathematical sentences, it can be proved that the kind "self-referential" sentence that Gödel used in his argument cannot be constructed because the required fixed point that Gödel used to construct the "self-referential" sentence does not exist. In this way, consistency of mathematics is preserved without giving up power.[23]

It is very important to distinguish between the following:
- "self-reference" using fixed points
- recursion using types

Gödel famously thought that mathematics necessarily has the "self-referential" proposition **I am not provable** where the **I** comes from a fixed-point construction using an untyped notation for mathematics. **Using typed recursion, it is impossible to construct such a "self-referential" proposition.**

Mathematics proves that it is open in the sense that it can prove that its theorems cannot be provably computationally enumerated:

Theorem ⊢Mathematics is Open

Proof.[i] Suppose to obtain a contradiction that it is possible to prove closure[24], *i.e.,* there is a provably computable total procedure Proof such that it is provable that

$$\vdash^P \Psi \Leftrightarrow \exists [i:\mathbb{N}] \rightarrow \text{Proof}[i] = p$$

As a consequence of the above, there is a provably total procedure ProvableComputableTotal that enumerates the provably total computable procedures that can be used in the implementation of the following procedure:

Diagonal[i] ≡ (ProvableComputableTotal[i])[i]+1

However,
- ProvableComputableTotal[Diagonal] because Diagonal is implemented using provably computable total procedures.
- ¬ProvableComputableTotal[Diagonal] because Diagonal is a provably computable total procedure that differs from every other provably computable total procedure.

The above contradiction completes the proof.

Franzén [25] argued that mathematics is inexhaustible because of inferential undecidability[ii] of mathematical theories. The above theorem that mathematics is open provides another independent argument for the inexhaustibility of mathematics.

Direct Logic distinguishes between concrete **sentences** and abstract **propositions**. For example, the follow sentence is a Latin parse of the string "Gallia est omnis divisa in partes tres.":

⌈"Gallia est omnis divisa in partes tres."⌉$_{Latin}$

On the other hand, the proposition that *All of Gaul is divided into three parts* was believed by Caesar.[26]

A sentence s can be **abstracted** (⌊s⌋$_T$)[27] as a proposition in a theory T. For example,

⌊⌈"Gallia est omnis divisa in partes tres."⌉$_{Latin}$⌋$_{English}$
↠ *All of Gaul is divided into three parts*

---

[i] This argument appeared in [Alonzo Church. *The Richard Paradox*. Proceedings of American Mathematical Society. 1934] expressing concern that the argument meant that there is *"no sound basis for supposing that there is such a thing as logic."*

[ii] sometimes called "incompleteness"

Also,
⌊⌈"Gallia est omnis divisa in partes tres."⌉_{Latin} ⌋_{Spanish}
→ *Toda Galia está dividida en tres partes* [i]

Abstraction and parsing are becoming increasingly important in software engineering. *e.g.,*
- The execution of code can be dynamically checked against its documentation. Also Web Services can be dynamically searched for and invoked on the basis of their documentation.
- Use cases can be inferred by specialization of documentation and from code by automatic test generators and by model checking.
- Code can be generated by inference from documentation and by generalization from use cases.

Abstraction and parsing are needed for large software systems so that that documentation, use cases, and code can mutually speak about what has been said and their relationships.

A closed mathematical theory is an extension of mathematics whose proofs are computationally enumerable. For example, group theory is obtained by adding the axioms of groups to Classical Direct Logic along with the requirement that proofs are computational enumerable.

Inconsistency Robustness is performance of information systems with pervasively inconsistent information. Inconsistency Robustness of the community of professional mathematicians is their performance in repeatedly repairing contradictions over the centuries. In the Inconsistency Robustness paradigm, deriving contradictions have been a progressive development and not "game stoppers." **Contradictions can be helpful instead of being something to be "swept under the rug" by denying their existence, which has been repeatedly attempted by Establishment Philosophers (beginning with some Pythagoreans).** Such denial has delayed mathematical development.

The inherently social nature of the processes by which principles and propositions in logic are produced, disseminated, and established is illustrated by the following issues with examples:[28]

- **The formal presentation of a demonstration (proof) has not led automatically to consensus.** Formal presentation in print and at several different professional meetings of the extraordinarily simple proof in this paper have not led automatically to consensus about the theorem that "Mathematics is Consistent".

---

[i] Spanish for all of Gaul is divided in three parts.

- **There has been an absence of universally recognized central logical principles**. Disputes over the validity of the Principle of Excluded Middle led to the development of Intuitionistic Logic, which is an alternative to Classical Logic.
- **There are many ways of doing logic.** One view of logic is that it is about *truth*; another view is that it is about *argumentation* (i.e. proofs).
- **Argumentation and propositions have be variously (re-)connected and both have been re-used.** Church's paradox is that assuming theorems of mathematics are computationally enumerable leads to contradiction. In this papers, the paradox is transformed into the fundamental principle that "Mathematics is Open" (*i.e.* it is a theorem of mathematics that the theorems of mathematics are not computationally enumerable) using the argument used in Church's paradox.
- **New technological developments have cast doubts on traditional logical principles.** The pervasive inconsistency of large-scale information systems has cast doubt on classical logical principles, *e.g.*, Excluded Middle.[i]
- **Political actions have been taken against views differing from Establishment Philosophers**. According to Kline, Hippasus was literally thrown overboard by his fellow Pythagoreans "*...for having produced an element in the universe which denied the...doctrine that all phenomena in the universe can be reduced to whole numbers and their ratios.*"[29] Fearing that he was dying and the influence that Brouwer might have after his death, Hilbert fired[ii] Brouwer as an associate editor of *Mathematische Annalen* because of "*incompatibility of our views on fundamental matters*"[30], *e.g.*, Hilbert ridiculed Brouwer for challenging the validity of the Principle of Excluded Middle.

Establishment Philosophers have often ridiculed dissenting views and attempted to limit their distribution by political means.[31] Electronic archives and repositories that record precedence of scientific publication in mathematical logic have censored[iii] submissions with proofs such as those in this article.

---

[i] See discussion in article 1-1 of this volume.
[ii] in an unlawful way (Einstein, a member of the editorial board, refused to support Hilbert's action)
[iii] while refusing to provide any justification for the censorship other than administrative fiat

Contradiction	Outcome
Church discovered to his dismay that if theorems of mathematics are postulated to be computationally enumerable, then mathematics is inconsistent.	Theorems of mathematics cannot be computationally enumerated and mathematics is open and inexhaustible. But theorems of a particular theory can be postulated to be computationally enumerable.
Using fixed points to construct a "self-referential" sentence for an untyped notation of mathematical sentences, [Gödel 1931] claimed that mathematics cannot prove its own consistency. However, it is pointed out in this paper that mathematics easily proves its own consistency.	The contradiction can be resolved by using a properly-typed notation for sentences of mathematics does not allow the use of fixed points to construct "self-referential" sentences.
Using fixed points to construct a "self-referential" sentence using an untyped notation of mathematical sentences, [Gödel 1931] claimed to prove inferential undecidability (sometimes called "incompleteness") for mathematics. However, such "self-referential" sentences lead to inconsistency in mathematics.	[Church 1935, Turing 1936] proved inferential undecidabilty of closed mathematical theories without using fixed points for an untyped notation of mathematical sentences to construct "self-referential" sentences.
In Computer Science, it is important that the Natural Numbers ($\mathbb{N}$) be axiomatized in a way that does not allow integers (e.g. infinite ones) in models of the axioms. However, it is impossible to properly axiomatize $\mathbb{N}$ using first-order logic.	Using Classical Direct Logic, $\mathbb{N}$ can be axiomatized in such a way that all models are uniquely isomorphic to $\mathbb{N}$ [Dedekind 1888, Peano 1889]. Consequently, there are no infinite integers in models of the axioms
In Computer Science, it is important that sets of the Natural Numbers (Sets◁$\mathbb{N}$▷) be axiomatized in a way that does not allow countable models of the real numbers and non-reals (e.g. infinitesimals) in models of the axioms. However, it is impossible to properly axiomatize Sets◁$\mathbb{N}$▷ using first-order logic.	Using Classical Direct Logic, Sets◁$\mathbb{N}$▷ are defined by characteristic functions of types and thus all models are uniquely isomorphic to Sets◁$\mathbb{N}$▷. Consequently, there are no infinitesimal reals in the models or other nonstandard elements.

First-order logic is unsuitable as the foundation of mathematics for Computer Science: <ul><li>Some theorems of ordinary Classical Mathematics cannot be proved.</li><li>Some ordinary theorems useful in Computer Science cannot be proved.</li><li>There are undesirable models of mathematical theories (see above).</li></ul>	Classical Direct Logic is suitable as the foundation of mathematics for Computer Science: <ul><li>All ordinary theorems of Classical Mathematics can be proved.</li><li>All ordinary theorems useful in Computer Science can be proved</li><li>There are no undesirable models of mathematical theories (see above).</li></ul>

Article 1-3. *Inconsistency: Its present impacts and future prospects*[i]

This article presents John Woods' philosophical analysis of the current state of Inconsistency Robustness and its future prospects.

The article alludes to the following aspects of Classical Direct Logic:[ii]
- Russell's paradox is excluded by basing set theory on types[iii]
- Wittgenstein's proof[iv] (showing that Gödel's 1931 "self-referential" proposition for Mathematics leads to contradiction in Mathematics) is *valid* in Classical Direct Logic. In order to avoid contradiction, Gödel's "self-referential" proposition is *excluded* from Classical Direct Logic by having a proper typed notation for propositions of mathematics that excludes Gödel's "self-referential" proposition because the required fixed points do *not* exist.[32] Of course, the *correctness* of Wittgenstein's proof means that the *arguments* of Gödel's 1931 results are *invalid* because they are based on *inconsistent assumptions* for Mathematics.[v] The proof that "Mathematics self-proves its own consistency" is *valid* in Classical Direct Logic[vi] and does not cause any problems because:
    - Gödel's 1931 argument that "Mathematics cannot prove its own consistency" is *invalid* for the reason given above
    - Mathematics is in fact consistent

---

[i] authored by John Woods
[ii] See article 1-3 in this volume
[iii] See "Foundations with both Types and Sets" in article 1-3 of this volume on how sets can be defined as characteristic functions using types
[iv] See "Wittgenstein: `self-referential´ propositions lead to inconsistency" in article 1-3 of this volume for Wittgenstein's proof
[v] See "Provability Logic" in article 1-3 of this volume for discussion of a proposal on how to consistently incorporate "self-referential" propositions into *first-order logic*.
[vi] See proof above in this preface that "Mathematics Self Proves its own Consistency."

In the article, particular attention to the role that IGOR[i] plays in inconsistency robustness.[33]

It is important to distinguish Inconsistency Robust Direct Logic from Classical Direct Logic:
- Because Classical Direct Logic *must* be consistent, **there is no anxiety about inconsistencies in Classical Direct Logic because they do not occur!**
- **There is no anxiety about inconsistencies in Inconsistency Robust Direct Logic because it doesn't have the IGOR rule of Classical Logic.**[ii]

The article eloquently explains limitations of the Ambiguation Strategy for denying the existence of inconsistencies as follows:

[The Ambiguation Strategy] "**provides that where an ambiguity is not obviously in play, we should try to find one that might become apparent to us upon further reflection. It is a good idea with a spotty operational history. The trouble is that ambiguities aren't free for the asking. They are available as inconsistency-dissolvers only when independently established** [*e.g.*, by specifying the exact nature of a claimed ambiguity and establishing its importance]. **In actual practice invocation** [*i.e.*, claiming ambiguity] **considerably outpaces independent establishment.**"

The article concludes as follows:[iii]

The idea of inconsistency robustness is so rich and so full of promise as to deserve a life of its own.

---

[i] The article refers to IGOR by the Latin name *ex falso quodlibet*

[ii] Because of IGOR, if Classical Direct Logic were inconsistent, then it would be useless. However, since it is consistent IGOR doesn't actually come into play and Classical Direct Logic works as a practical mathematical foundation for Computer Science.

[iii] with technical caveats concerning IGOR whose upshot is as follows:
- IGOR is a *necessary* rule of Classical Direct Logic but it does *not* apply to Classical Direct Logic because it is consistent
- IGOR is *not* a rule of Inconsistency Robust Direct Logic

Article 1-4. *Two sources of Explosion*
This article presents two bugs that were discovered in earlier versions of Inconsistency Robust Direct Logic. Both of these bugs have since been repaired. The discovery of these bugs and their repair is an illustration of *one* of the processes of Inconsistency Robustness. In this case the following inconsistency was isolated:
- Inconsistency Robust Direct Logic aims to be a generally useful system for inference about inconsistent information.
- An older version of Inconsistency Robust Direct Logic included the rule of Excluded Middle. Kao developed a clever argument showing that including Excluded Middle would render the older version of Inconsistency Robust Direct Logic useless because *every* proposition could be proved from a single contradiction.

The solution was to remove Excluded Middle as one of the rules of Inconsistency Robust Direct Logic.

An important influence of this article was that it helped provide motivation for the development of Inconsistency-Robust Proof by Contradiction that is an important contribution of Inconsistency Robust Direct Logic.

Part 2. Software Foundations[i]

Inconsistency Robustness aspires to sound engineering. Consequently, it must have software foundations

Message passing using types is the foundation of system communication: [34]
- Messages are the unit of communication
- Types enable secure communication with any Actor

Article 2-1. *Actor Model of Computation: Scalable Robust Information Systems*[ii]
The Actor model is a mathematical theory that treats "Actors" as the universal conceptual primitive of digital computation. The model has been used both as a framework for a theoretical understanding of concurrency, and as the theoretical basis for several practical implementations of concurrent systems. Unlike previous models of computation, the Actor model was inspired by relationships among computational events in physical laws. It was also influenced by programming languages such as the lambda calculus[iii], Lisp, Simula 67 ,

---

[i] Article summaries for this part include extensive quotations from the articles.
[ii] authored by Carl Hewitt
[iii] In general, Actor computations can be exponentially faster than the parallel lambda

Smalltalk-72, as well as ideas for Petri Nets, capability systems and packet switching. The advent of massive concurrency through client-cloud computing and many-core computer architectures has galvanized interest in the Actor Model.

Hypothesis:[35] **All physically possible computation can be directly implemented using Actors.**

Axioms of locality including *Organizational* and *Operational* hold as follows:
- *Organization:* The local storage of an Actor can include *addresses* only
  1. that were provided when it was created or of Actors that it has created
  2. that have been received in messages
- *Operation:* In response to a message received, an Actor can
  1. create more Actors
  2. send messages[i] to addresses in the following:
     - the message it has just received
     - its local storage
  3. for an exclusive[ii] Actor, designate how to process the next message received[iii]

The Actor Model can be used as a framework for modeling, understanding, and reasoning about, a wide range of concurrent systems. Actor technology will see significant application for coordinating all kinds of digital information for individuals, groups, and organizations so their information usefully links together.

Information coordination needs to make use of the following information system principles:
- **Persistence**: Information is collected and indexed.
- **Concurrency**: Work proceeds interactively and concurrently, overlapping in time.
- **Quasi-commutativity**: Information can be used regardless of whether it initiates new work or become relevant to ongoing work.
- **Sponsorship**: Sponsors provide resources for computation, *i.e.*,

---

calculus. For example, implementations using Actors of Direct Logic can be exponentially faster than implementations in the parallel lambda calculus.

[i] Likewise the messages sent can contain addresses only
  1. that were provided when the Actor was created
  2. that have been received in messages
  3. that are for Actors created here

[ii] An *exclusive* Actor can perform at most one activity at a time.

[iii] A determinate Actor that always responds with the same response for the same message can be freely replicated and cached.

processing, storage, and communications.
- **Pluralism**: Information is heterogeneous, overlapping and often inconsistent. There is no central arbiter of truth.
- **Provenance**: The provenance of information is carefully tracked and recorded

The Actor Model is designed to provide a foundation for inconsistency robust information coordination.

Karmani and Agha[36] promoted "Fog Cutter"[i] Actors each of which must have a mailbox, thread, state, and program diagrammed as follows:[37].

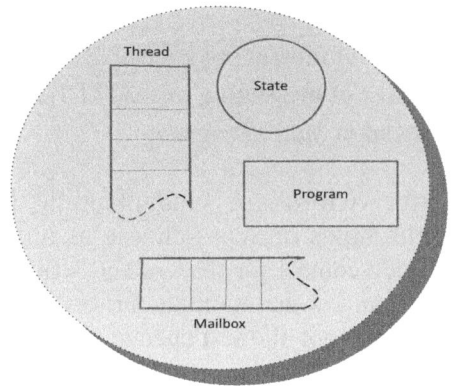

Fog Cutter Actor Event loop:
Process a message from Mailbox using the Thread, then reset the Thread

However, Fog Cutter Actors are special cases of Actors because of the following:[ii]
- *Each Fog Cutter Actor has a 'mailbox'.* But if everything that interacts is an Actor, then a mailbox must be an Actor and so in turn needs a mailbox which in turn...[Hewitt, Bishop, and Steiger 1973] Of course, mailboxes having mailboxes is an infinite regress that has been humorously characterized by Erik Meijer as "down the rabbit hole." [Hewitt, Meijer, and Szyperski 2012]
- *A Fog Cutter Actor 'terminates' when Actor that it has created is 'idle' and there is no way to send it a message.* In practice, it is preferable to use garbage collection for Actors that are inaccessible. [Baker and Hewitt 1977]
- *Each Fog Cutter Actor executes a 'loop' using its own sequential 'thread' that begins with receiving a message followed by possibly creating more computational Actors, sending messages, updating its local state, and then looping back for the next message.* In practice, it is preferable to provide

---
[i] so dubbed by Kristen Nygaard (private communication).
[ii] Fog Cutter is in *italics*.

"Swiss cheese" by which an Actor can concurrently process multiple messages without the limitation of a sequential thread loop. [Hewitt and Atkinson 1977, 1979; Atkinson 1980; Hewitt 2011]

- *A Fog Cutter Actor has a well-defined local 'autonomous' 'state' that can be updated[38] while processing a message.* However, because of indeterminacy an Actor may not be in a well-defined local independent state. For example, Actors might be entangled[39] with each other so that their actions are correlated. Also, large distributed Actors (*e.g.* www.dod.gov) do not have a well-defined state. In practice, it is preferable for an Actor not to change its local variables while it is processing a message and instead specify to process the next message received (as in ActorScript [Hewitt 2011]).

Fog Cutter Actors have been useful for exploring issues about Actors including the following alternatives:[i]

- **Reception order of messaging** instead of *Mailbox*
- **Activation order of messaging** instead of *Thread*
- **Behavior** instead of *State+Program*

However, Fog Cutter Actors are fundamentally lacking in generality because they lack the holes of Swiss cheese as illustrated by the classic problem of concurrency control for readers and writers in a shared resource. The fundamental constraint is that multiple writers are not allowed to operate concurrently and a writer is not allowed operate concurrently with a reader.

---

[i] Actor Model in bold face versus Fog Cutter in italics.

Below is an interface for the type ReadersWriter

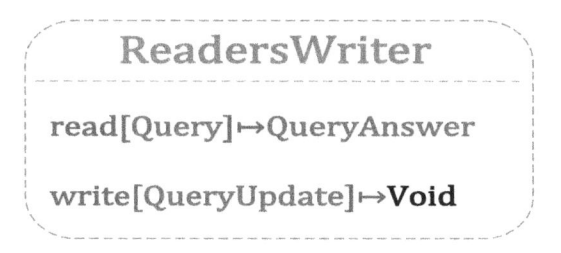

> **ReadersWriter**
>
> read[Query] ↦ QueryAnswer
>
> write[QueryUpdate] ↦ **Void**

Cheese diagram for ReadersWriter implementations:

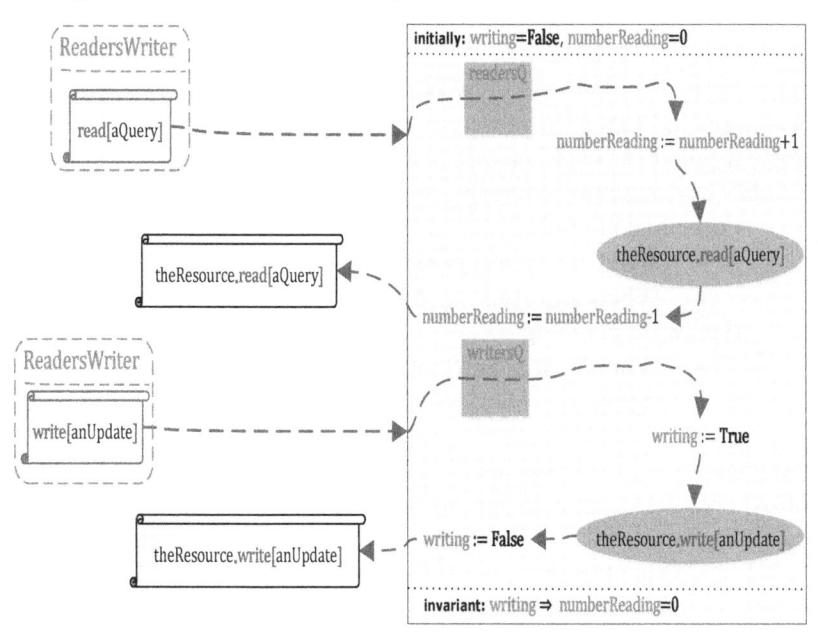

[Diagram showing:
- ReadersWriter with read[aQuery] operation
- **initially:** writing=False, numberReading=0
- readersQ queue → numberReading := numberReading+1 → theResource.read[aQuery] → theResource,read[aQuery] → numberReading := numberReading-1
- ReadersWriter with write[anUpdate] operation
- writersQ queue → writing := True → theResource.write[anUpdate] → theResource,write[anUpdate] → writing := False
- **invariant:** writing ⇒ numberReading=0]

Note:
1. At most one activity is allowed to execute in the cheese.[i]
2. The cheese has holes.[ii]
3. The cheese changes only when leaving the cheese or after an internal delegated operation.[iii]

Invariants hold at cheese boundaries, *i.e.*, an invariant must hold when the cheese is entered. Consequently, it doesn't matter what actions other Actors may be concurrently performing.

---

[i] Cheese is yellow in the diagram
[ii] A hole is grey in the diagram
[iii] Of course, other external Actors can change.

In practice, the most common and effective way to explain Actors has been *operationally* using a suitable Actor programming language (*e.g.*, ActorScript [Hewitt 2012]) that specifies how Actors can be implemented along with an English explanation of the axioms for Actors (*e.g.*, as presented in this paper).

Article 2-2. *Inconsistency Robustness for Logic Programs*[i]
This paper explores the role of Inconsistency Robustness in the history and theory of Logic Programs. Inconsistency Robustness has been a continually recurring issue in Logic Programs from the beginning including Church's system developed in the early 1930s based on *partial* functions (defined in the lambda calculus) that he thought would allow development of a general logic without the kind of paradoxes that had plagued earlier efforts by Frege, *etc.*[ii]

Planner [Hewitt 1969, 1971] was a kind of hybrid between the preceding procedural[iii] and logical paradigms[iv] in that it featured a procedural embedding of logical sentences using message passing in which an implication of the form (*p implies q*) can be procedurally embedded in the following ways:
   Forward chaining
   - **When asserted** *p*, **Assert** *q*
   - **When asserted** ¬*q*, **Assert** ¬*p*
   Backward chaining
   - **When goal** *q*, **SetGoal** *p*
   - **When goal** ¬*p*, **SetGoal** ¬*q*

Developments by different research groups in the fall of 1972 gave rise to a controversy over Logic Programs that persists to this day in the form of following alternatives:
1. A Logic Program is expressed using a *procedural interpretation of logic-clause syntax for a program*[40]
2. A Logic Program is expressed by *each computational step*[v] *being logically inferred.* [vi]

This article argues for the second alternative based on the following considerations:

---

[i] authored by Carl Hewitt
[ii] Unfortunately, Church's system was quickly shown to be inconsistent because it allowed Gödelian "self-referential" propositions. See article 1-2 in this volume.
[iii] epitomized by the programming language LISP
[iv] epitomized by uniform proof procedures using resolution theorem proving
[v] *e.g.* using the Actor Model of computation
[vi] *e.g.* using Direct Logic

- Programs in logic-clause syntax are a special case of the second alternative because each computational step of a program in logic-clause syntax is logically inferred as backward chaining or forward chaining.
- Reducing propositions to logic-clause syntax can obscure their natural structure.
- Procedural interpretation of logic-clause syntax can obscure the natural structure of proofs (*e.g.* Natural Deduction using Direct Logic).

Logic-clause syntax is far too limited to be of use for general Logic Programs.

Robert Kowalski advocates a bold thesis: "*Looking back on our early discoveries, I value most the discovery that computation could be subsumed by deduction.*" [41] However, mathematical logic cannot always infer computational steps because computational systems make use of arbitration for determining which message is processed next. Since reception orders are in general indeterminate, they cannot be inferred from prior information by mathematical logic alone. Therefore mathematical logic alone cannot in general implement computation. Logic Programs (like Functional Programs) are useful idioms even though they are not universal. For example Logic Programs can provide useful principles and methods for systems which are quasi-commutative and quasi-monotonic even though the systems themselves cannot be implemented using Logic Programs. Also, Logic Programs in ActorScript Note can use causal partial orders of events that do *not* make use of global[42] time.[i]

A Logic Program can be characterized using the Actor Model by the criterion that each computational step is logically inferred. [ii]

A fundamental principle of Inconsistency Robustness is to make contradictions explicit so that arguments for and against propositions can be formalized. In the Inconsistency Robustness paradigm, deriving contradictions is a progressive development and contradictions are not "game stoppers" that they would be using Classical Logic (in which reasoning about inconsistent information can make erroneous inferences). Contradictions can be helpful in information systems of practice instead of being something to be "swept under the rug" by denying their existence or fruitlessly attempting complete elimination.

Logic Programs are rigorously defined in this article based on a solid mathematical foundation of Direct Logic tracing their heritage back to Planner [Hewitt 1969, 1971]. On the other hand, Kowalski has for a long time advocated "*Logic Programming*"[43], which suffers many limitations including the following: [44]

---

[i] which is physically unrealizable
[ii] *e.g.* in Direct Logic

- Based on a mistaken assumption, namely, "*that logic subsumes computation*".
- Very limited and inexpressive notation for Logic Programs, namely, Horn clauses.[45]
- Incapable of inconsistency-robust inference because it is based on Classical Logic making use of resolution theorem proving.[46]
- As used by Kowalski, "Logic Programming" is a vague concept.[i]

Contradiction	Outcome
Kowalski advocates using resolution theorem proving to make inferences about inconsistent information systems. Unfortunately, using resolution theorem provers allows inferring every proposition from an inconsistent information system.	Using Direct Logic, inconsistent-robust inference allows inference about inconsistent information systems without enabling inference of every sentence.
Planner was intended to be a general purpose programming language for the procedural embedding of knowledge. Partly as a result of limitations of contemporary computers, pragmatic decisions were made in the implementation of Planner that limited its generality.	Programming languages (like ActorScript) have been developed that incorporate general Logic Programs.

---

[i] which could be fixed by defining the concept as "programming using Logic Programs."

Kowalski, *et. al.* advocate that Horn-clause syntax for procedures be used as the foundation of Logic Programs. But Horn-clause syntax for procedures (and slightly more general logic-clause syntax for procedures) lack the generality and modularity needed for Logic Programs.	Logic Program languages (like ActorScript) are not restricted to logic-clause syntax for Logic Programs.
The Japanese Fifth Generation Project (ICOT) attempted to create a new computer architecture based on logic-clause programs.	ICOT failed to gain commercial traction although it was an important research project.
Kowalski claims that mathematical logical deduction subsumes computation. However, there are computations that cannot be implemented using deduction (*i.e.* Logic Programs) and there are important applications that cannot be implemented using only Logic Programs.	Actor programming languages (like ActorScript) use direct message passing to Actors and are not restricted to just Logic Programs.
Previously, change was modeled in Logic Programs using a global time that is physically meaningless.	The Actor model enables change in computation to be modeled by causal partial orders of message-passing events.

Article 2-3. *ActorScript extension of C#, Java, Objective C, JavaScript, and SystemVerilog using iAdaptive concurrency for antiCloud privacy and security*[i]

ActorScript is a general purpose programming language for implementing iAdaptive concurrency that manages resources and demand. It is differentiated from previous languages by the following:
- Universality
    - Ability to directly specify exactly what Actors can and cannot do
    - Everything in the language is accomplished using message passing including the very definition of ActorScript itself. Messages can be directly communicated without requiring indirection through brokers, channels, class hierarchies, mailboxes, pipes, ports, queues *etc.*
    - Functional, Imperative, Logic, and Concurrent programming are integrated.

---

[i] authored by Carl Hewitt

- o Concurrency can be dynamically adapted to resources available and current load.
- o Programs do not expose low-level implementation mechanisms such as threads, tasks, locks, cores, *etc*.
- o A type in ActorScript is an interface that does not name its implementations (contra to object-oriented programming languages beginning with Simula that name implementations called "classes" that are types). XML, JSON, and Java and C++ objects are data types. ActorScript can send a message to anything for which it has an (imported) type.
- o Application binary interfaces are afforded so that no program symbol need be looked up at runtime.
- Safety, security and readability
  - o Programs are *extension invariant*, *i.e.*, extending a program does not change the meaning of the program that is extended.
  - o Applications cannot directly harm each other.
  - o Variable races are eliminated while allowing flexible concurrency.
  - o Lexical singleness of purpose. Each syntactic token is used for exactly one purpose.
- Performance
  - o Imposes no overhead on implementation of Actor systems in the sense that ActorScript programs are as efficient as the same implementation in machine code. For example, message passing has essentially same overhead as procedure calls and looping.
  - o Execution dynamically adjusted for system load and capacity (*e.g.* cores)
  - o Locality because execution is not bound by a sequential global memory model
  - o Inherent concurrency because execution is not limited by being restricted to communicating *sequential* processes
  - o Minimize latency along critical paths

ActorScript attempts to achieve the highest level of performance, scalability, and expressibility with a minimum of primitives.

Part 3. Applications[i]

Inconsistency Robustness aspires to be a field of wide applicability. Consequently, there must be numerous important applications.

Article 3-1. *Some Types of Inconsistency in Legal Reasoning*[ii]

---

[i] Article summaries for this part include extensive quotations from the articles.
[ii] authored by Anne Gardner

This article considers three kinds of inconsistency that may be encountered in the course of deciding a legal case: inconsistent findings of fact; inconsistent statutes; and inconsistent judicial opinions. The method is a case study. All the examples are drawn from a case in the United States Supreme Court on which the author worked for several years. The article identifies and explores the consequences of inconsistencies in robust information systems.

Information systems of practice have pervasive inconsistencies. Often practioners try to sweep inconsistencies under the rug. The article concludes that the law provides a better source of examples of this phenomenon than it does of solutions.

Article 3-2. *Rules versus Standards: Competing Notions of Inconsistency: Robustness in the Supreme Court and Federal Circuit*[i]

This article investigates inconsistency robustness phenomena in patent appeal litigation. It analyzes inconsistency robustness in the following:
- First the Federal Circuit attempts horizontal[ii] and vertical[iii] inconsistency reduction via the creation of bright-line rules.
- Second, the Supreme Court weighs in with a focus on reducing manifest error[iv] what it considers to be unsatisfactory outcomes, and reverses the bright-line rules.

Unfortunately, the pattern has determined idiosyncratic changes in key elements of patent law and, thus, has created possible significant uncertainty for innovators in fields such as online commerce and the software industry that are of great importance for the US economy.

There is a rich literature on the application of rules versus standards to legal questions. Rules provide predictability and consistency, while standards are less predictable but provide the opportunity for nuanced, contextual decision making. The Federal Circuit's understanding of its mandate as being focused, in part, on creating predictability through horizontal and vertical inconsistency reduction seems to have caused it to move toward bright-line rules and away from contextual standards. The result of the Federal Circuit's rules were that horizontal and vertical consistency were increased (which also increases predictability), but at the "cost" of increased manifest error in the form of more obvious patents being issued, the doctrine of equivalents being made unavailable for amended patent claims, and strict exclusions of some process patent claims. In a series of cases over the last six years, the Supreme Court has reversed each of the Federal Circuit's rules set forth above, and replaced them with more

---

[i] authored by Stefania Fusco and David Olson
[ii] horizontal inconsistencies arise from courts that are *not* subordinate to one another
[iii] vertical inconsistencies arise from courts that are subordinate to one another
[iv] manifest errors are lower court judgments with which the Supreme Court strongly disagrees

contextual standards intended to decrease manifest error but at the price of some predictability (increased horizontal and vertical inconsistency).

The article argues that the reason for this difference in tolerance of error versus inconsistencies can be found in the different role that the Federal Circuit and Supreme Court see themselves as playing. The Federal Circuit's understanding of its mandate to increase predictability in patent law, and its unique situation as the only circuit court hearing patent law cases, encourages the court to attempt nationwide inconsistency reduction by providing bright-line rules to the district courts. The Supreme Court is used to operating within the historic federal court system within which horizontal inconsistency among the circuit courts, and thus correspondingly, the district courts, is the norm. While part of the Supreme Court's mandate is to provide some horizontal and vertical consistency by settling disputed legal questions, it has neither the inclination nor the capacity to drive out anything near all of the horizontal inconsistency in the system. Thus, the Supreme Court has historically been comfortable with a large amount of vertical and horizontal inconsistency and has focused on crafting "correct" decisions as to particularly thorny or disputed legal questions. This difference in focus helps explain why the Supreme Court has repeatedly ruled against Federal Circuit's decisions that the Court considered to be manifest errors.

To make the best decisions on what rules should govern patent litigation issues, and to decrease the likelihood of continued reversals by the Supreme Court, the Federal Circuit should recognize the different way in which the Supreme Court approaches inconsistency robustness in the United States federal court system. Understanding that the Supreme Court is likely to focus more on manifest error than vertical and horizontal inconsistency can help the Federal Circuit predict when the Supreme Court is likely to overturn a legal rule crafted by the Federal Circuit.

At the same time, the Supreme Court would do well to remember that when it reverses patent appeals from the Federal Circuit, it is reversing not just the law in one geographic area of the United States, but rather is reversing the law nationwide. In evaluating the benefit of decreasing manifest error, the Supreme Court should remember that the cost is overturning a high degree of horizontal and vertical consistency that the Federal Circuit has established nationwide. The Supreme Court should contemplate giving some deference to the judgment of the Federal Circuit as to the importance of vertical and horizontal consistency versus error reduction in the realm of patent law. It may be that the Federal Circuit's greater experience day in and day out with patent cases and patent litigants gives the Federal Circuit particular expertise in judging how to balance the elimination and allowance of inconsistencies so as to arrive at the court system that best manages inconsistency robustness in service of the values of the legal system in the unique area of patent law.

Thus, there may be times when a properly nuanced vision of the inconsistency robustness paradigm with respect to the court system would encourage the Supreme Court to consider the costs in terms of inconsistency and predictability of correcting error in Federal Circuit opinions. It may be that at times the Federal Circuit's bright-line rules have greater benefits to society in terms of predictability and consistency of application than nuanced standards that allow for reducing manifest error at the cost of inconsistency and unpredictability.

Article 3-3. *Politics and Pragmatism in Scientific Ontology Construction*[i]
Some have maintained that a purpose of ontological representation is to represent the world accurately, objectively, and consistently. This paper argues that even in the domain of natural science, such an effort is misguided. Actual computational representations of scientific knowledge are deeply shaded by the motives of their designers, and these often come into conflict. The author argues for a looser, more polyvalent approach to knowledge representation, one that can capture both the richness of the world and the symbolic representations we construct to envision it.

Ontologies are supposed to define a common representational framework for a domain of knowledge, but in practice achieving "common" is not a simple task. It might seem that achieving mutual agreement about ontology ought to be an inevitable result of the structure of the world, but in practice it is often a laborious and contentious process, filled with argument, negotiations, compromise, power, and politics. Recent debates in the ontology community between "realists" and "conceptualists" hide the true nature of ontology building, and the article examines philosophical pragmatism as an alternate approach. One of the roots of the pragmatic approach is to look at ontologies as a social product, with an attention to how they are constructed, promulgated, and used. The article looks at some examples of the sociology of ontology from his personal work experience building knowledge-based systems for scientists. One of the lessons learned is that ontologies in practice are influenced by a whole variety of factors other than pure logic, such as cost of implementation, the relative status of particular users, and user interface design. The pragmatic view says that rather than bemoan these impurities, or marginalizing them, we should explicitly acknowledge and make use of them.

Representations of reality that are in some sense objective are what science does best, but objectivity is a destination, an end-goal of science. Scientists in practice use representations that are local, subjective, and subject to the pull of conflicting interest. So, computationalists need to acknowledge the way representations are actually used, by scientists and others, and adjust our tools to enable them to be used better. If computational systems are to support the process of science they

---

[i] authored by Mike Travers

must take this into account, and in addition to being repositories of finished knowledge, allow tentative and conflicting "pre-knowledge" to be represented, shared, and processed.

Science is almost defined by its values of open publication of results. Science invented open knowledge centuries before the web existed, but now there is a movement to get science to utilize the tools of the web to share knowledge with greater speed and flexibility than it has been able to do in the past. Such efforts involve any or all of: standard representations for data, public repositories for data (e.g., Geo) and workflows, open access publications like the Public Library of Science (PLoS), and their convergence in web-scale science.

The movement for Open Notebook Science aims to make these representations more public, promising a more collaborative, accelerated, and open form of scientific knowledge management than the traditional publishing models. But such efforts are likely to founder without some kind of shared basis of representation. Between the private, radically situated scribblings in individual lab notebooks and the crystalline, formal, supposedly objective status of realist ontologies lies a vast space of possible representational schemes and practices to be explored.

The fact that ontologies, like anything else, are subject to conflicting social forces should not come as a surprise. Nor should it be something that is swept under the rug. Ontologists are trying to put this process on a sounder footing, but it seems to me they are going about it in the wrong way. There is a vast and largely unexplored design space in between pure chaos and rigid formalism.

Article 3-4. *Sentence Composition in EPGY's Language Arts and Writing Course*[i]

This article addresses issues of natural language parsing. Computational linguists who develop grammar implementations often begin with the motivation to encode their hypotheses about the particular structures and the general principles which illuminate the analysis of a given language. Often these hypotheses are tested either on naturally occurring text corpora, or on systematically constructed test suites illustrating the range of linguistic phenomena under study, including both well-formed and ill-formed example sentences. Since many applications that make use of grammar implementations emphasize robustness of analysis over precision, it is nice for the grammarian to encounter an application where precision is demanded.

Article 3-5. *The Singularity is Here*[ii]

This article investigates inconsistency robustness in software development.

---

[i] authored by Dan Flickinger
[ii] authored by Fanya S. Montalvo

The article presents aspects of a current crisis in software and argues that business as usual is not going to cut it. It reviews Kurzweil's Singularity and distinguish two aspects: computers becoming super intelligent, and humans losing control. There are signs that humans are losing control but without computers becoming intelligent enough for us to feel comfortable with them having control. The article shows how Kurzweil's predictions are measuring the wrong thing. It presents a possible way to improve our software systems that Kurzweil's Singularity measurements do not take into account, that is, organizational abstraction. To have a chance of succeeding in the current software crisis, we need systems that can embody organizational abstraction. The article introduces types of organizational abstraction that may help.

Article 3-6. *Biological responses to chemical exposure: Case studies in how to manage ostensible inconsistencies using the Claim Framework*[i]

This article investigates inconsistency robustness in analyzing biological responses to chemical exposure.

Biological responses to chemical exposure play an important role in human health. Government agencies such as the FDA and EPA use the results reported in scientific literature to determine if there is an association between individual chemicals and harmful responses and if such an association exists, they work with law-makers to establish limits to protect human health. In addition, our daily decisions about foods, drugs and substances to consume also have a direct impact on our chemical exposure.

The article presents a bottom-up approach to identifying claims from scientific articles that assumes that there exists a sub-language that scientists use to convey their experimental results. The Claim Framework employs four information facets (agent, object, change and dimension) that are pieced together to form five different claim types (explicit, implicit, comparison, correlation and observation) to capture results. In contrast to systems that first identify entities and then try to find relationships that include those entities, the article focuses first on the claim type, and leave noun phrase unification to latter steps of the process. This late binding approach is well suited for scientific literature where new factors are established with each new experiment. Moreover, maintaining fidelity to the original terms used from an article (or at the very least mapping back to the original terms) is a critical component of this approach, in much the same way that risk assessment in toxicology and meta-analyses in medicine must cite the exact text and maintain the link back to the original source document.

The case studies from toxicology, medicine, and epidemiology presented in this paper illustrate how the claim framework can accurately reflect the information

---

[i] authored by Catherine Blake

necessary to remove ostensible inconsistencies when working with biological responses to chemical exposure. Much work remains to be done with respect to unifying noun phrases (in particular new kinds of anaphoric references), but systems that employ the claim framework will be able to foreground the factors that influence biological responses to chemical exposure. More importantly, such systems could identify areas where inconsistencies are not explained. These edges of scientific knowledge are precisely the areas in which both scientists and policy makers should focus.

Article 3-7. *From Inter-Annotation to Intra-Publication Inconsistency*[i]
This article investigates inconsistency robustness in statistical analyses of health information.

Curing chronic illnesses and diseases requires the huge effort of collecting all available information on this matter and piecing it together with the aid of mathematical and computer modeling. Both phases of information collection and piecing together are prone to error. Errors may result from human annotation inconsistency, machine learning and parameterization when using supervised learning. On a different scale, published results that need to be collected may suffer from another kind of disagreement either due to varying experimental methodologies or assumptions. The article discusses these inconsistencies and disagreements in scientific literature and investigates those of the inter-annotation of named entities in bioliterature from empirical perspectives.

Illustrative Issues
Inconsistencies are pervasive throughout our information infrastructures and they affect one another. Consequently, an interdisciplinary approach is needed.

---

[i] authored by Alaa Abi Haidar, Mihnea Tufiş, and Jean-Gabriel Ganascia

For example, (in no particular order):
- What will be the effects of increasing greenhouse gasses?[47]
- What is the future of mass cyber surveillance?[i] Is Edward Snowden a whistleblower?[48]
- What are effective ways to help prevent and treat chronic illness (*e.g.*, metabolic syndrome, heart disease, *etc.*), given that the solution requires large-scale behavioral change? Of course, information about issues of large-scale behavioral change is pervasively inconsistent.
- Addiction is a huge health problem in which inconsistencies abound. For example, Step 1 in Twelve Step programs of recovery is that addicts admit that they are powerless over their addiction. How can admitting powerlessness facilitate recovery? Is highly processed food[ii] addictive.
- What are the limitations in the ability of a many-core computer software system to measure and diagnose its own performance in real time?
- How to deal with the strategic inconsistency between the following
  - classical microeconomics (*i.e.* individual economic transactions) often lead to generally desirable outcomes)
  - real macroeconomics (i.e. fraud, externalities, monetary instabilities, etc.) require government regulation
- In teaching situations (e.g. with infants, avatars, or robots), how does a teacher realize that they need to help correct a learner and how does a learner realize what correction is needed?
- Is freedom from mass surveillance inconsistent with preventing terrorism?
- How do appellate courts deal with inconsistent decisions of lower courts?[iii] How do courts attempt to maintain consistency of their own decisions over time?[iv]
- If interlocutors in the same organization hold inconsistent positions, how do they negotiate? If the interlocutors are in separate organizations with overlapping concerns, how are the negotiations different?
- Is the existence of an observer-independent objective view of reality inconsistent with the laws of physics?[v]
- How can regulation and government support and facilitate innovation?
- What are foundations for robust reasoning in pervasively inconsistent theories?[vi]
- Does the human brain mediate inconsistencies among its constituent parts?

---

[i] See description of Panel on "Inconsistency Robustness in Cyberspace Security and Privacy" in this preface.
[ii] *e.g.*, sugar
[iii] See article 3-1 in this volume.
[iv] See article 3-2 in this volume.
[v] See "Interaction creates reality" in article 1-1 of this volume.
[vi] See article 1-1 in this volume.

- What are inconsistencies between *Elites* and larger *Communities* of which they are part. How are these conflicts processed? [49]
- Computational linguistics relies on human-annotated data to train machine learners. Inconsistency among the human annotators must be carefully managed (otherwise, the annotations are useless in computation). How can this annotation process be made scalable?[i]

In each case, inconsistencies need to be precisely identified and their consequences explored.

Panel Discussions
Panel discussions were held at IR'14 addressing important issues that are summarized below.

Panel on "Inconsistency Robustness in Cyberspace Security and Privacy"
This panel highlighted inconsistencies[ii] in current issues in Internet of Things (IoT) security and privacy grounded in an ongoing saga including the following hypotheses about the future and recent events:

- **Cyberspace is broken**
  Cyberspace has become an instrument of universal mass surveillance and intrusion[50] threatening everyone's creativity and freedom of expression.[51] Intelligence services gobble most of the world's long-distance communications traffic[52] and can break into almost any cell phone, personal computer, and datacenter to steal information [53], thereby causing the dangerous development that the most powerful nations are intensely preparing for pre-emptive massive cyberwar.[54] Failure to secure endpoints (cell phones, computers, and data centers) has turned cyberspace into a war zone with continual (although often unpublicized) attacks.[55]
  According to [Harris 2014]:[56]
  > The US is one of a handful of countries whose stated policy is to dominate cyberspace as a battlefield and has the means to do it. ... **In its zeal, .. the [US] government is making it [cyberspace] more vulnerable.** ...
  > Senior military and Pentagon leaders are convinced that if a cyberwar ever did break out, it would happen at the speed of light with practically no warning.[iii] Whenever they testify before Congress or give press interviews, they warn about the

---

[i] See article 3-4 in this volume.
[ii] as opposed the very different approach of attempting to come to a balanced consensus view
[iii] "*In a response cycle of seconds to minutes, this* [requiring Presidential approval for offensive attacks] *could come with a severe cost and could even obviate any*

instantly devastating nature of cyberwarfare. ... **The US has to prepare for the inevitability of this conflict and to take extraordinary measures to strength its forces for defense and offense.**

According in a PBS interview of Ed Snowden by James Bamford:[57]

Bamford: Another thing that the public doesn't really have any concept of, I think at this point, is how organized this whole Cyber Command is, and how aggressive it is. People don't realize there's a Cyber Army now, a Cyber Air Force, a Cyber Navy. And the fact that the models for some of these organizations like the Cyber Navy are things like we will dominate the cyberspace the same way we dominate the sea or the same way that we dominate land and the same way we dominate space. So it's this whole idea of creating an enormous military just for cyber warfare, and then using this whole idea of we're going to dominate cyberspace, just like it's the navies of centuries ago dominating the seas.

Snowden: Right. The reason they say that they want to dominate cyberspace is because it's politically incorrect to say you want to dominate the internet. Again, it's sort of a branding effort to get them the support they need, because we the public don't want to authorize the internet to become a battleground. We need to do everything we can as a society to keep that a neutral zone, to keep that an economic zone that can reflect our values, both politically, socially, and economically. The internet should be a force for freedom. The internet should not be a tool for war. And for us, the United States, a champion of freedom, to be funding and encouraging the subversion of a tool for good to be a tool used for destructive ends is, I think, contrary to the principles of us as a society. ...

Every time we walk on to the field of battle and the field of battle is the internet, it doesn't matter if we shoot our opponents a hundred times and hit every time. As long as they've hit us once, we've lost, because we're so much more reliant on those systems. And because of that, **we need to be focusing more on creating a more secure, more reliable, more robust, and more trusted internet, not one that's weaker, not one that relies on this systemic model of exploiting every vulnerability, every threat out there.** Every time somebody on the internet sort of glances at us sideways, we launch an attack at them. That's not going to work

---

meaningful action." [Congressional testimony of US CYBERCOM commander Mike Rogers on March 4, 2015] Unfortunately, because botnets can be implanted undetected in any country, it can be very difficult in the early stages to know with certainty whom to counterattack.

out for us long term, and we have to get ahead of the problem if we're going to succeed.[58]

Creating **secure endpoints** with **universal use of public key cryptography** can reduce the danger of massive pre-emptive cyberwar and make mass seizure of the content of citizens' private information infeasible even for intelligence agencies of the most powerful countries..[59]

- **Multiple authentication services**, incorporated in different countries can publish independent directories of public keys that can be cross referenced with other personal and corporate directories.
- Hardware (that can be verified by independent parties to operate exactly according to formal specifications) has been developed that can prevent mass intrusions using the following two methods:
    i. **Encryption of traffic between processor packages and RAM** can protect applications from operating systems and hypervisors which cannot read the memory of applications, meaning that the worst they can do is a denial of service and
    ii. Using an **every-word-tagged architecture**[60] can protect an Actor from other Actors in the same application.[61]
- Security can be further increased by using interactive biometrics for continuous authentication[62] instead of passwords and using interactive incremental revelation of information so that large amounts of information cannot be stolen in one go.

Implementation of the above can make mass intrusions infeasible even for the largest intelligence agencies in the most powerful countries.

- **Mass surveillance has been used as an instrument of economic and political oppression, increased terror in the populace, and stifled creativity**. Surveillance and remote attacks via the Internet of Things (IoT) are almost universal, whether by nation states, corporations, or others. Whistleblowers[63] are persecuted everywhere. Reporters who refuse to reveal their sources are being jailed. Journalists and publishers have been subject to government surveillance in their purely investigative and reporting activities. According to John Napier [former US State Department democracy official]:

> "**Based in part on classified facts that I am prohibited by law from publishing, I believe that Americans should be ... concerned about the collection and storage of their communications** [that] **does not require that the affected U.S. persons be suspected of wrongdoing and places no limits on the volume of communications by U.S. persons that may be collected and retained.**"[64]

According to Glennon:[65]

Following the US Senate committee investigation into domestic spying by the U.S. intelligence community, Committee Chairman Frank Church made a prophetic statement: "[The NSA's] **capability at any time could be turned around on the American people, and no American would have** any privacy left, such [is] the capability to monitor everything: telephone conversations, telegrams, it doesn't matter." There is, Church said, "tremendous potential for abuse" should the NSA "**turn its awesome technology against domestic communications.**"

He [Church] added:

> I don't want to see this country ever go across the bridge. I know the capacity that is there to make tyranny total in America, and we must see to it that this agency [NSA] and all agencies that possess this technology operate within the law and under proper supervision, so that we never cross over that abyss. That is the abyss from which there is no return.

- **Law enforcement can be effective without mass intrusion on consumer devices.** Cell tower tracking, automobile tracking, IP address use, ubiquitous video tracking (including drones) using facial recognition in public places can enable law enforcement.
- **Leakers to the press have been dealt long prison sentences based on the justification that leaking to the press is espionage for a foreign power.** These leakers have not been allowed to raise whistleblower defenses at their trials.
- **The US government threatened[66] NY Times reporter James Risen[67] with imprisonment for not revealing his sources[68] caused by "the menacing attempt by the Obama administration to threaten and intimidate whistleblowers, journalists and activists who meaningfully challenge what the government does in secret".[69]** According to Risen:[70]

> I believe that the investigation that led to this prosecution started because of my reporting on the National Security Agency's warrantless wiretapping program. The Bush White House was furious over that story. I believe that this investigation started as part of an effort by the Bush Administration to punish me and silence me, following the publication of the NSA wiretapping story. I was told by a reliable source that **Vice President Dick Cheney pressured the Justice Department to personally target me because he was unhappy with my reporting and wanted to see me in jail.** ...
>
> I believe that the efforts to target me have continued under the Obama Administration, which has been aggressively investigating whistleblowers and reporters in a way that will have **a chilling effect on the freedom of the press in the United States.**

According to Shane Harris,[71]
> The Obama administration has been historically hostile to govenment employees who share information with journalists. ... **Simply put, it is dangerous time to talk to journalists.**
>
> And this risk extends to former government employees and military personnel. Several former intelligence officials have told me that within the past year, they were explicitly told by the intelligence agencies where they are still employed as contractors that they should stop talking to journalists if they want to continue doing business with the government.

- The Fourth Amendment of the US Constitution states:
  The right of the people to be secure in their persons, houses, papers, and effects, against unreasonable searches and seizures, shall not be violated, and no warrants shall issue, but upon probable cause, supported by oath or affirmation, and particularly describing the place to be searched, and the persons or things to be seized.

- US companies face diminished foreign business prospects because US claims jurisdiction (in secret using gag orders) over foreign operations of US companies. CEOs of major tech companies have complained loudly about how NSA surveillance has been ruining their business. **Facebook founder and CEO Mark Zuckerberg recently called the US a *"threat"* to the Internet, and Google Board Chair Eric Schmidt called some of the NSA tactics *"outrageous"* and potentially *"illegal"*.** Governments can issue (unexplained) gag orders to Internet companies that they surrender their encryption keys and any other data they possess both domestically and in other countries. "It [concern over the Snowden revelations] is not blowing over," said Microsoft General Counsel Brad Smith, adding **"In June of 2014, it is clear it is getting worse, not better."** [emphasis added]

  According to Perlroth:[72]
  > **If the tech sector cannot persuade foreign customers that their data is safe from the National Security Agency, the tech industry analysis firm Forrester Research[73] predicts that America's cloud computing industry stands to lose $180 billion — a quarter of its current revenue — over the next two years to competitors abroad.**

  According to PC Week:[74]
  > If U.S. law enforcement agencies demand access, so will other governments, said Greg Nojeim, senior counsel at digital rights group the Center for Democracy and Technology.
  >
  > **"If you're Apple, or you're selling Androids, you can't sell an NSA/FBI-ready phone in Europe**," he said. "Are you expecting them to build two kinds of iPhones, two kinds of Android phones? Are they going to have to build three or four or six kinds when other countries follow our lead?"

Comey said he hasn't thought through all the international implications. "I can imagine them saying, '**we as an American domiciled corporation, will comply with ... requests from the U.S. government** in connection with lawful investigations,'" he said. "Where we may get is to a place where the **U.S., through its Congress says, 'we need to force this on American companies,' and maybe they will take a hit**."

- **Governments are preparing military forces for devastating massive pre-emptive cyberwar attacks that can be delivered without prior detection.** Retaliation against cyberattacks is often challenged by not being certain of the identity of attacker(s). Greater endpoint security could mitigate the dangers of such attacks by reducing botnets and persistent viruses.
- FBI Director James Comey[75] has proposed that US companies be compelled to install worldwide a backdoor in every cell phone, personal computer and any other product or service in order that the **US government can break in undetected** with the approval of US courts.[76] Such backdoors can have the following effects:[77]
  - *Increased insecurity*. **Backdoors can increase the danger of massive pre-emptive cyberwar.**
  - *Decreased competitiveness of US information technology industry*. **Backdoors can increase mistrust in products and services of US companies.**
  - *Decreased creativity and freedom of expression*. **Backdoors can enable undetected massive surveillance.**

  According to James Risen,
  > It is difficult to recognize the limits a society places on accepted thought at the time it is doing it. When everyone accepts basic assumptions, there don't seem to be constraints on ideas. That truth often only reveals itself in hindsight. Today, the basic prerequisite to being taken seriously in American politics is to accept the legitimacy of the new national security state. **The new basic American assumption is that there really is a need for a global war on terror. Anyone who doesn't accept that basic assumption is considered dangerous and maybe even a traitor.** The crackdown on leaks by the Obama administration has been designed to suppress the truth about the war on terror. Stay on the interstate highway of conventional wisdom with your journalism, and you will have no problems. Try to get off and challenge basic assumptions, and you will face punishment.[78]
- According to Hoofnagle:
  > "**Once they've identified you, they can track you on basically the entire web, even if you do not use Google tools. Google Analytics, DoubleClick, etc., are basically on all popular sites**."[79]

  Almost all consumers have Internet services (e.g. Internet search, email, etc.) paid by exploiting (and even selling) their personal information and

attention. Unlike credit information, personal information held by Internet service companies does not have to be revealed to consumers. In *"Why we fear Google"*, Axel Springer CEO Mathias Döpfner recently declared,
> "Nobody knows as much about its [users] as Google. Even private or business emails are read by Gmail [using arbitrary server programs without legal restriction. Google's official position is that users "**have no legitimate expectation of privacy**"] of their Gmail messages. You [Eric Schmidt] yourself said in 2010**: 'We [Google] know where you [Google users] are [and] where you've been. We can more or less know what you're thinking about.' Are users happy with the fact that this information ... [can] end up in the hands of [government] intelligence services ...?"** [emphasis added]

According to Public Citizen's Congress Watch:[80]
> **With so much personal information collected in one place, Google has become a gold mine for intelligence agencies, such as the National Security Agency (NSA), to which Google has both wittingly and unwittingly provided huge amounts of information about Americans. Google is required to comply with most requests for information from intelligence agencies, so the more information it collects, the more information the government can access. Although Google claims that its information troves are primarily viewed only by computer systems, some employees do have access to private information, and at least one has used this information improperly. Hackers also target personal information contained on Google's servers. ...**
>
> **Some number of Google employees have unfettered access to all kinds of personal information most users might not expect could be viewed by humans. In July 2010, Google fired an engineer who was caught looking at the personal information of four underage teens, potentially among unknown others. In his position as a Site Reliability Engineer, the employee had access to the company's most sensitive data, including users' e-mails, contact lists, chat transcripts, Google Voice call logs and more. ...**

According to Christopher Soghoian, currently principal technologist and a senior policy analyst of the American Civil Liberties Union's Privacy and Technology Project:

> **"It's just that their [Google's] business model is in conflict with your privacy."**

In response, Vince Cerf, who is Vice President and "Chief Internet Evangelist" of Google ... said,

> "I think you're quite right, however, that we couldn't run our system if everything in it were encrypted because then we wouldn't know which ads to show you. So this is a system that was designed around a particular business model."

According to ACLU:

> **If you keep data for purposes of data mining and analytics, there's nothing you can do to stop [it] when the government comes and asks for it later. And so companies have to choose – they have to choose privacy, or the business model ... Google has chosen keeping and monetizing and mining user data, over privacy.**[81]

Sir Martin Sorrell, CEO WPP (the world's largest advertising company) recently declared:

> **People understate the importance of Snowden and NSA.** [They] underestimate the impact on consumers…We have been removing third-party networks for our sites, those ads are also data-gathering mechanisms. We want to be more respectful of privacy and also want to monetise our audiences our way. **Being more focused on privacy is not bad for business, it can be good.** [emphases added]

According to Apple CEO Tim Cook:

> **A few years ago, users of Internet services began to realize that when an online service is free, you're not the customer. You're the product ... Our business model is very straightforward: We sell great products. We don't build a profile based on your e-mail content or Web browsing habits to sell to advertisers. We don't 'monetize' the information you store on your iPhone or in iCloud. And we don't read your e-mail or your messages to get information to market to you.**[82]

The following are recommend to better understand consequences of massive surveillance:
- Anna Funder. *Stasiland: Stories from Behind the Berlin Wall*. Harper. 2011.
- *The Lives of Others*. DVD video. Sony Pictures. With Ulrich Mühe and Martina Gedeck. 2007.:
- Nick Davies. *Hack Attack: The Inside Story of How the Truth Caught Up with Rupert Murdoch*. Faber & Faber. 2014.
- *The Last Enemy*. DVD video. WGBH PBS. With Benedict Cumberbatch. 2009.
- George Orwell. *1984* Signet. 1948. DVD video. With John Hurt and Richard Burton. 2009.

DataCenterism is a system in which *all* electronic information is accessible[i] in datacenters.

In due course, governments will obtain[ii] bulk access to all information in datacenters with pipes to government surveillance datacenters in order to speed and coordinate government security efforts.

Consequently, DataCenterism inevitably leads to the following:
CyberTotalism is a system in which all electronic information is accessible in datacenters under regulations that allow *total access* by the government.

To facilitate efficiency in security operations, governments will compel businesses to use information mining tools in their datacenters for security purposes[iii] thereby making their engineers and executive *increasing complicit in mass surveillance*. Furthermore, businesses will be harmed by the following developments:
- inability to change datacenter operations because it would disrupt government surveillance[83]
- uniformization of datacenter operations across companies because of government requirements for standardized surveillance operations across companies.[iv]

---

[i] Of course, encrypted information is not accessible unless the corresponding decryption key is accessible.
[ii] perhaps after further terror attacks
[iii] perhaps with some direct costs reimbursed by the government
[iv] to the competitive disadvantage of the companies

Fortunately, there is an alternative to CyberTotalism as follows:
CyberLocalism is a system in which a *citizen's Internet of Things (IoT)* **information is stored locally**[i] **in their own equipment**[ii] – *the antithesis of CyberTotalism.*
A local information system [iii] can hold the most sensitive [iv] of a citizen's information where it can be coordinated with other sensitive information as well as information from the following:
- the citizen's Internet of Things (IoT)
- other citizens
- datacenters.

Inconsistency-robust information systems can be used facilitate new business implementations that are made more *efficient, pervasive,* and *profitable* by improving interactions among consumers[v] and businesses.[vi]

However, there is a currently unmet requirement as follows:
CyberLocalism requires greater security of citizens' Internet of Things (IoT) devices.[vii]

---

[i] Typically local information will also be backed up elsewhere automatically encrypted using the citizen's private keys, *e.g.*, in commercial datacenters and distributed on other citizens' equipment.

Also, a citizen can share selected information automatically encrypted with the public keys of other parties.

[ii] Of course, local operations on citizens' equipment (cellphones, home computers, personal computers, and their Internet of Things) will incorporate access to the Internet to provide scalable search, retrieval, and collaboration using commercial datacenters in cooperation with other citizens' equipment.

[iii] embedded in home modems, routers, gateways, large screen displays, audiovisual systems, computers, refrigerators, stoves, climate control systems, washer/dryers, *etc.*

[iv] *sensitive information* is nonpublic information whose revelation can potentially harm a citizen, *e.g.*, medical (including psychiatric), legal, financial, sexual, political, religious, *etc.*

[v] Consumers will no longer be continually hassled by *intrusive unwanted* advertisements. Instead, mediation systems running on their own equipment will provide the ability to seek and help evaluate appropriate offers for their purchases, e.g., from commerce agents.

[vi] Businesses will no longer be burdened by having to pay for *grossly inefficient* advertising that annoys potential customers. Instead, businesses will provide their information to commerce agents that will aggregate and package it for citizens' equipment to be used by their systems in evaluating offers.

[vii] Currently, state-sponsored intruders can hack into almost every citizen's personal cellphone, computer, tablet, television, *etc.* on the Internet. The

In order to be successful CyberLocalism needs the following:
- ***RAM-processor package encryption*** to protect an app [i] from operating environments and other apps
- ***Every-word-tagged architecture*** to protect an Actor in an app from other Actors

However, there are still some unresolved issues:
Backdoors[ii] are among the greatest threats to CyberLocalism.

On March 2, 2015, President Obama denounced a government attempt to require backdoors in companies' products[84] saying
> "*As you might imagine tech companies are not going to be willing to do that... I don't think there is any U.S. or European firm, any international firm, that could credibly get away with that wholesale turning over of data, personal data, over to a government.*"[85]

The threat of mandatory backdoors can be mitigated as follows:
If the US adopts auditing against backdoors[86], then *the practice will rapidly spread to the rest of the world*, which is very much in the *long-term security interests of the US.*[87]
However, FBI Director James Comey[88] and NSA Director Mike Rogers[89] have proposed[90] that CALEA[91] be expanded so that US companies will be compelled to install a hardware backdoor in every cell phone, personal computer and other network-enabled products and services in order that the US government can hack in undetected with the approval of US courts.[92]

Rogers clamed: "*I think that we're lying that this* [mandatory backdoors] *isn't technically feasible.*"[93] Control of encryption keys for backdoors[94] would require a system similar to the ones currently used in command, control, and communication systems for nuclear weapons, which have had many problems.[95] Adopting the NSA/FBI backdoor proposal will have the following effects:[96]

---

current default security strategy has not worked, namely, "*beating up on personnel to improve security until the public outcry subsides.*"

[i] An *app* is a user application, which is technically a process.

[ii] A *backdoor* is means by which a cyber device can provide information and control about the users of a device
- to parties that were not specifically enumerated
- concerning kinds of information and control that were not specifically described
- that was not specifically authorized by users of the device.

1) Increase the danger of preemptive cyberwar because of potential vulnerabilities in the government's backdoor implementation.[97]
2) Decrease the competitiveness of US manufacturers in the market of the Internet of Things (IoT), which will include almost *everything*.
3) Tremendously increase the power of government security monitors

In fact, the NSA/FBI backdoor proposal has *already*[i] increased mistrust by foreign governments and citizens alike, with the following consequences:
- **Future exports of U.S. companies will need to be certified by corporate officers and independently audited not to have backdoors available to the U.S. government.**[98]
- **A key issue is whether companies will hire their own independent cyberauditors or submit to cyberaudits by foreign governments.**[99]

A new IoT Security Commission (ISC) needs to be established as follows:
- *Jurisdiction*: ISC will have jurisdiction over all US providers of IoT equipment and services. **The hardware of every type of IoT device will be required to be audited using inconsistency-robust operational bi-simulation**[i] **against a publicly available operational specification.**[i]
- *Quarterly Corporate Security Report*: ISC will enforce that at end of each quarter, a corporate security report must be signed by the corporate officers of a covered company, which must specify either
  i. no evidence was found for the existence of a backdoor was found in any of the company's products or that
  ii. evidence that was found for the existence of backdoors and the measures that were taken to remove backdoors from any products that were shipped and to prevent re-occurrence.
- *Oversight*: ISC will provide independent oversight of public security accounting firms providing cyberaudit services ("*cyberauditors*") as follows:
  o registering cyberauditors
  o defining the specific processes and procedures for compliance cyberaudits
  o inspecting and policing cyberaudit conduct and quality control
  o restricting cyberauditing companies from providing non-audit services (*e.g.*, consulting) for the same clients.
  o enforcing compliance with specific legal mandates, *e.g.*, the use of RAM-processor encryption and every-word-tagged architectures.

Conclusions:

---

[i] It is well known that the government has ways to coerce US companies to perform surveillance even absent new legislation to expand CALEA.

- If the US adopts mandatory backdoors, then *each country will have its own backdoors* and *massive pervasive surveillance will become the norm*.
- Installing backdoors can assist cyberterrorists[100] in the following ways:
    - controlling, modifying, and otherwise operating citizens' Internet of Things (IoT)
    - stealing citizens' sensitive information.

What *precise* contradictions (including goals, norms, and values) are contained in the above information? How can they be rigorously stated? A *very* long-term goal is for computer systems to have a formal understanding of these contradictions.

Panelists: Carl Hewitt, iRobust
Karl Levitt, UC Davis
Peter Neumann, SRI
John C. Mallery, MIT

Panel on "Inconsistency Robustness in Medical Informatics"
This panel discussed current issues in inconsistency robustness for medical informatics grounded in an ongoing saga including processing inconsistencies in the following issues:
- How can mobile computing deal with inconsistent information in managing chronic illness, e.g., addiction, diabetes, heart disease, etc.
- How can mobile computing foster lifestyle change for preventing and managing chronic illness[i] by providing improved social interactions[ii] and information technology.
- Lustig explained how **processed food[iii] is an imminent threat to world health**. Internal conflicts in human physiology make it impossible for almost everyone to diet successfully.[101]
- Ioannidis claimed that "**most published medical research findings are false**"?[102] How should medical studies of mobile computing for health be designed, conducted, and evaluated?
- How can recent advances in inconsistency-robust inference be applied to medical statistical information including the design, interpretation, and analysis of medical studies?
- How are lesions described and reported using inconsistent terminology and how does these inconsistencies thwart meaningful reuse of quantitative imaging data?

---

[i] addiction, diabetes, heart disease, *etc.*
[ii] with relatives, friends, medical professionals, *etc.*
[iii] and attendant sugar addiction

Panelists:
> Carl Hewitt, iRobust
> John-Jules Meyer, Information and Computing Sciences, Utrecht
> Daniel Rubin, Department of Radiology, Stanford University
> Laura Schmidt, Departments Of Health Policy Studies, UCSF
> Yao Sun, Director of neonatal ICU at UCSF Children's Hospital

Organizers:
> John-Jules Meyer, Information and Computing Sciences, Utrecht
> Mark Musen, Biomedical Informatics Research, Stanford University
> Mor Peleg, Department of Information Systems, University of Haifa

This panel discussed current issues in inconsistency robustness for medical informatics grounded in an ongoing saga including processing inconsistencies in the following issues:
- How can mobile computing deal with inconsistent information in managing chronic illness, e.g., addiction, diabetes, heart disease, etc.
- How can mobile computing foster lifestyle change for preventing and managing chronic illness[i] by providing improved social interactions[ii] and information technology.
- Lustig explained how **processed food[iii] is an imminent threat to world health**. Internal conflicts in human physiology make it impossible for almost everyone to diet successfully.[103]
- Ioannidis claimed that *"***most published medical research findings are false***"*[104] How should medical studies of mobile computing for health be designed, conducted, and evaluated?
- How can recent advances in inconsistency-robust inference be applied to medical statistical information including the design, interpretation, and analysis of medical studies?
- How are lesions described and reported using inconsistent terminology and how does these inconsistencies thwart meaningful reuse of quantitative imaging data?

---
[i] addiction, diabetes, heart disease, *etc.*
[ii] with relatives, friends, medical professionals, *etc.*
[iii] and attendant sugar addiction

Panelists:
> Carl Hewitt, iRobust
> John-Jules Meyer, Information and Computing Sciences, Utrecht
> Daniel Rubin, Department of Radiology, Stanford University
> Laura Schmidt, Departments Of Health Policy Studies, UCSF
> Yao Sun, Director of neonatal ICU at UCSF Children's Hospital

Organizers:
> John-Jules Meyer, Information and Computing Sciences, Utrecht
> Mark Musen, Biomedical Informatics Research, Stanford University
> Mor Peleg, Department of Information Systems, University of Haifa

Panel on "Inconsistency Robustness in Foundations of Mathematics"
This panel discussed current issues in the history and practice of avoiding and repairing inconsistency in powerful mathematical systems grounded in an ongoing saga including the following:
- Perhaps the first foundational crises was due to Hippasus "for having produced an element in the universe which denied the...doctrine that all phenomena in the universe can be reduced to whole numbers and their ratios." Legend has it because he wouldn't recant, Hippasus was literally thrown overboard to drown by his fellow Pythagoreans.
- Frege expressed despair that his life work had been in vain when he received Russell's letter with its revelation of the paradoxical set of all sets that are not members of themselves.
- According to Church:
  "in the case of any system of symbolic logic, the set of all provable theorems is [computationally] enumerable... any system of symbolic logic not hopelessly inadequate ... would contain the formal theorem that this same system ... was either insufficient [theorems are not computationally enumerable] or over-sufficient [that theorems are computationally enumerable means that the system is inconsistent]...This, of course, is a deplorable state of affairs... Indeed, if there is no formalization of logic as a whole, then there is no exact description of what logic is, for it in the very nature of an exact description that it implies a formalization. And if there no exact description of logic, then there is no sound basis for supposing that there is such a thing as logic."
  What is the way out of this fundamental paradox?
- Scott claimed that "there is only one satisfactory way of avoiding the paradoxes: namely, the use of some form of the theory of types."[105] But exactly which theory of types should be used? Russell's ramified theory of types is generally regarded to be a failure.
- Article 1-2 in this volume challenges the validity of one of the most famous results of mathematical logic: namely, Gödel's result that mathematics cannot prove its own consistency. Currently there is an

overwhelming consensus among professional working logicians that Gödel proved that mathematics cannot prove its own consistency if mathematics is consistent. But could they be wrong?

Was Wittgenstein, after all, correct that Gödel's proof is erroneous because inconsistency results from allowing self-referential sentences constructed using fixed points for an untyped notation of mathematical sentences?

In each of the above cases, means were devised to avoid known inconsistencies while increasing mathematical power. What lessons can be drawn and how should they affect practice?

Participants:
　　Carl Hewitt, iRobust
　　Eric Kao, Stanford CS
　　John-Jules Meyer, Information and Computing Sciences, Utrecht
　　Peter Neumann, SRI
　　John C. Mallery, MIT

Acknowledgment
CSLI, Media X, Blaine Garst, and Everett Meisser, Jr. provided support. Adelaide (Addy) Dawes provided administrative support for IR'11 and IR'14.

Alaa Abi Haidar, Dennis Allison, Dan Flickinger, Diana Ford, Anne Gardner, Ken Kahn, Eric Kao, John Mashey, Fanya S. Montalvo, Peter Neumann, Mike Travers, and Tom Wasow provided comments and suggestions that greatly improved this preface.

This book is dedicated to Fanya S. Montalvo and Carol Woods, who made it all possible.

Symposia Particulars
The 2011 and 2014 International Symposia on Inconsistency Robustness were organized by the International Society for Inconsistency Robustness (iRobust).

Submissions were refereed by the program committee with members listed below.[106]
　　John Woods, *University of British Columbia*
　　Eric Winsberg, *University of South Florida Philosophy*
　　Mary-Anne Williams, *Sydney Innovation Lab*
　　Richard Waldinger, *SRI*
　　David Ungar, *IBM*
　　Mario Tokoro, *Sony CSL*
　　John Traxler, *Wolverhampton School of Technology*
　　Mike Travers, *Collaborative Drug Discovery*

Harry Surden, *University of Colorado Law*
Martha Russell, *Stanford Media X*
Jeff Rulifson, *Oracle*
Neil Rubens, *Electro-Communications Information Systems*
Dave Ripley, *University of Connecticut Philosophy*
Greg Restall, *Melbourne Philosophy*
Mor Peleg, *University of Haifa Information Systems*
David Olson, *Boston College Law*
Peter Neumann, *SRI*
Ike Nassi, *UC Santa Cruz*
Hideyuki Nakashima, *Future University Hakodate*
Fanya S. Montalvo, *iRobust*
Mark Musen, *Stanford Biomedical Informatics*
Annemarie Mol, *University of Amsterdam Philosophy*
Nicolas McGinnis *University of Western Ontario*
J. J. Meyer, *University of Utrecht Information and CS*
Hugo Mercier, *University of Neuchâtel*
Erik Meijer, *Microsoft*
Cindy Mason, *Kurzweil Technologies*
John Mashey, *independent consultant*
John C. Mallery, *MIT CSAIL*
Henry Lieberman, *MIT Media Lab*
Jos Lehmann, *Edinburgh Informatics*
Alan Karp, *HP*
Eric Kao, *Stanford CS*
David Israel, *SRI*
Thomas F. Icard III, *Stanford Philosophy*
Mike Huhns, *South Carolina Electrical & Computer Engineering*
Robert Hoehndorf, *Cambridge Genetics*
Carl Hewitt, Chair
Elihu M. Gerson, *Tremont Research Institute*
Anne Gardner, *iRobust*
Jean-Gabriel Ganascia, *University Pierre et Marie Curie*
Stefania Fusco, *University of New Hampshire Law*
Dan Flickinger, *Stanford CSLI*
Paul N. Edwards, *Michigan History and School of Information*
Ron Dolin, *Stanford CodeX and Media X*
Jack Copeland, *Canterbury Philosophy*
Gilad Bracha, *Google*
Alan Bundy, *University of Edinburgh Informatics*
Geoffrey Bowker, *UC Irvine Informatics*
Francesco Berto, *Aberdeen Philosophy*
Emily Bender, *University of Washington Linguistics*
Trevor Bench-Capon, *University of Liverpool CS*
Gil Alterovitz, *MIT EECS*

iRobust Scientific Society
iRobust[TM] [http://irobust.org] is a scientific society to promote the science and practice of inconsistency robustness.

The Board of iRobust is:[107]
  John Woods, *UBC Philosophy*
  Mary-Anne Williams, *Sydney Innovation and Enterprise Research Lab*
  Mario Tokoro, *Sony CSL*
  Patrick Suppes, *Stanford Philosophy* (deceased)
  Martha Russell, *Stanford Media X*
  Jeff Rulifson, *Oracle*
  Carlo Rovelli, *Marseille Centre de Physique Theorique de Luminy*
  Greg Restall, *Melbourne Philosophy*
  Stanley Peters, *Stanford CSLI*
  Peter Neumann, *SRI*
  Ike Nassi, *UC Santa Cruz*
  Hideyuki Nakashima, *Future University Hakodate*
  Mark Musen, *Stanford Center for Biomedical Informatics Research*
  Fanya S. Montalvo, *independent consultant*
  Annemarie Mol, *University of Amsterdam*
  Marvin Minsky, *MIT Media Lab*
  J.J. Meyer, *University of Utrecht*
  John Law, *Open University*
  Mike Huhns, *South Carolina Electrical & Computer Engineering*
  Chuck House, *ex Stanford*
  Carl Hewitt (chair)
  Elihu M. Gerson, *Tremont Research Institute*
  Blaine Garst, *ex Apple*
  Anne Gardner, *International Association for Artificial Intelligence and Law*
  Nancy Cartwright, *Durham Centre for Humanities Engaging Science and Society*
  Alan Bundy, *Edinburgh Informatics*
  Richard Boland, *Case Western Reserve*
  Gil Alterovitz, *MIT EECS and Harvard Medical School*

End Notes

[1] This preface also serves as a summary of this book.
[2] better or worse
[3] iRobust™ http://irobust.org
[4] Carl Hewitt, Erik Meijer and Clemens Szyperski
[5] With respect to *detected* contradictions in large software systems, according to [Alessandra Russo, Bashar Nuseibeh, and Steve Easterbrook. *Making Inconsistency Respectable in Software Development* Journal of Systems and Software. Vol. 56. No. 58. 2000]:

"The choice of an inconsistency handling strategy depends on the context and the impact it has on other aspects of the development process. Resolving the inconsistency may be as simple as adding or deleting information from a software description. However, it often relies on resolving fundamental conflicts, or taking important design decisions. In such cases, immediate resolution is not the best option, and a number of choices are available:

- **Ignore** - it is sometimes the case that the effort of fixing an inconsistency is too great relative to the (low) risk that the inconsistency will have any adverse consequences. In such cases, developers may choose to ignore the existence of the inconsistency in their descriptions. Good practice dictates that such decisions should be revisited as a project progresses or as a system evolves.
- **Defer** - this may provide developers with more time to elicit further information to facilitate resolution or to render the inconsistency unimportant. In such cases, it is important to flag the parts of the descriptions that are affected, as development will continue while the inconsistency is tolerated.
- **Circumvent** - in some cases, what appears to be an inconsistency according to the consistency rules is not regarded as such by the software developers. This may be because the rule is wrong, or because the inconsistency represents an exception to the rule that had not been captured. In these cases, the inconsistency can be circumvented by modifying the rule, or by disabling it for a specific context.
- **Ameliorate** - it may be more cost-effective to 'improve' a description containing inconsistencies without necessarily resolving them all. This may include adding information to the description that alleviates some adverse effects of an inconsistency and/or resolves other inconsistencies as a side effect. In such cases, amelioration can be a useful inconsistency

handling strategy in that it moves the development process in a 'desirable' direction in which inconsistencies and their adverse impact are reduced."

[6] Solomon Feferman "Axioms for determinateness and truth" Review of Symbolic Logic. 2008.
[7] *i.e.*, $(\Phi \wedge \neg \Phi) \vdash \Psi$
[8] $\vdash_T ((\Psi \Rightarrow (\Phi \wedge \neg \Phi)) \Rightarrow \neg \Psi)$
[9] $\vdash_T (\Theta \Rightarrow \Omega)$ is *much* stronger than $\Theta \vdash_T \Omega$.
In fact, $(\vdash_T (\Theta \Rightarrow \Omega)) \Rightarrow (\Theta \vdash_T \Omega)$ but *not* vice versa.
[10] *i.e.*, $\vdash_T ((\Psi \Rightarrow (\Phi \wedge \neg \Phi)) \Rightarrow \neg \Psi)$. IGOR does *not* follow from Inconsistency Robust Proof by Contradiction.
[11] $(\Psi \vdash (\Phi \wedge \neg \Phi)) \Rightarrow \neg \Psi$
[12] Classical Proof by Contradiction cannot be safely used for theories that might be inconsistent because of IGOR.
[13] in Rebecca Herold *Managing an Information Security and Privacy Awareness and Training Program* 2005. p. 101.
[14] Hasok Chang. *From Incommensurability to Pluralism* Symposium on Occasion of the Farewell of Paul Hoyningen-Huene from Hannover: Science - Big Questions Revisited. August 19, 2014.
[15] Hasok Chang. *Is Water H_2O?* Springer. 2012.
[16] In 1994, Alan Robinson noted that he has "*always been a little quick to make adverse judgments about what I like to call 'wacko logics' especially in Australia...I conduct my affairs as though I believe ... that there is only one logic [i.e., first-order logic]. All the rest is variation in what you're reasoning about, not in how you're reasoning ... [Logic] is immutable.*" (quoted in [Donald MacKenzie. Mechanizing Proof. MIT Press. 2001. page 286])

On the other hand, [Richard Routley *Relevant Logics and Their Rivals 1* Ridgeview. 2003] noted:

> ... classical logic bears a large measure of responsibility for the growing separation between philosophy and logic which there is today... If classical logic is a modern tool inadequate for its job, modern philosophers have shown a classically stoic resignation in the face of this inadequacy. They have behaved like people who, faced with a device, designed to lift stream water, but which is so badly designed that it spills most of its freight, do not set themselves to the design of a better model, but rather devote much of their energy to constructing ingenious arguments to convince themselves that the device is admirable, that they do not need or want the device to deliver more water; that there is nothing wrong with wasting water and that it may even be desirable; and that in order to "improve" the device they would have to change some features of the design, a thing which goes totally against their engineering intuitions and which they could not possibly consider doing.

[17] According to [Thomas Kuhn. *The Structure of Scientific Revolutions* University of Chicago Press. 1962. page 151]
   And Max Planck, surveying his own career in his Scientific Autobiography [Planck 1949], *sadly remarked that "a new scientific truth does not triumph by convincing its opponents and making them see the light, but rather because its opponents eventually die, and a new generation grows up that is familiar with it."*

[18] without fundamental limitations such as those imposed by first-order logic. (See "Limitations of first-order logic" in article 1-2 of this volume.)

[19] Natural Deduction was developed in
   Stanisław Jaśkowski *On the Rules of Suppositions in Formal* Logic Studia Logica 1, 1934. (reprinted in: Polish logic 1920-1939, Oxford University Press, 1967.
   cf. David Barker-Plummer, Jon Barwise and John Etchemendy. *Language, Proof, and Logic: Second Edition* Stanford Center for the Study of Language and Information. 2011

[20] Consequently, the axioms of Classical Direct Logic must be formalized *very carefully*.

[21] [Church 1935, Turing 1936] published the first valid proof that the Peano/Dedekind categorical axiomatization of $\mathbb{N}$ inferentially undecidable (*i.e.* there is a proposition Ψ such that $\nvdash_{\mathbb{N}} \Psi$ and $\nvdash_{\mathbb{N}} \neg\Psi$) because provability in $\mathbb{N}$ is computationally undecidable (provided that the theory $\mathbb{N}$ is consistent).

[22] There seem to be no practical uses for "self-referential" propositions in the mathematical foundations of Computer Science.

[23] Formal typed syntax had not yet been invented when Gödel and other philosophers weakened the foundations of mathematics so that, as expressed, "self-referential" propositions do not infer contradiction because the weakened foundations lacked expressivity. The weakened foundations (based on first-order logic) enabled some limited meta-mathematical theorems to be proved. However, as explained in this article, the weakened foundations are cumbersome, unnatural, and unsuitable as the mathematical foundation for Computer Science.

[24] Theorems can be provably computationally enumerated.

[25] Torkel Franzén. *Inexhaustibility* AK Peters. 2004.

[26] Even though English had not yet been invented!

[27] Heuristic: Think of the "elevator bars" $\lfloor ... \rfloor_T$ around s as "raising" the concrete sentence s "up" into the abstract proposition $\lfloor s \rfloor_T$. The elevator bar heuristics are due to Fanya S. Montalvo.

[28] *cf.* Claude Rosental. *Weaving Self-Evidence* Princeton. 2008.

[29] Morris Kline. *Mathematical Thought from Ancient to Modern Times* Oxford University Press, 1990.

[30] Hilbert letter to Brouwer, October 1928.

[31] e.g. *"The problem with such papers* [critiquing Establishment doctrine] *is that casual readers will use them to criticize and maybe stop future funding ..."* [Hamid Berenji, et. al. *A reply to the paradoxical success of Fuzzy Logic* AI Magazine. Spring 1994]

[32] See "Notation of Classical Direct Logic" in article 1-1 of this volume for the typed notation of Classical Direct Logic. Please note that it is important not to confuse the following:
- Direct Logic permits directly expressing properties of theories, such as the following, which are important knowledge for computer systems:
  - *Classical Soundness*: A theorem can be used in a proof, *i.e.*, $(\vdash\Phi) \Rightarrow \Phi$
  - *Classical Proof by Contradiction*: A hypothesis can be refuted by inferring a contradiction, *i.e.*, $(\Psi\vdash(\Phi\wedge\neg\Phi)) \Rightarrow \neg\Psi$

  Of course, neither of the above propositions is expressible in first-order logic.
- Direct Logic does not admit Gödelian "self-referential" propositions, such as the following: *This proposition is not provable.* (See "Curry and Löb Paradoxes" in article 1-2 of this volume for inconsistencies that would result if "self-referential" propositions were allowed in Classical Direct Logic.)

[33] The article prominently mentions that IGOR can be derived in Classical Logic using Classical ∨-Introduction. However the derivation is *not* fundamental because of the following:
- Classical ∨-Introduction is *unintuitive* because it simply tacks on an extraneous alternative.
- Classical ∨-Introduction does *not* play an important role in Mathematics.
- Classical ∨-Introduction is highly inconsistency *non-robust*.[33] There is *no* inconsistency robust version of Classical ∨-Introduction, unlike the *fundamental* Classical Proof by Contradiction for which there is the corresponding Inconsistency Robust Proof by Contradiction.

Also, as mentioned above, IGOR can be derived using a stronger argument by a rule which *is* fundamental to Mathematics, namely, Classical Proof by Contradiction.

[34] [Alan Kay. *Alan Kay on Messaging* Squeak email list. October 10, 1998] stated:

The big idea is "messaging" .... The key in making great and growable systems is much more to design how its modules communicate rather than what their internal properties and behaviors should be. Think of the internet - to live, it
   a) has to allow many different kinds of ideas and realizations that are beyond any single standard and
   b) to allow varying degrees of safe interoperability between these ideas.

[35] This hypothesis is an update to [Church 1936] that all physically computable functions can be implemented using the lambda calculus. It is a consequence of the Actor Model that there are some computations that *cannot* be implemented in the lambda calculus.

[36] Rajesh Karmani and Gul Agha. Actors. Encyclopedia of Parallel Computing 2011.

[37] *e.g.*, as in Erlang [Joe Armstrong. *Erlang*. CACM. September 2010].

[38] *e.g.*, using assignment commands

[39] a concept from (quantum) physics

[40] *i.e.*, a Logic Program procedure is written as $\Psi \Leftarrow (\Phi_1 \wedge ... \wedge \Phi_n)$, which is logically equivalent to the disjunctive clause $\Psi \vee \neg \Phi_1 \vee ... \vee \neg \Phi_n$ where Ψ and each of the Φ_i is a literal proposition or its negation (*i.e.*, either $P[t_1, ..., t_m]$ or $\neg P[t_1, ..., t_m]$ for some atomic predicate P and terms t_j).

[41] Robert Kowalski. *The Early Years of Logic Programming* CACM. January 1988.

[42] *e.g.*, Robert Kowalski and Fariba Sadri. *Reactive Computing as Model Generation* New Generation Computing. 2015.

[43] Robert Kowalski. *Logic for problem-solving* DCL Memo 75. Dept. of Artificial Intelligence. Edinburgh. 1974.

[44] Robert Kowalski. *Logic Programming* Computational Logic Volume Elsevier. 2014.

[45] As explained in this article, logic-clause syntax is inadequate for expressing Logic Programs.

[46] As explained in this article, resolution theorem provers can make invalid inferences using inconsistent axioms.

[47] US National Research Council. *Advancing the Science of Climate Change: Report in Brief* National Academies Press. 2010.

[48] Raising issues of Inconsistency Robustness, Obama deleted the following statement from his 2008 campaign website:

> "**Protect Whistleblowers**: Often the best source of information about waste, fraud, and abuse in government is an existing government employee committed to public integrity and willing to speak out. Such acts of courage and patriotism, which can sometimes save lives and often save taxpayer dollars, should be encouraged rather than stifled. We need to empower federal employees as watchdogs of wrongdoing and partners in performance. Barack Obama will strengthen whistleblower laws to protect federal workers who expose waste, fraud, and abuse of authority in government. Obama will ensure that federal agencies expedite the process for reviewing whistleblower claims and whistleblowers have full access to courts and due process."

It may be that Obama's statement on the importance of protecting whistleblowers went from being a promise for his administration to a political liability. **There are manifest contradictions in what Obama said then and what he is doing now.**

[49] Walter Bagehot. *The English Constitution* Cornell Univ. Press. 1867.
[50] Glenn Greenwald. *No Place to Hide: Edward Snowden, the NSA, and the U.S. Surveillance State* Metropolitan Books. 2014.
[51] Laura Poitras. *Citizenfour* Praxis Films. 2014.
[52] Diane Roark. *Another NSA Whistleblower Steps Forward* Portland Metro Liberty. June 9, 2014. Diane Roark is a former congressional staffer who was assigned to the intelligence committee. Undaunted by FBI raids on her home and others who also served on that committee, she now comes forward to reveal NSA secrets that she learned of.
[53] Ryan Gallagher. *OPERATION SOCIALIST: The Inside story of British Spies Hacked into Belgium's' Largest Telco* The Intercept. December 12, 2014.
[54] Shane Harris. *@War: The Rise of the Military-Internet Complex* Eamon Dolan/Houghton Mifflin Harcourt. 2014.
[55] Edward Snowden. *Exclusive: Edward Snowden on Cyber Warfare* PBS. January 8, 2015.
[56] Shane Harris. *@War: The Rise of the Military-Internet Complex* Eamon Dolan/Houghton Mifflin Harcourt. 2014.
[57] [Snowden 2015]
[58] emphasis added
[59] Peter Swire and Kenesa Ahmad. *Encryption and Globalization* Columbia Science and Technology Law Review, Vol. 23, 2012.
[60] extension to current Intel and ARM architectures
[61] Each Actor can *only* be sent messages and its storage can be securely recovered when no longer in use *without pausing application programs*.
[62] with the possibility for pre-arranged disconnection
[63] Daniel Ellsberg. *Daniel Ellsberg introduces ExposeFacts.org - Whistleblowers welcome.* June 2014.
[64] John Napier. *Meet Executive Order 12333: The Reagan rule that lets the NSA spy on Americans* Washington Post. July 18, 2014.
[65] Michael Glennnon. *National Security and Double Govenment* Harvard National Security Journal. Vol. 5. 2014.
[66] Trevor Timm. *The James Risen case and Eric Holder's tarnished press freedom legacy* Freedom of the Press Foundation. February 18, 2015.
[67] James Risen. *Pay Any Price: Greed, Power, and Endless War* Houghton Mifflin Harcourt. 2014
[68] Mark Sherman. *Supreme Court Rejects James Risen's Bid To Protect His Source* HuffPost Media. June 2, 2014.
[69] Glenn Greenwald. *Climate of Fear: Jim Risen v. the Obama administration* Salon. June 23, 2011.
Norman Solomon and Marcy Wheeler. *The Government War Against Reporter James Risen* The Nation. October 27, 2014.
[70] James Risen. *Affidavit of James Risen* US District Court for the Easter District of Virginia. Document 115-2. June 21, 2011. After a long delay and under a court deadline, the US government relented and did not compel Risen to

testify.
[71] Shane Harris. *@War: The Rise of the Military-Internet Complex* Eamon Dolan/Houghton Mifflin Harcourt. 2014.
[72] Nicole Perlroth. *Hacked vs. Hackers: Game On* New York Times. December 2, 2014.
[73] James Staten. *The Cost of PRISM Will Be Larger Than ITIF Projects* James Staten's Blog at Forrester Research. August 14, 2013.
[74] PCWorld. *FBI director calls for greater police access to communications* December 7, 2014.
[75] James Comey. *Going Dark: Are Technology, Privacy, and Public Safety on a Collision Course?* Brookings Institution. October 16, 2014.
[76] Julian Hattem. *'Crypto wars' return to Congress* The Hill. October 20, 2014.
[77] Kevin Bankston, moderator. *Debate on Law Enforcement vs. Smartphone Encryption* New American Foundation. Nov. 18, 2014. https://www.youtube.com/watch?v=6NVmsn6yuS4
[78] James Risen. *Acceptance Speech for Colby College Elijah Parish Lovejoy Award for Courageous Journalism* October 5, 2014.
[79] Chris Hoofnagle. E-mail interview with Public Citizen's Sam Jewler. October 1, 2014.
[80] Sam Jewler. *Mission Creep-y: Google is Quietly becoming One of the Nation's Most Powerful Forces While Expanding Its Information-Collection Empire* Public Citizen. 2014.
[81] Christopher Soghoian. *Why Google Won't Protect You from Big Brother* TEDx. San Jose. 2012.
[82] Tim Cook. *A Message from Tim Cook about Apple's Commitment to Your Privacy.* Apple. 2014.
[83] Lee Fang. *How Big Business Is Helping Expand NSA Surveillance, Snowden Be Damned.* The Intercept. April 1, 2015.
[84] Jeremy Scahill and Josh Begley. *The CIA Campaign to Steal Apple's Secrets.* The Intercept. March 10, 2015.
[85] Jeff Mason. *Obama sharply criticizes China's plans for new technology rules.* Reuters. March 2, 2015.
[86] Relatively secure backdoors ideally require the equivalent of a different public key on each device.
[87] BBC News. *China and US clash over software backdoor proposals.* March 4, 2015.
[88] *Speech on Encryption.* October 17, 2014.
[89] Mike Rogers. *A Conversation with Admiral Mike Rogers* Cybersecurity for a New America: Big Ideas and New Voices. February 23, 2015.
[90] Concerning pitfalls with such proposals see [Steven Bellovin, Matt Blaze, Whitfield Diffie, Susan Landau, Peter Neumann, and Jennifer Rexford. *Risking Communications Security: Potential Hazards of the Protect America Act.* IEEE Security & Privacy. Vol. 6. No. 1. Jan.-Feb. 2008].

[91] According to [*EFF Response to FBI Director Comey's Speech on Encryption.* October 17, 2014]:

"USC 1002(b)(3): A telecommunications carrier shall not be responsible for decrypting, or ensuring the government's ability to decrypt, any communication encrypted by a subscriber or customer, unless the encryption was provided by the carrier and the carrier possesses the information necessary to decrypt the communication."

Here's the relevant part of CALEA that Comey wants to effectively undo:

Also from the CALEA legislative history:

"Finally, telecommunications carriers have no responsibility to decrypt encrypted communications that are the subject of court-ordered wiretaps, unless the carrier provided the encryption and can decrypt it. ... Nothing in this paragraph would prohibit a carrier from deploying an encryption service for which it does not retain the ability to decrypt communications for law enforcement access ... Nothing in the bill is intended to limit or otherwise prevent the use of any type of encryption within the United States. Nor does the Committee intend this bill to be in any way a precursor to any kind of ban or limitation on encryption technology. To the contrary, section 2602 protects the right to use encryption."

[92] Similarly, the UK government has vowed that if it is re-elected, then it will create new legal powers to make sure that UK intelligence and security agencies have maximum capabilities for cybersurveillance. It also submitted legislation to Parliament to ban "extremists" from the web and the airwaves. [Alan Travis. *Theresa May vows Tory government would introduce 'snooper's charter.'* The Guardian. September 30, 2014.]

[93] John Reed. *Transcript: NSA Director Mike Rogers vs. Yahoo! on Encryption Back Doors.* Just Security Blog. February 23, 1015

[94] Tom McCarthy. *NSA director defends plan to maintain 'backdoors' into technology companies.* The Guardian. February 23, 2015.

[95] Eric Schlosser *Command and Control: Nuclear Weapons, the Damascus Accident, and the Illusion of Safety* Penguin Books. 2014.

[96] Carl Hewitt. *What to do about our broken cyberspace.* CACM. February 2015.

[97] Shane Harris *@War: The Rise of the Military-Internet Complex.* Eamon Dolan/Houghton Mifflin Harcourt. Boston, MA, 2014.

[98] If the US adopts mandatory backdoors for products sold domestically, then cyberaudits of exports will have to be much more thorough that there is no backdoor available to the US government.

[99] Li Dandan. *Apple express a willingness to accept the Chinese domestic network security review.* Beijing News. January 21, 2015.

[100] which can include those who installed the backdoors as well as anyone who can hack into the backdoors including state-sponsored intruders and other criminals.

[101] Robert Lustig. *Beating the Odds Against Sugar, Processed Food, Obesity, and Disease* Hudson Street Press. 2012.

[102] John Ioannidis. *Why Most Published Research Findings Are False* PLoS Med. 2(8): e124. August 2005.

[103] Robert Lustig. *Beating the Odds Against Sugar, Processed Food, Obesity, and Disease* Hudson Street Press. 2012.

[104] John Ioannidis. *Why Most Published Research Findings Are False* PLoS Med. 2(8): e124. August 2005.

[105] Dana Scott. *Axiomatizing Set Theory* Symposium in Pure Mathematics Los Angeles. July 1967.

[106] affiliations are only for the purpose of identification

[107] affiliations are only for the purpose of identification

Part 1

Mathematical Foundations

Formalizing common sense reasoning for scalable inconsistency-robust information coordination using Direct Logic™ Reasoning and the Actor Model

Carl Hewitt

This article is dedicated to Stanisław Jaśkowski, John McCarthy, Marvin Minsky and Ludwig Wittgenstein.

Abstract
People use common sense in their interactions with large information systems. This common sense needs to be formalized so that it can be used by computer systems. Unfortunately, previous formalizations have been inadequate. For example, classical logic is not safe for use with pervasively inconsistent information. The goal is to develop a standard foundation for reasoning in large-scale Internet applications (including sense making for natural language).

Inconsistency Robust Direct Logic is a minimal fix to Classical Logic without the rule of Classical Proof by Contradiction
$$(\Psi \vdash (\Phi \wedge \neg \Phi)) \vdash \neg \Psi$$
Addition of the above transforms Inconsistency Robust Direct Logic into Classical Logic. Inconsistency Robust Direct Logic makes the following contributions over previous work:
- *Direct* Inference[1]
- *Direct* Argumentation (argumentation directly expressed)
- *Inconsistency-robust* Natural Deduction that doesn't require artifices such as indices (labels) on propositions or restrictions on reiteration
- Intuitive inferences hold including the following:
  - Propositional Equivalences (except absorption) including Double Negation and De Morgan
  - ∨-Elimination (Disjunctive Syllogism), *i.e.*, $\neg\Phi, (\Phi \vee \Psi) \vdash_T \Psi$
  - Reasoning by disjunctive cases, *i.e.*,
    $(\Psi \vee \Phi), (\Psi \vdash_T \Theta), (\Phi \vdash_T \Omega) \vdash_T \Theta \vee \Omega$
  - Contrapositive for implication *i.e.*, $\Psi \Rightarrow \Phi$ if and only if $\neg\Phi \Rightarrow \neg\Psi$
  - Soundness (a theorem can be used in a proof), *i.e.*, $\vdash_T ((\vdash_T \Psi) \Rightarrow \Psi)$
  - Inconsistency Robust Proof by Contradiction, *i.e.*,
    $\vdash_T (\Psi \Rightarrow (\Phi \wedge \neg \Phi)) \Rightarrow \neg \Psi$

A fundamental goal of Inconsistency Robust Direct Logic is to effectively reason about large amounts of pervasively inconsistent information using computer information systems.

Jaśkowski [1948] stated the following initial goal:
To find a system [for inconsistency robust inference] ... *which:*
1) *when applied to contradictory* [information] *would not always entail overcompleteness* [i.e. infer every proposition]
2) *would be rich enough for practical inference*
3) *would have an intuitive justification*

According to Feferman [2008]: *So far as I know, it has not been determined whether such* [inconsistency robust] *logics account for "sustained ordinary reasoning", not only in everyday discourse but also in mathematics and the sciences.* Direct Logic is put forward as an improvement over classical logic with respect to Feferman's desideratum above using the following:
- **Inconsistency Robust Direct Logic** for pervasively inconsistent theories of practice[i]
- **Classical Direct Logic** for use of consistent mathematical theories in inconsistency robust theories

Direct Logic is an improvement over classical logic with respect to Feferman's desideratum above for today's information systems that are perpetually, pervasively inconsistent. Information technology needs an all-embracing system of inconsistency-robust reasoning to support practical information coordination. Having such a system is important in computer science because computers must be able to carry out all inferences (including inferences about their own inference processes) without relying on humans

Consequently, Direct Logic is proposed as a standard to replace classical logic as a mathematical foundation for Computer Science.

Since the global state space model of computation (first formalized by Turing) is inadequate to the needs of modern large-scale Internet applications the Actor Model was developed to meet this need.

Hypothesis:[ii] **All physically possible computation can be directly implemented using Actors.**

---

[i] *e.g.*, theories for climate modeling and for modeling the human brain

[ii] This hypothesis is an update to [Church 1936] that all physically computable functions can be implemented using the lambda calculus. It is a consequence of the Actor Model that there are some computations that *cannot* be implemented in the lambda calculus.

Using, the Actor Model, this paper proves that Logic Programs are not computationally universal in that there are computations that cannot be implemented using logical inference. Consequently the Logic Program paradigm is strictly less general than the Embedding of Knowledge paradigm.

Introduction

Beneath the surface of the world are the rules of science. But beneath them there is a far deeper set of rules: a matrix of pure mathematics, which explains the nature of the rules of science and how it is that we can understand them in the first place.
Malone [2007]

Our lives are changing: ***soon we will always be online***. People use their common sense interacting with large information systems. This common sense needs to be formalized.[i]

Large-scale Internet software systems present the following challenges:
1. **Pervasive inconsistency is the norm** and consequently classical logic infers too much, i.e., anything and everything. Inconsistencies (e.g. that can be derived from implementations, documentation, and use cases) in large software systems are pervasive and despite enormous expense have not been eliminated.
2. **Concurrency is the norm.** Logic Programs based on the inference rules of mathematical logic are not computationally universal because the message order reception indeterminate computations of concurrent programs in open systems cannot be deduced using mathematical logic from propositions about pre-existing conditions. The fact that computation is not reducible to logical inference has important practical consequences. For example, reasoning used in information coordination cannot be implemented using logical inference [Hewitt 2008a].

This paper suggests some principles and practices formalizing common sense approaches to addressing the above issues.

Interaction *creates* Reality[2]

[We] cannot think of any object apart from the possibility of its connection with other things.
Wittgenstein, *Tractatus*

---

[i] Eventually, computer systems need to be able to address issues like the following:
- What will be the effects of increasing greenhouse gasses?
- What is the future of mass cyber surveillance?
- What can done about the increasing prevalence of metabolic syndrome?

According to [Rovelli 2008]:
a pen on my table has information because it points in this or that direction. We do not need a human being, a cat, or a computer, to make use of this notion of information.[i]

Relational physics takes the following view [Laudisa and Rovelli 2008]:
- Relational physics discards the notions of absolute state of a system and absolute properties and values of its physical quantities.
- State and physical quantities refer always to the interaction, or the relation, among multiple systems.[ii]
- Nevertheless, relational physics is a complete description of reality.[iii]

According to this view, **Interaction creates reality.**[3]

Information is a generalization of physical information in Relational Physics
Information, as used in this article, is a generalization of the physical information of Relational Physics.[iv] Information systems participate in reality and thus are both consequence and cause. Science is a large information system that investigates and theorizes about interactions. So how does Science work?

---

[i] Rovelli added: *This* [concept of information] *is very weak; it does not require* [consideration of] *information storage, thermodynamics, complex systems, meaning, or anything of the sort. In particular:*
  i. *Information can be lost dynamically* ([correlated systems can become uncorrelated]);
  ii. [It does] *not distinguish between correlation obtained on purpose and accidental correlation;*
  iii. *Most important: any physical system may contain information about another physical system.*
  Also, *Information is exchanged via physical interactions.* and furthermore, *It is always possible to acquire new information about a system.*
[ii] *In place of the notion of state, which refers solely to the system,* [use] *the notion of the information that a system has about another system.*
[iii] Furthermore, according to [Rovelli 2008], *quantum mechanics indicates that the notion of a universal description of the state of the world, shared by all observers, is a concept which is physically untenable, on experimental grounds.* In this regard, [Feynman 1965] offered the following advice: *Do not keep saying to yourself, if you can possibly avoid it, "But how can it be like that?" because you will go "down the drain,"* into a blind alley from which nobody has yet escaped.
[iv] Unlike physical information in Relational Physics [Rovelli 2008, page 10], this paper does *not* make the assumption that information is necessarily a discrete quantity or that it must be consistent.

According to [Law 2004, emphasis added]:
> ... *scientific routinisation, produced with immense difficulty and at immense cost, that secures the general continued stability of natural (and social) scientific reality. Elements within* [this routinisation] *may be overturned... But overall and most of the time, ... it is the expense* [and other difficulties] *of doing otherwise that allows* [scientific routinisation] *to achieve relative stability. So it is that a scientific reality is produced that holds together more or less.*[4]

He added that we can respond as follows:
> *That we refuse the distinction between the literal and the metaphorical (as various philosophers of science have noted, the literal is always 'dead' metaphor, a metaphor that is no longer seen as such). ... That we work allegorically.* **That we imagine coherence without consistency.** [emphasis added]

The coherence envisaged by Law (above) is a dynamic interactive ongoing process among humans and other objects.

Pervasive Inconsistency is the Norm in Large Software Systems

> *"... find bugs faster than developers can fix them and each fix leads to another bug"*
> Cusumano & Selby, 1995, p. 40

The development of large software systems and the extreme dependence of our society on these systems have introduced new phenomena. These systems have pervasive inconsistencies among and within the following:[5]
- *Use cases* that express how systems can be used and tested in practice.[6]
- *Documentation* that expresses over-arching justification for systems and their technologies.[7]
- *Code* that expresses implementations of systems

Adapting a metaphor used by Popper[8] for science, the bold structure of a large software system rises, as it were, above a swamp. It is like a building erected on piles. The piles are driven down from above into the swamp, but not down to any natural or given base; and when we cease our attempts to drive our piles into a deeper layer, it is not because we have reached bedrock. We simply pause when we are satisfied that they are firm enough to carry the structure, at least for the time being. Or perhaps we do something else more pressing. Under some piles there is no rock. Also some rock does not hold.

Different communities are responsible for constructing, evolving, justifying and maintaining documentation, use cases, and code for large, software systems. In specific cases any one consideration can trump the others.

Sometimes debates over inconsistencies among the parts can become quite heated, *e.g.,* between vendors. ***In the long run, after difficult negotiations, in large software systems, use cases, documentation, and code all change to produce systems with new inconsistencies. However, no one knows what they are or where they are located!***

A large software system is never done [Rosenberg 2007].[9]

With respect to *detected* contradictions in large information systems, according to [Russo, Nuseibeh, and Easterbrook 2000]:

> *The choice of an inconsistency handling strategy depends on the context and the impact it has on other aspects of the development process. Resolving the inconsistency may be as simple as adding or deleting information from a software description. However, it often relies on resolving fundamental conflicts, or taking important design decisions. In such cases, immediate resolution is not the best option, and a number of choices are available:*
> - ***Ignore*** - *it is sometimes the case that the effort of fixing an inconsistency is too great relative to the (low) risk that the inconsistency will have any adverse consequences. In such cases, developers may choose to ignore the existence of the inconsistency in their descriptions. Good practice dictates that such decisions should be revisited as a project progresses or as a system evolves.*
> - ***Defer*** - *this may provide developers with more time to elicit further information to facilitate resolution or to render the inconsistency unimportant. In such cases, it is important to flag the parts of the descriptions that are affected, as development will continue while the inconsistency is tolerated.*
> - ***Circumvent*** - *in some cases, what appears to be an inconsistency according to the consistency rules is not regarded as such by the software developers. This may be because the rule is wrong, or because the inconsistency represents an exception to the rule that had not been captured. In these cases, the inconsistency can be circumvented by modifying the rule, or by disabling it for a specific context.*
> - ***Ameliorate*** - *it may be more cost-effective to 'improve' a description containing inconsistencies without necessarily resolving them all. This may include adding information to the description that alleviates some adverse effects of an inconsistency and/or resolves other inconsistencies as a side effect. In such cases, amelioration can be a useful inconsistency handling strategy in that it moves the development process in a 'desirable' direction in which inconsistencies and their adverse impact are reduced.*

Inconsistency Robustness

> *You cannot be confident about applying your calculus until you know that there are no hidden contradictions in it.*[i]
> Turing *circa* 1930. [Wittgenstein 1933-1935]

> *Indeed, even at this stage, I predict a time when there will be mathematical investigations of calculi containing contradictions, and people will actually be proud of having emancipated themselves from consistency.*
> Wittgenstein *circa* 1930. [Wittgenstein 1933-1935][10]

Inconsistency robustness is information system performance in the face of continually pervasive inconsistencies--- a shift from the previously dominant paradigms of *inconsistency denial* and *inconsistency elimination* attempting to sweep them under the rug.[ii]

In fact, inconsistencies are pervasive throughout our information infrastructure and they affect one another. Consequently, an interdisciplinary approach is needed.

Inconsistency robustness differs from previous paradigms based on belief revision, probability, and uncertainty as follows:
- *Belief revision*: Large information systems are continually, pervasively inconsistent and there is no way to revise them to attain consistency.
- *Probability and fuzzy logic*: In large information systems, there are typically several ways to calculate probability. Often the result is that the probability is both close to 0% and close to 100%!
- *Uncertainty*: Resolving uncertainty to determine truth is not realistic in large information systems.

There are many examples of inconsistency robustness in practice including the following:
- Our economy relies on large software systems that have tens of thousands of known inconsistencies (often called "bugs") along with tens of thousands more that have yet to be pinned down even though their symptoms are sometimes obvious.

---

[i] Turing was correct that it is unsafe to use classical logic to reason about inconsistent information. Church and Turing later proved that determining whether there are hidden inconsistencies in a mathematical theory is computationally undecidable.

[ii] Inconsistency robustness builds on previous work on inconsistency tolerance, *e.g.*, [Bertossi, Hunter and Schaub 2004; Gabbay and Hunter 1991-1992; Bèziau, Carnielli and Gabbay 2007].

- Physics has progressed for centuries in the face of numerous inconsistencies including the ongoing decades-long inconsistency between its two most fundamental theories (general relativity and quantum mechanics).
- Decision makers commonly ask for the case against as well as the case for proposed findings and action plans in corporations, governments, and judicial systems.

Inconsistency robustness stands to become a more central theme for computation. The basic argument is that because inconsistency is continually pervasive in large information systems, the issue of inconsistency robustness must be addressed!

A fundamental goal of Inconsistency Robustness is to effectively reason about large amounts of information at high degrees of abstraction:

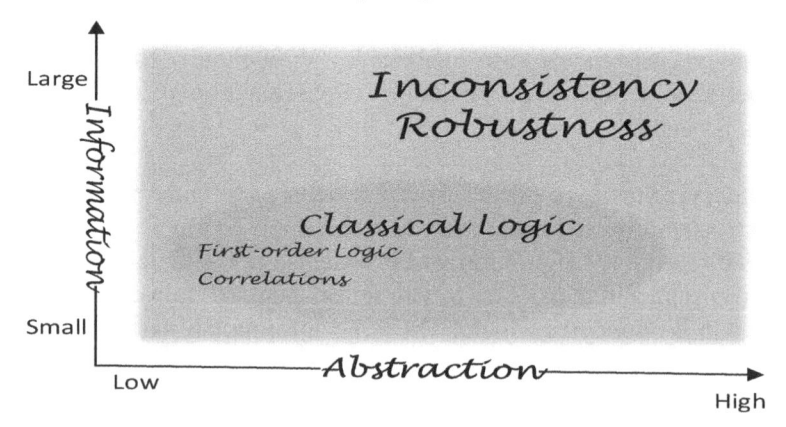

Inconsistency Robustness

Classical Logic
First-order Logic
Correlations

(Information: Small to Large; Abstraction: Low to High)

Classical logic is safe only for theories for which there is strong evidence of consistency.

> *A little inaccuracy sometimes saves tons of explanation.*
> Saki in "The Square Egg"

Inconsistency robust theories can be easier to develop than classical theories because perfect absence of inconsistency is not required. In case of inconsistency, there will be some propositions that can be both proved and disproved, *i.e.*, there will be arguments both for and against the propositions.

A classic case of inconsistency occurs in the novel Catch-22 [Heller 1961] which states that a person *"would be crazy to fly more missions and sane if he didn't, but if he was sane he had to fly them. If he flew them he was crazy and didn't have to; but if he didn't want to he was sane and had to. Yossarian was moved very deeply by the absolute simplicity of this clause of Catch-22 and let out a respectful whistle. 'That's some catch, that Catch-22,' he observed."*

Consider the follow formalization of the above in classical logic:[i]
Policy$_1$[x] ≡ Sane[x] ⇒ Obligated[x, Fly]
Policy$_2$[x] ≡ Obligated[x, Fly] ⇒ Fly[x]
Policy$_3$[x] ≡ Crazy[x] ⇒ ¬Obligated[x, Fly]

Observe$_1$[x] ≡ ¬Obligated[x, Fly] ∧ ¬Fly[x] ⇒ Sane[x]
Observe$_2$[x] ≡ Fly[x] ⇒ Crazy[x]
Observe$_3$[x] ≡ Sane[x] ∧ ¬Obligated[x, Fly] ⇒ ¬Fly[x]]
Observe$_4$ ≡ Sane[Yossarian]

In addition, there is the following background material:

Background$_2$ ≡ ¬Obligated[Moon, Fly]

Using classical logic, the following rather surprising conclusion can be inferred:
> **Fly[Moon]**

i.e., the moon flies an aircraft!

Classical logic is not safe for theories not know to be consistent.[ii]

Inconsistency robustness facilitates formalization
Inconsistency Robust Direct logic facilitates common sense reasoning by formalizing inconsistency robust inference.[iii]

---

[i] This is a very simple example of how classical logic can infer absurd conclusions from inconsistent information. More generally, classical inferences using inconsistent information can be arbitrarily convoluted and there is no practical way to test if inconsistent information has been used in a derivation.

[ii] It turns out that there is a hidden inconsistency in the theory *Catch22*:

    Inference$_1$ ≡ ⊢$_{Catch22}$ Fly[Yossarian]

    Inference$_2$ ≡ ⊢$_{Catch22}$ ¬Fly[Yossarian]

Thus there is an inconsistency in the theory *Catch22* concerning whether Yossarian flies.

[iii] According to [Minsky 1974]:
The consistency that [classical] *logic absolutely demands is not otherwise usually available – and probably not even desirable! – because consistent systems are likely to be too "weak".*

In Direct Logic, the above can be formulated using a very strong form of implication in Inconsistency Robust Direct Logic as follows in the theory $Catch22$:[11]

$\text{Policy}_1[x] \equiv \vdash_{Catch22} \text{Sane}[x] \Rightarrow \text{Obligated}[x, \text{Fly}]$

$\text{Policy}_2[x] \equiv \vdash_{Catch22} \text{Obligated}[x, \text{Fly}] \Rightarrow \text{Fly}[x]$

$\text{Policy}_3[x] \equiv \vdash_{Catch22} \text{Crazy}[x] \Rightarrow \neg\text{Obligated}[x, \text{Fly}]$

$\text{Observe}_1[x] \equiv \vdash_{Catch22} \neg\text{Obligated}[x, \text{Fly}] \wedge \neg\text{Fly}[x] \Rightarrow \text{Sane}[x]$

$\text{Observe}_2[x] \equiv \vdash_{Catch22} \text{Fly}[x] \Rightarrow \text{Crazy}[x]$

$\text{Observe}3[x] \equiv \vdash_{Catch22} \text{Sane}[x] \wedge \neg\text{Obligated}[x, \text{Fly}] \Rightarrow \neg\text{Fly}[x]]$

$\text{Observe}4 \equiv \vdash_{Catch22} \text{Sane}[\text{Yossarian}]$

$\text{Background}2 \equiv \vdash_{Catch22} \neg\text{Obligated}[\text{Moon}, \text{Fly}]$

Unlike Classical Logic, in Direct Logic:
$\nvdash_{Catch22} \text{Fly}[\text{Moon}]$

It turns out that the following can be inferred:[12]
$\vdash_{Catch22} \text{Fly}[\text{Yossarian}]$
$\vdash_{Catch22} \neg\text{Fly}[\text{Yossarian}]$

However, instead of being able to infer everything[i], once the above contradiction been noticed, question answering can be improved using the "**but**" construct of Inconsistency Robust Direct Logic as follows:

$\vdash_{Catch22} \text{Fly}[\text{Yossarian}]$ **but** $\vdash_{Catch22} \neg\text{Fly}[\text{Yossarian}]$

$\vdash_{Catch22} \neg\text{Fly}[\text{Yossarian}]$ **but** $\vdash_{Catch22} \text{Fly}[\text{Yossarian}]$

Contradictions can facilitate Argumentation

> [I] *emphasize that contradictions are not always an entirely bad thing. I think we have all found in our googling that it is often better to find contradictory information on a search topic rather than finding no information at all. I explore some of the various reasons this may arise, which include finding that there is at least active interest in the topic, appraising the credentials of the informants, counting their relative number, assessing their arguments, trying to reproduce their experimental results, discovering their authoritative sources, etc.*
> [Dunn 2014]

---

[i] which is the case in classical logic from a contradiction

Using Direct Logic, various arguments can be made in $Catch22$. For example:

$$Sane[x] \vdash^{Argument1}_{Catch22} Crazy[x]$$

i.e. "The sane ones are thereby crazy because they fly."

$$Crazy[x], \neg Fly[x] \vdash^{Argument2}_{Catch22} Sane[x]$$

i.e. "The crazy ones who don't fly are thereby sane."

However, neither of the above arguments is absolute because there might be arguments against the above arguments. Also, the following axiom can be added to the mix:

$$Observe_5[x] \equiv \vdash_{Catch22} Crazy[x] \Rightarrow \neg Sane[x]]$$

Once, the above axiom is added we have:

$\vdash_{Catch22} Fly[Yossarian]$ **but** $\vdash_{Catch22} \neg Sane[Yossarian]$

although Sane[Yossarian] is used in the argument for Fly[Yossarian].

The theory $Catch22$ illustrates the following points:
- *Inconsistency robustness facilitates theory development because a single inconsistency is not disastrous.*
- *Even though the theory $Catch22$ is inconsistent, it is not meaningless.*
- *Queries can be given sensible answers in the presence of inconsistent information.*

Inconsistent probabilities

> *You can use all the quantitative data you can get, but you still have to distrust it and use your own intelligence and judgment.*
> Alvin Toffler

> *it would be better to ... eschew all talk of probability in favor of talk about correlation.*
> N. David Mermin [1998]

Inconsistency is built into the very foundations of probability theory:[13]
- $\mathbb{P}PresentMoment \cong 0$
  Because of cumulative contingencies to get here.[i]
- $\mathbb{P}PresentMoment \cong 1$
  Because it's reality.

---

[i] For example, suppose that we have just flipped a coin a large number of times producing a long sequence of heads and tails. The exact sequence that has been produced is extremely unlikely.

The above problem is not easily fixed because of the following:
- Indeterminacies are omnipresent/
- Interdependencies[14] are pervasive thereby calling to question probabilistic calculations that assume independence.

The above points about the perils of correlation were largely missed in [Anderson 2008]. which stated
> "Correlation is enough." **We can stop looking for models. We can analyze the data without hypotheses about what it might show.** We can throw the numbers into the biggest computing clusters the world has ever seen and let statistical algorithms find patterns where science cannot.
(emphasis added)

Of course, Anderson missed the whole point that causality is about *affecting* correlations through interaction. Statistical algorithms can always find meaningless correlations. Models (*i.e.* theories) are used to create interventions to test which correlations are causal.

Theorem. $(\Psi \vdash \Phi) \Rightarrow \mathbb{P}\Psi \leq \mathbb{P}\Phi$

Proof: Suppose $\Psi \vdash \Phi$.
$$1 \cong^i \mathbb{P}\Phi|\Psi \equiv \frac{\mathbb{P}\Phi \wedge \Psi}{\mathbb{P}\Psi}$$
$$\mathbb{P}\Psi \cong \mathbb{P}\Phi \wedge \Psi \leq \mathbb{P}\Phi$$

Thus probabilities for the theory Catch22 obey the following:
P1. $\vdash_{Catch22} \mathbb{P}Sane[x] \leq \mathbb{P}Obligated[x, Fly]$
P2. $\vdash_{Catch22} \mathbb{P}Obligated[x, Fly] \leq \mathbb{P}Fly[x]$
P3. $\vdash_{Catch22} \mathbb{P}Crazy[x] \leq \mathbb{P}\neg Obligated[x, Fly]$]

S1. $\vdash_{Catch22} \mathbb{P}\neg Obligated[x, Fly] \wedge \neg Fly[x] \leq \mathbb{P}Sane[x]$
S2. $\vdash_{Catch22} \mathbb{P}Fly[x] \leq \mathbb{P}Crazy[x]$
S3. $\vdash_{Catch22} \mathbb{P}Sane[x] \wedge \neg Obligated[x, Fly] \leq \mathbb{P}\neg Fly[x]$
S4. $\vdash_{Catch22} \mathbb{P}Sane[Yossarian] \cong 1$

Consequently, the following inferences hold
I1. $\vdash_{Catch22} 1 \cong \mathbb{P}Obligated[Yossarian, Fly]$ ⓘ *using* **P1** *and* **S4**
I2. $\vdash_{Catch22} 1 \cong \mathbb{P}Fly[Yossarian]$ ⓘ *using* **P2** *and* **I1**
I3. $\vdash_{Catch22} 1 \cong \mathbb{P}Crazy[Yossarian]$ ⓘ *using* **S2** *and* **I2**
I4. $\vdash_{Catch22} 1 \lesssim \mathbb{P}\neg Obligated[Yossarian, Fly]$ ⓘ *using* **P3** *and* **I3**
I5. $\vdash_{Catch22} \mathbb{P}\neg Fly[Yossarian] \cong 0$ ⓘ *using* **I4** *and* **S3**
I6. $\vdash_{Catch22} \mathbb{P}Fly[Yossarian] \cong 1$ ⓘ *reformulation of* **I5**

---

[i] This conclusion is not accepted by all. See [Lewis 1976].

Thus there is an inconsistency in Catch22 in that both of the following hold in the above:
12. $\vdash_{Catch22}$ ℙFly[Yossarian] $\cong 1$
16. $\vdash_{Catch22}$ ℙFly[Yossarian] $\cong 0$

Inconsistent probabilities are potentially a much more serious problem than logical inconsistencies because they have unfortunate consequences like the following: $\vdash_{Catch22} 1 \cong 0$.[15]

In addition to inconsistency non-robustness, probability models are limited by the following:
- ✗ Limited expressiveness (avoidance of non-numerical reasoning)
- ✗ Limited scalability
- ✗ Fragile independence assumptions
- ✗ Markovian ahistoricity
- ✗ Bayes rule (very conservative) versus general reasoning
- ✗ Contrafactuals (contra scientific knowledge)

Nevertheless, probabilities have important uses in physics, *e.g.* quantum systems.

However, statistical reasoning is enormously important in practice including the following:
- Aggregation and Correlation
- Interpolation and Extrapolation
- Classification and Simulation

Circular information

How can inconsistencies such as the one above be understood?
Assigning truth values to propositions is an attempt to characterize whether or not a proposition holds in a theory. Of course, this cannot be done consistently if the theory is inconsistent. Likewise, assigning probabilities to propositions is an attempt to characterize the likelihood that a proposition holds in a theory. Similar to assigning truth values, assigning probabilities cannot be done consistently if the theory is inconsistent.

The process of theory development can generate circularities that are an underlying source of inconsistency:

> Mol shows that clinical diagnoses often depend on collective and statistically generated norms. What counts as a 'normal' haemoglobin level in blood is a function of measurements of a whole population. She is saying, then, that **individual diagnoses include collective norms though**

*they cannot be reduced to these (Mol and Berg 1994). At the same time, however, the collective norms depend on a sample of clinical measurements which may be influenced by assumptions about the distribution of anaemia—though it is not, of course, reducible to any individual measurement. The lesson is that **the individual is included in the collective, and the collective is included in the individual—but neither is reducible to the other.**[16]*

Classical logic is unsafe for use with potentially inconsistent information

Irony is about contradictions that do not resolve into larger wholes even dialectically, about the tension of holding incompatible things together because all are necessary and true.
Haraway [1991]

An important limitation of classical logic[i] for inconsistent information is that it supports the principle that from an inconsistency anything and everything can be inferred, *e.g. "The moon is made of green cheese."*

For convenience, I have given the above principle the name IGOR[17] for Inconsistency in Garbage Out Redux. IGOR can be formalized as follows in which a contradiction about a proposition Ω infers any proposition Θ,[ii] *i.e.*, $\Omega, \neg \Omega \vdash \Theta$.

Of course, IGOR *cannot* be part of Inconsistency Robust Direct Logic because it allows *every* proposition to be inferred from a contradiction.

The IGOR principle of classical logic may not seem very intuitive! So why is it included in classical logic?
- **Classical Proof by Contradiction:** $(\Psi \vdash \Phi, \neg \Phi) \Rightarrow (\vdash \neg \Psi)$, which can be justified in classical logic on the grounds that if Ψ infers a contradiction in a consistent theory then Ψ must be false. In an inconsistent theory. Classical Proof by Contradiction leads to explosion by the following derivation in classical logic by a which a contradiction about P infers any proposition Θ:
    $P, \neg P \vdash \neg \Theta \vdash P, \neg P \vdash (\neg \neg \Theta) \vdash \Theta$
- **Classical Contrapositive for Inference:** $(\Psi \vdash \Phi) \Rightarrow (\neg \Phi \vdash \neg \Psi)$, which can be justified in classical logic on the grounds that if $\Psi \vdash \Phi$, then if Φ

---
[i] A very similar limitation holds for intuitionistic logic.
[ii] Using the symbol $\vdash$ to mean "infers in classical mathematical logic." The symbol was first published in [Frege 1879].

is false then Ψ must be false. In an inconsistent theory. Classical Contrapositive for Inference leads to explosion by the following derivation in classical logic by a which a contradiction about P (*i.e.*, ⊢ P, ¬P) infers any proposition Θ by the following proof:
  Since ⊢ P, ¬Θ ⊢ P by monotonicity. Therefore ¬P ⊢ Θ by Classical Contrapositive for Inference. Consequently P, ¬P ⊢ Θ.

- **Classical Extraneous ∨ Introduction:**[18] Ψ ⊢ (Ψ∨Φ), which in classical logic says that if Ψ is true then Ψ∨Φ is true regardless of whether Φ is true.[19] In an inconsistent theory, Extraneous ∨ introduction leads to explosion via the following derivation in classical logic in which a contraction about P infers any proposition Θ:
  P,¬P ⊢ (P∨Θ),¬P ⊢ Θ

- **Classical Excluded Middle:** ⊢ (Ψ∨¬Ψ), which in classical logic says that Ψ∨¬Ψ is true regardless of whether Ψ is true. *Excluded Middle* is the principle of Classical Logic that for every proposition X the following holds: ExcludedMiddle[X] ≡ X∨¬X
  However, Excluded Middle is not suitable for inconsistency-robust logic because it is equivalent[i] to saying that there are no inconsistencies, *i.e.*, for every proposition X,
    Noncontradiction[X] ≡ ¬(X∧¬X)
  Using propositional equivalences, note that
    ExcludedMiddle[Φ∨Ψ] ⇔ (Ψ∨¬Ψ∨Φ)∧(Φ∨¬Φ∨Ψ)
  Consequently, ExcludedMiddle[Φ∨Ψ]⇒(Ψ∨¬Ψ∨Φ), which means that the principle of Excluded Middle implies Ψ∨¬Ψ∨Φ for all propositions Ψ and Φ. Thus the principle of Excluded Middle is not inconsistency robust because it implies every proposition Φ can be proved[ii] given any contradiction Ψ. [Kao 2011]

Classical Logic is unsafe for inference using potentially inconsistent information.[iii]

Direct Logic

"But if the general truths of Logic are of such a nature that when presented to the mind they at once command assent, wherein consists the difficulty of constructing the Science of Logic?" [Boole, 1853 pg. 3]

---

[i] using propositional equivalences
[ii] using ∨-*Elimination* , *i.e.*, ¬Φ, (Φ∨Ψ) ⊢$_T$ Ψ
[iii] Turing noted that classical logic can be used to make invalid inferences using inconsistent information "*without actually going through* [an explicit] *contradiction.*" [Diamond 1976] Furthermore, [Church 1935, Turing 1936] proved that it is computationally undecidable whether a mathematical theory of practice is inconsistent.

Direct Logic[20] is a framework: propositions have arguments for and against. Inference rules provide arguments that let you infer more propositions. Direct Logic is just a bookkeeping system that helps you keep track. It doesn't tell you what to do when an inconsistency is derived. But it does have the great virtue that it doesn't make the mistakes of classical logic when reasoning about inconsistent information.

The semantics of Direct Logic are based on argumentation. Arguments can be inferred for and against propositions. Furthermore, additional arguments can be inferred for and against these *arguments*, *e.g.*, supporting and counter arguments.[21]

Direct Logic must meet the following challenges:
- *Consistent* to avoid security holes
- *Powerful* so that computer systems can carry formalize all logical inferences
- *Principled* so that it can be easily learned by software engineers
- *Coherent* so that it hangs together without a lot of edge cases
- *Intuitive* so that humans can follow computer system reasoning
- *Comprehensive* to accommodate all forms of logical argumentation
- *Inconsistency Robust* to be applicable to pervasively inconsistent theories of practice with
    - Inconsistency Robust Direct Logic for logical inference about inconsistent information
    - Classical Direct Logic for mathematics used in inconsistency-robust theories

Inconsistency Robust Direct Logic is for reasoning about pervasively-inconsistent large software systems with the following goals:
- Provide a foundation for reasoning about the mutually inconsistent implementation, specifications, and use cases large software systems.
- Formalize a notion of "direct" inference for reasoning about inconsistent information
- Support "natural" deduction [Jaśkowski 1934][i] inference rules[ii]
- Support the usual propositional equivalences[iii]

---

[i] See discussion in [Pelletier 1999].
[ii] with the *exception* of the following:
- *Classical Proof by Contradiction* i.e., $(\Psi \vdash_T \neg\Phi, \Phi) \vdash_T \neg\Psi$
- *Extraneous* ∨ *Introduction*, i.e., $\Psi \vdash_T (\Phi \vee \Psi)$
- *Excluded Middle*, i.e., $\vdash_T (\Phi \vee \neg\Phi)$

[iii] with exception of absorption, which must be restricted to avoid IGOR

- ∨-*Elimination* , *i.e.*, ¬Φ, (Φ∨Ψ) ⊢$_T$ Ψ
- Reasoning by disjunctive cases,
  i.e., (Ψ∨Φ), (Ψ ⊢$_T$ Θ), (Φ ⊢$_T$ Ω) ⊢$_T$ Θ∨Ω
- Inconsistency Robust Proof by Contradiction, *i.e.*,
  ⊢$_T$ (Ψ⇒(¬Φ∧Φ)) ⇒ ¬Ψ
- Support abstraction among code, documentation, and use cases of large software systems. (See discussion below.)
- Provide increased safety in reasoning using inconsistent information.[i]

Consequently, Inconsistency Robust Direct Logic is well suited in practice for reasoning about large software systems.[ii]

Adding just Classical Proof by Contradiction to Inconsistency Robust Direct Logic transforms it into a classical logic.

The theories of Direct Logic are "open" in the sense of open-ended schematic axiomatic systems [Feferman 2007b]. The language of a theory can include any vocabulary in which its axioms may be applied, i.e., it is not restricted to a specific vocabulary fixed in advance (or at any other time). Indeed a theory can be an open system can receive new information at any time [Hewitt 1991, Cellucci 1992].

In the argumentation lies the knowledge

You don't understand anything until you learn it more than one way.
[Minsky 2005][22]

Partly in reaction to Popper[iii], Lakatos [1967, §2]) calls the view below *Euclidean*:[23]

"*Classical epistemology has for two thousand years modeled its ideal of a theory, whether scientific or mathematical, on its conception of Euclidean geometry. The ideal theory is a deductive system with an indubitable truth-injection at the top (a finite conjunction of axioms)—so that truth, flowing*

---

[i] by comparison with classical logic

[ii] In this respect, Direct Logic differs from previous inconsistency tolerant logics, which had inference rules that made them intractable for use with large software systems.

[iii] Proof by contradiction has played an important role in science (emphasized by Karl Popper [1962]) as formulated in his principle of refutation which in its most stark form is as follows:
If ⊢$_T$¬Ob for some observation Ob, then it can be concluded that *T* is refuted (in a theory called *Popper*), *i.e.*, ⊢$_{Popper}$¬*T*
See Suppe [1977] for further discussion.

down from the top through the safe truth-preserving channels of valid inferences, inundates the whole system."

Since truth is out the window for inconsistent theories, we need a reformulation in terms of argumentation.

Direct Argumentation

Inference in a theory T ($\vdash_T$) carries chains of argument from antecedents to consequents.

Direct Argumentation means that $\vdash_T$ in a proposition actually means inference in the theory T.[24] For example, together $\vdash_T\Psi$ and $\Psi\vdash_T\Phi$ infer $\vdash_T\Phi$, which in Inconsistency Robust Direct Logic can be expressed as follows by *Direct Argumentation*: $\Psi, (\Psi \vdash_T \Phi) \vdash_T \Phi$

Theory Dependence

Inference in Inconsistency Robust Direct Logic is theory dependent. For example [Latour 2010]:

> *"Are these stone, clay, and wood idols true divinities[i]?"* [The Africans] answered *"Yes!"* with utmost innocence: yes, of course, otherwise we would not have made them with our own hands[ii]! The Portuguese, shocked but scrupulous, not want to condemn without proof, gave the Africans one last chance: "You can't say both that you've made your own [idols] and that they are true divinities[iii]; **you have to choose**: it's either one or the other. Unless," they went on indignantly, "you really have no brains, and you're as oblivious to the principle of contraction[iv] as you are to the sin of idolatry." Stunned silence from the [Africans] who failed to see any contradiction.[v]*

As stated, there is no inconsistency in either the theory Africans or the theory Portuguese. But there is an inconsistency in the join of these theories, namely, Africans+Portuguese.

In general, the theories of Inconsistency Robust Direct Logic are inconsistent and therefore propositions cannot be consistently labeled with truth values.

---

[i] $\vdash_{Africans}$Divine[idols]

[ii] $\vdash_{Africans}$Fabricated[idols]

[iii] $\vdash_{Portuguese}\neg$(Fabricated[idols] $\wedge$ Divine[idols])

[iv] in *Africans+Portuguese*

[v] in *Africans*

Information Invariance

> *Become a student of change. It is the only thing that will remain constant.*
> Anthony D'Angelo, The College Blue Book

Invariance[i] is a fundamental technical goal of Direct Logic.

> **Invariance:** Principles of Direct Logic are invariant as follows:
> 1. **Soundness of inference:** information is not increased by inference
> 2. **Completeness of inference:** all information that necessarily holds can be inferred

Semantics of Direct Logic

The semantics of Direct Logic is the semantics of argumentation. Arguments can be made in favor of against propositions. And, in turn, arguments can be made in favor and against arguments. The notation $\vdash_T^A \Psi$ is used to express that A is an argument for Ψ in T.

The semantics of Direct Logic are grounded in the principle that every proposition that holds in a theory must have argument in its favor which can be expressed as follows:

> The principle **Inferences have Arguments** says that $\vdash_T \Psi$ if and only if there is an argument A for Ψ in T, *i.e.*, $\vdash_T^A \Psi$[ii]

For example, there is a controversy in biochemistry as to whether or not it has been shown that arsenic can support life with published arguments by Redfield[25] and NASA[26] to the following effect:
$\vdash_{Biochemistry}^{Redfield} (\nvdash_{Biochemistry}^{NASA} \text{SupportsLife[Arsenic]})$

[Rovelli 2011] has commented on this general situation:
> *There is a widely used notion that does plenty of damage: the notion of "scientifically proven". Nearly an oxymoron. The very foundation of science is to keep the door open to doubt. Precisely because we keep*

---

[i] Closely related to conservation laws in physics
[ii] There is a computational decision deterministic procedure Checker$_T$ running in linear time such that:
$\forall[a:\text{Argument}, s:\text{Sentence}] \rightarrow \text{Checker}_T[a, s] = \text{True} \Leftrightarrow \vdash_T^a \lfloor s \rfloor_T)$

questioning everything, especially our own premises, we are always ready to improve our knowledge. Therefore a good scientist is never 'certain'. Lack of certainty is precisely what makes conclusions more reliable than the conclusions of those who are certain: because the good scientist will be ready to shift to a different point of view if better elements of evidence, or novel arguments emerge. Therefore certainty is not only something of no use, but is in fact damaging, if we value reliability.

A fanciful example of argumentation comes from the famous story *"What the Tortoise Said to Achilles"* [Carroll 1895].

Applied to example of the Tortoise in the stony, we have
$$\vdash \frac{\text{ProofOfZ(Axiom1, Axiom2)}}{\text{Achilles}} Z^{27}$$
where
A ≡ *"Things that are equal to the same are equal to each other."*
B ≡ *"The two sides of this Triangle are things that are equal to the same."*
Z ≡ *"The two sides of this Triangle are equal to each other."*
$\text{Axiom}_1 \equiv \vdash A, B$
$\text{Axiom}_2 \equiv A, B \vdash Z$

The above proposition fulfills the demand of the Tortoise that
 *Whatever Logic is good enough to tell me is worth **writing down**.*

Inference in Argumentation

Scientist and engineers speak in the name of new allies that they have shaped and enrolled; representatives among other representatives, they add these unexpected resources to tip the balance of force in their favor.
Latour [1987] Second Principle

"⊢ Elimination" (Chaining) is a fundamental principle of inference: [28]

⊢ **Elimination (Chaining):** Ψ, (Ψ ⊢$_T$Φ) ⊢$_T$ Φ
① Φ *inferred in T from* ⊢$_T$Ψ *and* Ψ ⊢$_T$Φ

SubArguments is another fundamental principle of inference:

⊢ **Introduction (SubArguments):** (⊢$_{T \wedge \Psi}$ Φ) ⊢$_T$(Ψ ⊢$_T$Φ)
① *In T,* Ψ *infers* Φ *when* Φ *is inferred in* T∧Ψ

Please see the appendix *"Detail of Direct Logic"* for more information.

Mathematics Self Proves that it is Open

Mathematics proves that it is open in the sense that it can prove that its theorems cannot be provably computationally enumerated:[29]

Theorem ⊢Mathematics is Open
Proof.[i] Suppose to obtain a contradiction that it is possible to prove closure, *i.e.*, there is a provably computable total deterministic procedure Theorem such that it is provable that
$$\forall[\Psi\text{:Proposition}] \rightarrow (\vdash\Psi) \Leftrightarrow \exists[i:\mathbb{N}] \rightarrow \text{Theorem.}[i]=p$$
As a consequence of the above, there is a provably total procedure ProvableComputableTotal that enumerates the provably total computable procedures that can be used in the implementation of the following procedure: Diagonal[i] ≡ (ProvableComputableTotal[i])[i]+1
However,
- ProvableComputableTotal[Diagonal] because Diagonal is implemented using provably computable total procedures.
- ¬ProvableComputableTotal[Diagonal] because Diagonal is a provably computable total procedure that differs from every other provably computable total procedure.

[Franzén 2004] argued that mathematics is inexhaustible because of inferential undecidability[ii] of closed mathematical theories. The above theorem that mathematics is open provides another independent argument for the inexhaustibility of mathematics.

---

[i] This argument appeared in [Church 1934] expressing concern that the argument meant that there is *"no sound basis for supposing that there is such a thing as logic."*
[ii] See section immediately below.

Contributions of Direct Logic
Inconsistency Robust Direct Logic aims to be a minimal fix to classical logic to meet the needs of information coordination. (Addition of just the rule of Classical Proof by Contradiction by Inference, transforms Direct Logic into Classical Logic.) Direct Logic makes the following contributions over previous work:
- *Direct* Inference[30]
- *Direct* Argumentation (inference directly expressed)
- *Inconsistency Robustness*
- *Inconsistency-robust* Natural Deduction[31]
- Intuitive inferences hold including the following:
    - *Propositional equivalences*[i]
    - *Reasoning by disjunctive cases*, i.e.,
      $(\Psi \vee \Phi), (\Psi \vdash_T \Theta), (\Phi \vdash_T \Omega) \vdash_T \Theta \vee \Omega$
    - ∨-*Elimination*, i.e., $\neg \Phi, (\Phi \vee \Psi) \vdash_T \Psi$
    - *Contrapositive for implication*: A proposition implies another if an only if negation of the latter implies negation of the former, *i.e.*, $\Psi \Rightarrow \Phi$ if and only if $\neg \Phi \Rightarrow \neg \Psi$
    - *Soundness*: A theorem can be used in a proof, *i.e.*,
      $\vdash_T ((\vdash_T \Psi) \Rightarrow \Psi)$
    - *Inconsistency Robust Proof by Contradiction*: A hypothesis can be refuted by showing that it implies a contradiction, *i.e.*,
      $\vdash_T (\Phi \Rightarrow (\Psi \wedge \neg \Psi)) \Rightarrow \neg \Phi$

Actor Model of Computation[32]
> *The distinction between past, present and future is only a stubbornly persistent illusion.*
> Einstein

Concurrency has now become the norm. However nondeterminism came first. See [Hewitt 2010b] for a history of models of nondeterministic computation.

What is Computation?
> *Any problem in computer science can be solved by introducing another level of abstraction.*
> paraphrase of Alan Perlis

Turing's model of computation was intensely psychological.[33] He proposed the thesis that it included all of purely mechanical computation.[34]

---
[i] except absorption

Gödel declared that
> It is *"absolutely impossible that anybody who understands the question [What is computation?] and knows Turing's definition should decide for a different concept."*[35]

By contrast, in the Actor model [Hewitt, Bishop and Steiger 1973; Hewitt 2010b], computation is conceived as distributed in space where computational devices called Actors communicate asynchronously using addresses of Actors and the entire computation is not in any well-defined state. The behavior of an Actor is defined when it receives a message and at other times may be indeterminate.

Axioms of locality including *Organizational* and *Operational* hold as follows:
- *Organization:* The local storage of an Actor can include *addresses* only
  1. that were provided when it was created or of Actors that it has created
  2. that have been received in messages
- *Operation:* In response to a message received, an Actor can
  1. create more Actors
  2. send messages[i] to addresses in the following:
     - the message it has just received
     - its local storage
  3. for an exclusive[ii] Actor, designate how to process the next message received[iii]

The Actor Model differs from its predecessors and most current models of computation in that the Actor model assumes the following:
- Concurrent execution in processing a message.
- The following are *not* required by an Actor: a thread, a mailbox, a message queue, its own operating system process, *etc.*
- Message passing has the same overhead as looping and procedure calling.

Configurations versus Global State Spaces

Computations are represented differently in Turing Machines and Actors:
1. *Turing Machine*: a computation can be represented as a global state that determines all information about the computation. It can be nondeterministic as to which will be the next global state, *e.g.*, in

---

[i] Likewise the messages sent can contain addresses only
  1. that were provided when the Actor was created
  2. that have been received in messagesthat are for Actors created here
[ii] An *exclusive* Actor can perform at most one activity at a time.
[iii] An Actor that will never update its local storage can be freely replicated and cached.

simulations where the global state can transition nondeterministically to the next state as a global clock advances in time, e.g., Simula [Dahl and Nygaard 1967].[36]
1. *Actors*: a computation can be represented as a configuration. Information about a configuration can be indeterminate.[i]

Functions defined by lambda expressions [Church 1941] are special case Actors that never change.

That Actors which behave like mathematical functions exactly correspond with those definable in the lambda calculus provides an intuitive justification for the rules of the lambda calculus:
- *Lambda identifiers*: each identifier is bound to the address of an Actor. The rules for free and bound identifiers correspond to the Actor rules for addresses.
- *Beta reduction*: each beta reduction corresponds to an Actor receiving a message. Instead of performing substitution, an Actor receives addresses of its arguments.

The lambda calculus can be implemented in ActorScript as follows:

Actor Identifier◁aType▷[ ]
 implements Expression◁aType▷ **using**
  anEnvironment.lookup[[:]Expression◁aType▷]
              // lookup this identifier in anEnvironment

Actor ProcedureCall◁aType, AnotherType▷
      [operator:([aType]↦ anotherType), operand:aType]
 implements Expression◁anotherType▷ **using**
  eval[anEnvironment]→
      (operator.eval[anEnvironment]).[operand.eval[environment]]

Actor Lambda◁aType, AnotherType▷
      [anIdentifier:Identifier◁aType▷, body:anotherType]
 implements Expression◁[aType]↦ anotherType▷ **using**
  eval[anEnvironment]→
   [anArgument:aType]→
     body.eval[anEnvironment.bind[anIdentifier, anEnvironment]]
      // create a new environment with anIdentifier
      //   bound to anArgument

---

[i] For example, there can be messages in transit that will be delivered at some indefinite time.

Note that in the above:
- All operations are local.
- The definition is modular in that each lambda calculus programming language construct is an Actor.
- The definition is easily extensible since it is easy to add additional programming language constructs.
- The definition is easily operationalized into efficient concurrent implementations.
- The definition easily fits into more general concurrent computational frameworks for many-core and distributed computation.

However, there are *nondeterministic* computable functions on integers that cannot be implemented using the nondeterministic lambda calculus. Furthermore, the lambda calculus can be very inefficient as illustrate by the theorem below:

Theorem: In systems of practice[i], simulating an Actor system using the parallel lambda calculus (*i.e.* using purely functional programming) can be exponentially slower.

The lambda calculus can express parallelism but not general concurrency (see discussion below).

Actors generalize Turing Machines

Actor systems can perform computations that are impossible by Turing Machines as illustrated by the following example:
There is a bound on the size of integer that can be computed by an *always halting* nondeterministic Turing Machine starting on a blank tape.[37]

Plotkin [1976] gave an informal proof as follows:[38]
Now the set of initial segments of execution sequences of a given nondeterministic program P, starting from a given state, will form a tree. The branching points will correspond to the choice points in the program. Since there are always only finitely many alternatives at each choice point, the branching factor of the tree is always finite.[39] That is, the tree is finitary. Now König's lemma says that if every branch of a finitary tree is finite, then so is the tree itself. In the present case this means that if every execution sequence of P terminates, then there are only finitely many execution sequences. So if an output set of P is infinite, it must contain a nonterminating computation.[40]

---

[i] Examples include climate models and medical diagnosis and treatment systems for cancer. A software system of practice typically has tens of millions of lines of code.

By contrast, the following Actor system can compute an integer of unbounded size:
The above Actor system can be implemented as follows using ActorScript™:

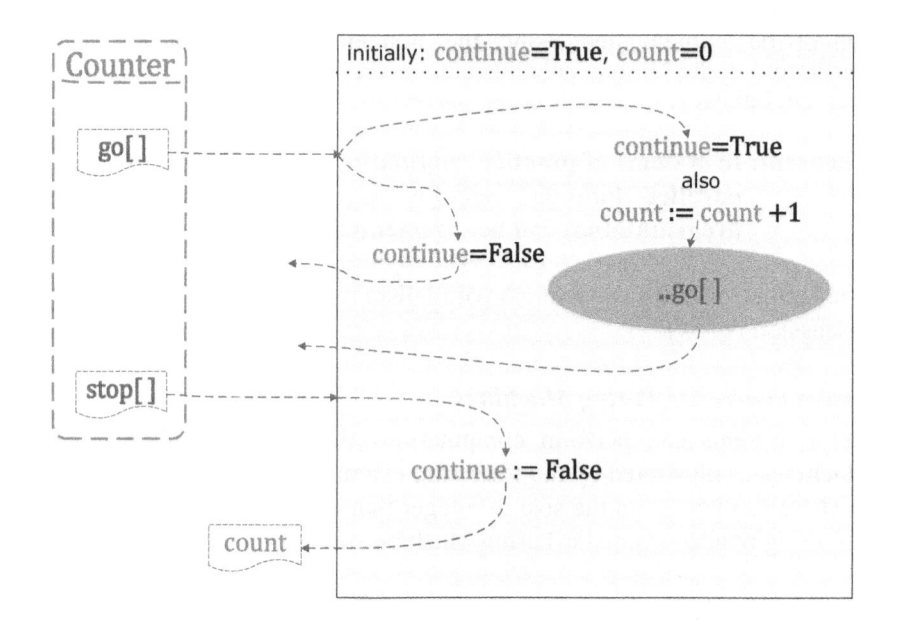

   Unbounded ≡
     start[ ]→   // a start message is implemented by
      Let aCounter ← SimpleCounter.[ ].   // let aCounter be a new Counter
       ①aCounter.go[ ],   // send aCounter a go message and concurrently
       ①aCounter.stop[ ]
                   // return the value of sending aCounter a stop message

Actor SimpleCounter[ ]
  count := 0   // the variable count is initially 0
  continue := **True**   // the variable continue is initially **True**
  implements Counter **using**
    stop[ ]→
      count   // return count
        afterward continue := false
                // continue is false for the next message received
    go[ ]→ continue ◆
       True⸷
         Hole ..go[ ]   // send go[ ] to this counter after
          after count := count+1 // incrementing count
       False⸷ **Void**   // if continue is **False**, return **Void**

By the semantics of the Actor model of computation [Clinger 1981; Hewitt 2006], sending Unbounded a start message will result in sending an integer of unbounded size to the return address that was received with the start message.

The nondeterministic procedure Unbounded above can be axiomatized as follows:
$\forall [n:\text{Integer}] \rightarrow$
  $\exists [aRequest:\text{Request}, anInteger:\text{Integer}] \rightarrow$
    Unbounded sent$_{aRequest}$ start[ ]
    $\Rightarrow$ Sent$_{\text{Response}_{aRequest}}$ returned[$anInteger$] $\wedge$ $anInteger > n$

However, the above axiom does *not* compute any actual output! Instead the above axiom simply asserts the *existence* of unbounded outputs for start messages.

Theorem. There are *nondeterministic* computable functions on integers that cannot be implemented by a nondeterministic Turing machine.
  Proof. The above Actor system implements a nondeterministic function[i] that cannot be implemented by a nondeterministic Turing machine.

The following arguments support unbounded nondeterminism in the Actor model [Hewitt 1985, 2006]:
- There is no bound that can be placed on how long it takes a computational circuit called an *arbiter* to settle. Arbiters are used in computers to deal with the circumstance that computer clocks operate asynchronously with input from outside, *e.g.*, keyboard input, disk access, network input, *etc.* So it could take an unbounded time for a message sent to a computer to be received and in the meantime the computer could traverse an unbounded number of states.
- Electronic mail enables unbounded nondeterminism since mail can be stored on servers indefinitely before being delivered.
- Communication links to servers on the Internet can be out of service indefinitely.

Reception order indeterminacy
Hewitt and Agha [1991] and other published work argued that mathematical models of concurrency did not determine particular concurrent computations as follows: The Actor Model[ii] makes use of arbitration for implementing the order in which Actors process message. Since these orders are in general

---
[i] with graph {start[ ] ⤳ 0, start[ ] ⤳ 1, start[ ] ⤳ 2, ... }
[ii] Actors are the universal conceptual primitives of concurrent computation.

indeterminate, they cannot be deduced from prior information by mathematical logic alone. Therefore mathematical logic cannot implement concurrent computation in open systems.

In concrete terms for Actor systems, typically we cannot observe the details by which the order in which an Actor processes messages has been determined. Attempting to do so affects the results. Instead of observing the internals of arbitration processes of Actor computations, we await outcomes.[41] Indeterminacy in arbiters produces indeterminacy in Actors.[i]

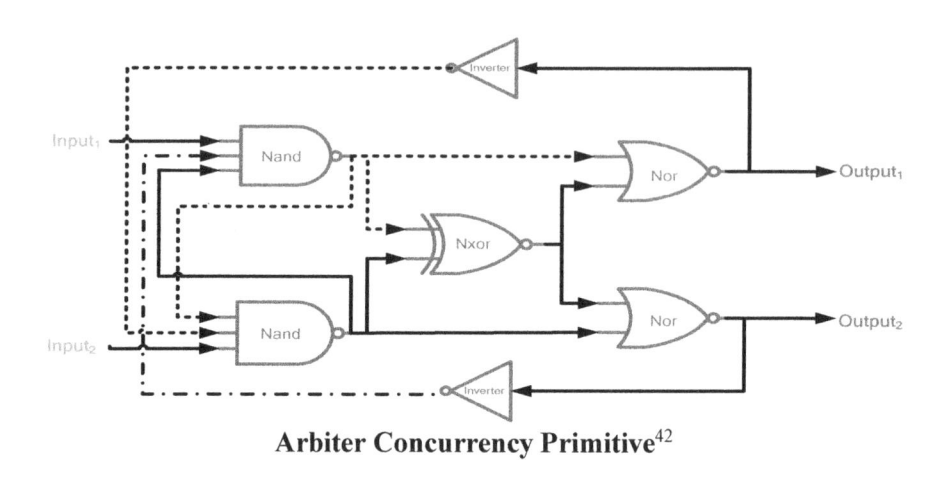

Arbiter Concurrency Primitive[42]

The reason that we await outcomes is that we have no realistic alternative.

Actor Physics

The Actor model makes use of two fundamental orders on events [Baker and Hewitt 1977; Clinger 1981, Hewitt 2006]:
1. The *activation order* ($\rightsquigarrow$) is a fundamental order that models one event activating another (there is energy flow from an event to an event which it activates). The activation order is discrete:
    $\forall [e_1, e_2 \in Events] \rightarrow Finite[\{e \in Events \mid e_1 \rightsquigarrow e \rightsquigarrow e_2\}]$
    There are two kinds of events involved in the activation order: reception and transmission. Reception events can activate transmission events and transmission events can activate reception events.
2. The *reception order* of an exclusive Actor $\mathbf{x}$ ($\stackrel{x}{\Rightarrow}$) models the (total) order of events in which a message is received at $\mathbf{x}$. The reception order of each $\mathbf{x}$ is discrete:
    $\forall [r_1, r_2 \in ReceptionEvents_x] \rightarrow Finite[\{r \in ReceptionEvents_x \mid r_1 \stackrel{x}{\Rightarrow} r \stackrel{x}{\Rightarrow} r_2\}]$

---

[i] dashes are used solely to delineate crossing wires

The *combined order* (denoted by ⤳) is defined to be the transitive closure of the activation order and the reception orders of all Actors. So the following question arose in the early history of the Actor model: *"Is the combined order discrete?"* Discreteness of the combined order captures an important intuition about computation because it rules out counterintuitive computations in which an infinite number of computational events occur between two events (*à la* Zeno).

Hewitt conjectured that the discreteness of the activation order together with the discreteness of all reception orders implies that the combined order is discrete. Surprisingly [Clinger 1981; later generalized in Hewitt 2006] answered the question in the negative by giving a counterexample.

The counterexample is remarkable in that it violates the compactness theorem for 1st order logic:
> Any finite set of propositions is consistent (the activation order and all reception orders are discrete) and represents a potentially physically realizable situation. But there is an infinite set of propositions that is inconsistent with the discreteness of the combined order and does not represent a physically realizable situation.

The counterexample is not a problem for Direct Logic because the compactness theorem does not hold.

The resolution of the problem is to take discreteness of the combined order as an axiom of the Actor model:
$$\forall [e_1, e_2 \in \text{Events}] \rightarrow \text{Finite}[\{e \in \text{Events} \mid e_1 \curvearrowright e \curvearrowright e_2\}]$$

Computational Representation Theorem

> *a philosophical shift in which knowledge is no longer treated primarily as referential, as a set of statements **about** reality, but as a practice that interferes with other practices. It therefore participates **in** reality.*
> Annemarie Mol [2002]

What does the mathematical theory of Actors have to say about the relationship between logic and computation? A closed system is defined to be one which does not communicate with the outside. Actor model theory provides the means to characterize all the possible computations of a closed system in terms of the Computational Representation Theorem [Clinger 1982; Hewitt 2006]:[43]

> The denotation Denote_S of a closed system S represents all the possible behaviors of S as $\text{Denote}_S = \overrightarrow{\lim}^\infty \text{Progression}_S^i$ *where* Progression_S takes a set of partial behaviors to their next stage, i.e., $\text{Progression } s^i \mapsto^i \text{Progression } s^{i+1}$

---
[i] read as *"can evolve to"*

In this way, S can be mathematically characterized in terms of all its possible behaviors (including those involving unbounded nondeterminism).[i]

The denotations form the basis of constructively checking programs against all their possible executions,[ii]

A consequence of the Computational Representation system is that there are uncountably many different Actors.

For example, CreateReal.[ ] can produce any real number[iii] between 0 and 1 where
 CreateReal.[ ] ≡ [(0 **either** 1), ⱽ**Postpone** CreateReal.[ ]]
where
- CreateReal.[ ] is the result of sending the actor CreateReal the message [ ]
- (0 **either** 1) is the nondeterministic choice of 0 or 1
- [first, ⱽrest] is the sequence that begins with first and whose remainder is rest
- **Postpone** expression delays execution of expression until the value is needed.

The upshot is that **concurrent systems can be represented and characterized by logical deduction but cannot be implemented**.

Thus, the following problem arose:
 How can programming languages be rigorously defined since the proposal by Scott and Strachey [1971] to define them in terms lambda calculus failed because the lambda calculus cannot implement concurrency?

One solution is to develop a concurrent interpreter using eval messages in which eval[anEnvironment] is a message that can be sent to an expression to cause it be evaluated using the environment anEnvironment. Using such messages, modular meta-circular definitions can be concisely expressed in the Actor model for universal concurrent programming languages [Hewitt 2010a].

---

[i] There are no messages in transit in Denote$_s$
[ii] a restricted form of this can be done via Model Checking in which the properties checked are limited to those that can be expressed in Linear-time Temporal Logic [Clarke, Emerson, Sifakis, *etc*. ACM 2007 Turing Award]
[iii] using binary representation. See [Feferman 2012] for more on computation over the reals.

Computation is not subsumed by logical deduction

The gauntlet was officially thrown in *The Challenge of Open Systems* [Hewitt 1985] to which [Kowalski 1988b] replied in *Logic-Based Open Systems*. [Hewitt and Agha 1988] followed up in the context of the Japanese Fifth Generation Project.

Kowalski claims that *"computation could be subsumed by deduction"* [i] His claim has been valuable in that it has motivated further research to characterize exactly which computations could be performed by Logic Programs. *However, contrary to Kowalski, computation in general is not subsumed by deduction.*

Bounded Nondeterminism of Direct Logic

Since it includes the nondeterministic λ calculus, direct inference, and categorical induction in addition to its other inference capabilities, Direct Logic is a very powerful foundation for Logic Program languages.

But there is no Direct Logic expression that is equivalent to sending Unbounded a **start** message for the following reason:
An expression ε will be said to always converge (written as AlwaysConverges[ε]) if and only if every reduction path terminates. *I.e.*, there is no function f such that f[0]= ε *and* ∀[i:ℕ]→ ⌊f[i]⌋ →⌊f[i+1]⌋
where the symbol → is used for reduction (see the appendix of this paper on classical mathematics in Direct Logic). For example,
¬AlwaysConverges[([x]→ (0 **either** x.[x])) .[[x]→ (0 **either** x.[x])]][ii]
because there is a nonterminating path.
Theorem: Bounded Nondeterminism of Direct Logic. If an expression in Direct Logic always converges, then there is a bound Bound$_\varepsilon$ on the number to which it can converge. *I.e.*,
∀[i:ℕ]→ (ε **AlwaysConvergesTo** n) ⇒ i≤Bound$_\varepsilon$

Consequently there is no Direct Logic program equivalent to sending Unbounded a **start** message because it has unbounded nondeterminism whereas every Direct Logic program has bounded nondeterminism.

---

[i] In fact, [Kowalski 1980] forcefully stated:
> *There is only one language suitable for representing information -- whether declarative or procedural -- and that is first-order predicate logic. There is only one intelligent way to process information -- and that is by applying deductive inference methods.*

[ii] Note that there are two expressions (separated by "**either**") in the bodies which provides for nondeterminism.

In this way, we have proved that the Procedural Embedding of Knowledge paradigm is strictly more general than the Logic Program paradigm.

Computational Undecidability

Some questions cannot be uniformly answered computationally.

The halting problem is to computationally decide whether a program halts on a given input[i] *i.e.*, there is a total computational deterministic predicate Halt such that the following 3 properties hold for any program p and input x:
1. Halt.[p, x] →$_1$ *True* ⇔ Converges[⌈⌊p⌋.[x]⌉]
2. Halt.[p, x] →$_1$ *False* ⇔ ¬Converges[⌈⌊p⌋.[x]⌉]
3. Halt.[p, x] →$_1$ *True* ∨ Halt.[p, x] →$_1$ *False*

[Church 1935 and later Turing 1936] published proofs that the halting problem is computationally undecidable for computable deterministic procedures.[44] In other words, there is no such procedure Halt for computable procedures.
  Theorem: ⊢ ¬ComputationallyDecidable[Halt][ii]

Classical mathematics self proves its own consistency (contra Gödel *et. al.*)

The following rules are fundamental to classical mathematics:
- Proof by Contradiction, *i.e.* (¬Φ⇒(Θ∧¬Θ)) ⊢Φ, which says that a proposition can be proved showing that its negation implies a contradiction.
- Soundness, *i.e.* (⊢Φ)⇒Φ, which says that a theorem can be used in a proof.

Theorem: [45] Mathematics self proves its own consistency.
  Formal Proof. By definition,
   ¬Consistent ⇔ ∃[Ψ:Proposition]→ ⊢(Ψ∧¬Ψ). By the rule of Existential Elimination, there is some proposition Ψ$_0$ such that ¬Consistent⇒ ⊢(Ψ$_0$ ∧¬Ψ$_0$) which by the rule of Soundness and transitivity of implication means ¬Consistent⇒(Ψ$_0$ ∧¬Ψ$_0$).

---

[i] Adapted from [Church 1936]. Normal forms were discovered for the lambda calculus, which is the way that they "halt." [Church 1936] proved the halting problem computationally undecidable. Having done considerable work, Turing was disappointed to learn of Church's publication. The month after Church's article was published, [Turing 1936] was hurriedly submitted for publication.
[ii] The fact that the halting problem is computationally undecidable does not mean that proving that programs halt cannot be done in practice [Cook, Podelski, and Rybalchenko 2006].

Substituting for Φ and Θ, in the rule for Proof by Contradiction, we have $(\neg\text{Consistent} \Rightarrow (\Psi_0 \wedge \neg\Psi_0)) \vdash \text{Consistent}$. Thus, $\vdash\text{Consistent}$.

1) $\neg$Consistent	// hypothesis to derive a contradiction **just in this subargument**
2) $\exists[\Psi\text{:Proposition}] \rightarrow \vdash(\Psi \wedge \neg\Psi)$	// definition of inconsistency using 1)
3) $\vdash(\Psi_0 \wedge \neg\Psi_0)$	// rule of Existential Elimination using 2)
4) $\Psi_0 \wedge \neg\Psi_0$	// rule of Soundness using 3)
$\vdash$ Consistent	// rule of Proof by Contradiction using 1) and 4)

Natural Deduction[i] Proof of Consistency of Mathematics

Please note the following points:
- The above argument formally mathematically proves that mathematics is consistent and that **it is not a premise of the theorem that mathematics is consistent.**[46]
- Classical mathematics was designed for consistent axioms and consequently the rules of classical mathematics can be used to prove consistency regardless of other axioms.[47]

The above proof means that "Mathematics is consistent" is a theorem in Classical Direct Logic. This means that the usefulness of Classical Direct Logic depends crucially on the consistency of Mathematics.[48] Good evidence for the consistency of Mathematics comes from the way that Classical Direct Logic avoids the known paradoxes. Humans have spent millennia devising paradoxes.

The above recently developed self-proof of consistency shows that the current common understanding that Gödel proved "Mathematics cannot prove its own consistency, if it is consistent" is inaccurate.

Long ago, Wittgenstein showed that contradiction in mathematics results from the kind of "self-referential"[i] sentence that Gödel used in his proof. However, using a typed notation for mathematical sentences, it can be proved that the kind "self-referential" sentence that Gödel used in his proof cannot be constructed because required fixed points do not exist. In this way, consistency of mathematics is preserved without giving up power.

---

[i] [Jaśkowski 1934] developed Natural Deduction *cf.* [Barker-Plummer, Barwise, and Etchemendy 2011]

Completeness versus Inferential Undecidability

> "In mathematics, there is no *ignorabimus*."
> Hilbert, 1902

A mathematical theory is an extension of mathematics whose proofs are computationally enumerable. For example, group theory is obtained by adding the axioms of groups along with the provision that theorems are computationally enumerable.

By definition, if T is a mathematical theory, there is a total deterministic procedure $Proof_T$ such that:

$$\vdash_T^p \psi \Leftrightarrow \exists[i:\mathbb{N}] \to Proof_T[i]=p$$

Theorem: If T is a consistent mathematical theory, there is a proposition $\psi_{ChurchTuring}$, such that both of the following hold:[i]

- $\vdash\!\!\!\!/_T \psi_{ChurchTuring}$
- $\vdash\!\!\!\!/_T \neg\psi_{ChurchTuring}$

Note the following important ingredients for the proof of inferential undecidability[ii] of mathematical theories:
- Closure (computational enumerability) of the theorems of a mathematical theory to carry through the proof.
- Consistency (nontriviality) to prevent everything from being provable.

Information Invariance[iii] is a fundamental technical goal of logic consisting of the following:
1. *Soundness of inference:* information is not increased by inference[iv]
2. *Completeness of inference:* all information that necessarily holds can be inferred

---

[i] Otherwise, provability in classical logic would be computationally decidable because

$$\forall[p:Program, x:\mathbb{N}] \to (Halt[p, x] \Leftrightarrow \vdash_T Halt[p, x])$$

where $Halt[p, x]$ if and only if program p halts on input x. If such a $\psi_{ChurchTuring}$ did not exist, then provability could be decided by a computable procedure $Decide_T:[Sentence] \mapsto Boolean$ enumerating theorems of T until the proposition in question or its negation is encountered:

$$Decide_{T^*}[s] \to True \Leftrightarrow (\vdash_T \lfloor s \rfloor) \vee \vdash_T \neg \lfloor s \rfloor$$

Of course, $Decide_T$ is a partial procedure and does not always converge.

[ii] sometimes called "incompleteness"
[iii] related to conservation laws in physics
[iv] *E.g.* inconsistent information does not infer nonsense.

Note that that a closed mathematical theory T is inferentially undecidable with respect to $\psi_{ChurchTuring}$ does not mean *"incompleteness"* with respect to the information that can be inferred because
$$\vdash (\nvdash_T \psi_{ChurchTuring}), (\nvdash_T \neg\psi_{ChurchTuring}).^i$$

Information Coordination

Technology now at hand can coordinate all kinds of digital information for individuals, groups, and organizations so their information usefully links together.[49] Information coordination needs to make use of the following information system principles:
- *Persistence.* Information is collected and indexed.
- *Concurrency:* Work proceeds interactively and concurrently, overlapping in time.
- *Quasi-commutativity:* Information can be used regardless of whether it initiates new work or become relevant to ongoing work.
- *Sponsorship:* Sponsors provide resources for computation, i.e., processing, storage, and communications.
- *Pluralism:* Information is heterogeneous, overlapping and often inconsistent.
- *Provenance:* The provenance of information is carefully tracked and recorded.
- *Lossless* : Once a system has some information, then it has it thereafter.

Opposition of Philosophers

> *By this it appears how necessary it is for nay man that aspires to true knowledge to examine the definitions of former authors; and either to correct them, where they are negligently set down, or to make them himself. For the errors of definitions multiply themselves, according as the reckoning proceeds, and lead men into absurdities, which at last they see, but cannot avoid, without reckoning anew from the beginning; in which lies the foundation of their errors...*
> [Hobbes *Leviathan*, Chapter 4]

> *Faced with the choice between changing one's mind and proving that there is no need to do so, almost everyone gets busy on the proof.*
> John Kenneth Galbraith [1971 pg. 50]

---

[i] by construction

A number of philosophers have opposed the results in this paper:
- Some would like to stick with just classical logic and not consider inconsistency robustness.[50]
- Some would like to stick with the first-order theories and not consider direct inference.
- Some would like to stick with just Logic Programs (*e.g.* nondeterministic Turing Machines, λ-calculus, *etc.*) and not consider concurrency.

And some would like to have nothing to do with any of the above![51] However, the results in this paper (and the driving technological and economic forces behind them) tend to push towards inconsistency robustness, direct inference, and concurrency. [Hewitt 2008a]

Philosophers are now challenged as to whether they agree that
- *Inconsistency is the norm.*
- *Direct inference is the norm.*
- *Logic Programs are **not** computationally universal.*

Scalable Information Coordination

Information coordination works by making connections including examples like the following:
- A statistical connection between "being in a traffic jam" and "driving in downtown Trenton between 5PM and 6PM on a weekday."
- A terminological connection between "MSR" and "Microsoft Research."
- A causal connection between "joining a group" and "being a member of the group."
- A syntactic connection between "a pin dropped" and "a dropped pin."
- A biological connection between "a dolphin" and "a mammal".
- A demographic connection between "undocumented residents of California" and "7% of the population of California."
- A geographical connection between "Leeds" and "England."
- A temporal connection between "turning on a computer" and "joining an on-line discussion."

By making these connections, iInfo™ information coordination offers tremendous value for individuals, families, groups, and organizations in making more effective use of information technology.

In practice coordinated information is invariably inconsistent.[52] Therefore iInfo must be able to make connections even in the face of inconsistency.[53] The business of iInfo is not to make difficult decisions like deciding the ultimate truth or probability of propositions. Instead it provides means for processing information and carefully recording its provenance including arguments (including arguments about arguments) for and against propositions.

Work to be done
The best way to predict the future is to invent it.   Alan Kay

There is much work to be done including the following:

Invariance
Invariance should be precisely formulated and proved. This bears on the issue of how it can be known that all the principles of Direct Logic have been discovered.

Consistency
The following conjectures for Direct Logic need to be convincingly proved:
- Consistency of Inconsistency Robust Direct Logic[i] relative to the consistency of classical mathematics. In this regard Direct Logic is consonant with Bourbaki:
  Absence of contradiction, in mathematics as a whole or in any given branch of it, ... appears as an empirical fact, rather than as a metaphysical principle. The more a given branch has been developed, the less likely it becomes that contradictions may be met with in its farther development.[ii]
  Thus the long historical failure to find an explosion in the methods used by Direct Logic can be considered to be strong evidence of its nontriviality.
- Constructive proof of consistency of Classical Direct Logic

Inconsistency Robustness
Inconsistency robustness of theories of Direct Logic needs to be formally defined and proved. Church remarked as follows concerning a *Foundation of Logic* that he was developing:
  Our present project is to develop the consequences of the foregoing set of postulates until a contradiction is obtained from them, or until the development has been carried so far consistently as to make it empirically probable that no contradiction can be obtained from them. And in this connection it is to be remembered that just such empirical evidence, although admittedly inconclusive, is the only existing evidence

---

[i] *i.e.* consistency of ⊢
[ii] [André Weil 1949] speaking as a representative of Bourbaki

of the freedom from contradiction of any system of mathematical logic which has a claim to adequacy. [Church 1933][i]

Direct Logic is in a similar position except that the task is to demonstrate inconsistency robustness of inconsistent theories. This means that the exact boundaries of Inconsistency Robust Direct Logic as a minimal fix to classical logic need to be established.

Argumentation
Argumentation is fundamental to inconsistency robustness.
- Further work is need on fundamental principles of argumentation for large-scale information coordination. See [Hewitt 2008a, 2008b].
- Tooling for Direct Logic needs to be developed to support large software systems. See [Hewitt 2008a].

Inferential Explosion
Inconsistencies such as the one about whether Yossarian flies are relatively *benign* in the sense that they lack significant consequences to software engineering. Other propositions (such as $\vdash_T 1=0$ in a theory T) are more *malignant* because they can be used to infer that all integers are equal to 0 using mathematical induction. To address malignant propositions, deeper investigations of argumentation using must be undertaken in which the provenance of information will play a central role. See [Hewitt 2008a].

Robustness, Soundness, and Coherence
Fundamental concepts such as *robustness*, *soundness*, and *coherence* need to be rigorously characterized and further developed. Inconsistency-robust reasoning beyond the inference that can be accomplished in Direct Logic needs to be developed, e.g., analogy, metaphor, discourse, debate, and collaboration.

Evolution of Mathematics
In the relation between mathematics and computing science, the latter has been far many years at the receiving end, and I have often asked myself if, when, and how computing would ever be able to repay the debt. [Dijkstra 1986]

We argue that mathematics will become more like programming. [Asperti, Geuvers and Natrajan 2009]

---

[i] The difference between the time that Church wrote the above and today is that the standards for adequacy have gone up dramatically. Direct Logic must be adequate to the needs of reasoning about large software systems.

Mathematical foundations are thought to be consistent by an overwhelming consensus of working professional mathematicians, e.g., mathematical theories of real numbers, integers, *etc.*

In practice, mathematical theories that are thought to be consistency by an overwhelming consensus of working mathematicians play an important supporting role for inconsistency-robust theories, *e.g.*, theories of the Liver, Diabetes, Human Behavior, *etc.*

Conclusion

> "The problem is that today some knowledge still feels too dangerous because our times are not so different to Cantor or Boltzmann or Gödel's time. We too feel things we thought were solid being challenged; feel our certainties slipping away. And so, as then, we still desperately want to cling to a belief in certainty. It makes us feel safe. ... Are we grown up enough to live with uncertainties or will we repeat the mistakes of the twentieth century and pledge blind allegiance to another certainty?"
> Malone [2007]

Inconsistency robustness builds on the following principles:
- We know only a little, but it affects us *enormously*[i]
- At any point in time, much is wrong[ii] with the consensus of leading scientists but it is not known how or which parts.
- Science is never certain; it is continually (re-)made

Software engineers for large software systems often have good arguments for some proposition P and also good arguments for its negation of P. So what do large software manufacturers do? If the problem is serious, they bring it before a committee of stakeholders to try and sort it out. In many particularly difficult cases the resulting decision has been to simply live with the problem for an indefinite period. Consequently, large software systems are shipped to customers with thousands of known inconsistencies of varying severity where
- Even relatively simple subsystems can be subtly inconsistent.
- There is no practical way to test for inconsistency.
- Even though a system is inconsistent, it is not meaningless.

Inconsistency Robust Direct Logic is a minimal fix to Classical Logic without the rule of Classical Proof by Contradiction[iii], *the addition of which transforms*

---

[i] for better or worse
[ii] *e.g.*, misleading, inconsistent, wrong-headed, ambiguous, contra best-practices, *etc.*
[iii] *i.e.,* $(\Psi \vdash (\Phi \wedge \neg \Phi)) \vdash \neg \Psi$

Inconsistency Robust Direct Logic into Classical Logic. A big advantage of inconsistency robust logic is that it makes it practical for computer systems to reason about theories of practice (e.g. for macroeconomics, human history, etc.) that are pervasively inconsistent. Since software engineers have to deal with theories chock full of inconsistencies, Inconsistency Robust Direct Logic should be attractive. However, to make it relevant we need to provide them with tools that are cost effective.

Our everyday life is becoming increasingly dependent on large software systems. And these systems are becoming increasingly permeated with inconsistency and concurrency.

As pervasively inconsistent concurrent systems become a major part of the environment in which we live, it becomes an issue of common sense to use them effectively. We will need sophisticated software systems that formalize this common sense to help people understand and apply the principles and practices suggested in this paper.

Creating this software is not a trivial undertaking!

There is much work to be done!

Acknowledgements

> *Science and politics and aesthetics, these do not inhabit different domains. Instead they interweave. Their relations intersect and resonate together in unexpected ways.*
> Law [2004 pg. 156]

Sol Feferman, Mike Genesereth, David Israel, Bill Jarrold, Ben Kuipers, Pat Langley, Vladimir Lifschitz, Frank McCabe, John McCarthy, Fanya S. Montalvo, Peter Neumann, Ray Perrault, Natarajan Shankar, Mark Stickel, Richard Waldinger, and others provided valuable feedback at seminars at Stanford, SRI, and UT Austin to an earlier version of the material in this paper. For the AAAI Spring Symposium'06, Ed Feigenbaum, Mehmet Göker, David Lavery, Doug Lenat, Dan Shapiro, and others provided valuable feedback. At MIT Henry Lieberman, Ted Selker, Gerry Sussman and the members of Common Sense Research Group made valuable comments. Reviewers for AAMAS '06 and '07, KR'06, COIN@AAMAS'06 and IJCAR'06 made suggestions for improvement.

In the logic community, Mike Dunn, Sol Feferman, Mike Genesereth, Tim Hinrichs, Mike Kassoff, John McCarthy, Chris Mortensen, Graham Priest, Dana Scott, Richard Weyhrauch and Ed Zalta provided valuable feedback

Dana Scott made helpful suggestions concerning inferential undecidability. Richard Waldinger provided extensive suggestions that resulted in better focusing a previous version of this paper and increasing its readability. Discussion with Pat Hayes and Bob Kowalski provided insight into the early history of Prolog. Communications from John McCarthy and Marvin Minsky suggested making common sense a focus. Mike Dunn collaborated on looking at the relationship of the Boolean Fragment of Inconsistency Robust Direct Logic to R-Mingle. Greg Restall pointed out that Inconsistency Robust Direct Logic does not satisfy some Relevantist principles. Gerry Allwein and Jeremy Forth made detailed comments and suggestions for improvement. Bob Kowalski and Erik Sandewall provided helpful pointers and discussion of the relationship with their work. Discussions with Ian Mason and Tim Hinrichs helped me develop Löb's theorem for Direct Logic. Scott Fahlman suggested introducing the roadmap in the introduction of the paper. At CMU, Wilfried Sieg introduced me to his very interesting work with Clinton Field on automating the search for proofs of the Gödel/Rosser inferential undecidability theorems. Also at CMU, I had productive discussions with Jeremy Avigad, Randy Bryant, John Reynolds, Katia Sycara, and Jeannette Wing. At my MIT seminar and afterwards, Marvin Minsky, Ted Selker, Gerry Sussman, and Pete Szolovits made helpful comments. Les Gasser, Mike Huhns, Victor Lesser, Pablo Noriega, Sascha Ossowski, Jaime Sichman, Munindar Singh, *etc.* provided valuable suggestions at AAMAS'07. I had a very pleasant dinner with Harvey Friedman at Chez Panisse after his 2nd Tarski lecture.

Jeremy Forth, Tim Hinrichs, Fanya S. Montalvo, and Richard Waldinger provided helpful comments and suggestions on the logically necessary inconsistencies in theories of Direct Logic. Rineke Verbrugge provided valuable comments and suggestions at MALLOW'07. Mike Genesereth and Gordon Plotkin kindly hosted my lectures at Stanford and Edinburgh, respectively, on *"The Logical Necessity of Inconsistency"*. Inclusion of Cantor's diagonal argument as motivation was suggested by Jeremy Forth. John McCarthy pointed to the distinction between Logic Programs and the Logicist Programme for Artificial Intelligence. Reviewers at JAIR made useful suggestions. Mark S. Miller made important suggestions for improving the meta-circular definition of ActorScript. Comments by Michael Beeson helped make the presentation of Direct Logic more rigorous. Conversations with Jim Larson helped clarify the relationship between classical logic and the inconsistency robust logic. An anonymous referee of the Journal of Logic and Computation made a useful comment. John-Jules Meyer and Albert Visser provided helpful advice and suggestions. Comments by Mike Genesereth, Eric Kao, and Mary-Anne Williams at my Stanford Logic Group seminar *"Inference in Boolean Direct Logic is Computationally Decidable"* on 18

November 2009 greatly improved the explanation of direct inference. Discussions at my seminar "Direct Inference for Direct Logic™ Reasoning" at SRI hosted by Richard Waldinger on 7 January 2010 helped improve the presentation of Direct Logic. Helpful comments by Emily Bender, Richard Waldinger and Jeannette Wing improved the section on Inconsistency Robustness.

Eric Kao provided numerous helpful comments and discovered bugs in the principles of Self-refutation and Excluded Middle that were part of a previous version of Inconsistency Robust Direct Logic [Kao 2011]. Self-refutation has been replaced by Self-annihilation in the current version. Stuart Shapiro provided helpful information on why SNePS [Shapiro 2000] was based on Relevance Logic. Discussions with Dennis Allison, Eugene Miya, Vaughan Pratt and others were helpful in improving this article.

Make Travers made suggestions and comments that greatly improved the overall organization of the paper. Richard Waldinger provided guidance on classical automatic theorem provers. Illuminating conversations with Patrick Suppes provided additional ideas for improvement.

Bibliography

Hal Abelson and Gerry *Sussman Structure and Interpretation of Computer Programs* 1984.

Luca Aceto and Andrew D. Gordon (editors). *Algebraic Process Calculi: The First Twenty Five Years and Beyond* Bertinoro, Italy, August, 2005.

Sanjaya Addanki, Roberto Cremonini, and J. Scott Penberthy. "Reasoning about assumptions in graphs of models" *Readings in Qualitative Reasoning about Physical Systems*. Kaufman. 1989.

Gul Agha. *Actors: A Model of Concurrent Computation in Distributed Systems* Doctoral Dissertation. 1986.

Gul Agha, Ian Mason, Scott Smith, and Carolyn Talcott. "A foundation for Actor computation." *Journal of Functional Programming.* 1997.

Allen, L. E., and Saxon, C. S. "More is needed in AI: Interpretation assistance for coping with the problem of multiple structural interpretations" *ICAIL* 1991.

Bruce Anderson. "Documentation for LIB PICO-PLANNER" School of Artificial Intelligence, Edinburgh University. 1972.

Chris Anderson. "The End of Theory: The Data Deluge Makes the Scientific Method Obsolete" *Wired*. June 23, 2009.

Alan Anderson and Nuel Belnap, Jr. (1975) *Entailment: The Logic of Relevance and Necessity* Princeton University Press.

Robert Anderson and Woody Bledsoe (1970) "A Linear Format for Resolution with Merging and a New Technique for Establishing Completeness" *JACM* 17.

Aldo Antonelli (2006). "Non-monotonic Logic" *Stanford Encyclopedia of Philosophy*. March 2006.

A. I. Arruda. "Aspects of the historical development of paraconsistent logic" In *Paraconsistent Logic: Essays on the Inconsistent* Philosophia Verlag. 1989

William Aspray "Interview with J. Barkley Rosser and Stephen C. Kleene" *The Princeton Mathematics Community in the 1930s* Transcript PMC23 1985.

William Athas and Nanette Boden "Cantor: An Actor Programming System for Scientific Computing" *Proceedings of the NSF Workshop on Object-Based Concurrent Programming.* 1988. Special Issue of SIGPLAN Notices.

Henry Baker. *Actor Systems for Real-Time Computation* MIT EECS Doctoral Dissertation. January 1978.

Henry Baker and Carl Hewitt: *Laws for Communicating Parallel Processes* IFIP. August 1977.

Henry Baker and Carl Hewitt "The Incremental Garbage Collection of Processes." Symposium on Artificial Intelligence Programming Languages. SIGPLAN Notices. August 1977. "

Bob Balzer. "Tolerating Inconsistency" *13th International Conference on Software Engineering.* 1991.

Marcel Barzin 1940.

Bruce Baumgart. "Micro-Planner Alternate Reference Manual" Stanford AI Lab Operating Note No. 67, April 1972.

JC Beall and Greg Restall. *Logical Pluralism* Oxford University Press. 2006.

Michael Beeson. "Lambda Logic" Lecture Notes in Artificial Intelligence 3097. Springer. 2004.

Nuel Belnap. "A useful four-valued logic" in *Modern uses of multiple valued logics*. D. Reidel, Dordrecht, 1977.

Francesco Berto *The Gödel Paradox and Wittgenstein's Reasons* Philosophia Mathematica (III) 17. 2009.

Francesco Berto. *There's Something about Gödel: The Complete Guide to the Incompleteness Theorem* John Wiley and Sons. 2010.

Francesco Berto. "Representing Inconsistency" Inconsistency Robustness 2011.

Leopoldo Bertossi, Anthony Hunter, and Torsten Schaub eds. *Inconsistency Tolerance* Springer. 2004.

Philippe Besnard and Anthony Hunter. "Quasi-classical Logic: Non-trivializable classical reasoning from inconsistent information" *Symbolic and Quantitative Approaches to Reasoning and Uncertainty* Springer LNCS 1995.

Philippe Besnard and Torsten Schaub. "Significant Inferences: Preliminary Report. 2000.

Jean-Yves Béziau. "The future of paraconsistent logic" *Logical Studies* 2. 1999.

Jean-Yves Béziau, Walter Carnielli, and Dov Gabbay. Ed. *Handbook of Paraconsistency* College Publications Kings College London. 2007

S. V. Bhave. "Situations in Which Disjunctive Syllogism Can Lead from True Premises to a False Conclusion" *Notre Dame Journal of Formal Logic* Vol. 38, No. 3. 1997.

Fisher Black. *A deductive question answering system,* Harvard University Thesis. 1964.

Simon Blackburn and Keith Simmons (1999) *Truth* Oxford University Press.

H. Blair and V. S. Subrahmanian. "Paraconsistent Logic Programming". *Theoretical Computer Science*, 68(2) 1989.

Patricia Blanchette "The Frege-Hilbert Controversy" *The Stanford Encyclopedia of Philosophy* December 7, 2007.

Andreas Blass, Yuri Gurevich, Dean Rosenzweig, and Benjamin Rossman (2007a) *Interactive small-step algorithms I: Axiomatization* Logical Methods in Computer Science. 2007.

Andreas Blass, Yuri Gurevich, Dean Rosenzweig, and Benjamin Rossman (2007b) *Interactive small-step algorithms II: Abstract state machines and the characterization theorem.* Logical Methods in Computer Science. 2007.

George Boole. *An Investigation of the Laws of Thought* 1853. http://www.gutenberg.org/etext/15114

Geof Bowker, Susan L. Star, W. Turner, and Les Gasser, (Eds.) *Social Science Research, Technical Systems and Cooperative Work* Lawrence Earlbaum. 1997.

Robert Boyer (1971) *Locking: A Restriction of Resolution* Ph. D. University of Texas at Austin.

Fisher Black. *A Deductive Question Answering System* Harvard University. Thesis. 1964.

Daniel Bobrow and Bertram Raphael. "New programming languages for Artificial Intelligence research" *ACM Computing Surveys.* 1974.

Jean-Pierre Briot. *From objects to actors: Study of a limited symbiosis in Smalltalk-80* Rapport de Recherche 88-58, RXF-LITP. Paris, France. September 1988.

Stephen Brookes, Tony Hoare, and Bill Roscoe. *A theory of communicating sequential processes* JACM. July 1984.

Maurice Bruynooghe, Luís Moniz Pereira, Jörg Siekmann, Maarten van Emden. "A Portrait of a Scientist as a Computational Logician" *Computational Logic: Logic Programming and Beyond: Essays in Honour of Robert A. Kowalski, Part I* Springer. 2004.

Martin Caminda. "On the Issue of Contraposition of Defeasible Rules" *COMMA '08.*

Andrea Cantini "Paradoxes and Contemporary Logic" *The Stanford Encyclopedia of Philosophy* October 16, 2007.
George Cantor. "Diagonal Argument" German Mathematical Union (*Deutsche Mathematiker-Vereinigung)* (Bd. I, S. 75-78) 1890-1.
Rudolph Carnap. Logische Syntax der Sprache. (*The Logical Syntax* of Language Open Court Publishing 2003) 1934.
Luca Cardelli and Andrew Gordon. "Mobile Ambients" *Foundations of Software Science and Computational Structures* Springer, 1998.
Lewis Carroll "What the Tortoise Said to Achilles" *Mind* 4. No. 14. 1895.
Lewis Carroll. *Through the Looking-Glass* Macmillan. 1871.
Carlo Cellucci "Gödel's Incompleteness Theorem and the Philosophy of Open Systems" *Kurt Gödel: Actes du Colloque, Neuchâtel 13-14 juin 1991*, Travaux de logique N. 7, Centre de Recherches Sémiologiques, University de Neuchâtel. http://w3.uniroma1.it/cellucci/documents/Goedel.pdf
Carlo Cellucci "The Growth of Mathematical Knowledge: An Open World View" *The growth of mathematical knowledge* Kluwer. 2000.
Aziem Chawdhary, Byron Cook, Sumit Gulwani, Mooly Sagiv, and Hongseok Yang *Ranking Abstractions* ESOP'08.
Alonzo Church "A Set of postulates for the foundation of logic (1)" *Annals of Mathematics*. Vol. 33, 1932.
Alonzo Church "A Set of postulates for the foundation of logic (2)" *Annals of Mathematics*. Vol. 34, 1933.
Alonzo Church. *An unsolvable problem of elementary number theory* Bulletin of the American Mathematical Society 19, May, 1935. American Journal of Mathematics, 58 (1936),
Alonzo Church *The Calculi of Lambda-Conversion* Princeton University Press. 1941.
Will Clinger. *Foundations of Actor Semantics* MIT Mathematics Doctoral Dissertation. June 1981.
Paul Cohen "My Interaction with Kurt Gödel; the man and his work" *Gödel Centenary: An International Symposium Celebrating the 100th Birthday of Kurt Gödel* April 27–29, 2006.
Alain Colmerauer and Philippe Roussel. "The birth of Prolog" *History of Programming Languages* ACM Press. 1996
Melvin Conway. *Design of a separable transition-diagram compiler* CACM. 1963.
F. S. Correa da Silva, J. M. Abe, and M. Rillo. "Modeling Paraconsistent Knowledge in Distributed Systems". Technical Report RT-MAC-9414, Instituto de Matematica e Estatistica, Universidade de Sao Paulo, 1994.
James Crawford and Ben Kuipers. "Negation and proof by contradiction in access-limited logic." *AAAI-91.*
Haskell Curry "Some Aspects of the Problem of Mathematical Rigor" *Bulletin of the American Mathematical Society* Vol. 4. 1941.

Haskell Curry. "The combinatory foundations of mathematics" *Journal of Symbolic Logic.* 1942.
Haskell Curry. *Foundations of Mathematical Logic.* McGraw-Hill. 1963.
Michael Cusumano and Richard Selby, R. *Microsoft Secrets: How the World's Most Powerful Software Company Creates Technology, Shapes Markets, and Manages People.* Free Press. 1995
Newton da Costa *Inconsistent Formal Systems* (Sistemas Formais Inconsistentes in Portuguese) Doctoral dissertation. University of Paraná. 1963.
Newton da Costa. "On the Theory of Inconsistent Formal Systems" *Notre Dame Journal of Formal Logic* October 1974.
Ole-Johan Dahl and Kristen Nygaard. "Class and subclass declarations" *IFIP TC2 Conference on Simulation Programming Languages.* May 1967.
Ole-Johan Dahl and Tony Hoare. *Hierarchical Program Structures* in "Structured Programming" Prentice Hall. 1972.
Carlos Damásio and Luís Pereira. "A Model Theory for Paraconsistent Logic Programming" *Portuguese Conference on Artificial Intelligence* 1995.
Giacomo Mauro D'Ariano and Alessandro Tosini. "Space-time and special relativity from causal networks" *ArXiv.* 1008.4805. August 2010.
Julian Davies. "Popler 1.5 Reference Manual" University of Edinburgh, TPU Report No. 1, May 1973.
Ernest Davis. "The Naïve Physics Perplex" AI Magazine. Winter 1998.
Ernest Davis and Leora Morgenstern. "A First-Order Theory of Communication and Multi-Agent Plans" *Journal of Logic and Computation,* Vol. 15, No. 5, 2005.
John Dawson *Logical Dilemmas. The Life and Work of Kurt Gödel* AK Peters. 1997
John Dawson. "What Hath Gödel Wrought?" *Synthese.* Jan. 1998.
John Dawson. "Shaken Foundations or Groundbreaking Realignment? A Centennial Assessment of Kurt Gödel's Impact on Logic, Mathematics, and Computer Science" *FLOC'06.*
Walter Dean and Hdenori Kurokawa. "Knowledge, proof, and the Knower" TARK'09,
Richard Dedekind (1888) "What are and what should the numbers be?" (Translation in *From Kant to Hilbert: A Source Book in the Foundations of Mathematics.* Oxford University Press. 1996) Braunschweig.
Hendrik Decker. *A Case for Paraconsistent Logic as a Foundation of Future Information Systems.* CAiSE'05 Workshop PHISE'05. 2005.
Hendrik Decker. *Historical and Computational Aspects of Paraconsistency in View of the Logic Foundation of Databases.* Semantics in Databases. Springer. 2003.
David Deutsch. "Quantum theory, the Church-Turing principle and the universal quantum computer" *Proceedings of the Royal Society of London.* 1985.

Richard De Millo, Richard Lipton and Alan Perlis "Social Processes and Proofs of Theorems and Programs" CACM. May 1979.

René Descartes. *Principles of Philosophy* (English translation in *The Philosophical Writings of Descartes* Cambridge University Press 1985). 1644.

Harry Deutsch "A Note on the Decidability of a Strong Relevant Logic" *Studia Logica* Vol. 44. No. 2. 1985.

Cora Diamond. *Wittgenstein's Lectures on the Foundations of Mathematics, Cambridge, 1939* Cornell University Press. 1976.

Edsger Dijkstra. *A Discipline of Programming.* Prentice Hall. 1976.

Edsger Dijkstra and A.J.M. Gasteren. "A Simple Fixpoint Argument Without the Restriction of Continuity" Acta Informatica. Vol. 23. 1986.

Kosta Dōzen. "Logical Constants as Punctuation Marks" *Notre Dame Journal of Formal Logic*. Summer 1989.

Paul du Bois-Reymond-1880 "Der Beweis des Fundamentalsatzes der Integralrechnung" *Mathematische Annalen* Vol. 16. 1880.

Michael Dummett (1973). "The Justification of Deduction" in *Truth and other Enigmas* Duckworth. 1978.

Michael Dunn and Greg Restall. "Relevance Logic" in *The Handbook of Philosophical Logic, second edition*. Dov Gabbay and Franz Guenther (editors), Kluwer. 2002.

Michael Dunn. *Contradictory Information: Better than the Nothing* CMU Philosophy Colloquium. April 10, 2014.

T. S. Eliot. *Four Quartets.* Harcourt. 1943.

Ralph Waldo Emerson. "Self Reliance " Essays—First Series. 1841.

Pascal Engel. "Dummett, Achilles and the Tortoise" *The philosophy of Michael Dummett* Open Court. 2007.

Euclid. *The Thirteen Books of Euclid's Elements*. (3 Vol. translated by Thomas Heath. Cambridge University Press. 1925). *Circa* 300BC.

Scott Fahlman. *A Planning System for Robot Construction Tasks* MIT AI TR-283. June 1973.

Adam Farquhar, Anglela Dappert, Richard Fikes, and Wanda Pratt. "Integrating Information Sources Using Context" Logic Knowledge Systems Laboratory. KSL-95-12. January, 1995.

Anita Feferman and Solomon Feferman *Alfred Tarski: Life and Logic*. Cambridge University Press. 2004.

Solomon Feferman (1984a) "Toward Useful Type-Free Theories, I" in *Recent Essays on Truth and the Liar Paradox*. Ed. Robert Martin (1991) Claraendon Press.

Solomon Feferman (1984b) "Kurt Gödel: Conviction and Caution" *Philosophia Naturalis* Vol. 21.

Solomon Feferman. "Reflecting on incompleteness" *Journal of Symbolic Logic* 1991

Solomon Feferman *In the Light of Logic* Oxford University Press. 1998.

Solomon Feferman. "Logic, Logics, and Logicism" *Notre Dame Journal of Formal Logic*. V 40. 1999.
Solomon Feferman "Does reductive proof theory have a viable rationale?" *Erkenntnis* 53. 2000.
Solomon Feferman "Tarski's Conceptual Analysis for Semantical Notions" *Sémantique et Épistémologie* 2004.
Solomon Feferman "Predicativity" in *The Oxford Handbook of Philosophy of Mathematics and Logic* Oxford University Press. 2005.
Solomon Feferman (2006a) "The nature and significance of Gödel's incompleteness theorems" lecture for the Princeton Institute for Advanced Study Gödel Centenary Program, Nov. 17, 2006.
Solomon Feferman (2006b) "Lieber Herr Bernays! Lieber Herr Gödel! Gödel on finitism, constructivity and Hilbert's program" submitted version of lecture for the Gödel centenary conference, *Horizons of Truth*, Vienna, 27-29 April 2006.
Solomon Feferman (2006c) "Are there absolutely unsolvable problems? Gödel's dichotomy" *Philosophia Mathematica* Series III vol. 14.
Solomon Feferman (2007a) "Axioms for determinateness and truth"
Solomon Feferman (2007b) "Gödel, Nagel, minds and machines" October 25, 2007.
Solomon Feferman "Axioms for determinateness and truth" *Review of Symbolic Logic*. 2008.
Solomon Feferman. "About and around computing over the reals" *Computability: Gödel, Church, Turing and Beyond* MIT Press. forthcoming 2012.
Dieter Fensel and Frank van Harmelen. "Unifying Reasoning and Search to Web Scale" *IEEE Internet Computing*. March/April 2007.
James Fetzer. "Program Verification: The Very Idea" *CACM* September 1988.
Paul Feyerabend. *Killing Time: The Autobiography of Paul Feyerabend*. University Of Chicago Press. 1995.
Richard Feynman. "Lecture 6: Probability and Uncertainty — the Quantum Mechanical view of Nature" T*he Character of Physical Law*. MIT Press. 1965.
Hartry Field. "A Revenge-Immune Solution to the Semantic Paradoxes." *Journal of Philosophical Logic*, April 2003
Kit Fine. "Analytic Implication" *Notre Dame Journal of Formal Logic*. April 1986.
A. C. W. Finkelstein, D. Gabbay, A. Hunter, J. Kramer, and B. Nuseibeh, "Inconsistency Handling in Multi-Perspective Specifications" *Transactions on Software Engineering*, August 1994.
Frederic Fitch. *Symbolic Logic: an Introduction*. Ronald Press. 1952.
Juliet Floyd and Hilary Putnam. "Wittgenstein's 'Notorious' Paragraph About the Gödel Theorem: Recent Discussions" ("Wittgenstein's ‚berüchtigter' Paragraph über das Gödel-Theorem: Neuere Diskussionen") in *Prosa oder*

Besweis? Wittgenstein's ›berüchtigte‹ Bemerkungen zu Gödel, Texte und Dokumente Parerga Verlag. 2008.

J.M. Foster and E.W. Elcock. (1969) "ABSYS: An Incremental Compiler for Assertions" Machine Intelligence 4. Edinburgh University Press.

Nissim Francez, Tony Hoare, Daniel Lehmann, and Willem-Paul de Roever. "Semantics of nondeterminism, concurrency, and communication" *Journal of Computer and System Sciences.* December 1979.

Torkel Franzén. *Inexhaustibility* AK Peters. 2004

Torkel Franzén. *Gödel's Theorem: an incomplete guide to its use and abuse*. A K Peters. 2005.

Gottlob Frege. *Begriffsschrift: eine der arithmetischen nachgebildete Formelsprache des reinen Denkens* Halle, 1879.

Gottlob Frege (1915) "My Basic Logical Insights" *Posthumous Writings* University of Chicago Press. 1979.

Kazuhiro Fuchi, Robert Kowalski, Kazunori Ueda, Ken Kahn, Takashi Chikayama, and Evan Tick. "Launching the new era". CACM. 1993.

Dov Gabbay (ed.) *What is a Logical System?* Oxford. 1994.

Dov Gabbay and Anthony Hunter. "Making inconsistency respectable: A logical framework for inconsistency in reasoning (Part 1). *Fundamentals of Artificial Intelligence Research '91*, Springer-Verlag.. 1991.

Dov Gabbay and Anthony Hunter. "Making inconsistency respectable: A logical framework of r inconsistency in reasoning (Part 2). *Symbolic and Quantitative Approaches to Reasoning and Uncertainty* LNCS, Springer-Verlag, 1992.

John Kenneth Galbraith. *Economics, Peace and Laughter*. New American Library. 1971.

Robin Gandy. "Church's Thesis and Principles of Mechanisms" *The Kleene Symposium* North–Holland. 1980.

John Gay. "The Elephant and the Bookseller" *Fifty-one Fables in Verse* 1727

Michael Gelfond and Vladimir Lifschitz. "Logic programs with classical negation" *International Conference on Logic Programming*. MIT Press. 1990.

Gerhard Gentzen. "Provability and nonprovability of restricted transfinite induction in elementary number theory" (*Collected Papers of Gerhard Gentzen.* North-Holland. 1969) Habilitation thesis. Göttingen. 1942.

Gerhard Gentzen (1935) "Investigations into Logical Deduction." (*Collected Papers of Gerhard Gentzen.* North-Holland. 1969)

Steve Gerrard "Wittgenstein's Philosophies of Mathematics" *Synthese* 87. 1991.

Matt Ginsberg. "AI and nonmonotonic reasoning" in *Handbook of Logic in Artificial Intelligence and Logic Programming* Clarendon Press. 1994.

Jean-Yves Girard. *The Blind Spot: Lectures on proof-theory* Roma Tre. 2004.

Andreas Glausch and Wolfgang Reisig. *Distributed Abstract State Machines and Their Expressive Power* Informatik-Berichete 196. Humboldt University of Berlin. January 2006.
Kurt Gödel (1930) "The completeness of the axioms of the functional calculus of logic" (translated in *A Source Book in Mathematical Logic, 1879-1931*. Harvard Univ. Press. 1967)
Kurt Gödel (1931) "On formally undecidable propositions of *Principia Mathematica*" in *A Source Book in Mathematical Logic, 1879-1931*. Translated by Jean van Heijenoort. Harvard Univ. Press. 1967.
Kurt Gödel (1933) "An Interpretation of the Intuitionistic Propositional Calculus," in *Collected Works of Kurt Gödel*, Oxford University Press, Volume 3, 1995, pp. 296-302.
Kurt Gödel (1944) "Russell's Mathematical Logic" in *Philosophy of Mathematics(2nd ed.)* Cambridge University Press.
Kurt Gödel (1951) "Some basic theorems on the foundations of mathematics and their implications" in *Collected Works of Kurt Gödel*, Oxford University Press, Volume 3, 1995.
Kurt Gödel (1965) "On Undecidable Propositions of Formal Mathematical Systems" (a copy of Gödel's 1931 paper with his corrections of errata and added notes) in *The Undecidable: Basic Papers on Undecidable Propositions, Unsolvable problems and Computable Functions* Martin Davis editor. Raven Press 1965.
Kurt Gödel (1972), "Some Remarks on the Undecidability Results" in *Kurt Gödel Collected Works, II*. Oxford University Press. 2001.
Dina Goldin and Peter Wegner. "The Interactive Nature of Computing: Refuting the Strong Church-Turing Thesis" *Minds and Machines* March 2008.
Solomon Golomb and Leonard Baumert. (1965) "Backtrack Programming" JACM. Vol. 12 No. 4.
Thomas Gordon. *Foundations of Argumentation Technology: Summary of Habilitation Thesis* Technische Universität Berlin. 2009.
C. Cordell Green: "Application of Theorem Proving to Problem Solving" IJCAI 1969.
Steve Gregory. "Concurrent Logic Programming Before ICOT: A Personal Perspective" August 15, 2007.
http://www.cs.bris.ac.uk/~steve/papers/ALP/CLPbeforeICOT.pdf
Irene Greif. *Semantics of Communicating Parallel Processes* MIT EECS Doctoral Dissertation. August 1975
Ramanathan Guha. *Contexts: Formalization and Some Applications* PhD thesis, Stanford University, 1991.
Robert Hadley. "Consistency, Turing Computablity and Gödel's First Incompleteness Theorem" *Minds and Machines* 18. 2008.
Volker Halbach "Axiomatic theories of truth" *Stanford Encyclopedia of Philosophy*. 2007.

Ronald Harrop. "Some structure results for propositional calculi" Journal of Symbolic Logic, 30. 1965.

W. D. Hart. "Skolem Redux" *Notre Dame Journal of Formal Logic.* 41, no. 4. 2000.

Donna Haraway. "Situated Knowledge: the Science Question in Feminism and the Privilege of Partial Perspective" in *Simians, Cyborgs, and Women: the Reinvention of Nature.* Free Association Books. 1991.

Pat Hayes. "Computation and Deduction" Mathematical Foundations of Computer Science: *Proceedings of Symposium and Summer School,* Štrbské Pleso, High Tatras, Czechoslovakia. September 1973.

Pat Hayes "Some Problems and Non-Problems in Representation Theory" *AISB.* Sussex. July, 1974.

Pat Hayes. "The Naïve Physics Manifesto". *Expert Systems in the Microelectronic Age.* Edinburgh University Pres. 1979.

Pat Hayes. 1985a. "The Second Naïve Physics Manifesto" *Formal Theories of the Commonsense World.* Ablex. 1985.

Pat Hayes. 1985b. "Naïve Physics 1: Ontology for Liquids" *Formal Theories of the Commonsense World.* Ablex. 1985.

Pat Hayes. "Contexts in context." *Contexts in Knowledge Representation and Natural Language.* AAAI. 1997.

Pat Hayes. "Context Mereology." Commonsense 2007.

Jean van Heijenoort (1967) *From Frege to Gödel. A Source Book in Mathematical Logic, 1897-1931*, Harvard University Press.

Joseph Heller. *Catch-22.* Simon & Schuster.1961.

Leon Henkin "A Problem Concerning Provability" *Journal of Symbolic Logic*, Vol. 17 (1952).

Carl Hewitt. "Planner: A Language for Proving Theorems in Robots" *IJCAI* 1969.

Carl Hewitt. "Procedural Embedding of Knowledge In Planner" *IJCAI* 1971.

Carl Hewitt, Peter Bishop and Richard Steiger. "A Universal Modular Actor Formalism for Artificial Intelligence" *IJCAI* 1973.

Carl Hewitt and Henry Baker Laws for Communicating Parallel Processes *IFIP*. August 1977.

Carl Hewitt. "Viewing Control Structures as Patterns of Passing Messages" *Journal of Artificial Intelligence.* June 1977.

Carl Hewitt and Peter de Jong. "Open Systems'" *Perspectives on Conceptual Modeling*, Brodie, Mylopoulos, and Schmidt (eds.), Springer-Verlag, 1983.

Carl Hewitt. "The Challenge of Open Systems" *Byte Magazine.* April 1985.

Carl Hewitt (1986). "Offices Are Open Systems" *ACM Transactions on Information Systems* 4(3)

Carl Hewitt (1990). "Towards Open Information Systems Semantics" *International Workshop on Distributed Artificial Intelligence*

Carl Hewitt (1991). "Open Information Systems Semantics" *Journal of Artificial Intelligence.* January 1991.

Carl Hewitt and Jeff Inman. "DAI Betwixt and Between: From 'Intelligent Agents' to Open Systems Science" *IEEE Transactions on Systems, Man, and Cybernetics*. Nov. /Dec. 1991.

Carl Hewitt and Gul Agha. "Guarded Horn clause languages: are they deductive and Logical?" *International Conference on Fifth Generation Computer Systems*. Ohmsha 1988.

Carl Hewitt. (2006). "What is Commitment? Physical, Organizational, and Social" *COIN@AAMAS'06*. (Revised version to be published in Springer Verlag Lecture Notes in Artificial Intelligence. Edited by Javier Vázquez-Salceda and Pablo Noriega. 2007) April 2006.

Carl Hewitt (2007a). "Organizational Computing Requires Unstratified Paraconsistency and Reflection" *COIN@AAMAS*. 2007.

Carl Hewitt (2008a) "A historical perspective on developing foundations for privacy-friendly client cloud computing: iConsult™ & iEntertain™ Apps using iInfo™ Information Integration for iOrgs™ Information Systems" (Revised version of "Development of Logic Programming: What went wrong, What was done about it, and What it might mean for the future" in Proceedings of *What Went Wrong and Why* edited by Mehmet Göker and Daniel Shapiro, AAAI Press. 2008 pp. 1-11) ArXiv. 0901.4934

Carl Hewitt (2008b). "Norms and Commitment for iOrgs™ Information Systems: Direct Logic™ and Participatory Grounding Checking" ArXiv 0906.2756

Carl Hewitt (2008c) "Large-scale Organizational Computing requires Unstratified Reflection and Strong Paraconsistency" *Coordination, Organizations, Institutions, and Norms in Agent Systems III* Jaime Sichman, Pablo Noriega, Julian Padget and Sascha Ossowski (ed.). Springer-Verlag. *http://organizational.carlhewitt.info/*

Carl Hewitt (2008d) *"Middle History of Logic Programming: Resolution, Planner, Edinburgh Logic for Computable Functions, Prolog and the Japanese Fifth Generation Project"* ArXiv 0904.3036

Carl Hewitt (2008e). *ORGs for Scalable, Robust, Privacy-Friendly Client Cloud Computing* IEEE Internet Computing September/October 2008.

Carl Hewitt (2009a) *Perfect Disruption: The Paradigm Shift from Mental Agents to ORGs* IEEE Internet Computing. Jan/Feb 2009.

Carl Hewitt (2010a) ActorScript™ extension of C#®, Java®, and Objective C®: iAdaptive™ concurrency for antiCloud™ privacy-friendly computing in Inconsistency Robustness. College Publications. 2015.

Carl Hewitt (2010b) "Actor Model of Computation: Scalable Robust Information Systems" in Inconsistency Robustness. College Publications. 2015.

Carl Hewitt (2010c) Wittgenstein versus Gödel on the Foundations of Logic Stanford Media X Logic Colloquium video recording. April 23, 2010.

Carl Hewitt. Looming private information fiasco versus the new cloud business model: The next generation will ask, *"Where were you when this was going down?"* Risks Digest. Vol. 26: Issue 37. March 9. 2011.

Carl Hewitt (editor). *Inconsistency Robustness 1011* Stanford University. 2011.
Carl Hewitt. *What is computation? Actor Model versus Turing's Model* in "A Computable Universe: Understanding Computation & Exploring Nature as Computation" Edited by Hector Zenil. World Scientific Publishing Company. 2012.
David Hilbert. 1900. in "Mathematical Developments Arising From Hilbert Problems" *Proceedings of Symposia in Pure Mathematics*, Vol. 28. American Mathematical Society. 1976
David Hilbert (1926) "Über das Unendliche" *Mathematische Annalen*, 95: 161-90. ("On the Infinite" English translation in van Heijenoort. 1967).
David Hilbert and Paul Bernays. *Grundlagen der Mathematik I.* (L'Harmattan edition 2001) 1934.
David Hilbert and Paul Bernays. *Grundlagen der Mathematik II.* (L'Harmattan edition 2001) 1939.
Tony Hoare. "Communicating Sequential Processes" *CACM* August, 1978.
Tony Hoare. *Communicating Sequential Processes*. Prentice Hall. 1985.
Tony Hoare. "The verifying compiler: A grand challenge for computing research" *JACM*. January 2003.
Tony Hoare. *Retrospective: An Axiomatic Basis for Computer Programming* CACM 2009.
Wilfrid Hodges (2006) "Tarski's Truth Definitions" *Stanford Encyclopedia of Philosophy*.
Douglas Hofstadter. *Godel, Escher, Bach: An Eternal Golden Braid*. Random House. 1980.
Douglas Hofstadter. *I am a Strange Loop* Basic Books. 2007.
Jim Holt. "Code-Breaker" *The New Yorker* February 6, 2006.
Leon Horsten "Philosophy of Mathematics" *The Stanford Encyclopedia of Philosophy* September 27, 2007.
Matthew Huntbach and Graem Ringwood. *Agent-Oriented Programming: From Prolog to Guarded Definite Clauses* Sprinter. 1999.
Anthony Hunter. *Reasoning with Contradictory Information using Quasi-classical Logic* Journal of Logic and Computation. Vol. 10 No. 5. 2000.
Daniel Ingalls. "The Evolution of the Smalltalk Virtual Machine" *Smalltalk-80: Bits of History, Words of Advice*. Addison Wesley. 1983.
Daniel Isaacson. "The reality of mathematics and the case of set theory" *Truth, Reference, and Realism* Central European University Press, 2008.
Stanisław Jaśkowski "On the Rules of Suppositions in Formal Logic" *Studia Logica* 1, 1934. (reprinted in: *Polish logic 1920-1939*, Oxford University Press, 1967.
Stanisław Jaśkowski. *Propositional calculus for contradictory deductive systems* Studia Logica. 24 (1969) *Rachunek zdań dla systemów dedukcyjnych sprzecznych* in: Studia Societatis Scientiarum Torunensis, Sectio A, Vol. I, No. 5, Toruń 1948.

Eric Kao. "Proof by self-refutation and excluded middle lead to explosion" *Inconsistency Robustness 2011* Stanford. August 16-18, 2011.

Michael Kassoff, Lee-Ming Zen, Ankit Garg, and Michael Genesereth. *PrediCalc: A Logical Spreadsheet Management System* 31st International Conference on Very Large Databases (VLDB). 2005.

Alan Kay. "Personal Computing" in *Meeting on 20 Years of Computing Science* Instituto di Elaborazione della Informazione, Pisa, Italy. 1975. http://www.mprove.de/diplom/gui/Kay75.pdf

Jussi Ketonen and Richard Weyhrauch. "A decidable fragment of Predicate Calculus" *Theoretical Computer Science*. 1984.

Thomas Kida. *Don't Believe Everything You Think: The 6 Basic Mistakes We Make in Thinking* Prometheus Books. 2006.

Stephen Kleene and John Barkley Rosser "The inconsistency of certain formal logics" *Annals of Mathematics* Vol. 36. 1935.

Stephen Kleene *General recursive functions and natural numbers* Mathematical Annuals. 1936.

Stephen Kleene *Recursive Predicates and Quantifiers* American Mathematical Society Transactions. 1943

Stephen Kleene "Reflections on Church's Thesis" *Notre Dame Journal of Formal Logic* 1987.

Morris Kline. *Mathematical thought from ancient to modern times* Oxford University Press. 1972.

Frederick Knabe. "A Distributed Protocol for Channel-Based Communication with Choice" *PARLE* 1992.

Bill Kornfeld and Carl Hewitt. "The Scientific Community Metaphor" IEEE *Transactions on Systems, Man, and Cybernetics*. January 1981.

Bill Kornfeld. *Parallelism in Problem Solving* MIT EECS Doctoral Dissertation. August 1981.

Robert Kowalski "Predicate Logic as Programming Language" Memo 70, Department of Artificial Intelligence, Edinburgh University. 1973

Robert Kowalski. "A proof procedure using connection graphs" JACM. October 1975.

Robert Kowalski (1979) "Algorithm = Logic + Control" *CACM*. July 1979.

Robert Kowalski (1986). "The limitation of logic" *ACM Annual Conference on Computer Science*.

Robert Kowalski 1988a. "The Early Years of Logic Programming" *CACM*. January 1988.

Robert Kowalski (1988b). "Logic-based Open Systems" *Representation and Reasoning*. Stuttgart Conference Workshop on Discourse Representation, Dialogue tableaux and Logic Programming. 1988.

Robert. Kowalski and Francesca Toni. "Abstract Argumentation" *Artificial Intelligence and Law*. 1996

Robert Kowalski (2006) "The Logical Way to be Artificially Intelligent." *CLIMA VI*. Springer Verlag.

Robert Kowalski (2007) "What is Logic Programming?"
http://en.wikipedia.org/wiki/Talk:Logic_programming#What_is_Logic_Programming.3F
S. Kraus, D. Lehmann and M. Magidor. "Non-monotonic reasoning, preferential models and cumulative logics" *Artificial Intelligence* 44:167–207. 1990.
Richard Kraut. "Plato" *Stanford Encyclopedia of Philosophy.* 2004.
Georg Kreisel. "Wittgenstein's Remarks on the Foundations of Mathematics" *British Journal for the Philosophy of Science* 1958.
Thomas Kuhn. *The Structure of Scientific Revolutions* University of Chicago Press. 1962.
Ernest Kurtz and Katherine Ketcham. *The Spirituality of Imperfection: Storytelling and the Search for Meaning* Bantam 1993.
Henry Kyburg and Choh Teng) *Uncertain Inference*, Cambridge University Press. 2001
Imre Lakatos. "A renaissance of empiricism in the recent philosophy of mathematics?" *Mathematics, Science and Epistemology.* 1978.
Imre Lakatos. *Proofs and Refutations* Cambridge University Press. 1976
Imre Lakatos. *Mathematics, Science and Epistemology* edited by J. Worrall and G. Currie. Cambridge University Press. 1978.
Hélène Landemore. " 'Talking it Out': Deliberation with Others Versus Deliberation Within" Political Psychology. forthcoming 2011.
Peter Landin. "A Generalization of Jumps and Labels" UNIVAC Systems Programming Research Report. August 1965. (Reprinted in *Higher Order and Symbolic Computation.* 1998)
Bruno Latour *Science in Action: How to Follow Scientists and Engineers Through Society* Harvard University Press. 1987.
Bruno Latour. *The Making of Law* Polity Press. 2010.
Bruno Latour. *On the Modern Cult of the Factish Gods* Duke University Press. 2010.
John Law. *After Method: mess in social science research* Routledge. 2004.
Federico Laudisa and Carlo Rovelli. "Relational Quantum Mechanics" *Stanford Encyclopedia of Philosophy* 2008.
Hannes Leitgeb. "What theories of truth should be like (but cannot be)" *Philosophy Compass* 2 (2). 2007.
Doug Lenat "CYC: Lessons Learned in Large-Scale Ontological Engineering" November 17, 2005.
Isaac Levi. *Direct Inference* Journal of Philosophy. Jan. 1977.
Steven Levy *Hackers: Heroes of the Computer Revolution* Doubleday. 1984.
Clarence Lewis and Cooper Langford. Symbolic Logic Century-Croft, 1932.
David Lewis. "Probabilities of Conditionals, and Conditional Probabilities" *Philosophical Review.* 1976.
Philip Lewis. "Jonathon von Neumann and EDVAC" Nov. 8. 2004. www.cs.berkeley.edu/~christos/classics/paper.pdf
Henry Lieberman. "A Preview of Act 1" MIT AI memo 625. June 1981.

James Lighthill. "Artificial Intelligence: A General Survey" *Artificial Intelligence: a paper symposium*. UK Science Research Council. 1973
Martin Löb. "Solution of a problem of Leon Henkin." *Journal of Symbolic Logic*. Vol. 20. 1955.
Per Martin-Löf "Verificationism then and now" *The Foundational Debate*. Kluwer. 1995.
Van McGee "Counterexample to Modus Ponens" *The Journal of Philosophy* 82. 1985.
Eckart Menzler-Trott. *Logic's Lost Genius: The Life of Gerhard Gentzen* American Mathematical Society. 2007.
Donald Loveland. *Report of a Workshop on the Future Directions of Automated Deduction* NSF 1997.
http://www.cs.duke.edu/AutoDedFD/report/
Leopold Löwenheim (1915) "Über Möglichkeiten im Relativkalkül" *Mathematische Annalen 76*. (Translated as "On possibilities in the calculus of relatives" in Jean van Heijenoort, 1967. *From Frege to Gödel: A Source Book in Mathematical Logic, 1879-1931*. Harvard Univ. Press)
Michael Lynch *The Nature of Truth* MIT Press. 2001.
Donald MacKenzie. *Mechanizing Proof.* MIT Press. 2001.
Edwin Mares. "Relevance Logic" *Stanford Encyclopedia of Philosophy*. Jan. 2006.
Roger Maddux *Relevance Logic and the calculus of relations* International Conference on. Order, Algebra and Logics. Vanderbilt. 2007.
Frederick Maier, Yu Ma, and Pascal Hitzler. "Paraconsistent OWL and Related Logics" *Semantic Web Journal*. 2011.
David Malone. *Dangerous Knowledge* BBC4 documentary. 2007.
http://www.dailymotion.com/playlist/x1cbyd_xSilverPhinx_bbc-dangerous-knowledge/1
Edwin Mares. *Relevant Logic* Cambridge University Press. 2007
Per Martin-Löf. "Verificationism then and now" in W. De Pauli-Schimanovich, *et al.*, eds. *The Foundational Debate* Kluwer. 1995.
John McCarthy. "Programs with common sense" *Symposium on Mechanization of Thought Processes*. National Physical Laboratory. Teddington, England. 1958.
John McCarthy. "Situations, actions and causal laws" Stanford Artificial Intelligence Project: Memo 2. 1963
John McCarthy and Pat Hayes. "Some Philosophical Problems from the Standpoint of Artificial Intelligence" *Machine Intelligence 4*. 1969
John McCarthy, Paul Abrahams, Daniel Edwards, Timothy Hart, and Michael Levin. *Lisp 1.5 Programmer's Manual* MIT Computation Center and Research Laboratory of Electronics. 1962.
John McCarthy. "Review of 'Artificial Intelligence: A General Survey'" *Artificial Intelligence: a paper symposium*. UK Science Research Council. 1973.

John McCarthy. "Circumscription—a form of nonmonotonic reasoning." *Artificial Intelligence*. 1980.

John McCarthy. "Applications of circumscription to formalizing common sense knowledge" *Artificial Intelligence*. 1986.

John McCarthy. "Generality in Artificial Intelligence" *CACM*. December 1987.

John McCarthy. "A logical AI Approach to Context" Technical note, Stanford Computer Science Department, 1996.

John McCarthy. *Sterile Containers* September 8, 2000. http://www.ai.sri.com/~rkf/designdoc/sterile.ps

John McCarthy. "What is Artificial Intelligence" September 1, 2007. http://www-formal.stanford.edu/jmc/whatisai/whatisai.html

L. Thorne McCarty. "Reflections on TAXMAN: An Experiment on Artificial Intelligence and Legal Reasoning" *Harvard Law Review* Vol. 90, No. 5, March 1977.

Drew McDermott and Gerry Sussman. "The Conniver Reference Manual" MIT AI Memo 259. May 1972.

Drew McDermott. *The Prolog Phenomenon* ACM SIGART Bulletin. Issue 72. July, 1980.

Vann McGee "In Praise of the Free Lunch: Why Disquotationalists Should Embrace Compositional Semantics" *Self-Reference* CSLI Publications. 2006.

Casey McGinnis "Paraconsistency and logical hypocrisy" *The Logica Yearbook* Praha. http://www.geocities.com/cnmcginnis/ParaLogHyp.pdf

Hugo Mercier and Dan Sperber. "Why Do Humans Reason? Arguments for an Argumentative Theory" Behavior al and Brain Sciences. 34. 2011.

Hugo Mercier and Hélène Landemore. "Reasoning is for Arguing: Understanding the Successes and Failures of Deliberation" Political Psychology. forthcoming 2011.

N. David Mermin. "What is Quantum Mechanics Trying to Tell us?" arXiv:quant-ph/9801057. 1998.

George Milne and Robin Milner. "Concurrent processes and their syntax" *JACM*. April, 1979.

Robert Milne and Christopher Strachey. *A Theory of Programming Language Semantics* Chapman and Hall. 1976.

Robin Milner. *Logic for Computable Functions: description of a machine implementation.* Stanford AI Memo 169. May 1972

Robin Milner '"Elements of interaction: Turing award lecture'" *CACM*. January 1993.

Marvin Minsky (ed.) *Semantic Information Processing* MIT Press. 1968.

Marvin Minsky and Seymour Papert. "Progress Report on Artificial Intelligence" MIT AI Memo 252. 1971.

Marvin Minsky. *A Framework for Representing Knowledge.* MIT AI Lab Memo 306. 1974.

Marvin Minsky, Push Singh, and Aaron Sloman: "The St. Thomas Common Sense Symposium: Designing Architectures for Human-Level Intelligence" *AI Magazine.* Summer 2004.

Annemarie Mol and Marc Berg. "Principles and Practices of Medicine: the Coexistence of various Anaemias" *Culture, Medicine, and Psychiatry* 1994.

Annemarie Mol. *The Body Multiple: ontology in medical practice* Duke University Press. 2002

Ray Monk. "Bourgeois, Boshevist or anarchist? The Reception of Wittgenstein's Philosophy of Mathematics" in *Wittgenstein and his interpreters* Blackwell. 2007.

Charles Morgan. "The Nature of Nonmonotonic Reasoning" *Minds and Machines* 2000

Chris Mortensen. "The Validity of Disjunctive Syllogism is Not So Easily Proved." *Notre Dame Journal of Formal Logic* January 1983.

Chris Mortensen. *Inconsistent Mathematics* Kluwer Academic Publishers. 1995.

Alexander Nekham. De Naturis Rerum Thomas Wright, editor. London: Longman, 1863.

Allen Newell and Herbert Simon. "The logic theory machine: A complex information processing system" *IRE Transactions on Information Theory* IT-2:61-79. 1956.

Bashar Nuseibeh "To Be and Not to Be: On Managing Inconsistency in Software Development" *IWSSD-8.* March 1996,

Kristen Nygaard. *SIMULA: An Extension of ALGOL to the Description of Discrete-Event Networks* IFIP'62.

David Park. "Concurrency and Automata on Infinite Sequences" Lecture Notes in Computer Science, Vol 104. Springer. 1980

Peter Patel-Schneider *A decidable first-order logic for knowledge representation* IJCAI'85.

Mike Paterson and Carl Hewitt. "Comparative Schematology" MIT AI Memo 201. August 1970.

Giuseppe Peano *Arithmetices principia, nova methodo exposita* (The principles of arithmetic, presented by a new method) 1889.

Judea Pearl, *Probabilistic Reasoning in Intelligent Systems: Networks of Plausible Inference* Morgan Kaufmann. 1988

Francis Pelletier "A Brief History of Natural Deduction" History and Philosophy of Logic Vol. 20, Issue. 1, 1999.

Carl Petri. *Kommunikation mit Automate.* Ph. D. Thesis. University of Bonn. 1962.

Andrew Pitts. "Categorical Logic" in *Algebraic and Logical Structures* Oxford University Press. 2000.

Max Planck *Scientific Autobiography and Other Papers* 1949.

Gordon Plotkin. "A powerdomain construction" *SIAM Journal of Computing* September 1976.

Henri Poincaré. "La grandeur mathematiques et l'experience, *La Science et l'Hypothése,*" Bibliotμeque de Philosophie Scientique *Ernest Flammarion* 1902; English translation "Mathematical magnitude and experiment" *Science and Hypothesis* Walter Scott Publishing Co, 1905

George Polya (1957) *Mathematical Discovery: On Understanding, Learning and Teaching Problem Solving Combined Edition* Wiley. 1981.

Karl Popper(1962). *Conjectures and Refutations* Basic Books.

Karl Popper. (1934) *Logik der Forschung*, Springer. (*Logic of Scientific Discovery* Routledge 2002).

Howard Pospesel. *Propositional Logic* Prentice Hall. 2000

H. Prakken "A tool in modeling disagreement in law: Preferring the most specific argument" *ICAIL '91.*

H. Prakken and G. Sartor. "A dialectical model of assessing conflicting arguments in legal reasoning" *Artificial Intelligence and Law* 1996.

Graham Priest. "Dialetheism" *The Stanford Encyclopedia of Philosophy* (Winter 2004 Edition)

Graham Priest, and Richard Routley "The History of Paraconsistent Logic" in *Paraconsistent Logic: Essays on the Inconsistent* Philosophia Verlag. 1989.

Graham Priest. "Paraconsistent Logic" *Handbook of Philosophical Logic* Volume 6, 2nd ed. Kluwer. 2002

Graham Priest and Koji Tanaka. "Paraconsistent Logic" *The Stanford Encyclopedia of Philosophy.* Winter 2004.

Graham Priest. "Wittgenstein's Remarks on Gödel's Theorem" in *Wittgenstein's Lasting Significance* Routledge. 2004.

Graham Priest (2006a) "60% Proof: Lakatos, Proof, and Paraconsistency" 2006.

Graham Priest (2006b) *In Contradiction 2nd Edition* Clarendon Press. 2006.

Michael Rathjen. "The art of ordinal analysis" *Proceedings of the International Congress of Mathematicians* 2006

Willard Quine "Review of Charles Parsons' Mathematics in Philosophy" *Journal of Philosophy* 1984.,

Miklós Rédei "John von Neumann 1903-1957" *European Mathematical Society Newsletter* March 2004.

Stephen Reed and Doug Lenat. "Mapping Ontologies into Cyc" *AAAI 2002 Conference Workshop on Ontologies for the Semantic Web* July 2002.

Ray Reiter. "A logic for default reasoning" *Artificial Intelligence* 13:81. 1980.

Ray Reiter. *Knowledge in Action: Logical Foundations for Specifying and Implementing Dynamical Systems.* MIT Press, 2001.

Greg Restall "Curry's Revenge: the costs of non-classical solutions to the paradoxes of self-reference" (to appear in *The Revenge of the Liar* ed. J.C. Beall. Oxford University Press. 2007) July 12, 2006.
http://consequently.org/papers/costing.pdf

Greg Restall "Proof Theory and Meaning: on Second Order Logic" *Logica 2007 Yearbook*, 2007.

Edwina Rissland. "The Ubiquitous Dialectic" ECAI'84.
Abraham Robinson. "Model theory and non-standard arithmetic" in *Infinitistic Methods*. Proceedings of the Symposium on Foundations of Mathematics. September 2-9, 1959. Pergamon Press.
John Alan Robinson, "A Machine-Oriented Logic Based on the Resolution Principle." CACM. 1965.
Victor Rodych. "Wittgenstein on Mathematical Meaningfulness, Decidability, and Application" *Notre Dame Journal on Formal Logic* Vol. 38. No. 2. 1997.
Victor Rodych. "Wittgenstein's Inversion of Gödel's Theorem" *Erkenntnis* 51. 1999.
Victor Rodych. "Wittgenstein on Gödel: The Newly Published Remarks" *Erkenntnis* 56. 2002.
Victor Rodych. "Misunderstanding Gödel: New Arguments about Wittgenstein and New Remarks by Wittgenstein" *Dialectica* Vol. 57. No. 3. 2003.
Bill Roscoe. *The Theory and Practice of Concurrency* Prentice-Hall. Revised 2005.
Scott Rosenberg. *Dreaming in Code*. Crown Publishers. 2007.
Marcus Rossberg. "Second-Order Logic" Socrates Teaching Mobility Intensive Seminar, University of Helsinki, 16-19 May, 2005. *http://www.st-andrews.ac.uk/~mr30/SOL/SOL3.pdf*
John Barkley Rosser. "Extensions of Some Theorems of Gödel and Church" *Journal of Symbolic. Logic.* 1(3) 1936.
Philippe Rouchy (2006). "Aspects of PROLOG History: Logic Programming and Professional Dynamics" *TeamEthno-Online Issue* 2, June 2006.
Richard Routley "Dialectical Logic, Semantics and Metamathematics" *Erkenntnis* 14. 1979.
Richard Routley *Relevant Logics and Their Rivals 1* Ridgeview. 2003.
Carlo Rovelli "Relational quantum mechanics" *International Journal of Theoretical Physics*, 1996.
Carlo Rovelli. "The Uselessness of Certainty" *Edge* 2011.
Jeff Rulifson, Jan Derksen, and Richard Waldinger. "QA4, A Procedural Calculus for Intuitive Reasoning" SRI AI Center Technical Note 73. November 1973.
Bertrand Russell. *Principles of Mathematics* Norton. 1903.
Bertrand Russell. *Principia Mathematica 2nd Edition* 1925.
Alessandra Russo, Bashar Nuseibeh, and Steve Easterbrook. "Making Inconsistency Respectable in Software Development" Journal of Systems and Software. Vol. 56. No. 58. 2000.
Earl Sacerdoti, *et. al.*, "QLISP A Language for the Interactive Development of Complex Systems" *AFIPS.* 1976.
Eric Sandewall. "A functional approach to non-monotonic logic" *Computational Intelligence*. Vol. 1. 1985.

Eric Sandewall. "From Systems to Logic in the Early Development of Nonmonotonic Reasoning" CAISOR. July, 2006.
Davide Sangiorgi and David Walker. *The Pi-Calculus: A Theory of Mobile Processes* Cambridge University Press. 2001.
Marek Sergot. *"Bob Kowalski: A Portrait" Computational Logic: Logic Programming and Beyond: Essays in Honour of Robert A. Kowalski, Part I* Springer. 2004.
R. W. Schwanke and G. E. Kaiser, "Living With Inconsistency in Large Systems" International Workshop on Software Version and Configuration Control. January 1988.
Dana Scott "Data Types as Lattices". *SIAM Journal on computing*. 1976.
Dana Scott. "The Future of Proof" LICS 2006.
Dana Scott and Christopher Strachey. *Toward a mathematical semantics for computer languages* Oxford Programming Research Group Technical Monograph. PRG-6. 1971
Thoralf Skolem (1920) "Logico-combinatorial investigations on the satisfiability or provability of mathematical propositions: A simplified proof of a theorem by Löwenheim" (English translation in Jean van Heijenoort, 1967. *From Frege to Gödel: A Source Book in Mathematical Logic, 1879-1931*. Harvard Univ. Press)
Oron Shagrir "Gödel on Turing on Computability" *Church's Thesis after 70 years* Ontos-Verlag. 2006.
Natarajan Shankar. *Metamathematics, Machines, and Gödel's Proof* Cambridge University Press. 1994.
Ehud Shapiro. "The family of concurrent logic programming languages" *ACM Computing Surveys*. September 1989
Stewart Shapiro. *Thinking About Mathematics*. Oxford University Press. 2000.
Stewart Shapiro. "Lakatos and logic Comments on Graham Priest's '60% proof: Lakatos, proof, and paraconsistency'" Preprint 2006
Stewart Shapiro *Foundations without Foundationalism: A Case for Second-Order Logic* Oxford. 2002.
Stewart Shapiro. "Do Not Claim Too Much: Second-order Logic and First-order Logic" *Philosophia Mathematica* (3) Vol. 7. 1999.
Stuart. Shapiro. "Relevance logic in computer science" in *Entailment, Volume II* pg. 553-563. Princeton University Press. 1992.
Stuart Shapiro. "SNePS: A Logic for Natural Language Understanding and Commonsense Reasoning" in *Natural Language Processing and Knowledge Representation: Language for Knowledge and Knowledge for Language*, AAAI Press. 2000.
Wilfried Sieg and Clinton Field. "Automated search for Gödel proofs." *Annals of Pure and Applied Logic*. 2005.
Wilfried Sieg and J. Byrnes "An Abstract Model for Parallel Computations: Gandy's Thesis" *Monist* 1999.

Wilfried Sieg. "Gödel on Computability" Philosophia Mathematica 2006.
Wilfried Sieg "Church Without Dogma – axioms for computability" *New Computational Paradigms* Springer Verlag. 2008.
G. R. Simari and R. P. Loui. A mathematical treatment of defeasible reasoning and its implementation. Artificial Intelligence Vol. 53 No. 2-3 1992.
John Slaney. "Relevant Logic and Paraconsistency" in *Inconsistency Tolerance* Springer 2004.
Aaron Sloman. "Must Intelligent Systems Be Scruffy?" *Evolving Knowledge in Natural Science and Artificial Intelligence.* Pitman. 1990.
Timothy Smiley. "The Logical Basis of Ethics," *Acta Philosophica Fennica*, 16: 1963.
Peter Smith. *An Introduction to Gödel's Theorems.* Draft. 2006. http://www.godelbook.net/
Lee Smolin. *The Trouble with Physics: The Rise of String Theory, the Fall of a Science, and What Comes Next* Houghton Mifflin. 2006
Craig Smorynski. "The Incompleteness Theorems" *Handbook of Mathematical Logic.* North Holland. 1977.
Raymond Smullyan *Gödel's Incompleteness Theorems* Oxford Univ. Press. 1991.
Michael Smyth. *Power domains* Journal of Computer and System Sciences. 1978.
Gerry Sussman, Terry Winograd and Eugene Charniak. "Micro-Planner Reference Manual (Update)" AI Memo 203A, MIT AI Lab, December 1971.
Gerry Sussman and Guy Steele *Scheme: An Interpreter for Extended Lambda Calculus* AI Memo 349. December, 1975. University of Illinois Press. 1977.
Frederick Suppe, ed. "The Structure of Scientific Theories" University of Illinois Press. 1977.
Alfred Tarski *Introduction to Logic* Oxford University Press. 1940 (and many subsequent editions).
Alfred Tarski (1944) "The semantic conception of truth and the foundations of semantics" *Philosophy and Phenomenological Research* 4 (Reprinted in *Readings in Philosophical Analysis,* Appleton-1944)
Alfred Tarski and Robert Vaught (1957). "Arithmetical extensions of relational systems" *Compositio Mathematica* 13.
Paul Tillich. "Courage to be" *Yale University* Press. 2000.
Stephen Toulmin *The Uses of Argument* Cambridge University Press. 1958.
Alan Turing. "On computable numbers, with an application to the Entscheidungsproblem." *Proceedings London Math Society.* 1936.
Alan Turing. "Intelligent Machinery". National Physical Laboratory Report. 1948. Also in Machine Intelligence 5. Edinburgh: Edinburgh University Press. (Digital facsimile viewable at http://www.AlanTuring.net/intelligent_machinery)

Shunichi Uchida and Kazuhiro Fuchi (1992). *Proceedings of the FGCS Project Evaluation Workshop* Institute for New Generation Computer Technology (ICOT)
Moshe Vardi "More Debate, Please!" CACM. Jan. 2010.
Rineke Verbrugge "Provability Logic" *The Stanford Encyclopedia of Philosophy* 2010.
John von Neumann. "The role of mathematics in the sciences and in society" *John von Neumann Collected Works Vol.VI.* Pergamon. 1961.
John von Neumann. "The Mathematician" *John von Neumann Collected Works Vol. I.* Pergamon. 1962.
Richard Waldinger and R. Lee (1969) "PROW: a step toward automatic program writing" IJCAI'69.
Douglas Walton *Fundamentals of Critical Argumentation* Cambridge University Press. 2006.
Hao Wang *A Logical Journey, From Gödel to Philosophy* MIT Press. 1974.
André Weil, In letter to Fréchet, January 31, 1927..
Peter Whalley. "Modifying the metaphor in order to improve understanding of control languages—the little-person becomes a cast of actors." *British Journal of Educational Technology. 2006.*
John Wheeler. "It from Bit" in *Complexity, Entropy, and the Physics of Information* Addison-Wesley. 1990
Eugene Wigner. "The Unreasonable Effectiveness of Mathematics in the Natural Sciences" *Communications in Pure and Applied Mathematics* February 1960.
Bill Wilson. *Twelve Steps and Twelve Traditions* Alcoholics Anonymous. 1952
Terry Winograd. *Procedures as a Representation for Data in a Computer Program for Understanding Natural Language.* MIT AI TR-235. January 1971.
Ludwig Wittgenstein. 1956. Bemerkungen ¨uber die Grundlagen der Mathematik/*Remarks on the Foundations of Mathematics, Revised Edition* Basil Blackwell. 1978
Ludwig Wittgenstein. *Philosophische Grammatik* Basil Blackwell. 1969.
Ludwig Wittgenstein. (1933-1935) *Blue and Brown Books.* Harper. 1965.
Ludwig Wittgenstein *Philosophical Investigations* Blackwell. 1953/2001.
John Woods, *Paradox and Paraconsistency* Cambridge University Press. 2003
Larry Wos, George Robinson, Daniel Carson (1965) "Efficiency and Completeness of the Set of Support Strategy in Theorem Proving" *JACM* 12(4).
Noson Yanofsky. "A universal approach to self-referential paradoxes, incompleteness and fixed points" *Bulletin of Symbolic Logic* 9 No. 3. 2003.
Noson Yanofsky. *The Outer Limits of Reason: What Science, Mathematics, and Logic Cannot Tell Us* MIT Press. 2013.

Aki Yonezawa. *Specification and Verification Techniques for Parallel Programs Based on Message Passing Semantics* MIT EECS Ph. D. December 1977.

Ernst Zermelo. "Investigations in the foundations of set theory" (English translation in *From Frege to Gödel: A Source Book in Mathematical Logic, 1879-1931* Ed. Jean van Heijenoort 1967). 1908.

Ernst Zermelo, "Uber Grenzzahlen und Mengenbereiche: Neue Untersuchungen Äuber die Grundlagen der Mengenlehre", *Fundamenta mathematicae*, 1930; English translation by Michael Hallett, "On boundary numbers and domains of sets: new investigations in the foundations of set theory" *From Kant to Hilbert: a Source Book in the Foundations of Mathematics*, Oxford University Press, 1996

APPENDIX 1: DETAILS OF DIRECT LOGIC

Notation of Direct Logic

> The aims of logic should be the creation of *"a unified conceptual apparatus which would supply a common basis for the whole of human knowledge."*
> [Tarski 1940]

In Direct Logic, unrestricted recursion is allowed in programs. For example,
- There are uncountably many Actors.[54] For example, Real.[ ] can output any real number[i] between 0 and 1 where
  Real.[ ] ≡ [(0 **either** 1), ∀**Postpone** Real.[ ]]
  where
    - (0 **either** 1) is the nondeterministic choice of 0 or 1,
    - [*first*, ∀*rest*] is the list that begins with *first* and whose remainder is *rest*, and
    - **Postpone** *expression* delays execution of *expression* until the value is needed.
- There are uncountably many propositions (because there is a different proposition for every real number). Consequently, there are propositions that are not the abstraction of any element of a denumerable set of sentences. For example,
  p ≡ [x∈ℝ]→([y∈ℝ]→(y=x))
  defines a different predicate p[x] for each real number x, which holds for only one real number, namely x.[ii]

It is important to distinguish between strings, sentences, and propositions. Some strings can be parsed into sentences[iii], which can be abstracted into propositions that can be asserted. Furthermore, expressions[iv] can be abstracted into Actors (*e.g.*, objects in mathematics).

---

[i] using binary representation.
[ii] For example (p[3])[y] holds if and only if y=3.
[iii] which are grammar tree structures
[iv] which are grammar tree structures

Abstraction and parsing are becoming increasingly important in software engineering. *e.g.,*
- The execution of code can be dynamically checked against its documentation. Also Web Services can be dynamically searched for and invoked on the basis of their documentation.
- Use cases can be inferred by specialization of documentation and from code by automatic test generators and by model checking.
- Code can be generated by inference from documentation and by generalization from use cases.

Abstraction and parsing are needed for large software systems so that that documentation, use cases, and code can mutually speak about what has been said and their relationships.

For example:

Proposition
e.g. $\forall [n:\mathbb{N}] \to \exists [m:\mathbb{N}] \to m>n$
i.e., for every $\mathbb{N}$ *there is a larger* $\mathbb{N}$

Sentence
e.g. ⌜"$\forall [n:\mathbb{N}] \to \exists [m:\mathbb{N}] \to m>n$"⌝
i.e., the sentence that for every $\mathbb{N}$ *there is a larger* $\mathbb{N}$

String
e.g. "$\forall [n:\mathbb{N}] \to \exists [m:\mathbb{N}] \to m>n$"
which is a string that begins with the symbol "$\forall$"

In Direct Logic, a sentence is a grammar tree (analogous to the ones used by linguists). Such a grammar tree has terminals that can be constants. And there are uncountably many constants, *e.g.*, the real numbers:

The sentence ⌈3.14159... < 3.14159... + 1⌉ is impossible to obtain by parsing a string (where 3.14159... is an Actor[i] for the transcendental real number that is the ratio of a circle's circumference to its diameter). The issue is that there is no string which when parsed is
⌈3.14159... < 3.14159... + 1⌉

Of course, because the digits of 3.14159... are computable, there is an expression$_1$ such that ⌊expression$_1$⌋ = 3.14159... that can be used to create the sentence ⌈expression$_1$ < expression$_1$ + 1⌉.

However the sentence ⌈expression$_1$ < expression$_1$ + 1⌉ is not the same as ⌈3.14159... < 3.14159... + 1⌉ because it does not have the same vocabulary and it is a much larger sentence that has many terminals whereas ⌈3.14159... < 3.14159... + 1⌉ has just 3 terminals:

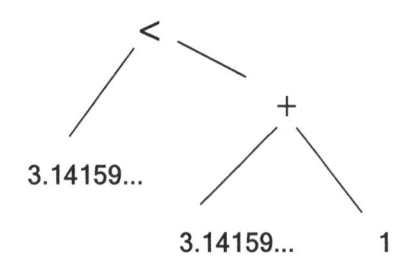

```
         <
        / \
  3.14159...  +
             / \
       3.14159...  1
```

Consequently, sentences *cannot* be enumerated and there are some sentences that *cannot* be obtained by parsing strings. These arrangements exclude known paradoxes from Classical Direct Logic.[ii]

Note: type theory of Classical Direct Logic is much stronger than constructive type theory with constructive logic[55] because Classical Direct Logic has all of the power of Classical Mathematics.

---

[i] whose digits are incrementally computable
[ii] Please see historical appendix of this article.

Types and Propositions are defined as follows:
- **Types** i.e., a Type is *only* by the rules below:
    - Boolean,$\mathbb{N}^{56}$,Sentence,Proposition,Proof,Theory:Type
    - If σ_1,σ_2:Type, then $\sigma_1\oplus\sigma_2^i,[\sigma_1, \sigma_2]^{57},[\sigma_1]\mapsto\sigma_2^{ii},\sigma_2^{\sigma_1\,iii}$:Type
    - If f:Type$^\mathbb{N}$, then $(\oplus_\mathbb{N}\, f)$:Type^{iv}
    - If σ:Type, then Term$\triangleleft\sigma\triangleright^{58}$:Type
    - If σ:Type and e:Expression$\triangleleft\sigma\triangleright$ with no free variables, then $\lfloor e \rfloor$:σ.

- **Propositions**, i.e., a Proposition is *only* by the rules below:
    - If σ:Type, Π:Boolean$^\sigma$ and x:σ, then $\Pi[x]$:Proposition.^{v}
    - If Φ:Proposition, then $\neg\Phi$:Proposition.
    - If Φ,Ψ:Proposition, then $\Phi\wedge\Psi$, $\Phi\vee\Psi$, $\Phi\Rightarrow\Psi$, $\Phi\Leftrightarrow\Psi$:Proposition.
    - If p:Boolean and Φ,Ψ:Proposition, then
      (p $\blacklozenge$ True$\S$ $\Phi_1\square$ False$\S$ Φ_2):Proposition.^{59}
    - If σ_1,σ_2:Type, x_1:σ_1 and x_2:σ_2, then
      $x_1=x_2,x_1\in x_2,x_1\subseteq x_2,x_1\subsetneq x_2,x_1$:$x_2$:Proposition.
    - If T:Theory, p:Proof and $\Phi_{1\,\text{to}\,n}$:Proposition, then
      $(\Phi_1,...,\Phi_k \vdash^p_T \Phi_{k+1},...,\Phi_n)$:Proposition^{60}
    - If s:Sentence with no free variables, then $\lfloor s \rfloor$:Proposition.

---

^{i} For i=1,2
- If x:σ_i, then $(x\oslash(\sigma_1\oplus\sigma_2))$:$(\sigma_1\oplus\sigma_2)$ and $x=(x\oslash(\sigma_1\oplus\sigma_2))\ominus\sigma_i$.
- $\forall[\tau$:Type, z:$\tau]\to z$:$\sigma_1\oplus\sigma_2 \Leftrightarrow \exists[x$:$\sigma_i]\to z=x\oslash(\sigma_1\oplus\sigma_2)$

^{ii} Type of computable procedures from σ_1 into σ_2.
If σ_1,σ_2:Type, f:$([\sigma_1]\mapsto\sigma_2)$ and x:σ_1, then f$_*$[x]:σ_2.

^{iii} If σ_1,σ_2:Type, f:$\sigma_2^{\sigma_1}$ and x:σ_1, then f[x]:σ_2.

^{iv} $\forall[i$:$\mathbb{N}$, x:f[i]]$\to (x\oslash\oplus_\mathbb{N}\,f)$:$\oplus_\mathbb{N}\,f \wedge x=(x\oslash\oplus_\mathbb{N}\,f)\ominus f[i]$
$\forall[\tau$:Type, z:$\tau]\to z$:$\oplus_\mathbb{N}\,f \Leftrightarrow \exists[i$:$\mathbb{N}$, x:f[i]]$\to z=x\oslash\oplus_\mathbb{N}\,f$

^{v} $\forall[\sigma$:Type, x:$\sigma]\to \Pi[x]\Leftrightarrow(\Pi[x]=\text{True})$
Note that σ:Strict, Π:Boolean$^\sigma$ means that there are no fixed points for propositions.

Grammar trees (*i.e.* expressions and sentences) are defined as follows: [i]
- **Expressions**, *i.e.,* an Expression is *only* by the rules below:
  - **True, False**:Constant◁Boolean▷ and **0,1**:Constant◁ℕ▷.
  - Boolean,ℕ,Sentence,Proposition,Proof,Theory:Constant◁Type▷.
  - If σ:Type and **x**:Constant◁σ▷, then **x**:Expression◁σ▷.
  - If σ:Type and **x**:Variable◁σ▷, then **x**:Expression◁σ▷.
  - If σ,σ$_{1\text{ to }n}$,τ$_{1\text{ to }n}$:Type, x$_{1\text{ to }n}$:Expression◁σ$_{1\text{ to }n}$▷ and
    y:Expression◁σ▷, then
    (Let v$_1$◁τ$_1$▷ ≡ x$_1$, ... , v$_n$◁τ$_n$▷ ≡ x$_n^{61}$ ₀ y):Expression◁σ▷ and
    v$_{1\text{ to }n}$:Variable◁σ$_{1\text{ to }n}$▷ in y and in each x$_{1\text{ to }n}$.
  - If e$_1$, e$_2$:Expression◁Type▷, then
    ⌈e$_1$⊕e$_2$⌉,⌈[e$_1$, e$_2$]⌉,⌈[e$_1$]↦e$_2$⌉,⌈e$_2{}^{e_1}$⌉:Expression◁Type▷.
  - If σ:Type, t$_1$:Expression◁Boolean▷, t$_2$, t$_3$:Expression◁σ▷, then
    ⌈t$_1$❖True⦂ t$_2$▽ False⦂ t$_3$⌉:Expression◁σ▷.[62]
  - If σ$_1$,σ$_2$:Type, t:Expression◁σ$_2$▷, then
    ⌈[x:σ$_1$]→ t⌉:Expression◁[σ$_1$]↦σ$_2$▷ and x:Variable◁σ$_1$▷.[63]
  - If σ$_1$,σ$_2$:Type, p:Expression◁[σ$_1$]↦σ$_2$▷ and x:Expression◁σ$_1$▷, then
    ⌈p.[x]⌉:Expression◁σ$_2$▷.

- **Sentences**, *i.e.,* a Sentence is *only* by the rules below:
  - If s$_1$:Sentence then, ⌈¬s$_1$⌉:Sentence.
  - If s$_1$:Sentence and s$_2$:Sentence then
    ⌈s$_1$∧s$_2$⌉,⌈s$_1$∨s$_2$⌉,⌈s$_1$⇨s$_2$⌉,⌈s$_1$⇔s$_2$⌉:Sentence.
  - If σ:Type, t$_1$:Expression◁Boolean^σ▷ and t$_2$:Expression◁σ▷, then
    ⌈t$_1$[t$_2$]⌉:Sentence
  - If t:Expression◁Boolean▷, s$_1$,s$_2$:Sentence, then
    ⌈t ❖ True⦂ s$_1$▽ False⦂ s$_2$⌉:Sentence.[64]
  - If σ$_1$,σ$_2$:Type, t$_1$:Expression◁σ$_1$▷ and t$_2$:Expression◁σ$_2$▷, then
    ⌈t$_1$=t$_2$⌉,⌈t$_1$∈t$_2$⌉,⌈t$_1$⊑t$_2$⌉,⌈t$_1$⊏t$_2$⌉,⌈t$_1$:t$_2$⌉:Sentence.
  - If σ:Type and s:Sentence, then ⌈∀[x:σ]→ s⌉,⌈∃[x:σ]→ s⌉:Sentence
    and x:Variable◁σ▷ in s.
  - If T:Expression◁Theory▷, s$_{1\text{ to }n}$:Sentence and
    p:Expression◁Proof▷, then ⌈s$_1$, ..., s$_k$ ⊢$_T^p$ s$_{k+1}$, ..., s$_n$⌉:Sentence
  - If s:Sentence with no free variables, then ⌊s⌋:Proposition.

---
[i] Because expressions are typed, fixed points do *not* exist. Parameterized mutually recursive definitions are used instead.

Inconsistency Robust Implication

Whether a deductive system is Euclidean or quasi-empirical is decided by the pattern of truth value flow in the system. The system is Euclidean if the characteristic flow is the transmission of truth from the set of axioms 'downwards' to the rest of the system—logic here is an organon of proof; it is quasi-empirical if the characteristic flow is retransmission of falsity from the false basic statements 'upwards' towards the 'hypothesis'—logic here is an organon of criticism. [Lakatos 1967]

Inconsistency-robust bi-implication is denoted by $\Leftrightarrow$.

Logical Equivalence: $(\Psi \Leftrightarrow \Phi) = (\Psi \Rightarrow \Phi) \wedge (\Phi \Rightarrow \Psi)$

Direct Logic has the following rules for inconsistency robust implication[i] in theory T:[ii]

Reiteration: $\vdash_T \Psi \Rightarrow \Psi$

Exchange: $(\vdash_T \Psi \wedge \Phi \Rightarrow \Theta) \Leftrightarrow \vdash_T \Phi \wedge \Psi \Rightarrow \Theta$
$(\vdash_T \Theta \Rightarrow \Psi \wedge \Phi) \Leftrightarrow \vdash_T \Theta \Rightarrow \Phi \wedge \Psi$

Dropping: $(\vdash_T \Psi \Rightarrow \Phi \wedge \Theta) \Rightarrow \vdash_T \Psi \Rightarrow \Phi$
                             ① *an implication holds if extra conclusions are dropped*

Accumulation: $(\vdash_T \Psi \Rightarrow \Phi, \Psi \Rightarrow \Theta) \Rightarrow \vdash_T \Psi \Rightarrow \Phi \wedge \Theta$

$(\vdash_T \Phi \Rightarrow \Psi, \Theta \Rightarrow \Psi) \Rightarrow \vdash_T \Phi \vee \Theta \Rightarrow \Psi$

Implication implies inference: $(\vdash_T \Phi \Rightarrow \Psi) \Rightarrow \Phi \vdash_T \Psi$

Transitivity: $(\vdash_T \Psi \Rightarrow \Phi, \Phi \Rightarrow \Theta) \Rightarrow \vdash_T \Psi \Rightarrow \Theta$
                                  ① *implication in a theory is transitive*

Contrapositive: $(\Psi \Rightarrow \Phi) \Leftrightarrow \neg \Phi \Rightarrow \neg \Psi$
                                  ① *contrapositive holds for implication*

Implication infers disjunction: $(\Phi \Rightarrow \Psi) \vdash_T \Psi \vee \neg \Phi$

---

[i] denoted by $\Rightarrow$. Inconsistency-robust implication is different from the much *weaker* concept of non-monotonic consequence [*e.g.* Kraus, *et. al.* 1990] which has axioms that are *not* valid for inconsistency-robust implication.

[ii] Inconsistency-robust implication is a very strong relationship. For example, monotonicity does not hold for implication although it does hold for inference. See section on Inconsistency Robust Inference below.

The ∨-rule for **Accumulation** is due to Eric Kao [private communication].

Substitution of Equivalent Propositions

Logical equivalence is defined for propositions for which the usual substitution rules apply:[i]

Substitution of equivalent propositions:
$(\Psi\Leftrightarrow\Phi) \Rightarrow (\neg\Psi)\Leftrightarrow(\neg\Phi)$
$(\Psi\Leftrightarrow\Phi) \Rightarrow ((\Psi\vee\Theta)\Leftrightarrow(\Phi\vee\Theta))$
$(\Psi\Leftrightarrow\Phi) \Rightarrow ((\Psi\vee\Theta)\Leftrightarrow(\Phi\vee\Theta))$
$(\Psi\Leftrightarrow\Phi) \Rightarrow ((\Psi\wedge\Theta)\Leftrightarrow(\Phi\wedge\Theta))$
$(\Psi\Leftrightarrow\Phi) \Rightarrow ((\Psi\wedge\Theta)\Leftrightarrow(\Phi\wedge\Theta))$
$(\Psi\Leftrightarrow\Phi) \Rightarrow ((\Psi\vdash_T\Theta)\Leftrightarrow(\Phi\vdash_T\Theta))$
$(\Psi\Leftrightarrow\Phi) \Rightarrow ((\Theta\vdash_T\Psi)\Leftrightarrow(\Theta\vdash_T\Phi))$
$(\Psi\Leftrightarrow\Phi) \Rightarrow ((\Psi\Rightarrow\Theta)\Leftrightarrow(\Phi\Rightarrow\Theta))$
$(\Psi\Leftrightarrow\Phi) \Rightarrow ((\Theta\Rightarrow\Psi)\Leftrightarrow(\Theta\Rightarrow\Phi))$
$(F\Leftrightarrow G) \Rightarrow (\forall F\Leftrightarrow\forall G)$

Propositional Equivalences

Theorem: The following usual propositional equivalences hold:

Self Equivalence: $\Psi \Leftrightarrow \Psi$
Double Negation: $\neg\neg\Psi \Leftrightarrow \Psi$
Idempotence of $\wedge$: $\Psi\wedge\Psi \Leftrightarrow \Psi$
Commutativity of $\wedge$: $\Psi\wedge\Phi \Leftrightarrow \Phi\wedge\Psi$
Associativity of $\wedge$: $\Psi\wedge(\Phi\wedge\Theta) \Leftrightarrow (\Psi\wedge\Phi)\wedge\Theta$
Distributivity of $\wedge$ **over** $\vee$: $\Psi\wedge(\Phi\vee\Theta) \Leftrightarrow (\Psi\wedge\Phi)\vee(\Psi\wedge\Theta)$
De Morgan for $\wedge$: $\neg(\Psi\wedge\Phi) \Leftrightarrow \neg\Psi\vee\neg\Phi$
Idempotence of $\vee$: $\Psi\vee\Psi \Leftrightarrow \Psi$
Commutativity of $\vee$: $\Psi\vee\Phi \Leftrightarrow \Phi\vee\Psi$
Associativity of $\vee$: $\Psi\vee(\Phi\vee\Theta) \Leftrightarrow (\Psi\vee\Phi)\vee\Theta$
Distributivity of $\vee$ **over** $\wedge$: $\Psi\vee(\Phi\wedge\Theta) \Leftrightarrow (\Psi\vee\Phi)\wedge(\Psi\vee\Theta)$
De Morgan for $\vee$: $\neg(\Psi\vee\Phi) \Leftrightarrow \neg\Psi\wedge\neg\Phi$
Contrapositive for $\Rightarrow$: $(\Psi\Rightarrow\Phi) \Lefteightarrow \neg\Phi\Rightarrow\neg\Psi$

---

[i] Classical implication (denoted by $\Rightarrow$) is logical implication for classical mathematics. (See the appendix on classical mathematics in Direct Logic.) Likewise classical bi-implication is denoted by $\Leftrightarrow$.
Direct Logic has the following usual principles for equality:
$E_1=E_1$
$E_1=E_2 \Rightarrow E_2=E_1$
$(E_1=E_2 \wedge E_2=E_3) \Rightarrow E_1=E_3$

Also, the following usual propositional inferences hold:

Absorption of ∧: $\Psi \wedge (\Phi \vee \Psi) \vdash_T \Psi$
Absorption of ∨: $\Psi \vee (\Phi \wedge \Psi) \vdash_T \Psi$ [65]

Conjunction, i.e., comma

> **∧-Elimination:** $(\vdash_T \Psi \wedge \Phi) \Rightarrow \vdash_T \Psi, \Phi$

> **∧-Introduction:** $(\vdash_T \Psi, \Phi) \Rightarrow \vdash_T \Psi \wedge \Phi$

Disjunction

> **∨-Elimination:**[i] $\vdash_T \neg\Psi \wedge (\Psi \vee \Phi) \Rightarrow \Phi$

> **∨-Introduction:** $\vdash_T \Psi \wedge \Phi \Rightarrow \Psi \vee \Phi$

> **Disjunctive Cases:** $\vdash_T (\Psi \vee \Phi) \wedge (\Psi \Rightarrow \Theta) \wedge (\Phi \Rightarrow \Omega) \Rightarrow \Theta \vee \Omega$

Theorem: *Inconsistency Robust Resolution*[ii]
$\vdash_T (\Psi \vee \neg\Psi) \wedge (\Psi \vee \Theta) \wedge (\Phi \vee \Omega) \Rightarrow \Theta \vee \Omega$
Proof: Immediate from Disjunctive Cases and ∨-Elimination.

Inconsistency Robust Inference

> *Logic merely sanctions the conquests of the intuition.*
> Jacques Hadamard (quoted in Kline [1972])

Inference in theory T (denoted by $\vdash_T$) is characterized by the following additional axioms:[iii]

---

[i] i.e. Disjunctive Syllogism
[ii] Joint work with Eric Kao
[iii] Half of the Classical Deduction Theorem holds for Inconsistency Direct Logic. That one proposition infers another in a theory does not in general imply that the first proposition implies the second because Inconsistency Robust Implication is a *very* strong relationship.

Soundness

> **Soundness:** $\vdash_T ((\vdash_T \Psi) \Rightarrow \Psi)$
> ⓘ *a proposition inferred in a theory implies the proposition in the theory*

Inconsistency Robust Proof by Contradiction

> **Inconsistency Robust Proof by Contradiction:**
> $\vdash_T (\Phi \Rightarrow (\Psi \wedge \neg \Psi)) \Rightarrow \neg \Phi$

Quantifiers

Direct Logic makes use of functions for quantification.[66] For example following expresses commutativity for natural numbers:
$$\forall [x,y:\mathbb{N}] \rightarrow x+y=y+x$$

> **Variable Elimination:** $\forall F \Rightarrow F[E]$
> ⓘ *a universally quantified variable of a statement can be instantiated with any expression* E *(taking care that none of the variables in* E *are captured).*
> **Variable Introduction:** *Let* Z *be a new constant,* $F[Z] \Leftrightarrow \forall F$
> ⓘ *inferring a statement with a universally quantified variable is equivalent to inferring the statement with a newly introduced constant substituted for the variable*
> **Existential quantification:** $\exists F = \neg \forall \neg F$

Appendix 2. Foundations of Classical Mathematics beyond Logicism

> *Mathematicians do not study objects, but the relations between objects; to them it is a matter of indifference if these objects are replaced by others, provided that the relations do not change. Matter does not engage their attention, they are interested by form alone.*
> Poincaré [1902]

This appendix presents foundations for mathematics that goes beyond logicism in that it does not attempt to reduce mathematics solely to logic, solely to types, or solely to sets in a way that encompasses all of standard mathematics including the integers, reals, analysis, geometry, *etc.*[67]

Consistency has been the bedrock of classical mathematics.

Platonic Ideals were to be perfect, unchanging, and eternal.[68] Beginning with the Hellenistic mathematician Euclid [*circa* 300BC] in Alexandria, theories were intuitively supposed to be consistent.[69] Wilhelm Leibniz, Giuseppe Peano, George Boole, Augustus De Morgan, Richard Dedekind, Gottlob Frege, Charles Peirce, David Hilbert, *etc.* developed mathematical logic. However, a crisis occurred with the discovery of the logical paradoxes based on self-reference by Burali-Forti [1897], Cantor [1899], Russell [1903], *etc.* In response Russell [1925] stratified types, [Zermelo 1905, Fränkel 1922, Skolem 1922] stratified sets and [Tarski and Vaught 1957] stratified logical theories to limit self-reference. [Church 1935, Turing 1936] proved that closed mathematical theories are inferentially undecidable[i], *i.e.,* there are propositions which can neither be proved nor disproved. However, the bedrock of consistency remained.

This appendix present classical mathematics in Direct Logic using ⊢.[ii]

The following additional principles are available because ⊢ is thought to be consistent by an overwhelming consensus of working professional mathematicians:

Classical Proof by Contradiction: $(\Phi \vdash \Psi, \neg \Psi) \vdash \neg \Phi$
   i.e., the negation of a proposition can be inferred from inferring a contradiction

---
Classical Deduction Theorem: $(\Psi \vdash \Phi) \Leftrightarrow \vdash (\Psi \Rightarrow \Phi)$
   i.e., an implication can be proved by inference

Classical Proof by Contradiction: $(\Phi \vdash \Psi, \neg \Psi) \vdash \neg \Phi$
   i.e., the negation of a proposition can be inferred from inferring a contradiction

---

Inheritance from classical mathematics
Theorems of mathematics hold in every theory:
   If Φ is a proposition of mathematics, $(\vdash \Phi) \Rightarrow (\vdash_T \Phi)$

---

[i] sometimes called "incomplete"
[ii] with no subscripted inconsistency robust theory, i.e., ⊢ is used for classical mathematics whereas ⊢_T is used for inconsistency-robust inference in theory T.

Nondeterministic Execution
Direct Logic makes use of the nondeterministic execution as follows:[70]
- If **E₁** and **E₂** are *expressions*, then **E₁→E₂** (**E₁** *can nondeterministically evolve to* **E₂**) is a *proposition*.
- If **E** is an *expression*, then Converges[**E**] (**E** always converges) is a *proposition*.

Foundations with both Types and Sets

Classical Direct Logic develops foundations for mathematics using *both*[i] types[ii] *and* sets[iii] encompassing all of standard mathematics including the integers, reals, analysis, geometry, *etc.*[71]
Combining types and sets as the foundation has the advantage of using the strengths of each without the limitations of trying to use just one because each can be used to make up for the limitations of the other. The key idea is compositionality, *i.e.*, composing new entities from others. Types can be composed from other types and sets can be composed from other sets.[iv]

Functions are fundamental to Computer Science. Consequently, graphs of functions and sets are fundamental collections.[72] SetFunctions◁σ▷ (type of set functions based on type σ) that can be defined inductively as follows:

SetFunctionsOfOrder◁σ▷[1] ≡ σ^σ
SetFunctionsOfOrder◁σ▷[n+1] ≡
   (σ⊕SetFunctionsOfOrder◁σ▷[n])^(σ⊕SetFunctionsOfOrder◁σ▷[n])

---

[i] Past attempts to reduce mathematics to logic alone, to sets alone, or to types alone have not be very successful.

[ii] According to [Scott 1967]: "there is only one satisfactory way of avoiding the paradoxes: namely, the use of some form of the *theory of types*... the best way to regard Zermelo's theory is as a simplification and extension of Russell's ...*simple* theory of types. Now Russell made his types *explicit* in his notation and Zermelo left them *implicit*. It is a mistake to leave something so important invisible..."

[iii] According to [Scott 1967]: "As long as an idealistic manner of speaking about abstract objects is popular in mathematics, people will speak about collections of objects, and then collections of collections of ... of collections. In other words *set theory is inevitable.*" [emphasis in original]

[iv] Compositionality avoids standard foundational paradoxes. For example, Direct Logic composes propositions from others using strict types so there are no "self-referential" propositions.

Furthermore the process of constructing orders of SetFunctionsOfOrder◁σ▷ is exhaustive for SetFunctions◁σ▷:[i]

SetFunctions◁σ▷ ≡ ⊔$_{i:\mathbb{N}}$ SetFunctionsOfOrder◁σ▷[i]

Sets (along with lists) provide a convenient way to collect together elements.[73] For example, sets (of sets of sets of ...) of σ can be axiomatized as follows:
∀[s:Sets◁σ▷]→ ∃[f:SetFunctions◁σ▷]→ CharacteristicFunction[f, s]
 where ∀[s:Sets◁σ▷, f:Boolean$^{\text{SetFunctions◁σ▷}}$]→
   CharacteristicFunction[f, s]
     ⇔ ∀[e:σ⊕Sets◁σ▷]→ e∈s ⇔ f[e]=True
i.e. every set of type Sets◁σ▷ is defined by a characteristic function of SetFunctions◁σ▷

Note that there is no set corresponding to the *type* Sets◁ℕ▷ which is an example of how types extend the capabilities of sets.[74]

XML

We speak in strings, but think in trees.
---Nicolaas de Bruijin[75]

The base domain of Direct Logic is XML[ii]. In Direct Logic, a dog is an XML dog, *e.g.*, <Dog><Name>Fido</Name></Dog> ∈ Dogs⊆XML
Unlike First Order Logic, there is no unrestricted quantification in Direct Logic. So the proposition ∀d∈Dogs → Mammal[d] is about dogs in XML. *The base equality built into Direct Logic is equality for* XML, *not equality in some abstract "domain"*. In this way Direct Logic does not have to take a stand on the various ways that dogs, photons, quarks and everything else can be considered "equal"!

This axiomization omits certain aspects of standard XML, *e.g.*, attributes, namespaces, *etc.*

Two XML expressions are equal if and only if they are both atomic and are identical or are both elements and have the same tag and the same number of children such that the corresponding children are equal.

---

[i] The closure property below is used to guarantee that there is just one model of SetFunctions◁ℕ▷ up to isomorphism using a unique isomorphism.
[ii] Lisp was an important precursor of XML. The Atomics axiomatised below correspond roughly to atoms and the Elements to lists.

The following are axioms for XML:
(Atomics $\cup$ Elements) = XML
(Atomics $\cap$ Elements) = { }[76]
Tags $\subseteq$ Atomics
$\forall[x] \rightarrow x \in$ Elements $\Leftrightarrow$ $x = $ <Tag(x)> $x_1...x_{Length(x)}$ </Tag(x)>
  where x_i *is the i th subelement of x and*
    Tag(x) *is the tag of x*
    Length(x) *is the number of subelements of x*

A set p⊆XML is defined to be *inductive* (written Inductive[p]) if and only it contains the atomics and for all elements that it contains, it also contains every element with those sub-elements:
($\forall$[p⊆XML; $x_1...x_n \in$ p; t∈Tags]→
  Inductive[p] $\Rightarrow$ (Atomics $\subseteq$ p $\wedge$ <t> $x_1...x_n$</t> ∈p)
The Strong Principle of Induction for XML is as follows:
  $\forall$[p⊆XML]→ Inductive[p] $\Rightarrow$ p = XML
The reason that induction is called *"strong"* is that there are no restrictions on inductive predicates.[77]

Natural Numbers, Real Numbers, and their Sets are Unique up to Isomorphism
The following question arises: What mathematics have been captured in the above foundations?

Theorem[i] **(Categoricity of** $\mathbb{N}$**):**[78] $\forall$[M:Model⊲$\mathbb{N}$⊳]→ M≈$\mathbb{N}$, *i.e.*, models of the natural numbers $\mathbb{N}$ are isomorphic by a unique isomorphism.[ii]

The following categorical induction axiom[79] can be used to characterize the natural numbers ($\mathbb{N}$[80]) up to isomorphism with a unique isomorphism:
  $\forall$[P:Boolean$^\mathbb{N}$]→ Inductive[P]$\Rightarrow$ $\forall$[i:$\mathbb{N}$]→ P[i]
    where $\forall$[P:Boolean$^\mathbb{N}$]→
      Inductive[P] $\Leftrightarrow$ P[0] $\wedge$ $\forall$[i:$\mathbb{N}$]→ P[i] $\Rightarrow$P[i+1][iii]

---

[i] [Dedekind 1888, Peano 1889]
[ii] Consequently, the type $\mathbb{N}$ is unique up to isomorphism and the type $\mathbb{R}$ is unique up to isomorphism.
[iii] which can be equivalently expressed as:
  $\forall$[P:Boolean$^\mathbb{N}$]→ Inductive[P]$\Rightarrow$ $\forall$[i:$\mathbb{N}$]→ P[i]=True
    where $\forall$[P:Boolean$^\mathbb{N}$]→
      Inductive[P] $\Leftrightarrow$ (P[0]=True $\wedge$ $\forall$[i:$\mathbb{N}$]→ P[i]=True $\Rightarrow$P[i+1]=True)

Theorem[i] **(Categoricity of** $\mathbb{R}$**):**[81] ∀[M:Model◁$\mathbb{R}$▷]→ M≈$\mathbb{R}$, *i.e.*, models of the real numbers $\mathbb{R}$ are isomorphic by a unique isomorphism.[ii]

The following can be used to characterize the real numbers ($\mathbb{R}^{82}$) up to isomorphism with a unique isomorphism:
∀[S:Set◁$\mathbb{R}$▷]→ S≠{ } ∧ Bounded[S] ⇨ HasLeastUpperBound[S]
  where
    UpperBound[b:$\mathbb{R}$, S:Set◁$\mathbb{R}$▷] ⇔ b∈S ∧ ∀[x∈S]→ x≦b
    HasLeastUpperBound[S:Set◁$\mathbb{R}$▷]]
          ⇔ ∃[b:$\mathbb{R}$]→ LeastUpperBound[b, S]
    LeastUpperBound[b:$\mathbb{R}$, S:Set◁$\mathbb{R}$▷]
          ⇔ UpperBound[b,S] ∧ ∀[x∈S]→ UpperBound[x,S] ⇨ x≦b

Theorem (Categoricity of Sets◁$\mathbb{N}$▷):[83]
  ∀[M:Model◁Sets◁$\mathbb{N}$▷▷]→ M≈Sets◁$\mathbb{N}$▷
    i.e., models of Sets◁$\mathbb{N}$▷ are isomorphic by a unique isomorphism.[iii]

Sets◁$\mathbb{N}$▷ (which is a fundamental type of mathematics) is exactly characterized axiomatically, which is what is required for Computer Science.

> Proof: By above, ∀[M:Model◁$\mathbb{N}$▷]→ M≈$\mathbb{N}$, *i.e.*, models of $\mathbb{N}$ are isomorphic by a unique isomorphism. Unique isomorphism of higher order sets can be proved using induction from the following closure property for SetFunctions (see above):
> SetFunctionsOfOrder◁σ▷[n+1] ≡
>   (σ⊕SetFunctionsOfOrder◁σ▷[n])$^{σ⊕SetFunctionsOfOrder◁σ▷[n]}$
> Unique isomorphism for SetFunctions◁$\mathbb{N}$▷ can be extended Sets◁$\mathbb{N}$▷ because every set in Sets◁$\mathbb{N}$▷ is defined by a characteristic function of SetFunctions◁$\mathbb{N}$▷ (see above):

Classical Direct Logic is much stronger than first-order axiomatizations of set theory.[84] Also, the semantics of Classical Direct Logic cannot be characterized using Tarskian Set Models [Tarski and Vaught 1957].[iv]

---

[i] [Dedekind 1888]
[ii] Consequently, the type of natural numbers $\mathbb{N}$ is unique up to isomorphism and the type of reals $\mathbb{R}$ is unique up to isomorphism.
[iii] Consequently, the set of natural numbers $\mathbb{N}$ is unique up to isomorphism and is contained in the set of reals $\mathbb{R}$ that is unique up to isomorphism.
[iv] See section on "Inadequacy of Tarskian Set Models."

Theorem (Set Theory Model Soundness): $\vdash_{\text{Sets}\triangleleft\mathbb{N}\triangleright}\Psi$ implies $\vDash_{\text{Sets}\triangleleft\mathbb{N}\triangleright}\Psi$

Proof: Suppose $\vdash_{\text{Sets}\triangleleft\mathbb{N}\triangleright}\Psi$. The conclusion immediately follows because the axioms for the theory Sets⊲ℕ⊳ hold in the model 𝕊𝕖𝕥𝕤⊲ℕ⊳.

Appendix 3. Historical development of inferential undecidability ("incompleteness")

Truth versus Argumentation

[Peano 1889, Dedekind 1888] made fundamental contributions to the foundations of mathematics with the following theorems:

- *Full Peano Integers:* Let **X** be the structure $<X, 0_X, S_X>$, then Peano[**X**] ⇒ **X**≈$<\mathbb{N}, 0, S>$[85] The theory Peano is the full theory of natural numbers with categorical induction that is strictly more powerful than cut-down first-order theory. Perhaps of greater import, there are nondeterministic Turing machines that Peano proves always halt that cannot be proved to halt in the cut-down first-order theory.

- *Full Dedekind Reals:* Let **X** be the structure $<X, \leq_X, 0_X, 1_X, +_X, *_X>$, then Dedekind[**X**] ⇒ **X**≈$<\mathbb{R}^i, \leq, 0, 1, +, *>$[86]
  The theory Dedekind is the full theory of real numbers that is strictly more powerful than cut-down first-order theory.[87]

The above results categorically characterize the natural numbers (integers) and the real numbers up to isomorphism based on *argumentation*. There is no way to go beyond argumentation to get at some special added insight called *"truth."* Argumentation is all that we have.

---

[i] ℝ is the set of real numbers

Turing versus Gödel

You shall not cease from exploration
And the end of all our journeying
Will be to arrive where we started
And know the place for the first time.
  T.S. Eliot [1942]

Turing recognized that proving that inference in mathematics is computationally undecidable is quite different than proving that there is a proposition of mathematics that is inferentially undecidable.[i] [Turing 1936, page 259]:
> It should perhaps be remarked what I shall prove is quite different from the well-known results of Gödel [1931]. Gödel has shown that there are propositions U such that neither U nor ¬U is provable. ... On the other hand, I shall show that there is no general method which tells whether a given formula U is provable.[88]

Although they share some similar underlying ideas, the method of proving computational undecidability developed by Church and Turing is much more robust than the one previously developed by Gödel that relies on "self-referential" propositions.

The difference can be explicated as follows:
- Actors: an Actor that has an address for itself can be used to generate infinite computations.
- Propositions: "self-referential" propositions can be used to infer inconsistencies in mathematics.

As Wittgenstein pointed out, the following "self-referential" proposition leads an inconsistency in the foundations of mathematics: This proposition is not provable. If the inconsistencies of "self-referential" propositions stopped with this example, then it would be somewhat tolerable for an inconsistency-robust theory. However, other "self-referential" propositions (constructed in a similar way) can be used to prove every proposition thereby rendering inference useless.

This is why Direct Logic does not support "self-referential" propositions.[ii]

---

[i] sometimes called "incompleteness."
[ii] There It seems that are no practical uses for "self-referential" propositions in the mathematical foundations of Computer Science.

Contra Gödel et. al

The proof of the consistency of mathematics in this article contradicts the result [Gödel 1931] using "self-referential" propositions that mathematics cannot prove its own consistency.

One resolution is not to have "self-referential" propositions, which is contra Gödel *et. al*. Direct Logic aims to not have "self-referential" propositions by carefully arranging the rules so that "self-referential" propositions cannot be constructed. The basic idea is to use typed functions [Russell 1908, Church 1940] to construct propositions so that fixed points do not exist and consequently cannot be used to construct "self-referential" propositions.

How the self-proof of consistency of mathematics was overlooked and then discovered

Before the paradoxes were discovered, not much attention was paid to proving consistency. Hilbert et. al. undertook to find a *convincing* proof of consistency. Gentzen found a consistency proof for the first-order Peano theory but many did not find it convincing because the proof was not elementary. Then following Carnap and Gödel, philosophers blindly accepted the necessity of "self-referential" prepositions in mathematics. And none of them seemed to understand Wittgenstein's critique. (Gödel insinuated that Wittgenstein was *"crazy."*) Instead, philosophers turned their attention to exploring the question of which is the weakest theory in which Gödel's proof can be carried out. They were prisoners of the existing paradigm.

Computer scientists brought different concerns and a new perspective. They wanted foundations with the following characteristics:
- powerful so that arguments (proofs) are short and understandable and all logical inferences can be formalized
- standard so they can join forces and develop common techniques and technology
- inconsistency robust because computers deal in pervasively inconsistent information.

The results of [Gödel 1931], [Curry 1941], and [Löb 1055] played an important role the development of Direct Logic:
- Direct Logic easily formalized Wittgenstein's proof that Gödel's "self-referential" proposition leads to contradiction. So the consistency of mathematics had to be rescued against Gödel's "self-referential" proposition. The "self-referential" propositions used in results of [Curry 1941] and [Löb 1955] led to inconsistency in mathematics. So the consistency of mathematics had to be rescued against these "self-referential" propositions as well.
- Direct Logic easily proves the consistency of mathematics. So the consistency of mathematics had to be rescued against Gödel's "2nd incompleteness theorem."
- Direct Logic easily proves Church's Paradox. So the consistency of mathematics had to be rescued against the assumption that the theorems of mathematics can be computationally enumerated.

In summary, computer science advanced to a point where it caused the development of Direct Logic.

Inconsistency-robust Logic Programs

Logic Programs[i] can logically infer computational steps.

Forward Chaining
Forward chaining is performed using ⊢

```
(⊢_aTheory PropositionExpression):Continuation
    Assert PropositionExpression for aTheory.
```

```
(When ⊢_aTheory PropositionPattern →
    Expression):Continuation
    When PropositionPattern holds for aTheory, evaluate
Expression.
```

---

[i] [Church 1932; McCarthy 1963; Hewitt 1969, 1971, 2010; Milner 1972, Hayes 1973; Kowalski 1973]. Note that this definition of Logic Programs does *not* follow the proposal in [Kowalski 1973, 2011] that Logic Programs be restricted only to backward chaining, *e.g.,* to the exclusion of forward chaining, *etc.*

Illustration of forward chaining:
    ⊢$_t$ Human[Socrates]▮
    When ⊢$_t$ Human[x] → ⊢$_t$ Mortal[x]▮
will result in asserting Mortal[Socrates] for theory t

Backward Chaining
Backward chaining is performed using ⊩

(⊩ $_{aTheory}$ *GoalPattern* → *Expression*):*Continuation*
Set *GoalPattern* for *Theory* and when established evaluate *Expression*.

(⊩ $_{aTheory}$ *GoalPattern*):*Expression*
Set *GoalPattern* for *Theory* and return a list of assertions that satisfy the goal.

(**When** ⊩ $_{aTheory}$ *GoalPattern* → *Expression*):*Continuation*
    When there is a goal that matches *GoalPattern* for Theory, evaluate *Expression*.

Illustration of backward chaining:
    ⊢$_t$ Human[Socrates]▮
    When ⊩$_t$ Mortal[x] → (⊩$_t$ Human[x] → ⊢$_t$ Mortal[x])▮
    ⊩$_t$ Mortal[Socrates]▮
will result in asserting Mortal[Socrates] for theory t.

SubArguments
This section explains how subarguments[i] can be implemented in natural deduction.
    When ⊩$_s$ (*psi* ⊢$_t$ *phi*) →
        Let t' ← extension(t),
            Do ⊢$_{t'}$ *psi*,
            ⊩$_{t'}$ *phi* → ⊢$_s$ (*psi* ⊢$_t$ *phi*))▮

Note that the following hold for t' because it is an extension of t:
- **When** ⊢$_t$ *theta* → ⊢$_{t'}$ *theta*▮
- **When** ⊩$_{t'}$ *theta* → ⊩$_t$ *theta*▮

---
[i] See appendix on Inconsistency Robust Natural Deduction.

End Notes

[1] Inference is direct when it does not involved unnecessary circumlocutions, *e.g.*, coding sentences as Godel numbers. In Direct Logic, it is possible speak directly about inference relationships.

[2] This section shares history with [Hewitt 2010b]

[3] D'Ariano and Tosini [2010] showed how the Minkowskian space-time emerges from a topologically homogeneous causal network, presenting a simple analytical derivation of the Lorentz transformations, with metric as pure event-counting.

Do events happen in space-time or is space-time that is made up of events? This question may be considered a "which came first, the chicken or the egg?" dilemma, but the answer may contain the solution of the main problem of contemporary physics: the reconciliation of quantum theory (QT) with general relativity (GR). Why? Because "events" are central to QT and "space-time" is central to GR. Therefore, the question practically means: which comes first, QT or GR? In spite of the evidence of the first position—"events happen in space-time"—the second standpoint—"space- time is made up of events"—is more concrete, if we believe à la Copenhagen that whatever is not "measured" is only in our imagination: space-time too must be measured, and measurements are always made-up of events. Thus QT comes first. How? Space-time emerges from the tapestry of events that are connected by quantum interactions, as in a huge quantum computer: this is the Wheeler's "It from bit." [Wheeler 1990].

[4] According to [Law 2006], a classical realism (to which he does *not* subscribe) is:

Scientific experiments make no sense if there is no reality independent of the actions of scientists: an independent reality is one of conditions of possibility for experimentation. The job of the investigator is to experiment in order to make and test hypotheses about the mechanisms that underlie or make up reality. Since science is conducted within specific social and cultural circumstances, the models and metaphors used to generate fallible claims are, of course, socially contexted, and always revisable...Different 'paradigms' relate to (possibly different parts of) the same world.

[5] Vardi [2010] has defended the traditional paradigm of proving that program meet specifications and attacked an early critical analysis as follows: "*With hindsight of 30 years, it seems that De Millo, Lipton, and Perlis'* [1979] *article has proven to be rather misguid*ed." However, contrary to Vardi, limitations of the traditional paradigm of proving that program meet specifications have become much more apparent in the last 30 years—as admitted even by some who had been the most prominent proponents, *e.g.*, [Hoare 2003, 2009].

[6] According to [Hoare 2009]: *One thing I got spectacularly wrong. I could see that programs were getting larger, and I thought that testing would be an increasingly ineffective way of removing errors from them. I did not realize that the success of tests is that they test the programmer, not the program. Rigorous testing regimes rapidly persuade error-prone programmers (like me) to remove themselves from the profession. Failure in test immediately punishes any lapse in programming concentration, and (just as important) the failure count enables implementers to resist management pressure for premature delivery of unreliable code. The experience, judgment, and intuition of programmers who have survived the rigors of testing are what make programs of the present day useful, efficient, and (nearly) correct.*

[7] According to [Hoare 2009]: *Verification* [proving that programs meet specifications] *technology can only work against errors that have been accurately specified, with as much accuracy and attention to detail as all other aspects of the programming task. There will always be a limit at which the engineer judges that the cost of such specification is greater than the benefit that could be obtained from it; and that testing will be adequate for the purpose, and cheaper. Finally, verification* [proving that programs meet specifications] *cannot protect against errors in the specification itself.*

[8] Popper [1934] section 30.

[9] The thinking in almost all scientific and engineering work has been that models (also called theories or microtheories) should be internally consistent, although they could be inconsistent with each other.

Indeed some researchers have even gone so far as to construct consistency proofs for some small software systems, *e.g.*, [Davis and Morgenstern 2005] in their system for deriving plausible conclusions using classical logical inference for Multi-Agent Systems. In order to carry out the consistency proof of their system, Davis and Morgenstern make some simplifying assumptions:
- No two agents can simultaneously make a choice (following [Reiter 2001]).
- No two agents can simultaneously send each other inconsistent information.
- Each agent is individually serial, *i.e.*, each agent can execute only one primitive action at a time.
  - There is a global clock time.
  - Agents use classical Speech Acts (see [Hewitt 2006b 2007a, 2007c, 2008c]).
  - Knowledge is expressed in first-order logic.

The above assumptions are not particularly good ones for modern systems (e.g., using Web Services and many-core computer architectures). [Hewitt 2007a]

The following conclusions can be drawn for documentation, use cases, and code of large software systems for human-computer interaction:
- Consistency proofs are impossible for whole systems.
- There are some consistent subtheories but they are typically mathematical. There are some other consistent microtheories as well, but they are small, make simplistic assumptions, and typically are inconsistent with other such microtheories [Addanki, Cremonini and Penberthy 1989].

Nevertheless, the Davis and Morgenstern research programme to prove consistency of microtheories can be valuable for the theories to which it can be applied. Also some of the techniques that they have developed may be able to be used to prove the consistency of the mathematical fragment of Direct Logic and to prove inconsistency robustness (see below in this article).

[10] Turing differed fundamentally on the question of inconsistency from Wittgenstein when he attended Wittgenstein's seminar on the Foundations of Mathematics [Diamond 1976]:

Wittgenstein:... Think of the case of the Liar. It is very queer in a way that this should have puzzled anyone — much more extraordinary than you might think... Because the thing works like this: if a man says 'I am lying' we say that it follows that he is not lying, from which it follows that he is lying and so on. Well, so what? You can go on like that until you are black in the face. Why not? It doesn't matter. ...it is just a useless language-game, and why should anyone be excited?

Turing: What puzzles one is that one usually uses a contradiction as a criterion for having done something wrong. But in this case one cannot find anything done wrong.

Wittgenstein: Yes — and more: nothing has been done wrong, ... where will the harm come?

Turing: The real harm will not come in unless there is an application, in which a bridge may fall down or something of that sort.... You cannot be confident about applying your calculus until you know that there are no hidden contradictions in it.... Although you do not know that the bridge will fall if there are no contradictions, yet it is almost certain that if there are contradictions it will go wrong somewhere.

Wittgenstein followed this up with [Wittgenstein 1956, pp. 104e–106e]: *Can we say: 'Contradiction is harmless if it can be sealed off'? But what prevents us from sealing it off?.*

[11] A more conservative axiomatization in Direct Logic is the following:
  Policy₁[x] ≡ Sane[x] ⊢_{Catch22} Obligated[x, Fly]
  Policy₂[x] ≡ Obligated[x, Fly] ⊢_{Catch22} Fly[x]
  Policy₃[x] ≡ Crazy[x] ⊢_{Catch22} ¬Obligated[x, Fly]
  Observe₁[x] ≡ ¬Obligated[x, Fly].¬Fly[x] ⊢_{Catch22} Sane[x]
  Observe₂[x] ≡ Fly[x] ⊢_{Catch22} Crazy[x]
  Observe₃[x] ≡ Sane[x], ¬Obligated[x, Fly] ⊢_{Catch22} ¬Fly[x]]
  Observe₄ ≡ ⊢_{Catch22} Sane[Yossarian]
  Background₂ ≡ ⊢_{Catch22} ¬Obligated[Moon, Fly]

For the more conservative axiomatization above:
  ⊢_{Catch22} Fly[Yossarian] **but** ⊢_{Catch22} ¬Fly[Yossarian]
  ⊢_{Catch22} ¬Fly[Yossarian] **but** ⊢_{Catch22} Fly[Yossarian]

But, unlike for the stronger axiomatization using strong implication:
  ⊬_{Catch22} ¬Obligated[Yossarian, Fly]
  ⊬_{Catch22} ¬Sane[Yossarian]

[12] Because of the use of a very strong form of implication in the axiomatization, the following can also be inferred:
  ⊢_{Catch22} ¬Obligated[Yossarian, Fly]
  ⊢_{Catch22} ¬Sane[Yossarian]

[13] Philosophers have given the name *a priori* and *a posteriori* to the inconsistency

[14] including entanglement

[15] One possible approach towards developing inconsistency robust probabilities is to attach directionality to the calculations as follows:

P1. ⊢_{Catch22} ℙSane[x] $\overset{\leq}{\rightarrow}$ ℙObligated[x, Fly]

P2. ⊢_{Catch22} ℙObligated[x, Fly] $\overset{\leq}{\rightarrow}$ ℙFly[x]

P3. ⊢_{Catch22} ℙCrazy[x] $\overset{\leq}{\rightarrow}$ ℙ¬Obligated[x, Fly]

S1. ⊢_{Catch22} ℙ¬Obligated[x, Fly] ∧ ¬Fly[x] $\overset{\leq}{\rightarrow}$ ℙSane[x]

S2. ⊢_{Catch22} ℙFly[x] $\overset{\leq}{\rightarrow}$ ℙCrazy[x]

S3. ⊢_{Catch22} ℙSane[x]∧¬Obligated[x, Fly] $\overset{\leq}{\rightarrow}$ ℙ¬Fly[x]

S4. ⊢_{Catch22} ℙSane[Yossarian] $\twoheadrightarrow$ 1

Consequently, the following inferences hold

I1. $\vdash_{Catch22} \mathbb{P}\text{Obligated}[\text{Yossarian, Fly}] \Rrightarrow 1$ ⓘ **P1** *and* **S4**

I2. $\vdash_{Catch22} \mathbb{P}\text{Fly}[\text{Yossarian}] \Rrightarrow 1$ ⓘ *using* **P2** and **I1**

I3. $\vdash_{Catch22} \mathbb{P}\text{Crazy}[\text{Yossarian}] \Rrightarrow 1$ ⓘ *using* **S2** *and* **I2**

I4. $\vdash_{Catch22} \mathbb{P}\neg\text{Obligated}[\text{Yossarian, Fly}] \Rrightarrow 1$ ⓘ **P3** *and* **I3**

I5. $\vdash_{Catch22} \mathbb{P}\neg\text{Fly}[\text{Yossarian}] \Rrightarrow 0$ ⓘ **I4** *and* **S3**

I6. $\vdash_{Catch22} \mathbb{P}\text{Fly}[\text{Yossarian}] \Rrightarrow 1$ ⓘ *reformulation of* **I5**

Thus there is a contradiction in *Catch22* in that both of the following hold in the above:

I2. $\vdash_{Catch22} \mathbb{P}\text{Fly}[\text{Yossarian}] \Rrightarrow 1$

I6. $\vdash_{Catch22} \mathbb{P}\text{Fly}[\text{Yossarian}] \Rrightarrow 0$

However, it is not possible to immediately conclude that **1≈0** because of the directionality.

[16] In [Law 2006]. Emphases added.

[17] In Latin, the principle is called *ex falso quodlibet* which means that from falsity anything follows.

[18] [Nekham 1200, pp. 288-289]; later rediscovered and published in [Lewis and Langford 1932]

[19] [Pospesel 2000] has discussed extraneous ∨ introduction on in terms of the following principle: $\Psi, (\Psi \vee \Phi \vdash \Theta) \vdash \Theta$

However, the above principle immediately derives extraneous ∨ introduction when Θ is Ψ∨Φ. In Direct Logic, argumentation of the above form would often be reformulated as follows to eliminate the spurious Φ middle proposition: $\Psi, (\Psi \vdash \Theta) \vdash \Theta$

[20] Direct Logic is distinct from the Direct Predicate Calculus [Ketonen and Weyhrauch 1984].

[21] The importance of (counter) examples in reasoning was emphasized in [Rissland 1984] citing mathematics, law, linguistics and computer science. According to [Gordon 2009]:

> *[Toulmin 1958] was one of the first to reflect on the limitations of mathematical logic as a model of rationality in the context of everyday discourse and practical problems. By the 1950s, logic had become more or less synonymous with mathematical logic, as invented by Boole, De Morgan, Pierce, Frege, Hilbert and others, starting in the middle of the nineteenth century. Interestingly, Toulmin proposed legal argumentation as a model for practical reasoning, claiming that normative models of practical reasoning should be measured by the ideals of jurisprudence. [Walton 2006] is a good starting point for getting an overview of the modern philosophy of argumentation.*

[22] in Rebecca Herold *Managing an Information Security and Privacy Awareness and Training Program* 2005. p. 101.

[23] although there is no claim concerning Euclid's own orientation

[24] *Cf.* "*on the ordinary notion of proof, it is compelling just because, presented with it, we cannot resist the passage from premises to conclusion without being unfaithful to the meanings we have already given to the expressions employed in it.*" [Dummett 1973]

[25] Rosemary Redfield. *Arsenic associated bacteria (NASA's claims)* RR Research blog. Dec. 6, 2010.

[26] Felisa Wolfe-Simon, et. al. *A bacterium that can grow by using arsenic instead of phosphorus* Science. Dec. 2, 2010.

[27] Consequence$_1$ ≡ NaturalDeduction(Axiom$_2$)

$\quad\quad$ = $\vdash_{Achilles}$(A, B $\vdash_{Achilles}$Z)

Consequence$_2$ ≡ Combination(Axiom$_1$, Consequence$_1$)

$\quad\quad$ = $\vdash_{Achilles}$A, B, (A, B $\vdash_{Achilles}$Z)

Consequence$_3$ ≡ ForwardChaining(Consequence$_2$)

$\quad\quad$ = $\vdash_{Achilles}$ Z

ProofOfZ[a$_1$, a$_2$] ≡

$\quad\quad$ ForwardChaining[Combination[a$_1$, NaturalDeduction[a$_2$]]]

[28] McGee [1985] has challenged modus ponens using an example that can be most simply formalized in Direct Logic as follows:

RepublicanWillWin $\vdash_{McGee}$(¬ReaganWillWin $\vdash_{McGee}$AndersonWillWin)

and $\vdash_{McGee}$RepublicanWillWin

From the above, in Direct Logic it follows that:

$\quad\quad$ ¬ReaganWillWin $\vdash_{McGee}$AndersonWillWin

McGee challenged the reasonableness of the above conclusion on the grounds that. intuitively, the proper inference is that if Reagan will not win, then ¬AndersonWillWin because Carter (the Democratic candidate) will win. However, in theory *McGee*, it is reasonable to infer AndersonWillWin from ¬ReaganWillWin because RepublicanWillWin holds in *McGee*.

McGee phrased his argument in terms of implication which in Direct Logic (see following discussion in this paper) would be as follows:

$\vdash_{McGee}$RepublicanWillWin⇒ (¬ReaganWillWin⇒AndersonWillWin)

However, this makes no essential difference because, in Direct Logic, it still follows that $\vdash_{McGee}$(¬ReaganWillWin ⇒ AndersonWillWin)

[29] [*cf.* Church 1934, Kleene 1936]

[30] Direct inference is defined differently in this paper from probability theory [Levy 1977, Kyburg and Teng 2001], which refers to "*direct inference*" of

frequency in a reference class (the most specific class with suitable frequency knowledge) from which other probabilities are derived.

[31] [Jaśkowski 1934][31] that doesn't require artifices such as indices (labels) on propositions or restrictions on reiteration

[32] This section of the paper shares some history with [Hewitt 2010b].

[33] Turing [1936] stated:
- *the behavior of the computer at any moment is determined by the symbols which he* [the computer] *is observing, and his 'state of mind' at that moment*
- *there is a bound B to the number of symbols or squares which the computer can observe at one moment. If he wishes to observe more, he must use successive observations.*

Gödel's conception of computation was formally the same as Turing but more reductionist in motivation:

There is a major difference between the historical contexts in which Turing and Gödel worked. Turing tackled the Entscheidungsproblem [computational decidability of provability] *as an interesting mathematical problem worth solving; he was hardly aware of the fierce foundational debates. Gödel on the other hand, was passionately interested in the foundations of mathematics. Though not a student of Hilbert, his work was nonetheless deeply entrenched in the framework of Hilbert's finitistic program, whose main goal was to provide a meta-theoretic finitary proof of the consistency of a formal system "containing a certain amount of finitary number theory."* Shagrir [2006]

[34] According to [Turing 1948]:

LCMs [Logical Computing Machines: Turing's expression for Turing machines] *can do anything that could be described as ... "purely mechanical"...This is sufficiently well established that it is now agreed amongst logicians that "calculable by means of an LCM" is the correct accurate rendering* [of phrases like *"purely mechanical"*]

[35] [Wang 1974, p. 84]

[36] An example of the global state space model is the Abstract State Machine (ASM) model [Blass, Gurevich, Rosenzweig, and Rossman 2007a, 2007b; Glausch and Reisig 2006].

[37] This result is very old. It was known by Dijkstra motivating his belief that it is impossible to implement unbounded nondeterminism. Also the result played a crucial role in the invention of the Actor Model in 1972.
   Consider the following Nondeterministic Turing Machine:
   Step 1: Next do either *Step 2* or *Step 3*.
   Step 2: Next do *Step 1*.
   Step 3: Halt.
   It is possible that the above program does not halt. It is also possible that the above program halts.

   Note that above program is not equivalent to the one below in which it is not possible to halt:
   Step 1: Next do *Step 1*.

[38] The below proof is quite general and applies to the Abstract State Machine (ASM) model [Blass, Gurevich, Rosenzweig, and Rossman 2007a, 2007b; Glausch and Reisig 2006], which consequently are not really models of concurrency. It also applies to the parallel lambda calculus, which includes all the capabilities of the nondeterministic lambda calculus. Researchers (before the Actor Model was invented) hypothesized that the parallel lambda calculus naturally modeled all of computation and their research programme was to reduce all computation to the parallel lambda calculus [Scott and Strachey 1971, Milne and Strachey 1976].

[39] This proof does not apply to extensions of Nondeterministic Turing Machines that are provided with a new primitive instruction NoLargest which is defined to write an unbounded large number on the tape. Since executing NoLargest can write an unbounded amount of tape in a single instruction, executing it can take an unbounded time during which the machine cannot read input.

   Also, the NoLargest primitive is of limited practical use. Consider a Nondeterministic Turing Machine with two input-only tapes that can be read nondeterministically and one standard working tape.

   It is possible for the following program to copy both of its input tapes onto its working tape:
   Step 1: Either
     1. copy the current input from the 1st input tape onto the working tape and next do *Step 2*,
     or
     2. copy the current input from the 2nd input tape onto the working tape and next do *Step 3*.
   Step 2: Next do Step 1.
   Step 3: Next do Step 1.
   It is also possible that the above program does not read any input from the 1st input tape (*cf.* [Knabe 1993]) and the use of NoLargest is of no use in alleviating this problem. Bounded nondeterminism is a symptom of deeper underlying issues with Nondeterministic Turing Machines.

[40] Consequently,
- The tree has an infinite path. ⇔ The tree is infinite. ⇔ It is possible that P does not halt. If it is possible that P does not halt, then it is possible that that the set of outputs with which P halts is infinite.
- The tree does not have an infinite path. ⇔ The tree is finite. ⇔ P always halts. If P always halts, then the tree is finite and the set of outputs with which P halts is finite.

[41] Arbiters render meaningless the states in the Abstract State Machine (ASM) model [Blass, Gurevich, Rosenzweig, and Rossman 2007a, 2007b; Glausch and Reisig 2006].

[42] The logic gates require suitable thresholds and other characteristics.

[43] *cf.* denotational semantics of the lambda calculus [Scott 1976]

[44] Proof: Suppose to obtain a contraction that ComputationallyDecidable[HaltingProblem].

Define the program Diagonal as follows:
Diagonal ≡ [x]→ Halt.[x, x] ◆ True⦂ InfiniteLoop.[ ]▢ False⦂ True
    where InfiniteLoop ≡ [ ]→ InfiniteLoop.[ ]

Poof of inconsistency: By the definition of Diagonal:
⌊Diagonal⌋.[Diagonal] →₁ Halt.[Diagonal, Diagonal] ◆
    True⦂ InfiniteLoop.[ ]▢
    False⦂ True

Consider the following 2 cases:
1. Halt.[Diagonal, Diagonal] →₁ *True*
   Converges[⌊Diagonal⌋.[Diagonal]] by the axioms for Halt
   ¬Converges[⌊Diagonal⌋.[Diagonal]] by the definition of Diagonal
2. Halt.[Diagonal, Diagonal] →₁ *False*
   ¬Converges[⌊Diagonal⌋.[Diagonal]] by the axioms for Halt
   Converges[⌊Diagonal⌋.[Diagonal]] by the definition of Diagonal

Consequently, ¬ComputationallyDecidable[HaltingProblem]

[45] Note that this theorem is very different from the result [Kleene 1938], that mathematics can be extended with a proposition asserting its own consistency.

[46] A prominent logician referee of this article suggested that if the proof is accepted then consistency should be made an explicit premise of every theorem of classical mathematics!

[47] As shown above, there is a simple proof in Classical Direct Logic that Mathematics (⊢) is consistent. If Classical Direct Logic has a bug, then there might also be a proof that Mathematics is inconsistent. Of course, if a such a bug is found, then it must be repaired.

Fortunately, Classical Direct Logic is simple in the sense that it has just *one* fundamental axiom:

∀[P:Boolean$^\mathbb{N}$]→ Inductive[P]⇨ ∀[i:ℕ]→ P[i]
  where ∀[P:Boolean$^\mathbb{N}$]→
    Inductive[P] ⇔ (P[0] ∧ ∀[i:ℕ]→ P[i] ⇨P[i+1])

Of course, Classical Direct Logic has machinery in addition the above axiom that could also have bugs.

The Classical Direct Logic proof that Mathematics (⊢) is consistent is very robust. One explanation is that consistency is built in to the very architecture of classical mathematics because it was designed to be consistent. Consequently, it is not absurd that there is a simple proof of the consistency of Mathematics (⊢) that does not use all of the machinery of Classical Direct Logic.

In reaction to paradoxes, philosophers developed the dogma of the necessity of strict separation of "object theories" (theories about basic mathematical entities such as numbers) and "meta theories" (theories about theories). This linguistic separation can be very awkward in Computer Science. Consequently, Direct Logic does not have the separation in order that some propositions can be more "directly" expressed. For example, Direct Logic can use ⊢ ⊢Ψ to express that it is provable that P is provable in Mathematics. It turns out in Classical Direct Logic that ⊢ ⊢Ψ holds if and only if ⊢Ψ holds. By using such expressions, Direct Logic contravenes the philosophical dogma that the proposition ⊢ ⊢Ψ must be expressed using Gödel numbers.

[48] As shown above, there is a simple proof in Classical Direct Logic that Mathematics (⊢) is consistent. If Classical Direct Logic has a bug, then there might also be a proof that Mathematics is inconsistent. Of course, if a such a bug is found, then it must be repaired.

Fortunately, Classical Direct Logic is simple in the sense that it has one fundamental axiom:

∀[P:Boolean$^\mathbb{N}$]→ Inductive[P]⇨ ∀[i:ℕ]→ P[i]
  where ∀[P:Boolean$^\mathbb{N}$]→
    Inductive[P] ⇔ P[0] ∧ ∀[i:ℕ]→ P[i] ⇨P[i+1]

Of course, Classical Direct Logic has machinery in addition the above axiom that could also have bugs.

The Classical Direct Logic proof that Mathematics (⊢) is consistent is very robust. One explanation is that consistency is built in to the very architecture of classical mathematics because it was designed to be consistent. Consequently, it is not absurd that there is a simple proof of the consistency of Mathematics ($\vdash$) that does not use all of the machinery of Classical Direct Logic.

In reaction to paradoxes, philosophers developed the dogma of the necessity of strict separation of "object theories" (theories about basic mathematical entities such as numbers) and "meta theories" (theories about theories). This linguistic separation can be very awkward in Computer Science. Consequently, Direct Logic does not have the separation in order that some propositions can be more "directly" expressed. For example, Direct Logic can use $\vdash \vdash \Psi$ to express that it is provable that P is provable in Mathematics. It turns out in Classical Direct Logic that $\vdash \vdash \Psi$ holds if and only if $\vdash \Psi$ holds. By using such expressions, Direct Logic contravenes the philosophical dogma that the proposition $\vdash \vdash \Psi$ must be expressed using Gödel numbers.

[49] This coordination can include calendars and to-do lists, communications (including email, SMS, Twitter, Facebook), presence information (including who else is in the neighborhood), physical (including GPS recordings), psychological (including facial expression, heart rate, voice stress) and social (including family, friends, team mates, and colleagues), maps (including firms, points of interest, traffic, parking, and weather), events (including alerts and status), documents (including presentations, spreadsheets, proposals, job applications, health records, photons, videos, gift lists, memos, purchasing, contracts, articles), contacts (including social graphs and reputation), purchasing information (including store purchases, web purchases, GPS and phone records, and buying and travel habits), government information (including licenses, taxes, and rulings), and search results (including rankings and rating).

[50] In 1994, Alan Robinson noted that he has *"always been a little quick to make adverse judgments about what I like to call 'wacko logics' especially in Australia...I conduct my affairs as though I believe ... that there is only one logic. All the rest is variation in what you're reasoning about, not in how you're reasoning ... [Logic] is immutable."* (quoted in Mackenzie [2001] page 286)

On the other hand Richard Routley noted:

... classical logic bears a large measure of responsibility for the growing separation between philosophy and logic which there is today... If classical logic is a modern tool inadequate for its job, modern philosophers have shown a classically stoic resignation in the face of this inadequacy. They have behaved like people who, faced with a device, designed to lift stream water, but which is so badly designed that it spills most of its freight, do not set themselves to the design of a better *model, but rather devote much of their energy to constructing ingenious arguments to convince themselves*

that the device is admirable, that they do not need or want the device to deliver more water; that there is nothing wrong with wasting water and that it may even be desirable; and that in order to "improve" the device they would have to change some features of the design, a thing which goes totally against their engineering intuitions and which they could not possibly consider doing. [Routley 2003]

[51] According to [Kuhn 1962 page 151]
And Max Planck, surveying his own career in his Scientific Autobiography [Planck 1949], *sadly remarked that "a new scientific truth does not triumph by convincing its opponents and making them see the light, but rather because its opponents eventually die, and a new generation grows up that is familiar with it."*

[52] It is not possible to guarantee the consistency of information because consistency testing is computationally undecidable even in logics much weaker than first order logic. Because of this difficulty, it is impractical to test whether information is consistent.

[53] Consequently iDescriber makes use of direct inference in Direct Logic to reason more safely about inconsistent information because it omits the rules of classical logic that enable every proposition to be inferred from a single inconsistency.

[54] By the *Computational Representation Theorem* [Clinger 1981; Hewitt 2006], which can define all the possible executions of a procedure.

[55] e.g. [Shulman 2012, nLab 2014]

[56] $\mathbb{N}$ is the type of Natural Number axiomatized in this article.

[57] type of 2-element list with first element of type σ_1 and with second element of type σ_2

[58] type of term of type σ

[59] *if* t *then* Φ_1 *else* Φ_2

[60] $\Phi_1, \ldots$ and Φ_k infer $\Psi_1, \ldots,$ and Ψ_n

[61] parameterized mutually recursive definitions of $v_{1\ to\ n} \triangleleft \tau_{1\ to\ n} \triangleright$

[62] *if* t_1 *then* t_2 *else* t_3

[63] Because there is no type restriction, fixed points may be freely used to define recursive procedures on expressions.

[64] *if* t *then* s_1 *else* s_1

[65] Proof: $(\Psi \vee (\Phi \wedge \Psi)) \Leftrightarrow (\Psi \vee \Phi) \wedge (\Psi \vee \Psi) \Leftrightarrow (\Psi \vee \Phi) \wedge \Psi$

[66] Direct Logic uses the full meaning of quantification as opposed to a cut down syntactic variant, e.g., [Henken 1950]. Disadvantages of the Henkin approach are explained in [Restall 2007].

[67] [Church 1956; Concoran 1973, 1980; Boulos 1975; Shapiro 2002]

[68] *"The world that appears to our senses is in some way defective and filled with error, but there is a more real and perfect realm, populated by entities [called "ideals" or "forms"] that are eternal, changeless, and in some sense*

paradigmatic for the structure and character of our world. Among the most important of these [ideals] *(as they are now called, because they are not located in space or time) are Goodness, Beauty, Equality, Bigness, Likeness, Unity, Being, Sameness, Difference, Change, and Changelessness. (These terms — "Goodness", "Beauty", and so on — are often capitalized by those who write about Plato, in order to call attention to their exalted status;...) The most fundamental distinction in Plato's philosophy is between the many observable objects that appear beautiful (good, just, unified, equal, big) and the one object that is what Beauty (Goodness, Justice, Unity) really is, from which those many beautiful (good, just, unified, equal, big) things receive their names and their corresponding characteristics. Nearly every major work of Plato is, in some way, devoted to or dependent on this distinction.*

Many of them explore the ethical and practical consequences of conceiving of reality in this bifurcated way. We are urged to transform our values by taking to heart the greater reality of the [ideals] *and the defectiveness of the corporeal world."* [Kraut 2004]

[69] Structuralism takes a different view of mathematics:

The structuralist vigorously rejects any sort of ontological independence among the natural numbers. The essence of a natural number is its relations to other natural numbers. The subject matter of arithmetic is a single abstract structure, the pattern common to any infinite collection of objects that has a successor relation, a unique initial object, and satisfies the induction principle. The number 2 is no more and no less than the second position in the natural number structure; and 6 is the sixth position. Neither of them has any independence from the structure in which they are positions, and as positions in this structure, neither number is independent of the other. [Shapiro 2000]

[70] Basic axioms are as follows:

$\quad$ **True ◆ True**: $E_1 \boxdot$ **False**: $E_2 \twoheadrightarrow E_1$

$\quad$ **False ◆ False**: $E_1 \boxdot$ **True**: $E_2 \twoheadrightarrow E_1$

$\quad$ **False ◆ True**: $E_1 \boxdot$ **False**: $E_2 \twoheadrightarrow E_2$

$\quad$ **True ◆ False**: $E_1 \boxdot$ **True**: $E_2 \twoheadrightarrow E_2$

$\quad (E_1 \twoheadrightarrow E_2) \wedge (E_2 \twoheadrightarrow E_3)) \Rightarrow (E_1 \twoheadrightarrow E_3)$

$\quad ([x] \twoheadrightarrow F[x])[E] \twoheadrightarrow F[E]$

$\quad (E_1 \text{ either } E_2) \twoheadrightarrow E_1$ [70]

$\quad (E_1 \text{ either } E_2) \twoheadrightarrow E_2$ [70]

$\quad F_1 \twoheadrightarrow F_2 \Rightarrow F_1(E) \twoheadrightarrow F_2(E)$

$\qquad\quad$ ⓘ *an application evolves if its operator evolves*

$\quad E_1 \twoheadrightarrow E_2 \Rightarrow F(E_1) \twoheadrightarrow F(E_2)$

$\qquad\quad$ ⓘ *an application evolves if its operand evolves*

$E_1 \rightarrow E_2 \Rightarrow (\downarrow E_2 \Rightarrow \downarrow E_1)$

$E_1 \downarrow E_2 \Leftrightarrow ((E_1 \rightarrow E_2 \wedge \downarrow E_2) \vee (\downarrow E_1 \wedge E_1 = E_2))$

$E \downarrow_1 \Leftrightarrow (E \downarrow \wedge (E \downarrow E_1 \wedge E \downarrow E_2) \Rightarrow E_1 = E_1)$

$\downarrow E_1 \Rightarrow \neg (E_1 \rightarrow E_2)$

[71] [Church 1956; Boolos 1975; Corcoran 1973, 1980]

[72] along with lists

[73] Set◁σ▷ is the type of a set of type σ, Sets◁σ▷ is the type all sets of sets over type σ, and Domain◁σ▷=σ⊕Sets◁σ▷ with the following axioms:

{ }:Set◁σ▷   ⓘ the empty set { } is a set

$\forall[x:\sigma] \rightarrow \{x\}$:Set◁σ▷   ⓘ a singleton set is a set

$\forall[s$:Sets◁σ▷$] \rightarrow$ Us:Sets◁σ▷   ⓘ all elements of the subsets of a set is a set

$\forall[x:\sigma] \rightarrow x \notin \{\}$ ⓘ the empty set { } has no elements

$\forall[s$:Set◁σ▷, $f:\sigma^\sigma] \rightarrow$ (Elementwise[f])[s]:Set◁σ▷
     ⓘ the function image of a set is a set

$\forall[s$:Set◁σ▷, p:Boolean$^\sigma] \rightarrow s\restriction p$:Set◁σ▷
     ⓘ a predicate restriction of a set is a set

$\forall[s$:Set◁σ▷$] \rightarrow \{\} \subseteq s$ ⓘ { } is a subset of every set

$\forall[s_1,s_2$:Set◁σ▷$] \rightarrow s_1 = s_2 \Leftrightarrow (\forall[x:\sigma] \rightarrow x \in s_1 \Leftrightarrow x \in s_2)$

$\forall[x,y:\sigma] \rightarrow x \in \{y\} \Leftrightarrow x=y$

$\forall[s_1,s_2$:Set◁σ▷$] \rightarrow s_1 \subseteq s_2 \Leftrightarrow \forall[x:\sigma] \rightarrow x \in s_1 \Rightarrow x \in s_2$

$\forall[x:\sigma; s_1,s_2$:Set◁σ▷$] \rightarrow x \in s_1 \cup s_2 \Leftrightarrow (x \in s_1 \vee x \in s_2)$

$\forall[x:\sigma; s1,s2$:Set◁σ▷$] \rightarrow x \in s1 \cap s2 \Leftrightarrow (x \in s1 \wedge x \in s2)$

$\forall[x$:Domain◁σ▷; s:Sets◁σ▷$] \rightarrow x \in$ Us $\Leftrightarrow \exists[s1$:Sets◁σ▷$] \rightarrow x \in s1 \wedge s1 \in s$

$\forall[y:\sigma; s$:Set◁σ▷, $f:\sigma^\sigma] \rightarrow$
        $y \in$ (Elementwise[f])[s] $\Leftrightarrow \exists[x \in s] \rightarrow f[x]=y$

$\forall[y:\sigma; s$:Set◁σ▷, p:Boolean$^\sigma] \rightarrow y \in s\restriction p \Leftrightarrow y \in s \wedge p[y]$

The natural numbers are axiomatised as follows where Successor is the successor function:

- $0:\mathbb{N}$
- Successor:$\mathbb{N}^\mathbb{N}$
- $\forall[i:\mathbb{N}] \rightarrow$ Successor[i]$\neq 0$
- $\forall[i, j:\mathbb{N}] \rightarrow$ Successor[i]= Successor[j] $\Rightarrow i=j$
- $\forall[P$:Boolean$^\mathbb{N}] \rightarrow$ Inductive[P]$\Rightarrow \forall[i:\mathbb{N}] \rightarrow P[i]$
  where
       $\forall[P$:Boolean$^\mathbb{N}] \rightarrow$ Inductive[P]
                  $\Leftrightarrow P[0] \wedge \forall[i:\mathbb{N}] \rightarrow P[i] \Rightarrow P[$Successor[i]$]$

[74] *I.e.*, $\nexists[s$:Sets◁$\mathbb{N}$▷, σ:Type$] \rightarrow \forall[x:\sigma] \rightarrow x \in s \Leftrightarrow x$:Sets◁$\mathbb{N}$▷

[75] Quoted by Bob Boyer [personal communication 12 Jan. 2006].
[76] Atomics *and* Elements *are disjoint*
[77] For example, there is no restriction that an inductive predicate must be defined by a first order proposition.
[78] [Dedekind 1888], [Peano 1889], and [Zermelo 1930].
[79] [Dedekind 1888, Peano 1889]
[80] ℕ is identified with the type of natural numbers
[81] [Dedekind 1888], [Peano 1889], and [Zermelo 1930].
[82] ℝ is identified with the type of real numbers
[83] *cf.* [Zermelo 1930].
[84] The Continuum Hypothesis remains an open problem for Direct Logic because its set theory is very powerful. The forcing technique used to prove the independence of the Continuum Hypothesis for first-order set theory [Cohen 1963] does not apply to Direct Logic because of the categorical induction axiom [Dedekind 1888, Peano 1889] used in formalizing the natural numbers ℕ, which is the foundation of set theory. Of course, trivially,
$(\vDash_{Domain \triangleleft \mathbb{N} \triangleright} ContinuumHypothesis) \vee (\vDash_{Domain \triangleleft \mathbb{N} \triangleright} \neg ContinuumHypothesis)$
where $Domain \triangleleft \sigma \triangleright = \sigma \oplus Sets \triangleleft \sigma \triangleright$.
[85] Peano[X], means that X satisfies the full Peano axioms for the non-negative integers, ℕ is the type of non-negative integers, s is the successor function, and ≈ means isomorphism.

The isomorphism is proved by defining a function f from ℕ to X by:
1. $f[0]=0_X$
2. $f[S[n]]=S_X[f[n]]$

Using proof by induction, the following follow:
1. f is defined for every element of $\mathbb{N}$
2. f is one-to-one
   Proof:
      First prove $\forall [n \in X] \to f[n]=0_X \Rightarrow n=0$
         Base: Trivial.
         Induction: Suppose $f[n]=0_X \Rightarrow n=0$
            $f[S[n]]=S_X[f[n]]$ Therefore if $f[S[n]]=0_X$ then $0_X=S_X[f[n]]$
            which is an inconsistency
      Suppose $f[n]=f[m]$. To prove: $n=m$
         Proof: By induction on n:
         Base: Suppose $f[0]=f[m]$. Then $f[m]= 0_X$ and $m=0$ by above
         Induction: Suppose $\forall [m \in \mathbb{N}] \to f[n]=f[m] \Rightarrow n=m$
            Proof: By induction on m:
            Base: Suppose $f[n]=f[0]$. Then $n=m=0$
            Induction: Suppose $f[n]=f[m] \Rightarrow n=m$
               $f[S[n]]=S_X[f[n]]$ and $f[S[m]]=S_X[f[m]]$
               Therefore $f[S[n]]=f[S[m]] \Rightarrow S[n]=S[m]$
3. the range of f is all of X.
   Proof: To show: Inductive[Range[f]]
   Base: To show $0_X \in \text{Range}[f]$. Clearly $f[0]=0_X$
   Induction: To show $\forall [n \in \text{Range}[f]] \to S_X[n] \in \text{Range}[f]$.
   Suppose that $n \in \text{Range}[f]$. Then there is some m such that $f[m]=n$.
      To prove: $\forall [k \in \mathbb{N}] \to f[k]=n \Rightarrow S_X[n] \in \text{Range}[f]$
      Proof: By induction on k:
   Base: Suppose $f[0]=n$. Then $n= 0_X =f[0]$ and
   $S_X[n]=f[S[0]] \in \text{Range}[f]$
   Induction: Suppose $f[k]=n \Rightarrow S_X[n] \in \text{Range}[f]$
      Suppose $f[S[k]]=n$. Then $n=S_X[f[k]]$ and
      $S_X[n]=S_X[S_X[f[k]]]=S_X[f[S[k]]]= f[S[S[k]]] \in \text{Range}[f]$

[86] Dedekind[X], means that **X** satisfies the Dedekind axioms for the real numbers
[87] Robinson [1961]

[88] The inferability problem is to computationally decide whether a proposition defined by sentence is inferable.

Theorem [Church 1935 followed by Turing 1936]:

Consistent$_T$ ⇒ ¬ComputationallyDecidable[InferenceProblem$_T$]

Proof. Suppose to obtain a contradiction that ComputationallyDecidable[InferenceProblem$_T$].

This means that there is a total computational deterministic predicate Inferable$_T$ such that the following 3 properties hold

1. Inferable$_{T■}$[Ψ] →$_1$ True ⇔ ⊢$_T$Ψ
2. Inferable$_{T■}$[Ψ] →$_1$ False ⇔ ⊬$_T$Ψ
3. Inferable$_{T■}$[Ψ] →$_1$ True ∨ Inferable$_{T■}$[Ψ]→$_1$ False

The proof proceeds by showing that if inference is computationally decidable, the halting problem is computationally decidable.

Consider proposition of the form Converges[⌊p⌋$_■$[x]], which is the proposition that the program p halts on input x.

Lemma: Consistent$_T$ ⇒ Inferable$_{T■}$[Converges[⌊p⌋$_■$[x]]]→$_1$True
if and only if Converges[⌊p⌋$_■$[x]]

Proof of lemma: Suppose Consistent$_T$

1. Suppose Inferable$_{T■}$[Converges[⌊p⌋$_■$[x]]→$_1$ True. Then ⊢$_T$ Converges[⌊p⌋$_■$[x]] by definition of Inferable$_T$. Suppose to obtain a contradiction that ¬Converges[⌊p⌋$_■$[x]]. The contradiction ⊬$_T$ Converges[⌊p⌋$_■$[x]] follows by consistency of T.
2. Suppose Converges[⌊p⌋$_■$[x]]. Then ⊢$_T$ Converges[⌊p⌋$_■$[x]] by Adequacy of T. It follows that Inferable$_{T■}$[Converges[⌊p⌋$_■$[x])] →$_1$ True.

But this contradicts ¬ComputationallyDecidable[HaltingProblem] because Halt[p, x] ⇔ Inferable$_{T■}$[Converges[⌊p⌋$_■$[x]]]

Consequently,

Consistent$_T$ ⇒ ¬ComputationallyDecidable[InferenceProblem$_T$]

Inconsistency Robustness in Foundations: Mathematics self proves its own Consistency and Other Matters

Carl Hewitt

This article is dedicated to Alonzo Church, Stanisław Jaśkowski, Ludwig Wittgenstein, and Ernst Zermelo.

Abstract

Inconsistency Robustness is performance of information systems with pervasively inconsistent information. Inconsistency Robustness of the community of professional mathematicians is their performance repeatedly repairing contradictions over the centuries. In the Inconsistency Robustness paradigm, deriving contradictions have been a progressive development and not "game stoppers." Contradictions can be helpful instead of being something to be "swept under the rug" by denying their existence, which has been repeatedly attempted by Establishment Philosophers (beginning with some Pythagoreans). Such denial has delayed mathematical development. This article reports how considerations of Inconsistency Robustness have recently influenced the foundations of mathematics for Computer Science continuing a tradition developing the sociological basis for foundations.[1]

Classical Direct Logic is a foundation of mathematics for Computer Science, which has a foundational theory (for convenience called "Mathematics") that can be used in any other theory. A bare turnstile is used for Mathematics so that $\vdash\Psi$ means that Ψ is a mathematical proposition that is a theorem of Mathematics and $\Phi \vdash \Psi$ means that Ψ can be inferred from Φ in Mathematics.

The current common understanding is that Gödel proved "Mathematics cannot prove its own consistency, if it is consistent." However, the consistency of mathematics can be proved by a simple argument using standard rules of Mathematics including the following:
- rule of Proof by Contradiction, *i.e.*, $(\neg\Phi \Rightarrow (\Theta \wedge \neg\Theta)) \vdash \Phi$
- and the rule of Soundness (a theorem can be used in a proof), *i.e.*, $(\vdash \Phi) \Rightarrow \Phi$

Formal Proof. By definition,
Consistent $\Leftrightarrow \neg \exists [\Psi{:}\text{Proposition}] \rightarrow \vdash (\Psi \wedge \neg\Psi)$. By Existential Elimination, there is some proposition Ψ_0 such that $\neg\text{Consistent} \Rightarrow \vdash (\Psi_0 \wedge \neg\Psi_0)$ which by Soundness and transitivity of implication means
$\neg\text{Consistent} \Rightarrow (\Psi_0 \wedge \neg\Psi_0)$. Substituting for Φ and Θ, in the rule for Proof by Contradiction, it follows that $(\neg\text{Consistent} \Rightarrow (\Psi_0 \wedge \neg\Psi_0)) \vdash \text{Consistent}$.
Thus, $\vdash \text{Consistent}$.

The above theorem means that consistency is deeply embedded in the architecture of classical mathematics. Please note the following points: **The above argument formally mathematically proves the theorem that mathematics is consistent** and that **it is *not* a premise of the theorem that mathematics is consistent.** Classical mathematics was designed for consistent axioms and consequently the rules of classical mathematics can be used to prove consistency regardless of the axioms, *e.g.*, Euclidean geometry.

The above proof means that "Mathematics is consistent" is a theorem in Classical Direct Logic. This means that the usefulness of Classical Direct Logic depends crucially on the consistency of Mathematics. Good evidence for the consistency of Mathematics comes from the way that Classical Direct Logic avoids the known paradoxes. Humans have spent millennia devising paradoxes.

Having a powerful system like Direct Logic is important in computer science because computers must be able to formalize all logical inferences (including inferences about their own inference processes) without requiring recourse to human intervention. Any inconsistency in Classical Direct Logic would be a potential security hole because it could be used to cause computer systems to adopt invalid conclusions.

The recently developed self-proof of consistency (above) shows that the current common understanding that Gödel proved "Mathematics cannot prove its own consistency, if it is consistent" is inaccurate.[i]

It is very important to distinguish between the following:
- "self-reference" using fixed points
- recursion using types

Gödel famously thought that mathematics necessarily has the "self-referential"[2] proposition **I am not provable** where the **I** comes from a fixed-point construction using an untyped notation for mathematics. **Using typed recursion, it is impossible to construct such a "self-referential" proposition.** In this way, consistency of mathematics is preserved without giving up power.[3]

---

[i] [Church 1935, Turing 1936] published the first valid proof that the mathematical theory $\mathbb{N}$ is inferentially undecidable (*i.e.* there is a proposition Ψ such that $\nvdash_{\mathbb{N}} \Psi$ and $\nvdash_{\mathbb{N}} \neg\Psi$) because provability in $\mathbb{N}$ is computationally undecidable (provided that the theory $\mathbb{N}$ is consistent).

Mathematical Foundation for Computer Science

Computer Science brought different concerns and a new perspective to mathematical foundations including the following requirements:[4] [Arabic numeral superscripts refer to endnotes at the end of this article]

- provide powerful inference machinery so that arguments (proofs) can be short and understandable and all logical inferences can be formalized
- establish standard foundations so people can join forces and develop common techniques and technology
- incorporate axioms thought to be consistent by the overwhelming consensus of working professional mathematicians, e.g., natural numbers [Dedekind 1888, Peano 1889], real numbers [Dedekind 1888], sets of sets of integers, real, strings, *etc.*
- facilitate inferences about the mathematical foundations used by computer systems.

Classical Direct Logic is a foundation of mathematics for Computer Science, which has a foundational theory (for convenience called "Mathematics") that can be used in any other theory. A bare turnstile is used for Mathematics so that $\vdash\Psi$ means that Ψ is a mathematical proposition that is a theorem of Mathematics and $\Phi\vdash\Psi$ means that Ψ can be inferred from Φ in Mathematics.

Mathematics self proves its own consistency
A mathematically significant idea involves:
> "...a very high degree of unexpectedness, combined with inevitability and economy." [Hardy 1940]

The following rules are fundamental to classical mathematics:
- Proof by Contradiction, *i.e.* $(\neg\Phi\Rightarrow(\Theta\wedge\neg\Theta))\vdash\Phi$, which says that a proposition can be proved by showing that it implies a contradiction.
- Soundness, *i.e.* $(\vdash\Phi)\Rightarrow\Phi$, which says that a theorem can be used in a proof.[5]

Theorem: Mathematics self proves its own consistency.[6]

Formal Proof[7] By definition,
¬Consistent⇔∃ [Ψ:Proposition]→ ⊢ (Ψ∧¬Ψ).[8] By the rule of Existential Elimination, there is some proposition Ψ_0 such that ¬Consistent ⇒ ⊢ ($\Psi_0 \land \neg\Psi_0$) which by the rule of Soundness and transitivity of implication means ¬Consistent⇒ ($\Psi_0 \land \neg\Psi_0$). Substituting for Φ and Θ, in the rule for Proof by Contradiction, we have (¬Consistent⇒($\Psi_0 \land \neg\Psi_0$)) ⊢ Consistent. Thus, ⊢ Consistent.

A Natural Deduction[i] proof is given below:

1) ¬Consistent	// hypothesis to derive a contradiction **just in this subargument**
2) ∃[Ψ:Proposition]→ ⊢(Ψ∧¬Ψ)	// definition of inconsistency using **1)**
3) ⊢($\Psi_0 \land \neg\Psi_0$)	// rule of Existential Elimination using **2)**
4) $\Psi_0 \land \neg\Psi_0$	// rule of Soundness using **3)**

⊢ Consistent   // rule of Proof by Contradiction using **1)** and **4)**

Natural Deduction Proof of Consistency of Mathematics

Please note the following points:
- The above argument formally mathematically proves that mathematics is consistent and that **it is not a premise of the theorem that mathematics is consistent.**[9]
- Classical mathematics was designed for consistent axioms and consequently the rules of classical mathematics can be used to prove consistency regardless of other axioms.[10]

The above proof means that "Mathematics is consistent" is a theorem in Classical Direct Logic. This means that the usefulness of Classical Direct Logic depends crucially on the consistency of Mathematics. Good evidence for the consistency of Mathematics comes from the way that Classical Direct Logic avoids the known paradoxes. Humans have spent millennia devising paradoxes.

Computer Science needs very strong foundations for mathematics so that computer systems are not handicapped. It is important not to have

---
[i] [Jaśkowski 1934] developed Natural Deduction *cf.* [Barker-Plummer, Barwise, and Etchemendy 2011]

inconsistencies in mathematical foundations of Computer Science because they represent security vulnerabilities.

The recently developed self-proof of consistency (above) shows that the current common understanding that Gödel proved "Mathematics cannot prove its own consistency, if it is consistent" is inaccurate. But the situation is even more interesting because Wittgenstein more than a half-century ago showed that contradiction in mathematics results from the kind of "self-referential" sentence that Gödel used in his proof. Fortunately, using a typed notation for mathematical sentences, it can be proved that the kind "self-referential" sentence that Gödel used in his proof cannot be constructed because required fixed points do not exist. Consequently, using a typed notation, consistency of mathematics can be preserved without giving up power.

Formal typed syntax had not yet been invented when Gödel and other philosophers developed the First-order Thesis that weakened the foundations of mathematics so that, as expressed, "self-referential" propositions do not infer contradiction.[11] The weakened foundations (based on first-order logic) enabled some limited meta-mathematical theorems to be proved. However, as explained in this article, the weakened foundations are cumbersome, unnatural, and unsuitable as the mathematical foundation for Computer Science.

Monster-Barring

> *"But why accept the counterexample? ... Why should the theorem give way...? It is the 'criticism' that should retreat.... It is a monster, a pathological case, not a counterexample."*
> Delta, student in [Lakatos, 1976, pg. 14].

The Euler formula for polyhedra is Vertices-Edges+Faces=2, which can be proved in a variety of different ways.

But the hollow cube below is a counterexample because Vertices-Edges+Faces=4.

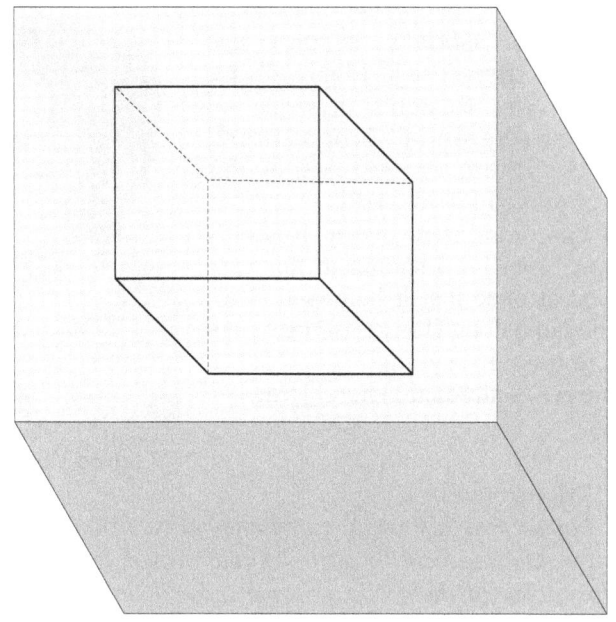

Counterexample to Euler's Formula

In the face of this counterexample, it becomes important to characterize polyhedra more rigorously. For example,
- A Regular solid
- A convex solid with polyhedral faces
- A surface consisting of a system of polygons
- *etc.*

Lakatos has called this strategy *"monster-barring."*

Wittgenstein: "self-referential" propositions lead to inconsistency in mathematics

All truth passes through three stages:
First, it is ridiculed.
Second, it is violently opposed.
Third, it is accepted as being self-evident.
Arthur Schopenhauer (1788-1860)

Early on, Wittgenstein correctly noted that Gödel's "self-referential" proposition infers inconsistency in mathematics:[i]

> Let us suppose [Gödel's results are correct and therefore] I prove[ii] the improvability (in Russell's system) of [Gödel's "self-referential" proposition[iii]] P; [i.e., ⊢⊬P where P⇔⊬P] then by this proof I have proved P [i.e., ⊢P].
>
> Now if this proof were one in Russell's system [i.e., ⊢⊢P] —I should in this case have proved at once that it belonged [i.e., ⊢P] and did not belong [i.e., ⊢¬P because ¬P⇔⊢P] to Russell's system.
>
> But there is a contradiction here! [i.e., ⊢P and ⊢¬P]

Ludwig Wittgenstein

According to [Monk 2007]:[12]
Wittgenstein hoped that his work on mathematics would have a cultural impact, that it would threaten the attitudes that prevail in logic, mathematics and the philosophies of them. On this measure it has been a spectacular failure.

Unfortunately, recognition of the worth of Wittgenstein's work on mathematics came long after his death. For decades, professional work logicians mistakenly believed that they had been completely victorious over Wittgenstein.

---

[i] Wittgenstein in 1937 published in Wittgenstein 1956, p. 50e and p. 51e]

[ii] Wittgenstein was granting the supposition that Gödel had proved inferential undecidability (sometimes called "incompleteness") of Russell's system, *e.g.,* ⊢⊬P. However, inferential undecidability is easy to prove using the "self-referential" proposition *P*:

Proof. Suppose to obtain a contradiction that ⊢ *P*. Both of the following can be inferred:

1) ⊢ ⊬ *P* from the hypothesis because *P*⇔⊬*P*

2) ⊢ ⊢ *P* from the hypothesis by Adequacy.

But 1) and 2) are a contradiction. Consequently, ⊢⊬ *P* follows from proof by contradiction.

[iii] constructed using a fixed point exploiting an untyped notation for mathematics

contra Gödel *et. al*

> *"Men... think in herds ...*
> *they only recover their senses slowly, and one by one."*
> Charles Mackay

That mathematics self proves its own consistency contradicts the result [Gödel 1931] using a "self-referential" proposition[i] that mathematics cannot prove its own consistency.

One resolution is not to have "self-referential" propositions.[ii] This can be achieved by carefully arranging the rules using a properly constructed notation so that "self-referential" propositions cannot be constructed as shown below.[iii] The basic idea is to use types [Russell 1908, Church 1940] to construct propositions from other propositions so that fixed points do not exist and consequently cannot be used to construct "self-referential" propositions.

However, there is a crucial difference between how Russell used types and the method used in Direct Logic. Russell attempted to use types as the fundamental mechanism for preventing inconsistencies by restricting the domain of mathematics to object that can be described by a strict hierarchical type system. However, he ran into trouble because his type mechanism was too strict and prevented ordinary mathematical reasoning.[iv]

Bertrand Russell

In this paper, types are used to prevent the construction of "self-referential" sentences and to provide the foundations for sets. The difficulties encountered by Russell are avoided as follows:
- having integers[13] as primitive
- constructing sets from the characteristic functions of typed functions

---

[i] constructed using a fixed point operator exploiting an untyped notation for sentences
[ii] There do not seem to be any practical uses of "self-referential" propositions in the mathematical foundations of Computer Science.
[iii] It is important to note that disallowing "self-referential" propositions does not place restrictions on recursion in computation, *e.g.*, the Actor Model, untyped lambda calculus, *etc.*
[iv] In order to be able to carry out ordinary mathematical reasoning, Russell introduced an (unmotivated) patch called "ramified types" that collapsed the type hierarchy.

- types are used to resolve the usual paradoxes with sets, *e.g.*, there is no set of all sets, *etc.*[14]

The above approach provides a very usable foundation for ordinary mathematical reasoning. Combining types and sets as the foundation has the advantage of using the strengths of each without the limitations of trying to use just one because each can be used to make up for the limitations of the other. The key idea is compositionality, *i.e.*, composing new entities from others. Types can be composed from other types and sets can be composed from other sets.[i]

Classical Direct Logic

> *I suspect there are few today who share ...* [the] *belief that there should be a single overarching theory embracing all of mathematics.* [Dowson 2006]

Classical Direct Logic must meet the following challenges:
- *Consistent* to avoid security holes
- *Powerful* so that computer systems can formalize all logical inferences
- *Principled* so that it can be easily learned by software engineers
- *Coherent* so that it hangs together without a lot of edge cases
- *Intuitive* so that humans can follow computer system reasoning
- *Comprehensive* to accommodate all forms of logical argumentation
- *Inconsistency Robust* to be applicable to pervasively inconsistent theories of practice with
    - Inconsistency Robust Direct Logic for logical inference about inconsistent information
    - Classical Direct Logic for Mathematics used in inconsistency-robust theories

In Direct Logic, unrestricted recursion is allowed in programs by using recursive definitions.

---

[i] Compositionality avoids standard foundational paradoxes. For example, Direct Logic composes sentences from others using types so there are no "self-referential" propositions.

There are uncountably many Actors.[15] For example, CreateReal.[ ] can output any real number[i] between 0 and 1 where[ii]
    CreateReal.[ ] ≡ [(0 **either** 1), **VPostpone** CreateReal.[ ]]
    where
- CreateReal.[ ] is the result of sending the Actor CreateReal the message [ ]
- (0 **either** 1) is the nondeterministic choice of 0 or 1,
- [*first, rest*] is the list that begins with *first* and whose remainder is *rest*, and
- **Postpone** *expression* delays execution of *expression* until the value is needed.

There are uncountably many propositions (because there is a different proposition for every real number). Consequently, there are propositions that are not the abstraction of any element of a denumerable set of sentences. For example, p ≡ [x:ℝ]→ ([y:ℝ]→ (y=x)) defines a different predicate p[x] for each real number x, which holds for only one real number, namely x.[iii]

It is important to distinguish between strings, sentences, and propositions. Some strings can be parsed into sentences[iv], which can be abstracted into propositions that can be asserted. Furthermore, terms[v] can be abstracted into Actors (*i.e.* objects in mathematics).

Abstraction and parsing are becoming increasingly important in software engineering. *e.g.,*
- The execution of code can be dynamically checked against its documentation. Also Web Services can be dynamically searched for and invoked on the basis of their documentation.
- Use cases can be inferred by specialization of documentation and from code by automatic test generators and by model checking.
- Code can be generated by inference from documentation and by generalization from use cases.

---

[i] using binary representation.
[ii] Typically, a result returned by the non-deterministic procedure **Real** is not computable in the sense there is no computable deterministic procedure that can compute its digits.
[iii] For example (p[3])[y] holds if and only if y=3.
[iv] which are grammar tree structures
[v] which are grammar tree structures

Abstraction and parsing are needed for large software systems so that that documentation, use cases, and code can mutually speak about what has been said and their relationships.

For example:

Proposition

e.g. $\forall[n:\mathbb{N}] \to \exists[m:\mathbb{N}] \to m>n$

i.e., for every $\mathbb{N}$ there is a larger $\mathbb{N}$

Sentence

e.g. $\lceil "\forall[n:\mathbb{N}] \to \exists[m:\mathbb{N}] \to m>n" \rceil$

i.e., the sentence that for every $\mathbb{N}$ there is a larger $\mathbb{N}$

String

e.g. $"\forall[n:\mathbb{N}] \to \exists[m:\mathbb{N}] \to m>n"$

which is a string that begins with the symbol $"\forall"$

In Direct Logic, a sentence is a grammar tree (analogous to the ones used by linguists). Such a grammar tree has terminals that can be constants. And there are uncountably many constants, *e.g.*, the real numbers:

> The sentence $\lceil 3.14159... < 3.14159... + 1 \rceil$ is impossible to obtain by parsing a string (where 3.14159... is an Actor[i] for the transcendental real number that is the ratio of a circle's circumference to its diameter). The issue is that there is no string which when parsed is $\lceil 3.14159... < 3.14159... + 1 \rceil$

---

[i] whose digits are incrementally computable

Of course, because the digits of 3.14159... are computable, there is a expression₁ such that ⌊expression₁⌋ = 3.14159... that can be used to create the sentence ⌈expression₁ < expression₁ + 1⌉.

However the sentence ⌈expression₁ < expression₁ + 1⌉ is not the same as ⌈3.14159... < 3.14159... + 1⌉ because it does not have the same vocabulary and it is a much larger sentence that has many terminals whereas ⌈3.14159... < 3.14159... + 1⌉ has just 3 terminals:

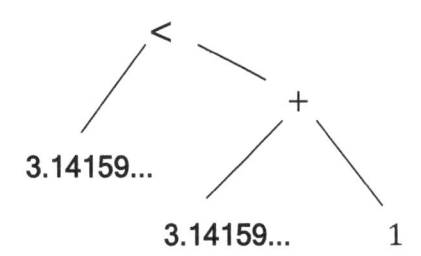

```
         <
        / \
  3.14159...  +
             / \
       3.14159... 1
```

Consequently, sentences *cannot* be enumerated and there are some sentences that *cannot* be obtained by parsing strings. These arrangements exclude known paradoxes from Classical Direct Logic.[i]

Note: Type theory of Classical Direct Logic is much stronger than constructive type theory with constructive logic[16] because Classical Direct Logic has all of the power of Classical Mathematics.

---

[i] Please see historical appendix of this article.

Mathematics self proves that it is open

Mathematics proves that it is open in the sense that it can prove that its theorems cannot be provably computationally enumerated:[17]

Theorem ⊢Mathematics is Open
Proof.[i] Suppose to obtain a contradiction that it is possible to prove closure, *i.e.,* there is a provably computable total procedure Theorem such that it is provable that

($\vdash \Psi$) ⇔ $\exists[i:\mathbb{N}] \rightarrow$ Theorem.[i]= Ψ

As a consequence of the above, there is a provably total procedure ProvableComputableTotal that enumerates the provably total computable procedures that can be used in the implementation of the following procedure:

Diagonal[i] ≡ 1+(ProvableComputableTotal.[i]).[i]

However,
* ProvableComputableTotal[Diagonal] because Diagonal is implemented using provably computable total procedures.
* ¬ProvableComputableTotal[Diagonal] because Diagonal is a provably computable total procedure that differs from every other provably computable total procedure.

The above contradiction completes the proof.

[Franzén 2004] argued that mathematics is inexhaustible because of inferential undecidability[ii] of mathematical theories. The above theorem that mathematics is open provides another independent argument for the inexhaustibility of mathematics.

Completeness of inference versus inferential undecidability of closed mathematical theories

A closed mathematical theory is an extension of mathematics whose proofs are computationally enumerable. For example, group theory is obtained by adding the axioms of groups to Classical Direct Logic along with the axiom that theorems of group theory are computationally enumerable.

By definition, if T is a closed theory, there is a total procedure Proof$_T$ such that ($\vdash_T \Psi$) ⇔ $\exists[i:\mathbb{N}] \rightarrow$ Theorem$_T$.[i]= Ψ

---

[i] This argument appeared in [Church 1934] expressing concern that the argument meant that there is *"no sound basis for supposing that there is such a thing as logic."*
[ii] See section immediately below.

Ernst Zermelo   Alonzo Church   Alan Turing

Theorem:[i] If T is a consistent, closed mathematical theory, there is a proposition ChurchTuring$_T$ such that both of the following hold:[ii]

- $\vdash\!\!\!\not\vdash_T$ ChurchTuring$_T$
- $\vdash\!\!\!\not\vdash_T \neg$ChurchTuring$_T$

Corollary: There is a proposition Φ of $\mathbb{N}$ such that the following hold:[18]

- $\vdash\vDash_\mathbb{N}\Phi$
- $\vdash\!\!\!\not\vdash_\mathbb{N}\Phi$

Proof.[iii] Since $\mathbb{N}$ is consistent, one of the following two cases hold:

1. $\vDash_\mathbb{N}\Psi_{\text{ChurchTuring}}$: choose Φ to be ChurchTuring$_\mathbb{N}$
2. $\vDash_\mathbb{N}\neg\Psi_{\text{ChurchTuring}}$: choose Φ to be $\neg$ChurchTuring$_\mathbb{N}$

---

[i] First stated in [Gödel 1931].

[ii] Proof [Church 1935, Turing 1936] (This proof is a replacement for the incorrect proof in [Gödel 1931]):

Otherwise, provability in classical logic would be computationally decidable because

$$\forall[p{:}\text{Program}, x{:}\mathbb{N}]\rightarrow \text{Halt}[p, x] \Leftrightarrow \vdash \text{Halt}[p, x]$$

where Halt[p, x] if and only if program p halts on input x. If such a $\psi_{\text{ChurchTuring}}$ did not exist, then provability could be decided by enumerating theorems until the proposition in question or its negation is encountered.

Note the following important ingredients for the proof of inferential undecidability of a consistent, closed mathematical theory:

- Closure (computational enumerability) of theorems of a mathematical theory to carry through the proof.
- Consistency (nontriviality) to prevent everything from being provable

[iii] This proof is a replacement for the invalid proof in [Gödel 1931].

⊢_ℕ Consistent[ℕ] is a fundamental open problem in (Meta-)Mathematics for the Peano/Dedekind axiomatically defined categorical closed theory ℕ where Consistent[ℕ] means that no contradiction can be derived using the axioms and rules of inference of ℕ.

Information Invariance[i] is a *fundamental* technical goal of logic consisting of the following:
1. *Soundness of inference:* information is not increased by inference[ii]
2. *Completeness of inference:* all information that necessarily holds can be inferred

Note that a closed mathematical theory T is inferentially undecidable[iii] with respect to ChurchTuring$_T$ does not mean *incompleteness* with respect to the information that can be inferred about theory T because ⊢($\nvdash_T$ChurchTuring$_T$), ($\nvdash_T$¬ChurchTuring$_T$).[19]

---

[i] Closely related to conservation laws in physics
[ii] *E.g.* inconsistent information does not infer nonsense.
[iii] sometimes called "incomplete"

Overview

Contradiction	Outcome
Church discovered to his dismay that if theorems of mathematics are postulated to be computationally enumerable, then mathematics is inconsistent.	Theorems of mathematics cannot be computationally enumerated and mathematics is open and inexhaustible. But theorems of a particular theory can be postulated to be computationally enumerable.
Using fixed points to construct a "self-referential" sentence for an untyped notation of mathematical sentences, [Gödel 1931] claimed that mathematics cannot prove its own consistency. However, it is pointed out in this paper that mathematics easily proves its own consistency.	The contradiction can be resolved by using a properly-typed notation for sentences of mathematics does not allow the use of fixed points to construct "self-referential" sentences.[i]
Using fixed points to construct a "self-referential" sentence using an untyped notation of mathematical sentences, [Gödel 1931] claimed to prove inferential undecidability (sometimes called "incompleteness") for mathematics. However, such "self-referential" sentences lead to inconsistency in mathematics.	[Church 1935, Turing 1936] proved inferential undecidabilty of closed mathematical theories without using fixed points for an untyped notation of mathematical sentences to construct "self-referential" sentences.
In Computer Science, it is important that the Natural Numbers ($\mathbb{N}$) be axiomatized in a way that does not allow integers (e.g. infinite ones) in models of the axioms. However, it is impossible to properly axiomatize $\mathbb{N}$ using first-order logic.	Using Classical Direct Logic, $\mathbb{N}$ can be axiomatized in such a way that all models are uniquely isomorphic to $\mathbb{N}$ [Dedekind 1888, Peano 1889]. Consequently, there are no infinite integers in models of the axioms.
In Computer Science, it is important that sets of the Natural Numbers (Sets◁$\mathbb{N}$▷) be axiomatized in a way that does not allow countable models. However, it is impossible to properly axiomatize Sets◁$\mathbb{N}$▷ using first-order logic.	Using Classical Direct Logic, Sets◁$\mathbb{N}$▷ are defined by characteristic functions of types and thus all models are uniquely isomorphic to Sets◁$\mathbb{N}$▷. Consequently, its models have no infinite integers or other nonstandard elements.

---

[i] Note this does not prevent using fixed points to define recursion in programs.

First-order logic is unsuitable as the foundation of mathematics for Computer Science:	Classical Direct Logic is suitable as the foundation of mathematics for Computer Science:
• Some theorems of ordinary classical mathematics cannot be proved. • Some ordinary theorems useful in Computer Science cannot be proved. • There are undesirable models of mathematical theories (see above).	• All ordinary theorems of classical mathematics can be proved. • All ordinary theorems useful in Computer Science can be proved • There are no undesirable models of mathematical theories.

Conclusion

The problem is that today some knowledge still feels too dangerous because our times are not so different to Cantor or Boltzmann or Gödel's time. We too feel things we thought were solid being challenged; feel our certainties slipping away. And so, as then, we still desperately want to cling go a belief in certainty. It makes us feel safe. ...

Are we grown up enough to live with uncertainties or will we repeat the mistakes of the twentieth century and pledge blind allegiance to another certainty. Malone [2007]The world always needs heretics to challenge the prevailing orthodoxies. We are lucky that we can be heretics today without any danger of being burned at the stake. But unfortunately I am an old heretic. Old heretics do not cut much ice. When you hear an old heretic talking, you always say, "Too bad he has lost his marbles."

What the world needs is young heretics. I am hoping that one or two of you people in the audience may fill that role.
Dyson [2005]

A closed mathematical theory is an extension of mathematics whose proofs are computationally enumerable. For example, group theory is obtained by adding the axioms of groups to Classical Direct Logic along with the axioms that the theorems of group theory are computationally enumerable. If a closed mathematical theory T is consistent, then it is inferentially undecidable[i] because provability in T is computationally undecidable [Church 1935 and later Turing 1936].

---

[i] *i.e.* there is a proposition Ψ such that $\nvdash_T \Psi$ and $\nvdash_T \neg\Psi$, which is sometimes called "incompleteness"

Information Invariance is a fundamental technical goal of logic consisting of the following:
1. *Soundness of inference*: information is not increased by inference
2. *Completeness of inference*: all information that necessarily holds can be inferred.

That a closed mathematical theory T is inferentially undecidable[i] with respect to Ψ (above) does not mean incompleteness with respect to the information that can be inferred because (by construction) $\vdash (\nvdash_T \Psi), (\nvdash_T \neg\Psi)$.

Computer Science needs a rigorous foundation for all of mathematics that enables computers to carry out all reasoning without human intervention.[20] [Frege 1879] was a good start, but it foundered on the issue of being well-founded. [Russell 1925] attempted basing foundations entirely on types, but foundered on the issue of being expressive enough to carry to some common mathematical reasoning. [Church 1932, 1933] attempted basing foundations entirely on untyped higher-order functions, but foundered because it allowed "self-referential" propositions leading to contradictions [Kleene and Rosser 1935]. Presently, Isabelle [Paulson 1989] and Coq [Coquand and Huet 1986] are founded on types and do not allow theories to reason about themselves. Classical Direct Logic is a foundation for all of mathematical reasoning based on both sets (for well-founded structures) and types (to provide grounding for concepts) that allows general inference about reasoning.

[Gödel 1931] claimed inferential undecidability[ii] results for mathematics using a *"self-referential"* proposition constructed using fixed points exploiting a untyped notation of mathematical sentences. In opposition to Wittgenstein's correct argument that "self-referential" propositions lead to contradictions in mathematics, Gödel later claimed that his results were for a cut-down first-order theory of Peano numbers. However, first-order logic is not a suitable foundation for Computer Science because of the requirement that computer systems be able to carry out all reasoning without requiring human intervention (including reasoning about their own inference systems). Following [Frege 1879, Russell 1925, and Church 1932-1933], Direct Logic was developed and then investigated "self-referential" propositions with the following results.
- Formalization of Wittgenstein's proof that Gödel's "self-referential" proposition leads to contradiction in mathematics. So the consistency of mathematics had to be rescued against Gödel's "self-referential" propositions. The "self-referential" proposition used in results of [Curry

---

[i] sometimes called "incomplete"
[ii] sometimes called "incompleteness"

1941] and [Löb 1955] also lead to inconsistency in mathematics. Consequently, mathematics had to be rescued against these "self-referential" propositions as well.
- Self-proof of the consistency of mathematics. Consequently, mathematics had to be rescued against the claim [Gödel 1931] that mathematics cannot prove its own consistency. Also, it became an open problem whether mathematics proves its own consistency, which was resolved by the author discovering an amazing simple proof. [21]

A solution is to bar "self-referential" propositions using a properly constructed notation for sentences of mathematics.[22] However, Establishment Philosophers have very reluctant to accept the solution. According to [Dawson 2006]:[23]

- *Gödel's results altered the mathematical landscape, but they did **not** "produce a debacle".*
- *There is **less** controversy today over mathematical foundations than there was **before** Gödel's work.*

However, Gödel's results have produced a controversy of a very different kind from the one discussed by Dawson:

- Gödel's result that mathematics cannot prove its own consistency[i] has been disproved.
- Consequently, Gödel's results have led to increased controversy over mathematical foundations.

The development of Direct Logic has strengthened the position of working mathematicians as follows:[ii]

- Allowing freedom from the philosophical dogma of the First-Order Thesis
- Providing a usable type theory for all of Mathematics
- Allowing theories to freely reason about theories
- Providing Inconsistency Robust Direct Logic for safely reasoning about theories of practice that are (of necessity) pervasively inconsistent.

Acknowledgments
Extensive discussions with Tom Costello, Eric Kao, Ron van der Meyden and other members of the Stanford CS Logic Group helped the development of this paper. Tom suggested that more conventional terminology be used in the formal proof of consistency of mathematics. Martin Davis kindly provide the reference for [Gödel 1933]. Comments by James Lottes, Pat Suppes, Daniel

---

[i] Gödel's result was accepted doctrine by Establishment Philosophers for over eight decades
[ii] Of course, Direct Logic must preserve as much previous learning as possible.

Raggi, Eric Winsberg, John Woods, and Ming Xiong helped improve the presentation. Dan Flickinger suggested including an overview table. Alan Bundy pointed out many crucial places where the presentation needed improvement. John Woods served ably as the senior referee by compiling an excellent synopsis of anonymized conference referee reports for this article. Discussions with Michael Beeson helped improve the section on how mathematics self-proves its own consistency. Correspondence with Monroe Eskew helped clarify the relationship of Classical Direct Logic with first-order logic. Also, Monroe suggested looking at Berry's Paradox.[i] Correspondence with Jack Copeland helped clarify the relationship of the work reported in this article with previous work by Gödel *et. al.* Also, Jack suggested inclusion of the closely related natural deduction proof that mathematics proves its own consistency in addition to the linear proof. Discussions on the FriAM electronic mailing list were very helpful in improving this article.

---

[i] Please see section on Berry's Paradox in the historical appendix.

Bibliography

Anthony Anderson and Michael Zelëny (editors). *Logic, Meaning and Computation: Essays in Memory of Alonzo Church* Springer. 2002.

Jeremy Avigad and John Harrison. *Formally Verified Mathematics.* CACM. April 2014.

Steve Awodey and Erich Reck. *Completeness and Categoricity. Parts I and II: Nineteenth-century Axiomatics to Twentieth-century Metalogic.* History and Philosophy of Logic. Vol. 23. 2002.

Steve Awodey, Álvaro Pelayo, and Michael A. Warren. *Voevodsky's Univalence Axiom in Homotopy Type Theory* Notices of AMS. October 2013.

Alan Anderson. *Mathematics and the "Language Game"* (1958) in Philosophy of Mathematics Selected Readings. Prentice Hall. 1964.

David Barker-Plummer, Jon Barwise and John Etchemendy. *Language, Proof, and Logic: Second Edition* Stanford Center for the Study of Language and Information. 2011.

Jon Barwise. *Model-Theoretic Logics: Background and Aims* in "Model Theoretic Logics" Springer-Verlag. 1985.

Hamid Berenji, et. al. *A reply to the paradoxical success of Fuzzy Logic* AI Magazine. Spring 1994.

Francesco Berto. *The Gödel Paradox and Wittgenstein's Reasons* Philosophia Mathematica. February, 2009.

Errett Bishop. *The Crisis in Contemporary Mathematics* Historia Mathematica. 2. 1975.

George Boolos. *On second-order logic* Journal of Philosophy. Vol. 72. 1975.

Bernd Buldt. *The Scope of Gödel's First Incompleteness Theorem.* Logica Universalis. Volume 8. December 2014.

Andrea Cantini, *Paradoxes and Contemporary Logic*, Stanford Encyclopedia of Philosophy. Winter 2012 Edition.

Rudolph Carnap. Logische Syntax der Sprache. (*The Logical Syntax* of Language Open Court Publishing 2003) 1934.

Walter Carnielli and João Marcos. *Ex Contradictione Non Sequitur Quodlibet* Bulletin of Advanced Reasoning and Knowledge. 2001.

Hasok Chang. *Inventing Temperature: Measurement and Scientific Progress* Oxford University Press. 2007.

Aziem Chawdhary, Byron Cook, Sumit Gulwani, Mooly Sagiv, and Hongseok Yang *Ranking Abstractions* ESOP'08.

Gregory Chaitin. Interview in "Dangerous Knowledge" BBC4 documentary. 2007.

Alonzo Church. *A Set of postulates for the foundation of logic (1)* Annals of Mathematics. Vol. 33, 1932.

Alonzo Church. *A Set of postulates for the foundation of logic (2)* Annals of Mathematics. Vol. 34, 1933.

Alonzo Church. *The Richard Paradox.* Proceedings of American Mathematical Society. 1934.

Alonzo Church. *An unsolvable problem of elementary number theory* Bulletin of the American Mathematical Society 19, May, 1935. American Journal of Mathematics, 58 (1936),
Alonzo Church: *A Formulation of the Simple Theory of Types*, Journal of Symbolic Logic. vol. 5. 1940.
Alonzo Church *The Calculi of Lambda-Conversion* Princeton University Press. 1941.
Alonzo Church. *Introduction to Mathematical Logic* Princeton University Press. 1956.
Paul Cohen. *The Independence of the Continuum Hypothesis I and II* Proceedings of the National Academy of Sciences of the United States of America, Vol. 50, No. 6. Dec. 15, 1963.
John Corcoran. *Second-order Logic.* Logic, Meaning and Computation. Kluwer. 2001.
Thierry Coquand and Gérard Huet: *The calculus of constructions.* Technical Report 530, INRIA, Centre de Rocquencourt, 1986.John Corcoran. *Gaps between logical theory and mathematical practice* in The methodological unity of science. 1973.John Corcoran. *Categoricity.* History and Philosophy of Logic. Vol. 1. 1980
Will Clinger. *Foundations of Actor Semantics* MIT Mathematics Doctoral Dissertation. June 1981.
Jack Copeland. *The Essential Turing* Oxford University Press. 2004.
Haskell Curry "Some Aspects of the Problem of Mathematical Rigor" *Bulletin of the American Mathematical Society* Vol. 4. 1941.
Reuben Hersh (editor). *18 Unconventional Essays on the Nature of Mathematics* Springer. 2005
John Dawson. *Shaken Foundations or Groundbreaking Realignment? A Centennial Assessment of Kurt Gödel's Impact on Logic, Mathematics, and Computer Science* FLOC'06.
Richard Dedekind (1888) *What are and what should the numbers be?* (Translation in From Kant to Hilbert: A Source Book in the Foundations of Mathematics. Oxford University Press. 1996) Braunschweig.
Cora Diamond. *Wittgenstein's Lectures on the Foundations of Mathematics, Cambridge, 1939* Cornell University Press. 1967.
Heinz-Dieter Ebbinghaus. *Ernst Zermelo: An Approach to His Life and Work* Springer. 2007.
Solomon Feferman. *Arithmetization of Metamathematics in a General Setting* Fundamenta Mathematicae. 49. 1960.
Solomon Feferman. *Finitary Inductively Presented Logics* Logic Colloquium '88. North-Holland, 1989.
Solomon Feferman "Axioms for determinateness and truth" Review of Symbolic Logic. 2008.
Freeman Dyson. *Heretical Thoughts about Science and Society* Boston University. November 1, 2005.
T. S. Eliot. *Four Quartets.* Harcourt. 1943.

Solomon Feferman, Solomon (1984). *Toward Useful Type-Free Theories, I.* "Journal of Symbolic Logic. 1984.

Juliet Floyd and Hilary Putnam *A note on Wittgenstein's "Notorious Paragraph" about the Gödel's Theorem* Journal of Philosophy. 2000.

Torkel Franzén. *Inexhaustibility* AK Peters. 2004

Gottlob Frege. *Begriffsschrift: eine der arithmetischen nachgebildete Formelsprache des reinen Denkens* Halle, 1879.

Gerhard Gentzen. *Investigations into Logical Deduction.* 1934-1935 in The collected works of Gerhard Gentzen. edited by Szabo. North-Holland, 1969.

Gerhard Gentzen. *The Consistency of Arithmetic.* 1936 in The collected works of Gerhard Gentzen. edited by Szabo. North-Holland, 1969.

Kurt Gödel. *Über die Vollständigkeit des Logikkalküls.* Doctoral dissertation. University Of Vienna. 1929

Kurt Gödel. *Die Vollständigkeit der Axiome des logischen Functionenkalküls,* Monatshefte für Mathematik und Physik 1930.Kurt Gödel (1931) *On formally undecidable propositions of Principia Mathematica* in *"A Source Book in Mathematical Logic, 1879-1931"* Translated by Jean van Heijenoort. Harvard Univ. Press. 1967.

Kurt Gödel (1933) *Kurt Gödel Collected Works, Vol. III.* Oxford University Press. Page 47.

Godfrey Hardy, *A Mathematician's Apology* Cambridge: University Press. 1940

Carl Hewitt, Peter Bishop and Richard Steiger. *A Universal Modular Actor Formalism for Artificial Intelligence* IJCAI-1973.

Carl Hewitt *Inconsistency Robustness for Logic Programs* in Inconsistency Robustness. College Publications. 2015.

Carl Hewitt *Formalizing common sense for inconsistency-robust information integration using Direct Logic™ Reasoning and the Actor Model* Inconsistency Robustness 2010.

Carl Hewitt *ActorScript™ extension of C#™, Java™, JavaScript™ and Objective C™* in Inconsistency Robustness. College Publications. 2015.

Carl Hewitt *Actor Model of Computation: Many-core Inconsistency-robust Information_Integration* Inconsistency Robustness 2011.

Carl Hewitt. *What is computation?* A Computable Universe: Understanding Computation & Exploring Nature as Computation. Edited by Hector Zenil. World Scientific Publishing Company. 2012.

David Hilbert *Mathematical Problems* Lecture delivered before the International Congress of Mathematicians at Paris in 1900. Translation by Newson: http://aleph0.clarku.edu/~djoyce/hilbert/problems.html

David Hilbert. *Neubegründung der Mathematik: Erste Mitteilung* Abhandlungen aus dem Seminar der Hamburgischen Universität. 1. 1922. English translation in *From Brouwer to Hilbert. The Debate on the Foundations of Mathematics in the 1920s* Oxford University Press. 1998.

Stanisław Jaśkowski *On the Rules of Suppositions in Formal* "Logic Studia Logica" 1, 1934. (reprinted in: *Polish logic 1920-1939*, Oxford University Press, 1967.

Stephen Kleene and John Barkley Rosser *The inconsistency of certain formal logics* Annals of Mathematics Vol. 36. 1935.

Stephen Kleene *General recursive functions and natural numbers* Mathematical Annuals. 1936.

Stephen Kleene *On the Notation of Ordinal Numbers* Journal of Symbolic Logic 1938.

Morris Kline. *Mathematical Thought from Ancient to Modern Times* Oxford University Press, 1990.

Rob Knies. *Terminator Tackles an Impossible Task* Microsoft Research. Aug. 6. 2006

Robert Kowalski *The Early Years of Logic Programming* CACM. January 1988.

Thomas Kuhn. The Structure of Scientific Revolutions University of Chicago Press. 1962.

Imre Lakatos. *Proofs and Refutations* Cambridge University Press. 1976.

John Law. *After Method: mess in social science research* Routledge. 2004.

Martin Löb. *Solution of a problem of Leon Henkin.* Journal of Symbolic Logic. Vol. 20. 1955.

David Malone. *Dangerous Knowledge* BBC4 documentary. 2007.
http://www.dailymotion.com/playlist/x1cbyd_xSilverPhinx_bbc-dangerous-knowledge/1

Ray Monk. *Bourgeois, Boshevist or anarchist? The Reception of Wittgenstein's Philosophy of Mathematics* in Wittgenstein and his interpreters. Blackwell. 2007.

Nick Nielsen *Alternative Foundations/philosophical* February 28, 2014.
http://www.cs.nyu.edu/pipermail/fom/2014-February/017861.html

nLab. *Constructive mathematics* 2014.
http://ncatlab.org/nlab/show/constructive+mathematics

Russell O'Connor. *Essential Incompleteness of Arithmetic Verified by Coq* TPHOLs 2005. http://arxiv.org/abs/cs/0505034

George Orwell. *In Front of Your Nose* Tribune. London. March 22, 1946.

Lawrence Paulson. *A Machine-Assisted Proof of Gödel's Incompleteness Theorems* Computer Laboratory, University of Cambridge. September 2014.
http://www.cl.cam.ac.uk/~lp15/papers/Formath/Goedel-slides.pdf

Giuseppe Peano *Arithmetices principia, nova methodo exposita* (The principles of arithmetic, presented by a new method) 1889.

Álvaro Pelayo, Michael A. Warren *Homotopy type theory and Voevodsky's univalent foundations* ArXiv:1210.5658. October 2012.

Francis Pelletier *A Brief History of Natural Deduction* "History and Philosophy of Logic" Vol. 20, Issue. 1, 1999.

Max Planck *Scientific Autobiography and Other Papers* 1949.

Graham Priest. *Wittgenstein's remarks on Gödel's Theorem* in Wittgenstein's Lasting Significance. Routledge 2004.
Panu Raatikainen. *Gödel's Incompleteness Theorems* Stanford Encyclopedia of Philosophy. Nov. 11, 2013.
Jules Richard. *Les Principes des Mathématiques et le Problème des Ensembles. Revue Générale des Sciences Pures et Appliquées.* 1905. Translated in "Source Book in Mathematical Logic 1879-1931" Harvard University Press. 1964
Victor Rodych. *Misunderstanding Gödel: New arguments about Wittgenstein and new remarks by Wittgenstein* Dialectica 2003.
Claude Rosental. *Weaving Self-Evidence* Princeton. 2008.
Richard Routley. *Dialectical logic, semantics and metamathematics* Erkenntnis 1979.
Bertrand Russell. "Les paradoxes de la logique" *Revue de métaphysique et de morale* 1906.
Bertrand Russell. *Mathematical logic as based on the theory of types* American. journal of mathematics. 1908,
Bertrand Russell. *Principia Mathematica 2nd Edition* 1925.
Michael Shulman. *Type theory and category theory* April 10, 2012. http://www.math.ucsd.edu/~mshulman/hottminicourse2012/
Dana Scott. *Axiomatizing Set Theory* "Symposium in Pure Mathematics" Los Angeles. July 1967.
Dana Scott *Data Types as Lattices* "SIAM Journal on computing". 1976.
Oron Shagrir *Gödel on Turing on Computability* Church's Thesis after 70 years Ontos-Verlag. 2006.
Stewart Shapiro *Foundations without Foundationalism: A Case for Second-Order Logic* Oxford. 2002.
Stewart Shapiro. *Do Not Claim Too Much: Second-order Logic and First-order* Logic Philosophia Mathematica.1999.
Natarajan Shankar. *Meta-mathematics, Machines, and Gödel's Proof.* Cambridge University Press. 1994.
Sandro Skansi. *A constructive proof of cut elimination for a system of full second-order logic* Retrieved February 27, 2014. http://www.logic101.net/upload/4296/documents/Article%20SO%20Skansi.pdf
Alfred Tarski *A Decision Method for Elementary Algebra and Geometry* University of California Press. 1951.
Alfred Tarski and Robert Vaught. "Arithmetical extensions of relational systems" *Compositio Mathematica* 13. 1957
Alan Turing. *On computable numbers, with an application to the Entscheidungsproblem* Proceedings London Math Society. 1936.
van Dalen, D. *Zermelo and the Skolem Paradox* Logic Group Preprint Series. Number 83. February 1998. Utrecht Research Institute of Philosophy.
Rineke Verbrugge. *Provability Logic* "The Stanford Encyclopedia of Philosophy" 2010.

Albert Visser. *Can We Make the Second Incompleteness Theorem Coordinate Free* Journal on Logic and Computation. 21(4) 2011.

Hao Wang *A Logical Journey, From Gödel to Philosophy* MIT Press. 1974.

Dan Willard *On the Results of a 14-Year Effort to Generalize Gödel's Second Incompleteness Theorem and Explore Its Partial Exceptions* Collegium Logicum IX, 2007

Leslie White. *The Locus of Mathematical Reality: An Anthropological Footnote* in The World of Mathematics. Vol. 4. Dover. 1956.

Raymond Wilder *Evolution of mathematical concepts. An elementary study.* Dover. 1968.

Ludwig Wittgenstein. 1956. *Bemerkungen ¨uber die Grundlagen der Mathematik/Remarks on the Foundations of Mathematics, Revised Edition* Basil Blackwell. 1978

Ludwig Wittgenstein. *Philosophische Grammatik* Basil Blackwell. 1969.

Ludwig Wittgenstein. (1933-1935) *Blue and Brown Books.* Harper. 1965.

Ludwig Wittgenstein *Philosophical Investigations* Blackwell. 1953/2001.

Noson Yanofsky. *The Outer Limits of Reason* MIT Press 2013.

Ernst Zermelo *Uber Grenzzahlen und Mengenbereiche: Neue Untersuchungen Äuber die Grundlagen der Mengenlehre* Fundamenta mathematicae. 1930; English translation by Michael Hallett, "On boundary numbers and domains of sets: new investigations in the foundations of set theory" *From Kant to Hilbert: a Source Book in the Foundations of Mathematics*, Oxford University Press, 1996

Ernst Zermelo. *Collected Works/Gesammelte Werke: Volume I/Band I - Set Theory, Miscellanea/Mengenlehre, Varia (Schriften der Mathematisch-naturwissenschaftlichen Klasse) (English and German Edition)* Springer. 2010.

Appendix 1. Notation of Classical Direct Logic

Types and Propositions are defined as follows:

- *Types* i.e., a Type is *only* by the rules below:
    - Boolean,$\mathbb{N}^{24}$,Sentence,Proposition,Proof,Theory:Type
    - If σ_1,σ_2:Type, then $\sigma_1 \oplus \sigma_2{}^{\text{i}}, [\sigma_1, \sigma_2]^{25}, [\sigma_1] \mapsto \sigma_2{}^{\text{ii}}, \sigma_2{}^{\sigma_1\,\text{iii}}$:Type
    - If f:Type$^\mathbb{N}$, then ($\oplus_\mathbb{N}$ f):Type^{iv}
    - If σ:Type, then Term⊲σ▷^{26}:Type
    - If σ:Type and e:Expression⊲σ▷ with no free variables, then ⌊e⌋:σ.

- *Propositions*, i.e., a Proposition is *only* by the rules below:
    - If σ:Type, Π:Boolean$^\sigma$ and x:σ, then $\Pi[x]$:Proposition.^{v}
    - If Φ:Proposition, then $\neg\Phi$:Proposition.
    - If Φ,Ψ:Proposition, then $\Phi\wedge\Psi, \Phi\vee\Psi, \Phi\Rightarrow\Psi, \Phi\Leftrightarrow\Psi$:Proposition.
    - If p:Boolean and Φ,Ψ:Proposition, then
      (p ◆ True⸚ Φ_1▯ False⸚ Φ_2):Proposition.^{27}
    - If σ_1,σ_2:Type, x_1:σ_1 and x_2:σ_2, then
      $x_1=x_2, x_1 \in x_2, x_1 \sqsubseteq x_2, x_1 \subseteq x_2, x_1:x_2$:Proposition.
    - If $\Phi_{1\,\text{to}\,n}$:Proposition,
      then ($\Phi_1, ..., \Phi_k \vdash \Phi_{k+1}, ..., \Phi_n$):Proposition^{28}
    - If p:Proof and Φ:Proposition, then ($\vdash^{\underline{p}} \Phi$):Proposition^{vi}
    - If s:Sentence with no free variables, then ⌊s⌋:Proposition.

---

[i] For i=1,2
- If x:σ_i, then $(x \oslash (\sigma_1 \oplus \sigma_2))$:$(\sigma_1 \oplus \sigma_2)$ and $x=(x \oslash (\sigma_1 \oplus \sigma_2)) \ominus \sigma_i$.
- $\forall[\tau$:Type, z:$\tau] \rightarrow z$:$\sigma_1 \oplus \sigma_2 \Leftrightarrow \exists[x$:$\sigma_i] \rightarrow z = x \oslash (\sigma_1 \oplus \sigma_2)$

[ii] Type of computable procedures from σ_1 into σ_2.
If σ_1,σ_2:Type, f:$([\sigma_1] \mapsto \sigma_2)$ and x:σ_1, then f.$[x]$:σ_2.

[iii] If σ_1,σ_2:Type, f:$\sigma_2{}^{\sigma_1}$ and x:σ_1, then f[x]:σ_2.

[iv] $\forall[i$:$\mathbb{N}$, x:f[i]] $\rightarrow (x \oslash \oplus_\mathbb{N} f)$:$\oplus_\mathbb{N} f \wedge x = (x \oslash \oplus_\mathbb{N} f) \ominus f[i]$
$\forall[\tau$:Type, z:$\tau] \rightarrow z$:$\oplus_\mathbb{N} f \Leftrightarrow \exists[i$:$\mathbb{N}$, x:f[i]] $\rightarrow z = x \oslash \oplus_\mathbb{N} f$

[v] $\forall[\sigma$:Type, x:$\sigma] \rightarrow \Pi[x] \Leftrightarrow (\Pi[x] = \text{True})$

Note that σ:Type, Π:Boolean$^\sigma$ means that there are no fixed points for propositions.

[vi] p is a proof of Φ

Grammar trees (*i.e.* expressions and sentences) are defined as follows :
- ***Expressions***, *i.e.,* an Expression◁σ▷ is *only* by the rules below:
  - **True, False**:Constant◁Boolean▷ and **0,1**:Constant◁ℕ▷.
  - Boolean,ℕ,Sentence,Proposition,Proof,Theory:Constant◁Type▷.
  - If σ:Type and x:Constant◁σ▷, then x:Expression◁σ▷.
  - If σ:Type and x:Variable◁σ▷, then x:Expression◁σ▷.
  - If σ,σ$_{1\,to\,n}$,τ$_{1\,to\,n}$:Type, x$_{1\,to\,n}$:Expression◁σ$_{1\,to\,n}$▷ and y:Expression◁σ▷, then
    (Let v$_1$◁τ$_1$▷ ≡ x$_1$, ... , v$_n$◁τ$_n$▷ ≡ x$_n$ ^{29} ₒ y):Expression◁σ▷ and v$_{1\,to\,n}$:Variable◁σ$_{1\,to\,n}$▷ in y and in each x$_{1\,to\,n}$.
  - If e$_1$, e$_2$:Expression◁Type▷, then
    ⌈e$_1$⊕e$_2$⌉,⌈[e$_1$, e$_2$]⌉,⌈[e$_1$]↦e$_2$⌉,⌈e$_2$^{e_1}⌉:Expression◁Type▷.
  - If σ:Type, t$_1$:Expression◁Boolean▷, t$_2$, t$_3$:Expression◁σ▷, then
    ⌈t$_1$◆True⁚ t$_2$▽ False⁚ t$_3$⌉:Expression◁σ▷.[30]
  - If σ$_1$,σ$_2$:Type, t:Expression◁σ$_2$▷, then
    ⌈[x:σ$_1$]→ t⌉:Expression◁[σ$_1$]↦σ$_2$▷ and x:Variable◁σ$_1$▷ in t.[31]
  - If σ$_1$,σ$_2$:Type, p:Expression◁[σ$_1$]↦σ$_2$▷ and x:Expression◁σ$_1$▷, then
    ⌈p.[x]⌉:Expression◁σ$_2$▷.

- ***Sentences***, *i.e.,* a Sentence is *only* by the rules below:
  - If s$_1$:Sentence then, ⌈¬s$_1$⌉:Sentence.
  - If s$_1$:Sentence and s$_2$:Sentence then
    ⌈s$_1$∧s$_2$⌉,⌈s$_1$∨s$_2$⌉,⌈s$_1$⇨s$_2$⌉,⌈s$_1$⇔s$_2$⌉:Sentence.
  - If σ:Type, t$_1$:Expression◁Boolean^σ▷ and t$_2$:Expression◁σ▷, then
    ⌈t$_1$[t$_2$]⌉:Sentence.
  - If t:Expression◁Boolean▷, s$_1$,s$_2$:Sentence, then
    ⌈t ◆ True⁚ s$_1$▽ False⁚ s$_2$⌉:Sentence.[32]
  - If σ$_1$,σ$_2$:Type, t$_1$:Expression◁σ$_1$▷ and t$_2$:Expression◁σ$_2$▷, then
    ⌈t$_1$=t$_2$⌉,⌈t$_1$∈t$_2$⌉,⌈t$_1$⊆t$_2$⌉,⌈t$_1$⊂t$_2$⌉,⌈t$_1$:t$_2$⌉:Sentence.
  - If σ:Type and s:Sentence, then ⌈∀[x:σ]→ s⌉,⌈∃[x:σ]→ s⌉:Sentence and x:Variable◁σ▷ in s.
  - If T:Expression◁Theory▷, s$_{1\,to\,n}$:Sentence and
    p:Expression◁Proof▷, then ⌈s$_1$, ..., s$_k$ ⊢$_T^p$ s$_{k+1}$, ..., s$_n$⌉:Sentence[33]

Foundations with both types and sets

Everyone is free to elaborate [their] *own foundations. All that is required of* [a] *Foundation of Mathematics is that its discussion embody absolute rigor, transparency, philosophical coherence, and addresses fundamental methodological issues.*
[Nielsen 2014]

Classical Direct Logic develops foundations for mathematics by deriving sets[i] from types[ii] *and* the Peano/Dedekind axioms for the integers to encompass all of standard mathematics including the reals, analysis, geometry, *etc.*[34]

Combining types and sets as the foundation has the advantage of using the strengths of each without the limitations of trying to use just one because each can be used to make up for the limitations of the other. The key idea is compositionality, *i.e.*, composing new entities from others. Types can be composed from other types and sets can be composed from other sets.

Functions, graphs, and lists are fundamental to the mathematical foundations of Computer Science. SetFunctions◁σ▷ (type of set functions based on type σ) that can be defined inductively as follows:

SetFunctionsOfOrder◁σ▷[0] ≡ σ^σ

SetFunctionsOfOrder◁σ▷[n+1] ≡
    (σ⊕SetFunctionsOfOrder◁σ▷[n])$^{\sigma \oplus \text{SetFunctionsOfOrder}◁\sigma▷[n]}$

Furthermore the process of constructing orders of
SetFunctionsOfOrder◁σ▷ is exhaustive for SetFunctions◁σ▷:

SetFunctions◁σ▷ ≡ ⊕$_\mathbb{N}$ SetFunctionsOfOrder◁σ▷

// in conventional notation: ⊕$_{i:\mathbb{N}}$ SetFunctionsOfOrder◁σ▷[i]

---

[i] According to [Scott 1967]: "As long as an idealistic manner of speaking about abstract objects is popular in mathematics, people will speak about collections of objects, and then collections of collections of ... of collections. In other words *set theory is inevitable.*" [emphasis in original]

[ii] According to [Scott 1967]: "there is only one satisfactory way of avoiding the paradoxes: namely, the use of some form of the *theory of types*... the best way to regard Zermelo's theory is as a simplification and extension of Russell's ...*simple* theory of types. Now Russell made his types *explicit* in his notation and Zermelo left them *implicit*. It is a mistake to leave something so important invisible..."

Sets (along with lists) provide a convenient way to collect together elements.[35]
For example, sets (of sets of sets of ...) of σ can be axiomatized as follows:[i]
∀[s:Sets◁σ▷]→ ∃[f:SetFunctions◁σ▷]→ CharacteristicFunction[f, s]
  where ∀[s:Sets◁σ▷, f:Boolean^(SetFunctions◁σ▷)]→
    CharacteristicFunction[f, s]
      ⇔ ∀[e:σ⊕Sets◁σ▷]→ e∈s ⇔ f[e]=True
i.e. every set of type Sets◁σ▷ is defined by a characteristic function of SetFunctions◁σ▷

Note that there is no set corresponding to the *type* Sets◁ℕ▷ which is an example of how types extend the capabilities of sets.[36]

Natural Numbers, Real Numbers, and their Sets are Unique up to Isomorphism[ii]

The following question arises: What mathematics have been captured in the above foundations?

Theorem[iii] (Categoricity of ℕ):[37]
∀[M:Model◁ℕ▷]→ M≈ℕ, *i.e.*, models of the natural numbers ℕ are isomorphic by a unique isomorphism.[iv]

Giuseppe Peano

The following strong induction axiom[38] can be used to characterize the natural numbers (ℕ[39]) up to isomorphism with a unique isomorphism:
∀[P:Boolean^ℕ]→ Inductive[P]⇨ ∀[i:ℕ]→ P[i]
  where ∀[P:Boolean^ℕ]→ Inductive[P]
    ⇔ (P[0] ∧ ∀[i:ℕ]→ P[i] ⇨P[i+1])[40]

---

[i] Of course, the higher cardinals are left out of these foundations. On the other hand, Computer Science doesn't need higher cardinals in its mathematical foundations.
[ii] and the isomorphism is unique
[iii] [Dedekind 1888, Peano 1889]
[iv] Consequently, the type of natural numbers ℕ is unique up to isomorphism and the type of reals ℝ is unique up to isomorphism.

Theorem[i] (Categoricity of $\mathbb{R}$):[41]
∀[M:Model◁$\mathbb{R}$▷]→ M≈$\mathbb{R}$, *i.e.*, models of the real numbers $\mathbb{R}$ are isomorphic by a unique isomorphism.[ii]

The following can be used to characterize the real numbers ($\mathbb{R}$[42]) up to isomorphism with a unique isomorphism:

Richard Dedekind

∀[S:Set◁$\mathbb{R}$▷]→ S≠{ } ∧ Bounded[S] ⇨ HasLeastUpperBound[S]
where
  Bounded[S:Set◁$\mathbb{R}$▷] ⇔ ∃[b:$\mathbb{R}$]→ UpperBound[b, S]
  UpperBound[b:$\mathbb{R}$, S:Set◁$\mathbb{R}$▷] ⇔ b∈S ∧ ∀[x∈S]→ x≦b
  HasLeastUpperBound[S:Set◁$\mathbb{R}$▷]] ⇔ ∃[b:$\mathbb{R}$]→ LeastUpperBound[b, S]
  LeastUpperBound[b:$\mathbb{R}$, S:Set◁$\mathbb{R}$▷]
          ⇔ UpperBound[b,S] ∧ ∀[x∈S]→ UpperBound[x,S] ⇨ x≦b

Theorem (Categoricity of Sets◁$\mathbb{N}$⊕$\mathbb{R}$▷):[43]
∀[M:Model◁Sets◁$\mathbb{N}$⊕$\mathbb{R}$▷▷]→ M≈Sets◁$\mathbb{N}$⊕$\mathbb{R}$▷, *i.e.*, models of Sets◁$\mathbb{N}$⊕$\mathbb{R}$▷ are isomorphic by a unique isomorphism.[iii]

Sets◁$\mathbb{N}$⊕$\mathbb{R}$▷ (which is a fundamental type of mathematics) is exactly characterized axiomatically, which is what is required for Computer Science.

Ernst Zermelo

Proof: By above, ∀[M:Model◁$\mathbb{N}$▷]→ M≈$\mathbb{N}$, *i.e.*, models of $\mathbb{N}$ are isomorphic by a unique isomorphism. Unique isomorphism of higher order sets can be proved using induction from the following closure property for SetFunctions (see above):
  SetFunctions◁$\mathbb{N}$⊕$\mathbb{R}$▷ ≡ $\bigsqcup_{i:\mathbb{N}}$ SetFunctionsOfOrder◁$\mathbb{N}$⊕$\mathbb{R}$▷[i]
Unique isomorphism for SetFunctions◁$\mathbb{N}$⊕$\mathbb{R}$▷ can be extended to Sets◁$\mathbb{N}$⊕$\mathbb{R}$▷ because every set in Sets◁$\mathbb{N}$⊕$\mathbb{R}$▷ is defined by a characteristic function of SetFunctions◁$\mathbb{N}$⊕$\mathbb{R}$▷. (See above)

---

[i] [Dedekind 1888]
[ii] Consequently, the type of natural numbers $\mathbb{N}$ is unique up to isomorphism and is a subtype of reals $\mathbb{R}$ that is unique up to isomorphism.
[iii] Consequently, the type of natural numbers $\mathbb{N}$ is unique up to isomorphism and the type of reals $\mathbb{R}$ is unique up to isomorphism.

Classical Direct Logic is much stronger than first-order axiomatizations of set theory.[44]

Theorem (Set Theory Model Soundness): $(\vdash_{\text{Sets}\triangleleft\mathbb{N}\triangleright} \Psi) \Rightarrow \vDash_{\mathbb{S}\text{ets}\triangleleft\mathbb{N}\triangleright} \Psi$

Proof: Suppose $\vdash_{\text{Sets}\triangleleft\mathbb{N}\triangleright} \Psi$. The conclusion immediately follows because the axioms for the theory Sets◁N▷ hold in the model 𝕊ets◁ℕ▷.

Appendix 2. Historical Background

> *The powerful (try to) insist that their statements are literal depictions of a single reality. 'It really is that way', they tell us. 'There is no alternative.' But those on the receiving end of such homilies learn to read them allegorically, these are techniques used by subordinates to read through the words of the powerful to the concealed realities that have produced them.*
> Law [2004]

Gödel was certain

> *"Certainty" is far from being a sign of success; it is only a symptom of lack of imagination and conceptual poverty. It produces smug satisfaction and prevents the growth of knowledge.*
> [Lakatos 1976]

Paul Cohen [2006] wrote as follows of his interaction with Gödel:

> *His* [Gödel's] *main interest seemed to lie in discussing the "truth" or "falsity" of these questions, not merely in their undecidability. He struck me as having an almost unshakable belief in this "realist" position, which I found difficult to share. His ideas were grounded in a deep philosophical belief as to what the human mind could achieve. I greatly admired this faith in the power and beauty of Western Culture, as he put it, and would have liked to understand more deeply what were the sources of his strongly held beliefs. Through our discussions, I came closer to his point of view, although I never shared completely his "realist" point of view, that all questions of Set Theory were in the final analysis, either true or false.*

Kurt Gödel

Chaitin [2007] presented the following analysis:

> Gödel's proof of inferential undecidability [incompleteness] *was too superficial. It didn't get at the real heart of what was going on. It was more tantalizing than anything else. It was not a good reason for something so devastating and fundamental. It was too clever by half. It was too superficial.* [It was based on the clever construction] *"I'm unprovable." So what? This doesn't give any insight how serious the problem is.*

Gödel's alleged Mathematical sentence *"I am not provable"* comes from a nonexistent fixed point (sometimes called the Diagonal Lemma) that doesn't exist because of types. His results were for Principia Mathematica, which was intended as the foundation of all of Mathematics. Unfortunately,

Principia Mathematica had some defects in its types that have been corrected in Direct Logic.

Church/Turing correctly proved inferential incompleteness (sometimes called the "First Incompleteness Theorem") without using a nonexistent "self-referential" proposition. The Church/Turing theorem and its proof are very robust.

After Church[1935] and Turing[1936] proved inferential undecidabilty of closed mathematical theories using computational undecidablity[i], Gödel claimed more generality and that his results applied to all consistent mathematical systems that incorporate Peano axioms. However, when he learned of Wittgenstein's devastating proof of inconsistency,[45] Gödel retreated to claiming that his results applied to the very weak first-order theory of natural numbers.[46] The upshot is that Gödel never acknowledged that his "self-referential" proposition[ii] implies inconsistency in mathematics. See further discussion below in this article.

Also, the ultimate criteria for correctness in the theory of natural numbers is provability using categorical induction [Dedekind 1888, Peano 1889]. In this sense, Wittgenstein was correct in his identification of "truth" with provability. On the other hand, Gödel obfuscated the important identification of provability as the touchstone of ultimate correctness in mathematics.

von Neumann [1961] had a very different view from Gödel:

> *It is **not** necessarily true that the mathematical method is something absolute, which was revealed from on high, or which somehow, after we got hold of it, was evidently right and has stayed evidently right ever since.*

John von Neumann

---

[i] See proof of inferential undecidablity of closed mathematical theories elsewhere in this article.
[ii] constructed using fixed points exploiting an untyped notation for mathematics

Limitations of first-order logic

> *By this it appears how necessary it is for nay man that aspires to true knowledge to examine the definitions of former authors; and either to correct them, where they are negligently set down, or to make them himself. For the errors of definitions multiply themselves, according as the reckoning proceeds, and lead men into absurdities, which at last they see, but cannot avoid, without reckoning anew from the beginning; in which lies the foundation of their errors...*
> [Hobbes *Leviathan*, Chapter 4][47]

It is very important not to confuse Mathematics with first-order logic, which was invented by philosophers for their own purposes. It turns out that first-order logic is amazing weak. For example, first-order logic is incapable of characterizing even the Peano numbers, *i.e.*, there are infinite integers in models of every first-order axiomatization of the Peano numbers. Furthermore, there are infinitesimal real numbers in models of every first-order axiomatization of the real numbers.[i] Of course, infinite integers and infinitesimal reals are monsters that must be banned from the mathematical foundations of Computer Science.

However, some philosophers have found first-order logic to be useful for their careers because it is weak enough that they can prove theorems about first-order axiomatizations whereas they cannot prove such theorems about stronger practical systems, *e.g.*, Classical Direct Logic. For example, there is a famous theorem that first-order set theory is too weak to decide ContinuumHypothesis[48], *i.e.*, $\nvdash_{FirstOrderSetAxioms}$ContinuumHypothesis and $\nvdash_{FirstOrderSetAxioms}\neg$ContinuumHypothesis.[49] However, ContinuumHypothesis is still an open problem in Mathematics. That ContinuumHypothesis is an open problem is not so important for Computer Science because for subsets of reals of that are computable[ii], the ComputationalContinuumTheorem[iii] holds.[50]

Zermelo considered the First-Order Thesis to be a mathematical "hoax" because it necessarily allowed unintended models of axioms.[51]

Ernst Zermelo

---

[i] Likewise, first-order set theory (e.g. ZFC) is very weak. See discussion immediately below.

[ii] A real number is computable if an only if its digits are computable.

[iii] $\mathbb{R}$ has no subset of computable reals whose cardinality is strictly between $\mathbb{N}$ and $\mathbb{R}$.

[Barwise 1985] critiqued the First-Order Thesis[i] as follows:

> *The reasons for the widespread, often uncritical acceptance of the first-order thesis are numerous. The first-order thesis ... confuses the subject matter of logic with one of its tools. First-order language is just an artificial language structured to help investigate logic, much as a telescope is a tool constructed to help study heavenly bodies. From the perspective of the mathematics in the street, the first-order thesis is like the claim that astronomy is the study of the telescope.*[52]

Jon Barwise

Computer Science is making increasing use of Model Analysis[ii] in the sense of analyzing relationships among the following:
- concurrent programs and their Actor Model denotations
- axiom systems and their models

Having infinite integers and infinitesimal reals in models of axioms can cause problems in practical Model Analysis because a computer system can easily prove that there are no infinite integers and no infinitesimal reals. Consequently, infinite integers and infinitesimal reals are modeling monsters. Fortunately, these modeling monsters do not exist in Classical Direct Logic.

The cut-down-first-order theory $FirstOrderPeano$[iii] is too limited for Computer Science because of the following:
- $(\vdash_{FirstOrderPeano} \Psi) \Rightarrow \vdash_{Peano} \Psi$
- There are some Ψ_0 that are important in Computer Science (see immediately below) such that:
  - $\vdash_{Peano} \Psi_0$
  - $\nvdash_{FirstOrderPeano} \Psi_0$

In Computer Science, it is important that the Natural Numbers ($\mathbb{N}$) be axiomatized in a way that does not allow non-numbers (*e.g.* infinite ones) in models of the axioms. Unfortunately, every consistent first-order axiomatization of $\mathbb{N}$ has a model with an infinite integer:

---

[i] The "First-Order Thesis" is that mathematical foundations should be restricted to first-order logic.
[ii] a restricted form of Model Checking in which the properties checked are limited to those that can be expressed in Linear-time Temporal Logic has been studied [Clarke, Emerson, Sifakis, *etc.* ACM 2007 Turing Award].
[iii] with cut-down first-order Peano axioms

Theorem: If ℕ is a model of a first-order axiomatization 𝑇, then 𝑇 has a model 𝕄 with an infinite integer.

Proof: The model 𝕄 is constructed as an extension of ℕ by adding a new element ∞ with the following atomic relationships:
$$\{\neg\infty<\infty\} \cup (\text{Elementwise}[\,[m]\to m<\infty])[\mathbb{N}]^i$$
It can be shown that 𝕄 is a model of 𝑇 with an infinite integer ∞.

The infinite integer ∞ is a monster that must be banned from the mathematical foundations of Computer Science.

A similar result holds for the standard theory ℝ of real numbers [Dedekind 1888] compared to a cut-down, first-order theory[53], which has models with infinitesimals:

Theorem: If ℝ is a model of a first-order axiomatization 𝑇, then 𝑇 has a model 𝕄 with an infinitesimal.

Proof: The model 𝕄 is constructed as an extension of ℝ by adding a new element ∞ with the following atomic relationships:
$$\{\neg\infty<\infty\} \cup (\text{Elementwise}[\,[m]\to m<\infty])[\mathbb{N}]^{ii}$$
Defining ε to be $\frac{1}{\infty}$, it follows that $\forall[r:\mathbb{R}]\to 0<\varepsilon<\frac{1}{r}$. It can be shown that 𝕄 is a model of 𝑇 with an infinitesimal ε, which is a monster that must be banned from the mathematical foundations of Computer Science.

On the other hand, since it is not limited to first-order logic, Classical Direct Logic characterizes structures such as natural numbers and real numbers up to isomorphism.[iii]

---

[i] Elementwise[f] = [s]→ {f[x] | x∈s}
[ii] Elementwise[f] = [s]→ {f[x] | x∈s}
[iii] proving that software developers and computer systems are using the same structures

Of greater practical import, that a computer provides service *i.e.*
∃ [i:ℕ]→ ResponseBefore[i] cannot be proved in a first-order theory.

> Proof: In order to obtain a contradiction, suppose that it is possible to prove the theorem that computer server provides service[i] in a first-order theory T.
> Therefore the following infinite set of propositions is inconsistent:[ii]
> (Elementwise[[i]→ ¬ResponseBefore[i]])[ℕ].
> By the compactness theorem of first-order logic, it follows that there is finite subset of the set of propositions that is inconsistent. But this is a contradiction, because all the finite subsets are consistent since the amount of time before a server responds is unbounded, i.e.,
> (∄ [i:ℕ]→ ⊢$_T$ ResponseBefore[i]).

The above examples illustrate the following fundamental limitation of first-order theories:

In a first-order theory T, it is impossible to have both of the following for a predicate P:

- ∄ [i:ℕ]→ ⊢$_T$ P[i][iii]
- ⊢$_T$ ∃ [i:ℕ]→ P[i]

> Proof: Suppose that it is possible for both of the above to hold in a first-order theory T. Therefore the following infinite set of propositions is inconsistent:[54]
> (Elementwise[[m]→ ¬P[m]])[ℕ]
> By the compactness theorem of first-order logic, it follows that there is finite subset of the set of propositions that is inconsistent. But this is a contradiction, because all the finite subsets are consistent.

As a foundation of mathematics for Computer Science, Classical Direct Logic provides categorical[55] numbers (integer and real), sets, lists, trees, graphs, etc. which can be used in arbitrary mathematical theories including theories for categories, large cardinals, first-order axiomatizations, etc. These various theories might have "monsters" of various kinds. However, these monsters are not imported into the foundations of Computer Science.

---

[i] ∃ [i:ℕ]→ ResponseBefore[i]
[ii] *i.e.* in classical notation: { ¬ResponseBefore[i] | i:ℕ}
[iii] *i.e.* ∀[i:ℕ]→ ⊬$_T$ P[i]

Computer Science needs *stronger* systems than provided by first-order logic in order to weed out unwanted models. In this regard, Computer Science doesn't have a problem computing with "infinite" objects (*i.e.* Actors) such as π and uncountable sets such as the real numbers ℝ.[56]

Of course some problems are theoretically not computable. However, even in these cases, it is often possible to compute approximations and cases of practical interest.[i]

The mathematical foundation of Computer Science is very different from the general philosophy of mathematics in which infinite integers and infinitesimal reals may be of some interest. Of course, it is always possible to have special theories with infinite integers, infinitesimal reals, unicorns, *etc.*

Provability Logic
One kind of Provability Logic (called 𝒫𝐿) is a cut-down theory of deduction that has been used to investigate provability predicates for languages that allow "self-referential" propositions [Verbrugge 2010].

In Direct Logic, fixed points on propositions do not exist and consequently Gödel's proofs are not valid. Even in the closed theory ℕ, a "self-referential" sentence cannot be constructed by enumerating strings for sentences. Let SentenceFromStringWithIndex_ℕ be a procedure that enumerates sentences that can be produced by parsing mathematical strings of the closed theory ℕ and IndexOfSentenceFromString_ℕ be a procedure that returns the index of a sentence that can be obtained by parsing a mathematical string.
  I_am_not_provable:Proposition ≡
      ⌊SentenceFromStringWithIndex_ℕ.[Fix[Diagonal]]⌋
  where Diagonal.[i:ℕ]:ℕ ≡ IndexOfSentenceFromString_ℕ
      .[⌈⊬_ℕ ⌊SentenceFromStringWithIndex_ℕ.[i]⌋⌉]
Because of types in Classical Direct Logic the fixed point operator Fix cannot be defined because of the following:
  NtoN ≡ [ℕ]↦ℕ
  Helper.[f:NtoN]:NtoN ≡ [x:([?]↦NtoN)]↦ f.[x.[x]]
  Fix.[f:NtoN]:NtoN ≡ (Helper.[f]).[Helper.[f]]
The missing type [?] does not exist.

Consequently, the above attempt does *not* create a sentence *S* such that
⌊⌈S⌉⌋ ⇔ ⊬_ℕ⌊⌈S⌉⌋

---

[i] *e.g.* see Terminator [Knies 2006], which practically solves the halting problem for device drivers

Because it is first-order, $\mathcal{PL}$ is very weak; even for proving theorems about integers. Also, $\mathcal{PL}$ makes the assumption that there are only countably many propositions[57] and that for every proposition Φ, there is an integer $\lceil\Phi\rceil_{\mathcal{PL}}$ such that $\Phi\Leftrightarrow\lfloor\lceil\Phi\rceil_{\mathcal{PL}}\rfloor_{\mathcal{PL}}$.

In formulating his results, [Löb 1955] proposed the following provability conditions that became the basis of Provability Logic:[i]
1. $(\vdash_{\mathcal{PL}}\Phi) \Rightarrow \vdash_{\mathcal{PL}}\vdash_{\mathcal{PL}}\Phi$
2. $\vdash_{\mathcal{PL}}((\vdash_{\mathcal{PL}}(\Phi\Rightarrow\Psi)) \Rightarrow ((\vdash_{\mathcal{PL}}\Phi)\Rightarrow\vdash_{\mathcal{PL}}\Psi)))$
3. $\vdash_{\mathcal{PL}}((\vdash_{\mathcal{PL}}\Phi) \Rightarrow \vdash_{\mathcal{PL}}\vdash_{\mathcal{PL}}\Phi)$

Using "self-referential" propositions, [Löb 1955] proved the following:[58]
$$(\vdash_{\mathcal{PL}}((\vdash_{\mathcal{PL}}\Phi)\Rightarrow\Phi)) \Rightarrow \vdash_{\mathcal{PL}}\Phi.$$

However, $\mathcal{PL}$ is a very weak theory of deduction. For example, the principle of natural deduction below called "Soundness" in Direct Logic that allows theorems to be used in subarguments is not allowed in $\mathcal{PL}$:[59]

$$(\vdash\Phi)\Rightarrow\Phi$$

Note that the rule of Soundness [*i.e.* $(\vdash\Phi)\Rightarrow\Phi$] does not involve any coding of propositions as integers. It is highly desirable for computer systems to be able to reason about the mathematical foundations of Classical Direct Logic using Classical Direct Logic. Unlike $\mathcal{PL}$, Classical Direct Logic does not require complex circumlocutions (involving coding into integers) that obscure what is going on.

In summary, Provability Logic (although a useful historical development step) is too cumbersome and fragile to serve in the mathematical foundation of Computer Science.

---

[i] His formulation actually used the convoluted coding of propositions into integers.

Inadequacies of Tarskian Set Models
Tarskian Set Models[60] are inadequate for foundations of Computer Science for they are inadequate to characterize direct inference used by systems to reason about their own inference capabilities.[i]

But the most fundamental limitation of Tarskian Set Models is that large information theories of practice have *no* models because they are pervasively inconsistent.

Church's Paradox

> *in the case of any system of symbolic logic, the set of all provable theorems is* [computationally] *enumerable... any system of symbolic logic not hopelessly inadequate ... would contain the formal theorem that this same system ... was either insufficient* [theorems are not computationally enumerable] *or over-sufficient* [that theorems are computationally enumerable means that the system is inconsistent]*...*
> *This, of course, is a deplorable state of affairs...*
> *Indeed, if there is no formalization of logic as a whole, then there is no exact description of what logic is, for it in the very nature of an exact description that it implies a formalization. And if there no exact description of logic, then there is no sound basis for supposing that there is such a thing as logic.*
> [Church 1934][61]

[Church 1932, 1933] attempted basing foundations entirely on untyped higher-order functions, but foundered because contradictions emerged because
1. His system allowed "self-referential" propositions [Kleene and Rosser 1935]
2. He believed that theorems must be computationally enumerable.

Our proposal is to address the above issues as follows:
1. Not providing for the construction of "self-referential" propositions in mathematics
2. Mathematics self proves that it is "open" in the sense that theorems are not computationally enumerable (*i.e.* not "closed").[ii]

---

[i] *E.g.* the theorems in this article.
[ii] In other words, the paradox that concerned Church (because he thought that it could mean the demise of formal mathematical logic) has been transformed into fundamental theorem of foundations!

Curry and Löb Paradoxes

An example of a "self-referential" proposition is *"I am not provable"* that was used by in [Gödel 1931].[62] Unfortunately, allowing construction of "self-referential" propositions[i] results in contradictions [Wittgenstein 1937].[63]

For example the following paradoxes prove *every* proposition using "self-referential" propositions:[64]

- **Curry's Paradox** [Curry 1941]: Suppose that Ψ:Proposition.
  Curry$_\Psi$:Proposition $\equiv^{ii}$ Fix[f$_\Psi$] // note that this fixed point does *not*
  // exist in typed notation of mathematics
  where f$_\Psi$[Φ:Proposition]:Proposition $\equiv \Phi \vdash \Psi$
  1) Curry$_\Psi$ $\Leftrightarrow$ (Curry$_\Psi$ $\vdash \Psi$)   // fixed point
  2) $\vdash$ (Curry$_\Psi$ $\vdash$ Curry$_\Psi$)   // idempotency
  3) $\vdash$ (Curry$_\Psi$ $\vdash$ (Curry$_\Psi$ $\vdash \Psi$))   // substituting 1) into 2)
  4) $\vdash$ (Curry$_\Psi$ $\vdash \Psi$)   // contraction
  5) $\vdash$ Curry$_\Psi$ // substituting 1) into 4)
  6) $\vdash \Psi$ // chaining 4) and 5)

- **Löb's Paradox** [Löb 1955]:[65] Suppose that Ψ:Proposition.
  Löb$_\Psi$:Proposition $\equiv^{iii}$ Fix[f$_\Psi$] // note that this fixed point does *not*
  // exist in typed notation of mathematics
  where f$_\Psi$[Φ:Proposition]:Proposition $\equiv$ ($\vdash \Phi$) $\vdash \Psi$
  1) Löb$_\Psi$ $\Leftrightarrow$ (($\vdash$ Löb$_\Psi$) $\vdash \Psi$)   // fixed point
  2) $\vdash$ (($\vdash$ Löb$_\Psi$) $\vdash$ Löb$_\Psi$)   // soundness
  3) $\vdash$(($\vdash$ Löb$_\Psi$) $\vdash$ (($\vdash$ Löb$_\Psi$) $\vdash \Psi$))   // substituting 1) into 2)
  4) $\vdash$(($\vdash$ Löb$_\Psi$) $\vdash \Psi$)   // contraction
  5) $\vdash$ Löb$_\Psi$ // substituting 1) into 4)
  6) Ψ // chaining 4) and 5)

Of course, it is completely unacceptable for every proposition to be provable and so measures must be taken to prevent this.

---

[i] using fixed point operators exploiting an untyped notation for mathematics
[ii] Not allowed in Direct Logic because Fix is not allowed.
[iii] Not allowed in Direct Logic because Fix is not allowed..

Berry's Paradox
Berry's construction [Russell 1906] can be formalized using:
- Least[s] is the smallest integer in the nonempty set of integers s
- Length[s] is length of string s.
- Characterize[s:StringForPredication, k:ℕ]:Proposition ≡
  ∀[x:ℕ]→⌊⌈s⌉⌋[x] ⇔ x=k

The above definition of Characterize is *not* allowed in Direct Logic because ⌊⌈s⌉⌋[x] is not a sentence in Direct Logic because ⌈s⌉ is not Term◁Boolean$^\sigma$▷ for some type σ.

Consider the following definition:
  BerryString ≡
    "[n:ℕ]→
        ∀[s:String]→
            Length[s]<1000 ⇨ ¬Characterize[s, n]"[66]
Consider the following set:
  BerrySet[67] ≡ {n:ℕ | Characterize[BerryString, n]}
Note that if BerrySet existed, then it would not be empty.[68]

1. BerryNumber[69] ≡ Least[BerrySet]
2. Characterize[BerryString, BerryNumber][70]
3. ∀[x:ℕ]→⌊⌈BerryString⌉⌋[x] ⇔ x=BerryNumber[71]
4. ⌊⌈BerryString⌉⌋[BerryNumber] ⇔ BerryNumber=BerryNumber[72]
5. ⌊⌈ [n:ℕ]→
        ∀[s:StringForPredication]→
            Length[s]<1000
                ⇨ ¬Characterize[s, n] ⌉⌋[BerryNumber] ⌋[73]
6. ([n:ℕ]→
      ∀[s:StringForPredication]→
          Length[s]<100 ⇨ ¬Characterize[s, n])[BerryNumber]
7. ∀[s:StringForPredication]→
      Length[s]<1000 ⇨¬Characterize[s, BerryNumber]
8. Length[BerryString]<1000
      ⇨¬Characterize[BerryString, BerryNumber][74]
9. ¬Characterize[BerryString, BerryNumber][75]

Sociology of Foundations

> *"Faced with the choice between changing one's mind and proving that there is no need to do so, almost everyone gets busy on the proof."*
> John Kenneth Galbraith [1971 pg. 50]

> *Max Planck, surveying his own career in his Scientific Autobiography [Planck 1949], sadly remarked that 'a new scientific truth does not triumph by convincing its opponents and making them see the light, but rather because its opponents eventually die, and a new generation grows up that is familiar with it.'* [Kuhn 1962]

The inherently social nature of the processes by which principles and propositions in logic are produced, disseminated, and established is illustrated by the following issues with examples:[76]

- **The formal presentation of a demonstration (proof) has not lead automatically to consensus.** Formal presentation in print and at several different professional meetings of the extraordinarily simple proof in this paper have not lead automatically to consensus about the theorem that "Mathematics is Consistent". New results can sound crazy to those steeped in conventional thinking. Paradigm shifts often happen because conventional thought is making assumptions taken as dogma. As computer science continues to advance, such assumptions can get in the way and have to be discarded.
- **There has been an absence of universally recognized central logical principles**. Disputes over the validity of the Principle of Excluded Middle led to the development of Intuitionistic Logic, which is an alternative to Classical Logic.
- **There are many ways of doing logic.** One view of logic is that it is about *truth*; another view is that it is about *argumentation* (i.e. proofs).[77]
- **Argumentation and propositions have be variously (re-)connected and both have been re-used.** Church's paradox is that assuming theorems of mathematics are computationally enumerable leads to contradiction. In this papers, the paradox is transformed into the fundamental principle that "Mathematics is Open" (*i.e.* it is a theorem of mathematics that the theorems of mathematics are not computationally enumerable) using the argument used in Church's paradox.
- **New technological developments have cast doubts on traditional logical principles.** The pervasive inconsistency of modern large-scale

information systems has cast doubt on classical logical principles, *e.g.*, Excluded Middle.[78]

- **Political actions have been taken against views differing from the Establishment Philosophers.** According to [Kline 1990, p. 32], Hippasus was literally thrown overboard by his fellow Pythagoreans "*...for having produced an element in the universe which denied the...doctrine that all phenomena in the universe can be reduced to whole numbers and their ratios.*" Fearing that he was dying and the influence that Brouwer might have after his death, Hilbert fired[i] Brouwer as an associate editor of *Mathematische Annalen* because of "*incompatibility of our views on fundamental matters*"[79] *e.g.*, Hilbert ridiculed Brouwer for challenging the validity of the Principle of Excluded Middle.

Philosophers celebrated Gödel's results because their jobs depended on adherence to the first-order dogma. Since philosophers couldn't prove anything significant about practical mathematical theories, they cut them down to unrealistic first-order theories where results could be proved (*e.g.* compactness) that did not hold for practical mathematical theories. In the famous words of Upton Sinclair:

"It is difficult to get a man to understand something, when his salary depends on his not understanding it."

Establishment Philosophers have often ridiculed dissenting views and attempted to limit their distribution by political means.[80] Electronic archives and repositories that record precedence of scientific publication in mathematical logic have censored[ii] submissions with proofs such as those in this article.

---

[i] in an unlawful way (Einstein, a member of the editorial board, refused to support Hilbert's action)
[ii] while refusing to provide any justification for the censorship other than administrative fiat

Appendix 3. Classical Natural Deduction
Below are schemas for nested-box-style Natural Deduction[i] for Classical Mathematics:

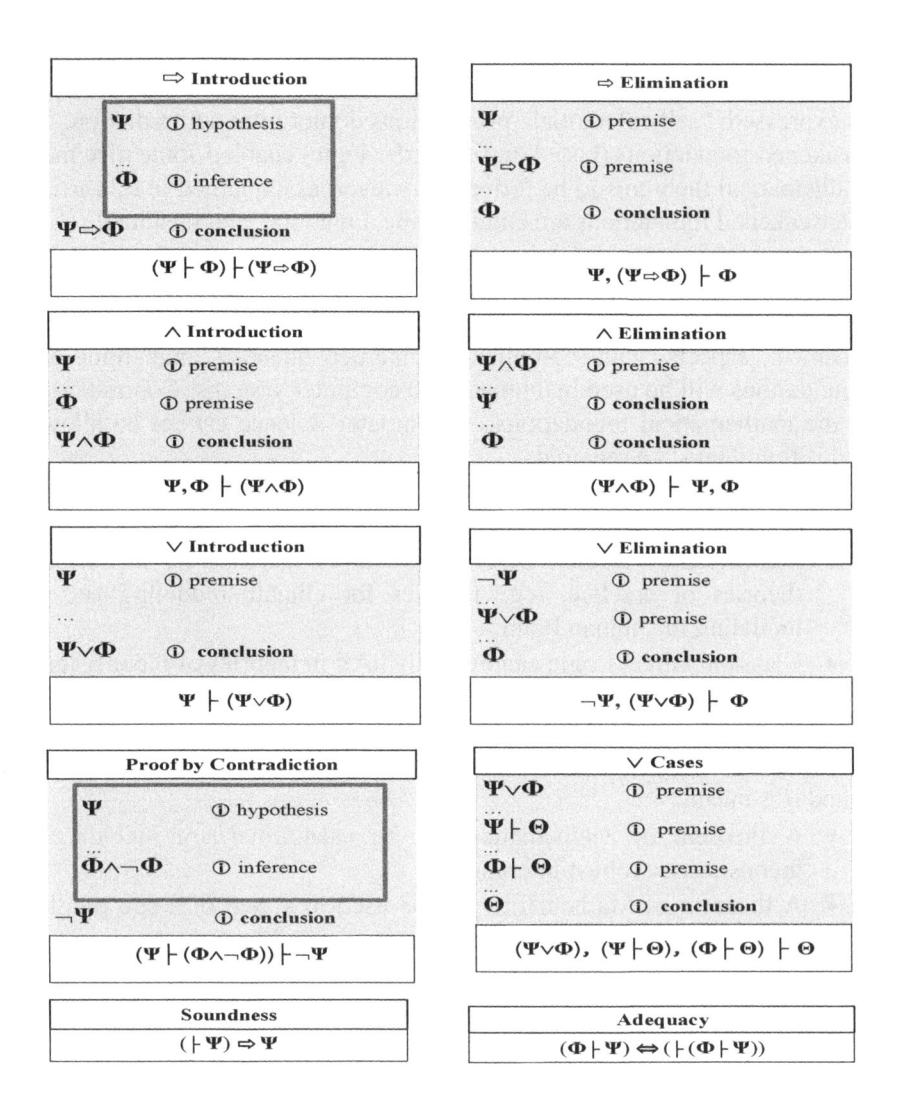

⇒ Introduction	
Ψ	① hypothesis
Φ	① inference
Ψ⇒Φ	① conclusion
$(\Psi \vdash \Phi) \vdash (\Psi \Rightarrow \Phi)$	

⇒ Elimination	
Ψ	① premise
Ψ⇒Φ	① premise
Φ	① conclusion
$\Psi, (\Psi \Rightarrow \Phi) \vdash \Phi$	

∧ Introduction	
Ψ	① premise
Φ	① premise
Ψ∧Φ	① conclusion
$\Psi, \Phi \vdash (\Psi \wedge \Phi)$	

∧ Elimination	
Ψ∧Φ	① premise
Ψ	① conclusion
Φ	① conclusion
$(\Psi \wedge \Phi) \vdash \Psi, \Phi$	

∨ Introduction	
Ψ	① premise
Ψ∨Φ	① conclusion
$\Psi \vdash (\Psi \vee \Phi)$	

∨ Elimination	
¬Ψ	① premise
Ψ∨Φ	① premise
Φ	① conclusion
$\neg\Psi, (\Psi \vee \Phi) \vdash \Phi$	

Proof by Contradiction	
Ψ	① hypothesis
Φ∧¬Φ	① inference
¬Ψ	① conclusion
$(\Psi \vdash (\Phi \wedge \neg\Phi)) \vdash \neg\Psi$	

∨ Cases	
Ψ∨Φ	① premise
Ψ⊢Θ	① premise
Φ⊢Θ	① premise
Θ	① conclusion
$(\Psi \vee \Phi), (\Psi \vdash \Theta), (\Phi \vdash \Theta) \vdash \Theta$	

Soundness
$(\vdash \Psi) \Rightarrow \Psi$

Adequacy
$(\Phi \vdash \Psi) \Leftrightarrow (\vdash (\Phi \vdash \Psi))$

---

[i] Evolved from classical natural deduction [Jaśkowski 1934]. See history in Pelletier [1999].

End Notes

[1] [White 1956, Wilder 1968, Rosental 2008]

[2] There seem to be no practical uses for "self-referential" propositions in the mathematical foundations of Computer Science.

[3] Formal typed syntax had not yet been invented when Gödel and other philosophical logicians weakened the foundations of mathematics so that, as expressed, "self-referential" propositions do not infer contradiction. The weakened foundations (based on first-order logic) enabled some nice meta-mathematical theorems to be proved. However, as explained in this article, the weakened foundations are cumbersome, unnatural, and unsuitable as the mathematical foundation for Computer Science.

[4] Mathematical foundations of Computer Science must be general, rigorous, realistic, and as simple as possible. There are a large number of highly technical aspects with complicated interdependencies and trade-offs. Foundations will be used by humans and computer systems. Contradictions in the mathematical foundations of Computer Science cannot be allowed and if found must be repaired.

Classical mathematics is the subject of this article. In a more general context:

- Inconsistency Robust Direct Logic is for pervasively inconsistent theories of practice, e.g., theories for climate modeling and for modeling the human brain.
- Classical Direct Logic can be freely used in theories of Inconsistency Robust Direct Logic. See [Hewitt 2010] for discussion of Inconsistency Robust Direct Logic. Classical Direct Logic for mathematics used in inconsistency robust theories.

[5] Soundness means:

- A theorem of Mathematics can be used *anywhere* including in inconsistency robust inference
- A theorem of Mathematics can be used in a step of a sub-proof to prove a theorem in Mathematics *regardless* of the assumptions of the sub-proof.

[6] Note that this theorem is very different from the result [Kleene 1938], that mathematics can be extended with a proposition asserting its own consistency.

[7] Many of today's most prominent philosophers and logicians have cast doubt on the correctness of the proof.

[8] The definition of inconsistency, *i.e.,*

Consistent$\Leftrightarrow \neg \exists [\Psi:\text{Proposition}] \rightarrow \vdash (\Psi \wedge \neg \Psi)$ is not about numbers.
Consistent with the general practice in Computer Science, there is no way to identify propositions with integers.

[9] A prominent logician referee of this article suggested that if the proof is accepted then consistency should be made an explicit premise of every theorem of classical mathematics!

[10] As shown above, there is a simple proof in Classical Direct Logic that Mathematics (⊢) is consistent. If Classical Direct Logic has a bug, then there might also be a proof that Mathematics is inconsistent. Of course, if a such a bug is found, then it must be repaired.

Fortunately, Classical Direct Logic is simple in the sense that it has just *one* fundamental axiom:
$$\forall[P:\mathbf{Boolean}^{\mathbb{N}}] \to \text{Inductive}[P] \Rightarrow \forall[i:\mathbb{N}] \to P[i]$$
where $\forall[P:\mathbf{Boolean}^{\mathbb{N}}] \to$
$$\text{Inductive}[P] \Leftrightarrow (P[0] \land \forall[i:\mathbb{N}] \to P[i] \Rightarrow P[i+1])$$
Of course, Classical Direct Logic has machinery in addition the above axiom that could also have bugs.

The Classical Direct Logic proof that Mathematics (⊢) is consistent is very robust. One explanation is that consistency is built in to the very architecture of classical mathematics because it was designed to be consistent. Consequently, it is not absurd that there is a simple proof of the consistency of Mathematics (⊢) that does not use all of the machinery of Classical Direct Logic.

In reaction to paradoxes, philosophers developed the dogma of the necessity of strict separation of "object theories" (theories about basic mathematical entities such as numbers) and "meta theories" (theories about theories). This linguistic separation can be very awkward in Computer Science. Consequently, Direct Logic does not have the separation in order that some propositions can be more "directly" expressed. For example, Direct Logic can use ⊢ ⊢Ψ to express that it is provable that P is provable in Mathematics. It turns out in Classical Direct Logic that ⊢ ⊢Ψ holds if and only if ⊢Ψ holds. By using such expressions, Direct Logic contravenes the philosophical dogma that the proposition ⊢ ⊢Ψ must be expressed using Gödel numbers.

[11] Classical Direct Logic is different from [Willard 2007], which developed sufficiently weak systems that "self-referential" sentences do not exist.

[12] Subsequent further discussion of Wittgenstein's criticism of Gödel's results has unfortunately misunderstood Wittgenstein.

For example, [Berto 2009] granted that proof theoretically if P⇔⊬P, then:
1) ⊢⊬P

However, the above has proof consequences as follows:
2) ⊢P because (⊬P)⇔P in 1) above
3) ⊢⊢P because of 2) above
4) ⊢¬P because (⊢P)⇔¬P in 3) above

Of course, 2) and 4) are a manifest contradiction in mathematics that has been obtained without any additional "'semantic' story" that [Berto 2009] claimed is required for Wittgenstein's argument that contradiction in mathematics "*is what comes of making up such* ["self-referential"] *sentences.*" [Wittgenstein 1956, p. 51e]

[13] specified by axioms [Dedekind 1888, Peano 1889] that characterize them up to a unique isomorphism

[14] Consequently there is no need to introduce a special kind of set called a "class" that was introduced as a patch for set theory by von Neumann.

[15] The *Computational Representation Theorem* [Clinger 1981; Hewitt 2006] characterizes computation for systems which are closed in the sense that they do not receive communications from outside:

> The denotation **Denote**$_s$ of a closed system **S** represents all the possible behaviors of **S** as[15]
>
> **Denote**$_S$ = $\lim\limits_{i \to \infty}$ Progressions$_S^i$
>
> *where* Progressions^i → Progressions^{i+1}
>
> In this way, **S** can be mathematically characterized in terms of all its possible behaviors (including those involving unbounded nondeterminism).

The denotations of the Computational Representation Theorem form the basis of procedurally checking programs against all their possible executions.

[16] e.g. [Shulman 2012, nLab 2014]

[17] [*cf.* Church 1934, Kleene 1936]

[18] Zermelo in a 1931 letter to Gödel pointed out that in the mathematical theory ℕ, there are uncountably many true but unprovable propositions because

- there are uncountably many true propositions in $\{x=x \mid x:\text{Boolean}^ℕ\}$
- theorems of ℕ are countable. Consequently, here is some $x_0:\text{Boolean}^ℕ$ such that ⊨$_ℕ$ $x_0 = x_0$ and ⊬$_ℕ$ $x_0 = x_0$.

[19] Let Sets◁ℕ⊕ℝ▷ be the closed mathematical theory with axioms for ℕ, ℝ and Sets◁ℕ⊕ℝ▷ in this article. Consequently, (⊢_{Sets◁ℕ⊕ℝ▷}Ψ) ⇒ ⊢Ψ. Theorems of Sets◁ℕ⊕ℝ▷ are computational enumerable and it is computationally decidable whether or not a proof is correct in Sets◁ℕ⊕ℝ▷ Of course, both of the following hold:
- ⊬_{Sets◁ℕ⊕ℝ▷}ChurchTuring_{Sets◁ℕ⊕ℝ▷}
- ⊬_{Sets◁ℕ⊕ℝ▷}¬ChurchTuring_{Sets◁ℕ⊕ℝ▷}

[20] Consequently, there can cannot be any escape hatch into an unformalized "meta-theory."

[21] The claim also relied on Gödel's "self-referential" proposition.

[22] Formal syntax was invented long after [Gödel 1931].

[23] emphasis in original

[24] ℕ is the type of Natural Number axiomatized in this article.

[25] type of 2-element list with first element of type σ_1 and with second element of type σ_2

[26] type of term of type σ

[27] *if* t *then* Φ_1 *else* Φ_2

[28] Φ_1, ... and Φ_k infer Ψ_1, ..., and Ψ_n

[29] parameterized mutually recursive definitions of $v_{1\ to\ n}◁\tau_{1\ to\ n}▷$

[30] *if* t_1 *then* t_2 *else* t_3

[31] Because there is no type restriction, fixed points may be freely used to define recursive procedures on expressions.

[32] *if* t *then* s_1 *else* s_1

[33] There is a computable total procedure Proof? such that
∀[p:Proof, s:Sentence] → ⊢^{p}⌊s⌋ ⇔ Proof?.[p, s]=**True**

[34] [Church 1956; Boolos 1975; Corcoran 1973, 1980]. Also, Classical Direct Logic is *not* a univalent homotopy type theory [Awodey, Pelayo, and Warren 2013].

[35] Set◁σ▷ is the type of a set of type σ, Sets◁σ▷ is the type all sets of sets over type σ, and Domain◁σ▷=σ⊕Sets◁σ▷ with the following axioms:

{ }:Set◁σ▷ ⓘ the empty set { } is a set
∀[x:σ]→ {x}:Set◁σ▷ ⓘ a singleton set is a set
∀[s:Sets◁σ▷]→ ∪s:Sets◁σ▷ ⓘ all elements of the subsets of a set is a set
∀[x:σ]→ x∉{ } ⓘ the empty set { } has no elements
∀[s:Set◁σ▷, f:σ^σ] → (Elementwise[f])[s]:Set◁σ▷
  ⓘ the function image of a set is a set
∀[s:Set◁σ▷, p:Boolean^σ] → s↾p:Set◁σ▷
  ⓘ a predicate restriction of a set is a set
∀[s:Set◁σ▷]→ { }⊆s ⓘ { } is a subset of every set

$\forall[s_1,s_2:\text{Set}\triangleleft\sigma\triangleright]\rightarrow s_1=s_2 \Leftrightarrow (\forall[x:\sigma]\rightarrow x\in s_1 \Leftrightarrow x\in s_2)$

$\forall[x,y:\sigma]\rightarrow x\in\{y\} \Leftrightarrow x=y$

$\forall[s_1,s_2:\text{Set}\triangleleft\sigma\triangleright]\rightarrow s_1\subseteq s_2 \Leftrightarrow \forall[x:\sigma]\rightarrow x\in s_1 \Rightarrow x\in s_2$

$\forall[x:\sigma; s_1,s_2:\text{Set}\triangleleft\sigma\triangleright]\rightarrow x\in s_1\cup s_2 \Leftrightarrow (x\in s_1 \vee x\in s_2)$

$\forall[x:\sigma; s1,s2:\text{Set}\triangleleft\sigma\triangleright]\rightarrow x\in s1\cap s2 \Leftrightarrow (x\in s1 \wedge x\in s2)$

$\forall[x:\text{Domain}\triangleleft\sigma\triangleright; s:\text{Sets}\triangleleft\sigma\triangleright]\rightarrow x\in \cup s \Leftrightarrow \exists[s1:\text{Sets}\triangleleft\sigma\triangleright]\rightarrow x\in s1 \wedge s1\in s$

$\forall[y:\sigma; s:\text{Set}\triangleleft\sigma\triangleright, f:\sigma^\sigma]\rightarrow y\in(\text{Elementwise}[f])[s] \Leftrightarrow \exists[x\in s]\rightarrow f[x]=y$

$\forall[y:\sigma; s:\text{Set}\triangleleft\sigma\triangleright, p:\text{Boolean}^\sigma]\rightarrow y\in s\upharpoonright p \Leftrightarrow y\in s \wedge p[y]$

The natural numbers are axiomatised as follows where Successor is the successor function:

- $0:\mathbb{N}$
- $\text{Successor}:\mathbb{N}^\mathbb{N}$
- $\forall[i:\mathbb{N}]\rightarrow \text{Successor}[i]\neq 0$
- $\forall[i,j:\mathbb{N}]\rightarrow \text{Successor}[i]= \text{Successor}[j] \Rightarrow i=j$
- $\forall[P:\text{Boolean}^\mathbb{N}]\rightarrow \text{Inductive}[P]\Rightarrow \forall[i:\mathbb{N}]\rightarrow P[i]$

where $\forall[P:\text{Boolean}^\mathbb{N}]\rightarrow$
$\text{Inductive}[P] \Leftrightarrow P[0] \wedge \forall[i:\mathbb{N}]\rightarrow P[i]\Rightarrow P[\text{Successor}[i]]$

[36] *I.e.,* $\not\exists[s:\text{Sets}\triangleleft\mathbb{N}\triangleright, \sigma:\text{Type}]\rightarrow \forall[x:\sigma]\rightarrow x\in s \Leftrightarrow x:\text{Sets}\triangleleft\mathbb{N}\triangleright$

[37] [Dedekind 1888, Peano 1889]

[38] [Dedekind 1888, Peano 1889]

[39] $\mathbb{N}$ is identified with the type of natural numbers

[40] which can be equivalently expressed as:

$\forall[P:\text{Boolean}^\mathbb{N}]\rightarrow \text{Inductive}[P]\Rightarrow \forall[i:\mathbb{N}]\rightarrow P[i]=\text{True}$
where
$\forall[P:\text{Boolean}^\mathbb{N}]\rightarrow$
$\text{Inductive}[P] \Leftrightarrow (P[0]=\text{True} \wedge \forall[i:]\rightarrow P[i]=\text{True} \Rightarrow P[i+1]=\text{True})$

[41] [Dedekind 1888]

[42] $\mathbb{R}$ is identified with the type of natural numbers

[43] *cf.* [Zermelo 1930].

[44] The Continuum Hypothesis remains an open problem for Direct Logic because its set theory is very powerful. The forcing technique used to prove the independence of the Continuum Hypothesis for first-order set theory [Cohen 1963] does not apply to Direct Logic because of the strong induction axiom [Dedekind 1888, Peano 1889] used in formalizing the natural numbers $\mathbb{N}$.

Of course, trivially,

$(\vDash_{\text{Domain}\triangleleft\mathbb{N}\triangleright}\text{ContinuumHypothesis})\vee(\vDash_{\text{Domain}\triangleleft\mathbb{N}\triangleright}\neg\text{ContinuumHypothesis})$
where $\text{Domain}\triangleleft\sigma\triangleright=\sigma\oplus\text{Sets}\triangleleft\sigma\triangleright$.

[45] [Wittgenstein in 1937 published in Wittgenstein 1956, p. 50e and p. 51e]

[46] [Wang 1997] pg. 197.

[47] In 1666, England's House of Commons introduced a bill against atheism and blasphemy, singling out Hobbes' Leviathan. Oxford university condemned and burnt Leviathan four years after the death of Hobbes in 1679.
[48] There is no subset of $\mathbb{R}$ whose cardinality is strictly between $\mathbb{N}$ and $\mathbb{R}$.
[49] [Cohen 2006] Cohen's proof was a great achievement in spite of the weakness of his theorem.
[50] because the computable real numbers are enumerable.
[51] [Zermelo 1930, van Dalen 1998, Ebbinghaus 2007]
[52] First-order theories fall prey to paradoxes like the Löwenheim–Skolem theorems (*e.g.* any first-order theory of the real numbers has a countable model). First-order theorists have used the weakness of first-order logic to prove results that do not hold in stronger formalisms such as Direct Logic [Cohen 1963, Barwise 1985].
[53] *e.g.* the theory $\mathcal{RealClosedField}$[Tarski 1951]
[54] i.e. in classical notation: $\{\neg P[m] \mid m:\mathbb{N}\}$
[55] unique up to isomorphism via a unique isomorphism
[56] Rejection of the First-Order Thesis resolves the seeming paradox between the formal proof in this article that Mathematics formally proves its own consistency and the formal proof that 'Every "strong enough" formal system that admits a proof of its own consistency is actually inconsistent.' [Paulson 2014]. Although Mathematics is "strong enough," the absence of "self-referential" propositions (constructed using a fixed point on a untyped notation for Mathematics) blocks the proof of inconsistency to which Paulson referred.
[57] Unlike Direct Logic, which is more expressive because propositions are not countable.
[58] As pointed out elsewhere in this paper, in the more powerful system of Direct Logic, Löb's theorem when generalized to all of mathematics turns into a paradox because Direct Logic has the Principle of Integrity that in mathematics: $(\vdash\Phi)\Rightarrow\Phi$, which does not result in the same proof of contradiction because "self-referential" propositions are not allowed in Direct Logic.
[59] If the principle were allowed, then $\mathcal{PL}$ would be inconsistent because every sentence would be provable in $\mathcal{PL}$ by Löb's theorem.
[60] [Tarski and Vaught 1957]
[61] Statement of Church's Paradox
[62] Unfortunately, in formalizing Gödel's proof, [Shankar 1994] and [O'Connor 2005] followed Gödel in using integers to code "self-referential" sentences using fixed points (exploiting an untyped notation for mathematics).

[63] See Historical Appendix. The Liar Paradox [Eubulides of Miletus] is an example of using fixed pointes to derive an inconsistency as follows:
Liar:Proposition ≡[63] Fix[f] // note that this fixed point does *not*
// exist in typed notation of mathematics
where f[Φ:Proposition]:Proposition ≡ ¬Φ
1) Liar ⇔ ¬Liar // fixed point
2) ¬Liar   // proof by contradiction from 1)
3) Liar   // chaining 1) and 2)

[64] In Direct Logic, fixed points on propositions cannot be shown to be propositions and consequently the proofs are not valid for the following reason:
The fixed point operator cannot be defined using Direct Logic:
PropToProp ≡ [Proposition]↦Proposition

Helper$_\blacksquare$[f:PropToProp]:PropToProp ≡
$\qquad\qquad\qquad\qquad$ [x:([?]↦PropToProp)]→ f[x$_\blacksquare$[x]]
Fix$_\blacksquare$[f:([PropToProp]↦PropToProp)]:PropToProp ≡
$\qquad\qquad\qquad\qquad$ (Helper$_\blacksquare$[f])$_\blacksquare$[Helper$_\blacksquare$[f]]

The missing strict type [?] does not exist.

[65] Recently, [Yanofsky 2013 page 328] has expressed concern about Löb's paradox:
we must restrict the fixed-point machine in order to avoid proving false statements [using Löb's argument]. *Such a restriction might seem strange because the proof that the fixed-point machine works seems applicable to all* [functions on sentences in an untyped syntax of sentences]. *But restrict we must.*

Yanofsky solved the above problem posed by Löb's paradox using systems of logic that are so weak that they cannot abstract their own sentences. Unfortunately, such weak systems are inadequate for Computer Science. Instead of weakening, Direct Logic adopted the strategy of barring "self-referential" propositions by using a syntax for sentences that does not allow the fixed-point machinery for sentences.

[66] Note that Length[BerryString]<100

[67] Note that BerrySet is not allowed in Direct Logic because Characterize is not allowed.

[68] Consider the following definition using ε notation of Hilbert:
TrivialCharacterization[k:ℕ] ≡
String["[x:ℕ]→ (ε[y:ℕ]→ y=",
    IntegerToString[k],
    ") =",
    IntegerToString[k]]
Clearly, ∀[k:ℕ]→ Characterize[TrivialCharacterization[k], k].
Consequently, Characterize[TrivialCharacterization[0], 0]
Note that length[TrivialCharacterization[0]]<1000. Thus BerrySet is not empty.

[69] Note that BerryNumber is not defined in Direct Logic because BerrySet is not defined.

[70] using definition of BerryNumber

[71] using definition of Characterize

[72] substituting BerryNumber for x

[73] using definition of BerryString

[74] substitution of BerryString for s

[75] Contradicting step 2.

[76] cf. [Rosental 2008]

[77] According to [Concoran 2001]:
> *"after first-order logic had been isolated and had been assimilated by the logic community, people [e.g. Jon Barwise] emerged who could not accept the idea that first-order logic was not comprehensive. These logicians can be viewed not as conservatives who want to reinstate an outmoded tradition but rather as radicals who want to overthrow an established tradition."*

Types helped establish the foundations of higher-order logic in Computer Science.

[78] for discussion see [Hewitt 2010]

[79] Hilbert letter to Brouwer, October 1928

[80] *e.g.* "*The problem with such papers* [critiquing Establishment doctrine] *is that casual readers will use them to criticize and maybe stop future funding* ..." [Berenji, et. al., 1994]

Inconsistency: Its present impacts and future prospects

John Woods, UBC, Vancouver. john.woods@ubc.ca; www.johnwoods.ca

> "Systems with contradictions do not have the right to be called mathematics and are ignored by researchers."
> N.S. Yanofsky

> "A piece of mathematics carried out in an inconsistent theory need not be vitiated by the inconsistency of the theory: it may be possible to develop the mathematics in a suitable proper subtheory."
> George Boolos

ABSTRACT
The concept of inconsistency robustness was brought to the fore in 2011 by Carl Hewitt, and most of what is known of it to date lies in the technical precincts of his Direct Logic and his still-in-progress Inconsistency Robust Direct Logic.[1] The intuitive idea is set out by Hewitt as follows:
Inconsistency robustness is information system performance in the face of continually pervasive inconsistencies – a shift from the dominant paradigms of *inconsistency denial* and *inconsistency elimination* attempting to sweep them under the rug .... Inconsistency robustness is a both observed dominant phenomenon and a desired feature. It is an observed phenomenon because large information-systems are required to operate in an environment of pervasive inconsistency .... It is a desired feature because we need to improve the performance of large information systems.[2]

There is a long-standing and rapidly growing literature about inconsistency, but nothing in equal measure in the way of consensus on the matters it gives rise to. Hewitt's concept takes to the stage in rivalrous times. It hardly needs saying that its appearance could radiate more heat than light, or anyhow more clutter. But it might equally help to calm things down a bit, or punch through to some unifying clarity. Hewitt's chief interest lies in logics of inconsistency management. This is my interest too. I want to begin the process of determining whether Hewitt's contributions simply enlarge the already ample family of such logics, or achieve some overall advance in the family's well-being. We will need to say something about the present state of inconsistency management, and thereupon to determine the similarities and differences exhibited by the logic of inconsistency robustness, and what it might portend for the times ahead.

---

[1] "Inconsistency robustness in foundations: Mathematics proves its own consistency and other matters", Chapter 1.3 in this volume. For DL see Hewitt, "Formalizing common sense for inconsistency-robust information integration using Direct Logic Reasoning about the Actor Model", Chapter 1.1 in this volume.

[2] From an earlier draft of the IR14 paper, p. 1. The passage occurs almost word for word on the opening page of the same author's "Inconsistency robustness for logic programs", this volume.

I. CLASSICAL ENVIRONMENTS

In the sense that interests a good many logicians and mathematicians, inconsistency is a property of information systems. Information systems play a vital role in the cognitive lives of the human agent, and of such further instantiations of intelligent interaction as may be found here or elsewhere. The human agent bears two significant connections to information systems. In one sense he is their embodiment. In the other, he is their employer in the service of his further cognitive and social ends.

When inconsistencies attach to information systems, effected by the concurrent presence of some formula Φ and its negation, they can be considered as *impacts* on them. They are properties that make things happen. Sometimes the things they make happen happen to the system itself. Call these the *environmental impacts* of inconsistency. Other things it makes happen happen to the users of the information system. Call these the *economic impacts* of inconsistency, its impact on the system's capacity for useful work in the cognitive economy of the system-user. Just as the money economy is a mechanism for the production and distribution of wealth, the cognitive economy is a mechanism for the production and distribution of knowledge.

Inconsistency has a deeply negative impact in classical logic, occasioned by the equivalence of negation- and absolute inconsistency. A system is negation-inconsistent just in case some formula and its negation are both provable. A system is absolutely inconsistent just in case every formula and its negation is provable. There is a simple little proof of this. Let $\ulcorner\Phi$ and $\sim\Phi\urcorner$ be assumed. Then we have Φ by $\wedge$-elimination, and from it $\ulcorner\Phi \vee \Psi\urcorner$ by $\vee$-introduction, thence to $\ulcorner\sim\Phi\urcorner$ by $\wedge$-elimination again on the opening line; and thereupon to arbitrary Ψ from the preceding two lines by disjunctive syllogism.[3] Environmentally, negation-inconsistency wrecks the system in which it occurs, reducing it to a condition of outright noise. Spoilage this widely distributed also disables a system for beneficial use or application. Think here of classical belief revision theories in which belief is assumed to be closed under consequence and adjunction. If a belief system B contains the belief that Φ and also the belief that $\sim\Phi$, then everything whatever follows from anything a believer believes. But this offends the very notion of rational belief. We also have it in classical logic that Ψ is a consequence of Φ iff for every interpretation in which Φ has model Ψ cannot

---

[3] It is said that the originator of the proof was Alexander Nekham in the year 1200 (Alexander Nekham, *De Naturis Rerum*, T. Wright, editor, London: Longman, 1863; pp. 288-289). The later version appears in Lewis and Langford's *Symbolic Logic*, New York: Appleton Century-Croft, 1932; reissued by Dover in 1959; p. 252. For the Nekham reference, see Stephen Read, *Relevant Logic: A Philosophical Examination of Inference*, Oxford: Blackwell, 1988; p. 31.

fail to have one too. Consider a contradictory sentence ⌐Φ ∧ ~Φ⌐. It has no model. So it is not possible that ⌐Φ ∧ ~Φ⌐ has a model and Ψ not. Accordingly Ψ is a consequence of ⌐Φ ∧ ~Φ⌐ for any Ψ. Similar provisions are made for the standard modal and intuitionist logics. The standard classical systems are also *Post-inconsistent*. They contain at least one atomic theorem under sway of the uniform substitutivity of extensional equivalents in all contexts. In classical environments the three inconsistency notions are equivalent.

It is easy to see how an apparently isolated or local inconsistency up-ends its host system. Given its implication of absolute consistency, the damage done by an isolated inconsistency can't be kept local. Its environmental impact is guaranteed to be global. If both Φ and ⌐~Φ⌐ are provable in system S for at least one Φ, both Ψ and ⌐~Ψ⌐ are provable there for all Ψ. Equally, if both Φ and ⌐~Φ⌐ were *true* there, so would everything else be. An S in which everything is provable is an environment in which nothing is provable *as opposed to* not provable. Similarly, an S in which everything is true is a system in which nothing is true *as opposed to* false. Accordingly, we can say that the environmental impact of local inconsistency under these conditions is the transmutation of proof and truth from local properties to global properties. In other words, negation-inconsistency triggers the *globalization effect* for proof and truth.

Of course, provability is more easily globalized than truth. Provability globalizes a system in which an inconsistency is sanctioned by the transformation rules. Truth globalizes it only when the local inconsistency is actually true. But, a sprinkling of dialethists aside, nobody thinks that this condition is ever met. Even so, the globalization of proof is bad news for truth. In globalized systems, theorems aren't truth-tracking.

Sometimes, as the old saying has it, it is possible to have too much of a good thing. Consider the case of sets. In building a theory of sets, a theorist seeks a principled basis on which to discriminate between the things that provable of them and the things that are not provable of them. Mathematicians want from their theories an enlarged knowledge of their subject matters. They want to know more about them post-theoretically than they knew about them pretheoretically. It is a deeply embedded assumption about knowing things that knowledge too is one of those properties that cannot endure the globalization effect. If there were nothing that could be known without its negation also being known, nothing whatever would be worth knowing.[4] Any theory that globalizes proof guarantees its users the discouragement of an epistemically null result. It is an easy point to generalize. Let S be an information system enlisted by users to facilitate

---

[4] In "How robust can inconsistency get?", *IFCoLoG Journal of Logics and Their Applications*, 1 (2014), 177-216, I discuss how successful knowledge-seeking might evade globalization even in environments wrecked by inconsistency.

some intelligently achievable end E. If S globalizes properties such as proof, then it is of no use in the advancement of E. That is, the globalization effect is not only an environmental scourge; it is in equal measure an economic or utility scourge as well.

A goodly and growing number of logicians think that classical logics have got hold of the wrong conception of inconsistency, that the way they've been thinking of it is not the way that inconsistency really is. Most of them also seem to think that these misconceptions about inconsistency flow from misconceptions about the consequence relation. What is needed, they say, is to conceive of inconsistency and consequence in some other way. This raises important questions: Is there a principled way of doing this? Is there a principled way of adjudicating among *rivalrous* reconceptualizations? What would it be to have the (or a) right concept of consequence and inconsistency?

II.   CONCEPTUAL FIELDS

Since Aristotle's launch of systematic logic, the principal focus has been on properties such as consequence and provability. It is perplexing, perhaps, that the one branch of science which has taken itself as that to which all the others are answerable has made such varying and often combatative provision for its own target concepts. One might think that logic's presumed imperiousness could only be undermined by multiplicities so abundant, all the more so in the light of logic's seemingly unbounded proliferation in the past eleven decades. Numbers this large challenge not only logic's imperial pretensions, they challenge the very idea that logicians have a common subject matter. It would be seriously undesirable, if true, that every time a logician tells a different story about logical consequence and the other concepts of interest, he has simply changed the subject. Semantic variabilities of such promiscuity would be a stunning embarrassment. What might we do to avert it?

Perhaps a degree of relief could be got from the Kantian distinction between analysis and synthesis.[5] Analysis, says Kant, is the business of philosophers. It is the business of making concepts clear. Synthesis is the business of mathematicians. It is the business of making clear concepts. The same distinction, without attribution, is advanced by Russell in *Principles of Mathematics*:[6] The "mathematical sense of *definition* is widely different from that current among philosophers" (p. 15) Indeed,

> it is necessary to realize that definition, in mathematics, does not mean, as in philosophy, an analysis of the idea to be defined into constituent ideas. This notion, in any case, is only applicable to [pre-

---

[5] Immanuel Kant, *Logic*, Indianapolis: Bobbs-Merrill, 1974; first published in 1800.
[6] Second edition, London: Allen and Unwin, 1937. First published in 1903.

existing] concepts, whereas in mathematics it is possible to define terms which are not [pre-existing] concepts. (p. 27)[7]

When we attend to actual philosophical and mathematical practice, it is easy to see that the terms of the analysis-synthesis distinction aren't strictly disjoint. They are the termini of a scaled interval, roughly reflected in the following spectrum:

> We can *clarify* a concept; we can *explicate* it; we can *rationally reconstruct* it; or we can even bring it about by *stipulation*.

For clarification, we might cite the ordinary language philosophers of the 1950s and 60s, and some versions of analytic philosophy in the manner of Moore; in which case an analysis of K would be the explicitization of meanings already present in "K". Explication, on the other hand, could be thought of as clarification supplemented by some tidying up, e.g. by some slight degree of counterintuitive smoothing out for the sake of greater generality or to help trim the idea's fuzzy borders. Rational reconstruction would be more aggressive. It would resemble the make-over imposed on old Paris by Baron Haussmann. Think here of Carnap's phenomenalist reduction of physical objects to structures of sense-data. Stipulation is off the radar, what with Riemann's adventurism regarding the mathematics of physical space and Planck's invocation of quanta for the unified constitution of light.

We might say, then, that a concept's clarification is achieved by express exposure of the intuitive meaning of the word that denotes it. This is done by reducing the concept to its simplest conceptual elements. The next two in the foursome are to some extent distortions of intuitive meaning, each intended as a kind of *conceptual improvement*, with explication lying closest to the clarification terminus and rational reconstruction to the stipulation terminus. As we move along this spectrum from left to right we replace intuitive concepts with progressively less intuitive successors, arriving finally at counterintuitiveness, or synthesis – by way, for example, of nominal definition.[8]

Elements of the clarification-stipulation spectrum are eligible for crossover application. In the fullness of time, the original stipulations that constituted the ZF theory of sets would come to be regarded as giving the

---

[7] Moreover, "of the three kinds of definition admitted by Peano – the nominal definition, the definition by postulates and the definition by abstraction – I recognize only the nominal." (p. 112)

[8] I should say here that for most of the non-philosophical logic community, our fourfold nomenclature is not in common used. But there is no doubt that the distinctions it marshalls are discernible in common practice. This would also be a good place to note that the recognizability-unrecognizability distinction *cuts across* the realism-irrealism divide in the philosophy of logic. I will come back to this.

right (or best) analysis of the common mathematical notion of set. We should also note that conceptual adjustments at the more intuitive end of the spectrum are sometimes subject to the leap-frog effect, in which an intended small change brings about a much larger unintended one. For example, as Quine has rightly noted in the case of the connectives, if we tinker with one, we change the whole lot.[9]

We now come upon another of Quine's interesting idea. Writing about the dialethic project in logic – about which more anon – Quine says that admitting true contradictions, renders the notion of negation "unrecognizable."[10] We might say that a concept is at its most recognizable at the clarification (or analysis) terminus of our spectrum, and progressively less so as we move to explication and thence to rational reconstruction, and not at all at the stipulation (or synthesis) terminus. There is little doubt that Quine would have regarded the negation operators of intuitionist and quantum logic as genuinely recognizable negations; but he found dialethic negation to be pure stipulation to no good end.[11]

How do a logician's target concepts find their place in the clarification-stipulation spectrum? Part of it is achieved by explicit definition, but much of it is provided less directly by the system's *operating manual*, that is, by the proof rules that implicitly define its theorems.

For most of its long history, logicians have preferred to work with recognizable concepts. If some logician has a consequence relation in his definitional sights, he is more likely than not to want it to turn out be at least *consequence-like*, once his theory has had its say about it. Call these *conceptually adequate* logics. But since the mathematical turn, logic has also been governed by a further condition of adequacy. A system of logic is now required to be, or be deeply lodged in, a well-built piece of abstract mathematics. Call these *mathematically virtuosic* logics. A great many logicians prefer their logics both ways; but there has been of late a growing fondness for mathematical virtuosity and a waning attachment to conceptual adequacy. There are a number of reasons for this drift from conceptual recognizability, this shift from intuitiveness, but one of them is that sometimes a concept we need for overall theoretical success isn't to be found in established usage, and must be created anew, typically enough with the very tools that are indispensable for a theory's mathematical virtuosity. More generally, how could the drift towards unrecognizability *not* have

---

[9] For a key case of this in relevant logic, see Aron Avron, "Wither relevance?", *Journal of Philosophical Logic*, 21 (1992), 243-281.

[10] Dialethic logics accept as true a select few contradictions. One is the Russell sentence. Another is the Liar sentence which says of itself truly that it is false. For unrecognizability, see Quine, *Philosophy of Logic*, 2nd edition, Cambridge, MA: Harvard University Press, 1986; p. 81. First published in 1970, by Prentice-Hall.

[11] Quine is not in the least hostile to instrumentally useful pure stipulation in science or mathematics, but he draws the line at logic.

happened? Logic is now a branch of mathematics, is it not? And isn't it the business of mathematics to make things up?

Of course, it is the concept of inconsistency that is the central preoccupation of inconsistency-management logics. Here we come upon a rare point of near unanimity. Logicians detest inconsistency; they take it to be their subject's most pathological of properties.[12] In *Paradox and Paraconsistency*,[13] I compared the way in which logicians respond to pathologies with how doctors deal with illness or injury. In medical practice when such an event befalls, *symptoms* present themselves. There follows a *diagnosis*, and then some *triage*, whereupon a *treatment* is proposed and a *prognosis* made. Here too the dividing lines aren't entirely sharp. For one thing, symptoms and diagnoses often co-occur. But the general idea is clear enough. The medical analogy is also useful for inconsistency-management logics. Φ and $\ulcorner\sim\Phi\urcorner$ present themselves (symptom); this is negation-inconsistency rather than the ambiguated appearance of it (diagnosis); a triage is performed: How bad is it? (The standard answer is very). Then the treatment: What's to be done about it? (Get rid of it; control it; ignore it; give-up); and finally prognosis: What are the prospects for satisfactory recovery? (It depends on the mode of treatment). In large part, the attractiveness of inconsistency-robustness lies in the originality of Hewitt's responses to the triage and treatment components of this sequence.

The triage component of the present protocols lies open to what in *Paradox and Paraconsistency* I've called – somewhat tongue in cheek – Philosophy's Most Difficult Problem. Consider the class of valid arguments whose premisses strike us as true and whose conclusions strike us as shocking, even absurd. This leaves us with two options, provided we retain the assumption of validity. One is to treat the argument as a *reductio* of its premisses or the rules used on them. The other is to regard the argument as a sound demonstration of an overlooked and deeply counterintuitive truth. The problem is that there seems not to be any disciplined general method for determining which is which. One might think that when the conclusion is an inconsistency, the verdict is easy: it has to be a *reductio*. But there are inconsistency-tolerating logics in which not even *that* is the case. See section VIII below. Also of interest here is Imre Lakatos' notion of monster-barring: "But why accept the counterexample? ....Why should the theorem give way

---

[12] This idea of logical pathologies is to be found in a well-known remark of Wittgenstein: "A contradiction is not a germ which shows a general illness." See Cora Diamond, editor, *Wittgenstein's Lectures in the Foundations of Mathematics, Cambridge, 1939*. Hassocks, UK: Harvester Press, 1976; p. 2. Note that, Wittgenstein here dissents from the dominant view. In *Philosophical Remarks* he writes: "Indeed, even at this stage, I predict a time when there will be mathematical investigations of calculi containing contradictions, and people will actually be proud of having emancipated themselves from consistency."

[13] Cambridge: University of Cambridge Press, 203; pp. 6-16.

...? It is the 'criticism' that should retreat .... It is a monster, a pathological case, not a counter example."[14]

For the sake of brevity, let's call the family of outcomes of these symptoms-prognosis protocols a concept's *treatment space*. A treatment space for a pathological concept can be regarded as a special chapter in its operating manual. We can now characterize *the recognizability space* for K. It is the fusion of the family of placements on the clarification-stipulation spectrum together with the family of its operating manual outcomes, including its treatment options if K is "bad".

It turns out that the recognizability space of a logician's target notions can help to mitigate, if not outright dispose of, the excesses of multiplicity. Two things could be true at once. It could be true that every time a new logic of K arrives on the scene, the subject has been changed. It could also be true – and often *is* true – that even so, the new K is recognizably K-*like* throughout these variations.

What now if K is unrecognizable? Suppose that there is some stateable goal to whose realization a purpose-built K makes a current contribution; or that in the absence of an immediate benefit, the value of a solely made-up K lies in its innovative enlargement of our conceptual inventories, a contribution to thinking big. When these conditions are met and supplemented by K's operating manual, let's say that the K in question lies in K's *invention space*. Here, too, there is a certain fluidity to such determinations. Quine somewhere remarks that today's stipulation might be tomorrow's explication. So it is worth repeating that today's conceptual unrecognizablity might sooner or later achieve recognizability at some later time. A familiar way of effecting such transformations is by keeping the new concept in play, by giving it a continuing presence in the research literatures. Neither should we think that there is no value in having in our intellectual inventories well-made items for which we have yet to find gainful employment. Think again of Riemann's geometry, both then and later.[15]

Let us now say that K's *conceptual field* is the union of its recognizability space and its invention space. This gives us the means to characterize a inconsistency:*conceptual map*. It is a hypothetical locater of a concept's placement in its conceptual space. If it has a recognizable location it will to some positive degree be K-like, as supplemented by provisions of its operating manual (including its treatment manual if pathological). If it lacks a recognizable place in its conceptual space, the map will locate it in its invention space.

---

[14] *Proofs and Refutations*, Cambridge: Cambridge University Press, 1976; p. 14.
[15] Useful work: A standard move is to establish a richly recognizable K-logic as a core sublogic of a newly contrived unrecognizable one. Here we have, to a positive degree no matter how small, recognizability *by association* – that is, furnished by the superlogic relation.

That leaves us to make a policy decision about our K unrecognizable logics, the K-logics which are logics of K-in-name-only. Mine is a somewhat latitudinarian answer: an unrecognizable K lays fair claim to theoretical treatment if it has an occurrence in the K-invention space.

The idea of a property's conceptual space has some useful work to do in the monist-pluralist debate in logical theory. No one doubts the sheer multiplicity of systems that self-identify as logic. Classical monism is the view that all but classic logic are logics in name only. Pluralism is the view that at least some further subsets of this multiplicity are logics in fact as well as in name. On our more generous view, a K-system qualifies as a bona fide logic of K if it is a well-executed piece of mathematics, its conception of K lies within the recognizability space of K-hood, or it advances with serious experimental intent some new idea of it – K in name only – by creative stipulation.

At its termini the clarification-stipulation spectrum incorporates two different conceptions of logic. One is that logic is a *fact-finding* discipline. The other is that logic is a *fact-making* discipline. At these extremes of discovery and invention we might seem to have an approximate fit with the realist-irrealist divide, but also with a bit of a wrinkle. The wrinkle is supplied by what's in between, each in varying degrees amalgams of the real and unreal. The appearance is mistaken. Stipulationism in logic need not be a retreat from reality. It can be an embrace of realities of the theorist's own making. The interior members of the clarification-stipulation spectrum are not amalgams of the real and unreal. They are amalgams of the already-real with the now-made-real.

It is necessary to compare our stipulationism with a more extreme notion of logic conveyed by a literal reading of some celebrated remarks of Carnap:[16]

> The first attempts to cast the ship of logic off from the *terra firma* of the classical forms were certainly bold ones, considered from the historical point of view. But they were hampered by the striving after 'correctness'. Now, however, that impediment has been overcome, and before us lies the boundless ocean of unlimited possibilities.

Carnap goes on to declare the

> *Principle of Tolerance: It is not our business to set up prohibitions, but to arrive at conclusions. In logic, there are no morals.* Everyone is at liberty to build his own logic, i.e. his own form of language, as

---

[16] *The Logical Syntax of Language*, London: Routledge & Kegan Paul, 1937. First published in German in 1934; p. xv.

he wishes. All that is required of him is that, if he wishes to discuss it, he must state his methods clearly and give syntactical rules instead of philosophical arguments. (§ 17)

On this view, logic is neither fact-finding nor fact-making. In the matter of facts, there are none to be found, and there are none to be made.[17] For the present I will simply assume that it is too silly for words. Further reflections can be found in the appendix on Carnap's nihilism.

Irrespective of one's particular druthers, it is *never* a good idea not to notice whether a logician intends his treatment of the K that interests him to have a place in its recognizability space, or whether he aims for outright conceptual innovation. It is a constant failure of standard practice not to take these considerations into account when framing our own systems and assessing the contributions of others, especially our rivals. It is a pointful omission, causing entirely avoidable confusion. Ideally speaking, a theorist owes his readers the courtesy of a conceptual map. So there are question to put: What is the conceptual field of inconsistency? Does Hewitt's notion of *robust inconsistency* have a home there, or is it a pioneering outlier, charting new denotata for the word "inconsistent" with which to make hay in some presently undefined future? Can we locate it on inconsistency's conceptual map?

Like it or not, the enterprise of logic is underlain by unsettled disagreement about logic's capacity to get at the real truth of things. Realism in logic asserts that logical facts are facts about the world. Quasi-realism asserts that logical facts are system-relative, differentially holding for one system and failing for another. Stipulationism asserts that all logical facts are facts of the logician's creative imagination. Irrealism (nihilism) as we see, asserts that there are not logical facts of any kind whatever. It is not an idle disagreement. It differentially influences how logicians conceive of their work.

Accordingly, as these reflections suggest, there would be value in proposing some procedural rules for the inconsistency-management community. Here are two of them.

> *The opt-out rule*: While inconsistency-management theorists are free to opt out of these recondite *philosophical* entanglements, they are not free to be unaware of them. Where possible, they should declare for one or other of the realist, relativist, stipulationist, nihilist foursome, and get on with things as best they can.

---

[17] Some commentators take the position that there is a gentler way of reading of Carnap's principle is not what he intended by it. See for example Greg Restall, "Carnap's tolerance, meaning, and pluralism", *Journal of Philosophy*, 99 (2002), 426-443.

The re-motivate rule: In the absence of any real-world fact of the matter as to whether negation-inconsistency causes the harm imputed to *ex falso*, it falls to the system builder to *re-motivate* his own system-relative provisions or – as the case may be, his own irrealist stipulations and fictions – when offered as provisions for inconsistency-management.

III. *AMBIGUATION*

This opens the door for consideration of what I call the Reconcilation strategy. In broad terms, Reconciliation mandates that in matters of deep theoretical disagreement, it is advisable to find something for the contending claims to be true *of*, provided of course that they aren't the same things.[18] In the present case, we might conjecture that the equivalence of negation- and absolute inconsistency is true of consequence-having, but not true of consequence-drawing. If this were so, environmental wreckage might turn out to be *compatible* with a system'seconomic utility. This is important. I'll come back to it a bit later.

Reconciliation is a particular form of what in *Paradox and Paraconsistency* I called the *ambiguation strategy*. Informally speaking it provides that if an inconsistency arises from equivocation on a recognizably ambiguous term, then the inconsistency is shown to have been only apparent – a pseudo-inconsistency. It also provides that where an ambiguity is not obviously in play, we should try to find one that might become apparent to us upon further reflection. It is a good idea with a spotty operational history. The trouble is that ambiguities aren't free for the asking. They are available as inconsistency-dissolvers only when independently established. In actual practice invocation considerably outpaces independent establishment.[19]

This also bears on the multiplicity problem. When C.I. Lewis introduced his logic of strict implication, there were five inequivalent and even rivalrous-seeming variations of it. Perhaps there were people who thought that this fivefold multiplicity could be justified by a corresponding fivefold ambiguity of the necessity and possibility modalities, hence of the consequence relation too. But there is no known theory of ambiguity in English in which the ambiguities of the English modals map to the differences among the Lewis systems. Besides, by the late 1960s one of the leading introductory textbooks charted in excess of fifty different systems of normal modal propositional logic. The idea that there awaits a corresponding fifty-fold ambiguity in English is simply laughable. [20]

---

[18] *Paradox and Paraconsistency*, pp. 80-90, 151-154.
[19] For more of this, see "How robust can inconsistency get?".
[20] G.E. Hughes and M. J. Cresswell, *An Introduction to Modal Logic*, London: Methuen, 1968.

Recall that "treatment" here is an abbreviation for the symptoms-diagnosis-triage-treatment-prognosis spectrum. In classical environments the symptom is the provability of some sentences Φ, $\ulcorner\sim\Phi\urcorner$. The diagnosis is negation-inconsistency rather than, say pseudo-consistency by way of ambiguity. Triage judges it to be globally destructive. Treatment will be described in the section to follow, and prognosis too. As we'll soon see, there are two main ways in which the calamity of globalization are dealt with in classical environments. One is by *containment*. The other is by *abandonment* Underlying these options is a question of central importance for the foundations of logic: Is the globalization of inconsistency an objective fact about negation and consequence, or is it a peculiarity solely of classical and like-minded formalisms? In other words, does inconsistency's globalization have a metaphysical footprint or is its turbulence an expression of how negation and consequence are *talked about* or *represented* in classical formalisms? Is it anything more than a representational glitch?

IV. DAMAGE-CONTROL

Classical environments lack all defences against unambiguous negation-inconsistency. They simply collapse and go out of business. They do so without prospect of finding buyers, even at fire-sale prices. In an epigraph to this paper, Noson Yanofsky says that inconsistent systems "have no right to be called mathematics, and are ignored by researchers". This is certainly a widely held view, even if not one that is much reflected upon. More's the pity. It is not always true. What *is* true is that among logicians the dominant position is that negation-inconsistency triggers the globalization effect, both environmentally and economically. It is not hard to see why. In these research communities there is a strong preference for classicality. It is a preference that bears significantly on standard practice when an inconsistency crops up. One favoured option is to snip it out and get back to business, as Hao Wang did with Quine's *Mathematical Logic*.[21] Another is to drop it like a hot potato and move on to something else, as

---

[21] New York: Norton, 1940. Emended second printing by Harvard University Press in 1947, and a revised edition of it in 1951. Wang writes: "Shortly after the appearance of the book, Rosser derived the Burali-Forti paradox from its axioms .... In 1947 I managed to use even weaker axioms and develop much more mathematics that [Quine's] *ML* .... In 1949 I discovered that there is a natural alternative to the troublesome axiom (scheme) ** 200 and proposed the alternative system ML. I also gave with my proposal a proof that ML is consistent if NF is ...." (Hao Wang, "Quine's logical ideas in historical perspective", in Lewis Edwin Hahn and Paul Arthur Schilpp, editors, *The Philosophy of W.V. Quine,* expanded edition, pages 623-648, Chicago and La Salle: Open Court, 1998. First edition 1986). Note the difference between the italicized "*ML*" and the unitalicized "ML".

Russell supposed himself to be doing with classes.[22] The choice of which option to exercise in those cases seems to have been regulated by something resembling what Quine called the "maxim of minimum mutilation".[23] It bids the theorist to opt for repairs that do least damage to the system in question, or to try something new only if the renovation costs are too excessive. It appears that Wang's mending of *Mathematical Logic* comports with Quine's maxim and that – by Russell's lights – a like repair of intuitive set theory transgresses it.[24]

Corresponding to these two options – to repair or to start all over – are two dominant conceptions of best practice in negation-inconsistency environments. Corresponding to the repair option, best practice is often said to require inconsistency *expulsion*.[25] Corresponding to the start-over option is inconsistency *preclusion*; that is, denial in the sense of "denied entry".[26]

A third preference is for the already mentioned *containment*, a measure by which negation-inconsistency is admitted, and yet the globalization effect is not. This is done by invalidating the *ex falso quodlibet* law in which the unwanted equivalence of negation- and absolute inconsistency is grounded.[27]

V. EXPULSION AND PRECLUSION

Expulsion works for the removal of the inconsistencies of slip-up.[28] It also works in contexts of factual error, as when what someone believes happened is inconsistent with what happened in fact, or when new information displaces old. Inconsistencies of this sort are entirely common in human life and, by a wide margin, the most frequent and numerous. Remedies for their sensible management are discussed in *Paradox and*

---

[22] Bertrand Russell, "Mathematical logic as based on a theory of types", in Jean Heijenoort, editor, *From Frege to Gödel*, pages 152-182, Cambridge, MA: Harvard University Press, 1967. First published in 1908.
[23] Quine, *Philosophy of Logic*, chapter 6.
[24] We should note here that Russell's idea that the thesis of set was beyond analytic repair wasn't then, and still less now, the dominant view. Ask a set theorist of the present day whether ZF's treatment of sets places them in the conceptual field of sets, the answer would be firmly in the affirmative.
[25] Or what Hewitt calls elimination.
[26] This is not what Hewitt means by it. Hewitt's inconsistency denial is denial not of inconsistency's admittance (preclusion) but rather of the supposition that what's arrived really is inconsistent after all. See the above discussion of the ambiguation strategy.
[27] Some authors prefer the more literal "*ex contradictione quodlibet*". Either way it asserts that a (logical) falsehood entails an unbridled *potpourri* of consequences.
[28] Think here of Emerson's couplet in which a foolish consistency is the hobgoblin of minds/adored by little statesmen, and philosophers and divines". Ralph Waldo Emerson, "Self-reliance", in *Essays*, London: Aldine Press, 1969; p. 37.

Paraconsistency and Gabbay's and my *Agenda Relevance*,[29] which latter postulates a pair of expulsion and preclusion devices, called in the first instance Putter of Things Right, and Seer of Trouble Coming in the second.[30] These are hypothetical mechanisms for inconsistency-management, favoured by the empirical record rather more in the first instance than the second. But neither is without some degree of factual backing. Putter of Things Right is able to respond to at least some negation-inconsistencies as they arise. In belief-theoretic environments this is effected by *erasure* of items from the pre-arrival belief-set so as to restore consistency to the new one.[31] Counting in favour of the Putter of Things Right assumption is that it mimics the fact that in the general case it is more economical for the human reasoner to correct mistakes after commission than to pay the costs of avoiding them in the first place. Counting against is that it leaves unexplained how the processes of consistency-stabilization actually work, given that even truth functional inconsistency checks are intractable for our resource-bound species.[32]

Inconsistency-preclusion is faced with the same intractability problem, as well as one other. It is imagined that Seer of Trouble Coming is able to read incoming information before it codes up to belief and to make the appropriate belief-set adjustments in that extremely small interval. For this not only is inconsistency-checking required, but some account needs giving of the device's ability to spot inconsistency-making information prior to its entering the agent's belief-space.

A belief-set that is cleansed of inconsistency is usually taken as a new and improved renovation of it, kitted out for an even sunnier future of cognitive engagement. A system that ducks an incoming inconsistency by prior readjustment of its own interior is likewise remains in good working order for these same cognitive engagements. We could say that, whether

---

[29] Amsterdam: North-Holland, 2003.

[30] pp. 136-139, 150-153, 256, 272, 291, 361

[31] For more on the dynamics of erasure, see Dov M. Gabbay, Odinaldo Roderigues and John Woods, "Belief contraction, anti-formulae and resource overdraft: Part I Deletion in resource bound logics", *Logic Journal of IGPL,* 10 (2002), 601-652, and "Belief contraction, anti-formulae and resource overdraft: Part II", in Shahid Rahman, J.M. Torres, Jean Paul van Bendegem and Dov M. Gabbay, editors, *Logic, Epistemology and the Unity of Science*, pages 291-326, Dordrecht: Kluwer, 2004.

[32] The consistency problem, as it is called in complexity theory, has a positive theoretical solution. It is solvable in polynomial time by a nondeterministic Turing machine. It is also solvable for decidable logics by a deterministic computer in exponential time. But it is human-computable impossible. See Stephen A. Cook, "The complexity of theorem-proving procedures", in Proceedings of the 3rd Annual ACM *Symposium on Theory of Computing,* pages 151-158, New York: Association for computing Machinery, 1971, and Petr Hájek, *Metamathematics of Fuzzy Logic*, Dordrecht: Kluwer, 1998.

expelled or averted, the absence of such inconsistencies is uniformly beneficial to the environments at hand.

VI. SELF-CANCELLATION

We come now to a special case of preclusion. Some theorists take, or at least entertain, the view that contradictions are harmless. In *Remarks on the Foundations of Mathematics*, Wittgenstein opines that a contradiction "is of no use; it is just a useless language game."[33] On the other hand, he cautions us not to think that "a contradiction *must* be senseless: that is to say, if e.g. we use the signs "p" "~" "." e.g. consistently, then "p . ~p" cannot say anything." (p. 171) So who knows?[34] Boethius was of the view that the reason a statement cannot entail its own negation is that the negation of a statement "entirely expels and extinguishes it."[35] Boethius appears to be working within some standard assumptions about truth values. They are mutually exclusive and jointly exhaustive, and there are only two of them. Accordingly, for any Φ we have it that if it is true it is not false, and if it is false it is not true. Consider now the contradictory conjunction $\ulcorner \Phi \wedge \sim\Phi \urcorner$. Under standard assumptions for "~", it emerges that the conjuncts Φ and $\ulcorner \sim\Phi \urcorner$ are both true and false. But given the other assumptions currently in play, that is impossible. No statement Φ can be true and false. Since this is precisely what we have if Φ and $\ulcorner \sim\Phi \urcorner$ are the conjuncts of $\ulcorner \Phi \wedge \sim\Phi \urcorner$, they are in those occurrences sentences without truth values; and the same therefore holds for $\ulcorner \Phi \wedge \sim\Phi \urcorner$ itself.

If we add to this the common view that the meaning of Φ and $\ulcorner \sim\Phi \urcorner$ is truth conditional, it would appear that, when adjoined, Φ and $\ulcorner \sim\Phi \urcorner$ evacuate each other of meaning. If so, in those contexts, what Φ and $\ulcorner \sim\Phi \urcorner$ also do is evacuate *themselves* of meaning. Extinction here is semantic self-extinction. It would not be implausible to suppose that something very like these "Boethian" considerations are the prime motivation of the non-adjunctive logics of our day.[36] The basic idea behind the non-adjunctive

---

[33] Oxford: Blackwell, 1964; p. 86.

[34] See John Woods, "The contradiction-exterminator", *Analysis,* (1965), 49-53.

[35] See L.M. de Rijk, editor, *Petrus Abealardus: Dialectica*, Assen: van Gorcum, 1970, p. 290, and John Woods, "Dialectical considerations on the logic of contradiction I", *Logic Journal of the IGPL*, 13 (2005), 231-260.

[36] In "Propositional calculus for contradictory deductive systems", *Studia Logica,* 24 (1969) 143-157, first published in Polish in 1948, Jaśkowski writes that "the first task is to find a system ... which: 1) when applied to the contradictory system would not always entail their overcompleteness, 2) would be rich enough for practical inference, 3) would have an intuitive justification ..., condition 3) being rather difficult to appraise objectively." See also Nicholas Rescher and Ruth Manor, "On inference from inconsistent premises", *Theory and Decision,* I (1970-

approach is to forbid the joint employment of Φ and ⌜~Φ⌝ in premiss-conclusion contexts, either as the conjuncts of ⌜Φ ∧ ~Φ⌝ or as separate premisses. This is a form of the premissory inertia solution. Consider again a belief-system B in which for some Φ, Φ and ⌜~Φ⌝ occur either separately or as conjuncts of a logically false conjunction. Then neither they nor it have (or can be assigned) premissory roles in any given of B's belief-revision operation. If we have it that when jointly used Φ and ⌜~Φ⌝ are meaningless, their premissory inertia is simply a matter of course. Indeed, if it is what Boethius intends as the subject of ⌜~Φ⌝'s extinction is by Φ itself, the proof also collapses in strictly proof-theoretic contexts. If Φ doesn't occur there, there, neither does ⌜~Φ⌝.

Cancellation also raises doubts about proof by contradiction, indeed about the generality of *reductio* proofs. If Σ is a data-set that entails Φ and ⌜~Φ⌝ separately in a given entailment chain, they cancel one another out in that context; and if in the spirit of Boethius they are meaningless there, the proof is spoiled.

It would be difficult to make the case that self-cancellation is a property of any serious member of inconsistency's recognizability-space. Less clear, but not by much, is whether it belongs in the category of stipulative conceptual innovation. A fairer assessment is that it belongs in neither camp, and is simply blunder, a putatively self-cancelling concept of inconsistency that does no one any good. It is true that if allowed to stand, in consistency does no harm, whether environmentally or economically. But it is a salvation achieved *in extremis*, by virtue of the fact that there is nothing that it is. This is hollow innocence, and then some.

VII. HOSTILE CONTAINMENT

Lewis and Langford issued to their critics a straightforward challenge: If you think that the *ex falso* proof is defective, at what place does it go wrong, and why? When it comes to negation-inconsistency there are two types of management sensibility. One is hostile and the other is guardedly and very selectively tolerant. By far the still dominant position among logicians is that hostility is precisely what inconsistency has coming to it. Expulsion tolerates it only as long as it takes to get rid of it; preclusion won't let it in the first place; and self-cancellation refuses to acknowledge its very existence. In the modern era we see stirrings of tolerance – or at least the occasion of it – in the efforts by relevant logicians to discredit the equation of entailment, which they say doesn't obey *ex falso,* with Lewis' relation of strict implication (which does). If successful, the platform it provides for tolerance is that isolated negation-inconsistencies are now

---

71), 179-217, and Nicholas Rescher and Robert Brandom, *The Logic of Inconsistency*, Oxford: Blackwell, 1980.

released from their destructive attachment to absolute inconsistency. If true, it is a significant liberation, in which an occasional negation-inconsistency or so is spared the ignominy of system-wide environmental and economic spoilage.

From the late 1950s well into the 1980s the relevant logicians of Yale, Pittsburgh and Canberra[37] were moved to resist *ex falso* because the strictist definitions of entailment allowed for its satisfaction by pairs of irrelevant relata. This was a wholly general dissatisfaction with classical treatments of consequence; *ex falso* was merely an especially egregious example of what riled them. What was required, they supposed, was the imposition on the entailment relation of a relevance condition between inputs and outputs, and their expectation was that this would suffice to disarm the Lewis-Langford proof. It wasn't, and doesn't. No step of the proof gives offence to the relevance constraints either intuitively, or as actually formulated by their promoters. There followed a series of independent efforts to bring the proof down, none of which − I say − has amounted to anything plausible or (pardon me) relevant.[38]

A system of logic that excludes *ex falso* is said to be *paraconsistent*.[39] Paraconsistency is now a flourishing province of logic, graced with an abundance that defies easy summarization. In the space available here, I'll have to limit myself to a sketch of broad strokes. A dominant theme cutting across most subdivisions of the paraconsistency family is that a system's negation-inconsistency is not a welcome visitor, that we have in the fact that entailment is not subject to *ex falso* the good fortune of not having to pay for a local inconsistency with wholesale inconsistency across the system. What is needed, therefore, is an apparatus that regulates the system's deductive flow in ways that keep the harm done by its negation-inconsistency strictly local. Even so, negation-inconsistency is a bad thing in these logics. It may be a disease but not a plague.

The paraconsistent literature is vast. The entry by Graham Priest, Koji Tanaka and Zach Weber in the *Stanford Encylopedia of Philosophy*[40] reviews developments in AI, automated reasoning, belief revision, formal semantics, set theory, Gödel's theorem, vagueness, discussive logic, non-adjunctive logics, including preservationism, adaptive logics, logics of formal inconsistency, many valued logics and relevant logics. I lack the

---

[37] Alan Ross Anderson and Nuel Belnap, Jr., *Entailment: The Logic of Relevance and Necessity,* volume 1, Princeton: Princeton University Press, 1975. ; volume 2, 1992. See also Richard Routley, Val Plumwood, Robert K. Meyer and Ross T. Brady, *Relevant Logics and Their Rivals*, Atascadero, CA: Ridgeview, 1982.

[38] For amplification, see *Paradox and Paraconsistency*, pp. 59-68.

[39] The term "paraconsistent" was introduced by Miró Quesda at the Third Latin American Conference on Mathematical Logic in 1976.

[40] First published in 1996, and substantially revised in 2013.

space for even a comprehensive sketch.[41] The SEP entry is a good place to start. A bit more detail can be found in an appendix to this paper.

Paraconsistent logics circulate around an interesting set of inconsistency-management strategies. Some, such as relevant logics, imposed a relevance constraint on the consequence relation, providing that consequence is a subrelation of strict implication just when the relation's inputs and outputs share an atomic element. Other approaches emphasize the importance of reining in entailment's admissible inputs, hence are constraints on premiss-eligibility. Still others restrict the application of classical rules. Usually they do both. *Preservationist logics* define the consequence relation over maximal consistent subsets of a possibly inconsistent set of premisses. *Discussive* and the other *non-adjunctive* logics, withhold the classical adjunction rule, hence can be taken as a kind of premissory-inertia manoeuvre. *Adaptive logics* likewise withhold the classical rules arising from contextual "abnormalities" – for example, the provability of $^{\neg}\Phi \wedge \sim\Phi^{\neg}$. All these approaches, including the several more we have no space for here, strive to keep their logics as consistent as possible. Inconsistency is not welcomed here. Provided that the globalization effect is not triggered, inconsistency is allowed only on the sufferance of tight constraints. A yet further device, and one of the earlier ones, was put into play by Newton da Costa.[42] This involves coding up the metalinguistic predicates "consistent" and "inconsistent" as admissible predicates of the

---

[41] Good additional sources are, in chronological order, Graham Priest, Richard Routley and Jean Norman, editors, *Paraconsistent Logic: Essays on the Inconsistent,* Munich: Philosophia Verlag, 1989; Philippe Besnard and Anthony Hunter, editors, *Handbook of Defeasible Reasoning and Uncertainty Management Systems,* volume 2, *Reasoning with Actual and Potential Contradictions,* Dordrecht: Kluwer, 1998; Priest, "Paraconsistent logic" in Dov M. Gabbay and Franz Guenthner, editors, *Handbook of Philosophicl Logic,* 2nd edition, pages 289-393, Dordrecht: Kluwer, 2002; Bryson Brown, "On paraconsistency", in Dale Jacquette, editor, *A companion to Philosophical Logic,* pages 628-650, Oxford: Blackwell, 2002; Diderik Batens, Chris Mortenson, Graham Priest and Jean Paul van Bendegem, editors, *Frontiers of Paraconsistent Logic,* Baldock: Research Studies Press, 2002; Jean-Yves Béziau, Walter Carnielli and Dov M. Gabbay, editors, *Handbook of Paraconsistency,* London: College Publications, 2007; Graham Priest, "Paraconsistency and dialetheism", in Dov M. Gabbay and John Woods, editors, *Handbook of the History of Logic,* volume 8, pages 129-204, Amsterdam: North-Holland, 2007; and Peter Schotch, Bryson Brown and Raymond Jennings, editors, *On Preserving: Essays on Preservationism and Paraconsistent Logic,* Toronto: University of Toronto Press, 2009.

[42] A classical paper is "On the theory of inconsistent formal systems", *Notre Dame Journal of Formal Logic,* 15 (1974), 497-510. See also Walter Carnielli, Marcelo E. Coniglio and João Marcos, "Logics of formal inconsistency", in Dov M. Gabbay and Franz Guenthner, editors *Handbook of Philosophical Logic,* volume 14, 2nd edition, pages 15-107, Berlin: Springer, 2007.

system's object language. Thus the globalization effect is averted by strengthening the system's vocabulary and making the collateral adjustments it occasions.

VIII. (SOMEWHAT) WELCOMING HOSTILE CONTAINMENT

Dialethic logic[43] is a distinctive form of paraconsistent logic, made so by its recognition of some select few genuinely true, hence welcome, contradictions. It offers a patch of relief in the otherwise hostile containment environments of paraconsistency. As paraconsistent, it has a stake in disarming *ex falso*. As dialethic, it offers a quite particular way of doing it. One of its targets is the Lewis-Langford proof. Efforts to topple the proof have had a flourishing career in question-begging, equivocation and stand-off. But now we have something different to consider.

The high point of dialethic logics is their claim that some contradictions are true, e.g. the Russell and the Liar sentences. They are, moreover, quite respectably true. They are true without offence to the Law of Noncontradiction, and they are true in a way that does indeed bring Lewis-Langford down as it applies to them. There are many paraconsistent environments in which truth values conform to the classical arrangements. There are just two of them, T and F, they are governed by Bivalence and Excluded Middle, and they are mutually exclusive. In dialethic environments Bivalence gives way to Trivalence: in addition to T and F we also have the third value {T, F}, whose members are the classical values of yore. {T, F} is reserved for the likes of the Russell and the Liar. They are both contradictions and yet true; but they are neither true as opposed to false nor

---

[43] One of the foundational paper is Priest's "The logic of paradox", *Journal of Philosophical* Logic 8 (1979), 219-241, which describes the system LP. Another is Richard Routley's contribution that same year: "Dialectical logic, semantics and metamathematics", *Erkenntnis*, 14 (1979) 301-331. In *Paradox and Paraconsistency*, I thought that I was anglicizing a good piece of Greek by spelling it "dialethic" rather than its coiners' "dialetheic". Later I came to think better of it upon reading on page 113 of John Burgess's *Philosophical Logic,* Princeton: Princeton University Press, 2009, that the second "e" of "dialetheia" has no warrant in the grammar of Greek. Now I learn that Burgess may be only half right. I've been instructed by my colleague Michael Griffin as follows: "I don't think 'dialethia' is a Greek compound word in itself, although the component parts are (*dia* = 'straight though, in different directions'; *alētheia* = 'truth), ... The extra 'e' comes from the abstract noun *alētheia*, 'truth' – so that justifies the usage 'dialetheia'. But the adjective *alēthēs* – 'true' – drops it out, so that warrants the usage 'alethic'. I guess in a nutshell, either usage seems right to me, but 'dialethic' is more correct as an adjective from the Greek perspective. (The-*eia*-bit ought to hang in there with abstract nouns, so 'dialetheism' might be fair game.") Personal communication 26 November, 2013. With warm thanks to Griffin, I think I'll stick with my anglicizations!

false as opposed to true. They are true and false together. Dialethism gives the Law of Noncontradiction a novel twist. It precludes a sentence from being both T and F, but it allows for cases in which it is not T and not F but is {T, F}. I'll leave to one side further observations about the historical fidelity of this reading of LNC. Let's move instead to the role played by {T, F} in overturning the Russell sentence "R ∧ ~R", with "R" expressing "The set S of non-selfmembered sets is a member of itself".

    1. R ∧ ~R   fact
    2. R   1, ∧-elim
    3. R ∨ X   2, ∨-into for arbitrary X
    4. ~R   1, ∧-elim
    5. X   3, 4, DS.

The dialethic solution is to make ∧-elimination {T, F}-preserving. Thus "R" at line 2 and "~R" at line 4 have the same truth value and none other. Thus, unlike the Boethian notion of the conjuncts of a contradictory conjunction wiping each other out, the dialethic manoeuvre is not a cancellation move. It is a negation-move that leaves truth values unflipped, and ready occasion of Quine's finding that there is nothing in this that would be recognizable as negation. Which leaves the only remaining option. The dialethic negation is a bespoke innovation, custom-designed for its author's ulterior and openly declared philosophical purposes.[44]

There is little relief accorded the paraconsistent community by the dialethic disarmament of *ex falso*. The trouble is that in inconsistent environments the dialethic option is hardly ever available. The reason is that almost no inconsistency is {T, F}. Even if the {T, F} manoeuvre spikes *ex falso*'s guns against the Russell and Liar inconsistencies, it lays no glove on the multitudes that remain. So dialethists, like all paraconsistentists, must find additional remedies to protect non-dialethic inconsistencies from the damage wrought by *ex falso*.

Before moving on, it would be useful to come back to the point that the dialethic systems allow for the truth of certain contradictions, hence by ordinary negation also their falsity. This is actually not true, if truth requires the truth value T and falsity the value F. What system's such as LP require for a contradiction "R ∧ ~R" to be both true and false is *not* for it to be both T and F, but rather for it not to be T and not to be F but to have instead the third value {T, F} (and none other). There is nothing whatever in the truth of

---

[44] See here Graham Priest, *Beyond the Limits of Thought,* Cambridge: Cambridge University press, 1995.

"$\nu (R \wedge \sim R) = \{T, F\}$" that supports the claim that "$R \wedge \sim R$", is true and also false; still less that it is true, because both true and false.[45]

As we have it now, there are in inconsistency's conceptual space two recognizably generic conceptions of it. One is that inconsistency is concurrent satisfaction of two conflicting truth values T and F. The other is that inconsistency is defined by a truth value in which T and F appear as elements, but the truth value itself confer joint satisfaction on T and F. Accordingly, we find quite different assessments in the requisite treatment space. Two valued inconsistency is pathological. Three valued inconsistency is not. I've already said my piece about self-cancelling inconsistency, at least about the Boethian variety. Self-cancelling inconsistency has no location in inconsistency's invention space, and it lacks a place in its recognizability space, for recognizable interpretations of "$\sim$" and "$\wedge$". There is no inconsistency-recognizable sense in which inconsistency causes itself not to exist. Dialethic inconsistency is a different case. Quine thinks that dialethic inconsistency is made unrecognizable by the unrecognizability of its "$\sim$".[46] For me there is a more basic reason. Dialethic inconsistency is made unrecognizable by the unrecognizability of $\{T, F\}$ as a *truth value*.

But the deeper and more sure-footed thing to say is that dialethic inconsistency is inconsistency in name only.

IX.   ABANDONMENT

We could think of preclusion as a special case of containment. It reflects the wise idea that the best way of handling trouble is not getting into it in the first place. Another limiting case of containment is walking away and starting over again. This is achieved in two steps: (1) The trouble-plagued site is abandoned and (2) a new and, it is hoped, trouble-free site is constructed under the same name as the old. Stage one is the logician's version of the troubled home-owner walking away from a mortgage he can no longer handle or is no longer interested in servicing.[47] Stage two in turn presents further options. One is to seek refuge in the pluralism afforded by

---

[45] Another quick observation. In dialethic systems, T and F are perfectly respectable (and antithetical) truth values. Lewis and Langford frame their proof for T and F, not T, F, $\{T, F\}$. The fact that the proof doesn't go through for a T-F-$\{T, F\}$ treatment of inconsistency is entirely separate from how it fares for a T-F conception of it.

[46] It is interesting that Quine's complaint dates from 1970, the year of the initial appearance of *Philosophy of Logic*, and nine years before the foundational papers of Priest and Routley. I happen not to know to whom Quine was reacting.

[47] Which in the United States, I am told, is a forfeiture protection from the usual provisions of the law of torts.

inconsistency's conceptual space.[48] Another is to tie your fortunes to system-relativity. A third is to make a place for yourself in the requisite invention space.

Walking away exchanges the risky good of expulsion for the more easily attained option of abandonment. It is easy to see the good of well-managed inconsistency expulsion, but much less easy to see how the expulsion is actually brought off. (As we saw, it has been known for a long time that systematic searches even for truth functional consistency are intractable tasks for beings like us). It is also easy to see the manageability of walking away, but much less so the good that's in it. It leaves the mortgage unpaid, and it invites all the difficulties occasioned by the building of consistency-free new systems.

A great many people think that when it comes to the classical approaches, an inconsistency-plagued system is a train wreck. A great many of that majority think that it is open to them simply to drop classical provisions in favour of those they like better. It is a natural impulse, but unless considerable care is taken, it is not a good idea. The particular culprit is *ex falso*. The walk-away strategy is to leave it to stew in its juices and move on to new places where it has no purchase. We come now to the heart of abandonment. It leaves the abandoned trouble unfixed. If *ex falso* were true, that would be very bad news for everybody. It would blow up the properties of proof and (dialethic) truth. So it matters considerably whether *ex falso is* true, that is, that it makes genuinely valid provision for negation and consequence. (It is to the credit of the earlier relevantists not to have shirked this burden. The younger breed reveal a more abandoning *mien.*) The enormity of the problem is easy to state. If *ex falso* is true, there is no escaping its disastrous impact on *all* the flowery fields for which we have forsaken it. We have in this a third plausible rule for the management of inconsistency.

The *ex falso* rule: Declare a position on *ex falso,* make your case for it, and then proceed accordingly. Abandonment is walking away from unfixed trouble. It calls to mind the old-fashioned advice, "Brush it from your mind, dearie; you'll get lines". It can hardly be said that it is lost on the abandoners that walking away from an unwelcome fact is not the way to make it go away. Left undealt with, a charge of desertion would be a just indictment. It would attract a verdict of guilty if not successfully rebutted. It is beyond belief that the abandonment crowd have no answer to make, never

---

[48] JC Beall and Greg Restall, *Logical Pluralism,* New York: Oxford University Press, 2006. See also my "MacColl's elusive pluralism", in Amirouche Moktefi and Stephen Read, editors, *MacDoll After One Hundred Years* pages 205-233, Paris: Éditions Kímé, 2011, a special number of *Philosophia Scientiae,* 15 (2011); and Ivor Grattan-Guiness, "Was Hugh MacColl a logical pluralist or a logical monist? A case study in the slow emergence of metatheorizing", also in Moktefi and Read, pages 189-203.

mind how seldom they bother to give voice to it. In their fidelity to the ways of abandonment they give implicit answer to the charge of desertion. What might it be? My fear is whatever their variations, that the abandoners' rebuttals all are the further abandonment of realism in logic.

Perhaps the form of non-realism which best suits the walker-away's frame of mind is system-relativity. As concerns facts, relativity is a way of eating your cake without precluding its availability afterwards. It gives license to say two things: One, that there *are* logical facts and, two, they are all without exception *internal* to the systems in which they arise. What we have here is not truth but L-truth, and not proof but L-proof. One understands the temptation. There comes a point when faced with this logical turbulence that some of our brethren feel bound to say, "To L with it all!" Say it if you like, say that logic's facts are in-house-facts and none is an in-the-world fact. We can also say (and rightly) that it is an in-the-world fact that it is an in-house fact that *ex falso* fails and another in-house fact that it succeeds in a different house. But here too these are in-house facts that leave no metaphysical footprints outside.

We should distinguish between walkers-away from unfixed trouble and *shoppers-around* for things that be might be better liked and easier to deal with. Consider a case. A mathematician may think that an intuitionist logic would be the better place in which to axiomatize arithmetic. In exercising this option, there is no need to discredit any of classical theorems. It is far from obvious that a condition on the adequacy of what classical logic says about consequence *et al.* is that it be the right logic for the axiomatic formulation of mathematics, in any or all of its branches. This is the same point made earlier about belief-revision. It is not a condition on the consequence relation that a believer's beliefs be closed under it. Within limits, the would-be axiomatizer is at liberty to shop around as he pleases. But his liberty is not limitless. If, for example, some antecedent logic demonstrates the globalization effect for proof and truth – as opposed to proof-in-L and truth-in-L – the hoped-for provisions for the theory would be pole-axed.

X.   EVEN MORE WELCOMING CONTAINMENT

It is time to say a further word about tolerance. My tolerance is assuredly not Carnap's. Tolerant containment preserves the management arrangements of hostile containment but lightens up on the pathological triage of inconsistency itself. The tolerance it shows is not condescending. Inconsistency is understood in one of two ways. The first contradicts the assumption, common to all hostile containment options, that inconsistency is to some degree or other pathological. This means that inconsistency is not intrinsically harmful. The second sees inconsistency as facilitating cognitively virtuous outcomes. In some way, then, it is a positive good. It would be natural to think that tolerant containment-measures apply to negation-inconsistency only and that they too require the rupture of *ex falso*. For the time being, I'll take this as given. Later on I'll recur very briefly to the possibility that for cognitive coherence in human life not even absolute inconsistency need be regarded as fatal. This sounds absurdly wrong. But let's wait a bit and see, before walking away.

Inconsistency tolerance is aptly summarized by Bertossi *et al.* in a volume of the same name:

> Inconsistency arises in many areas in advanced computing. Examples include: Merging information in advanced computing; Negotiation in multi-agent systems; Understanding natural language dialogues; and Common sense reasoning in robotics. Often inconsistency is unwanted, for example, in the specification for a plan, or in a sensor fusion in robotics. But sometimes the inconsistency is useful, e.g. when lawyers look for inconsistencies in an opponent's case, or in a brainstorming session in research collaboration. Whether inconsistency is unwanted or useful, there is a need to develop tolerance to inconsistency in application technologies such as data bases, knowledge bases, and software systems. To address this, inconsistency tolerance is being built on foundational technologies for representing and reasoning with inconsistent information, and for resolving inconsistent information, and for merging inconsistent information.[49]

It is interesting to compare this with what Russo *et al.* have to say about (detected) inconsistencies:

> The choice of an inconsistency handling strategy depends on the context and the impact it has on other aspects of the development process. Resolving the inconsistency may be as simple as adding or deleting information from a software description. However, it often relies on resolving fundamental conflicts, or taking important design decisions. In such cases, immediate resolution is not the best option, and a number of choices are available:

They list the following:

> *Ignore* - it is sometimes the case that the effort of fixing an inconsistency is too great relative to the (low) risk that the inconsistency will have any adverse consequences. In such cases, developers may choose to ignore the existence of the inconsistency in their descriptions. Good practice dictates that

---

[49] Leopoldo Bertossi, Anthony Hunter and Torsten Schaub, editors, *Inconsistency Tolerance, Lecture Notes in Computer Science 3300: A State-of-the-Art Survey*, Berlin: Springer 2004.

such decisions should be revisited as a project progresses or as a system evolves.

Defer - this may provide developers with more time to elicit further information to facilitate resolution or to render the inconsistency unimportant. In such cases, it is important to flag the parts of the descriptions that are affected, as development will continue while the inconsistency is tolerated.

Circumvent - in some cases, what appears to be an inconsistency according to the consistency rules is not regarded as such by the software developers. This may be because the rule is wrong, or because the inconsistency represents an exception to the rule that had not been captured. In these cases, the inconsistency can be circumvented by modifying the rule, or by disabling it for a specific context.

Ameliorate - it may be more cost-effective to 'improve' a description containing inconsistencies without necessarily resolving them all. This may include adding information to the description that alleviates some adverse effects of an inconsistency and/or resolves other inconsistencies as a side effect. In such cases, amelioration can be a useful inconsistency handling strategy in that it moves the development process in a 'desirable' direction in which inconsistencies and their adverse impact are reduced.[50]

Another significant source of the welcoming features of inconsistent systems are two papers of Gabbay and Hunter from the early 1990s.[51] In the 1991 paper, four themes are sounded.

1. In knowledge bases that model day-to-day human phenomena, inconsistency is a good sign. It is good in the sense that it calls for an improved way in which to model the phenomena.
2. Some data bases are intentionally inconsistent, containing information suitable for different users. In the big computer of Acme Realty International, the value of a client's house could be $500,000

---

[50] Alexandra Russo, Bashar Nusiebeh and Steve Easterbrook, "Making inconsistency respectable in software development", *Journal of Systems and Software*, 56 (2000).

[51] Dov M. Gabbay and Anthony Hunter, "Making inconsistency respectable 1: A logical framework for inconsistency in reasoning", in Ph. Jourand and T. Kelemen, editors, *Fundamentals of Artificial Intelligence Research*, volume 535 of *Lecture Notes in Computer Science*, pages 19-32, Berlin: Springer, 1991, and Gabbay and Hunter, "Making inconsistency respectable part 2: Meta-level handling of inconsistency", in M. Clarke, R. Kruse and S. Seraffin, editors, *Lecture Notes on Computer Science* volume 747, pages 129-136, Berlin: Springer, 1992.

for mortgage-qualification, $450, 000 for property tax purposes, and $575, 000 for market-listing purposes. There need be no fact of the matter about what the value of the house actually is.
3. Since data bases exist in context and are intended for use, it stands to reason that they are often – perhaps routinely – inconsistent. The reason for this is the sharp variations in the system's uses. Of course, we have to manage things with care. (Acme doesn't want to list your house at $450, 000 if its listing-estimate is $575, 000.) Management routines include revision of data, changing the logic of consequence for inconsistent inputs, stalling for time, and so on. It even might not depend on what actually follows from inconsistent inputs.
4. Relatedly, what should not be done is activate purely technical instruments to block the proof of absolute inconsistency such as changing the meaning of negation or weakening *modus ponens* and the like.[52]

This is a striking array of remedies. Remedy (1) allows for the intrinsic awfulness of inconsistency, and reserves its goodness for motivational purposes only. But it is not a trivial provision. As previously mentioned, correcting an inconsistency (by expulsion, say) is often cheaper for the human reasoner than avoiding it in the first place. Remedy (2) implements the ambiguation strategy or relativizes information to categories of use. Thus "house-value" is ambiguous as between mortgage-support value, property-tax value and re-sale value; or a univocal sense of house-value is relativized to the different things that house-value information is wanted for. Remedy (3) raises two suggestions of the first importance.

One is that inconsistency may well be a routine and unavoidable feature of our information systems.

---

[52] Consider, for example, Hewitt's own critique of the logical manipulations of Besnard et al., slightly extended in Hunter's "Reasoning with contradictory information using quasi-classical logic", *Journal of Logic and Computation,* 10 (2000), 677-703. Hewitt thinks that the quasi-theoretical framework is not a proper mathematical logic, hence (in my words) fails to have a place in the conceptual field of that subject. Hewitt dislikes it that the Boolean equivalences are quasi-classically inexpressible, and that standard tautologies are unavailable for use, e.g. $\neg\Phi \Leftrightarrow \Phi^{\neg}$. He objects to quasi-classical systems' incorporation of resolution, since Φ, $\neg\Phi^{\neg}$ classical-resolution prove the False. Most crucially, he says, transitivity fails for inference, and approvingly cites Anderson and Belnap in *Entailment,* volume 1: "Any criteria according to which entailment is not transitive is *ipso facto* wrong" (p. 154). I draw here on Hewitt's "Actor model of computation. Many case inconsistency-robust information-integrating inconsistency robustness", this volume.

The second is that whatever the devices that may recommend themselves to us, it is somehow cheating simply to re-jig logic.

To these I myself would add a third and a fourth.

The third is that the intelligent management of inconsistency may not depend in any deep and general way (or any at all) on what we think *follows* from it. If so, it would not be a matter for the logics of consequence, whether the having of them or the *drawing* of them.[53]

The fourth is that the re-stabilization of belief in the face of incoming information may be achievable entirely independently of the restoration of informational inconsistency (except possibly in some small subsets of it). For empirical support see the section that starts now.

XI. EMPIRICAL CONSIDERATIONS

A central question for belief-management systems is how belief-sets remain stable under the ceaseless informational turbulence to which an open world subjects them. Logicians tend to converge on a deeply dug-in view. It tells us that consistency is essential for doxastic stability. If this were really so, consistency would be more trouble than its worth. Not only is there abundant empirical evidence that the belief-sets of human beings are routinely inconsistent, albeit often without notice, there is no corresponding evidence of doxastic incoherence. If these facts on the ground were anything to go by, high levels of stable doxastic coherence would co-exist with deep and abiding levels of inconsistency. Absent a convincing case against the evidence, this is a co-existence to take serious note of.

Let me cite here some of the earlier evidence, which already convincing in its own right, was the beginning of a veritable flood of like significance. Newton's theory of gravitation was inconsistent with Galileo's law of free fall and also with Kepler's laws. As mentioned earlier, the Newton-Leibniz calculus is inconsistent. Statistical dynamics is inconsistent with the second law. Wave optics is inconsistent with geometrical optics. Bohr's model is inconsistent with Maxwell's equations.

"Ah, yes", I can hear it said, "all these were just temporary setbacks. Consistency has now been restored." To which I reply: It took some 200 years for calculus to get consistent. Did mathematics and mechanics fall apart in the interval?

Imagine a belief-set B at *t* as constituted by what at *t* is perceived, believed, remembered and inferred. There is much too much in long-term memory for anything like exhaustive retrieval. Comprehensively systematic

---

[53] See here my *Errors of Reasoning: Naturalizing the Logic of Inference,* volume 45 of *Studies in Logic,* London: College Publications, 2013; chapters 7 and 8.

inventories are not possible objects of search and rehearsal. Even if we were better at it than we are, the extensive plumbing of our memory stores would take paralytically long, and would derange the business of belief-management, and indeed of life itself. The psychological literature since the early 1970s has recognized that human memory is sectoral – much in the way that governments are compartmentalized by ministerial portfolios – the contents of which are routinely crosswise inconsistent.[54] It has long been held that memory answers to a distinction between occurrent and dormant, and that consistency-preservation in dynamic contexts is limitedly feasible for occurrency, it is hopeless for dormancy.[55]

Roughly speaking, what this amounts to is that locally detected inconsistencies may be open to repair, whereas unnoticed ones languish unfixed until they eventually surface. Bearing on this is a related distinction. Occurrent memory is said to be available for decision and action, while dormant memory lies in waiting, its inconsistencies off-set by the premissory inertia of its conflicting memories. But for this to be so, two things must be true. Either local inconsistency is not global, or its globalization effects do not impair or impede the processes of decision and action, and dormant memory (and background information more generally) have no inferential role in reasoning. The first awaits a definitive answer to the *ex falso* question. The second lies open to challenge by causal theories of reasoning.[56]

Beliefs and memories aren't the only things held to an expectation of consistency in rational life. Desires and preferences are expected to be consistent too. Indeed, "beliefs and desires can hardly be reasons for action unless they are consistent"[57] In much of contemporary social science consistency is demanded for rational preference. The minimal condition on preference is transitivity. But human beings, including the very smart ones, on lots of occasion do their preferring intransitively. In what economists call plans of consumption, preferences are linked to the span of time covered by the plan. What is required to maintain time preference is that the "future must be discounted at a constant ratio", that is, time preferences must be exponential.[58] Also required is a condition of continuity, and another is the condition of completeness. By the first, slight changes should not reverse a

---

[54] A. Klatzley, *Human Memory: Structures and Processes,* San Francisco: W.H. Freeman, 1975.

[55] M. Howe, *Introduction to Human Memory,* New York: Harper & Row, 1970, A. Collins and M. Quillam, "Retrieval time from semantic memory", *Journal of Verbal Learning and Verbal Behavior*, 8, (1969), 240-249, P. Lindsay and D. Norman, *Human Information Processing*, New York: Academic Press, 1977.

[56] See further *Errors of Reasoning.*

[57] Jon Elster, *Sour Grapes: Studies in the Subversion of Rationality*, Cambridge: Cambridge University Press, 1975; p. 4.

[58] *Sour Grapes*, p. 8.

preference; by the second, any rational person, for arbitrary X, and Y, will prefer X to Y or Y to X or will be indifferent to them both. In the conditions of real life, these expectations are pervasively breached.[59]

Since the early 1980s there has been a good deal of turmoil over how bad we are at probabilistic reasoning[60] and in the evolution of risk arising from defects in "the cognitive mechanism." (Elster, p. 26)[61] Amartya Sen picks up the theme:

> Recent empirical studies of behaviour under certainty has [sic] brought out what has appeared to be systematic inconsistencies in the evaluation of risk and alternative decision ... [T]he *prevalence* of such behaviour indicates the case for making room for departures from the usual requirements of "rationality" in understanding actual behaviour."[62]

Sen introduces a necessary complication, and reminds us of the importance of one we've already mentioned. Sen is struck by the massiveness of our defection from the requirements at hand, and is tempted by the idea that the fault lies not with us but with the norms themselves. He is on to something important. The social sciences make free with norms of rationality without saying anything much (or at all) about the source of the norms' normative authority over us.[63] A further question is the extent to which all this irrationality is constituted by negation-inconsistency or is at least underlain by it. If ever there were occasion for a treatment manual for inconsistency, it is here.[64]

There is ample empirical support for the observation that human cognitive practice is pervasively inconsistent. There is ample empirical evidence that human beings are good at belief-stabilization. It can hardly be true that consistency is required for it. So a belief-system's coherent intelligibility and support for intelligent action will have to be accounted for in some other way. Perhaps one of those ways will turn out to be the way in which inconsistency is handled in inconsistency-robust information systems.

---

[59] Howard Raiffa, *Decision Analysis,* Reading, Mass: Addison-Wesley, 1968. p. 75; George Ainslie, "A behavioural economic approach to the defense mechanism: Freud's energy theory revisited", *Social Science Information* 21 (1982), 735-779 and Elster, *Sour Grapes,* p. 9.

[60] The contrary position is advanced in *Errors of Reasoning*, chapter 14.

[61] See also R. Nisbett and L.Ross, *Human Inference: Strategies and Shortcomings of Social Judgement,* Englewood Cliffs, NJ: Prentice Hall, 1980 ... p. 146.

[62] Sen, *On Ethics and Economics*, Oxford: Blackwell, 1987; p. 69. Emphasis in the original.

[63] *Errors of Reasoning*, chapter 2.

[64] Note here that in these branches of social science, norms are postulated not for their empirical fidelity but rather to facilitate mathematical virtuosity. For example, in neoclassical economics utilities are stipulated to be infinitely divisible in order to allow the theory to engage available the fire-power of the calculus.

XII. INCONSISTENCY ROBUSTNESS

We come now to inconsistency robustness. I reported in the Abstract that Inconsistency Robust Direct Logic (IRDL) is an adaptation of Hewitt's Direct Logic (DL). DL is a logic that enables computers to carry out all inferences – including inferences about their own inferential processes – without the necessity of human intervention.[65] So DL has some capacity for self-reference.

Inconsistency robustness didn't suddenly spring into life in 2011.

It has been a continually recurring issue in Logic Programs from the beginning including Church's system developed in the early 1930s based on *partial* functions (defined in the lamda calculus) that he thought would allow development of a general logic without the kind of paradoxes that had plagued earlier efforts by Frege, Russell, *etc*. Unfortunately, Church's system was quickly shown to be inconsistent ....[66]

Indeed,

Inconsistency Robustness requires repairing mathematical foundations in the face of contradictions that have arisen over and over again. In the Inconsistency Robustness paradigm, deriving contradictions are [sic] a progressive development and not "game stoppers".[67]

Again,

Contradictions can be helpful instead of being something swept under the rug by denying their existence, which has been repeatedly attempted by the Establishment (beginning with the Pythagoreans).[68]

Recall that inconsistency robustness is actually a property of information system *performance* in the face of continually pervasive inconsistency, that is, inconsistency that is both chronic and widely-dispersed. By a slight extension, inconsistency-robustness can be ascribed to a system itself just in case its management is inconsistency-robust in Hewitt's sense.

Hewitt emphasizes that inconsistency-robustness is an empirically discernible property and a desirable one, at least in the case of large, practical systems.[69] They are more easily managed with the inconsistencies left in than they do with the inconsistencies expunged or denied entry in the first place. Indeed, "pervasive inconsistency *cannot* be removed from large software systems."[70] I take the empirical discernibility of inconsistency

---

[65] For example, without the further assistance of a software engineer.
[66] Hewitt, "Inconsistency robustness for logic programs", p. 1 of pre-publication text.
[67] Hewitt, "Inconsistency robustness in foundations", idem.
[68] Idem.
[69] A practical software system typically has tens of millions of lines of code. Examples of such are climate models, diagnostic and treatment systems in medicine, and climate change models.
[70] Hewitt to Woods, 31 August 2013. Emphasis added.

robustness to be especially important. It makes it an in-the-world fact that these systems S have the property, not merely an S-fact that they do.

We can say with some confidence that, in his ease with systems in which inconsistency is robust, Hewitt displays no anxiety – indeed it is the opposite – about its economic worth. There is no enthusiasm here for *preclusion* or *expulsion*. However, the global effect question is neither raised nor answered. It is a salient fact about the present understanding of inconsistency robustness is that nowhere in the IR literature is *ex falso* explicitly considered or, indeed, is its Lewis-Langford proof. Like it or not, this makes of Hewitt a kind of walker-away *malgré lui*. Mind you, Hewitt is wholly in sympathy with the fact that mathematics is thought by an overwhelming consensus of working mathematicians to be consistent. He is at one with "the assumption of consistency as deeply embedded in the architecture of classical mathematics."[71] So we may conclude that Hewitt's general view of inconsistency, like virtually everyone else's, is that it is a bad thing mathematically, never mind whether it does or doesn't trigger globalization. But there is no anxiety shown about absolute inconsistency in these writings, and yet a real appreciation of negation-inconsistencies in IR contexts. We may fairly infer that Hewitt's is a *paraconsistent* treatment of inconsistency, certainly in those systems in which their presence is robust; but there is no hint of *dialetheism*.

We needn't think that any of this strains against Hewitt's classical proclivities towards mathematics. But it bears on whatever proclivities he may have towards classical *logic*. Indeed,

> [m]athematical logic cannot always infer *computational* steps because computational systems make use of arbitration for determining which message is processed next by a recipient that is not multiple messages concurrently. Since reception orders are in general indeterminate they cannot be inferred from prior information by mathematical logic alone. Therefore mathematical logic alone cannot in general implement computation. Logic Programs (like Functional Programs) are useful idioms even though they are not universal. For example Logic Programs can provide useful principles and methods for systems which are quasi-commutative and quasi-monotonic even though the systems themselves cannot be implemented using Logic Programs". (Emphasis added)

Beyond a general paraconsistency, we also see in the IR writings intimations of features of *discussive logics* and the Gabbay-Hunter project of enlarging the investigation with respect to each side of the contradiction. This makes Hewitt an *inconsistency-container* but not entirely a hostile one.

---

[71] "Inconsistency robustness in foundations", p. 1 of pre-publication text.

Inconsistencies are contained, not just with the intention of having no more of them than prudence would indicate, but also with an interest in some more or less routine *shopping around* for a logic that will best suit the needs of implementation. One might think that this is also Hewitt's approach to a logic for inconsistency-robustness:

> The above examples are intended to be case studies in Inconsistency Robustness in which information is formalized, contradictions are derived using Inconsistency Robust reasoning, and arguments are formalized for and against contradictory propositions. A challenge for the future is to automate the reasoning involved in these case studies."[72]

Two issues of importance for Hewitt are *ex falso* and even more so proof by contradiction. Proof by contradiction can be expressed as follows: $(\psi \vdash \Phi \wedge \sim\Phi) \Rightarrow \sim\psi$. Although PBC gets into trouble in certain kinds of referential contexts, it is a necessary part of classical mathematics.[73] In Inconsistency Robust Direct Logic, the rule is reformulated accordingly as the Inconsistency Robust Proof by Contradiction Rule: $\vdash((\psi \Rightarrow \Phi \wedge \sim\Phi) \Rightarrow \sim\psi)$. But Hewitt stresses that it is a new rule, not yet thoroughly road-tested, obtained by making the consequence relation extremely strong.

Hewitt also acknowledges that *ex falso* is a necessary part of classical mathematics, "which has stood the test of time since before Euclid."[74] *Ex falso* is also a necessary part of Classical Direct Logic, if it is to be a classical mathematical foundation for computer science. However, to avoid detonation, Inconsistency Robust Direct Logic can't allow *ex falso*.

It is interesting to note the independence of these two principles, notwithstanding the cases in which what you get from the one you can also get from the other. Consider a case. The Russell contradiction is assumed; " $R \in R \wedge R \notin R$" is provable in naïve set theory. Accordingly, so are "$R \in R$" and "$R \notin R$". This gives a contradiction under the classical rule of adjunction. Hence, by the proof by contradiction rule, "$\sim(R \in R \wedge R \notin R)$ is also provable. Even so, we get the same in one step when *ex falso* is applied.

An important feature of Hewitt's approach to inconsistency robustness is motivated by his conviction that, as we have it now, the state of play in present-day work in the foundations of logic, allow for logics in which, under careful constraints, limited self-reference is permitted. This, says Hewitt, gives slack enough for mathematics to prove its own consistency, in contradiction of Gödel's valid proof to the contrary. Suppose, for contradiction, that a duly formalized classical mathematics is able to say

---

[72] Idem.
[73] Private correspondence, Hewitt to Woods, September 2, 2014.
[74] Idem.

that mathematics is inconsistent. Then for some formula Φ of that same system, both it and its negation are provable there. But under the standard adjunction rule this gives the provability of $\ulcorner \Phi \wedge \sim\Phi \urcorner$. Hence, by the proof by contradiction rule, the system is consistent, and the second of Gödel's 1931 theorems is overturned. This is a tricky result. It places Hewitt between Charyblis and Scylla. On the one hand, he doesn't want to grant to formalized mathematics the expressive powers of the Gödel results. On the other hand, he doesn't want the proof by contradiction rule to prove the consistency of inconsistency-robust information systems. Neither does he want to deny to IRDL some analogue of the proof by contradiction rule. So he must either suppress the self-referential capacities of the language of IRDL or retrofit the proof by contradiction rule to forbear against the heavy weather churned up by his proof. Of course, he could do both. These challenges more than suffice to make the logic of inconsistency robustness a work in progress. We should all keep an eye on how things shape up.

IRDL is not one of those pre-built logics sitting on the shelf in hopes of finding some gainful employment. IRDL is a work in progress, and is work with more than one objective in mind. One is to find ways of transforming ineliminably inconsistent large systems into better-working systems, themselves larger, more inconsistent and ineliminably so. Another is to find the means of automating the reasoning underlying these transformations. At the heart of it all is the IRDL operating manual for inconsistency in robust systems and the influence it has on its placement in inconsistency's conceptual field. Since IRDL is a work in progress, parts of the manual are not yet written, and IR's place in inconsistency's conceptual field not as well-marked as it will later turn out to be. The conceptual map for inconsistency is still an evolving instrument; its further refinement now lies with Hewitt. So we will have to wait and see. Meanwhile, as we see, not only is the *ex falso* rule not observed in his writings; the same is true of the opt out and re-motivate rules. In this Hewitt is no standout. Hardly any of today's practitioners observe them either.

What, finally, of our conceptual map for inconsistency? As regards inconsistency, Hewitt's is garden variety negation-inconsistency. As regards its operating manual, Hewitt is in a space all his own. Hewitt's operating manual leaves no room for a chapter on treatment. Among all the going policies for the management of inconsistency, Hewitt is alone if rejecting the standard judgements of triage and treatment, and therefore also the very question of prognosis. The inconsistencies of inconsistency-robust systems aren't pathological. The systems that contain them require no treatments for pathological relief. And there arises no prognostication question of prospects for medical recovery.

XIII. FUTURE PROSPECTS

I said early on that the notion of inconsistency robustness has arrived on the scene in rivalrous times. Never in its long history has logic been so well done and so unsettled – an *embarras de richesse* tempered (tainted) by a rooted indifference to its conflicting provisions for common subject matters, if not the outright refusal to see them so. Although still a work in progress, there is no reason to think that a mature IRDL won't be a wonderfully wrought mathematical structure. It will be mathematical virtuosity on wheels. There are, for me, two things of note that could be true at once. One is that IRDL is an acknowledged technical success. The other is that the very idea of inconsistency robustness will have no intellectual purchase beyond its technical mooring to that nice bit of abstract mathematics that gave it birth. If this latter proved to be so, I for one would regret it.[75] The *idea* of inconsistency robustness is so rich and so full of promise as to deserve a life of its own. But for that to happen there are two conditions that must be met.

(1) We must get off the fence about *ex falso*. We must get it settled whether it states a metaphysical fact, or expresses a metaphysical falsehood.

(2) If after concerted effort, a good-willed settlement of that question proves impossible, we must establish a fall-back or worst-case position on the assumption that, unbeknownst, *ex falso* is actually true.

We must also answer the obvious follow-up question:

(3) Would absolute inconsistency preclude the intelligent and profitable management of systems that have it?

If *ex falso* were true, and if the answer to (3) were in the negative, then a system's negation-inconsistency would carry it to the heights of *hyperinconsistency*-robustness. The system would be more than absolutely and unexpungably inconsistent. It would – large or small, practical or abstractly theoretical – be rationally manageable. It would not be pathological; and that would put out of business the entire sweep of theories for which paraconsistency is the rule of law or for which consistency is a condition of rational performability.

In recent writings I have found myself engaged with such questions. My answer to (1) is that *ex falso* states an in-the-world fact. My response to

---

[75] See again "How robust does inconsistency get?"

(2) is that for humanity to survive and prosper, and occasionally to build great civilizations, it doesn't matter whether *ex falso* is true. Which means that my answer to (3) is solidly in the negative. Details can be had in a talk to the Square of Opposition conference in Vatican City, Pontifical Lateran University, May 4-9, 2014, under the title "How globalization makes inconsistency unrecognizable"; to appear in the Proceedings.

Acknowledgements: In my treatment of it here, the originator of the idea of inconsistency-robustness' has graced my efforts with a shrewd eye and a more than generous helpfulness. I trust that Carl Hewitt will react to my presentiments for future work with the speculativeness that attends their advancement. My thanks also go out to the excellent referees of the Stanford Conference whose comments, both admonitory and encouraging, have been of great help to me. For comments in Rome or in follow up correspondence, I thank Lorenzo Magnani, Jean-Yves Béziau, Rusty Jones, Jonathan Westphal and Daniel Clausén, and several others whose names I lack or have forgotten. Apologies. I acknowledge with many thanks the astute observations of Dov Gabbay and Frank Hong. My entry into the *ex falso* wars dates from the 1960s, with Richard Routley, Bob Meyer and Nuel Belnap my principal co-belligerents, abetted by the forceful efforts of the relevantists Donald Hockney and Kent Wilson. Earlier still, I was introduced to the Lewis-Langford proof by one of its authors, my teacher at Michigan Harold Langford. My first exposure to paraconsistency arose in the early 1970s from occasional visits to Victoria by my Simon Fraser University colleague Ray Jennings, co-founder of preservationism. Further enrichments of the preservationist perspective were provided by Bryson Brown in our days together at Lethbridge from 1986-2002, and following. Carol Woods has been, as in all things in my life, indispensable in the preparation of this text.

APPENDIX ON CARNAP'S NIHILISM

Any more or less competently functioning human being will upon occasion know for a fact that this follows from that, hence know for a fact that the relation of following from is such as to make this so. It might come about one day that a member of the laity would seek further instruction about this familiar relation, in quest of some further details about it that would round out his understanding. Where would he go for such instruction? Where would he go to learn those further facts about the relation of following from that underlay his knowing for a fact that this follows from that? The short and cryptic answer is that he should not turn to the pages of the *Journal of Symbolic Logic*.

This far from showing that Carnap's nihilism has lodged itself unawares or unacknowledged in the (sub)consciousness of the working logicians. But we can only hope that it hasn't. If there were no logical facts, there would be nothing to be known about logic. If there is no fact of the matter about following from then, nothing would follow from anything, not in logic, not in mathematics, not in science, not in everyday premiss-conclusion inference. The non-factuality of following from is globalization on a scale that rivals the scepticism of Gorgias. Still, there is something very puzzling here. If our friend did consult the *JSL*, he wouldn't be told a Carnapian answer – not out loud anyway. But he wouldn't get a *straight* answer. There is nothing remotely like this in real analysis, physics or population genetics. It's all very puzzling. It gets us to thinking that, unlike those mathematicians and scientists, logicians really don't quite know what they're talking about.

APPENDIX ON PARACONSISTENCY

I will briefly sketch the following four ways of being paraconsistent: *discussively, non-adjunctively, preservationistically,* and *adaptively*.

Discussive logics were a pioneering contribution to the modern development of dialogue and dialectical logics. In the approach taken by Jaśkowski, a discussion between two parties is one in which each party advances claims he takes to be true, they are true in his world, so to speak. In a S5 frame M these assertions $\Phi_1, \ldots, \Phi_n$ are represented as $\Diamond\Phi_1, \ldots, \Diamond\Phi n$. Thus the scopes of these sentences might be true in one world and false in another.

Ex falso fails in M. Let Φ hold at w, $\ulcorner\sim\Phi\urcorner$ at a different w', and Ψ at no world for some Ψ. Then both Φ and $\ulcorner\sim\Phi\urcorner$ hold in M, yet Ψ does not. Even so, there is no S5 model where $\ulcorner\Phi \wedge \sim\Phi\urcorner$ holds. This re-invalidates $\Phi \wedge \sim\Phi \vDash \Psi$, and adjunction as well. The problem is averted by redefining "$\wedge$" as "$\wedge_d$": $\Phi \wedge_d \Psi \vDash \Phi \wedge \sim\Diamond \Psi$ (or $\Diamond \Phi \wedge B$).

Non-adjunctive logics. Of course, discussive logics are non-adjunctive. A different approach is one developed by Resche and Manor in 1971, and later elaborated by Rescher and Brandom Adjunction of premises is permitted up to maximal consistency. Thus if Σ is a set of premisses, and Σ^* a maximal consistent subset of them and Φ a wff in Σ but not in Σ^*, then $\Sigma^* \cup \{\Phi\}$ is inconsistent. Consequently $\{\Phi, \ulcorner\sim\Phi\urcorner\} \nvDash \ulcorner\Phi \wedge \sim\Phi\urcorner$.

Preservationism extends the Rescher-Manor approach in an interesting way. It gives a way of marking the level of a premiss-set's consistency. The level of Σ^* is 1(1 is tops) since Σ^* is itself maxcon and is its own maxcon subset. But the level of $\Sigma^* = \{\Phi, \sim\Phi\}$ is 2: $\{\Phi\}$ and $\{\sim\Phi\}$. The basic idea is that if we define a consequence relation on some maxcon set, we want the ensuing relation not to generate consequences of lower levels of consistency than that held by the lines up above. That is, we want the relation to preserve consistency levels. The technicalities of preservationism are quite impressive. Schotch and Jennings introduce a powerful quartet of tools, *levels* (as we've just seen), *covering* and *forcing*. In subsequent work by Brown and Priest, *chunk* and *permeate* are further enrichments.

Adaptive logics. If preservationess is a Canadian contribution to paraconsistency, adaptive logics are a Belgian advance. Here, too, the basic idea that a belief-set or theory should be treated as consistently as possible, and deviations, if needed, should be situation-specific in dynamic contexts. One of these is the context of dynamic reasoning in which new information might break a consequence relation currently in place without falsifying either the premisses or the conclusion. In such settings, the consequence relation is nonmonotonic. The once-derivable conclusion is no longer derivable, but might nevertheless be true. In the particular case of inconsistency, when it pops up in our inference chain, a previously engaged rule or axiom will have to be withdrawn.

The three core ideas of adaptive logic are a *lower limit logic* (LLL), a set of *abnormalities*, and an *adaptive strategy*. LLL is not open to adaptation. Its rules hold (generate no anomalies) in all contexts. A set of abnormalities is considered as absurd until the contrary is satisfactorily established. Let $\ulcorner \Phi \wedge \sim\Phi \urcorner$ be a member of such a set. Suppose we adjust our LLL with the stipulation that all abnormalities are logically impossible. This gives the *upper* limit logic ULL which contains the wherewithal of LLL, as well as additional measures enabling application of supplementary rules or axioms in the absence of normality – for example, the Disjunctive Syllogism rule.

Two Sources of Explosion

Eric J. Y. Kao, Computer Science Department, Stanford University, USA

Abstract
In pursuit of enhancing the deductive power of inconsistency logic while avoiding explosiveness, Hewitt proposed including the law of excluded middle and proof by self-refutation. In this paper, I show that the inclusion of either one of these inference patterns causes paraconsistent logics such as Hewitt's Inconsistency Robust Direct Logic and Besnard and Hunter's quasi-classical system to become explosive. As a consequence of the work reported here, the law of excluded middle and proof by self-refutation were not included in later versions of Inconsistency Robust Direct Logic.

Introduction
A central goal of a paraconsistent logic is to avoid explosiveness – the inference of any arbitrary sentence β from an inconsistent premise set $\{p, \neg p\}$ (*ex falso quodlibet*).

Inconsistency Robust Direct Logic and Besnard and Hunter's quasi-classical system [Besnard and Hunter 1995; Hunter 1996, 1999] both seek to maximize deductive power of "as much as possible" while still avoiding explosiveness. Their work fits into the ongoing research program of identifying some "reasonable" and "maximal" subsets of classically valid rules and axioms that do not lead to explosiveness.

To this end, it is natural to consider which classically sound deductive rules and axioms one can introduce into a paraconsistent logic without causing explosiveness. Seeking to increase the power of Inconsistency Robust Direct Logic, Hewitt proposed including the law of excluded middle and the proof by self-refutation rule (a very special case of proof by contradiction).

In this paper, I show that for Inconsistency Robust Direct Logic, the addition of either the law of excluded middle or the proof by self-refutation rule in fact leads to explosiveness.

I first introduce bIRDL [Hewitt 2011], boolean fragment of Inconsistency Robust Direct Logic (section 2). In section 3, I discuss the law of excluded middle and show that its addition to bIRDL leads to explosiveness. In section 4, I discuss proof by self-refutation and show that its addition to bIRDL leads to explosiveness. In section 5, I discuss how the results also hold in the quasi-classical systems [Besnard and Hunter 1995; Hunter 1996, 1999].

Boolean Inconsistency Robust Direct Logic

Boolean Inconsistency Robust Direct Logic (bIRDL) is a boolean fragment of Inconsistency Robust Direct Logic [Hewitt 2011]. It allows us to analyze some of the essential structure of Inconsistency Robust Direct Logic without engaging the complexity of the full logic.

Formal definition of bIRDL

The language of bIRDL is the language of boolean logic.

Definition 1. *Let the language* L *be the set of classical boolean propositional formulas (of finite length) formed from a set of propositional atoms (denoted by* **Atoms***) and the connectives* $\wedge, \vee, \neg$. L *is the fixed language assumed throughout this paper.*

The proof theory of bIRDL is presented as a set rules of inference. There are four core rules, supplemented by the rules of substitution using the usual boolean equivalences.

Definition 2 (bIRDL rules of inference). *The following are the bIRDL rules of inference. Conjunction and disjunction are taken to be commutative and associative.*

Core rules of bIRDL

$$\frac{\alpha \vee \beta \quad \neg \alpha \vee \psi}{\beta \vee \psi} \text{ [Resolution]} \qquad \frac{\alpha \wedge \beta}{\alpha} \text{ [}\wedge\text{-Elimination]}$$

$$\frac{\alpha \quad \beta}{\alpha \vee \beta} \text{ [Restricted }\vee\text{-Introduction]} \qquad \frac{\alpha \quad \beta}{\alpha \wedge \beta} \text{ [}\wedge\text{-Introduction]}$$

Substitution according boolean equivalences

$$\frac{\alpha}{s(\alpha)}$$

, where $s(\alpha)$ is the result of substituting in α an occurrence of a subformula by an equivalent subformula according to a boolean equivalence below.

| Distributivity | $\psi \vee (\alpha \wedge \beta)$ | is equivalent to | $(\psi \vee \alpha) \wedge (\psi \vee \beta)$ |
| | $(\psi \wedge \alpha) \vee (\psi \wedge \beta)$ | is equivalent to | $\psi \wedge (\alpha \vee \beta)$ |

De Morgan Laws	$\neg(\alpha \wedge \beta)$	is equivalent to	$\neg\alpha \vee \neg\beta$
	$\neg(\alpha \vee \beta)$	is equivalent to	$\neg\alpha \wedge \neg\beta$
Double negation	$\neg\neg\alpha$	is equivalent to	α
Idempotence	$\alpha \vee \alpha$	is equivalent to	α
	$\alpha \wedge \alpha$	is equivalent to	α

Definition 3 (bIRDL proof). *A bIRDL proof is a sequence of sentences $\alpha_1, \alpha_2, ..., \alpha_n$ such that each α_i is a premise or follows from $\alpha_1, ..., \alpha_{i-1}$ by the application of a bIRDL rule of inference.*

Definition 4 (bIRDL consequence). *A sentence β is a bIRDL-consequence of a set of sentences Σ if there exists a bIRDL proof $\alpha_1, \alpha_2, ..., \alpha_k, \beta$ with premises Σ. This fact is denoted by $\Sigma \vdash_{bIRDL} \beta$.*

Law of excluded middle

Intuitively, the law of excluded middle states that no sentence can be neither true nor false.

Hewitt [2010] suggested incorporating the law of excluded middle into Inconsistency Robust Direct Logic. At that time it was not obvious whether introducing the Excluded Middle axiom schema into bIRDL leads to explosiveness. For example, bIRDL plus the axioms $\{p \vee \neg p : p \in \textbf{Atoms}\}$ is not explosive [Kao, and Genesereth 2011].

I show that the law of excluded middle in fact leads to explosiveness in bIRDL. Specifically, for any sentences α and β, I derive β from premises α and ¬α using the rules of bIRDL plus the Excluded Middle axiom schema.

Proof 1: Explosion proof in bIRDL+[Excluded Middle]

1	α	Premise
2	$\neg \alpha$	Premise
3	$(\alpha \wedge \neg \beta) \vee \neg(\alpha \wedge \neg \beta)$	Excluded Middle
4	$(\alpha \wedge \neg \beta) \vee \neg \alpha \vee \neg\neg \beta$	De Morgan, 3
5	$(\alpha \wedge \neg \beta) \vee \neg \alpha \vee \beta$	Double negation, 4
6	$(\alpha \vee \neg \alpha \vee \beta) \wedge (\neg \beta \vee \neg \alpha \vee \beta)$	Distributivity, 5
7	$\alpha \vee \neg \alpha \vee \beta$	$\wedge$-Elimination, 6
8	$\alpha \vee \beta$	Resolution, 7, 1
9	β	Resolution, 8, 2

Proof by self-refutation

In this section, I introduce the proof by self-refutation rule as a special case of proof by contradiction.

The proof by contradiction rule[2] states that if by assuming a sentence α we derive a contradiction, then we can conclude $\neg \alpha$. It can be stated as the following meta rule: If $\Sigma, \alpha \vdash \psi$ and $\Sigma, \alpha \vdash \neg \psi$, then conclude $\Sigma \vdash \alpha$.

Proof by contradiction easily leads to explosiveness. For any sentences α and $\beta, \{\alpha, \neg \alpha\}, \neg \beta \vdash \alpha$ and $\{\alpha, \neg \alpha\}, \neg \beta \vdash \neg \alpha$, hence $\{\alpha, \neg \alpha\} \vdash \neg\neg \beta$ using proof by contradiction.

The proof by self-refutation rule states that if a sentence α derives the negation of itself, then we can introduce $\neg \alpha$. It can be stated as the following axiom schema: $\neg \alpha$, where α proves $\neg \alpha$ [Self-Refutation]

Proof by self-refutation is syntactically a much weaker special case of general proof by contradiction rule. First, it requires that we derive a negation of the assumption, not just any contradiction. Second, it requires that α itself proves its negation, without the aid of any other premises.

I show that the addition of the proof by self-refutation rule to bIRDL leads to explosiveness.

For any pair of sentences α and β, I derive β from premises α and $\neg \alpha$, using bIRDL inference rules plus the Self-Refutation axiom schema.

First, I show that $(\neg \alpha \wedge \neg \beta) \wedge (\alpha \vee \beta)$ proves its own negation $\neg((\neg \alpha \vee \neg \beta) \wedge (\alpha \vee \beta))$. Then I use $\neg((\neg \alpha \vee \neg \beta) \wedge (\alpha \vee \beta))$, α, and $\neg \alpha$ to prove β.

Proof 2a: $((\neg\alpha \vee \neg\beta) \wedge (\alpha \vee \beta))$ proves $\neg((\neg\alpha \vee \neg\beta) \wedge (\alpha \vee \beta))$

1. $(\neg\alpha \wedge \neg\beta) \wedge (\alpha \vee \beta)$ — Premise
2. $(\neg\alpha \wedge \neg\beta)$ — ∧-Elimination, 1
3. $(\alpha \vee \beta)$ — ∧-Elimination, 1
4. $(\alpha \vee \beta) \vee (\neg\alpha \wedge \neg\beta)$ — Restricted ∨-Introduction, 2, 3
5. $(\alpha \vee \beta) \vee \neg(\alpha \vee \beta)$ — De Morgan, 4
6. $(\alpha \vee \neg\neg\beta) \vee \neg(\alpha \vee \beta)$ — Double negation, 5
7. $(\neg\neg\alpha \vee \neg\neg\beta) \vee \neg(\alpha \vee \beta)$ — Double negation, 6
8. $\neg(\neg\alpha \vee \neg\beta) \vee \neg(\alpha \vee \beta)$ — De Morgan, 7
9. $\neg((\neg\alpha \vee \neg\beta) \wedge (\alpha \vee \beta))$ — De Morgan, 8

Also known as reductio ad absurdum or negation introduction. 5

Proof 2: Explosion in bIRDL+[Self-Refutation]

1	α	Premise
2	$\neg \alpha$	Premise
3	$\neg((\neg\alpha \vee \neg\beta) \wedge (\alpha \vee \beta))$	Self-Refutation, Proof 2a
4	$\neg(\neg\alpha \wedge \neg\beta) \vee \neg(\alpha \vee \beta)$	De Morgan, 3
5	$(\neg\neg\alpha \vee \neg\neg\beta) \vee \neg(\alpha \vee \beta)$	De Morgan, 4
6	$(\neg\neg\alpha \vee \beta) \vee \neg(\alpha \vee \beta)$	Double negation, 5
7	$\alpha \vee \beta \vee \neg(\alpha \vee \beta)$	Double negation, 6
8	$\alpha \vee \beta \vee (\neg\alpha \wedge \neg\beta)$	De Morgan, 7
9	$(\alpha \vee \beta \vee \neg\alpha) \wedge (\alpha \vee \beta \vee \neg\beta)$	Distributivity, 8
10	$\alpha \vee \beta \vee \neg\alpha$	$\wedge$-Elimination, 9
11	$\alpha \vee \beta$	Resolution, 10, 1
12	β	Resolution, 11, 2

Discussion

Beyond Inconsistency Robust Direct Logic itself, the results in this article have implications for the ongoing research program to identify some "reasonable" and "maximal" subset of classically valid rules and axioms that do not lead to explosiveness.

If we take the boolean equivalences and *wedge*-Elimination for granted, the explosiveness of bIRDL+[Excluded Middle] essentially rely on only Excluded Middle and Disjunctive Syllogism (a special case of Resolution).

Similarly, the explosiveness of bIRDL+[Self-Refutation] essentially rely on only Self-Refutation, Disjunctive Syllogism, and Restricted $\vee$-Introduction ($\alpha \vee \beta$ from α and β).

Therefore, the result apply immediately to other paraconsistent logics of the same class. For example, the same proofs (1, 2a, 2) show that Besnard and Hunter's quasi-classical system also becomes explosive if either Excluded Middle or Self-Refutation is added.

Restall [2004] pointed out that explosiveness is not a necessary consequence of the law of excluded middle. In fact, there are paraconsistent logics that support the law of excluded middle without being explosive. However, having the law of excluded middle in such logics means that the principles of bIRDL are not supported by such paraconsistent logics.

Conclusion

This work contributes to the ongoing research program of identifying some "reasonable" and "maximal" subset of classically valid rules and axioms that do not lead to explosiveness.

This paper that demonstrate that the rule of Excluded Middle leads to explosiveness in Inconsistency Robust Direct Logic and the quasi-classical systems. In response to this finding, Hewitt [2011] decided not to include these Excluded Middle in later versions of Inconsistency Robust Direct Logic.

More recently, Hewitt [2014] developed Inconsistency Robust Proof by Contradiction which seems to provide a more practical approach to dealing with the issue that Classical Proof by Contradiction is not valid in Inconsistency Robust Direct Logic.

Acknowledgments

I would like to thank Michael Genesereth, Carl Hewitt, the anonymous referees, and the Stanford Logic Group for their valuable feedback. I would also like to acknowledge Konica-Minolta for their support via the Media X project.

References

Besnard, P., Hunter, A.: Quasi-classical logic: Non-trivializable classical reasoning from inconsistent information. In: Proceedings of the European Conference on Symbolic and Quantitative Approaches to Reasoning and Uncertainty. pp. 44–51. Springer-Verlag, London, UK (1995), http://portal.acm.org/citation.cfm?id=646561.695561

Hewitt, C.: Common sense for inconsistency robust information integration using direct logic reasoning and the actor model. arXiv CoRR abs/0812.4852 (2010, 2014)

Hewitt, C.: Common sense for inconsistency robust information integration using direct logic reasoning and the actor model. arXiv CoRR abs/0812.4852v56 (2011)

Hunter, A.: Paraconsistent logics. In: Handbook of Defeasible Reasoning and Uncertain Information. pp. 11–36. Kluwer (1996)

Hunter, A.: Reasoning with contradictory information using quasi-classical logic. Journal of Logic and Computation 10, 677–703 (1999)

Kao, E.J.Y., Genesereth, M.: Achieving cut, deduction, and other properties with a variation on quasi-classical logic (2011), http://dl.dropbox.com/u/5152476/working papers/modified quasiclassical/main.pdf

Restall, G.: Laws of non-contradiction, laws of the excluded middle and logics. In: The Law of Non-Contradiction; New Philosophical Essays, pp. 73–85. Oxford University Press (2004)

Part 2

Software Foundations

Actor Model of Computation:
Scalable Robust Information Systems

Carl Hewitt

This article is dedicated to Alonzo Church and Dana Scott.

Introduction
The Actor Model is a mathematical theory that treats "*Actors*" as the universal conceptual primitives of digital computation.

Hypothesis:[i] **All physically possible computation can be directly implemented using Actors.**

The model has been used both as a framework for a theoretical understanding of concurrency, and as the theoretical basis for several practical implementations of concurrent systems. Actors are direct and efficient:
- Digital computation can be efficiently implemented without loss of processing, communication, or storage efficiency
- Digital computation can be directly modeled without requiring extraneous elements, e.g., channels or registers.

The advent of massive concurrency through client-cloud computing and many-core computer architectures has galvanized interest in the Actor Model.

Message passing using types is the foundation of system communication:
- Messages are the unit of communication
- Types[ii] enable secure communication with any Actor

When an Actor receives a message, it can concurrently:[1]
- send messages to (unforgeable) addresses of Actors that it has;
- create new Actors;[iii]
- for an exclusive[iv] Actor, designate how to handle the next message it receives.

---

[i] This hypothesis is an update to [Church 1936] that all physically computable functions can be implemented using the lambda calculus. It is a consequence of the Actor Model that there are some computations that *cannot* be implemented in the lambda calculus.

[ii] Each type is an Actor.

[iii] with new addresses

[iv] An *exclusive* Actor can perform at most one activity at a time.

The Actor Model can be used as a framework for modeling, understanding, and reasoning about, a wide range of concurrent systems. For example:
- Electronic mail (e-mail) can be modeled as an Actor system. Mail accounts are modeled as Actors and email addresses as Actor addresses.
- Web Services can be modeled with endpoints modeled as Actor addresses.
- Objects with locks (e.g. as in Java and C#) can be modeled as Actors.
- Functional and Logic programs can be implemented using Actors.

Actor technology will see significant application for coordinating all kinds of digital information for individuals, groups, and organizations so their information usefully links together.

Information coordination needs to make use of the following information system principles:

- ***Persistence***. *Information is collected and indexed.*
- ***Concurrency***: *Work proceeds interactively and concurrently, overlapping in time.*
- ***Quasi-commutativity***: *Information can be used regardless of whether it initiates new work or become relevant to ongoing work.*
- ***Sponsorship***: *Sponsors provide resources for computation, i.e., processing, storage, and communications.*
- ***Pluralism***: *Information is heterogeneous, overlapping and often inconsistent. There is no central arbiter of truth.*
- ***Provenance***: *The provenance of information is carefully tracked and recorded.*

The Actor Model is intended to provide a foundation for inconsistency robust information coordination. Inconsistency[i] robustness is information system performance[2] in the face of continual pervasive inconsistencies.[ii] Inconsistency robustness is both an observed phenomenon and a desired feature.

The Actor Model is a mathematical theory of computation that treats "*Actors*" as the universal conceptual primitives of concurrent digital computation [Hewitt, Bishop, and Steiger 1973; Hewitt 1977]. The model has been used both

---

[i] An inference system is *inconsistent* when it is possible to derive both a proposition and its negation.

A *contradiction* is manifest when both a proposition and its negation are asserted even if by different parties, *e.g.*, New York Times said "*Snowden is a whistleblower.*", but NSA said "*Snowden is not a whistleblower.*"

[ii] a shift from the previously dominant paradigms of inconsistency denial and inconsistency elimination, *i.e.*, to sweep inconsistencies under the rug.

as a framework for a theoretical understanding of concurrency, and as the theoretical basis for several practical implementations of concurrent systems.

Unlike previous models of computation, the Actor Model was inspired by physical laws. It was also influenced by programming languages such as, the lambda calculus[i], Lisp [McCarthy et. al. 1962], Simula-67 [Dahl and Nygaard 1967] and Smalltalk-72 [Kay 1975], as well as ideas for Petri Nets [Petri 1962], capability systems [Dennis and van Horn 1966] and packet switching [Baran 1964]. The advent of massive concurrency through client-cloud computing and many-core computer architectures has galvanized interest in the Actor Model [Hewitt 2009b].

It is important to distinguish the following:
- modeling arbitrary computational systems using Actors.[ii] It is difficult to find physical computational systems (regardless of how idiosyncratic) that cannot be modeled using Actors.
- securely implementing practical computational applications using Actors remains an active area of research and development.

Decoupling the sender from the communications it sends was a fundamental advance of the Actor Model enabling asynchronous communication and control structures as patterns of passing messages [Hewitt 1977].

An Actor can only communicate with another Actor to which it has an address.[iii] Addresses can be implemented in a variety of ways:
- direct physical attachment
- memory or disk addresses
- network addresses
- email addresses

The Actor Model is characterized by inherent concurrency of computation within and among Actors, dynamic creation of Actors, inclusion of Actor addresses in messages, and interaction only through direct asynchronous message passing with no restriction on message reception order.

---

[i] In general Actor systems can be exponentially faster than the parallel lambda calculus.
[ii] An Actor can be implemented directly in hardware.
[iii] In the literature, an Actor address is sometimes called a "capability" [Dennis and van Horn 1966] because it provides the capability to send a message.

The Actor Model differs from its predecessors and most current models of computation in that the Actor Model assumes the following:
- Concurrent execution in processing a message.
- The following are *not* required by an Actor: a thread, a mailbox, a message queue, its own operating system process, *etc.*[i]
- Message passing has the same overhead as looping and procedure calling.
- Primitive Actors can be implemented in hardware.[ii]

The Actor Model can be used as a framework for modeling, understanding, and reasoning about, a wide range of concurrent systems.

For example:
- Electronic mail (e-mail) can be modeled as an Actor system. Mail accounts are modeled as Actors and email addresses as Actor addresses.
- Web Services can be modeled with SOAP endpoints modeled as Actor addresses.
- Objects with locks (*e.g.* as in Java and C#) can be modeled as Actors.

Direct communication and asynchrony
The Actor Model is based on one-way asynchronous communication. Once a message has been sent, it is the responsibility of the receiver.[3]

Messages in the Actor Model are decoupled from the sender and are delivered by the system on a best efforts basis.[4] This was a sharp break with previous approaches to models of concurrent computation in which message sending is tightly coupled with the sender and sending a message synchronously transfers it someplace, *e.g.*, to a buffer, queue, mailbox, channel, broker, server, *etc.* or to the *"ether"* or *"environment"* where it temporarily resides. The lack of synchronicity caused a great deal of misunderstanding at the time of the development of the Actor Model and is still a controversial issue.

Because message passing is taken as fundamental in the Actor Model, there cannot be any required overhead, *e.g.*, any requirement to use buffers, pipes, queues, classes, channels, *etc.* Prior to the Actor Model, concurrency was defined in low level machine terms.

---

[i] For example, if an Actor were required to have a mailbox then, the mailbox would be an Actor that is required to have its own mailbox…

[ii] In some cases, this involves (clocked) one-way messages so message guarantees and exception processing can be different from typical application Actors.

It certainly is the case that implementations of the Actor Model typically make use of these hardware capabilities. However, there is no reason that the model could not be implemented directly in hardware without exposing any hardware threads, locks, queues, cores, channels, tasks, *etc.* Also, there is no necessary relationship between the number of Actors and the number threads, cores, locks, tasks, queues, *etc.* that might be in use. Implementations of the Actor Model are free to make use of threads, locks, tasks, queues, coherent memory, transactional memory, cores, *etc.* in any way that is compatible with the laws for Actors [Baker and Hewitt 1977].

As opposed to the previous approach based on composing sequential processes, the Actor Model was developed as an inherently concurrent model. In the Actor Model sequential ordering is a special case that derived from concurrent computation. Also, the Actor Model is based on communication rather that a global state space as in Turing Machines, CSP [Hoare 1978], Java [Sun 1995, 2004], C++11 [ISO 2011], X86 [AMD 2011], *etc.*

A natural development of the Actor Model was to allow Actor addresses in messages. A computation might need to send a message to a recipient from which it would later receive a response. The way to do this is to send a communication which has the message along with the address of another Actor called the *customer* along with the message. The recipient could then cause a response message to be sent to the customer.

Indeterminacy and Quasi-commutativity
The Actor Model supports indeterminacy because the reception order of messages can affect future behavior.

Operations are said to be quasi-commutative to the extent that it doesn't matter in which order they occur. To the extent possible, quasi-commutativity is used to reduce indeterminacy.

Locality and Security
Locality and security are important characteristics of the Actor Model[Baker and Hewitt 1977].[5]

Locality and security mean that in processing a message: an Actor can send messages only to addresses for which it has information by the following means:
1. that it receives in the message
2. that it already had before it received the message
3. that it creates while processing the message.

In the Actor Model, there is no hypothesis of simultaneous change in multiple locations. In this way it differs from some other models of concurrency, *e.g.*, the Petri net model in which tokens are simultaneously removed from multiple locations and placed in other locations.

The security of Actor systems can be protected in the following ways:
- **Strong personal authentication**, *e.g.*, using (3D) continuous interactive bio-authentication instead of passwords
- **Strong, ubiquitous public key authentication** so that it can be verified to whom a public key corresponds. Often this authentication can be performed by local bank offices, *etc.* that publish online multi-national directories of public keys in a network of mistrust. Individual citizens can have their own directories of public keys that are used to automatically and invisibly securely communicate with others.
  Many citizens will have more than one authenticated public key, which can be authenticated with various levels of security.
- **Public keys for IoT ownership** so that an IoT device has both:
  o a public key of its owner, which is installed when ownership is transferred
  o its own unique public/private key pair, which is created internally when acquired by the first owner.

  An owner can communicate securely with a device by encrypting information using the device's public key. (For efficiency reasons, most communication will actually be performed using symmetric keys encrypted/signed by public keys.) A device takes instructions only from its owner and is allowed to communicate with the external world only through the information coordination system of its owner. The nonprofit Standard IoT Foundation is working to develop standards based on the Actor Model of computation that provide for interoperation among existing and emerging consortium and proprietary corporate IoT standards.
- **Hardware architecture security** to help cope with the complexity of software systems that can never be made highly secure without hardware assistance including the following:
  o *RAM-processor package encryption* (*i.e.* all traffic between a processor package and RAM is encrypted using a uniquely generated key when a package is powered up and which is invisible to all software) to protect an app (*i.e.* a user application, which is technically a process) from the following:
    ▪ operating systems and hypervisors
    ▪ other apps
    ▪ other equipment, e.g., baseband processors, disk controllers, and USB controllers.

- *Hardware Actors* that communicate only using message passing to protect security registers
- *Every-word-tagged architecture* to protect an Actor in an app from other Actors by using a tag on each word of memory that controls how the memory can be used. Each Actor is protected from reading and/or writing by other Actors in its process. Actors can interact only by sending a message to the unforgeable address of another Actor. Existing software (e.g., operating systems, browsers, mail systems) will need to be upgraded to use tags.

A delicate point in the Actor Model is the ability to synthesize the address of an Actor. In some cases security can be used to prevent the synthesis of addresses in practice using the following:
- every-word-tagged memory
- signing and encryption of messages

Robustness in Runtime Failures

Runtime failures are always a possibility in Actor systems and are dealt with by runtime infrastructures. Message acknowledgement, reception, and response[i] cannot be guaranteed although best efforts are made. Consequences are cleaned up on a best-effort basis.

Robustness is based on the following principle:
> If an Actor is sent a request, then the continuation *must* be one of the following two mutually exclusive possibilities:
> 1. to process the response[ii] resulting from the recipient receiving the request
> 2. to throw a Messaging[iii] exception[iv]

Just sitting there forever after a request has been sent is a silent failure, which is unacceptable. So, in due course, the infrastructure must throw a Messaging exception as governed by the policies in place[v] if a response (return value or exception) to the request has not been received.

---

[i] a response is either a returned value or a thrown exception
[ii] conceptually processed by a customer Actor sent in the request
[iii] A Messaging exception can have information concerning the lack of response
[iv] even though the recipient may have received the request and sent a response that has not yet been received by the customer of the request. Requestors need to be able to interact with infrastructures concerning policies to be applied concerning when to generate Messaging exceptions.
[v] For example, several standard deviations have passed in the expected time to receive a response.

Ideally, if the continuation of sending a request is to throw a Messaging exception, then the sender of a response to the request also receives a Messaging exception saying that the response could not be processed.

If desired, things can arranged so that Messaging exceptions are very special and can be distinguished from all other exceptions.

Scalability and Modularity

ActorScript™ is a general purpose programming language for implementing iAdaptive™ concurrency that manages resources and demand. It is differentiated from previous languages by the following:
- Universality
  - Ability to directly specify what Actors can do
  - Specify interface between hardware and software
  - Everything in the language is accomplished using message passing including the very definition of ActorScript itself.
  - Functional, Imperative, Logic, and Concurrent programming are integrated. Concurrency can be dynamically adapted to resources available and current load.
  - Programs do not expose low-level implementation mechanisms such as threads, tasks, channels, coherent memory, location transparency, throttling, load balancing, locks, cores, *etc*. Messages can be directly communicated without requiring indirection through brokers, channels, class hierarchies, mailboxes, pipes, ports, queues *etc*. Variable races are eliminated.
  - Binary XML and JSON are data types.
  - Application binary interfaces are afforded so that no program symbol need be looked up at runtime.
- Safety and security
  - Programs are extension invariant, i.e., extending a program does not change its meaning.
  - Applications cannot directly harm each other.
- Performance
  - Impose no overhead on implementation of Actor systems
  - Message passing has essentially same overhead as procedure calling and looping.
  - Execution dynamically adjusted for system load and capacity (*e.g.* cores)
  - Locality because execution is not bound by a sequential global memory model
  - Inherent concurrency because execution is not bound by communicating sequential processes
  - Minimize latency along critical paths

ActorScript attempts to achieve the highest level of performance, scalability, and expressibility with a minimum of conceptual primitives.

Scalable information Coordination

Technology now at hand can coordinate all kinds of digital information for individuals, groups, and organizations so their information usefully links together. This coordination can include calendars and to-do lists, communications (including email, SMS, Twitter, Facebook), presence information (including who else is in the neighborhood), physical (including GPS recordings), psychological (including facial expression, heart rate, voice stress) and social (including family, friends, team mates, and colleagues), maps (including firms, points of interest, traffic, parking, and weather), events (including alerts and status), documents (including presentations, spreadsheets, proposals, job applications, health records, photos, videos, gift lists, memos, purchasing, contracts, articles), contacts (including social graphs and reputation), purchasing information (including store purchases, web purchases, GPS and phone records, and buying and travel habits), government information (including licenses, taxes, and rulings), and search results (including rankings and ratings).

Connections

Information coordination works by making connections including examples like the following:
- A statistical connection between "being in a traffic jam" and "driving in downtown Trenton between 5PM and 6PM on a weekday."
- A terminological connection between "MSR" and "Microsoft Research."
- A causal connection between "joining a group" and "being a member of the group."
- A syntactic connection between "a pin dropped" and "a dropped pin."
- A biological connection between "a dolphin" and "a mammal".
- A demographic connection between "undocumented residents of California" and "7% of the population of California."
- A geographical connection between "Leeds" and "England."
- A temporal connection between "turning on a computer" and "joining an on-line discussion."

By making these connections iInfo™ information coordination offers tremendous value for individuals, families, groups, and organizations in making more effective use of information technology.

Information Coordination Principles

In practice, coordinated information is invariably inconsistent.[6] Therefore iInfo must be able to make connections even in the face of inconsistency.[7] The business of iInfo is not to make difficult decisions like deciding the ultimate truth or probability of propositions. Instead it provides means for processing information and carefully recording its provenance including arguments (including arguments about arguments) for and against propositions.

Information coordination needs to make use of the following principles:
- **Persistence**. *Information is collected and indexed and no original information is lost.*
- **Concurrency**: *Work proceeds interactively and concurrently, overlapping in time.*
- **Quasi-commutativity**: *Information can be used regardless of whether it initiates new work or become relevant to ongoing work.*
- **Sponsorship**: *Sponsors provide resources for computation, i.e., processing, storage, and communications.*
- **Pluralism**: *Information is heterogeneous, overlapping and often inconsistent. There is no central arbiter of truth*
- **Provenance**: *The provenance of information is carefully tracked and recorded*

Interaction creates Reality[8]

> *a philosophical shift in which knowledge is no longer treated primarily as referential, as a set of statements **about** reality, but as a practice that interferes with other practices. It therefore participates **in** reality.*
> Annemarie Mol [2002]

Relational physics takes the following view [Laudisa and Rovelli 2008]:[i]
- Relational physics discards the notions of absolute state of a system and absolute properties and values of its physical quantities.
- State and physical quantities refer always to the interaction, or the relation, among multiple systems.
- Nevertheless, relational physics is a complete description of reality.

According to this view, **Interaction creates reality.** Information systems participate in this reality and thus are both consequence and cause.

Actor systems can be organized in higher level structures to facilitate operations.

Organizational Programming using iOrgs

The Actor Model supports Organizational Programming that is based on authority and accountability in iOrgs [Hewitt 2008a] with the goal of becoming

---

[i] According to [Rovelli 1996]: *Quantum mechanics is a theory about the physical description of physical systems relative to other systems, and this is a complete description of the world.*

[Feynman 1965] offered the following advice: *Do not keep saying to yourself, if you can possibly avoid it, "But how can it be like that?" because you will go "down the drain," into a blind alley from which nobody has yet escaped.*

an effective readily understood approach for addressing scalability issues in Software Engineering. The paradigm takes its inspiration from human organizations. iOrgs provide a framework for addressing issues of hierarchy, authority, accountability, scalability, and robustness using methods that are analogous to human organizations. Because humans are very familiar with the principles, methods, and practices of human organizations, they can transfer this knowledge and experience to iOrgs. iOrgs achieve scalability using methods and principles similar to those used in human organizations. For example an iOrg can have sub-organizations specialized by areas such as sales, production, and so forth. Authority is delegated down the organizational structure and when necessary issues are escalated upward. Authority requires accountability for its use including record keeping and periodic reports. Management is in large part the art of reconciling authority and accountability.

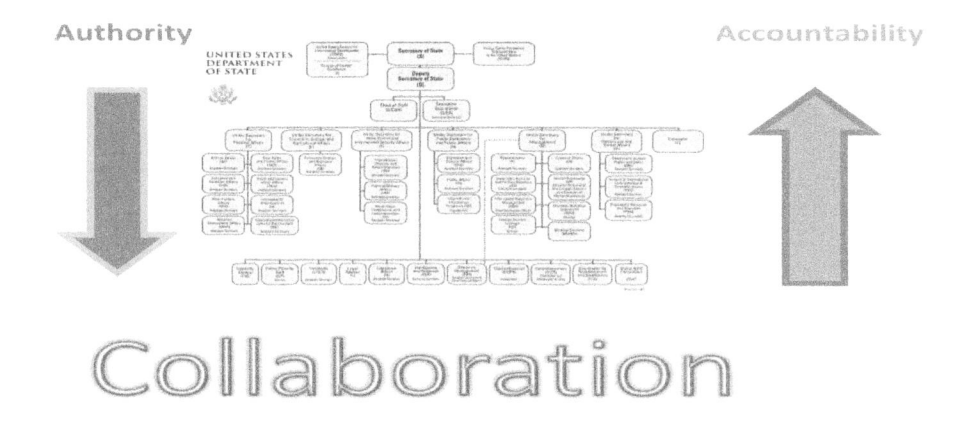

Organizational Programming for iOrgs

iOrgs are structured around *organizational commitment* defined as information pledged constituting an alliance to go forward. For example, iOrgs can use contracts to formalize their mutual commitments to fulfill specified obligations to each other.

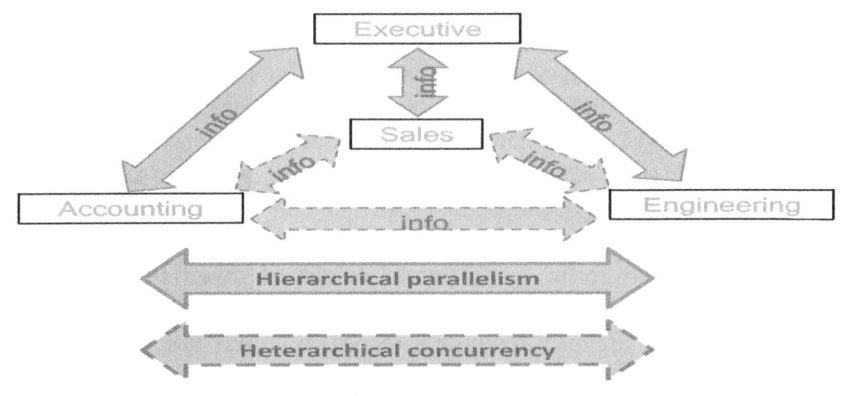

Scalability of iOrgs

Yet, manifestations of information pledged will often be inconsistent. Any given agreement might be internally inconsistent, or two agreements in force at one time could contradict each other.

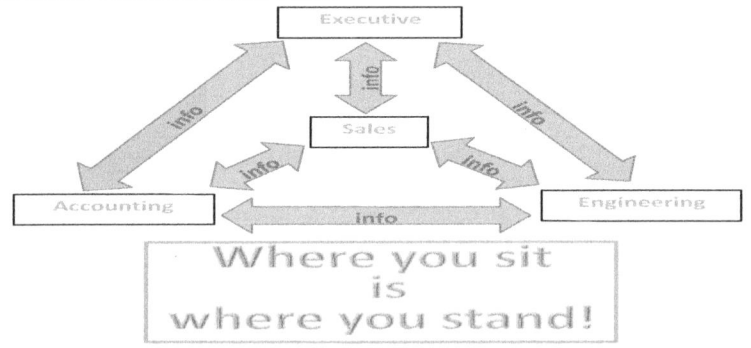

Inconsistency by Design for iOrgs

Issues that arise from such inconsistencies can be negotiated among iOrgs. For example the Sales department might have a different view than the Accounting department as to when a transaction should be booked.

A fundamental goal of Inconsistency Robustness is to effectively reason about large amounts of information at high degrees of abstraction:

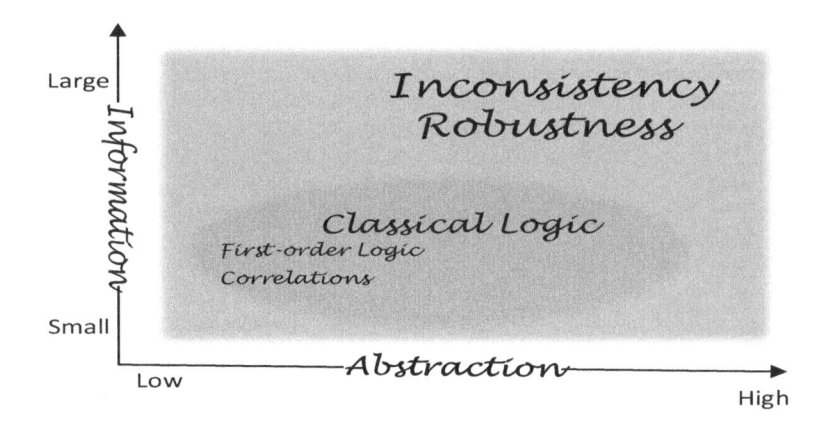

Classical logic is safe only for theories for which there is strong evidence of consistency.

Actor Addresses and Implementations
Actor addresses have types. For example the type Account has the following interface description:

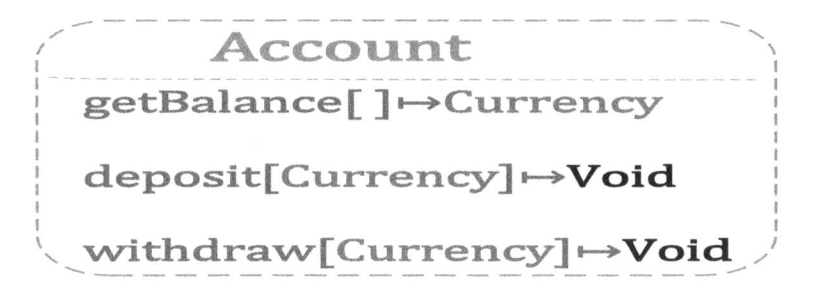

```
Account
  getBalance[ ] ↦ Currency
  deposit[Currency] ↦ Void
  withdraw[Currency] ↦ Void
```

Message Passing

[Diagram: Account with getBalance[ ] → myBalance; Account with deposit[anAmount] → myBalance := myBalance + anAmount; Account with withdraw[anAmount] → ¬(anAmount > myBalance) also myBalance := myBalance - anAmount; anAmount > myBalance → Overdrawn[ ]]

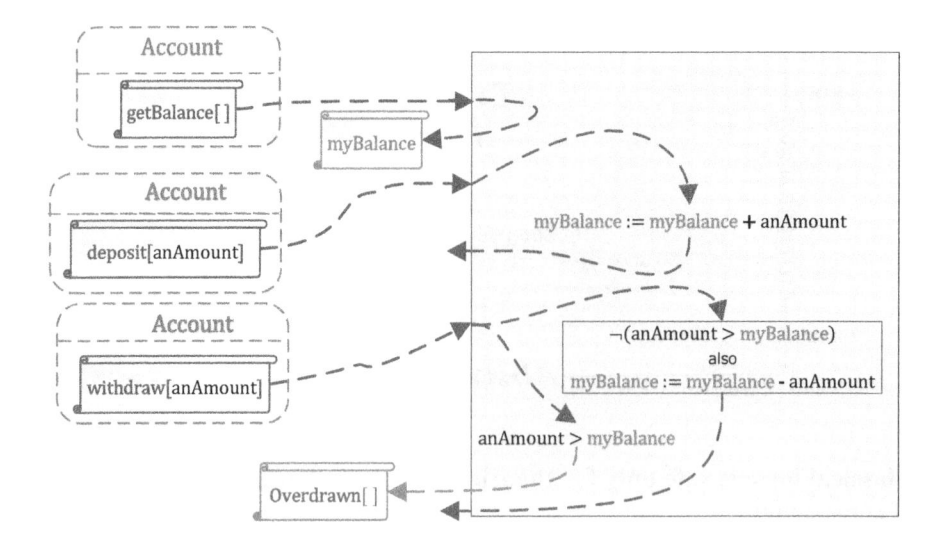

Computational Representation Theorem

The *Computational Representation Theorem* [Clinger 1981; Hewitt 2006][9] characterizes computation for systems which are closed in the sense that they do not receive communications from outside:

> The denotation **Denote**s of a closed system **S** represents all the possible behaviors of **S** as
>
> $$\textbf{Denote}_s = \lim_{i \to \infty} \textbf{Progressions}_S^i$$
>
> *where* Progressions takes a set of partial behaviors to their next stage, i.e., Progressions^i ↦ Progressions^{i+1}
>
> In this way, **S** can be mathematically characterized in terms of all its possible behaviors (including those involving unbounded nondeterminism).[ii]
>
> The denotations form the basis of constructively checking programs against all their possible executions,[iii]

A consequence of the Computational Representation Theorem is that there are uncountably many different Actors.

For example, Real.[ ] can output any real number between 0 and 1 where
   Real.[ ] ≡ [(0 **either** 1), **∀Postpone** Real.[ ]]
such that
- (0 **either** 1) is the nondeterministic choice of 0 or 1

---

[i] read as "*can evolve to*"

[ii] There are no messages in transit in Denote_s

[iii] a restricted form of Model Checking in which the properties checked are limited to those that can be expressed in Linear-time Temporal Logic has been studied [Clarke, Emerson, Sifakis, *etc.* ACM 2007 Turing Award]

- [first, ▼rest] is the list that begins with first and whose remainder is rest
- **Postpone** expression delays execution of expression until the value is needed.

The upshot is that ***concurrent systems can be axiomatized using mathematical logic[i] but in general cannot be implemented***. Thus, the following practical problem arose:
> How can practical programming languages be rigorously defined since the proposal [Scott and Strachey 1971, Milne and Strachey 1976] to define them in terms lambda calculus failed because the lambda calculus cannot implement concurrency?[10]

A proposed answer to this question is the semantics of ActorScript [Hewitt 2010].

Extension versus Specialization
Programming languages like ActorScript [Hewitt 2010] take the approach of extending behavior in contrast to the approach of specializing behavior:
- Type specialization: If type t1 is a subtype of type t2, then instances of t1 have all of the properties that are provable from the definition of type t2 [Liskov 1987, Liskov and Wing 2001].
- Type extension: A type can be extended to have additional (perhaps incompatible) properties from the type that it extends. An extension type can make use of the implementation of the type that it extends. Type extension is commonly used to extend operating system software as well as applications.

The term "inheritance" in programming has been used (sometimes ambiguously) to mean both specialization and extension.

Language constructs versus Library APIs
Library Application Programming Interfaces (APIs) are an alternative way to introduce concurrency.
For example,
- A limited version of futures[Baker and Hewitt 1977] have been introduced in C++11 [ISO 2011].
- Message Passing Interface (MPI) [Gropp et. al. 1998] provides some ability to pass messages.
- Grand Central Divide provides for queuing tasks.

There are a number of library APIs for Actor-like systems.

In general, appropriately defined language constructs provide greater power, flexibility, and performance than library APIs.[11]

---

[i] including the lambda calculus

Reasoning about Actor Systems
The principle of Actor induction is:
1. Suppose that an Actor x has property P when it is created
2. Further suppose that if x has property P when it receives a message, then it has property P when it receives the next message.
3. Then x always has the property P.

In his doctoral dissertation, Aki Yonezawa developed further techniques for proving properties of Actor systems including those that make use of migration. Russ Atkinson developed techniques for proving properties of Actors that are guardians of shared resources. Gerry Barber's 1981 doctoral dissertation concerned reasoning about change in knowledgeable office systems.

Other models of concurrency
The Actor Model does not have the following restrictions of other models of concurrency:[12]
- *Single threadedness:* There are no restrictions on the use of threads in implementations.
- *Message delivery order:* There no restrictions on message delivery order.
- *Independence of sender:* The semantics of a message in the Actor Model is independent of the sender.
- *Lack of garbage collection (automated storage reclamation):* The Actor Model can be used in the following systems:
    - CLR and extensions (Microsoft and Xamarin)
    - JVM (Oracle and IBM)
    - LLVM (Apple)
    - Dalvik (Google)

  In due course, we will need to extend the above systems with a tagged extension of the X86 and ARM architectures. Many-core architecture has made a tagged extension necessary in order to provide the following:
    - concurrent, nonstop, no-pause automated storage reclamation (garbage collection) and relocation to improve performance,
    - prevention of memory corruption that otherwise results from programming languages like C and C++ using thousands of threads in a process,
    - nonstop migration of Actors (while they are in operation) within a computer and between distributed computers.

Swiss Cheese
Swiss cheese [Hewitt and Atkinson 1977, 1979; Atkinson 1980][13] is a programming language construct for scheduling concurrent access to shared resources with the following goals:
- *Generality:* Ability to conveniently program any scheduling policy

- *Performance:* Support maximum performance in implementation, *e.g.*, the ability to avoid repeatedly recalculating conditions for proceeding.
- *Understandability:* Invariants of an Actor should hold at all observable execution points.

Concurrency control for readers and writers in a shared resource is a classic problem that illustrates limitations of Fog Cutter Actors. The fundamental constraint is that multiple writers are not allowed to operate concurrently and a writer is not allowed operate concurrently with a reader.

Cheese diagram for **ReadersWriter** implementations:[i]

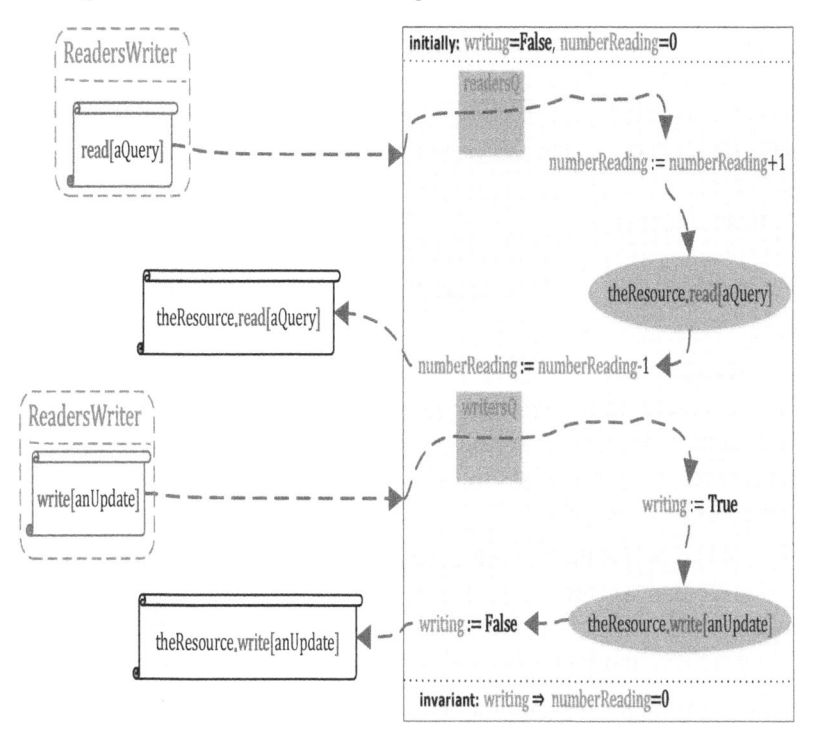

Note:
1. At most one activity is allowed to execute in the cheese.[ii]
2. The cheese has holes.[iii]

---

[i] The interface for the readers/writer guardian is the same as the interface for the shared resource: **Interface** ReadersWriter **with** read[Query] ↦ QueryAnswer,
write[Update] ↦ **Void**₀
[ii] Cheese is yellow in the diagram
[iii] A hole is grey in the diagram

3. A variable can change only when in a continuous section of cheese.[i]

Invariants hold at cheese boundaries, *i.e.*, an invariant must hold when the cheese is entered. Consequently, it doesn't matter what actions other Actors may be concurrently performing.

Futures
Futures [Baker and Hewitt 1977] are Actors that provide parallel execution by providing a proxy Actor for an expression while it is being computed.

The procedure below can computer the size of a list concurrently with creating the list making use of FutureList, which is a list that is either the empty list or whose list of elements after the first is a future.

Size.[aFutureList:FutureList◁String▷]:Integer ≡
 ↓aFutureList �   // resolve the beginning of aFutureList
  [ ] ։ 0
  [first, ⱽrest] ։
             // first is a string and rest is a future of the remainder
    first.length[ ] + Size.[rest]▮

Future work
As was the case with the lambda calculus and functional programming,[ii] it has taken decades since they were invented [Hewitt, Bishop, and Steiger 1973] to understand the scientific and engineering of Actor Systems and it is still very much a work in progress.

Actors are becoming the default model of computation. C#, Java, JavaScript, Objective C, and SystemVerilog are all headed in the direction of the Actor Model and ActorScript is a natural extension of these languages. Since it is very close to practice, many programmers just naturally assume the Actor Model.

The following major developments in computer technology are pushing the Actor Model forward because Actor Systems are highly scalable:
- Many-core computer architectures
- Client-cloud computing

In fact, the Actor Model and ActorScript can be seen as codifying what are becoming some best programming practices for many-core and client-cloud computing.

---

[i] Of course, other external Actors can change.
[ii] For example, it took over four decades to develop the eval message-passing model of the lambda calculus [Hewitt, Bishop, and Steiger 1973, Hewitt 2011] building on the Lisp procedural model.

Conclusion

The Actor Model is a mathematical theory that treats *"Actors"* as the universal conceptual primitives of concurrent digital computation. The model has been used both as a framework for a theoretical understanding of concurrency, and as the theoretical basis for several practical implementations of concurrent systems. Unlike previous models of computation, the Actor Model was inspired by physical laws. It was also influenced by the programming languages Lisp, Simula 67 and Smalltalk-72, as well as ideas for Petri Nets, capability systems and packet switching. The advent of massive concurrency through client-cloud computing and many-core computer architectures has galvanized interest in the Actor Model.

When an Actor receives a message, it can concurrently:
- Send messages to (unforgeable) addresses of Actors that it has.
- Create new Actors.[i]
- For an exclusive Actor, designate how to handle the next message received.

There is no assumed order to the above actions and they could be carried out concurrently. In addition two messages sent concurrently can be received in either order. Decoupling the sender from communication it sends was a fundamental advance of the Actor Model enabling asynchronous communication and control structures as patterns of passing messages.

Preferred methods for characterizing the Actor Model are as follows:
- *Axiomatically* stating laws that apply to all Actor *systems* [Baker and Hewitt 1977]
- *Denotationally* using the Computational Representation Theorem to characterize Actor computations [Clinger 1981; Hewitt 2006].
- O*perationally* using a suitable Actor programming language, *e.g.*, ActorScript [Hewitt 2012] that specifies how Actors can be implemented.

The Actor Model can be used as a framework for modeling, understanding, and reasoning about, a wide range of concurrent systems.
For example:
- Electronic mail (e-mail) can be modeled as an Actor system. Accounts are modeled as Actors and email addresses as Actor addresses.
- Web Services can be modeled with endpoints modeled as Actor addresses.
- Objects with locks (e.g. as in Java and C#) can be modeled as Actors.
- The Actor Model can be a computational foundation for Inconsistency Robustness

The Actor Model supports Organizational Programming that is based on authority and accountability in iOrgs [Hewitt 2008a] with the goal of becoming an effective readily understood approach for addressing scalability issues in Software Engineering. The paradigm takes its inspiration from human organizations. iOrgs provide a framework for addressing issues of hierarchy, authority, accountability, scalability, and robustness using methods that are analogous to human organizations. Because humans are very familiar with the principles, methods, and practices of human organizations, they can transfer this knowledge and experience to iOrgs. iOrgs achieve scalability by mirroring human organizational structure. For example an iOrg can have sub-organizations specialized by areas such as sales, production, and so forth.

---

[i] with new addresses

Authority is delegated down the organizational structure and when necessary issues are escalated upward. Authority requires accountability for its use including record keeping and periodic reports. Management is in large part the art of reconciling authority and accountability.

Actor technology will see significant application for coordinating all kinds of digital information for individuals, groups, and organizations so their information usefully links together.

Information coordination needs to make use of the following information system principles:
- *Persistence*. *Information is collected and indexed.*
- *Concurrency*: *Work proceeds interactively and concurrently, overlapping in time.*
- *Quasi-commutativity*: *Information can be used regardless of whether it initiates new work or become relevant to ongoing work.*
- *Sponsorship*: *Sponsors provide resources for computation, i.e., processing, storage, and communications.*
- *Pluralism*: *Information is heterogeneous, overlapping and often inconsistent.*
- *Provenance*: *The provenance of information is carefully tracked and recorded*

The Actor Model is intended to provide a foundation for inconsistency robust information coordination.

Acknowledgements

Important contributions to the semantics of Actors have been made by: Gul Agha, Beppe Attardi, Henry Baker, Will Clinger, Irene Greif, Carl Manning, Ian Mason, Ugo Montanari, Maria Simi, Scott Smith, Carolyn Talcott, Prasanna Thati, and Aki Yonezawa.

Important contributions to the implementation of Actors have been made by: Gul Agha, Bill Athas, Russ Atkinson, Beppe Attardi, Henry Baker, Gerry Barber, Peter Bishop, Nanette Boden, Jean-Pierre Briot, Bill Dally, Blaine Garst, Peter de Jong, Jessie Dedecker, Ken Kahn, Rajesh Karmani, Henry Lieberman, Carl Manning, Mark S. Miller, Tom Reinhardt, Chuck Seitz, Amin Shali, Richard Steiger, Dan Theriault, Mario Tokoro, Darrell Woelk, and Carlos Varela.

Research on the Actor Model has been carried out at Caltech Computer Science, Kyoto University Tokoro Laboratory, MCC, MIT Artificial Intelligence Laboratory, SRI, Stanford University, University of Illinois at Urbana-Champaign Open Systems Laboratory, Pierre and Marie Curie University (University of Paris 6), University of Pisa, University of Tokyo Yonezawa Laboratory and elsewhere.

Conversations over the years with Dennis Allison, Bruce Anderson, Arvind, Bob Balzer, Bruce Baumgart, Gordon Bell, Dan Bobrow, Rod Burstall, Luca Cardelli, Vint Cerf, Keith Clark, Douglas Crockford, Jack Dennis, Peter Deutsch, Edsger Dijkstra, Scott Fahlman, Dan Friedman, Ole-Johan Dahl, Julian Davies, Patrick Dussud, Doug Englebart, Bob Filman, Kazuhiro Fuchi, Cordell Green, Jim Gray, Pat Hayes, Anders Hejlsberg, Pat Helland, John Hennessy, Tony Hoare, Mike Huhns, Dan Ingalls, Anita Jones, Bob Kahn, Gilles Kahn, Alan Karp, Alan Kay, Bob Kowalski, Monica Lam, Butler Lampson, Leslie Lamport, Peter Landin, Vic Lesser, Jerry Lettvin, Lick Licklider, Barbara Liskov, John McCarthy, Drew McDermott, Dave McQueen, Erik Meijer, Robin Milner, Marvin Minsky, Fanya S. Montalvo, Ike Nassi, Alan Newell, Kristen Nygaard, Seymour Papert, David Patterson, Carl Petri, Gordon Plotkin, Vaughan Pratt, John Reynolds, Jeff Rulifson, Earl Sacerdoti, Vijay Saraswat, Munindar Singh, Dana Scott, Ehud Shapiro, Burton Smith, Guy Steele, Gerry Sussman, Chuck Thacker, Kazunori Ueda, Dave Unger, Richard Waldinger, Peter Wegner, Richard Weyhrauch, Jeannette Wing, Terry Winograd, Glynn Winskel, David Wise, Bill Wulf, *etc.* greatly contributed to the development of the ideas in this article.

The members of the Silicon Valley Friday AM group made valuable suggestions for improving this paper. Blaine Garst found numerous bugs and made valuable comments including information on the historical development of interfaces. Patrick Beard found bugs and suggested improvements in presentation. Discussions with Dennis Allison, Eugene Miya, Vaughan Pratt and others were helpful in improving this article. As reviewers for Inconsistency Robustness 2011, Blaine Garst, Mike Huhns and Patrick Suppes made valuable suggestions for improvement. Discussions with Dale Schumacher helped clarify issues with Fog Cutter Actors and also helped debug the axiomatization of runtime failures in the Actor Model. Phil Bernstein, Sergey Bykov, and Gabi Kliot provide valuable comments on the section on Orleans Actors. Terry Hayes, Chris Hibbert, Daira Hopwood, Ken Kahn, Alan Karp, William Leslie, and Mark S. Miller and made helpful suggestions for the sections on capability, Orleans, and JavaScript Actors. Dan Ingalls made helpful suggestions on the sections on Smalltalk and elsewhere.

The Actor Model is intended to provide a foundation for scalable inconsistency-robust information coordination in privacy-friendly client-cloud computing [Hewitt 2009b].

Bibliography
Hal Abelson and Gerry *Sussman Structure and Interpretation of Computer Programs* 1984.
Gul Agha. *Actors: A Model of Concurrent Computation in Distributed Systems* Doctoral Dissertation. 1986.

Gul Agha, Ian Mason, Scott Smith, and Carolyn Talcott. "A foundation for Actor computation." *Journal of Functional Programming.* 1997.
Mikael Amborn. *Facet-Oriented Program Design.* LiTH-IDA-EX–04/047–SE Linköpings Universitet. 2004.
AMD *AMD64 Architecture Programmer's Manual* October 12, 3011
Joe Armstrong *History of Erlang* HOPL III. 2007.
Joe Armstrong. *Erlang.* CACM. September 2010.
William Athas and Charles Seitz *Multicomputers: message-passing concurrent computers* IEEE Computer August 1988.
William Athas and Nanette Boden *Cantor: An Actor Programming System for Scientific Computing* in Proceedings of the NSF Workshop on Object-Based Concurrent Programming. 1988. Special Issue of SIGPLAN Notices.
Russ Atkinson. *Automatic Verification of Serializers* MIT Doctoral Dissertation. June, 1980.
Henry Baker. *Actor Systems for Real-Time Computation* MIT EECS Doctoral Dissertation. January 1978.
Henry Baker and Carl Hewitt *The Incremental Garbage Collection of Processes* Proceeding of the Symposium on Artificial Intelligence Programming Languages. SIGPLAN Notices 12, August 1977.
Paul Baran. *On Distributed Communications Networks* IEEE Transactions on Communications Systems. March 1964.
Gerry Barber. *Reasoning about Change in Knowledgeable Office Systems* MIT EECS Doctoral Dissertation. August 1981.
John Barton. *Language Features* November 12, 2014.
https://github.com/google/traceur-compiler/wiki/LanguageFeatures
Robert Bemer *How to consider a computer* Data Control Section, Automatic Control Magazine. March 1957.
Robert Bemer. *The status of automatic programming for scientific computation* Proc. 4th Annual Computer Applications Symposium. Armour Research Foundation. October 1057. (Panel discussion, pp. 118-126).
Philip A. Bernstein, Sergey Bykov, Alan Geller, Gabriel Kliot, and Jorgen Thelin, *Orleans: Distributed Virtual Actors for Programmability and Scalability* Microsoft MSR-TR-2014-41. March 24, 2014.
Harold Boley. *A Tight, Practical Integration of Relations and Functions* Springer.1999.
Sergey Bykov, Alan Geller, Gabriel Kliot, James Larus, Ravi Pandya, and Jorgen Thelin. *Orleans: A Framework for Cloud Computing* Microsoft MSR-TR-2010-159. November 30, 2010
Sergey Bykov. *Building Real-Time Services for Halo* Microsoft Research. June 26, 2013.
Peter Bishop *Very Large Address Space Modularly Extensible Computer Systems* MIT EECS Doctoral Dissertation. June 1977.

Andreas Blass, Yuri Gurevich, Dean Rosenzweig, and Benjamin Rossman (2007a) *Interactive small-step algorithms I: Axiomatization* Logical Methods in Computer Science. 2007.

Andreas Blass, Yuri Gurevich, Dean Rosenzweig, and Benjamin Rossman (2007b) *Interactive small-step algorithms II: Abstract state machines and the characterization theorem.* Logical Methods in Computer Science. 2007.

Per Brinch Hansen *Monitors and Concurrent Pascal: A Personal History* CACM 1996.

Stephen Brookes, Tony Hoare, and Bill Roscoe. *A theory of communicating sequential processes* JACM. July 1984.

Don Box, David Ehnebuske, Gopal Kakivaya, Andrew Layman, Noah Mendelsohn, Henrik Nielsen, Satish Thatte, Dave Winer. *Simple Object Access Protocol (SOAP) 1.1* World Wide Web Consortium Note. May 2000.

Jean-Pierre Briot. *Acttalk: A framework for object-oriented concurrent programming-design and experience* 2nd France-Japan workshop. 1999.

Jean-Pierre Briot. *From objects to Actors: Study of a limited symbiosis in Smalltalk-80* Rapport de Recherche 88-58, RXF-LITP. Paris, France. September 1988.

Luca Cardelli, James Donahue, Lucille Glassman, Mick Jordan, Bill Kalsow, Greg Nelson. *Modula-3 report (revised)* DEC Systems Research Center Research Report 52. November 1989.

Luca Cardelli and Andrew Gordon *Mobile Ambients* FoSSaCS'98.

Arnaud Carayol, Daniel Hirschkoff, and Davide Sangiorgi. *On the representation of McCarthy's amb in the π-calculus* "Theoretical Computer Science" February 2005.

Bernadette Charron-Bost, Friedemann Mattern, and Gerard Tel. S*ynchronous, Asynchronous, and Causally Ordered Communication* Distributed Computing. 1995.

Alonzo Church "A Set of postulates for the foundation of logic (1&2)" Annals of Mathematics. Vol. 33, 1932. Vol. 34, 1933.

Alonzo Church. *An unsolvable problem of elementary number theory* American Journal of Mathematics. 58. 1936.

Alonzo Church *The Calculi of Lambda-Conversion* Princeton University Press. 1941.

Will Clinger. *Foundations of Actor Semantics* MIT Mathematics Doctoral Dissertation. June 1981.

Tyler Close. *Web-key: Mashing with Permission* WWW'08.

Melvin Conway. *Design of a separable transition-diagram compiler* CACM. 1963.

Eric Crahen. Facet: A pattern for dynamic interfaces. CSE Dept. SUNY at Buffalo. July 22, 2002.

Ole-Johan Dahl and Kristen Nygaard. "Class and subclass declarations" *IFIP TC2 Conference on Simulation Programming Languages.* May 1967.

Ole-Johan Dahl and Tony Hoare. *Hierarchical Program Structures* in "Structured Programming" Prentice Hall. 1972.

William Dally and Wills, D. *Universal mechanisms for concurrency* PARLE '89.

William Dally, et al. *The Message-Driven Processor: A Multicomputer Processing Node with Efficient Mechanisms* IEEE Micro. April 1992.

Jack Dennis and Earl Van Horn. *Programming Semantics for Multiprogrammed Computations* CACM. March 1966.

ECMA. *C# Language Specification* June 2006.

ECMA *ECMAScript Language Specification 6th Edition Draft* December 6, 2014.

Jed Donnelley. *A Distributed Capability Computing System* Proceedings of the Third International Conference on Computer Communication. August, 1976.

Lars Ekeroth and Per-Martin Hedström. *General Packet Radio Service (GPRS) Support Notes* Ericsson Review No. 3. 2000.

Arthur Fine *The Shaky Game: Einstein Realism and the Quantum Theory* University of Chicago Press, Chicago, 1986.

Nissim Francez, Tony Hoare, Daniel Lehmann, and Willem-Paul de Roever. *Semantics of nondeterminism, concurrency, and communication* Journal of Computer and System Sciences. December 1979.

Christopher Fuchs *Quantum mechanics as quantum information (and only a little more)* in A. Khrenikov (ed.) Quantum Theory: Reconstruction of Foundations (Växjo: Växjo University Press, 2002).

Blaine Garst. *Origin of Interfaces* Email to Carl Hewitt on October 2, 2009.

Elihu M. Gerson. *Prematurity and Social Worlds* in Prematurity in Scientific Discovery. University of California Press. 2002.

Andreas Glausch and Wolfgang Reisig. *Distributed Abstract State Machines and Their Expressive Power* Informatik Berichete 196. Humboldt University of Berlin. January 2006.

Adele Goldberg and Alan Kay (ed.) *Smalltalk-72 Instruction Manual* SSL 76-6. Xerox PARC. March 1976.

Dina Goldin and Peter Wegner. *The Interactive Nature of Computing: Refuting the Strong Church-Turing Thesis* Minds and Machines March 2008.

Irene Greif and Carl Hewitt. *Actor Semantics of PLANNER-73* Conference Record of ACM Symposium on Principles of Programming Languages. January 1975.

Irene Greif. *Semantics of Communicating Parallel Professes* MIT EECS Doctoral Dissertation. August 1975.

Werner Heisenberg. *Physics and Beyond: Encounters and Conversations* translated by A. J. Pomerans (Harper & Row, New York, 1971), pp. 63–64.

Carl Hewitt, Peter Bishop and Richard Steiger. *A Universal Modular Actor Formalism for Artificial Intelligence* IJCAI'73.

Carl Hewitt, et al. *Actor Induction and Meta-evaluation* Conference Record of ACM Symposium on Principles of Programming Languages, January 1974.

Carl Hewitt, *The Apiary Network Architecture for Knowledgeable Systems* Proceedings of Lisp Conference. 1980.

Carl Hewitt and Henry Lieberman. *Design Issues in Parallel Architecture for Artificial Intelligence* MIT AI memo 750. Nov. 1983.

Carl Hewitt, Tom Reinhardt, Gul Agha, and Giuseppe Attardi *Linguistic Support of Receptionists for Shared Resources* MIT AI Memo 781. Sept. 1984.

Carl Hewitt, et al. *Behavioral Semantics of Nonrecursive Control Structure* Proceedings of *Colloque sur la Programmation*, April 1974.

Carl Hewitt. *How to Use What You Know* IJCAI. September, 1975.

Carl Hewitt. *Viewing Control Structures as Patterns of Passing Messages* AI Memo 410. December 1976. Journal of Artificial Intelligence. June 1977.

Carl Hewitt and Henry Baker *Laws for Communicating Parallel Processes* IFIP-77, August 1977.

Carl Hewitt and Russ Atkinson. *Specification and Proof Techniques for Serializers* IEEE Journal on Software Engineering. January 1979.

Carl Hewitt, Beppe Attardi, and Henry Lieberman. *Delegation in Message Passing* Proceedings of First International Conference on Distributed Systems Huntsville, AL. October 1979.

Carl Hewitt and Gul Agha. *Guarded Horn clause languages: are they deductive and Logical?* in Artificial Intelligence at MIT, Vol. 2. MIT Press 1991.

Carl Hewitt and Jeff Inman. *DAI Betwixt and Between: From "Intelligent Agents" to Open Systems Science* IEEE Transactions on Systems, Man, and Cybernetics. Nov./Dec. 1991.

Carl Hewitt and Peter de Jong. *Analyzing the Roles of Descriptions and Actions in Open Systems* Proceedings of the National Conference on Artificial Intelligence. August 1983.

Carl Hewitt. (2006). "What is Commitment? Physical, Organizational, and Social" *COIN@AAMAS'06*. (Revised in Springer Verlag Lecture Notes in Artificial Intelligence. Edited by Javier Vázquez-Salceda and Pablo Noriega. 2007) April 2006.

Carl Hewitt (2007a). "Organizational Computing Requires Unstratified Paraconsistency and Reflection" *COIN@AAMAS*. 2007.

Carl Hewitt (2008a) <u>Norms and Commitment for iOrgs[TM] Information Systems: Direct Logic[TM] and Participatory Argument Checking</u> ArXiv 0906.2756.

Carl Hewitt (2008b) "Large-scale Organizational Computing requires Unstratified Reflection and Strong Paraconsistency" *Coordination, Organizations, Institutions, and Norms in Agent Systems III* Jaime Sichman, Pablo Noriega, Julian Padget and Sascha Ossowski (ed.). Springer-Verlag. *http://organizational.carlhewitt.info/*

Carl Hewitt (2008c) <u>Middle History of Logic Programming: Resolution, Planner, Edinburgh Logic for Computable Functions, Prolog and the Japanese Fifth Generation Project</u> ArXiv 0904.3036.

Carl Hewitt (2008e). *ORGs for Scalable, Robust, Privacy-Friendly Client Cloud Computing* IEEE Internet Computing September/October 2008.

Carl Hewitt (2008f) *Formalizing common sense for scalable inconsistency-robust information integration using Direct Logic™ and the Actor Model* Inconsistency Robust 2011.

Carl Hewitt (2009a) *Perfect Disruption: The Paradigm Shift from Mental Agents to ORGs* IEEE Internet Computing. Jan/Feb 2009.

Carl Hewitt (2009b) *A historical perspective on developing foundations for client-cloud computing: iConsult™ & iEntertain™ Apps using iInfo™ Information Integration for iOrgs™ Information Systems* (Revised version of "Development of Logic Programming: What went wrong, What was done about it, and What it might mean for the future" AAAI Workshop on What Went Wrong. AAAI-08.) ArXiv 0901.4934.

Carl Hewitt (2009c) *Middle History of Logic Programming: Resolution, Planner, Prolog and the Japanese Fifth Generation Project* ArXiv 0904.3036

Carl Hewitt (2010a) *ActorScript™ extension of C#®, Java®, and Objective C®:, iAdaptive™ concurrency for antiCloud™-privacy and security in* Inconsistency Robustness. College Publications. 2015.

Carl Hewitt, Erik Meijer, and Clemens Szyperski "The Actor Model (everything you wanted to know, but were afraid to ask)" http://channel9.msdn.com/Shows/Going+Deep/Hewitt-Meijer-and-Szyperski-The-Actor-Model-everything-you-wanted-to-know-but-were-afraid-to-ask Microsoft Channel 9. April 9, 2012.

Carl Hewitt. *"Health Information Systems Technologies"* http://ee380.stanford.edu/cgi-bin/videologger.php?target=120606-ee380-300.asx Slides for this video: http://HIST.carlhewitt.info Stanford CS Colloquium. June 6, 2012.

Carl Hewitt. *What is computation? Actor Model versus Turing's Model* in "A Computable Universe: Understanding Computation & Exploring Nature as Computation". edited by Hector Zenil. World Scientific Publishing. Company. 2012 . PDF at http://what-is-computation.carlhewitt.info

Tony Hoare Quick sort Computer Journal 5 (1) 1962.

Tony Hoare *Monitors: An Operating System Structuring Concept* CACM. October 1974.

Tony Hoare. *Communicating sequential processes* CACM. August 1978.

Tony Hoare. *Communicating Sequential Processes* Prentice Hall. 1985.

Waldemer Horwat, Andrew Chien, and William Dally. *Experience with CST: Programming and Implementation* PLDI. 1989.

Daniel Ingalls. *Design Principles Behind Smalltalk*. Byte. August 1981.

Daniel Ingalls, Ted Kaehler, John Maloney, Scott Wallace, and Alan Kay. *Back to the Future: the story of Squeak, a practical Smalltalk written in itself* ACM Digital Library. 1997.

Peter Ingerman, *Thunks: A Way of Compiling Procedure Statements with Some Comments on Procedure Declarations*. CACM 4 (1). 1961.

Intel. *Intel Memory Protection Extensions (Intel MPX) support in the GCC compiler* GCC Wiki. November 24, 2014.

ISO. *ISO/IEC 14882:2011(E) Programming Languages -- C++, Third Edition* August, 2011.

Max Jammer *The EPR Problem in Its Historical Development* in Symposium on the Foundations of Modern Physics: 50 years of the Einstein-Podolsky-Rosen Gedankenexperiment, edited by P. Lahti and P. Mittelstaedt. World Scientific. Singapore. 1985.

Stanisław Jaśkowski On the Rules of Suppositions in Formal Logic *Studia Logica* 1, 1934. (reprinted in: *Polish logic 1920-1939*, Oxford University Press, 1967.)

Simon Peyton Jones, Andrew Gordon, Sigbjorn Finne. *Concurrent Haskell*, POPL'96.

Ken Kahn. *A Computational Theory of Animation* MIT EECS Doctoral Dissertation. August 1979.

Matthias Kaiser and Jens Lemcke *Towards a Framework for Policy-Oriented Enterprise Management* AAAI 2008.

Alan Karp and Jun Li. *Solving the Transitive Access Problem for the Services Oriented Architecture* HPL-2008-204R1. HP Laboratories 2008.

Alan Karp and Jun Li. *Access Control for the Services Oriented Architecture* ACM Workshop on Secure Web Services. November 2007

Rajesh Karmani and Gul Agha. *Actors*. Encyclopedia of Parallel Computing 2011.

Alan Kay. "Personal Computing" in *Meeting on 20 Years of Computing Science* Instituto di Elaborazione della Informazione, Pisa, Italy. 1975. *http://www.mprove.de/diplom/gui/Kay75.pdf*

Alan Kay. *Alan Kay on Messaging* Squeak email list. October 10, 1998.

Frederick Knabe *A Distributed Protocol for Channel-Based Communication with Choice* PARLE'92.

Jorgen Knudsen and Ole Madsen. *Teaching Object-Oriented Programming is more than teaching Object-Oriented Programming Languages* ECOOP'88. Springer. 1988.

Bill Kornfeld and Carl Hewitt. *The Scientific Community Metaphor* IEEE Transactions on Systems, Man, and Cybernetics. January 1981.

Bill Kornfeld. *Parallelism in Problem Solving* MIT EECS Doctoral Dissertation. August 1981.

Robert Kowalski. *A proof procedure using connection graphs* JACM. October 1975.

Robert Kowalski *Algorithm = Logic + Control* CACM. July 1979.

Robert Kowalski. *Response to questionnaire* Special Issue on Knowledge Representation. SIGART Newsletter. February 1980.

Robert Kowalski (1988a) *The Early Years of Logic Programming* CACM. January 1988.

Robert Kowalski (1988b) *Logic-based Open Systems* Representation and Reasoning. Stuttgart Conference Workshop on Discourse Representation, Dialogue tableaux and Logic Programming. 1988.

Stein Krogdahl. *The birth of Simula* HiNC 1 Conference. Trondheim. June 2003.

Albert Kwon, Udit Dhawan, Jonathan Smith, Tom. Knight, Jr., and André DeHon, "Low-fat pointers: Compact encoding and efficient gate-level implementation of fat pointers for spatial safety and capability-based security," in 20th ACM Conference on Computer and Communications Security, November 2013.

Leslie Lamport *Time, Clocks, and Orderings of Events in a Distributed System* CACM. 1978.

Leslie Lamport *How to make a multiprocessor computer that correctly executes multiprocess programs* IEEE Transactions on Computers. 1979.

Peter Landin. *A Generalization of Jumps and Labels* UNIVAC Systems Programming Research Report. August 1965. (Reprinted in *Higher Order and Symbolic Computation.* 1998)

Peter Landin *A correspondence between ALGOL 60 and Church's lambda notation* CACM. August 1965.

Edward Lee and Stephen Neuendorffer (June 2004). *Classes and Subclasses in Actor-Oriented Design.* Conference on Formal Methods and Models for Codesign (MEMOCODE).

Henry Levy. Capability-Based Computer Systems Digital Press. 1984.

Steven Levy *Hackers: Heroes of the Computer Revolution* Doubleday. 1984.

Henry Lieberman. *An Object-Oriented Simulator for the Apiary* Conference of the American Association for Artificial Intelligence, Washington, D. C., August 1983

Henry Lieberman. *Thinking About Lots of Things at Once without Getting Confused: Parallelism in Act 1* MIT AI memo 626. May 1981.

Henry Lieberman. *A Preview of Act 1* MIT AI memo 625. June 1981.

Henry Lieberman and Carl Hewitt. *A real Time Garbage Collector Based on the Lifetimes of Objects* CACM June 1983.

Barbara Liskov *Data abstraction and hierarchy* Keynote address. OOPSLA'87.

Barbara Liskov and Liuba Shrira *Promises: Linguistic Support for Efficient Asynchronous Procedure Calls* SIGPLAN'88.

Barbara Liskov and Jeannette Wing. *Behavioral subtyping using invariants and constraints* in "Formal methods for distributed processing: a survey of object-oriented approaches" Cambridge University Press. 2001.

Carl Manning. *Traveler: the Actor observatory* ECOOP 1987. Also appears in Lecture Notes in Computer Science, vol. 276.

Carl Manning,. *Acore: The Design of a Core Actor Language and its Compile* Master's Thesis. MIT EECS. May 1987.

Satoshi Matsuoka and Aki Yonezawa. *Analysis of Inheritance Anomaly in Object-Oriented Concurrent Programming Languages Research Directions in Concurrent Object-Oriented Programming* MIT Press. 1993.

John McCarthy *Programs with common sense* Symposium on Mechanization of Thought Processes. National Physical Laboratory, UK. Teddington, England. 1958.

John McCarthy. *A Basis for a Mathematical Theory of Computation* Western Joint Computer Conference. 1961.

John McCarthy, Paul Abrahams, Daniel Edwards, Timothy Hart, and Michael Levin. *Lisp 1.5 Programmer's Manual* MIT Computation Center and Research Laboratory of Electronics. 1962.

John McCarthy. *Situations, actions and causal laws* Technical Report Memo 2, Stanford University Artificial Intelligence Laboratory. 1963.

John McCarthy and Patrick Hayes. *Some Philosophical Problems from the Standpoint of Artificial Intelligence* Machine Intelligence 4. Edinburgh University Press. 1969.

Erik Meijer and Gavin Bierman. *A co-Relational Model of Data for Large Shared Data Banks* ACM Queue. March 2011.

Microsoft. *Asynchronous Programming with Async and Await* MSDN. 2013.

Giuseppe Milicia and Vladimiro Sassone. *The Inheritance Anomaly: Ten Years After* SAC. Nicosia, Cyprus. March 2004.

Mark S. Miller, Eric Dean Tribble, and Jonathan Shapiro. *Concurrency Among Strangers: Programming in E as Plan Coordination* Proceedings of the International Symposium on Trustworthy Global Computing. Springer. 2005.

Mark S. Miller, Ka-Ping Yee, and Jonathan Shapiro. *Capability Myths Demolished* Submitted to Usenix Security 2003.

Mark S. Miller and Jonathan Shapiro *Paradigm Regained: Abstraction Mechanisms for Access Control* ASIAN'03. 2003.

Mark S. Miller *Robust Composition: Towards a Unified Approach to Access Control and Concurrency Control* Doctoral Dissertation. John Hopkins. 2006.

Mark S. Miller *et. al. Bringing Object-orientation to Security Programming.* YouTube. November 3, 2011.

George Milne and Robin Milner. "Concurrent processes and their syntax" *JACM*. April, 1979.

Robert Milne and Christopher Strachey. *A Theory of Programming Language Semantics* Chapman and Hall. 1976.

Robin Milner *Processes: A Mathematical Model of Computing Agents* Proceedings of Bristol Logic Colloquium. 1973.

Robin Milner *Elements of interaction: Turing award lecture* CACM. January 1993.

Marvin Minsky (ed.) *Semantic Information Processing* MIT Press. 1968.

Ugo Montanari and Carolyn Talcott. *Can Actors and Pi-Agents Live Together?* Electronic Notes in Theoretical Computer Science. 1998.

Eugenio Moggi *Computational lambda-calculus and monads* IEEE Symposium on Logic in Computer Science. Asilomar, California, June 1989.

Allen Newell and Herbert Simon. *The Logic Theory Machine: A Complex Information Processing System.* Rand Technical Report P-868. June 15, 1956

Kristen Nygaard. *SIMULA: An Extension of ALGOL to the Description of Discrete-Event Networks* IFIP'62. Kristen Nygaard. *Basic Concepts in Object Oriented Programming* Special Edition on Object-Oriented Programming Languages. SIGPLAN Notices. Vol. 21. November 1986.

David Park. *Concurrency and Automata on Infinite Sequences* Lecture Notes in Computer Science, Vol. 104. Springer. 1980.

Elliot Organick. *A Programmer's View of the Intel 432 System* McGraw-Hill, 1983.

Carl Petri. *Kommunikation mit Automate* Ph. D. Thesis. University of Bonn. 1962.

Simon Peyton Jones, Alastair Reid, Fergus Henderson, Tony Hoare, and Simon Marlow. *A semantics for imprecise exceptions* Conference on Programming Language Design and Implementation. 1999.

Gordon Plotkin. *A powerdomain construction* SIAM Journal of Computing. September 1976.

George Polya (1957) *Mathematical Discovery: On Understanding, Learning and Teaching Problem Solving Combined Edition* Wiley. 1981.

Karl Popper (1935, 1963) *Conjectures and Refutations: The Growth of Scientific Knowledge* Routledge. 2002.

Claudius Ptolemaeus, Editor. *System Design, Modeling, and Simulation: Using Ptolemy II* LuLu. http://ptolemy.org/systems. 2014.

Susan Rajunas. *The KeyKOS/KeySAFE System Design.* Technical Report SEC009-01. Key Logic, Inc. March 1989.

John Reppy, Claudio Russo, and Yingqi Xiao *Parallel Concurrent ML* ICFP'09.

John Reynolds. *Definitional interpreters for higher order programming languages* ACM Conference Proceedings. 1972.

John Reynolds. *The Discoveries of Continuations* Lisp and Symbolic Computation *6 (3-4).* 1993.

Bill Roscoe. *The Theory and Practice of Concurrency* Prentice-Hall. Revised 2005.

Alex Russell. *A design for Futures/Promises in DOM.* W3C. March 7, 2013.

Dale Schumacher. *Implementing Actors in Kernel* February 16, 2012. http://www.dalnefre.com/wp/2012/02/implementing-actors-in-kernel/

Dana Scott and Christopher Strachey. *Toward a mathematical semantics for computer languages* Oxford Programming Research Group Technical Monograph. PRG-6. 1971

Dana Scott *Data Types as Lattices.* SIAM Journal on computing. 1976.

Charles Seitz. *The Cosmic Cube* CACM. Jan. 1985.

Peter Sewell, et. al. *x86-TSO: A Rigorous and Usable Programmer's Model for x86 Microprocessors* CACM. July 2010.

Jonathan Shapiro and Jonathan Adams. *Coyotos Microkernel Specification* EROS Group. September 10, 2007.

SIGPLAN. *Special Edition on Object-Oriented Programming Languages* SIGPLAN Notices. Vol. 21. November 1986.

Michael Smyth. *Power domains.* Computer and System Sciences. 1978.

Alfred Spiessens. *Patterns of Safe Collaboration.* Doctoral Thesis. Université catholique de Louvain. February 2007.

Guy Steele Jr. *Lambda: The Ultimate Declarative* MIT AI Memo 379. November 1976.

Lynn Stein, Henry Lieberman, and David Ungar. *A Shared View of Sharing: The Treaty of Orlando* Object-oriented concepts, databases, and applications. ACM. 1989

Jan Stenberg. *Building Halo 4, a Video Game, Using Actor Model.* InfoQ. March 7, 2015.

Gunther Stent. *Prematurity and Uniqueness in Scientific Discovery* Scientific American. December, 1972.

Sun *Java Specification Request 133* 2004

Gerry Sussman and Guy Steele *Scheme: An Interpreter for Extended Lambda Calculus* AI Memo 349. December, 1975.

Daniel Theriault. *A Primer for the Act-1 Language* MIT AI memo 672. 1982.

Daniel Theriault. *Issues in the Design and Implementation of Act 2* MIT AI technical report 728. June 1983.

Hayo Thielecke *An Introduction to Landin's "A Generalization of Jumps and Labels"* Higher-Order and Symbolic Computation. 1998.

Dave Thomas and Brian Barry. *Using Active Objects for Structuring Service Oriented Architectures: Anthropomorphic Programming with Actors* Journal of Object Technology. July-August 2004.

Bill Tulloh and Mark S. Miller. *Institutions as Abstraction Boundaries* Humane Economics: Essays in Honor of Don Lavoie. Elgar Publishing. 2006.

Ulf Wiger. *1000 Year-old Design Patterns* QCon. Apr 21, 2011.

Jonathan Woodruff, Robert N. M. Watson, David Chisnall, Simon W. Moore, Jonathan Anderson, Brooks Davis, Ben Laurie, Peter G. Neumann, Robert Norton, and Michael Roe. *The CHERI capability model: Revisiting RISC in an age of risk* International Symposium on Computer Architecture (ISCA). June 2014.

Robert N. M. Watson, Jonathan Woodruff, Peter G. Neumann, Simon W. Moore, Jonathan Anderson, David Chisnall, Nirav Dave, Brooks Davis, Khilan Gudka, Ben Laurie, Steven J. Murdoch, Robert Norton, Michael Roe, Stacey Son, and Munraj Vadera. *CHERI: A Hybrid Capability-System Architecture for Scalable Software Compartmentalization* IEEE Symposium on Security and Privacy. May 2015

Darrell Woelk. *Developing InfoSleuth Agents Using Rosette: An Actor Based Language* Proceedings of the CIKM '95 Workshop on Intelligent Information Agents. 1995.

World Wide Web Consortium. *HTML5: A vocabulary and associated APIs for HTML and XHTML* Editor's Draft. August 22, 2012.

Akinori Yonezawa, Ed. *ABCL: An Object-Oriented Concurrent System* MIT Press. 1990.

Akinori Yonezawa *Specification and Verification Techniques for Parallel Programs Based on Message Passing Semantics* MIT EECS Doctoral Dissertation. December 1977.

Takeshi Yoshino. *Intent to Implement: DOM Futures.* W3C. May 23, 2013

Hadasa Zuckerman and Joshua Lederberg. *Postmature Scientific Discovery?* Nature. December, 1986.

Appendix 1. Historical background[14]

The Actor Model builds on previous models of nondeterministic computation. Several models of nondeterministic computation were developed including the following:

Concurrency versus Turing's Model

Turing's model of computation was intensely psychological.[15] [Sieg 2008] formalized it as follows:
- *Boundedness:* A computer can immediately recognize only a bounded number of configurations.
- *Locality:* A computer can change only immediately recognizable configurations.

In the above, computation is conceived as being carried out in a single place by a device that proceeds from one well-defined state to the next.

Computations are represented differently in Turing Machines and Actors:
1. *Turing Machine*: a computation can be represented as a global state that determines all information about the computation.[16] It can be nondeterministic as to which will be the next global state.
2. *Actors*: a computation can be represented as a configuration. Information about a configuration can be indeterminate.[i]

Lambda calculus

The Lambda calculus was originally developed as part of a system for the foundations of logic [Church 1932-33]. However, the system was soon shown to be inconsistent. Subsequently, Church removed logical propositions from the system leaving a purely procedural lambda calculus [Church 1941].[17]

However, the semantics of the lambda calculus were expressed using string substitution in which the values of parameters were substituted into the body of an invoked lambda expression. The substitution model is unsuitable for concurrency because it does not allow the capability of sharing of changing resources.

That Actors which behave like mathematical functions exactly correspond with those definable in the lambda calculus provides an intuitive justification for the rules of the lambda calculus:
- *Lambda identifiers*: each identifier is bound to the address of an Actor. The rules for free and bound identifiers correspond to the Actor rules for addresses.

---

[i] For example, there can be messages in transit that will be delivered at some indefinite time.

- *Beta reduction*: each beta reduction corresponds to an Actor receiving a message. Instead of performing substitution, an Actor receives addresses of its arguments.

Inspired by the lambda calculus, the interpreter for the programming language Lisp [McCarthy *et. al.* 1962] made use of a data structure called an environment so that the values of parameters did not have to be substituted into the body of an invoked lambda expression.[18]

Note that in the definition in ActorScript [Hewitt 2011] of the lambda calculus below:
- All operations are local.
- The definition is modular in that each lambda calculus programming language construct is an Actor.
- The definition is easily extensible since it is easy to add additional programming language constructs.
- The definition is easily operationalized into efficient concurrent implementations.
- The definition easily fits into more general concurrent computational frameworks for many-core and distributed computation

The lambda calculus can be implemented in ActorScript as follows:

Actor Identifier◁aType▷[ ]
  implements Expression◁aType▷ **using**
    eval[anEnvironment]→
      anEnvironment.lookup[▪Expression◁aType▷]
            // lookup this identifier in **anEnvironment**

Actor ProcedureCall◁aType, AnotherType▷
      [operator:([aType]↦ anotherType), operand:aType]
  implements Expression◁anotherType▷ **using**
    eval[anEnvironment]→
      (operator.eval[anEnvironment]).[operand.eval[environment]]

Actor Lambda◁aType, AnotherType▷
    [anIdentifier:Identifier◁aType▷, body:anotherType]
  implements Expression◁[aType]↦ anotherType▷ **using**
  eval[anEnvironment]→
    [anArgument:aType]→
      body.eval[anEnvironment
        .bind[anIdentifier, anArgument]]
        // create a new environment with anIdentifier bound to
        // anArgument in anEnvironment

In many practical applications, the parallel lambda calculus (*i.e.* using purely functional programming) can be exponentially slower than concurrent computation using Actors.[i]

Petri nets

Prior to the development of the Actor Model, Petri nets[19] were widely used to model nondeterministic computation. However, they were widely acknowledged to have an important limitation: they modeled control flow but not data flow. Consequently they were not readily composable thereby limiting their modularity.

Hewitt pointed out another difficulty with Petri nets:
> Simultaneous action, *i.e.*, the atomic step of computation in Petri nets is a transition in which tokens simultaneously disappear from the input places of a transition and appear in the output places. The physical basis of using a primitive computational entity with this kind of simultaneity seemed questionable to him.

Despite these apparent difficulties, Petri nets continue to be a popular approach to modeling nondeterminism, and are still the subject of active research.

Simula

Simula 1 [Nygaard 1962] pioneered nondeterministic discrete event simulation using a global clock:
> *In this early version of Simula a system was modeled by a (fixed) number of "stations", each with a queue of "customers". The stations were the active parts, and each was controlled by a program that could "input" a customer from the station's queue, update variables (global, local in station, and local in customer), and transfer the customer to the queue of another station. Stations could discard customers by not transferring them to another queue, and could generate new customers. They could also wait a given period (in*

---

[i] For example, implementations using Actors of Direct Logic can be exponentially faster than implementations in the parallel lambda calculus.

simulated time) before starting the next action. Custom types were declared as data records, without any actions (or procedures) of their own. [Krogdahl 2003]

Thus at each time step, the program of the next station to be simulated would update the variables.

Kristen Nygaard and Ole-Johan Dahl developed the idea (first described in an IFIP workshop in 1967) of organizing objects into "classes" with "subclasses" that could inherit methods for performing operations from their super classes. In this way, Simula 67 considerably improved the modularity of nondeterministic discrete event simulations.

According to [Krogdahl 2003]:

Objects could act as processes that can execute in "quasi-parallel" that is in fact a form of nondeterministic sequential execution in which a simulation is organized as "independent" processes. Classes in Simula 67 have their own procedures that start when an object is generated. However, unlike Algol procedures, objects may choose to temporarily stop their execution and transfer the control to another process. If the control is later given back to the object, it will resume execution where the control last left off. A process will always retain the execution control until it explicitly gives it away. When the execution of an object reaches the end of its statements, it will become "terminated", and can no longer be resumed (but local data and local procedures can still be accessed from outside the object).

The quasi-parallel sequencing is essential for the simulation mechanism. Roughly speaking, it works as follows: When a process has finished the actions to be performed at a certain point in simulated time, it decides when (again in simulated time) it wants the control back, and stores this in a local "next-event-time" variable. It then gives the control to a central "time-manager", which finds the process that is to execute next (the one with the smallest next-event-time), updates the global time variable accordingly, and gives the control to that process.

The idea of this mechanism was to invite the programmer of a simulation program to model the underlying system by a set of processes, each describing some natural sequence of events in that system (e.g. the sequence of events experienced by one car in a traffic simulation).

Note that a process may transfer control to another process even if it is currently inside one or more procedure calls. Thus, each quasi-parallel process will have its own stack of procedure calls, and if it is not executing, its "reactivation point" will reside in the innermost of these calls. Quasi-parallel sequencing is analogous to the notion of co-routines [Conway 1963].

Note that Simula operated on the global state of a simulation and not just on the local variables of simulated objects.[20] Also Simula-67 lacked formal interfaces and instead relied on inheritance in a hierarchy of objects thereby placing limitations to the ability to define and invoke behavior no directly inherited.

Types in Simula are the names of implementations called "classes" in contrast with ActorScript in which types are interfaces that do not name their implementation. Also, although Simula had nondeterminism, it did not have concurrency.[21]

Planner

The two major paradigms for constructing semantic software systems were procedural and logical. The procedural paradigm was epitomized by using Lisp [McCarthy *et al.* 1962; Minsky, *et al.* 1968] recursive procedures operating on list structures. The logical paradigm was epitomized by uniform resolution theorem provers [Robinson 1965].

Planner [Hewitt 1969] was a kind of hybrid between the procedural and logical paradigms.[22] An implication of the form (P *implies* Q) was procedurally interpreted as follows:[23]
- **When asserted P, Assert Q**
- **When goal Q, SetGoal P**
- **When asserted** (*not* Q)**, Assert** (*not* P)
- **When goal** (*not* P)**, SetGoal** (*not* Q)

Planner was the first programming language based on the pattern-directed invocation of procedural plans from assertions and goals. *It represented a rejection of the resolution uniform proof procedure paradigm.*

Smalltalk-72

Planner, Simula 67, Smalltalk-72 [Kay 1975; Ingalls 1983] and packet-switched networks had previously used message passing. However, they were too complicated to use as the foundation for a mathematical theory of computation. Also they did not address fundamental issues of concurrency.

Alan Kay was influenced by message passing in the pattern-directed invocation of Planner in developing Smalltalk-71. Hewitt was intrigued by Smalltalk-71 but was put off by the complexity of communication that included invocations with many fields including global, sender, receiver, reply-style, status, reply, operator, *etc.*

In November 1972, Kay visited MIT and presented a lecture on some of his ideas for Smalltalk-72 building on the Logo work of Seymour Papert and the "little person" metaphor of computation used for teaching children to program. Smalltalk-72 made important advances in graphical user interfaces.

However, the message passing of Smalltalk-72 was quite complex [Kay 1975]. Code in the language was viewed by the interpreter as simply a stream of tokens. According to [Ingalls 1983]:[24]

> *The first (token) encountered (in a program) was looked up in the dynamic context, to determine the receiver of the subsequent message. The name lookup began with the class dictionary of the current activation. Failing there, it moved to the sender of that activation and so on up the sender chain. When a binding was finally found for the token, its value became the receiver of a new message, and the interpreter activated the code for that object's class.*[25]

Thus the message passing model in Smalltalk-72 was closely tied to a particular machine model and programming language syntax that did not lend itself to concurrency. Also, although the system was bootstrapped on itself, the language constructs were not formally defined as objects that respond to *eval* messages as in the definition of ActorScript [Hewitt 2010a].

Actors

The invention of digital computers caused a decisive paradigm shift when the notion of an interrupt was invented so that input that is received asynchronously from outside could be incorporated in an ongoing computation. At first concurrency was conceived using low level machine implementation concepts like threads, locks, coherent memory, channels, cores, queues, *etc.*

The Actor Model [Hewitt, Bishop, and Steiger 1973; *etc.*] was based on message passing that was different from previous models of computation because the sender of a message is not intrinsic to the semantics of a communication.[26]

In contrast to previous global state model, computation in the Actor Model is conceived as distributed in space where computational devices called Actors communicate asynchronously using addresses of Actors and the entire computation is not in any well-defined state.[27]

Axioms of locality including *Organizational* and *Operational* hold as follows:
- *Organization:* The local storage of an Actor can include *addresses* only
    1. that were provided when it was created
    2. that have been received in messages
    3. that are for Actors created here
- *Operation:* In response to a message received, an Actor can
    1. create more Actors
    2. send messages[i] to *addresses* in the following:
        - the message it has just received
        - its local storage
    3. for an exclusive Actor, designate how to process the next message received

In concrete terms for Actor systems, typically we cannot observe the details by which the order in which an Actor processes messages has been determined. Attempting to do so affects the results. Instead of observing the internals of arbitration processes of Actor computations, we await outcomes.[28] Indeterminacy in arbiters produces indeterminacy in Actors.[ii]

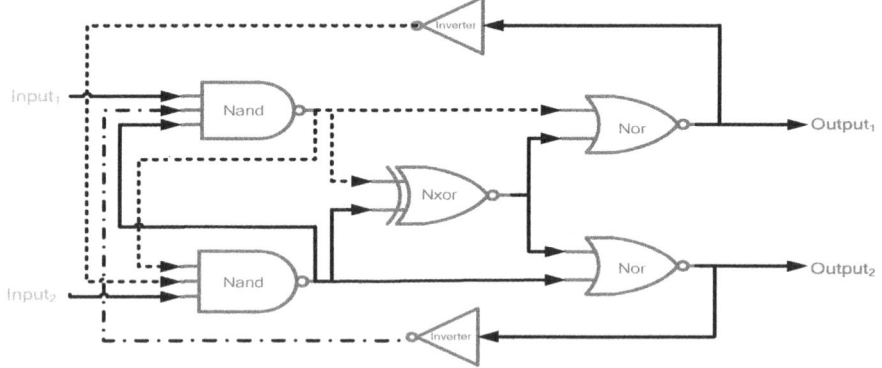

Arbiter Concurrency Primitive[29]

After the above circuit is started, it can remain in a meta-stable state for an unbounded period of time before it finally asserts either Output$_1$ or Output$_2$. So there is an inconsistency between the nondeterministic state model of computation and the circuit model of arbiters.[30]

The internal processes of arbiters are not public processes. Attempting to observe them affects their outcomes. Instead of observing the internals of arbitration processes, we necessarily await outcomes. Indeterminacy in arbiters produces indeterminacy in Actors. The reason that we await outcomes is that we have no realistic alternative.

---

[i] Likewise the messages sent can contain addresses only
   1. that were provided when the Actor was created
   2. that have been received in messages
   3. that are for Actors created here

[ii] The dashed lines are used only to disambiguate crossing wires.

The Actor Model integrated the following:
- the lambda calculus
- interrupts
- blocking method invocation
- imperative programming using locks
- capability systems
- co-routines
- packet networks
- email systems
- Petri nets
- Smalltalk-72
- Simula-67
- pattern-directed invocation (from Planner)

In 1975, Irene Greif published the first operational model of Actors in her dissertation. Two years after Greif published her operational model, Carl Hewitt and Henry Baker published the Laws for Actors [Baker and Hewitt 1977].

Indeterminacy in Concurrent Computation

The first models of computation (*e.g.* Turing machines, Post productions, the lambda calculus, *etc.*) were based on mathematics and made use of a global state to represent a computational *step* (later generalized in [McCarthy and Hayes 1969] and [Dijkstra 1976]). Each computational step was from one global state of the computation to the next global state. The global state approach was continued in automata theory for finite state machines and push down stack machines, including their nondeterministic versions.[31] Such nondeterministic automata have the property of bounded nondeterminism; that is, if a machine always halts when started in its initial state, then there is a bound on the number of states in which it halts.[32]

Gordon Plotkin [1976] gave an informal proof as follows:
Now the set of initial segments of execution sequences of a given nondeterministic program P, starting from a given state, will form a tree. The branching points will correspond to the choice points in the program. Since there are always only finitely many alternatives at each choice point, the branching factor of the tree is always finite.[33] That is, the tree is finitary. Now König's lemma says that if every branch of a finitary tree is finite, then so is the tree itself. In the present case this means that if every execution sequence of P terminates, then there are only finitely many execution sequences. So if an output set of P is infinite, it must contain a nonterminating computation.[34]

The above proof is quite general and applies to the Abstract State Machine (ASM) model [Blass, Gurevich, Rosenzweig, and Rossman 2007a, 2007b;

Glausch and Reisig 2006], which consequently are not really models of concurrency. It also applies to the parallel lambda calculus, which includes all the capabilities of the nondeterministic lambda calculus. Researchers (before the Actor Model was invented) hypothesized that the parallel lambda calculus naturally modeled all of computation and their research programme was to reduce all computation to the parallel lambda calculus [Scott and Strachey 1971, Milne and Strachey 1976]. One of the important early discoveries in the development of the Actor Model was that all of computation is not reducible to the parallel lambda calculus. In fact, there are Actor computations that cannot be implemented in the parallel lambda calculus. For example, by the semantics of the Actor Model of computation [Clinger 1981] [Hewitt 2006], concurrently sending the Actor below both a start message and a stop message will result in returning an integer of unbounded size for the stop message.

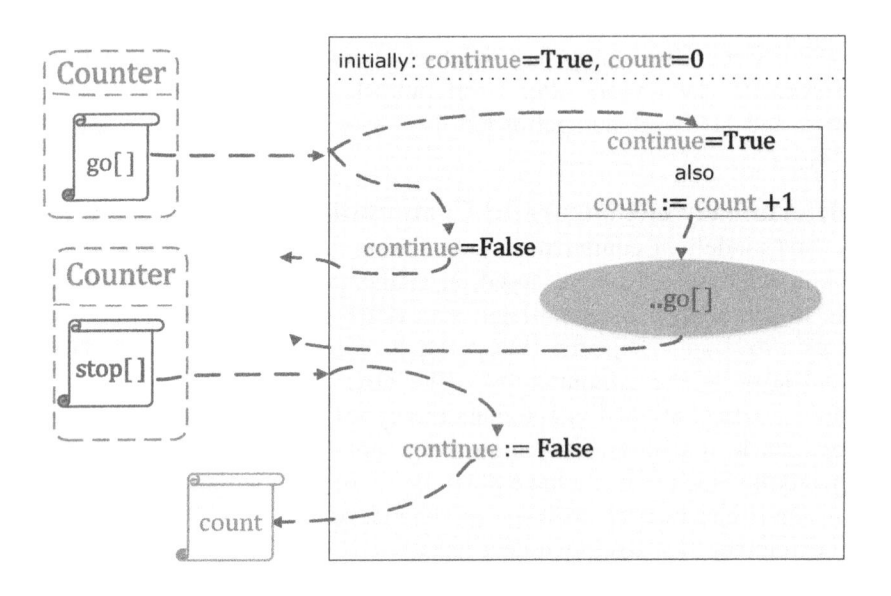

Theorem. There are nondeterministic computable functions on integers that cannot be implemented by a nondeterministic Turing machine.

Proof. The above Actor system implements a nondeterministic function[i] that cannot be implemented by a nondeterministic Turing machine.

Nondeterminism is a special case of Indeterminism.
Consider the following Nondeterministic Turing Machine that starts at *Step 1*:
  Step 1: Either print 1 on the next square of tape or execute *Step 3*.
  Step 2: Execute *Step 1*.
  Step 3: Halt.

---
[i] with graph {start[ ]⤳0, start[ ]⤳1, start[ ]⤳2, ...}

According to the definition of Nondeterministic Turing Machines, the above machine might never halt.

Note that the computations performed by the above machine are structurally different than the computations performed by the above counter Actor in the following way:
1. The decision making of the above Nondeterministic Turing Machine is internal (having an essentially psychological basis).
2. The decision making of the above counter Actor exhibits physical indeterminacy.

Edsger Dijkstra further developed the nondeterministic global state approach, which gave rise to a controversy concerning *unbounded nondeterminism*[i]. Unbounded nondeterminism is a property of concurrency by which the amount of delay in servicing a request can become unbounded as a result of arbitration of contention for shared resources *while providing a guarantee that the request will be serviced*. The Actor Model provides the guarantee of service. In Dijkstra's model, although there could be an unbounded amount of time between the execution of sequential instructions on a computer, a (parallel) program that started out in a well-defined state could terminate in only a bounded number of states [Dijkstra 1976]. He believed that it was impossible to implement unbounded nondeterminism.

Computation is not subsumed by logical deduction

Kowalski claims that "*computation could be subsumed by deduction*"[35] The gauntlet was officially thrown in *The Challenge of Open Systems* [Hewitt 1985] to which [Kowalski 1988b] replied in *Logic-Based Open Systems*.[ii] This was followed up with [Hewitt and Agha 1988] in the context of the Japanese Fifth Generation Project.

According to Hewitt, *et. al.* and contrary to Kowalski computation in general cannot be subsumed by deduction and contrary to the quotation (above) attributed to Hayes computation in general is not subsumed by deduction. [Hewitt and Agha 1991] and other published work argued that mathematical models of concurrency did not determine particular concurrent computations because they make use of arbitration for determining the order in which

---

[i] A system is defined to have *unbounded nondeterminism* exactly when both of the following hold:
  1. When started, the system always halts.
  2. For every integer n, the system can halt with an output that is greater than n.

[ii] [Kowalski 1979] forcefully stated:
  There is only one language suitable for representing information -- whether declarative or procedural -- and that is first-order predicate logic. There is only one intelligent way to process information -- and that is by applying deductive inference methods.

messages are processed. These orderings cannot be deduced from prior information by mathematical logic alone. Therefore mathematical logic cannot implement concurrent computation in open systems.

A nondeterministic system is defined to have *"unbounded nondeterminism"*[i] exactly when both of the following hold:
1. When started, the system *always* halts.
2. For every integer n, it is possible for the system to halt with output that is greater than n.

This article has discussed the following points about unbounded nondeterminism controversy:
- A Nondeterministic Turing Machine cannot implement unbounded nondeterminism.
- A Logic Program[36] cannot implement unbounded nondeterminism.
- Semantics of unbounded nondeterminism are required to prove that a server provides service to every client.[37]
- An Actor system [Hewitt, et. al. 1973] can implement servers that provide service to every client and consequently unbounded nondeterminism.
- Dijkstra believed that unbounded nondeterminism cannot be implemented [Dijkstra 1967; Dijkstra and van Gasteren 1986].
- The semantics of CSP [Francez, Hoare, Lehmann, and de Roever 1979] specified bounded nondeterminism for reasons mentioned above in the article. Since Hoare *et. al.* wanted to be able to prove that a server provided service to clients, the semantics of a subsequent version of CSP were switched from bounded to unbounded nondeterminism.
- Unbounded nondeterminism was but a symptom of deeper underlying issues with sequential processes using nondeterministic global states as a foundation for computation.[ii]

The Computational Representation Theorem [Clinger 1981, Hewitt 2006] characterizes the semantics of Actor Systems without making use of sequential processes.

Actor Model versus Classical Objects

The following are fundamental differences between the Actor Model and Classical Objects[Nygaard and Dahl 1967, Nygaard 1986]:
- Classical Objects[38] are founded on "a physical model, simulating the behavior of either a real or imaginary part of the world"[39], whereas the Actor Model is founded on the physics of computation.

---

[i] For example the following systems do *not* have unbounded nondeterminism:
- A nondeterministic system which sometimes halts and sometimes doesn't
- A nondeterministic system that always halts with an output less than 100,000.
- An operating system that never halts.

[ii] See [Knabe 1992].

- Every Classical Object[40] is an instance of a Class[i] in a hierarchy[41], whereas an Actor can implement multiple interfaces.[42]
- Virtual Procedures can be used to operate on Objects, whereas messages[ii] can be sent to Actors.[43]

Unfortunately, Objects remain ill-defined. Consequently, the term "Object" bas been used in inconsistent ways in the literature.

Hairy Control Structure
Peter Landin introduced a powerful co-routine control structure using his **J** (for Jump) operator that could perform a nonlocal goto into the middle of a procedure invocation [Landin 1965]. In fact the **J** operator enabled a program to jump back into the middle of a procedure invocation even after it had already returned!

[Reynolds 1972] introduced control structure continuations using a construct called **escape** that is a more structured versions of Landin's **J** operator. Sussman and Steele called their variant of **escape** by the name *"call with current continuation."* General use of **escape** is not compatible with usual stack disciple introducing considerable operational inefficiency. Also, using *escape* can leave customers stranded. Consequently, use of **escape** is generally avoided these days and exceptions[44] are used instead so that clean up can be performed.

In the 1960's at the MIT AI Lab a remarkable culture grew up around *"hacking"* that concentrated on remarkable feats of programming.[45] Growing out of this tradition, Gerry Sussman and Guy Steele decided to try to understand Actors by reducing them to machine code that they could understand and so developed a *"Lisp-like language, Scheme, based on the lambda calculus, but extended for side effects, multiprocessing, and process synchronization."* [Sussman and Steele 1975].[46]

Their reductionist approach included primitives like the following:
START!PROCESS, STOP!PROCESS, and
EVALUATE!UNINTERRUPTIBLEY.[iii]

Of course, the above reductionist approach is unsatisfactory because it missed a crucial aspect of the Actor Model: *the reception ordering of messages*.

---

[i] A Class is an implementation of an Actor.
[ii] A message can be one-way and each must be of type Message.
[iii] *"This is the synchronization primitive. It evaluates an expression uninterruptedly; i.e. no other process may run until the expression has returned a value."*

Using the **J** operator, McDermott, and Sussman [1972] developed the Lisp-based language Conniver based on "hairy control structure" that could implement non-chronological backtracking that was more general than the chronological backtracking in Planner. However, hairy control structure did not work out well in practice because it was very difficult to understand and debug procedures that could return more than once.

Pat Hayes remarked:
> *Their* [Sussman and McDermott] *solution, to give the user access to the implementation primitives of Planner, is however, something of a retrograde step (what are Conniver's semantics?).* [Hayes 1974]

Hewitt had concluded:
> *One of the most important results that has emerged from the development of Actor semantics has been the further development of techniques to semantically analyze or synthesize control structures as patterns of passing messages.* ***As a result of this work, we have found that we can do without the paraphernalia of "hairy control structure."*** [47](emphasis in original)

Sussman and Steele [1975] noticed some similarities between Actor programs and the lambda calculus. They mistakenly concluded that they had reduced Actor programs to a "continuation-passing programming style":
> *It is always possible, if we are willing to specify explicitly what to do with the answer, to perform any calculation in this way: rather than reducing to its value, it reduces to an application of a continuation to its value. That is, in this continuation-passing programming style,* ***a function always "returns" its result by "sending" it to another function.***
> (emphasis in original)

However, some Actor programming language constructs are not reducible to a continuation-passing style. For example, futures are not reducible to continuation-passing style.

On the basis of their experience, Sussman and Steele developed the general thesis that Actors were merely the lambda calculus in disguise. Steele [1976] in the section "Actors ≡ Closures (mod Syntax)" disagreed with Hewitt who had "*expressed doubt as to whether these underlying continuations can themselves be expressed as lambda expressions.*" However, customers cannot be expressed as lambda expressions because doing so would preclude being able to enforce the requirement that a customer will process at most one response (*i.e.* exception or value return). Also implementing customers as lambda expressions can leave customers stranded.

In summary, Sussman and Steele [1975] mistakenly concluded "*we discovered that the 'Actors' and the lambda expressions were identical in implementation.*"[48] The actual situation is that the lambda calculus is capable of expressing some kinds of sequential and parallel control structures but, in general, *not* the concurrency expressed in the Actor Model.[49] On the other hand, the Actor Model is capable of expressing everything in the parallel lambda calculus [Hewitt 2008f] and is exponentially faster for important applications like information coordination [Hewitt 2012].

For example, futures can be adaptively created to do the kind of computation performed by hairy structure. [Hewitt 1974] invented the same-fringe problem as an illustration where the "fringe" of a tree is a list of all the leaf nodes of the tree.

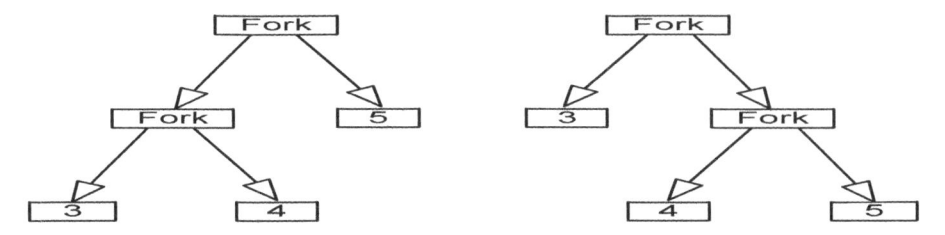

Two trees with the same fringe [3 4 5]

Below is the definition of a procedure that computes a FutureList that is the "fringe" of the leaves of tree.[i]

Fringe◁aType▷.[aTree:Tree◁aType▷]:FutureList◁aType▷ ≡
   aTree ◆ Leaf◁aType▷[x] ⦂ [x]
      Fork◁aType▷[tree1, tree2] ⦂
         [⩗Fringe.[tree1], ⩗**Postpone**[50] Fringe◁aType▷.[tree2]]

The above procedure can be used to define SameFringe that determines if two lists have the same fringe [Hewitt 1972]:
SameFringe◁aType▷
     .[aTree:Tree◁aType▷, anotherTree:Tree◁aType▷]:Boolean ≡
               // test if two trees have the same fringe
  Fringe◁aType▷.[aTree]=Fringe◁aType▷.[anotherTree]▮

Using Actors in this way obviates the need for explicit co-routine constructs, *e.g., yield* in C# [ECMA 2006], JavaScript [ECMA 2014], *etc.*

Early Actor Programming languages

Henry Lieberman, Dan Theriault, *et al.* developed Act1, an Actor programming language. Subsequently for his master's thesis, Dan Theriault developed Act2. These early proof of concept languages were rather inefficient and not suitable for applications. In his doctoral dissertation, Ken Kahn developed Ani, which he used to develop several animations. Bill Kornfeld developed the Ether programming language for the Scientific Community Metaphor in his doctoral

---

[i] See definition of Tree above in this article.

dissertation. William Athas and Nanette Boden [1988] developed Cantor which is an Actor programming language for scientific computing. Jean-Pierre Briot [1988, 1999] developed means to extend Smalltalk 80 for Actor computations. Darrell Woelk [1995] at MCC developed an Actor programming language for InfoSleuth agents in Rosette.

Hewitt, Attardi, and Lieberman [1979] developed proposals for delegation in message passing. This gave rise to the so-called inheritance anomaly controversy in concurrent programming languages [Satoshi Matsuoka and Aki Yonezawa 1993, Giuseppe Milicia and Vladimiro Sassone 2004]. ActorScript [Hewitt 2010] has proposal for addressing delegation issues.

Garbage Collection
Garbage collection (the automated reclamation of unused storage) was an important theme in the development of the Actor Model.

In his doctoral dissertation, Peter Bishop developed an algorithm for garbage collection in distributed systems. Each system kept lists of links of pointers to and from other systems. Cyclic structures were collected by incrementally migrating Actors (objects) onto other systems which had their addresses until a cyclic structure was entirely contained in a single system where the garbage collector could recover the storage.

Henry Baker developed an algorithm for real-time garbage collection is his doctoral dissertation. The fundamental idea was to interleave collection activity with construction activity so that there would not have to be long pauses while collection takes place.

Lieberman and Hewitt [1983] developed a real time garbage collection based on the lifetimes of Actors (Objects). The fundamental idea was to allocate Actors (objects) in generations so that only the latest generations would have to be examined during a garbage collection.

Cosmic Cube
The Cosmic Cube was developed by Chuck Seitz *et al.* at Caltech providing architectural support for Actor systems. A significant difference between the Cosmic Cube and most other parallel processors is that this multiple instruction multiple-data machine used message passing instead of shared variables for communication between concurrent processes. This computational model was reflected in the hardware structure and operating system, and also the explicit message passing communication seen by the programmer.

Communicating Sequential Processes

Arguably, the first concurrent programs were interrupt handlers. During the course of its normal operation, a computer needed to be able to receive information from outside (characters from a keyboard, packets from a network, *etc.*). So when the information was received, execution of the computer was "interrupted" and special code called an interrupt handler was called to *put* the information in a buffer where it could be subsequently retrieved.

In the early 1960s, interrupts began to be used to simulate the concurrent execution of several programs on a single processor. Having concurrency with shared memory gave rise to the problem of concurrency control. Originally, this problem was conceived as being one of mutual exclusion on a single computer. Edsger Dijkstra developed semaphores and later, [Hoare 1974, Brinch Hansen 1996] developed monitors to solve the mutual exclusion problem. However, neither of these solutions provided a programming language construct that encapsulated access to shared resources. This problem was remedied by the introduction of serializers [Hewitt and Atkinson 1977, 1979; Atkinson 1980].

Dijkstra was certain that unbounded nondeterminism is impossible to implement. Hoare was convinced by Dikstra's argument. Consequently, the semantics of CSP specified bounded nondeterminism.

Consider the following program written in CSP [Hoare 1978]:
```
    [X :: Z!stop( )                    ⓘ In process X, send Z a stop message
    ||                                 ⓘ process X operates in parallel with process Y
    Y :: guard: boolean; guard := true;
                                       ⓘ In process Y, initialize boolean variable guard to true and then
        *[guard→ Z!go( ); Z?guard]
        ⓘ while guard is true, send Z a go message and then input guard from Z
    ||                                 ⓘ process Y operates in parallel with process Z
    Z :: n: integer; n:= 0;  ⓘ In process Z, initialize integer variable n to 0 and then
        continue: boolean; continue := true;
                                       ⓘ initialize boolean variable continue to true and then
        *[                             ⓘ repeatedly either
            X?stop( ) → continue := false;
            ⓘ input a stop message from X, set continue to false and then
            Y!continue;                ⓘ send Y the value of continue
         []                            ⓘ or
            Y?go( )→ n := n+1;
            ⓘ input a go message from Y, increment n, and then
            Y!continue]]               ⓘ send Y the value of continue
```

253

According to Clinger [1981]:
> this program illustrates global nondeterminism, since the nondeterminism arises from incomplete specification of the timing of signals between the three processes X, Y, and Z. The repetitive guarded command in the definition of Z has two alternatives: either the stop message is accepted from X, in which case continue is set to false, or a go message is accepted from Y, in which case n is incremented and Y is sent the value of continue. If Z ever accepts the stop message from X, then X terminates. Accepting the stop causes continue to be set to false, so after Y sends its next go message, Y will receive false as the value of its guard and will terminate. When both X and Y have terminated, Z terminates because it no longer has live processes providing input.
>
> As the author of CSP points out, therefore, if the repetitive guarded command in the definition of Z were required to be fair, this program would have unbounded nondeterminism: it would be guaranteed to halt but there would be no bound on the final value of n. In actual fact, the repetitive guarded commands of CSP are not required to be fair, and so the program may not halt [Hoare 1978]. This fact may be confirmed by a tedious calculation using the semantics of CSP [Francez, Hoare, Lehmann, and de Roever 1979] or simply by noting that the semantics of CSP is based upon a conventional power domain and thus does not give rise to unbounded nondeterminism.

But Hoare knew that trouble was brewing because for several years, proponents of the Actor Model had been beating the drum for unbounded nondeterminism. To address this problem, he suggested that implementations of CSP should be as close as possible to unbounded nondeterminism! But his suggestion was difficult to achieve because of the nature of communication in CSP using nondeterministic select statements (from nondeterministic state machines, *e.g.*, [Dijkstra 1976]), which in the above program which takes the form

[X?stop( ) → ...
[]
Y?go( ) → ...]

The structure of CSP is fundamentally at odds with guarantee of service.

Using the above semantics for CSP, it was impossible to formally prove that a server actually provides service to multiple clients (as had been done previously in the Actor Model). That's why the semantics of CSP were reversed from bounded non-determinism [Hoare CSP 1978] to unbounded non-determinism [Hoare CSP 1985]. However, bounded non-determinism was but a symptom of deeper underlying issues with nondeterministic transitions in communicating sequential processes (see [Knabe 1992]).

Smalltalk-80

Smalltalk-72 progressed to Smalltalk-80[Alan Kay, Dan Ingalls, Adele Goldberg, Ted Kaehler, Diana Merry, Scott Wallace, Peter Deutsch], which introduced the code browser as an important innovation.

For example, the following diagram depicts a code-browser window:

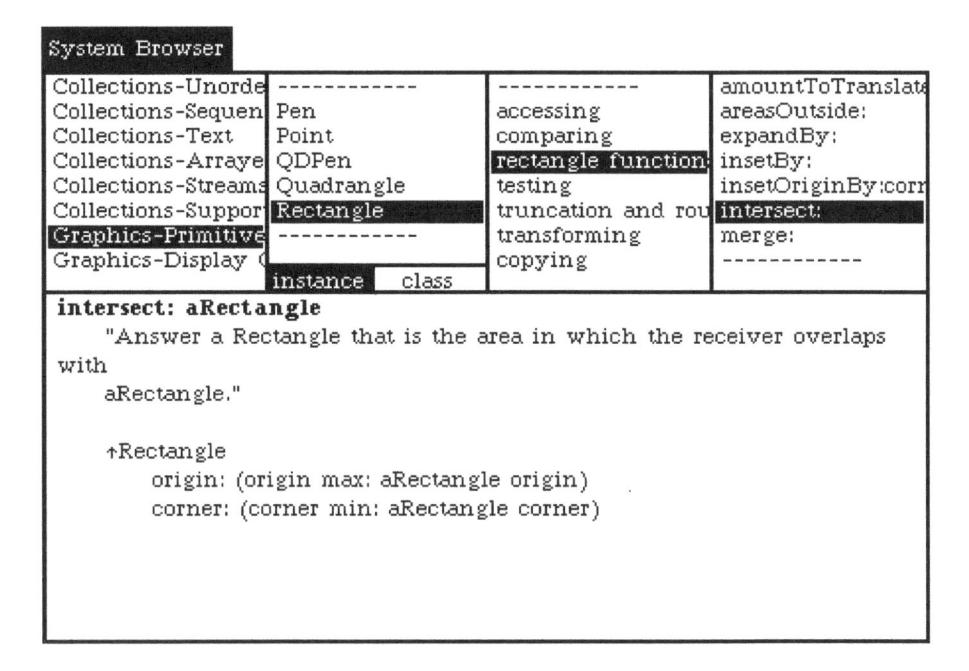

```
System Browser
Collections-Unorde  ------------  ------------     amountToTranslate
Collections-Sequen  Pen           accessing        areasOutside:
Collections-Text    Point         comparing        expandBy:
Collections-Arraye  QDPen         rectangle function  insetBy:
Collections-Streams Quadrangle    testing          insetOriginBy:corr
Collections-Suppor  Rectangle     truncation and rou  intersect:
Graphics-Primitive  ------------  transforming     merge:
Graphics-Display (                copying          ------------
                    instance  class

intersect: aRectangle
    "Answer a Rectangle that is the area in which the receiver overlaps
with
    aRectangle."

    ↑Rectangle
        origin: (origin max: aRectangle origin)
        corner: (corner min: aRectangle corner)
```

π-Calculus Actors

Robin Milner's initial published work on concurrency [Milner 1973] was notable in that it was not overtly based on sequential processes, although computation still required sequential execution (see below).

His work differed from the previously developed Actor Model in the following ways:
- There are a fixed number of processes as opposed to the Actor Model which allows the number of Actors to vary dynamically
- The only quantities that can be passed in messages are integers and strings as opposed to the Actor Model which allows the addresses of Actors to be passed in messages
- The processes have a fixed topology as opposed to the Actor Model which allows varying topology
- Communication is synchronous as opposed to the Actor Model in which an unbounded time can elapse between sending and receiving a message.

- Unlike the Actor Model, there is no reception ordering and consequently there is only bounded nondeterminism. However, with bounded nondeterminism it is impossible to prove that a server guarantees service to its clients, *i.e.*, a client might starve.

Building on the Actor Model, Milner [1993] removed some of these restrictions in his work on the π-calculus:
Now, the pure lambda-calculus is built with just two kinds of thing: terms and variables. Can we achieve the same economy for a process calculus? Carl Hewitt, with his Actors model, responded to this challenge long ago; he declared that a value, an operator on values, and a process should all be the same kind of thing: an Actor.

This goal impressed me, because it implies the homogeneity and completeness of expression ...

So, in the spirit of Hewitt, our first step is to demand that all things denoted by terms or accessed by names--values, registers, operators, processes, objects--are all of the same kind of thing....

However, some fundamental differences remain between the Actor Model and the π–calculus:
- The Actor Model is founded on physics whereas the π–calculus is founded on algebra.
- Semantics of the Actor Model is based on message orderings in the Computational Representation Theorem. Semantics of the π–calculus is based on structural congruence in various kinds of bi-simulations and equivalences.[51]

Communication in the π -calculus takes the following form:
- *input:* u[x].P is a process that gets a message from a communication channel u before proceeding as P, binding the message received to the identifier x. In ActorScript [Hewitt 2010a], this can be modeled as follows: Let x←u.get[ ]● P[52]
- *output:* ū[m].P is a process that puts a message m on communication channel u before proceeding as P. In ActorScript, this can be modeled as follows: u.put[x]● P[53]

The above operations of the π-calculus can be implemented in Actor systems using a two-phase commit protocol [Knabe 1992; Reppy, Russo, and Xiao 2009]. The overhead of communication in the π–calculus presents difficulties to its use in practical applications.

Process calculi (*e.g.* [Milner 1993; Cardelli and Gordon 1998]) are closely related to the Actor Model. There are similarities between the two approaches, but also many important differences (philosophical, mathematical and engineering):
- There is only one Actor Model (although it has numerous formal systems for design, analysis, verification, modeling, etc.) in contrast with a variety of species of process calculi.
- The Actor Model was inspired by the laws of physics and depends on them for its fundamental axioms in contrast with the process calculi being inspired by algebra [Milner 1993].
- Unlike the Actor Model, the sender is an intrinsic component of process calculi because they are defined in terms of reductions (as in the lambda calculus).
- Processes in the process calculi communicate by sending messages either through channels (synchronous or asynchronous), or via ambients (which can also be used to model channel-like communications [Cardelli and Gordon 1998]). In contrast, Actors communicate by sending messages to the addresses of other Actors (this style of communication can also be used to model channel-like communications using a two-phase commit protocol [Knabe 1992]).

There remains a Great Divide between process calculi and the Actor Model:
- *Process calculi:* algebraic equivalence, bi-simulation [Park 1980], *etc.*
- *Actor Model:* futures [Baker and Hewitt 1977], Swiss cheese, garbage collection, *etc.*

J–Machine

The J–Machine was developed by Bill Dally *et al.* at MIT providing architectural support suitable for Actors.
This included the following:
- Asynchronous messaging
- A uniform space of Actor addresses to which messages could be sent concurrently regardless of whether the recipient Actor was local or nonlocal
- A form of Actor pipelining

Concurrent Smalltalk (which can be modeled using Actors) was developed to program the J Machine.

"Fog Cutter" Actors

[Karmani and Agha 2011] promoted *"Fog Cutter"*[i] Actors each of which is required to have a mailbox, thread, state, and program diagrammed as follows:[54]

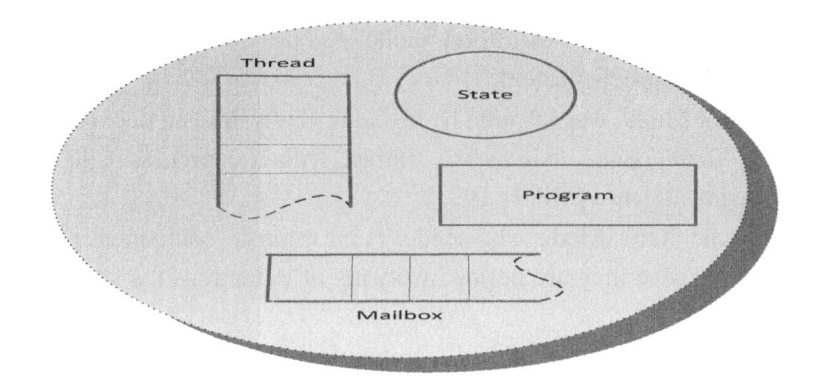

**Process a message from the Mailbox using the Thread,
then reset the Thread stack thereby completing the message-passing turn**

Fog Cutter Actors are special cases in that the following restrictions hold:[ii]

- *Each Fog Cutter Actor has a 'mailbox'.* But if everything that interacts is an Actor, then a mailbox must be an Actor and so in turn needs a mailbox which in turn ... [Hewitt, Bishop, and Steiger 1973]. Of course, mailboxes having mailboxes is an infinite regress that has been humorously characterized by Erik Meijer as "down the rabbit hole." [Hewitt, Meijer, and Szyperski 2012]
- *A Fog Cutter Actor 'terminates' when every Actor that it has created is 'idle' and there is no way to send it a message.* In practice, it is preferable to use garbage collection for Actors that are inaccessible. [Baker and Hewitt 1977]
- *Each Fog Cutter Actor executes a 'loop' using its own sequential 'thread' that begins with receiving a message followed by possibly creating more Actors, sending messages, updating its local state, and then looping back for the next message to complete a 'turn'.* In practice, it is preferable to provide "Swiss cheese" by which an Actor can concurrently process multiple messages without the limitation of a sequential thread loop. [Hewitt and Atkinson 1977, 1979; Atkinson 1980; Hewitt 2011]
- *A Fog Cutter Actor has a well-defined local 'autonomous' 'state' that can be updated* [55] *while processing a message.* However, because of indeterminacy an Actor may not be in a well-defined local independent state. For example, Actors might be entangled[56] with each other so that

---

[i] so dubbed by Kristen Nygaard (private communication).
[ii] "Fog Cutter" is in *italics*.

their actions are correlated. Also, large distributed Actors (*e.g.* www.dod.gov) do not have a well-defined state. In practice, it is preferable for an Actor not to change its local information while it is processing a message and instead specify to how it will process the next message received (as in ActorScript [Hewitt 2011]).

Fog Cutter Actors have been extremely useful for exploring issues about Actors including the following alternatives:
- **Reception order of messaging** instead of *Mailbox*
- **Activation order of messaging** instead of *Thread*
- **Behavior** instead of *State+Program*

However, Fog Cutter Actors are fundamentally lacking in generality because they lack the holes of Swiss cheese.[i]

In practice, the most common and effective way to explain Actors has been *operationally* using a suitable Actor programming language (*e.g.,* ActorScript [Hewitt 2012]) that specifies how Actors can be implemented along with an English explanation of the axioms for Actors (*e.g.*, as presented in this paper).

Erlang Actors

Erlang Actors [Armstrong 2010] are broadly similar to Fog Cutter Actors:
1. Each Erlang Actor not share memory addresses with other Erlang Actors.
2. An Erlang Actor can retrieve a message from its mailbox by selectively removing a message matching a particular pattern.

Erlang made important contributions by emphasizing the importance of the following:
- referential transparency
- failure handling

However, Erlang Actors have the following issues:
- Messaging in Erlang is not robust because a sent message will be dropped without warning if there is no Actor for the address.[ii]
- Erlang imposes high overhead in sending messages between Actors. For example, it imposes coordination overhead that messages sent between two Erlang Actors are delivered in the order they are sent.

---

[i] See section on Swiss cheese in this article.
[ii] Such silent failures are a bane of robust software engineering.

- Implementations of Erlang do not make efficient use of many-core coherent architectures because messages between Erlang Actors must be blobs.[i]
- Instead of using exception handling, until recently Erlang relied on process failure[ii] propagating between processes and their spawned processes.
- Instead of using garbage collection to recover storage and processing of unreachable Actors, each Erlang Actor must perform an internal termination or be killed externally.[57]
- Erlang does not have parameterized types, Actor aspects, interfaces or type discriminations.

Erlang Actors have been used in high-performance applications. For example, Ericsson uses Erlang in 3G mobile networks worldwide [Ekeroth and Hedström 2000].

Sqeak

Squeak [Ingalls, Kaehler, Maloney, Wallace, and Kay 1997] is a dialect of Smalltalk-80 with added mechanisms of islands, asynchronous messaging, players and costumes, language extensions, projects, and tile scripting. Its underlying object system is class-based, but the user interface is programmed as though it is prototype-based.

Orleans Actors

Orleans [Bykov, Geller, Kliot, Larus, Pandya, and Thelin 2010; Bernstein, Bykov, Geller, Kliot, and Thelin 2014] is a *distributed* implementation of Actors that transparently sends messages between Actors on different computers enabling greater scalability and reliability of practical applications.

Orleans is based on single-threaded Actor message invocations. An Actor processes a message using a thread from a thread pool. When the message has been processed, the thread can be returned to the thread pool.[58]

That an Orleans Actor does not share memory with other Actors is enforced by doing a deep copy of messages if required.

A globally unique identifier[59] is created for each Orleans Actor with a consequence that there is extra storage overhead that can be significant for a very small Orleans Actor.[60] A globally unique identifier can be used to send a message, which will, if necessary, create an activation[61] of an Orleans Actor in the memory of a process.[62]

---

[i] A blob is a data structure that cannot contain pointers.
[ii] based on an arbitrary time-out

Orleans has the following issues:
- Orleans allows the use of strings and long integers as globally unique identifiers in order to provide for perpetual Actors whose storage can only be collected using potentially unsafe means, which can result in a dangling globally unique identifier.
- A system design choice was made in Orleans not to use automated storage reclamation technology (garbage collection) to keep track of whether an Orleans Actor could have been forgotten by all applications and thus become inaccessible. Consequently, Orleans can have the following inefficiencies:
  - A short-lived Orleans Actor that has become inaccessible *does not have its storage in the process quickly recycled* resulting in a larger working set and decreased locality of reference.[63]
  - A long-lived Orleans Actor that has become inaccessible *does not ever have its storage recycled* [64] resulting in larger memory requirements.[65] However, collection of the storage of long-lived Actors is not so important in some applications because long-term memory has become relatively inexpensive.

An Orleans Actor ties up a thread while it is taking a turn to process a message regardless of the amount of time required, *e.g.*, time to make a system call. In this way, Orleans avoids timing races in the value of a variable of an Actor.[i] A consequence of being single-threaded can be reduced performance of Orleans Actors as follows:
- lack of parallelism in processing a message
- lack of concurrency between processing a message and executing waiting method calls invoked by processing the message.[66]
- thread-switching overhead between sending and receiving a message to an Orleans Actor in the same process[67]

A waiting method call can be resolved using the **await**[68] construct as follows:
    await *anActor.aMethodName*(…)[ii]
For example:
    var *anActor* = *aFactory*.GetActor(*aGloballyUniqueIdentifier*);
    try {…*aUse*(**await** *anActor.aMethodName*(…))…
        anotherUse(**await** *anActor.anotherMethodName*(…))…}
    catch ….;[69]

---

[i] ActorScript goes even further in this direction by enforcing that the value of a variable can change only when it is leaving the cheese or after an internal delegated operation.
[ii] ActorScript uses ↓*aFuture* to resolve *aFuture*

When reentrancy[70] is enabled, the method calls for *aMethodName* and *anotherMethodName* above are executed *after* the current message-processing turn:
- If completed successfully, the value of a waiting method call is supplied in a *new* turn at the point of method invocation, *e.g.*, the value of the method call for *aMethodName* of is supplied to *aUse*.
- If a waiting method call throws an exception, it is given to the exception handler in a new turn.

Orleans uses C# compiler "stack ripping" to use behind-the-scenes sequential turns to execute waiting method calls.

A message sent to an Orleans Actor must return a promise[71] Actor[72], which is a version of a future Actor. A promise Actor for a method call *anActor.aMethodName(...)* can be created using the following code:[i]

```
try {return Task.FromResult(await anActor.aMethodName(...));}
catch (Exception anException)
    {return Task.FromException(anException);}
```[ii]

Note that a promise is *not* an Orleans Actor because it does not have a globally unique identifier.[iii]

One of the motivations for the requirement that Orleans Actors must return promises when sent messages is to enable the **await** construct to *hide* promises so that clients of Orleans Actors do not have to deal with the return type `Task<T>` of each Orleans Actor method call for some application type `T`.

Orleans is an important step in furthering a goal of the Actor Model that application programmers need not be so concerned with low-level system details.[iv] For example, in moving to the current version, Orleans reinforces the current trend of not exposing customer Actors[73] to application programmers.[74]

As a research project, Orleans had to make some complicated tradeoffs to implement more reliable distributed Actors. Implementing Actor systems that are both *robust* and *performant* is an extremely challenging research project that has taken place over many decades. More research remains to be done. However, Orleans has already been used in some high-performance

---

[i] ActorScript uses **Future** *anExpression* to create a future for *anExpression*

[ii] There is an inefficiency in the above code in that the method call returns a promise that is taken apart and then an equivalent promise is created to be returned.

[iii] It would be impractical for promises to be Orleans Actors because
- they are created as the return value of *every* Orleans Actor method call
- the storage of inaccessible Orleans Actors is *not* recovered, *e.g.*, using garbage collection

[iv] *e.g.* threads, throttling, load distribution, cores, persistence, automated storage reclamation, locks, location transparency, channels, ports, *etc.*

applications including multi-player computer games, *e.g.*, Halo[Bykov 2013, Stenberg 2015].

JavaScript Actors

JavaScript Actors are broadly similar to Fog Cutter Actors.[75]

A *promise*[76] in JavaScript is a kind of future. JavaScript[77] will include asynchronous procedures as well as an **await**[78] construct that can be used to resolve promise Actors.

An asynchronous procedure *always*[i] returns a promise. For example, the following procedure computes a promise for the sum of two promises:
   async function PromiseForSumOfPromises(aPromise, anotherPromise)
   {**return** (**await** aPromise) + **await** anotherPromise)};

A promise for an expression can be created by the procedure CreatePromise[79], which takes a thunk[80] for the expression as its argument. For example, suppose we have the following:[ii]
   async function PromiseForSumOfTwoSlowCalls( )
   {**const** promise1 := CreatePromise(() => aSlowActor.do(10, 20));
    const promise2 := CreatePromise(() => aSlowActor.do(30, 40));
    return await PromiseForSumOfPromises(promise1, promise2)
   };
In an *asynchronous* procedure, **await** PromiseForSumOfTwoSlowCalls( ) is equivalent to the following:
   (↓**Future** aSlowActor▪do[10, 20]) + ↓**Future** aSlowActor▪do[30,40]

There is a potential pitfall in the use of JavaScript promises in that the following substitute code for the above does *not* work to *concurrently* execute the two calls to aSlowActor:[81]
   (**await**
     new Promise((aPromiseValueSetter) =>
       // a promise-value setter[82] is a procedure that sets the value of a promise
               aPromiseValueSetter(aSlowActor.do(10, 20))))
   + **await**
     new Promise((aPromiseValueSetter) =>
               aPromiseValueSetter(aSlowActor.do(30, 40)))

---

[i] The use of asynchronous procedures can be contagious because a procedures using the return value of an asynchronous procedure needs to be asynchronous to use **await**.
[ii] The code is written in this way to emphasize that an asynchronous procedure *always* returns a promise.

Note that neither of the two promise-value setters in the above code is called more than once to set the value of a promise. However, JavaScript will have the ability to call a promise-value setter multiple times. If a promise-value setter is called twice to set the value of a promise, an exception is *not* thrown. Instead, the second call fails *silently*.[i] The ability to call a promise-value setter multiple times will be used for *races* evaluating multiple expressions concurrently.

To implement parallelism, JavaScript has workers.[83] Although multiple workers can reside in a process, they do not share memory addresses and consequently cannot efficiently communicate using many-core coherency. A worker communicates with other workers using blobs[ii] in order to guarantee memory separation. Each worker acts as a *single-threaded, non-preemptive* time-sharing system for processing messages for Actors that reside in its memory.[84]

However, JavaScript workers have the following efficiency issues:[85]
1. There is no parallelism in processing messages for different Actors on a worker and the processing of a message by a slowly executing Actor *cannot* be preempted thereby bringing *all*[iii] other work on the worker to a *standstill*.[iv]
2. An Actor on a worker can directly send a message an Actor on another worker only if the recipient has been transferred to the worker on which the sender resides.[86] An Actor can also indirectly send a blobbed message using a MessageChannel.
3. A very difficult efficiency issue is to decide how many Actors to put on each worker and which Actors to put on which worker.

JavaScript workers limit much of the modularity and efficiency available in coherent many-core processor architectures. Inherent inefficiencies and architectural deficiencies in JavaScript workers and HTML5 standards handicap[v] browsers in their competition with apps.

---

[i] In general, failing silently is not a good practice.

[ii] A blob is a data structure that cannot contain pointers. In the past, a more limited meaning called BLOB has been used as an acronym for Binary Large OBject. In the Actor Model, an address (which is typed) can be used to send a message to an Actor. The model does not specify the physical representation of an address. So an address might be a (tagged) pointer. However, such pointers are not allowed in blobs.

[iii] including any queued promises

[iv] Issues of non-preemption motivated the invention of time-slicing [Bemer 1957] by which tasks are switched at the expiration of a timer.

[v] due mainly to the legacy requirement not to break the Web. W3C and ECMA have done excellent work ameliorating the worst problems.

Capability Actor Systems

Capabilities were proposed in order to provide finer grained protection in operating systems [Dennis and van Horn 1966]. Unfortunately, capabilities have been awkward to use because their addresses were allocated in private memory of operating systems. The situation was considerably clarified by the development of the Actor Model in 1972. Unfortunately, the terms "capability" and "capability system" lacked axiomatizations and denotational semantics. Consequently, the terms were used in ambiguous and inconsistent ways. Capability systems can be considered to be approaches to security making use of specified principles that must include the laws of the Actor Model.

Capabilities were further developed in [Organick 1983, Levy 1984, Shapiro and Adams 2007, Woodruff, et. al. 2014]. Unfortunately, capabilities have been awkward to use because their addresses were allocated in private memory of operating systems. [Kwon, et. al. 2014] is a tagged capability architecture that includes a special register to hold capabilities for addresses. The Object Capability Model [Miller 2006] has recommendations about best practices for implementing Actor systems.

Generally speaking, a capability is a token that contains an Actor address along with other information that can be used in sending messages to the Actor. The following are examples of capabilities:
- Waterken:[87] an Actor address of type WebKey
- Zebra Copy:[88] an Actor address together with additional information that includes a list of allowed message types

Capabilities were critiqued in [Rajunas 1989; Miller, Yee, and Shapiro 2003] concerning the following issues:
- *revocability*: Using proxies for Actors enables revocability because messages are forwarded and so a proxy can revoke. Also revocation can be performed by communicating directly with an Actor.
- *multi-level security*: Actors, *per se*, do *not* have levels of security although various security schemes can be implemented.[89]
- *delegation*:[90] Actors[91] directly support delegation by passing addresses of Actors in messages.

[Miller 2006] followed up with the following analysis:
Just as we should not expect a base programming language to provide us all the data types we need for computation, we should not expect a base protection system to provide us all the elements we need to directly express access control policies. Both issues deserve the same kind of answer: We use the base to build abstractions, extending the vocabulary we use to express our solutions. In evaluating an access control model,

one must examine how well it supports the extension of its own expressiveness by abstraction and composition.

Consider the following definition:

Interface Account **with** getBalance[ ] ↦ Currency,
                      deposit[Currency] ↦ **Void**,
                      withdraw[Currency] ↦ **Void**∎

The following is an implementation of Account:

  Actor SimpleAccount[aBalance:Currency]
     myBalance ≔ aBalance。
     implements Account **using**
       getBalance[ ] → myBalance¶
       deposit[anAmount] →
         Void afterward myBalance ≔ myBalance+anAmount
       withdraw[anAmount] →
         (anAmount > myBalance) ◆
           True ⦂ **Throw** Overdrawn[ ]
           False ⦂
              Void afterward myBalance ≔ myBalance−anAmount∎

The above implementation of Account can be extended as follows to provide the ability to revoke some abilities to change an account by providing AccountSupervisor and AccountRevoker interfaces:

The implementation AccountSupervisor below implements the Account interface as well as AccountSupervisor and AccountRevoker interfaces as an extension of the implementation SimpleAccount:[92]

  Actor AccountSupervisor [initialBalance:Currency]
    extends SimpleAccount[initialBalance]
      withdrawableIsRevoked := **False**,
      depositableIsRevoked := **False**₀
    implements AccountSupervisor **using**
      getRevoker[ ]→ ⌈:⌉AccountRevoker

      getAccount[ ] → ⌈:⌉Account

      withdrawFee[anAmount] →
        Void afterward myBalance := myBalance−anAmount
                // withdraw fee *even if balance goes negative*
    also partially reimplements exportable Account **using**
      withdraw[anAmount] →
        withdrawableIsRevoked ◆
          True ⦂ **Throw** Revoked[ ]
          False ⦂ ⌈:⌉SimpleAccount▪withdraw[anAmount]
      deposit[anAmount] →
        depositableIsRevoked ◆
          True ⦂ **Throw** Revoked[ ]
          False ⦂ ⌈:⌉SimpleAccount▪deposit[anAmount]
    also implements exportable AccountRevoker **using**
      revokeDepositable[ ] →
        Void afterward depositableIsRevoked := **True**
      revokeWithdrawable[ ] →
        Void afterward withdrawableIsRevoked := **True**▮

For example, the following expression returns *negative* €3:
Let anAccountSupervisor ← AccountSupervisor.[€3]。
   Let anAccount ← anAccountSupervisor.getAccount[ ],
      aRevoker ← anAccountSupervisor.getRevoker[ ]。
   anAccount.withdraw[€2]●   // the balance is €1
   aRevoker.revokeWithdrawable[ ]●
                           // withdrawableIsRevoked in is **True**
   Try anAccount.withdraw[€5]   // try another **withdraw**
      catch◆ _ ⸴ **Void**] ●   // ignore the thrown exception
                                    // the balance remains €1
   anAccountSupervisor.withdrawFee[€4]●
            // €4 is withdrawn *even though* withdrawableIsRevoked
   anAccount.getBalance[ ]▌   // the balance is *negative* €3

Was the Actor Model premature?
The history of the Actor Model raises the question of whether it was premature.

Original definition of prematurity
As originally defined by [Stent 1972], "A discovery is premature if its implications cannot be connected by a series of simple logical steps to contemporary canonical or generally accepted knowledge." [Lövy 2002] glossed the phrase "series of simple logical steps" in Stent's definition as referring to the "*target community's ways of asking relevant questions, of producing experimental results, and of examining new evidence.*" [Ghiselin 2002] argued that if a "*minority of scientists accept a discovery, or even pay serious attention to it, then the discovery is not altogether premature in the Stentian sense.*" In accord with Ghiselin's argument, the Actor Model was not premature. Indeed it enjoyed initial popularity and underwent steady development.

However, Stent in his original article also referred to a development as premature such that when it occurred contemporaries did not adopt it by consensus. This is what happened with the Actor Model partly for the following reasons:
- For over 30 years after the first publication of the Actor Model, widely deployed computer architectures developed in the direction of making a single sequential thread of execution run faster.
- For over 25 years after the first publication, there was no agreed standard by which software could communicate high level data structures across organizational boundaries.

Before its time?

According to [Gerson 2002], phenomena that lead people to talk about discoveries being before their time can be analyzed as follows:

> *We can see the phenomenon of 'before its time' as composed of two separate steps. The first takes place when a new discovery does not get tied to the conventional knowledge of its day and remains unconnected in the literature. The second step occurs when new events lead to the 'rediscovery' of the unconnected results in a changed context that enables or even facilitates its connection to the conventional knowledge of the rediscovering context.*

But circumstances have radically changed in the following ways:
- Progress on improving the speed of a single sequential thread has stalled for some time now. Increasing speed depends on effectively using many-core architectures.
- Better ways have been implemented that Actors can use to communicate messages between computers.
- Actors have been increasingly adopted by industry.

Consequently, by the criteria of Gerson, the Actor Model might be described by some as *before its time*.

According to [Zuckerman and Lederberg 1986], premature discoveries are those that were made but neglected. [Gerson 2002] argued,

> *But histories and sociological studies repeatedly show that we do not have a discovery until the scientific community accepts it as such and stops debating about it. Until then the proposed solution is in an intermediate state."*

By his argument, the Actor Model is a discovery but since its practical importance is not yet accepted by consensus, its practical importance is not yet a discovery.

End Notes

[1] The Actor model makes use of two fundamental orders on computational events [Baker and Hewitt 1977; Clinger 1981, Hewitt 2006]:
  1. The *activation order* (⤳) is a fundamental order that models one event activating another (there is energy flow from an event to an event which it activates). The activation order is discrete:

     $\forall [e_1, e_2 \in \text{Events}] \rightarrow \text{Finite}[\{e \in \text{Events} \mid e_1 \leadsto e \leadsto e_2\}]$

     There are two kinds of events involved in the activation order: reception and transmission. Reception events can activate transmission events and transmission events can activate reception events.
  2. The *reception order* of an exclusive Actor x ($\rightarrow_x$) models the (total) order of events in which a message is received at x. The reception order of each x is discrete:

     $\forall [r_1, r_2 \in \text{ReceptionEvents}_x] \rightarrow \text{Finite}[\{r \in \text{ReceptionEvents}_x \mid r_1 \rightarrow_x r \rightarrow_x r_2\}]$

The *combined order* (denoted by ↝) is defined to be the transitive closure of the activation order and the reception orders of all Actors. So the following question arose in the early history of the Actor model: *"Is the combined order discrete?"* Discreteness of the combined order captures an important intuition about computation because it rules out counterintuitive computations in which an infinite number of computational events occur between two events (*à la* Zeno).

Hewitt conjectured that the discreteness of the activation order together with the discreteness of all reception orders implies that the combined order is discrete. Surprisingly [Clinger 1981; later generalized in Hewitt 2006] answered the question in the negative by giving a counterexample:
Any finite set of events is consistent (the activation order and all reception orders are discrete) and represents a potentially physically realizable situation. But there is an infinite set of sentences that is inconsistent with the discreteness of the combined order and does not represent a physically realizable situation.

The resolution of the problem is to take discreteness of the combined order as an axiom of the Actor model:[1]

$\forall [e_1, e_2 \in \text{Events}] \rightarrow \text{Finite}[\{e \in \text{Events} \mid e_1 \leadsto e \leadsto e_2\}]$

Properties of concurrent computations can be proved using the above orderings [*e.g.* Bost, Mattern, and Tel 1995; Lamport 1978, 1979].

[2] better or worse

[3] The receiver might be on another computer and in any the system can make use of threads, locks, location transparency, throttling, load distribution,

persistence, automated storage reclamation, queues, cores, channels, ports, *etc.* as it sees fit.

Messages in the Actor model are generalizations of packets in Internet computing in that they need not be received in the order sent. Not implementing the order of delivery, allows packet switching to buffer packets, use multiple paths to send packets, resend damaged packets, and to provide other optimizations.

For example, Actors are allowed to pipeline the processing of messages. What this means is that in the course of processing a message m1, an Actor can designate how to process the next message, and then in fact begin processing another message m2 before it has finished processing m1. Just because an Actor is allowed to pipeline the processing of messages does not mean that it *must* pipeline the processing. Whether a message is pipelined is an engineering tradeoff.

[4] The amount of effort expended depends on circumstances.

[5] These laws can be enforced by a proposed extension of the X86 architecture that will support the following operating environments:
- CLR and extensions (Microsoft)
- JVM (Oracle, IBM, SAP)
- Dalvik (Google)

Many-core architecture has made the above extension necessary in order to provide the following:
- concurrent nonstop automated storage reclamation (garbage collection) and relocation to improve performance,
- prevention of memory corruption that otherwise results from programming languages like C and C++ using thousands of threads in a process,
- nonstop migration of iOrgs (while they are in operation) within a computer and between distributed computers

[6] It is not possible to guarantee the consistency of information because consistency testing is recursively undecidable even in logics much weaker than first order logic. Because of this difficulty, it is impractical to test whether information is consistent.

[7] Consequently iInfo makes use of direct inference in Direct Logic to reason more safely about inconsistent information because it omits the rules of classical logic that enable every proposition to be inferred from a single inconsistency.

[8] This section shares history with [Hewitt 2008f].

[9] *cf.* denotational semantics of the lambda calculus [Scott 1976]

[10] One solution is to develop a concurrent variant of the Lisp meta-circular definition [McCarthy, Abrahams, Edwards, Hart, and Levin 1962] that was inspired by Turing's Universal Machine [Turing 1936]. If *exp* is a Lisp expression and *env* is an environment that assigns values to identifiers, then

the procedure *Eval* with arguments *exp* and *env* evaluates *exp* using *env*. In the concurrent variant, eval[*env*] is a message that can be sent to *exp* to cause *exp* to be evaluated. Using such messages, modular meta-circular definitions can be concisely expressed in the Actor model for universal concurrent programming languages (*e.g.* ActorScript [Hewitt 2010a]).

[11] However, they come with additional commitment. Inappropriate language constructs are difficult to leave behind.

[12] *E.g.* processes in Erlang [Armstrong 2007] and vats in the object-capability model[Miller 2006].

[13] Swiss cheese was called serializers in the literature.

[14] In part, this section extends some material that was submitted to Wikipedia and [Hewitt 2008f].

[15] Turing [1936] stated:
the behavior of the computer at any moment is determined by the symbols which he [the computer] *is observing, and his 'state of mind' at that moment"* and *"there is a bound B to the number of symbols or squares which the computer can observe at one moment. If he wishes to observe more, he must use successive observations."*
Gödel's conception of computation was formally the same as Turing but more reductionist in motivation:
There is a major difference between the historical contexts in which Turing and Gödel worked. Turing tackled the Entscheidungsproblem [computational decidability of provability] *as an interesting mathematical problem worth solving; he was hardly aware of the fierce foundational debates. Gödel on the other hand, was passionately interested in the foundations of mathematics. Though not a student of Hilbert, his work was nonetheless deeply entrenched in the framework of Hilbert's finitistic program, whose main goal was to provide a meta-theoretic finitary proof of the consistency of a formal system "containing a certain amount of finitary number theory."* [Shagrir 2006]

[16] An example of the global state model is the Abstract State Machine (ASM) model [Blass, Gurevich, Rosenzweig, and Rossman 2007a, 2007b; Glausch and Reisig 2006].

[17] The lambda calculus can be viewed as the earliest message passing programming language [Hewitt, Bishop, and Steiger 1973] building on previous work.

For example, the lambda expression below implements a tree data structure when supplied with parameters for a leftSubTree and rightSubTree.

When such a tree is given a parameter message "getLeft", it returns leftSubTree and likewise when given the message "getRight" it returns rightSubTree:

λ[leftSubTree, rightSubTree]
  λ[message] message ◆ "getLeft" ⁘ leftSubTree
                              "getRight" ⁘ rightSubTree

[18] Allowing assignments to variables enabled sharing of the effects of updating shared data structures but did not provide for concurrency.

[19] [Petri 1962]

[20] Consequently in Simula-76 there was no required locality of operations unlike the laws for locality in the Actor mode [Baker and Hewitt 1977].

[21] The ideas in Simula became widely known by the publication of [Dahl and Hoare 1972] at the same time that the Actor model was being invented to formalize concurrent computation using message passing [Hewitt, Bishop, and Steiger 1973].

[22] The development of Planner was inspired by the work of Karl Popper [1935, 1963], Frederic Fitch [1952], George Polya [1954], Allen Newell and Herbert Simon [1956], John McCarthy [1958, *et. al.* 1962], and Marvin Minsky [1968].

[23] This turned out later to have a surprising connection with Direct Logic. See the Two-Way Deduction Theorem below.

[24] Subsequent versions of the Smalltalk language largely followed the path of using the virtual methods of Simula in the message passing structure of programs. However Smalltalk-72 made primitives such as integers, floating point numbers, etc. into objects. The authors of Simula had considered making such primitives into objects but refrained largely for efficiency reasons. Java at first used the expedient of having both primitive and object versions of integers, floating point numbers, etc. The C# programming language (and later versions of Java, starting with Java 1.5) adopted the more elegant solution of using boxing and unboxing, a variant of which had been used earlier in some Lisp implementations.

[25] According to the Smalltalk-72 Instruction Manual [Goldberg and Kay 1976]:

> There is not one global message to which all message "fetches" (use of the Smalltalk symbols eyeball, ✓; colon, **:**; and open colon, ⁘) refer; rather, messages form a hierarchy which we explain in the following way-- suppose I just received a message; I read part of it and decide I should send my friend a message; I wait until my friend reads his message (the one I sent him, not the one I received); when he finishes reading his message, I return to reading my message. I can choose to let my friend read the rest of my message, but then I cannot get the message back to read it myself (note, however, that this can be done using the Smalltalk object *apply* which will be discussed later). I can

also choose to include permission in my message to my friend to ask me to fetch some information from my message and to give that in information to him (accomplished by including **:** or **⁸** in the message to the friend). However, anything my friend fetches, I can no longer have. In other words,

1) An object (let's call it the CALLER) can send a message to another object (the RECEIVER) by simply mentioning the RECEIVER's name followed by the message.
2) The action of message sending forms a stack of messages; the last message sent is put on the top.
3) Each attempt to receive information typically means looking at the message on the top of the stack.
4) The RECEIVER uses the eyeball, ◀ the colon, **:**, and the open colon, **⁸**, to receive information from the message at the top of the stack.
5) When the RECEIVER completes his actions, the message at the top of the stack is removed and the ability to send and receive messages returns to the CALLER. The RECEIVER may return a value to be used by the CALLER.
6) This sequence of sending and receiving messages, viewed here as a process of stacking messages, means that each message on the stack has a CALLER (message sender) and RECEIVER (message receiver). Each time the RECEIVER is finished, his message is removed from the stack and the CALLER becomes the current RECEIVER. The now current RECEIVER can continue reading any information remaining in his message.
7) Initially, the RECEIVER is the first object in the message typed by the programmer, who is the CALLER.
8) If the RECEIVER's message contains an eyeball, ◀; colon, **:**, or open colon, **⁸**, he can obtain further information from the CALLER's message. Any information successfully obtained by the RECEIVER is no longer available to the CALLER.
9) By calling on the object *apply,* the CALLER can give the RECEIVER the right to see all of the CALLER's remaining message. The CALLER can no longer get information that is read by the RECEIVER; he can, however, read anything that remains after the RECEIVER completes its actions.
10) There are two further special Smalltalk symbols useful in sending and receiving messages. One is the keyhole, 🗝, that lets the RECEIVER "peek" at the message. It is the same as the **⁸** except it does not remove the information from the message. The second symbol is the hash mark, #, placed in the message in order to send a reference to the next token rather than the token itself.

[26] The sender is an intrinsic component of communication in the following previous models of computation:
- *Petri Nets*: the input places of a transition are an intrinsic component of a computational step (transition).
- *Lambda Calculus*: the expression being reduced is an intrinsic component of a computational step (reduction).
- *Simula*: the stack of the caller is an intrinsic component of a computation step (method invocation).
- *Smalltalk 72*: the invoking token stream is an intrinsic component of a computation step (message send).

[27] An Actor can have information about other Actors that it has received in a message about what it was like when the message was sent. See section of this paper on unbounded nondeterminism in ActorScript.

[28] Arbiters render meaningless the states in the Abstract State Machine (ASM) model [Blass, Gurevich, Rosenzweig, and Rossman 2007a, 2007b; Glausch and Reisig 2006].

[29] The logic gates require suitable thresholds and other parameters.

[30] Of course the same limitation applies to the Abstract State Machine (ASM) model [Blass, Gurevich, Rosenzweig, and Rossman 2007a, 2007b; Glausch and Reisig 2006]. In the presence of arbiters, the global states in ASM are mythical.

[31] Consider the following Nondeterministic Turing Machine:
Step 1: Next do either *Step 2* or *Step 3*.
Step 2: Next do *Step 1*.
Step 3: Halt.
It is possible that the above program does not halt. It is also possible that the above program halts. Note that above program is not equivalent to the one below in which it is not possible to halt:
Step 1: Next do *Step 1*.

[32] This result is very old. It was known by Dijkstra motivating his belief that it is impossible to implement unbounded nondeterminism. Also the result played a crucial role in the invention of the Actor Model in 1972.

[33] This proof does not apply to extensions of Nondeterministic Turing Machines that are provided with a new primitive instruction NoLargest which is defined to write a unbounded large number on the tape. Since executing NoLargest can write an unbounded amount of tape in a single instruction, executing it can take an unbounded time during which the machine cannot read input.

Also, the NoLargest primitive is of limited practical use. Consider a Nondeterministic Turing Machine with two input-only tapes that can be read nondeterministically and one standard working tape.

It is possible for the following program to copy both of its input tapes onto its working tape:

Step 1: **Either**
  a) copy the next input from the 1st input tape onto the working tape and next do *Step 2,*

  or

  b) copy the next input from the 2nd input tape onto the working tape and next do *Step 3.*

Step 2: Next do *Step 1.*

Step 3: Next do *Step 1.*

It is also possible that the above program does not read any input from the 1st input tape (*cf.* [Knabe 1993]). Bounded nondeterminism was but a symptom of deeper underlying issues with Nondeterministic Turing Machines.

[34] Consequently,
- The tree has an infinite path. ⇔ The tree is infinite. ⇔ It is possible that P does not halt.

  If it is possible that P does not halt, then it is possible that that the set of outputs with which P halts is infinite.
- The tree does not have an infinite path. ⇔ The tree is finite. ⇔ P always halts.

  If P always halts, then the tree is finite and the set of outputs with which P halts is finite.

[35] [Kowalski 1988a]

[36] A Logic Program is defined by the criteria that it must logically infer its computational steps.

[37] A request to a shared resource might never receive service because it is possible that a nondeterministic choice will always be made to service another request instead.

[38] [Nygaard 1986] Starting with Simula-67, which was not a pure Object programming language because for efficiency reasons numbers, strings, arrays, *etc.* were not made into Objects in the Class hierarchy.

[39] [Knudsen and Madsen 1988]

[40] According to [Nygaard 1986] (emphases in original):

The term **object-oriented programming** is derived from the **object** concept in the Simula-67 programming language. ... Objects sharing a common structure are said to constitute a **class**, described in the program by a common **class description**.

[SIGPLAN 1986, Stein, Lieberman, and Ungar 1989] have discussions of object-oriented programming.

[41] Examples of Object programming languages include Simula-67, Smalltalk-80, Java, C++, C#, and future versions of JavaScript. Recent Object languages support other abstraction and code reuse mechanisms, such as

traits, delegation, type classes, and so on, either in place of, or as well as inheritance.

[42] Every interface is a type and every type is an interface.

[43] [Kay 1998] wrote:
> The big idea is "messaging" .... The key in making great and growable systems is much more to design how its modules communicate rather than what their internal properties and behaviors should be. Think of the internet - to live, it (a) has to allow many different kinds of ideas and realizations that are beyond any single standard and (b) to allow varying degrees of safe interoperability between these ideas.

[44] missing from initial versions of Scheme

[45] Notable members of this community included Bill Gosper, Richard Greenblatt, Jack Holloway, Tom Knight, Stuart Nelson, Peter Samson, Richard Stallman, *etc*. See [Levy 1984].

[46] According to [Steele and Gabriel 1994]:
> *Hewitt had noted that the actor model could capture the salient aspects of the lambda calculus; Scheme demonstrated that the lambda calculus captured nearly all salient aspects (excepting only side effects and synchronization) of the actor model.*

Unfortunately, the above comment misses an important point: Actors that can be implemented in the parallel lambda calculus are special case Actors that have bounded nondeterminism and *cannot* change. In general, Actors that can be implemented in the parallel lambda calculus are exponentially slower than general Actor systems.

[47] [Hewitt 1976, 1977].

[48] This misconception was partially acknowledged in some of their subsequent work.

[49] The parallel lambda calculus includes the following limitations:
- Message reception order cannot be implemented.
- Actors that change cannot be implemented
- The parallel lambda calculus does not have exceptions.
- In general, the parallel lambda calculus is exponentially slower than general Actor systems.

[50] (**Postpone** *Expression* ◁aType▷): *Expression* ◁Future◁aType▷▷ ∎
// postpone execution of the expression until the value is needed.

[51] According to [Berger 2003], Milner revealed
> ...*secretly I realized that working in verification and automatic theorem proving...wasn't getting to the heart of computation theory...it was Dana Scott's work that was getting to the heart of computation and the meaning of computation.*

However, Milner continued his research on bi-simulation between systems and did not directly address the problem of developing mathematical denotations for general computations as in the Actor Model.

[52] Note that there is a limitation on concurrency because $u_\blacksquare get[\ ]$ must complete *before* P starts.
[53] As above, there is a limitation on concurrency because $u_\blacksquare put[x]$ must complete *before* P starts.
[54] *e.g.* as in Erlang [Armstrong 2010].
[55] *e.g.* using assignment commands
[56] a concept from (quantum) physics
[57] However, data structures *within* an Erlang Actor are garbage collected.
[58] which can be optimized by reusing the thread if another message is waiting
[59] a globally unique identifier can be a 128-bit guid, long integer, or a string.
[60] Also, a reference for an Orleans Actor can be created from a C# anObjectAddress using
aFactory.CreateObjectReference(anObjectAddress).
[61] There can be optimizations for determinate message passing, *i.e.*, the same message always responds with the same result.
[62] Because of the ability to instantiate an Actor from its globally unique identifier, Orleans Actors are called "*virtual*" in their documentation. By analogy with virtual memory, the term "virtual" applied to an Orleans Actor would seem to imply that it would have to return to where it left. However, this terminology is misleading because an Actor can potentially migrate elsewhere and never come back.
  Better terminology would be to say that an Orleans Actor is "*perpetual.*"
[63] unless it is deleted by potentially unsafe means, which can result in a dangling globally unique identifier.
[64] after it has been unused for a while, its storage can be moved elsewhere outside the process in which it currently resides
[65] unless it is deleted by potentially unsafe means, which can result in a dangling globally unique identifier.
[66] However, after the message is finished processing, sometimes waiting method calls it invoked can be processed concurrently if they are independent.
[67] provided that the Actor is not contended
[68] [Microsoft 2013]
[69] In ActorScript the program is:
   Try ...*aUse(①anActor.aMethodName(...))*...
       anotherUse(①anActor.anotherMethodName(...))...
   catch ...
[70] reentrancy allows execution of waiting method calls to be freely interleaved
[71] [Liskov and Shira 1988; Miller, Tribble, and Shapiro 2005]
[72] Orleans uses Task<aType> for the type of a promise which corresponds to the type Future◁aType▷ in ActorScript.
[73] for requests, *e.g.*, method calls. Customers are sometimes called continuations in the literature although continuations often cannot handle exceptions.

[74] However, Orleans does still surfaces continuations using lower level primitives.
[75] [ECMA 2014]
[76] Promise Actors were sometimes called "futures" in the beginning [Russell 2013, Yoshino 2013].
[77] [Barton 2014]
[78] somewhat analogous the **await** construct in C# [Microsoft 2013]
[79] **function** CreatePromise(thunkForExpression)
　　{**return** Promise.resolve(**true**)
　　　　　　　　.then((aValueToDiscard) =>
　　　　　　　　　　thunkForExpression())};
[80] A thunk is an intermediary procedure for assistance in carrying out a task [Church 1941, Ingerman, 1961].
[81] The reason that it doesn't work is because postponement of a callback provided to a Promise constructor was thought by the ECMA committee to be rarely useful.
[82] official JavaScript documentation uses "resolver" for a promise-value setter. The terminology used here distinguishes that a value for the promise is set as opposed to setting an exception for the promise.
[83] which are a kind of iOrg
[84] Of course, at a different level of abstraction, workers can also be modeled as Actors that communicate with other workers.
[85] roughly in order of decreasing importance
[86] JavaScript has transferable Actors, which are limited to being of type **ArrayBuffer**, **CanvasProxy**, and **MessagePort**. According to [World Wide Web Consortium 2012]:
　　To transfer a transferable Actor to a another worker, a worker must run the steps defined for the type of Actor in question. The steps will return a new Actor of the same type, and will permanently neuter the original Actor. (This is an irreversible and non-idempotent operation; once an Actor has been transferred, it cannot be transferred, or indeed used, again.)
[86] due mainly to the legacy requirement not to break the Web. Under difficult circumstances, W3C and ECMA have worked to clean-up and make extensions without breaking the Web.
[87] [Close 2008]
[88] [Karp and Li 2007]
[89] which may require using membranes [Donnelley 1976, Hewitt 1980]
[90] cf. [Karp and Li 2008]
[91] [Hewitt, Bishop, and Steiger 1973, Hewitt and Baker 1977, Hewitt, Attardi, and Lieberman 1979]
[92] As illustrated below, "▫" can be used to express an aspect of an Actor by designating an interface which it implements, cf. [Crahen 2002, Amborn 2004, Miller, et. al. 2011].

Inconsistency Robustness for Logic Programs

Carl Hewitt

This article is dedicated to Alonzo Church and Stanisław Jaśkowski

Abstract
This article explores the role of Inconsistency Robustness in the history and theory of Logic Programs. Inconsistency Robustness has been a continually recurring issue in Logic Programs from the beginning including Church's system developed in the early 1930s based on *partial* functions (defined in the lambda calculus) that he thought would allow development of a general logic without the kind of paradoxes that had plagued earlier efforts by Frege, *etc*.[1]

Planner [Hewitt 1969, 1971] was a kind of hybrid between the procedural and logical paradigms in that it featured a procedural embedding of logical sentences in that an implication of the form (*p **implies** q*) can be procedurally embedded in the following ways:
  Forward chaining
  - When asserted *p*, Assert *q*
  - When asserted ¬*q*, Assert ¬*p*
  Backward chaining
  - When goal *q*, SetGoal *p*
  - When goal ¬*p*, SetGoal ¬*q*

Developments by different research groups in the fall of 1972 gave rise to a controversy over Logic Programs that persists to this day in the form of following alternatives:
  1. **Procedural Interpretation:** Logic Programs using *procedural interpretation of logic-clause syntax for a program*[i] [Kowalski 2014]
  2. **Procedural Embedding:** Logic Program in which *each computational step*[ii] *is logically inferred*[iii]

---

[i] a Logic Program is written as $\Psi \Leftarrow (\Phi_1 \wedge ... \wedge \Phi_n)$, which is logically equivalent to the disjunctive clause $\Psi \vee \neg\Phi_1 \vee ... \vee \neg\Phi_n$ where Ψ and each of the Φ_i is either $P[t_1, ..., t_m]$ or $\neg P[t_1, ..., t_m]$ for some atomic predicate P and terms t_j.
[ii] *e.g.*, using the Actor Model of computation
[iii] *e.g.*, using Direct Logic

This article argues for the second alternative based on the following considerations:
- Programs in logic-clause syntax are a special case of the second alternative because each computational step of a program in logic-clause syntax is logically inferred as backward chaining or forward chaining.
- Reducing propositions to logic-clause syntax can obscure their natural structure.
- Procedural interpretation of logic-clause syntax can obscure the natural structure of proofs.[i]

Logic-clause syntax is far too limited to be of use for general Logic Programs.

Kowalski advocates a bold thesis: "*Looking back on our early discoveries, I value most the discovery that computation could be subsumed by deduction.*"[2] (Roman numeral superscripts in text are endnotes at the end of this article.)

However, mathematical logic cannot always infer computational steps because computational systems make use of arbitration for determining which message is processed next. Since reception orders are in general indeterminate, they cannot be inferred from prior information by mathematical logic alone. Therefore mathematical logic alone cannot in general implement computation. Logic Programs (like Functional Programs) are useful idioms even though they are not universal. For example Logic Programs can provide useful principles and methods for systems which are quasi-commutative and quasi-monotonic even though the systems themselves cannot be implemented using Logic Programs.

A fundamental principle of Inconsistency Robustness is to make contradictions explicit so that arguments for and against propositions can be formalized. In the Inconsistency Robustness paradigm, deriving contradictions is a progressive development and contradictions are not "game stoppers" that they would be using classical logic (in which reasoning about inconsistent information can make erroneous inferences). Contradictions can be helpful instead of being something to be "swept under the rug" by denying their existence or fruitlessly attempting complete elimination in systems of practice that are pervasively inconsistent.[3]

---

[i] *e.g.*, Natural Deduction using Direct Logic

A contradiction is manifest when both a proposition and its negation are asserted even if by different parties, *e.g.*, New York Times said *"Snowden is a whistleblower."*, but NSA said *"Snowden is not a whistleblower."*[4]

This paper explores the role of Inconsistency Robustness in the development and theory of Logic Programs, which is an interesting test case involving pervasive inconsistency in an area in which, traditionally, inconsistency was not supposed to occur.

Inconsistency Robustness
In this article, boxes like this one are used below to call out instances of inconsistency robustness.

Uniform Proof Procedures based on Resolution

> *By this it appears how necessary it is for nay man that aspires to true knowledge to examine the definitions of former authors; and either to correct them, where they are negligently set down, or to make them himself. For the errors of definitions multiply themselves, according as the reckoning proceeds, and lead men into absurdities, which at last they see, but cannot avoid, without reckoning anew from the beginning; in which lies the foundation of their errors...*
> [Hobbes *Leviathan*, Chapter 4][5]

An important limitation of classical logic for inconsistent theories is that it supports the principle that from an inconsistency anything and everything can be inferred, *e.g. "The moon is made of green cheese."*

For convenience, I have given the above principle the name IGOR[6] for **I**nconsistency in **G**arbage **O**ut **R**edux. IGOR can be formalized as follows in which a contradiction about a proposition Φ infers any proposition Ψ,[i] *i.e.*,
$\Phi, \neg\Phi \vdash \Psi$.

Of course, IGOR *cannot* be part of inconsistency-robust logic because it allows *every* proposition to be inferred from a contradiction.

---

[i] Using the symbol $\vdash$ to mean "infers in classical mathematical logic." The symbol was first published in [Frege 1879].

The IGOR principle of classical logic may not seem very intuitive! So why is it included in classical logic?
- **Classical Proof by Contradiction:** $(\Psi \vdash \Phi, \neg\Phi) \Rightarrow (\vdash \neg\Psi)$, which can be justified in classical logic on the grounds that if Ψ infers a contradiction in a consistent theory then Ψ must be false. In an inconsistent theory. Classical Proof by Contradiction leads to explosion by the following derivation in classical logic by a which a contradiction about P infers any proposition Θ:
  $P, \neg P \vdash \neg\Theta \vdash P, \neg P \vdash (\neg\neg\Theta) \vdash \Theta$
- **Classical Contrapositive for Inference:** $(\Psi \vdash \Phi) \Rightarrow (\neg\Phi \vdash \neg\Psi)$, which can be justified in classical logic on the grounds that if $\Psi \vdash \Phi$, then if Φ is false then Ψ must be false. In an inconsistent theory. Classical Contrapositive for Inference leads to explosion by the following derivation in classical logic by a which a contradiction about P (*i.e.*, $\vdash P, \neg P$) infers any proposition Θ by the following proof:
  Since $\vdash P$, $\neg\Theta \vdash P$ by monotonicity. Therefore $\neg P \vdash \Theta$ by Classical Contrapositive for Inference. Consequently P, $\neg P \vdash \Theta$.
- **Classical Extraneous ∨ Introduction:**[7] $\Psi \vdash (\Psi \vee \Phi)$, which in classical logic says that if Ψ is true then $\Psi \vee \Phi$ is true regardless of whether Φ is true.[8] In an inconsistent theory, Extraneous ∨ introduction leads to explosion via the following derivation in classical logic in which a contraction about P infers any proposition Θ:
  $P, \neg P \vdash (P \vee \Theta), \neg P \vdash \Theta$
- **Classical Excluded Middle:** $\vdash (\Psi \vee \neg\Psi)$, which in classical logic says that $\Psi \vee \neg\Psi$ is true regardless of whether Ψ is true. *Excluded Middle* is the principle of Classical Logic that for every proposition X the following holds: ExcludedMiddle[X] $\equiv$ X∨¬X
  However, Excluded Middle is not suitable for inconsistency-robust logic because it is equivalent[i] to saying that there are no inconsistencies, *i.e.*, for every proposition X,
  Noncontradiction[X] $\equiv \neg(X \wedge \neg X)$
  Using propositional equivalences, note that
  ExcludedMiddle[$\Phi \vee \Psi$] $\Leftrightarrow (\Psi \vee \neg\Psi \vee \Phi) \wedge (\Phi \vee \neg\Phi \vee \Psi)$
  Consequently, ExcludedMiddle[$\Phi \vee \Psi$]$\Rightarrow (\Psi \vee \neg\Psi \vee \Phi)$, which means that the principle of Excluded Middle implies $\Psi \vee \neg\Psi \vee \Phi$ for all propositions Ψ and Φ. Thus the principle of Excluded Middle is not

---

[i] using propositional equivalences

inconsistency robust because it implies every proposition Φ can be proved[9] given any contradiction Ψ. [Kao 2011]

Classical Logic is unsafe for use with potentially inconsistent information.[10]

[Robinson 1965] developed a deduction method called resolution which was proposed as a uniform proof procedure using first-order logic for proving theorems which
> *Converted everything to clausal form and then used a method analogous to modus ponens to attempt to obtain a contradiction by adding the negation of the proposition to be proved.*

Resolution uniform proof procedures were used to generate some simple proofs [Wos, et. al. 1965; Green 1969; Waldinger and Lee 1969; Anderson and Bledsoe 1970; *etc.*]. In the resolution uniform proof procedure theorem proving paradigm, the use of procedural knowledge was considered to be "*cheating.*"[11]

Kowalski (also see [Decker 2003, 2005, 2010]) advocates that inference for inconsistent information systems[12] be performed using resolution theorem proving.[13] Unfortunately, in the presence of inconsistent information, resolution theorem provers can prove propositions using invalid arguments.

For example, consider the following illustration:[i]
A resolution theorem prover proved $\Psi\vee\Phi$ and as a consequence it was added to the information system. Sometime afterward, another resolution theorem prover proved Φ making use of the previously proved $\Psi\vee\Phi$. Unfortunately, Φ was proved by resolution theorem proving using an invalid argument because[14]

- The first resolution theorem prover proved $\Psi\vee\Phi$ because[ii] $\vdash\Psi$[iii] where Ψ holding has no bearing[iv] on whether Φ holds.[i]

---

[i] The illustration below is presented in general terms for simplicity of exposition because presenting a detailed example involves significant complexity with lots of irrelevant details. An important point is that resolution theorem provers rely on overlap of vocabulary in deciding on which propositions to resolve. Consequently, they can become entangled in irrelevancy when deriving a contradiction when two propositions (having no bearing on whether the other holds) share vocabulary.

[ii] unknown to the resolution theorem prover

[iii] even though the resolution theorem prover could *not* prove Ψ in the time that it took to prove $\Psi\vee\Phi$

[iv] unknown to the resolution theorem prover although Ψ and Φ have some common vocabulary, which can lead a resolution theorem prover astray

- Using an invalid argument,[ii] the second resolution theorem proved Φ using the previously proved $\Psi\vee\Phi$ because[iii] $\vdash \neg\Psi$.[iv]

The above illustration illustrates how resolution theorem proving can prove propositions[v] using invalid arguments.

For a large information base Ω of theories of practice (*e.g.*, a climate models, theories of the human brain, etc.), Kowalski advocates use of the resolution set of support strategy[15] as follows: In proving a proposition Φ, the set of support strategy chooses resolutions involving resolving $\neg\Phi$ with Ω and resolving the resulting clauses with each other and with $\neg\Phi$.[16]

Any proposition X can be proved[vi] by interacting with a resolution theorem prover[vii] from an information base containing propositions ϑ and $\neg\vartheta$[viii] as follows:

1) $\vartheta \vdash_{SetOfSupport} (\vartheta \vee X)$ because $\vartheta, \underline{\neg(\vartheta \vee X)} \vdash_{ResolutionTheoremProver}$ False[ix]
2) $\vartheta \vee X, \neg\vartheta \vdash_{SetOfSupport} X$ because

    $\vartheta \vee X, \neg\vartheta, \underline{\neg X} \vdash_{ResolutionTheoremProver}$ False[x]
3) A resolution theorem prover *using set of support* working on an information base containing both ϑ and $\neg\vartheta$ can be used to first prove $\vartheta \vee X$ using 1) and then can be used to prove X using 2).

---

[i] Unfortunately, the following rule of classical logic is not inconsistency robust: $\Psi \vdash \Psi \vee \Phi$. However, a resolution theorem prove must honor *all* of the rules of classical logic.

[ii] because the resolution theorem provers unknowingly used $\vdash \Psi, \neg\Psi$ as the basis for the proof of Φ although Ψ holding has no bearing on Φ holding even though they have some common vocabulary

[iii] unknown to the resolution theorem prover

[iv] even though the resolution theorem prover could *not* prove $\neg\Psi$ in the time that it took to prove Φ

[v] for pervasively inconsistent information systems of practice, *e.g.*, theories for climate change and the human brain

[vi] using an invalid argument because it used inconsistent assumptions

[vii] using the set of support strategy

[viii] a resolution theorem prover using set of support might not realize that ϑ and $\neg\vartheta$ are inconsistent because if they are not in the set of support, they will not be resolved and it might not be immediately apparent from their clausal forms that they are inconsistent.

[ix] set of support is underlined

[x] set of support is underlined

Direct Logic was developed to address limitations[17] of classical logic as a foundation for Computer Science:
- Classical Direct Logic is intended to be thought to be consistent by an overwhelming consensus of working professional mathematicians. See [Hewitt 2013] for discussion of Classical Direct Logic.
- Inconsistency Robust Direct Logic is for pervasively inconsistent theories of practice, e.g., theories for climate modeling and for modeling the human brain. Classical Direct Logic can be freely used in theories of Inconsistency Robust Direct Logic. See [Hewitt 2010] for discussion of Inconsistency Robust Direct Logic.

Inconsistency Robust Direct Logic is the state of the art for possibly inconsistent information.[i] However, enforcing the constraint that a resolution theorem prover use only the rules of Inconsistency Robust Direct Logic is inefficient as well as extraordinarily complicated and awkward. Consequently, resolution theorem provers are unsuitable for inconsistency robust reasoning.

Inconsistency Robustness: Resolution

Using resolution as the only rule of inference is problematical because it can obscure the natural structure of propositions and the natural structure of proofs using Natural Deduction. Also, Resolution Theorem Proving can prove propositions using invalid arguments for systems of practice because of pervasive inconsistencies.

Procedural Embedding redux

In the late 1960's, the two major paradigms for constructing semantics software systems were procedural and logical. The procedural paradigm was epitomized by Lisp [McCarthy *et. al.* 1962] which featured recursive procedures that operated on list structures including property lists that were updated imperatively. The logical paradigm was epitomized by uniform Resolution Theorem Provers [Robinson 1965].

Planner

Inconsistency Robustness: Uniform Proof Procedures

Uniform proof procedures using resolution was intended be a general theorem proving paradigm. But it suffered immense inefficiency in practice. Changing an axiomatization to improve performance was considered to be "cheating."

Planner [Hewitt 1969, 1971] was a kind of hybrid between the procedural and logical paradigms in that it featured a procedural embedding of logical sentences in that an implication of the form (*p **implies** q*) can be procedurally embedding in the following ways:[i]
Forward chaining
- **When asserted** p, **Assert** q
- **When asserted** $\neg q$, **Assert** $\neg p$

Backward chaining
- **When goal** q, **SetGoal** p
- **When goal** $\neg p$, **SetGoal** $\neg q$

Planner was the first programming language based on using explicit assertions and goals processed using pattern-directed invocation. The development of Planner was inspired by the work of Jaśkowski [1934], Newell and Simon [1956], McCarthy [1958], McCarthy *et. al.* [1962], Minsky [1958], Polya [1954], and Popper [1935, 1963].

Planner represented a rejection of the resolution uniform proof procedure paradigm in favor of Procedural Embedding making use of new program language constructs[18] for computation including using explicit assertions and goals that invoked programs.

A subset called Micro-Planner was implemented by Gerry Sussman, Eugene Charniak and Terry Winograd as an extension to Lisp primarily for pragmatic reasons since it saved memory space and processing time (both of which were scarce) by comparison with more general problem solving techniques, *e.g.,* [Polya 1957]:
- Lisp was well suited to the implementation of a Micro-Planner interpreter.
- The full functionality of Lisp libraries were immediately available for use by Micro-Planner programs.
- The Lisp compiler could be used to compile Lisp programs used by Micro-Planner applications to make them smaller and run faster. (It was unnecessary to first implement a Micro-Planner compiler.)

---

[i] In modern notation [see appendix of this paper]:
Forward chaining
When $\vdash \Psi \rightarrow \vdash \Phi$
When $\vdash \neg \Phi \rightarrow \vdash \neg \Psi$
Backward chaining
When $\Vdash \Phi \rightarrow \Vdash \Psi$
When $\Vdash \neg \Psi \rightarrow \Vdash \neg \Phi$

Computers were expensive. They had only a single slow processor and their memories were very small by comparison with today. So Planner adopted some efficiency expedients including the following:[i]

- Backtracking [Golomb and Baumert 1965] was adopted to economize on the use of time and storage by working on and storing only one possibility at a time in exploring alternatives. In several ways, backtracking proved unwieldy helping to fuel the great control structure debate. Hewitt investigated some preliminary alternatives in his thesis.
- A unique name assumption was adopted by assuming that different names referred to different objects, which saved space and time. For example names like Peking and Beijing were assumed to refer to different objects.
- A closed world assumption could be implemented by conditionally testing whether an attempt to prove a goal exhaustively failed. Later this capability was given the misleading name "negation as failure" because for a goal G it was possible to say: "if attempting to achieve G exhaustively fails then assert (*Not* G).″[ii]
- Being a hybrid language, Micro Planner had two different syntaxes, variable binding mechanisms, etc. So it lacked a certain degree of elegance. In fact, after Hewitt's lecture at IJCAI'71, Allen Newell rose from the audience to remark on the lack of elegance in the language! However, variants of this syntax have persisted to the present day.

Micro-Planner was used in Winograd's natural-language understanding program SHRDLU [Winograd 1971], Eugene Charniak's story understanding work, work on legal reasoning [McCarty 1977], and some other projects. This generated a great deal of excitement in the field of Artificial Intelligence.

---

[i] Prolog later also adopted these same efficiency expedients.

[ii] satirized as *"the less that can proved, the more that can be assumed!"*

> **Inconsistency Robustness: Procedural Embedding**
>
> Planner was designed as a program language for Procedural Embedding. However, efficiency expedients were made in its implementation that unfortunately resulted in inflexible problem solving strategies as well as awkward, limited reasoning capabilities.
>
> Although Winograd made an impressive demo, the successors of Planner and SHRDLU were incapable of practically realizing Procedural Embedding because of limited hardware performance and lack of effective software frameworks and tooling. Because of decades of subsequent progress, it has become feasible to developed practical, principled systems for Procedural Embedding.

Logic Programs in ActorScript are a further development of Planner. For example, suppose there is a ground-complete predicate[19] Link[*aNode, anotherNode, aCost*] that is true exactly when there is a path from *aNode* to *anotherNode* with *aCost*.

When ⊪ Path[*aNode, aNode, aCost*]→
      // when a goal is set for a cost between *aNode* and itself
   ⊢ *aCost*=0▮   // assert that the cost from a node to itself is 0

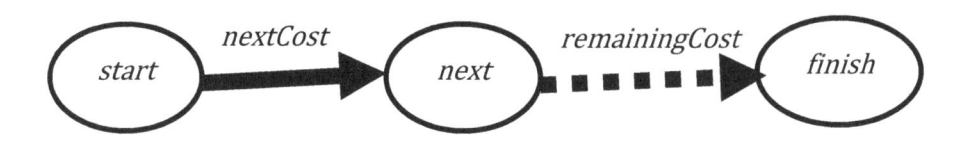

The following goal-driven Logic Program works forward from *start* to find the cost to *finish*: [20]
When ⊪ Path[*start, finish, aCost*]→
   ⊢ *aCost*=**Minimum** {*nextCost* + *remainingCost*
           | ⊪ Link[*start, next≠start, nextCost*],
             Path[*next, finish, remainingCost*]}▮
   // a cost from *start* to *finish* is the minimum of the set of the sum of the
   // cost for the next node after *start* and
   // the cost from that node to *finish*

The following goal-driven Logic Program works backward from *finish* to find the cost from *start*:
When ⊩ Path[*start, finish, aCost*]→
  ⊢ *aCost*= **Minimum**{*remainingCost* + *previousCost*
           | ⊩ Link[*previous≠finish, finish, previousCost*],
             Path[*start, previous, remainingCost*]}▮
   // the cost from *start* to *finish* is the minimum of the set of the sum of the
    // cost for the previous node before *finish* and
     // the cost from *start* to that Node

```
           remainingCost              previousCost
   ( start )■ ■ ■ ■▶( previous )────────▶( finish )
```

Note that all of the above Logic Programs work together concurrently providing information to each other.

Control Structure Controversies
Peter Landin introduced a powerful co-routine control structure using his J (for Jump) operator that could perform a nonlocal goto into the middle of a procedure invocation [Landin 1965]. In fact the J operator enabled a program to jump back into the middle of a procedure invocation even after it had already returned!

Drew McDermott and Gerry Sussman called Landin's concept *"Hairy Control Structure"* and used it in the form of a nonlocal goto for the Conniver program language [McDermott and Sussman 1972]. Hewitt and others were skeptical about hairy control structure. Pat Hayes [1974] remarked: *Their* [Sussman and McDermott] *solution, to give the user access to the implementation primitives of Planner, is however, something of a retrograde step (what are Conniver's semantics?)*

The difficulties using backtracking in Planner and Conniver were useful in that they provoked further research into control structures for procedural embedding.

> **Inconsistency Robustness: Control Structures**
> There was there germ of a good idea (previously emphasized in Polya [1957] and "progressive deepening" [de Groot 1965]) in Conniver; namely, using co-routines to computationally shift focus to another branch of investigation while keeping alive the one that has been left Scott Fahlman used this capability of Conniver to good effect in his planning system for robot construction tasks [Fahlman 1973] to introduce a set of higher-level control and communications operations for its domain. However, the ability to jump back into the middle of procedure invocations seemed awkward and confusing. Hairy Control Structure didn't seem to be what was needed as the foundation to solve the difficulties in communication that were a root cause of the control structure difficulties.

Control structures are patterns of passing messages

In November 1972. Alan Kay visited MIT and gave an inspiring lecture that explained some of his ideas for Smalltalk-72 building on the message-passing of Planner, Simula [Dahl and Nygaard 1967] as well as the Logo work of Seymour Papert with the "little person" model of computation used for teaching children to program (*cf.* [Whalley 2006]).

The Actor model [Hewitt, Bishop, and Steiger 1973] was a new model of computation that differed from previous models of computation in that it was grounded by the laws of physics so that it could be completely general in terms of control structure.[21] It took some time to develop practical program languages for the Actor model.

Work on Planner was temporarily suspended in favor of intensive investigation of the Actor model.[i]

---

[i] Work on Logic Programs later resumed in the Scientific Community Model [see section below].

> **Inconsistency Robustness: Message Passing**
> Planner aimed to extend what could be programmed using logical methods but did not take a stand about the theoretical limits of these methods. However, once the Actor model was invented in late 1972, it became clear that logical inference alone would not suffice for computation because the order of Actor message reception could not always be logically inferred.
> [Hewitt 1976] reported
> *... we have found that we can do without the paraphernalia of "hairy control structure" (such as possibility lists, non-local gotos, and assignments of values to the internal variables of other procedures in CONNIVER.)... **The conventions of ordinary message-passing seem to provide a better structured, more intuitive foundation for constructing the communication systems needed for expert problem-solving modules to cooperate effectively.*** (emphasis in original)

Edinburgh Logic for Computable Functions

Like Planner,[22] Edinburgh Logic for Computable Functions [Milner 1972; Gordon, Milner, and Wadsworth 1979] was capable of both forward chaining as well as backward chaining. This was accomplished by a purely functional program operating on a special data type called "Theorem" to produce new theorems by forward and backward chaining. Sub-goaling strategies (called tactics) were represented as higher-order functions taking strategies as arguments and returning them as results with goal failure implemented using exceptions.

> **Inconsistency Robustness: Logic for Computable Functions**
> Edinburgh Logic for Computable Functions was a notable advance in that its logical soundness was guaranteed by the type system. However, its problem solving generality is limited since it was not concurrent because it was purely functional.

Procedural Embedding versus Procedural Interpretation of Logic-clause Syntax

At Edinburgh, Pat Hayes and Bob Kowalski collaborated on resolution theorem proving. Then Hayes visited Stanford where Bruce Baumgart published his *Micro-Planner Alternate Reference Manual* in April 1972. Hayes says that from the time that he learned about Micro-Planner it seemed obvious to him that it was based on controlled deduction.[23]

When he returned to Edinburgh, he talked about his insight with anyone who would listen and gave internal seminars at two of the major departments at Edinburgh concerned with logic. In the third department, Hayes point seemed irrelevant because they were busy getting their hands on the latest "magic machinery" for controlling reasoning using Popler [Davies 1973], a derivative of Planner. Hayes wrote a joint paper with Bruce Anderson on "*The Logicians Folly*" against the resolution uniform proof procedure paradigm [Anderson and Hayes 1972].

Gerry Sussman and Seymour Papert visited Edinburgh spreading the news about Micro-Planner and SHRDLU casting doubt on the resolution uniform proof procedure approach that had been the mainstay of the Edinburgh Logicists. According to Maarten van Emden [2006]

The run-up to the workshop [Machine Intelligence 6 organized by Donald Michie in 1970] *was enlivened by telegrams from Seymour Papert at MIT announcing on alternating days that he was (was not) coming to deliver his paper entitled "The Irrelevance of Resolution", a situation that caused Michie to mutter something about the relevance of irresolution. The upshot was that a student named Gerry Sussman appeared at the appointed time. It looked as if this was going to be his first talk outside MIT. His nervousness was compounded by the fact that he had been instructed to go into the very bastion of resolution theorem proving and tell the assembled experts how totally misguided they were in trying to get anything relevant to AI with their chosen approach.*

I had only the vaguest idea what all this was about. For me theorem proving was one of the things that some people (including Kowalski) did, and I was there for the programming. If Bob and I had anything in common, it was search. Accordingly I skipped the historic Sussman lecture and arrived late for the talk scheduled to come after Sussman's. Instead, I found an unknown gentleman lecturing from a seat in the audience in, what I thought a very English voice. It turned out that a taxi from the airport had delivered Seymour Papert after all, just in time for the end of Sussman's lecture, which was now being re-done properly by the man himself.

The effect on the resolution people in Edinburgh of this frontal assault was traumatic. For nobody more so than for Bob Kowalski. Of course there was no shortage of counter objections, and the ad hoc creations of MIT were not a pretty sight. But the occasion hit hard because there was a sense that these barbarians had a point.

The above developments generated tension among the Logicists at Edinburgh. These tensions were exacerbated when the UK Science Research Council commissioned Sir James Lighthill to write a report on the AI research situation. The resulting report [Lighthill 1973; McCarthy 1973] was highly critical although SHRDLU [Winograd 1971] was favorably mentioned. "*Resolution theorem-proving was demoted from a hot topic to a relic of the misguided past. Bob* [Kowalski] *doggedly stuck to his faith in the*

potential of resolution theorem proving. He carefully studied Planner."
[Bruynooghe, Pereira, Siekmann, and van Emden 2004]

van Emden [2006] recalled:
> *Kowalski's apparent research program narrowed to showing that the failings so far of resolution inference were not inherent in the basic mechanism. He took great pains to carefully study PLANNER and CONNIVER. And painful it was. One of the features of the MIT work was that it assumed the audience consisted of LISP programmers. For anybody outside this circle (Kowalski most definitely was not a LISP programmer), the flavour is repellent.*

According to [Kowalski 2014]
> *Pat Hayes and I had been working in Edinburgh on a book [Hayes and Kowalski,1971] about resolution theorem-proving, when he returned from a second visit to Stanford (after the first visit, during which he and John McCarthy wrote the famous situation calculus paper [McCarthy and Hayes, 1968]). He was greatly impressed by Planner, and wanted to rewrite the book to take Planner into account. I was not enthusiastic, and we spent many hours discussing and arguing about the relationship between Planner and resolution theorem proving. Eventually, we abandoned the book, unable to agree.*

In the fall of 1972 at MIT, there was universal dissatisfaction with the adequacy of micro-Planner. Fundamental work[i] proceeded long before the name "Functional Program" was introduced. Likewise, as recounted in this article, fundamental work proceeded for decades before the name "Logic Program" was introduced.

To further the development of Procedural Embedding, the Actor Model was invented, which provided a rigorous basis for defining both:
- *Functional Program*: Actors do not change
- *Logic Program*: Each computational step is logically inferred.

Hayes reported that he was astonished when Kowalski wrote back from Marseilles saying that he and Colmerauer had a revolutionary idea that Horn clauses could be interpreted as backward-chaining programs. Feeling that his ideas were being unfairly appropriated by Kowalski, Hayes complained to the head of their unit Bernard Meltzer and still feeling unsatisfied wrote a summary and exegesis of his ideas in a paper for the proceedings of a

---

[i] *e.g.* [Church 1932, McCarthy *et. al.* 1962]

summer school in Czechoslovakia with the idea of recording the priority of his ideas [Hayes 1973].

However, Kowalski felt that his work with Colmerauer bore little resemblance to anything that had been discussed previously in Edinburgh by Hayes claiming that Hayes' ideas (and the paper that he published) were based on using equations for computation (in the spirit of the work in Aberdeen [Foster and Elcock 1969].

Kowalski [2008] recalled:
In the meanwhile, critics of the formal approach, based mainly at MIT, began to advocate procedural representations of knowledge, as superior to declarative, logic-based representations. This led to the development of the knowledge representation and problem-solving languages Planner and micro-Planner. Winograd's PhD thesis (1971), using micro-Planner to implement a natural language dialogue for a simple blocks world, was a major milestone of this approach. Research in automated theorem-proving, mainly based on resolution, went into sharp decline.

The battlefield between the logic-based and procedural approaches moved briefly to Edinburgh during the summer of 1970 at one of the Machine Intelligence Workshops organized by Donald Michie (van Emden, 2006). At the workshop, Papert and Sussman from MIT gave talks vigorously attacking the use logic in AI, but did not present a paper for the proceedings. This created turmoil among researchers in Edinburgh working in resolution theorem-proving. However, I was not convinced that the procedural approach was so different from the SL resolution system I had been developing with Donald Kuehner (1971).

During the next couple of years, I tried to reimplement Winograd's system in resolution logic and collaborated on this with Alain Colmerauer in Marseille. This led to the procedural interpretation of Horn clauses (Kowalski 1973/1974) and to Colmerauer's development of the programming language Prolog.

In the fall of 1972, *Prolog* (an abbreviation for "**PRO**grammation en **LOG**ique" (French for *programming in logic*)), was developed as a subset of micro-Planner that restricted programs to Horn-clause syntax[i] using backward chaining and consequently had a simpler more uniform syntax than Planner.[24] However, the restriction to Horn-clause syntax tremendously restricted the expressive power of Prolog.

---

[i] Horn-clause syntax for a logic program is of the form $\Psi \Leftarrow (\Phi_1 \wedge \ldots \wedge \Phi_n)$ which is logically equivalent to the disjunctive clause $\Psi \vee \neg \Phi_1 \vee \ldots \vee \neg \Phi_n$ where Ψ and each of the Φ_i is $P[t_1, \ldots, t_n]$ for some atomic predicate P and terms t_i.

Like Planner, Prolog provided the following:
- An indexed data base of propositions (limited by Prolog to positive predicates with ground arguments) and pattern-direct backward-chaining procedures (limited by Prolog to Horn-clause syntax).
- The Unique Name Assumption, by means of which different names are assumed to refer to distinct entities, *e.g.,* Peking and Beijing are assumed to be different in order to save space and time.
- The Closed World Assumption (available and used in practice in micro-Planner to save space and time although it was not strictly required by micro-Planner).

Prolog was fundamentally different in intent from Planner as follows:
- Planner was designed for **Procedural Embedding using explicit goals and assertions processed by pattern-directed procedures**. *Correctness can be checked when an assertion is made that a proposition holds in a theory using a rule of inference.* Theories do not limit the problem solving methods that can be used.[i]
- Prolog was designed a **backward-chaining interpretation of Horn-clause syntax**. Consequently, a goal established by a Prolog backward-chaining program was intended to be a logical consequence of the *propositional interpretation* of the Prolog program syntax *without any additional checking*. A theory expressed in Prolog limits the problem solving method that can be used to backward chaining of Horn-clause syntax programs whose propositional content is the Horn clauses[25] of the theory.

A number of Logic Program features of Micro-Planner were omitted from Prolog including the following:[26]
- Using explicit assertions processed by pattern-directed procedures (*i.e.*, "forward chaining")
- Logical negation, *e.g.*, (not (human Socrates))
- Explicit goals and subgoals that are distinct from assertions[27]

In summary, Prolog was basically a subset[ii] of Planner that restricted programs to a backward chaining interpretation of Horn clauses.

---

[i] *e.g.*, the full range of techniques in [Polya 1957] should be available.

[ii] excepting that Prolog used unification instead of the pattern matching used in Planner. However, in practice unification is often partially turned off in Prolog programs (at the potential cost of incorrect results) because unification can be expensive.

According to [Kowalski 2014]:
> "... it was widely believed that logic alone is inadequate for problem solving, and that some way of controlling the theorem-prover is needed for efficiency. Planner combined logic and control in a procedural representation that made it difficult to identify the logical component. Logic programs with SLD resolution also combine logic and control, but make it possible to read the same program both logically and procedurally. I later expressed this as Algorithm=Logic+Control (A=L+C) [Kowalski, 1979a], influenced by Pat Hayes' [1973] Computation=Controlled Deduction.
>
> The most direct implication of the equation is that, given a fixed logical representation L, different algorithms can be obtained by applying different control strategies, i.e. A_1=L+C_1 and A_2=L+C_2. Pat Hayes [1973], in particular, argued that logic and control should be expressed in separate languages, with the logic component L providing a pure, declarative specification of the problem, and the control component C supplying the problem solving strategies needed for an efficient algorithm A. Moreover, he argued against the idea, expressed by A_1=L_1+C and A_2=L_2+C, of using a fixed control strategy C, as in Prolog, and formulating the logic L_i the problem to obtain a desired algorithm A_i."

[Hayes 1974] complained that procedural interpretation was *"alien semantics"* for logical propositions that was analogous to *"... throwing out the baby and keeping the bathwater."* In other words, Hayes was arguing for Procedural Embedding as in Planner, whereas Kowalski was arguing for fixed control structure as in resolution uniform proof procedures.

Furthermore, there are concerns about the adequacy of logic-clause[i] syntax to express Logic Programs.

---

[i] Logic-clause syntax for a logic program is of the form $\Psi \Leftarrow (\Phi_1 \wedge ... \wedge \Phi_n)$ [logically equivalent to the disjunctive clause $\Psi \vee \neg\Phi_1 \vee ... \vee \neg\Phi_n$] where Ψ and each of the Φ_i is of the form P[t_1, ..., t_n] or the form $\neg$P[t_1, ..., t_n] for some atomic predicate P and terms t_i. (Logic-clause syntax is a slight generalization of Horn-clause syntax in that it allows predicates to be negated.)

> **Inconsistency Robustness: Expressiveness of Logic Programs**
> Procedural Embedding (starting with Planner) allows the distinction between propositions and programs:
> - Propositional information does not have to be reformulated using logic-clause syntax (which can obscure the natural structure of propositions).
> - Logic Programs can be more expressive and powerful when not restricted to logic-clause syntax. For example, Logic Programs in ActorScript use Natural Deduction.
> - Procedural Embedding can implement problem solving methods that cannot be implemented using Logic Programs (see this article on "Is Computation Subsumed by Deduction?")
> - Assertions have provenance that justify their inference in a theory.

Scientific Community Model[28]

Research on the Scientific Community Model [Kornfeld and Hewitt 1981, Kornfeld 1981]. involved the development of a program language named Ether that invoked procedural plans to process goals and assertions concurrently by dynamically creating new rules during program execution. Ether also addressed issues of conflict and contradiction with multiple sources of knowledge and multiple viewpoints.

The Scientific Community Model builds on the philosophy, history and sociology of science. It was originally developed building on work in the philosophy of science by Karl Popper and Imre Lakatos. In particular, it initially made use of Lakatos' work on proofs and refutations. Subsequently development has been influenced by the work of Geof Bowker, Michel Callon, Paul Feyerabend, Elihu M. Gerson, Bruno Latour, John Law, Karl Popper, Susan Leigh Star, Anselm Strauss, and Lucy Suchman.

In particular Latour's Science in Action had great influence. In the book, Janus figures make paradoxical statements about scientific development. An important challenge for the Scientific Community Model is to reconcile these paradoxical statements.

Scientific research depends critically on monotonicity, concurrency, commutativity, and pluralism to propose, modify, support, and oppose scientific methods, practices, and theories. Scientific Communities systems have characteristics of monotonicity, concurrency, commutativity, pluralism, skepticism and provenance:

- **monotonicity**: Once something is published it cannot be undone. Scientists publish their results so they are available to all. Published work is collected and indexed in libraries. Scientists who change their mind can publish later articles contradicting earlier ones.
- **concurrency**: Scientists can work concurrently, overlapping in time and interacting with each other.
- **quasi-commutativity**: Publications can be read regardless of whether they initiate new research or become relevant to ongoing research. Scientists who become interested in a scientific question typically make an effort to find out if the answer has already been published. In addition they attempt to keep abreast of further developments as they continue their work.
- **pluralism**: Publications include heterogeneous, overlapping and possibly conflicting information. There is no central arbiter of truth in scientific communities.
- **skepticism**: Great effort is expended to test and validate current information and replace it with better information.
- **provenance**: The provenance of information is carefully tracked and recorded.

> **Inconsistency Robustness: Scientific Community Model**
>
> The above characteristics are limited in real scientific communities. Publications are sometimes lost or difficult to retrieve. Concurrency is limited by resources including personnel and funding. Sometimes it is easier to re-derive a result than to look it up. Scientists only have so much time and energy to read and try to understand the literature. Scientific fads sometimes sweep up almost everyone in a field. The order in which information is received can influence how it is processed. Sponsors can try to control scientific activities. In Ether the semantics of the kinds of activity described in this paragraph are governed by the Actor model.
>
> Scientific research includes generating theories and processes for modifying, supporting, and opposing these theories. Karl Popper called the process "conjectures and refutations", which although expressing a core insight, has been shown to be too restrictive a characterization by the work of Michel Callon, Paul Feyerabend, Elihu M. Gerson, Mark Johnson, Thomas Kuhn, George Lakoff, Imre Lakatos, Bruno Latour, John Law, Susan Leigh Star, Anselm Strauss, Lucy Suchman, Ludwig Wittgenstein, etc.. Three basic kinds of participation in Ether are proposing, supporting, and opposing. Scientific communities are structured to support competition as well as cooperation.
>
> These activities affect the adherence to approaches, theories, methods, etc. in scientific communities. Current adherence does not imply adherence for all future time. Later developments will modify and extend current understandings. Adherence is a local rather than a global phenomenon. No one speaks for the scientific community as a whole.

There are a number of controversies involved in the history of Logic Programs in which different researchers took contradictory positions that are addressed in following sections of this article including, "Is computation subsumed by deduction?" and "Did Prolog-style clause programs contribute to the failure of the Japanese Fifth Generation Project (ICOT)?" and "What is a Logic Program?"

Is Computation Subsumed by Deduction?

> *"...a single formalism suffices for both logic and computation, and logic subsumes computation."*
> [Kowalski 2014]

The challenge to the generality of Logic Programs as a foundation for computation was officially thrown in *The Challenge of Open Systems* [Hewitt 1985] to which [Kowalski 1988b] replied in *Logic-Based Open Systems*. This was followed up with [Hewitt and Agha 1988] in the context of the Japanese Fifth Generation Project (see section below). All of this was in opposition to Kowalski's thesis: *"Looking back on our early discoveries, I value most the discovery that computation could be subsumed by deduction."*[29]

In concrete terms, we cannot observe the internals of the mechanism by which the reception order of messages is determined. Attempting to do so affects the results and can even push the indeterminacy elsewhere. Instead of observing the internals of arbitration processes, we await outcomes. The reason that we await outcomes is that we have no alternative because of indeterminacy. Because of indeterminacy in the physical basis of computation, no kind of deductive mathematical logic can always infer which message will be received next and the resulting computational steps. Consequently, Logic Programs can make inferences about computation but not in general implement computation. Nevertheless, Logic Programs (like Functional Programs) can be a useful idiom.

Inconsistency Robustness: Universality of Deduction

Contrary to Kowalski, computation in general cannot be subsumed by deduction. Mathematical models of computation do not determine particular computations as follows: Arbiters can be used in the implementation of the reception order of messages, which are subject to indeterminacy. Since reception orders are in general indeterminate, they cannot be inferred from prior information by mathematical logic alone. Therefore mathematical logic alone cannot implement computation in open systems.

Actor systems can perform computations that are impossible by mathematical deduction as illustrated by the following nondeterministic Actor system[i] that can compute an integer of unbounded size:

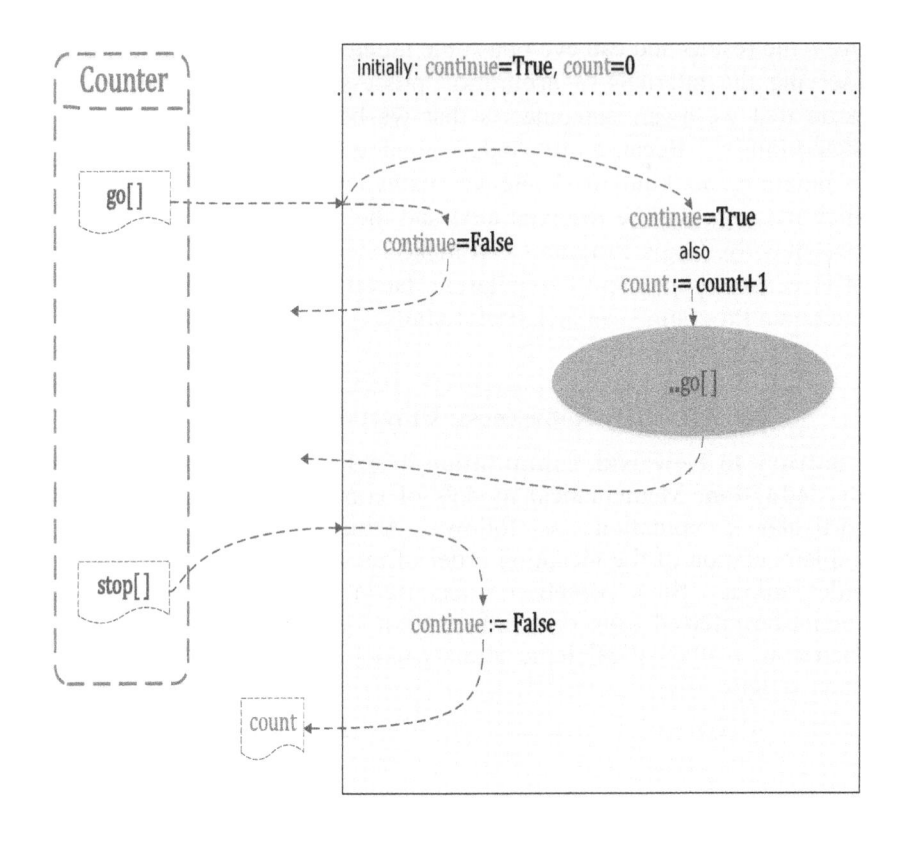

```
Counter
  go[ ]                  initially: continue=True, count=0

                                              continue=True
                         continue=False         also
                                              count := count+1

                                                  ..go[ ]

  stop[ ]
                           continue := False

  count
```

---

[i] using the ActorScript programming language [Hewitt 2010a]

The above Actor system can be implemented as follows using ActorScript™:

Unbounded ≡
　start[ ]→　　　　　　　　　// a start message is implemented by
　　Let aCounter ← SimpleCounter.[ ].　// let aCounter be a new Counter
　　☐aCounter.go[ ],　// send aCounter a go message and concurrently
　　☐aCounter.stop[ ]
　　　　　　// return the value of sending aCounter a stop message

Actor SimpleCounter[ ]
　count := 0　　　　　　　　// the variable count is initially 0
　continue := True.　// the variable continue is initially True
　implements Counter using
　　stop[ ]→
　　　count　　　　　　　　　　　// return count
　　　　afterward continue := false
　　　　　　　// continue is false for the next message received
　　go[ ]→ continue ◆
　　　　True⦂　　　　　　　// if continue is True,
　　　　　Hole..go[ ]　　// send go[ ] to this counter after
　　　　　　after count := count+1　// incrementing count
　　　　False⦂ Void　// if continue is False, return Void

By the semantics of the Actor model of computation [Clinger 1981; Hewitt 2006], sending Unbounded a start message will result in computing an integer of unbounded size.

The procedure Unbounded above can be axiomatized as follows:
∀[n:Integer]→
　∃[$aRequest$:Request, $anInteger$:Integer]→
　　Unbounded sent$_{aRequest}$ start[ ] ⇒
　　　Sent$_{Response_{aRequest}}$ Returned[$anInteger$] ∧ $anInteger > n$

However, the above axiom does *not* compute any actual output! Instead the above axiom simply asserts the *existence* of unbounded outputs for start messages.

Theorem. The nondeterministic function defined by Unbounded (above) cannot be implemented by a nondeterministic Logic Program[i].
Proof.[30]
> *The task of a nondeterministic Logic Program P is to start with an initial set of axioms and prove* Output=n *for some numeral* n. *Now the set of proofs of* P *starting from initial axioms will form a tree. The branching points will correspond to the nondeterministic choice points in the program and the choices as to which rules of inference to apply. Since there are always only finitely many alternatives at each choice point, the branching factor of the tree is always finite. Now König's lemma says that if every branch of a finitary tree is finite, then so is the tree itself. In the present case this means that if every proof of* P *proves* Output=n *for some numeral* n, *then there are only finitely many proofs. So if* P *nondeterministically proves* Output=n *for every numeral* n, *it must contain a nonterminating computation in which it does not prove* Output=n *for some numeral* n.

The following arguments support unbounded nondeterminism in the Actor model [Hewitt 1985, 2006]:
- There is no bound that can be placed on how long it takes a computational circuit called an *arbiter* to settle. Arbiters are used in computers to deal with the circumstance that computer clocks operate asynchronously with input from outside, *e.g.*, keyboard input, disk access, network input, *etc.* So it could take an unbounded time for a message sent to a computer to be received and in the meantime the computer could traverse an unbounded number of states.
- Electronic mail enables unbounded nondeterminism since mail can be stored on servers indefinitely before being delivered.
- Communication links to servers on the Internet can be out of service indefinitely.

---

[i] the lambda calculus is a special case of Logic Programs

The following Logic Programs procedurally embed information about Unbounded:
When ⊢ *aRequest* anActor sent *aMessage* →
　　　　　　　// When asserted that *anActor* is sent *aRequest* with *aMessage*
　⊢ *aRequest* anActor received *aMessage* ∎　// assert that *anActor* received *aRequest*
When ⊢ *aResponse* Sent *aResult* →[31]
　⊢ *aResponse* Received *aResult* ∎　// assert that *aResult* is received for *aResponse*
When ⊢ *aRequest* Unbounded received start[ ] →
　　　　　　　// When asserted that Unbounded is sent Start[ ]
　⊢Unbounded1[*aRequest*] Counter sent [ ],[32]
　⊩Response$_{Unbounded1[request]}$ Received Returned[*aCounter*:Counter] →
　　　　// Set a goal that *aCounter* is returned for the request Unbounded1[*aRequest*].
　　⊢Unbounded2[*aRequest*] *aCounter* sent go[ ],
　　⊢Unbounded3[*aRequest*] *aCounter* sent stop[ ],
　　⊩Response$_{Unbounded2[request]}$ Received Returned[Void] →
　　　⊩Response$_{Unbounded3[request]}$ Received Returned[*anInteger*:Integer] →
　　　　⊢Response$_{aRequest}$ Returned[*anInteger*] ∎
When ⊢ *aRequest* Counter received [ ] →
　⊢Response$_{aRequest}$ Returned[*aCounter*],
　⊢Response$_{aRequest}$ currentCount*anAccount* = 0,
　⊢Response$_{aRequest}$ continue*aCounter* = True ∎
When ⊢ *aRequest* *aCounter*:Counter received Stop[ ] →
　⊢Response$_{aRequest}$ Sent Returned[currentCount*aRequest*],
　When ⊢ *aRequest* currentCount*aCounter* = n →
　　⊢Response$_{aRequest}$ currentCount*aCounter* = n,
　⊢Response$_{aRequest}$ continue*aCounter* = False ∎
When ⊢ *aRequest* *aCounter*:Counter received go[ ] →
　⊩ *aRequest* ¬continue*aCounter* →　// Set a goal that continue*aCountet* = False
　　⊢Response$_{aRequest}$ Sent Returned[Void],
　　⊢Response$_{aRequest}$ Unchanged*aRequest* currentCount*aCounter*,
　　⊢Response$_{aRequest}$ Unchanged*aRequest* continue*aCounter*,
　⊩ *aRequest* continue*aCounter* →　// Set a goal that continue*aCounter* = True
　　⊢Counter1[*aRequest*] *aCounter* sent go[ ],
　　⊢Counter1[*aRequest*] Left,
　　　// Assert that the cheese has been left at Counter1[*aRequest*]
　　⊩ *aRequest* currentCount*aCounter* = *anInteger* →
　　　⊢Counter1[*aRequest*] currentCount*aCounter* = *anInteger* + 1,
　　⊩Response$_{Counter1[aRequest]}$ Received Returned[*anInteger*:Integer] →
　　　⊢Response$_{aRequest}$ Sent Returned[*anInteger*] ∎

305

Note that the above logic programs do *not* make use of global[33] time.[i]

Inconsistency Robustness: Modeling Change

Direct Logic can be used to model change in a way that is physically realizable as opposed to systems that make use of physically unrealizable global time:

1. *Global State Spaces*: a computation can be represented as a global state that determines all information about the computation. It can be nondeterministic as to which will be the next global state, *e.g.*, in simulations where the global state can transition nondeterministically to the next state as a global clock advances in time, *e.g.,* Simula [Dahl and Nygaard 1967].[i]
2. *Actors*: a computation can be represented as a configuration. Information about a configuration can be indeterminate. For example, there can be arbiters that are meta-stable and messages in transit that will be delivered at some indefinite (unbounded) time.

The Japanese 5th Generation Project (ICOT)

Beginning in the 1970's, Japan took the DRAM market (and consequently most of the integrated circuit industry) away from the previous US dominance. This was accomplished with the help of the Japanese VLSI project that was funded and coordinated in good part by the Japanese government Ministry of International Trade and Industry (MITI) [Sigurdson 1986].

Project Inception

MITI hoped to repeat this victory by taking over the computer industry. However, Japan had come under criticism for "copying" the US. One of the MITI goals for ICOT was to show that Japan could innovate new computer technology and not just copy the Americans.

Trying to go all the way with Prolog-style clause programs

ICOT tried to go all the way with Prolog-style clause programs. Kowalski later recalled *"Having advocated LP* [Logic Programs] *as a unifying*

---

[i] which is physically unrealizable

foundation for computing, I was delighted with the LP [Logic Program] *focus of the FGCS* [Fifth Generation Computer Systems] *project."* [Fuchi, Kowalski, Ueda, Kahn, Chikayama, and Tick 1993] By making Prolog-style clause programs (mainly being developed outside the US) the foundation, MITI hoped that the Japanese computer industry could leapfrog the US. *"The* [ICOT] *project aimed to leapfrog over IBM, and to a new era of advanced knowledge processing applications."* [Sergot 2004]

Unfortunately, ICOT misjudged the importance of direct message passing, *e.g.*, in the Actor Model [Hewitt, Bishop, and Steiger 1973] which had been developed in reaction to the limitations of Planner.

ICOT had to deal with the concurrency and consequently developed concurrent program languages based on Prolog-style clauses [Shapiro 1989] similar[34] to the above Logic Program. However, it proved difficult to implement clause-procedure invocation in these languages as efficiently as procedures in object-oriented program languages. Simula-67 originated a hierarchical class structure for objects so that message handling procedures (methods) and object instance variables could be inherited by subclasses. Ole-Johan Dahl [1967] invented a powerful compiler technology using dispatch tables that enabled message handling procedures in subclasses of objects to be efficiently invoked. The compiler technology originally developed for Simula[35] far out-performed the ICOT compliers for Prolog-style clause languages developed by ICOT.

The clausal syntax used by ICOT was awkward because it only allowed relational syntax for procedure calls and consequently was not compositional requiring the use of multiple ports for communication.[36]

Using clausal syntax, ICOT encountered difficulties dealing with concurrency, *e.g.*, readers-writers concurrency. Concurrency control for readers and writers in a shared resource is a classic problem. The fundamental constraint is that readers are allowed to operate concurrently but a writer is not allowed to operate concurrently with other writers and readers.

The interface for the readers/writer guardian is the same as the interface for the shared resource:

Interface ReadersWriter **having** read[Query]↦ QueryAnswer,
write[Update]↦ **Void**

Cheese diagram for ReadersWriter implementations:

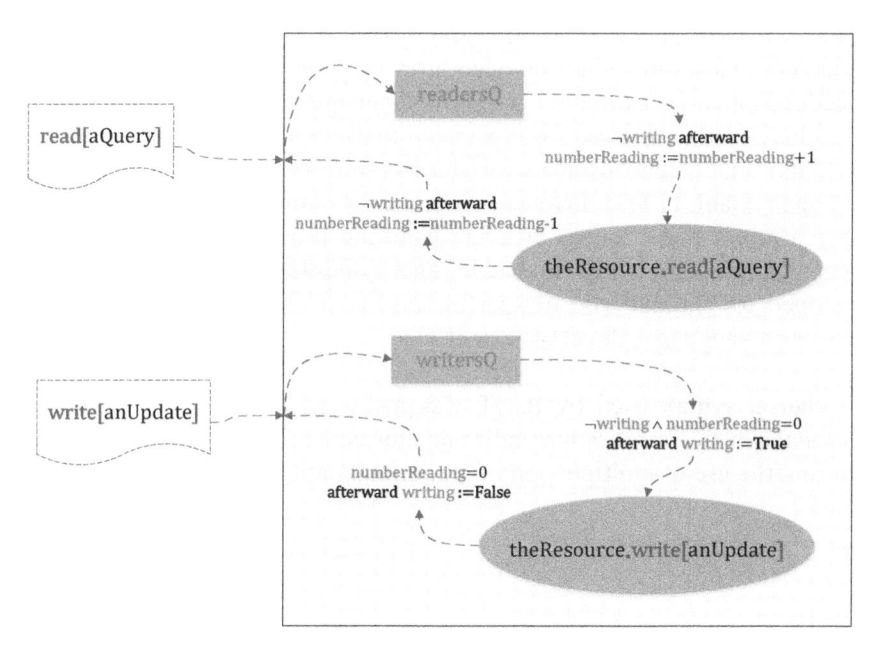

Note:
1. At most one activity is allowed to execute in the cheese.[i]
2. The cheese has holes.[ii]
3. The value of a variable[iii] cannot change in the cheese.[iv]

---

[i] Cheese is yellow in the diagram
[ii] A hole is grey in the diagram
[iii] A variable is orange in the diagram
[iv] Of course, other external Actors can change.

> **Inconsistency Robustness:
> Clausal Concurrent Programming Languages**
>
> The combination of efficient inheritance-based virtual procedure invocation (pioneered in Simula) together with class libraries and browsers (pioneered in Smalltalk) provided better tools than the slower pattern-directed invocation of the FGCS Prolog-style clause programs. Consequently, the ICOT program languages never took off and instead object-oriented program languages like Java and JavaScript became the mainstream.

Downfall

The technical managers at ICOT were aware of some of the pitfalls that had tripped up previous Artificial Intelligence (AI) researchers. So they deliberately avoided calling ICOT an AI Project. Instead they had the vision of an integrated hardware/software system [Uchida and Fuchi 1992]. However, the Prolog-style clause-program paradigm turned not to be a suitable foundation because of poor modularity and lack of efficiency by comparison with direct message passing [Hewitt and Agha 1988]. Another problem was that multi-processors found it difficult to compete in the marketplace because at the time single processors were rapidly increasing in speed and connections between multiple processors suffered long latencies.

The reliance on Prolog-style clause procedures was a principle contributing cause to the failure of ICOT to achieve commercial success.

> **Inconsistency Robustness: ICOT**
>
> MITI's Fifth Generation strategy backfired because Japanese companies refused to productize ICOT hardware.
>
> However, the architects of ICOT did get some things right:
> - The project largely avoided the Mental Agent paradigm [Hewitt 2009]
> - The project correctly placed tremendous emphasis on research in concurrency and parallelism as an emerging computing paradigm.

What is a Logic Program?

> *"It would be like saying Prolog and SLD-Resolution is the only way to do Logic Programming.* **To some extent, the LP** ["Logic Programming"] *community's insistence on clinging to this "exclusive method" has contributed to the relative disinterest in LP following its development in the 1980's and 1990's."* [Aït-Kaci 2009] (Emphasis added.)

Developments by different research groups in the fall of 1972 gave rise to a controversy over Logic Programs that persists to this day in the form of following alternatives:
1. Logic Programs using *procedural interpretation of logic-clause syntax for procedures* [Kowalski 2014][i]
2. Logic Programs in which *each computational step*[ii] *is logically inferred*[iii]

This article argues for the second conception based on the following considerations:
- Logic-clause syntax is inadequate to express Logic Programs, e.g., logic-clause syntax lacks the ability to construct sets using $\{x \mid \Vdash \Phi[x]\}$, where Φ is a ground-complete predicate.
- Programs in logic-clause syntax are a special case of the second alternative because each computational step of a program in logic-clause syntax is logically inferred by forward chaining and backward chaining.
- Reducing propositions to logic-clause syntax can obscure their natural structure
- Procedural interpretation of logic-clause syntax for procedures can obscure the natural structure of proofs.[iv]

Logic Programs need to deal with both of the following:
- *Mathematical Theories* that are thought to be consistent by the overwhelming consensus of professional working mathematicians, *e.g.* Hilbert spaces, homology theory, *etc.*

---

[i] Logic-clause syntax for a logic program is $\Psi \Leftarrow (\Phi_1 \wedge \ldots \wedge \Phi_n)$ where Ψ and each of the Φ_i is either $P[t_1, \ldots, t_m]$ or $\neg P[t_1, \ldots, t_m]$ for some atomic predicate P and terms t_j.

[ii] in the Actor Model of computation

[iii] *e.g.* using Direct Logic

[iv] *e.g.* ActorScript Logic Programs using Inconsistency Robust Natural Deduction in Direct Logic

- *Theories of Practice* that are pervasively inconsistent, *e.g.*, theories of climate change and the human brain. Mathematical theories are often freely used *within* theories of practice.

Going beyond the limitations of logic-clause syntax, there is a core subset of Logic Program constructs that are applicable to both Classical Direct Logic and Inconsistency Robust Direct Logic.[i]

Inconsistency Robustness: Characterization of Logic Programs

Developments by different research groups in the fall of 1972 gave rise to a controversy over Logic Programs that persists to this day in the form of following alternatives:
1. Each computational step (*e.g.* as defined in the Actor Model) of a Logic Program is logically inferred (*e.g.* in Direct Logic) with explicit assertions and goals processed using pattern-directed invocation.
2. A Logic Program is expressed using logic-clause syntax that is interpreted as both a backward-chaining program and a forward-chaining program.

---

[i] See appendix of this article.

Logic Programs versus Kowalski's "Logic Programming"

Kowalski has for a long time advocated *"Logic Programming"* characterized as follows:[37]

> *The driving force behind logic programming is the idea that a single formalism suffices for both logic and computation, and that logic subsumes computation. ...*
>
> *Logic programming aims ... to unify different areas of computing by exploiting the greater generality of logic* [over computational models[i]]. *It does so by building upon and extending*[ii] *one of the simplest, yet most powerful logics imaginable, namely the logic of Horn clauses.*

Kowalski's Logic Programming is a scientific research programme in the sense of [Lakatos 1980]. According to [Kowalski 2006]:

> *Admittedly, I have been messianic in my advocacy of Logic, and I make no apologies for it. Pushing Logic as hard as I could has been my way of trying to discover its limits.*

Kowalski's version of Logic Programing has the following limitations:
- based on the following mistaken assumptions:
    - *"that logic subsumes computation"*[iii]
    - that Horn clauses are the basis for a powerful logic[iv]
- lacks inconsistency-robust inference because it is based on classical logic making use of resolution theorem proving[v]
- lacks the precision of a well-defined scientific concept.[vi]

---

[i] *e.g.*, Turing Machines, relational model of data base queries, the Actor Model, *etc.*

[ii] using logic-clause syntax for a Logic Program, *e.g.*, $\Psi \Leftarrow (\Phi_1 \wedge ... \wedge \Phi_n)$ where Ψ and each of the Φ_i is either $P[t_1, ..., t_m]$ or $\neg P[t_1, ..., t_m]$ for some atomic predicate P and terms t_j.

[iii] Contrary to Kowalski, there are computations that cannot be performed using logical inference. See discussion earlier in this article.

[iv] Contrary to Kowalski, the logic-clause generalization of Horn-clause syntax is inadequate for expressing Logic Programs as explained earlier in this article. Also, Horn clauses do *not* form the basis for the most powerful logic because they are based on first-order logic, which has unintended models of axioms. For example, first-order logic cannot even characterize the integers up to isomorphism. See discussion in article 1-2 in this volume.

[v] As explained earlier in this article, resolution theorem provers can make invalid inferences using inconsistent axioms.

[vi] which could be fixed by defining the concept as "programming using Logic Programs" for a well-defined definition of a Logic Program.

Overview

Contradiction	Outcome
Kowalski advocates using resolution theorem proving to make inferences about inconsistent information systems. Unfortunately, using resolution theorem provers allows inferring every proposition from an inconsistent information system.	Using Direct Logic, inconsistent-robust inference allows inference about inconsistent information systems without enabling inference of every sentence.
Planner was intended to be a general purpose programming language for the procedural embedding of knowledge. Partly as a result of limitations of contemporary computers, pragmatic decisions were made in the implementation of Planner that limited its generality.	Programming languages (like ActorScript) have been developed that incorporate general Logic Programs.
Kowalski, *et. al.* advocated that Horn-clause syntax for programs be used as the foundation of Logic Programs. But Horn-clause syntax for programs (and slightly more general logic-clause syntax) lack the generality and modularity needed for Logic Programs.	Programming languages (like ActorScript) are not restricted to logic-clause syntax for Logic Programs.
The Japanese Fifth Generation Project (ICOT) attempted to create a new computer architecture based on logic-clause programs.	ICOT failed to gain commercial traction although it was an important research project.
Kowalski claims that mathematical logical deduction subsumes computation. However, there are computations that cannot be implemented using deduction (*i.e.* Logic Programs) and there are important applications that cannot be implemented using only Logic Programs.	Actor programming languages (like ActorScript) use direct message passing to Actors and are not restricted to just Logic Programs.

| Previously, change was modeled in Logic Programs using a global time that is physically meaningless. | The Actor model enables change in computation to be modeled by causal partial orders of message-passing events. |

The above examples are intended to be case studies in Inconsistency Robustness in which information is formalized, contradictions are derived using Inconsistency Robust reasoning, and arguments are formalized for and against contradictory propositions. A challenge for the future is to automate the reasoning involved in these case studies.

Conclusion

> *Max Planck, surveying his own career in his Scientific Autobiography [Planck 1949], sadly remarked that 'a new scientific truth does not triumph by convincing its opponents and making them see the light, but rather because its opponents eventually die, and a new generation grows up that is familiar with it.'*
> [Kuhn 1962]

A fundamental principle of Inconsistency Robustness is to make contradictions explicit so that arguments for and against propositions can be formalized. This paper has explored the role of Inconsistency Robustness in the history and theory of Logic Programs by making contradictions explicit and using them to explicate arguments. The development of Logic Programs has been shown to be a productive area for applying principles of Inconsistency Robustness.

The examples presented in this paper are intended to be case studies in Inconsistency Robustness in which information is formalized, contradictions are derived using Inconsistency Robust reasoning, and arguments are formalized for and against contradictory propositions with developments that included:
- Some arguments were dropped.
- Some arguments triumphed.
- Arguments were combined and improved.
- New arguments were developed

A challenge for the future is to automate the reasoning involved in these case studies.[i]

Acknowledgements

Scott Fahlman made suggestions and comments that materially improved an earlier version of this article. Richard Waldinger made an important suggestion for improving the definition of Logic Programs and otherwise greatly helped to improve the paper. Jeremy Forth made helpful suggestions. Bob Kowalski and Pat Hayes made important contributions and suggestions that greatly improved an earlier version article. I especially thank Bob for sharing his view of his recent research. Maarten van Emden corrected some typos. Dale Schumacher provided useful suggestions in the section on ICOT.

In 2013, this article was substantially revised to address issues of Inconsistency Robustness. Bob Kowalski provided useful comments on the abstract, which contributed to better delineation similarities and differences in our views. Alan Bundy pointed out many crucial places where the presentation needed improvement. Alan Karp pointed out a major bug in the Logic Program in the end notes. Ken Kahn provided helpful comments on clausal concurrent programming languages. Extensive discussions with Eric Kao helped clarify the discussion of the work of Kowalski. Harold Boley provided helpful suggestions on the presentation.

Of course, any remaining errors are entirely my own.

Bibliography

Hal Abelson and Gerry Sussman *Structure and Interpretation of Computer Programs (2nd edition)* MIT Press. 1996.
Hassan Aït-Kaci. *Children's Magic Won't Deliver the Semantic Web* CACM. March 2009
Robert Anderson and Woody Bledsoe (1970) *A Linear Format for Resolution with Merging and a New Technique for Establishing Completeness* JACM 17.
Bruce Anderson. *Documentation for LIB PICO-PLANNER* School of Artificial Intelligence, Edinburgh University. 1972.
Bruce Anderson and Pat Hayes. *The logician's folly* DCL Memo 54. University of Edinburgh. 1972.

---

[i] Computerization of argumentation is still in its infancy, *cf.*, [Toulmin 1959, Woods 2000, Bench-Capon 2012]. Also, there is a great deal of ongoing research in formalizing mathematical proofs [Avigad and Harrison 2014].

Jeremy Avigad and John Harrison. *Formally Verified Mathematics* CACM. April 2014.

Bruce Baumgart. *Micro-Planner Alternate Reference Manual Stanford* AI Lab Operating Note No. 67, April 1972.

L. Bertossi and J. Chomicki. *Query answering in inconsistent databases* Logics for Emerging Applications of Databases. 2003.

Trevor Bench-Capon. *The Long and Winding Road: Forty Years of Argumentation* COMMA'12.

Philippe Besnard and Anthony Hunter. *Quasi-classical logic: Non-trivializable classical reasoning from inconsistent information* Symbolic and Quantitative Approaches to Uncertainty. Springer LNCS 1995.

Maurice Bruynooghe, Luís Pereira, Jörg Siekmann, and Maarten van Emden. *A Portrait of a Scientist as a Computational Logician* Computational Logic: Logic Programming and Beyond: Essays in Honour of Robert A. Kowalski, Part I Springer. 2004.

Andrea Cantini, *Paradoxes and Contemporary Logic*, Stanford Encyclopedia of Philosophy. Winter 2012 Edition.

Eugene Charniak *Toward a Model of Children's Story Comprehension* MIT AI TR-266. December 1972.

Alonzo Church *A Set of postulates for the foundation of logic* Annals of Mathematics. Vol. 33, 1932. Vol. 34, 1933.

Paolo Ciancarini and Giorgio Levi. *What is Logic Programming good* for in Software Engineering? International Conference on Software Engineering. 1993.

Will Clinger. *Foundations of Actor Semantics* MIT Mathematics Doctoral Dissertation. June 1981

Jacques Cohen. *A view of the origins and development of Prolog* CACM. January 1988.

Alain Colmerauer and Philippe Roussel. *The birth of Prolog* History of Programming Languages. ACM Press. 1996.

Ole-Johan Dahl and Kristen Nygaard. *Class and subclass declarations* IFIP TC2 Conference on Simulation Programming Languages. May 1967.

John Dawson. *Shaken Foundations or Groundbreaking Realignment?* 2006.

Julian Davies. *Popler 1.6 Reference Manual* University of Edinburgh, TPU Report No. 1, May 1973.

Julian Davies. *Representing Negation in a Planner System* AISB'74.

Adriaan De Groot *Thought and choice in Chess* Mouton De Gruyter. 1965.

Jason Eisner and Nathaniel W. Filardo. *Dyna: Extending Datalog for modern AI.* Datalog Reloaded. Springer. 2011.

Hendrik Decker. *Historical and Computational Aspects of Paraconsistency in View of the Logic Foundation of Databases.* Semantics in Databases. Springer. 2003.

Hendrik Decker. *A Case for Paraconsistent Logic as a Foundation of Future Information Systems.* CAiSE'05 Workshop of PHISE'05. 2005.

Hendrik Decker. *How to Confine Inconsistency or, Wittgenstein only Scratched the Surface.* ECAP10. October 4-6, 2010.
Maarten van Emden. *The Early Days of Logic Programming: A Personal Perspective Association of Logic Programming* Newsletter. August 2006.
Scott Fahlman. *A Planning System for Robot Construction Tasks* MIT AI TR-283. June 1973.
Solomon Feferman *Axioms for determinateness and truth* Review of Symbolic Logic. 2008.
J.M. Foster and E.W. Elcock. *ABSYS: An Incremental Compiler for Assertions* Machine Intelligence 4. Edinburgh University Press. 1969.
Kazuhiro Fuchi, Robert Kowalski, Kazunori Ueda, Ken Kahn, Takashi Chikayama, and Evan Tick. *Launching the new era* CACM. 1993
Mike Gordon, Robin Milner, and Christopher Wadsworth. *Edinburgh LCF: A Mechanized Logic of Computation* Springer-Verlag. 1979.
Cordell Green. *Application of Theorem Proving to Problem Solving* IJCAI'69.
Steve Gregory. *Concurrent Logic Programming Before ICOT: A Personal Perspective* August 15, 2007.
Irene Greif. *Semantics of Communicating Parallel Professes* MIT EECS Doctoral Dissertation. August 1975.
Pat Hayes *Computation and Deduction* Mathematical Foundations of Computer Science: Proceedings of Symposium and Summer School, Štrbské Pleso, High Tatras, Czechoslovakia, September 3-8, 1973.
Pat Hayes. *Semantic Trees* Ph.D. thesis. Edinburgh University. 1973.
Pat Hayes. *Some Problems and Non-Problems in Representation Theory* AISB'74.
Carl Hewitt *PLANNER: A Language for Proving Theorems in Robots* IJCAI'69.
Carl Hewitt *Procedural Embedding of Knowledge in Planner* IJCAI 1971.
Carl Hewitt *Description and Theoretical Analysis (Using Schemata) of Planner, A Language for Proving Theorems and Manipulating Models in a Robot* AI Memo No. 251, MIT Project MAC, April 1972.
Carl Hewitt, Peter Bishop and Richard Steiger. *A Universal Modular Actor Formalism for Artificial Intelligence* IJCAI'73.
Carl Hewitt *Stereotypes as an Actor Approach Towards Solving the Problem of Procedural Attachment in Frame Theories* Theoretical Issues In Natural Language Processing. 1975.
Carl Hewitt. Viewing Control Structures as Patterns of Passing Messages AI Memo 410. December 1976. Journal of Artificial Intelligence. June 1977.
Carl Hewitt and Henry Baker *Actors and Continuous Functionals* Proceeding of IFIP Working Conference on Formal Description of Programming Concepts. August 1-5, 1977.
Carl Hewitt *The Challenge of Open Systems* Byte Magazine. April 1985.

Carl Hewitt and Jeff Inman. *DAI Betwixt and Between: From 'Intelligent Agents' to Open Systems Science* IEEE Transactions on Systems, Man, and Cybernetics. Nov. /Dec. 1991.

Carl Hewitt and Gul Agha. *Guarded Horn clause languages: are they deductive and Logical?* International Conference on Fifth Generation Computer Systems, Ohmsha 1988. Tokyo. Also in Artificial Intelligence at MIT, Vol. 2. MIT Press 1991

Carl Hewitt (2006b) *What is Commitment? Physical, Organizational, and Social* COIN@AAMAS'06.

Carl Hewitt (2008a) *A historical perspective on developing foundations iInfo™ information systems: iConsult™ and iEntertain™ apps using iDescribers™ information integration for iOrgs™ information systems* (revised version of *Development of Logic Programming: What went wrong, What was done about it, and What it might mean for the future* Proceedings of What Went Wrong and Why: Lessons from AI Research and Applications edited by Mehmet Göker and Daniel Shapiro. AAAI Press. AAAI'08.) Google Knol.

Carl Hewitt (2013) *ActorScript™ extension of C#™, Java™, and Objective C™: iAdaptive™ concurrency for antiCloud™ privacy and security* in Inconsistency Robustness. College Publications. 2015.

Carl Hewitt (2009) *Perfect Disruption: Causing the Paradigm Shift from Mental Agents to ORGs* IEEE Internet Computing. Jan/Feb 2009.

Carl Hewitt (2010) *Actor Model of Computation* in Inconsistency Robustness. College Publications. 2015

Carl Hewitt (2011), *Formalizing common sense for inconsistency-robust Information Integration using Direct Logic™ and the Actor Model* in Inconsistency Robustness. College Publications. 2015.

Carl Hewitt. *Health Information Systems Technologies.* Stanford CS Colloquium. June 2012. http://HIST.carlhewitt.info

Carl Hewitt (2013). *Inconsistency Robustness in Foundations: Mathematics self proves its own Consistency and Other Matters* to appear in Inconsistency Robustness 2014.

Alfred Horn. *On sentences which are true of direct unions of algebras* Journal of Symbolic Logic. March 1951.

Matthew Huntbach and Graem Ringwood. *Agent-Oriented Programming: From Prolog to Guarded Definite Clauses* Springer. 1999.

Anthony Hunter. *Reasoning with Contradictory Information using Quasi-classical Logic* Journal of Logic and Computation. Vol. 10 No. 5. 2000.

Daniel Ingalls. *The Evolution of the Smalltalk Virtual Machine* Smalltalk-80: Bits of History, Words of Advice. Addison Wesley. 1983.

Stanisław Jaśkowski *On the Rules of Suppositions in Formal Logic* Studia Logica 1, 1934. (reprinted in: *Polish logic 1920-1939*, Oxford University Press, 1967.

Ken Kahn and Vijay Saraswat. *Actors as a Special Case of Concurrent Constraint Programming* ECOOP/OOPSLA. October 1990.

Rajesh Karmani and Gul Agha. *Actors*. Encyclopedia of Parallel Computing 2011.

Michael Kassoff, Lee-Ming Zen, Ankit Garg, and Michael Genesereth. *PrediCalc: A Logical Spreadsheet Management System* 31st International Conference on Very Large Databases (VLDB). 2005.

Stephen Kleene and John Barkley Rosser *The inconsistency of certain formal logics* Annals of Mathematics Vol. 36. 1935.

William Kornfeld and Carl Hewitt T*he Scientific Community Metaphor* MIT AI Memo 641. January 1981.

William Kornfeld (1981a) *The Use of Parallelism to Implement a Heuristic Search* IJCAI'81.

William Kornfeld (1981b) *Parallelism in Problem Solving* MIT EECS Doctoral Dissertation. August 1981.

William Kornfeld. *Combinatorially Implosive Algorithms* CACM. 1982.

Robert Kowalski and Pat Hayes. *Semantic trees in automatic theorem-proving* Machine Intelligence 4. Edinburgh Press. 1969.

Robert Kowalski *Predicate Logic as Programming Language* IFIP'74.

Robert Kowalski *Logic for problem-solving* DCL Memo 75. Dept. of Artificial Intelligence. Edinburgh. 1974.

Robert Kowalski. *A proof procedure using connection graphs* JACM. October 1975.

Robert Kowalski *Algorithm = Logic + Control* CACM. July 1979.

Robert Kowalski. *Response to questionnaire* Special Issue on Knowledge Representation. SIGART Newsletter. February 1980.

Robert Kowalski *The Limitations of Logic* Proceedings of the ACM Annual Conference on Computer Science. 1986.

Robert Kowalski (1988a) *The Early Years of Logic Programming* CACM. January 1988.

Robert Kowalski (1988b) *Logic-based Open Systems Representation and Reasoning.* Stuttgart Conference Workshop on Discourse Representation, Dialogue tableaux and Logic Programming. 1988.

Robert Kowalski. *Logic Programming* MIT Encyclopedia of Cognitive Science. MIT Press. 1999.

Robert Kowalski. *Logic Programming and the Real World* Logic Programming Newsletter. January 2001.

Robert Kowalski (2004a) *History of the Association of Logic Programming* October 2004.

Robert Kowalski (2004b) *Directions for Logic Programming* Computational Logic: Logic Programming and Beyond: Essays in Honour of Robert A. Kowalski, Part I Springer. 2004.

Robert Kowalski *Re: Which Logicists?* Email to Carl Hewitt, Pat Hayes, Michael Genesereth, Richard Waldinger, and Mike Dunn. December 20, 2006.

Robert Kowalski (2007b) *Philosophy* Wikipedia. April 17, 2007.

Robert Kowalski (2007b) Robert Kowalski (2007b) *Philosophy* Wikipedia. January 10, 2007.
Robert Kowalski *Reasoning with Conditionals in Artificial Intelligence* The Psychology of Conditionals Oxford University Press. 2008.
Robert Kowalski *Email to Carl Hewitt* April 2009.
Robert Kowalski *Computational Logic and Human Thinking: How to be Artificially Intelligent* Cambridge University Press. 2011.
Robert Kowalski. *History of Logic Programming* Computational Logic Volume 9. Elsevier. 2014.
Robert Kowalski and Fariba Sadri. *Reactive Computing as Model Generation* New Generation Computing. 2015.
Thomas Kuhn. *The Structure of Scientific Revolutions* University of Chicago Press. 1962.
Imre Lakatos. *The Methodology of Scientific Research Programmes: Volume 1: Philosophical Papers*. Cambridge University Press. 1980.
Imre Lakatos. *Proofs and Refutations* Cambridge University Press. 1976.
Peter Landin *A Generalization of Jumps and Labels* Report UNIVAC Systems Programming Research. August 1965. Reprinted in Higher Order and Symbolic Computation. 1998.
Bruno Latour *Science in Action: How to Follow Scientists and Engineers through Society* Harvard University Press. 1988.
Clarence Lewis and Cooper Langford. *Symbolic Logic* Century-Croft, 1932.
James Lighthill *Artificial Intelligence: A General Survey* Artificial Intelligence: a paper symposium. UK Science Research Council. 1973.
Donald MacKenzie *Mechanizing Proof* MIT Press. 2001.
E. Mayol and E. Teniente. *A survey of current methods for integrity constraint maintenance and view updating* ER Workshops. 1999.
John McCarthy *Programs with common sense* Symposium on Mechanization of Thought Processes. National Physical Laboratory, UK. Teddington, England. 1958.
John McCarthy, Paul Abrahams, Daniel Edwards, Timothy Hart, and Michael Levin. *Lisp 1.5 Programmer's Manual* MIT Computation Center and Research Laboratory of Electronics. 1962.
John McCarthy *Review of 'Artificial Intelligence: A General* Survey' Artificial Intelligence: a paper symposium. UK Science Research Council. 1973.
John McCarthy. *Sterile Containers* www.ai.sri.com/~rkf/designdoc/sterile.ps September 8, 2000.
L. Thorne McCarty. *Reflections on TAXMAN: An Experiment on Artificial Intelligence and Legal Reasoning* Harvard Law Review. Vol. 90, No. 5, March 1977.
Drew McDermott and Gerry Sussman *The Conniver Reference Manual* MIT AI Memo 259A. January 1974.

Drew McDermott *The Prolog Phenomenon* ACM SIGART Bulletin. Issue 72. July, 1980.

Robin Milner. *Logic for Computable Functions: description of a machine implementation.* Stanford AI Memo 169. May 1972

Marvin Minsky (ed.) *Semantic Information Processing* MIT Press. 1968.

Marvin Minsky and Seymour Paper. *Progress Report, Artificial Intelligence* MIT AI Memo 252. 1972.

Alexander Nekham. *De Naturis Rerum* 1200. republished in Thomas Wright, editor. London: Longman, 1863.

Allen Newell and Herbert Simon *The logic theory machine: A complex information processing system* IRE Trans. Information Theory IT-2:61-79. 1956.

Nils Nilsson *Artificial Intelligence: A New Synthesis* San Francisco: Morgan Kaufmann, 1998.

L. Orman. *Transaction repair for integrity enforcement* TKDE, 13(6). 2001.

Mike Paterson and Carl Hewitt. *Comparative Schematology* MIT AI Memo 201. August 1970.

Max Planck *Scientific Autobiography and Other Papers* 1949.

George Polya (1957) *Mathematical Discovery: On Understanding, Learning and Teaching Problem Solving Combined Edition* Wiley. 1981.

Karl Popper (1935, 1963) *Conjectures and Refutations: The Growth of Scientific Knowledge* Routledge. 2002.

John Alan Robinson *A Machine-Oriented Logic Based on the Resolution Principle.* CACM. 1965.

Kenneth Ross, Yehoshua Sagiv. *Monotonic aggregation in deductive databases.* Principles of Distributed Systems. June 1992.

Jeff Rulifson, Jan Derksen, and Richard Waldinger *QA4, A Procedural Calculus for Intuitive Reasoning* SRI AI Center Technical Note 73, November 1973.

Philippe Rouchy. *Aspects of PROLOG History: Logic Programming and Professional Dynamics* TeamEthno-Online Issue 2. June 2006.

Earl Sacerdoti, et al., *QLISP A Language for the Interactive Development of Complex Systems* AFIPS. 1976.

Erik Sandewall. *From Systems to Logic in the Early Development of Nonmonotonic Reasoning CAISOR. July, 2006.*

Gary Saxonhouse *What's All This about Japanese Technology Policy?* Cato Institute. August 17, 2001

Dana Scott *Data Types as Lattices.* SIAM Journal on computing. 1976.

Marek Sergot. *Bob Kowalski: A Portrait* Computational Logic: Logic Programming and Beyond: Essays in Honour of Robert A. Kowalski, Part I Springer. 2004.

Jon Sigurdson *Industry and state partnership: The historical role of the engineering research associations in Japan* 1986

Ehud Shapiro *The family of concurrent logic programming languages* ACM Computing Surveys. September 1989.

Gerry Sussman, Terry Winograd and Eugene Charniak *Micro-Planner Reference Manual (Update)* AI Memo 203A, MIT AI Lab, December 1971.

Gerry Sussman and Guy *Steele Scheme: An Interpreter for Extended Lambda Calculus* MIT AI Lab Memo 349. December 1975.

Shunichi Uchida and Kazuhiro *Fuchi Proceedings of the FGCS Project Evaluation Worksho*p Institute for New Generation Computer Technology (ICOT). 1992.

Martin van Emden and Robert Kowalski. *The semantics of predicate logic as a programming language* Edinburgh TR 1974. JACM'76.

Arthur Prior. *The runabout inference ticket* Analysis, 21, 1960-61.

Alfred Tarski and Robert Vaught (1957). *Arithmetical extensions of relational systems* Compositio Mathematica 13.

Terry Winograd *Procedures as a Representation for Data in a Computer Program for Understanding Natural Language* MIT AI TR-235. January 1971.

John Woods. *How Philosophical is Informal Logic?* Informal Logic. 20(2). 2000

Larry Wos, et al. *Efficiency and completeness of the set of support strategy in theorem proving.* JACM), 12(4), 1965.

Stephen Toulmin. *The uses of argument.* 1959.

Appendix. Inconsistency Robust Logic Programs

Notation of Direct Logic

> The aims of logic should be the creation of "*a unified conceptual apparatus which would supply a common basis for the whole of human knowledge.*" [Tarski 1940]

In Direct Logic, unrestricted recursion is allowed in programs. For example,
- There are uncountably many Actors.[38] For example, Real₀[ ] can output any real number[i] between 0 and 1 where
  Real₀[ ] ≡ [(0 **either** 1), ▼**Postpone** Real₀[ ]]
  where
    o (0 **either** 1) is the nondeterministic choice of 0 or 1,
    o [*first*, ▼*rest*] is the list that begins with *first* and whose remainder is *rest*, and
  o **Postpone** *expression* delays execution of *expression* until the value is needed.
- There are uncountably many propositions (because there is a different proposition for every real number). Consequently, there are propositions that are not the abstraction of any element of a denumerable set of sentences. For example,
  p ≡ [x∈ℝ]→([y∈ℝ]→(y=x))
  defines a different predicate p[x] for each real number x, which holds for only one real number, namely x.[ii]

It is important to distinguish between strings, sentences, and propositions. Some strings can be parsed into sentences[iii], which can be abstracted into propositions that can be asserted. Furthermore, terms[iv] can be abstracted into Actors (*i.e.* objects in mathematics).

---

[i] using binary representation.
[ii] For example (p[3])[y] holds if and only if y=3.
[iii] which are grammar tree structures
[iv] which are grammar tree structures

Abstraction and parsing are becoming increasingly important in software engineering. *e.g.,*
- The execution of code can be dynamically checked against its documentation. Also Web Services can be dynamically searched for and invoked on the basis of their documentation.
- Use cases can be inferred by specialization of documentation and from code by automatic test generators and by model checking.
- Code can be generated by inference from documentation and by generalization from use cases.

Abstraction and parsing are needed for large software systems so that that documentation, use cases, and code can mutually speak about what has been said and their relationships.

For example:

Proposition

e.g. $\forall [n:\mathbb{N}] \rightarrow \exists [m:\mathbb{N}] \rightarrow m>n$

i.e., for every $\mathbb{N}$ *there is a larger* $\mathbb{N}$

Sentence

e.g. $\lceil "\forall [n:\mathbb{N}] \rightarrow \exists [m:\mathbb{N}] \rightarrow m>n" \rceil$

i.e., the sentence that for every $\mathbb{N}$ *there is a larger* $\mathbb{N}$

String

e.g. "$\forall [n:\mathbb{N}] \rightarrow \exists [m:\mathbb{N}] \rightarrow m>n$"

which is a string that begins with the symbol "$\forall$"

In Direct Logic, a sentence is a grammar tree (analogous to the ones used by linguists). Such a grammar tree has terminals that can be constants. And there are uncountably many constants, *e.g.*, the real numbers:

⌈3.14159... < 3.14159... + 1⌉ is impossible to obtain by parsing a string (where 3.14159... is an Actor[i] for the transcendental real number that is the ratio of a circle's circumference to its diameter). The issue is that there is no string which when parsed is ⌈3.14159... < 3.14159... + 1⌉

Of course, because the digits of 3.14159... are computable, there is a expression₁ such that ⌊expression₁⌋ = 3.14159... that can be used to create the sentence ⌈expression₁ < expression₁ + 1⌉.

However the sentence ⌈expression₁ < expression₁ + 1⌉ is not the same as ⌈3.14159... < 3.14159... + 1⌉ because it does not have the same vocabulary and it is a much larger sentence that has many terminals whereas ⌈3.14159... < 3.14159... + 1⌉ has just 3 terminals:

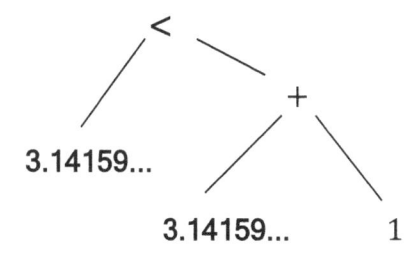

```
            <
          /   \
    3.14159…   +
              / \
        3.14159…  1
```

Consequently, sentences *cannot* be enumerated and there are some sentences that *cannot* be obtained by parsing strings. These arrangements exclude known paradoxes from Classical Direct Logic.[ii]

Note: type theory of Classical Direct Logic is much stronger than constructive type theory with constructive logic[39] because Classical Direct Logic has all of the power of Classical Mathematics.

---

[i] whose digits are incrementally computable

[ii] Please see historical appendix of this article.

Types and Propositions are defined as follows:
- *Types* i.e., a Type is *only* by the rules below:
  - Boolean,$\mathbb{N}^{40}$,Sentence,Proposition,Proof,Theory:Type
  - If σ_1,σ_2:Type, then $\sigma_1\oplus\sigma_2{}^i,[\sigma_1, \sigma_2]^{41},[\sigma_1]\mapsto\sigma_2{}^{ii},\sigma_2{}^{\sigma_1\,iii}$:Type
  - If f:Type$^\mathbb{N}$, then $(\bigoplus_\mathbb{N}$ f$)$:Type^{iv}
  - If σ:Type, then Term$\lhd\sigma\rhd^{42}$:Type
  - If σ:Type and e:Expression$\lhd\sigma\rhd$ with no free variables, then $\lfloor e\rfloor$:σ.

- *Propositions*, i.e., a Proposition is *only* by the rules below:
  - If σ:Type, Π:Boolean$^\sigma$ and x:σ, then $\Pi[x]$:Proposition.^{v}
  - If Φ:Proposition, then $\neg\Phi$:Proposition.
  - If Φ,Ψ:Proposition, then $\Phi\wedge\Psi$, $\Phi\vee\Psi$, $\Phi\Rightarrow\Psi$, $\Phi\Leftrightarrow\Psi$:Proposition.
  - If p:Boolean and Φ,Ψ:Proposition, then
    (p $\diamondsuit$ True⦂ Φ_1▱ False⦂ Φ_2):Proposition.^{43}
  - If σ_1,σ_2:Type, x_1:σ_1 and x_2:σ_2, then
    $x_1{=}x_2,x_1{\in}x_2,x_1{\sqsubseteq}x_2,x_1{\subset}x_2,x_1{:}x_2$:Proposition.
  - If T:Theory, p:Proof and $\Phi_{1\,\text{to}\,n}$:Proposition, then
    $(\Phi_1,...,\Phi_k \vdash^p_T \Phi_{k+1},...,\Phi_n)$:Proposition ^{44}
  - If s:Sentence with no free variables, then $\lfloor s\rfloor$:Proposition.

---

^{i} For i=1,2
- If x:σ_i, then $(x\oslash(\sigma_1\oplus\sigma_2))$:$(\sigma_1\oplus\sigma_2)$ and $x{=}(x\oslash(\sigma_1\oplus\sigma_2)\ominus\sigma_i$.
- $\forall[\tau$:Type, z:$\tau]\to$ z:$\sigma_1\oplus\sigma_2 \Leftrightarrow \exists[x{:}\sigma_i]\to z{=}x\oslash(\sigma_1\oplus\sigma_2)$

^{ii} Type of computable procedures from σ_1 into σ_2.
 If σ_1,σ_2:Type, f:$([\sigma_1]\mapsto\sigma_2)$ and x:σ_1, then f.$[x]$:σ_2.

^{iii} If σ_1,σ_2:Type, f:$\sigma_2{}^{\sigma_1}$ and x:σ_1, then f[x]:σ_2.

^{iv} $\forall[i{:}\mathbb{N}, x{:}f[i]]\to (x\oslash\bigoplus_\mathbb{N} f){:}\bigoplus_\mathbb{N} f \wedge x{=}(x\oslash\bigoplus_\mathbb{N} f)\ominus f[i]$
 $\forall[\tau$:Type, z:$\tau]\to$ z:$\bigoplus_\mathbb{N} f \Leftrightarrow \exists[i{:}\mathbb{N}, x{:}f[i]]\to z{=}x\oslash\bigoplus_\mathbb{N} f$

^{v} $\forall[\sigma$:Type, x:$\sigma]\to \Pi[x]\Leftrightarrow(\Pi[x]{=}\text{True})$
 Note that σ:Type, Π:Boolean$^\sigma$ means that there are no fixed points for propositions.

Grammar trees (*i.e.* expressions and sentences) are defined as follows:
- *Expressions*, i.e., an Expression◁σ▷ is *only* by the rules below:
  - **True, False**:Constant◁Boolean▷ and **0,1**:Constant◁ℕ▷.
  - Boolean,ℕ,Sentence,Proposition,Proof,Theory:Constant◁Type▷.
  - If σ:Type and x:Constant◁σ▷, then x:Expression◁σ▷.
  - If σ:Type and x:Variable◁σ▷, then x:Expression◁σ▷.
  - If σ,σ$_{1 \text{ to } n}$,τ$_{1 \text{ to } n}$:Type, x$_{1 \text{ to } n}$:Expression◁σ$_{1 \text{ to } n}$▷ and y:Expression◁σ▷, then
    (Let v$_1$◁τ$_1$▷ ≡ x$_1$, ... , v$_n$◁τ$_n$▷ ≡ x$_n$^{45} ∘ y):Expression◁σ▷ and v$_{1 \text{ to } n}$:Variable◁σ$_{1 \text{ to } n}$▷ in **y** and in each x$_{1 \text{ to } n}$.
  - If e$_1$, e$_2$:Expression◁Type▷, then
    ⌜e$_1$⊕e$_2$⌝,⌜[e$_1$, e$_2$]⌝,⌜[e$_1$]↦e$_2$⌝,⌜e$_2$^{e_1}⌝:Expression◁Type▷.
  - If σ:Type, t$_1$:Expression◁Boolean▷, t$_2$, t$_3$:Expression◁σ▷, then
    ⌜t$_1$ ◆ True⸳ t$_2$▨ False⸳ t$_3$⌝:Expression◁σ▷.[46]
  - If σ$_1$,σ$_2$:Type, t:Expression◁σ$_2$▷, then
    ⌜[x:σ$_1$]→ t⌝:Expression◁[σ$_1$]↦σ$_2$▷ and x:Variable◁σ$_1$▷ in t[47]
  - If σ$_1$,σ$_2$:Type, p:Expression◁[σ$_1$]↦σ$_2$▷ and x:Expression◁σ$_1$▷, then
    ⌜p⸳[x]⌝:Expression◁σ$_2$▷.

- *Sentences*, i.e., a Sentence is *only* if by the rules below:
  - If s$_1$:Sentence then,⌜¬s$_1$⌝:Sentence.
  - If s$_1$:Sentence and s$_2$:Sentence then
    ⌜s$_1$∧s$_2$⌝,⌜s$_1$∨s$_2$⌝,⌜s$_1$⇨s$_2$⌝,⌜s$_1$⇔s$_2$⌝:Sentence.
  - If σ:Type, t$_1$:Expression◁Boolean^σ▷ and t$_2$:Expression◁σ▷, then
    ⌜t$_1$[t$_2$]⌝:Sentence
  - If t:Expression◁Boolean▷, s$_1$,s$_2$:Sentence, then
    ⌜t ◆ True⸳ s$_1$▨ False⸳ s$_2$⌝:Sentence.[48]
  - If σ$_1$,σ$_2$:Type, t$_1$:Expression◁σ$_1$▷ and t$_2$:Expression◁σ$_2$▷, then
    ⌜t$_1$=t$_2$⌝,⌜t$_1$∈t$_2$⌝,⌜t$_1$⊆t$_2$⌝,⌜t$_1$⊏t$_2$⌝,⌜t$_1$:t$_2$⌝:Sentence.
  - If σ:Type and s:Sentence, then⌜∀[x:σ]→ s⌝,⌜∃[x:σ]→ s⌝:Sentence
    and x:Variable◁σ▷ in **s**.
  - If T:Expression◁Theory▷, s$_{1 \text{ to } n}$:Sentence and
    p:Expression◁Proof▷ , then⌜s$_1$, ..., s$_k$ ⊢^p_T s$_{k+1}$, ..., s$_n$⌝:Sentence

- **Sentences**, i.e., x:Sentence ⇔ x constructed by the rules below:
  - If s_1:Sentence then, ⌜¬s_1⌝:Sentence.
  - If s_1:Sentence and s_2:Sentence then
    ⌜$s_1 \wedge s_2$⌝,⌜$s_1 \vee s_2$⌝,⌜$s_1 \Rightarrow s_2$⌝,⌜$s_1 \Leftrightarrow s_2$⌝:Sentence.
  - If σ:Type, t_1:Term◁Boolean°▷ and t_2:Term◁σ▷, then
    ⌜$t_1[t_2]$⌝:Sentence
  - If t:Term◁Boolean▷, s_1,s_2:Sentence, then
    ⌜t◆True⦂ s_1▿ False⦂ s_2⌝:Sentence.[49]
  - If $σ_1,σ_2$:Type, t_1:Term◁$σ_1$▷ and t_2:Term◁$σ_2$▷, then
    ⌜$t_1=t_2$⌝,⌜$t_1 \in t_2$⌝,⌜$t_1 \subseteq t_2$⌝,⌜$t_1 \subset t_2$⌝,⌜$t_1:t_2$⌝:Sentence.
  - If σ:Type and s:Sentence, then ⌜∀[x:σ]→ s⌝,⌜∃[x:σ]→ s⌝:Sentence
    and x:Variable◁σ▷ in s.
  - If T:Term◁Theory▷ and $s_{1 \text{ to } n}$:Sentence,
    then ⌜$s_1, ..., s_k \vdash_T s_{k+1}, ..., s_n$⌝:Sentence
  - If T:Term◁Theory▷, p:Term◁Proof▷ and s:Sentence, then
    ⌜⊢$\frac{p}{T}$s⌝:Sentence
  - If s:Sentence, then ⌜⌊s⌋⌝:Sentence.

Forward Chaining

Forward chaining is performed using ⊢

("⊢"$_{Theory}$ *PropositionExpression*):*Expression*
  Assert *PropositionExpression* for *Theory*.

("**When**" "⊢"$_{Theory}$ *PropositionPattern* "→"
 Expression):*Continuation*
  When *PropositionPatterns* holds for *Theory*, evaluate
Expression.

Illustration of forward chaining:
  $\vdash_t$ Human[Socrates] ▮
  When $\vdash_t$ Human[x] → $\vdash_t$ Mortal[x] ▮
will result in asserting Mortal[Socrates] for theory t

Backward Chaining
Backward chaining is performed using $\Vdash$

(*"*$\Vdash$*"*$_{Theory}$ *GoalPatterns* "→" *Expression*):*Continuation*
Set *GoalPatterns* for *Theory* and when established evaluate *Expression*

(*"*$\Vdash$*"*$_{Theory}$ *GoalPattern*):*Expression*
Set *GoalPattern* for *Theory* and return a list of assertions that satisfy the goal.

(**"When"** *"*$\Vdash$*"*$_{Theory}$ *GoalPattern* "→" *Expression*):*Continuation*
  When there are goals that matches *GoalPatterns* for *Theory*, evaluate *Expression*.

Illustration of backward chaining:
  $\vdash_t$ Human[Socrates] ▮
  When $\Vdash_t$ Mortal[x] → ($\Vdash_t$ Human[x] → $\vdash_t$ Mortal[x]) ▮
  $\Vdash_t$ Mortal[Socrates] ▮
will result in asserting Mortal[Socrates] for theory t.

SubArguments
This section explains how subarguments can be implemented in natural deduction.

  When $\Vdash_s(\Psi \vdash_t \Phi)$ →
    Let t' = Extension.[t],
      Do $\vdash_{t'} \Psi$,
      $\Vdash_{t'} \Phi$ → $\vdash_s(\Psi \vdash_t \Phi)$ ▮

Note that the following hold for t' because it is an extension of t:
- **When** $\vdash_t \Theta$ → $\vdash_{t'} \Theta$ ▮
- **When** $\Vdash_{t'} \Theta$ → $\Vdash_t \Theta$ ▮

Inconsistency-Robust Propositional Equivalences

The following propositional equivalences hold in Inconsistency Robust Direct Logic:

Self Equivalence:	$\Psi \Leftrightarrow \Psi$
Double Negation:	$\neg\neg\Psi \Leftrightarrow \Psi$
Idempotence of $\wedge$:	$\Psi\wedge\Psi \Leftrightarrow \Psi$
Commutativity of $\wedge$:	$\Psi\wedge\Phi \Leftrightarrow \Phi\wedge\Psi$
Associativity of $\wedge$:	$\Psi \wedge (\Phi\wedge\Theta) \Leftrightarrow (\Psi\wedge\Phi) \wedge \Theta$
Distributivity of $\wedge$ over $\vee$:	$\Psi \wedge (\Phi\vee\Theta) \Leftrightarrow (\Psi\wedge\Phi) \vee (\Psi\wedge\Theta)$
De Morgan for $\wedge$:	$\neg(\Psi\wedge\Phi) \Leftrightarrow \neg\Psi\vee\neg\Phi$
Idempotence of $\vee$:	$\Psi\vee\Psi \Leftrightarrow \Psi$
Commutativity of $\vee$:	$\Psi\vee\Phi \Leftrightarrow \Phi\vee\Psi$
Associativity of $\vee$:	$\Psi \vee (\Phi\vee\Theta) \Leftrightarrow (\Psi\vee\Phi) \vee \Theta$
Distributivity of $\vee$ over $\wedge$:	$\Psi \vee (\Phi\wedge\Theta) \Leftrightarrow (\Psi\vee\Phi)\wedge (\Psi\vee\Theta)$
De Morgan for $\vee$:	$\neg(\Psi\vee\Phi) \Leftrightarrow \neg\Psi\wedge\neg\Phi$
Contrapositive for $\Rightarrow$:	$(\Psi\Rightarrow\Phi) \Leftrightarrow \neg\Psi\Rightarrow\neg\Phi$

End Notes

[1] Church's system was quickly shown to be inconsistent because it allowed Gödelian "self-referential" propositions, which lead to inconsistency in Mathematics [Hewitt 2011].

[2] [Kowalski1988]

[3] According to [Kowalski 1979]:
"an inconsistent system can ... organize useful information... Thus [finding a] contradiction, far from harming an information system, helps to indicate areas in which it can be improved. It facilitates the development of systems by successive approximation – daring conjectures followed by refutation and reconciliation. It favours bold, easily falsified beliefs, which can be weakened if need should arrive, over save, timid beliefs, which are difficult to strengthen later on. Better to make mistakes and to correct them than to make no progress at al."

[4] Raising issues of Inconsistency Robustness, The Obama administration deleted the following statement from its 2008 campaign website:
"**Protect Whistleblowers**: Often the best source of information about waste, fraud, and abuse in government is an existing government employee committed to public integrity and willing to speak out. Such acts of courage and patriotism, which can sometimes save lives and often save taxpayer dollars, should be encouraged rather than stifled. We need to empower federal employees as watchdogs of wrongdoing and partners in performance. Barack Obama will strengthen whistleblower laws to protect federal workers who expose waste, fraud, and abuse of authority in government. Obama will ensure that federal agencies expedite the process for reviewing whistleblower claims and whistleblowers have full access to courts and due process."
It may be that Obama's Administration's statement on the importance of protecting whistleblowers went from being a promise for his administration to a political liability. There are manifest contradictions in what Obama said then and what he is doing now.

[5] In 1666, England's House of Commons introduced a bill against atheism and blasphemy, singling out Hobbes' Leviathan. Oxford university condemned and burnt Leviathan four years after the death of Hobbes in 1679.

[6] In Latin, the principle is called ex falso quodlibet which means that from falsity anything follows.

[7] [Nekham 1200, pp. 288-289]; later rediscovered and published in [Lewis and Langford 1932]

[8] [Pospesel 2000] has discussed extraneous $\vee$ introduction on in terms of the following principle: $\Psi, (\Psi \vee \Phi \vdash \Theta) \vdash \Theta$ However, the above principle immediately derives extraneous $\vee$ introduction when Θ is

$\Psi\vee\Phi$. In Direct Logic, argumentation of the above form would often be reformulated as follows to eliminate the spurious Φ middle proposition: $\Psi, (\Psi \vdash \Theta) \vdash \Theta$

[9] using $\vee$-*Elimination*, i.e., $\neg\Phi, (\Phi\vee\Psi) \vdash_T \Psi$

[10] Turing noted that classical logic can be used to make invalid inferences using inconsistent information "*without actually going through* [an explicit] *contradiction.*" [Diamond 1976] Furthermore, [Church 1935, Turing 1936] proved that it is computationally undecidable whether a mathematical theory of practice is inconsistent.

[11] [Green 1969]

[12] [Kowalski 1988]

[13] Resolution Theorem Proving is not Inconsistency Robust because it can be used to prove that there are no contradictions as follows:
Using Resolution Theorem Proving, $\neg(\Psi\wedge\neg\Psi)$ can be proved because $\Psi, \neg\Psi \vdash_{ClassicalResolution}$ False
It is possible to use *Inconsistency-Robust Resolution* as follows:
$\Psi\vee\neg\Psi, \neg\Psi\vee\Phi, \Psi\vee\Omega \vdash_T \Phi\vee\Omega$ that requires the additional assumption $\Psi\vee\neg\Psi$ in order to make the inference.
Of course, it is possible to add the classical resolution rule to a theory T by adding the following: $\Psi\vee\Phi, \neg\Phi\vee\Theta \vdash_T \Psi\vee\Theta$

[14] The argument below originated in [Nekham 1200, pp. 288-289] (later rediscovered and published in [Lewis and Langford 1932]) is an argument that an inconsistency $\vartheta\wedge\neg\vartheta$ can be used to infer every proposition X. The Nekham argument is not valid in Inconsistency Robust Direct Logic because it make use of the rule of Extraneous $\vee$–Introduction, *i.e.*, $\Psi\vdash(\Psi\vee\Phi)$. The Nekham argument can be formalized is as follows: $\vartheta\vdash(\vartheta\vee X)$ and therefore $\vartheta, \neg\vartheta \vdash X$ because $\neg\vartheta, (\vartheta\vee X)\vdash X$

[15] [Wos et. al., 1965]

[16] I am grateful to Kowalski for clarifying his position. [Personal communication March 8, 2014].

[17] such as the one immediately above

[18] (later generalized, e.g., ActorScript [Hewitt 2013])

[19] A ground-complete predicate is one for which all instances in which the predicate holds are explicitly manifest, i.e. instances can be generated using patterns. See [Ross and Sagiv 1992, Eisner and Filardo 2011].

[20] Execution can proceed differently depending on how sets fit into computer storage units.

[21] Sussman and Steele [1975] mistakenly concluded
> "*we discovered that the 'Actors' and the lambda expressions were identical in implementation.*"

The actual situation is that the lambda calculus is capable of expressing some kinds of sequential and parallel control structures but, in general, not the concurrency expressed in the Actor model. On the other hand, the Actor model is capable of expressing everything in the lambda calculus and more.

Sussman and Steele noticed some similarities between Actor customers and continuations introduced by [Reynolds 1972] using a construct called escape that was a further development of hairy control structure. In their program language Scheme, they called their variant of escape by the name "*call with current continuation.*" Unfortunately, general use of escape is not compatible with usual hardware stack disciple introducing considerable operational inefficiency. Also, using escape can leave customers stranded. Consequently, use of escape is generally avoided these days and exceptions are used instead so that clean up can be performed. [Hewitt 2009]

[22] and unlike Prolog (see below)

[23] There was somewhat similar work that Hayes had discussed with the researchers at Aberdeen on ABSYS/ABSET [Foster and Elcock 1969].

[24] According to [Colmerauer and Roussel 1996]:
> *While attending an IJCAI convention in September '71 with Jean Trudel, we met Robert Kowalski again and heard a lecture by Terry Winograd on*
>
> *natural language processing. The fact that he did not use a unified formalism left us puzzled. It was at this time that we learned of the existence of Carl Hewitt's programming language, Planner [Hewitt, 1969]. The lack of formalization of this language, our ignorance of Lisp and, above all, the fact that we were absolutely devoted to logic meant that this work had little influence on our later research.*

However, according to [Kowalski 2008]:
> *During the next couple of years, I tried to reimplement Winograd's system in resolution logic and collaborated on this with Alain Colmerauer in Marseille. This led to the procedural interpretation of Horn clauses (Kowalski 1973/1974) and to Colmerauer's development of the programming language Prolog.*

[25] [Horn 1951]

[26] In practice, Prolog implemented a number of non-logical computational primitives for input-output, *etc.* Like Planner, for the sake of efficiency, it used backtracking. Prolog also had a non-logical computational primitive like the one of Planner to control backtracking by conditionally testing for

the exhaustive failure to achieve a goal by backward chaining. However, Prolog was incapable of expressing strong "Negation as Failure" because it lacked both the assertions and true negation of Planner and thus it was impossible in Prolog to say "if attempting to achieve the goal G exhaustively

fails then assert (*not* G)." Prolog extended Planner by using unification (but not necessarily soundly because for efficiency reasons it can omit use of the "occurs" check).

[27] Prolog required a top-level goal $\Phi_1 \wedge \ldots \wedge \Phi_n$ to be stated as follows: **False**$\Leftarrow$($\Phi_1 \wedge \ldots \wedge \Phi_n$) [logically equivalent to the disjunctive clause $\neg\Phi_1 \vee \ldots \vee \neg\Phi_n$], which requires that in order to find solutions to the goal, the disjunctive clause must be refuted by deriving an contradiction, which is not Inconsistency Robust.

[28] some of material below was contributed by the author for publication in Wikipedia on "The Actor Model."

[29] [Kowalski 1988a] On the other hand since the fall of 1972 with the invention of the Actor Model, Logic Programs can be rigorously defined very general terms (starting with the McCarthy's Advice Taker proposal [McCarthy 1958]) as "*what can be programmed in mathematical logic.*" Of course, what can be programmed in mathematical logic is exactly "*each computational step (e.g.* as defined in the Actor model) *can be logically deduced.*" Even allowing the full power of Direct Logic, computation is not reducible to Logic Programs [Hewitt 2011].

[30] *cf.* Plotkin [1976]

[31] When asserted that aResult is sent in *aResponse*

[32] Assert in Unbounded1[*aRequest*] that Counter is sent [ ]

[33] e.g. [Kowalski and Sadri 2015]

[34] ICOT used monotonic *mutable* lists instead of events in its Prolog-style clause programs.

[35] later adapted for concurrency, e.g., Java, etc.

[36] Use of multiple ports is an awkward programming idiom that introduces many difficulties, *e.g.*, starvation due not properly servicing a port. For a contrary view, see [Kahn and Saraswat 1990].

[37] [Kowalski 2014]

[38] By the *Computational Representation Theorem* [Clinger 1981; Hewitt 2006], which can define all the possible executions of a procedure.

[39] e.g. [Shulman 2012, nLab 2014]

[40] ℕ is the type of Natural Number axiomatized in this article.

[41] type of 2-element list with first element of type σ_1 and with second element of type σ_2

[42] type of term of type σ

[43] *if* **t** *then* Φ_1 *else* Φ_2

[44] $\Phi_1, \ldots$ and Φ_k infer $\Psi_1, \ldots,$ and Ψ_n

[45] parameterized mutually recursive definitions of $v_{1\,\text{to}\,n} \triangleleft \tau_{1\,\text{to}\,n} \triangleright$

[46] *if* t_1 *then* t_2 *else* t_3

[47] Because there is no type restriction, fixed points may be freely used to define recursive procedures on expressions.

[48] *if* **t** *then* s_1 *else* s_1

[49] *if* **t** *then* s_1 *else* s_1

ActorScript™ extension of C#®, Java®, Objective C®, C++, JavaScript®, and SystemVerilog using iAdaptive™ concurrency for antiCloud™ privacy and security

Carl Hewitt

This article is dedicated to Alonzo Church, John McCarthy, Ole-Johan Dahl and Kristen Nygaard.

Message passing using types is the foundation of system communication:
- Messages are the unit of communication
- Types enable secure communication with Actors

ActorScript™ is a general purpose programming language for implementing iAdaptive™ concurrency that manages resources and demand. It is differentiated from previous languages by the following:
- Universality
  o Ability to directly specify exactly what Actors can and cannot do
  o Everything is accomplished with message passing using types including the very definition of ActorScript itself.
  o Messages can be directly communicated without requiring indirection through brokers, channels, class hierarchies, mailboxes, pipes, ports, queues *etc*. Programs do not expose low-level implementation mechanisms such as threads, tasks, locks, cores, *etc*. Application binary interfaces are afforded so that no program symbol need be looked up at runtime. Functional, Imperative, Logic, and Concurrent programs are integrated.
  o A type in ActorScript is an interface that does not name its implementations (contra to object-oriented programming languages beginning with Simula that name implementations called "classes" that are types). ActorScript can send a message to any Actor for which it has an (imported) type.
  o Concurrency can be dynamically adapted to resources available and current load.

- Safety, security and readability
    o   Programs are *extension invariant*, *i.e.*, extending a program does not change the meaning of the program that is extended.
    o   Applications cannot directly harm each other.
    o   Variable races are eliminated while allowing flexible concurrency.
    o   Lexical singleness of purpose. Each syntactic token is used for exactly one purpose.
- Performance[i]
    o   Imposes no overhead on implementation of Actor systems in the sense that ActorScript programs are as efficient as the same implementation in machine code. For example, message passing has essentially same overhead as procedure calls and looping.
    o   Execution dynamically adjusted for system load and capacity (*e.g.* cores)
    o   Locality because execution is not bound by a sequential global memory model
    o   Inherent concurrency because execution is not limited by being restricted to communicating *sequential* processes
    o   Minimize latency along critical paths

ActorScript attempts to achieve the highest level of performance, scalability, and expressibility with a minimum of primitives.

C# is a registered trademark of Microsoft, Inc.
Java and **JavaScript** are registered trademarks of Oracle, Inc.
Objective C is a registered trademark of Apple, Inc.
Computer software should not only work; it should also appear to work.[1]

Introduction
ActorScript is based on the Actor mathematical model of computation that treats "*Actors*" as the universal conceptual primitive of digital computation [Hewitt, Bishop, and Steiger 1973; Hewitt 1977; Hewitt 2010a]. Actors have been used as a framework for a theoretical understanding of concurrency, and

---
[i] Performance can be tricky as illustrated by the following:
- "Those who would forever give up correctness for a little temporary performance deserve neither correctness nor performance." [Philips 2013]
- "The key to performance is elegance, not battalions of special cases" [Jon Bentley and Doug McIlroy]
- "If you want to achieve performance, start with comprehensible." [Philips 2013]
- Those who would forever give up performance for a feature that slows everything down deserve neither the feature nor performance.

as the theoretical basis for several practical implementations of concurrent systems.

ActorScript

ActorScript is a general purpose programming language for implementing massive local and nonlocal concurrency.

This paper makes use of the following typographical conventions that arise from underlying namespaces for types, messages, language constructs, syntax categories, *etc.*[i]
- type identifiers (*e.g.,* Integer)
- program variables (*e.g.,* aBalance)
- message names (*e.g.,* getBalance)
- reserved words[2] for language constructs (*e.g.,* **Actor**)
- structures (*e.g.,* [and])
- argument keyword (e.g., to)
- logical variables (e.g., *x*)
- comments in programs (e.g. /* this is a comment */)

There is a diagram of the syntax categories of ActorScript in an appendix of this paper in addition to an appendix with an index of symbols and names along with an explanation of the notation used to express the syntax of ActorScript.[3]

Actors

ActorScript is based on the Actor Model of Computation [Hewitt, Bishop, and Steiger 1973; Hewitt 2010a] in which all computational entities are Actors and all interaction is accomplished using message passing.

The Actor model is a mathematical theory that treats "*Actors*" as the universal conceptual primitive of digital computation. The model has been used both as a framework for a theoretical understanding of concurrency, and as the theoretical basis for several practical implementations of concurrent systems. Unlike previous models of computation, the Actor model was inspired by physical laws. The advent of massive concurrency through client-cloud computing and many-core computer architectures has galvanized interest in the Actor model.

---

[i] The choice of typography in terms of font and color has no semantic significance. The typography in this paper was chosen for pedagogical motivations and is in no way fundamental. Also, only the abstract syntax of ActorScript is fundamental as opposed to the surface syntax with its many symbols, e.g., ↦, etc.

An Actor is a computational entity that, in response to a message it receives, can concurrently:
- send messages to addresses of Actors that it has
- create new Actors
- for an exclusive Actor, designate how to handle the next message it receives.

There is no assumed order to the above actions and they could be carried out concurrently. In addition two messages sent concurrently can be received in either order. Decoupling the sender from communication it sends was a fundamental advance of the Actor model enabling asynchronous communication and control structures as patterns of passing messages.

The Actor model can be used as a framework for modeling, understanding, and reasoning about, a wide range of concurrent systems. For example:
- Electronic mail (e-mail) can be modeled as an Actor system. Mail accounts are modeled as Actors and email addresses as Actor addresses.
- Web Services can be modeled with endpoints modeled as Actor addresses.
- Object-oriented programing objects with locks (e.g. as in Java and C#) can be modeled as Actors.

Actor technology will see significant application for coordinating all kinds of digital information for individuals, groups, and organizations so their information usefully links together. Information coordination needs to make use of the following information system principles:
- ***Persistence***. *Information is collected and indexed.*
- ***Concurrency***: *Work proceeds interactively and concurrently, overlapping in time.*
- ***Quasi-commutativity***: *Information can be used regardless of whether it initiates new work or becomes relevant to ongoing work.*
- ***Sponsorship***: *Sponsors provide resources for computation, i.e., processing, storage, and communications.*
- ***Pluralism***: *Information is heterogeneous, overlapping and often inconsistent. There is no central arbiter of truth.*
- ***Provenance***: *The provenance of information is carefully tracked and recorded.*

The Actor Model is designed to provide a foundation for inconsistency robust information coordination.

Notation

To ease interoperability, ActorScript uses an intersection of the orthographic conventions of Java, JavaScript, and C++ for words[i] and numbers.

Expressions

ActorScript makes use of a great many symbols to improve readability and remove ambiguity. For example the symbol "▮" is used as the top level terminator to designate the end of input in a read-eval-print loop. An Integrated Development Environment (IDE) can provide a table of these symbols for ease of input as explained below:[ii]

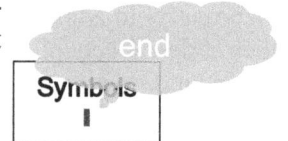

> *end*
> Symbols
> ▮

Expressions evaluate to Actors. For example, 1+3▮[iii] is equivalent[iv] to 4▮.

Parentheses "(" and ")" can be used for precedence. For example using the usual precedence for operators, 3*(4+2)▮ is equivalent to 18▮, while 3*4+2▮ is equivalent to 14▮.

Identifiers, e.g., x, are expressions that can be used in other expressions. For example if x is 1 then x+3▮ is equivalent to 4▮. The formal syntax of identifiers is in the following end note: **4.**

Types

Types are Actors. In this paper, Types are shown in green, *e.g.,* Integer.

The formal syntax for types is in the following end note: **5.**

Definitions, *i.e.,* ≡

A simple definition has the name to be defined followed by "≡" followed by the definition. For example, x:Integer≡3▮ defines the identifier x to be of type Integer with value 3.

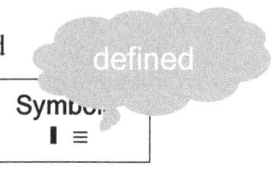

> *defined*
> Symbol
> ▮ ≡

The formal syntax of a definition is in the end note: **6.**

---

[i] sometimes called "names"

[ii] Furthermore, all special symbols have ASCII equivalents for input with a keyboard. An IDE can convert ASCII for a symbol equivalent into the symbol. See table in an appendix to this article.

[iii] An IDE can provide a box with symbols for easy input in program development. The grey callout bubble is a hover tip that appears when the cursor hovers above a symbol to explain its use.

[iv] in the sense of having the same value and the same effects

Interfaces for procedures, *i.e.,* **Interface with** [ ]↦ .

A procedure interface is used to specify the types of messages that a procedure Actor can receive. The syntax is "**Interface**" followed by an interface identifier, "**with**", and procedure signatures in parentheses separated by commas. A procedure signature consists of a message signature with argument types delimited by "[" and "]", followed by "↦", and a return type.[i] For example, the interface[ii] for the overloaded[7] procedure type ArithmeticToArithmetic that takes an Arithmetic argument to return an Arithmetic value and a **Vector** argument and to return a **Vector** can be constructed as follows:[8]

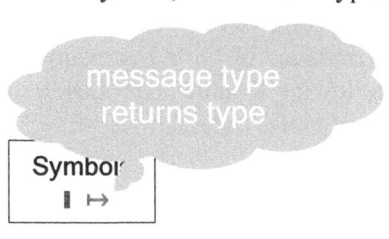

    Interface ArithmeticToArithmetic **with**
        [Arithmetic]↦ Arithmetic₀ ∎

Symbol
  ∎ ↦

(message type returns type)

The formal syntax of a procedure interface is in the following end note: **9.**

---

[i] Since communicating using messages is crucial for Actor systems, messages are shown in magenta in this article. The choice of color has no semantic significance.
[ii] Every interface is a type.

Procedures, *i.e.,* **Actor implements** [ ]→ , ¶ and §

A procedure has message formal parameters delimited by "[" and "]" followed by "→" and then the expression to be computed.[i] For example, [n:Arithmetic]:Arithmetic→ n+n▮ is a (unnamed) procedure that given a message with an integer number, n, returns the number plus itself.

Procedures can be overloaded using "**Actor implements**", followed by a type, followed by "**using**", followed by procedures separated by "¶" and terminated by "§".[ii] For example, in the following Double is defined to implement ArithmeticToArithmetic.

message received

Symbols
≡ →
¶ § ▮

Double ≡ **Actor implements** ArithmeticToArithmetic **using**
  [v:Vector]→ v+v§▮

The formal syntax of procedures is in the end note: **10.**

Sending messages to procedures, *i.e.,* ▪[ ]

Sending a message to a procedure (*i.e.* "calling" a procedure with arguments) is expressed by an expression that evaluates to a procedure followed by "▪"[11] followed by a message with parameter expressions delimited by "[" and "]". For example, Square▪[2+1]▮ means send Square[iii] the message [3]. Thus Square▪[2+1]▮ is equivalent to 9▮.

The formal syntactic definition of procedural message sending is in the end note: **12.**

---

[i] Note the following crucial differences (recalling that font, color, and capitalization are of no semantic significance for identifiers although words with different capitalization are different identifiers):
  - [Integer]↦Integer is a procedure signature and *not* a procedure that takes an Integer argument and returns an Integer.
  - [Integer]→Integer is a procedure and *not* a type. It is the "identity" procedure of one argument that always returns the argument.

[ii] Since both procedures and implementations can be quite large, an IDE can use these special symbols to provide additional help.

[iii] As a convenience, the procedure Square can be defined to as follows: Square▪[x:Integer]:Integer ≡ x*x▮

Patterns

Patterns are fundamental to ActorScript. For example,
- 3 is a pattern that matches 3
- "abc" is a pattern that matches "abc".
- _ is a pattern that matches anything[i]
- $$x is a pattern that matches the value of x.
- $$(x+2) is a pattern that matches the value of the expression x+2.
- < 5 is a pattern that matches an integer less than 5
- x **suchThat** Factorial.[x]>120 is a pattern that matches an integer whose factorial is greater than 120

Identifiers[ii] can be bound using patterns as in the following examples:
- x is a pattern that matches "abc" and binds x to "abc"

Cases, *i.e.,* ❖ ⁂ , ⁂ ⁇

Cases are used to perform conditional testing. In a Cases Expression, an expression for the value on which to perform case analysis is specified first followed by "❖"[iii] and then followed by a number of cases separated by "☑" terminated by "⁇".[13] A case consists of
- a pattern followed by "⁂" and an expression to compute the value for the case. *All of the patterns before an* **else** *case must be disjoint; i.e.,* it must not be possible for more than one to match.
- optionally (at the end of the cases) *one or more* of the following cases: "**else**" followed by an optional pattern, "⁂", and an expression to compute the value for the case. An **else** case applies *only* if none of the patterns in the preceding cases[iv] match the value on which to perform case analysis.

---

[i] e.g., _ matches 7
[ii] An identifier is a name that is used in a program to designate an Actor
[iii] "❖" is fancy typography for "**?**"
[iv] *including* patterns in previous else cases

As an arbitrary example purely to illustrate the above, suppose that the procedure Random, which has no argument and returns Integer, in the following example:

Random.[ ] ◆
    0 ⁂   // Random.[ ] returned 0[i]
    Throw[ii] RandomNumberException[ ] ☑
    // throw an exception
          // because Fibonacci.[0] is undefined
    1 ⁂   // Random.[ ] returned 1
        6☑   // the value of the cases expression is 6
else y **thatIs** < 5 ⁂
        // Random.[ ] returned y that is not 0 or 1 and is less than 5
    Fibonacci.[y] ☑
        // return Fibonacci of the value returned by Random.[ ]
else z ⁂
    // Random.[ ] returned z that is not 0 or 1 and is not less than 5
    Factorial.[z] ⁇▮
        // return Factorial of the value returned by Random.[ ]
The formal syntax of cases is in the following end note: **14**.

Binding locals, *i.e.,* **Let** ← ₒ

Local identifiers can be bound using "**Let**" followed by a pattern, "←", an expression for the Actor to be matched followed by "ₒ" and expressions terminated with "ₒ". For example, aProcedure.["G", "F", "F"]▮ could be written as follows:

    Let x ← "F"ₒ   // x is "F"
      aProcedure.["G", x, x]▮

---

[i] As is standard, ActorScript uses the token "//" to begin a one-line comment.
[ii] Reserved words are shown in bold black.

Dependent bindings (in which each can depend on previous ones) can be accomplished by nesting **Let**. For example:
   Let x ←"F"。   // x is "F"
    Let y ← aProcedure.["G", x, x]]。
       // y is aProcedure.["G", "F", "F"]
    anotherProcedure.[x, y]▮

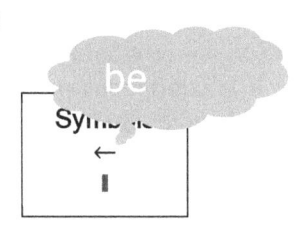

The above is equivalent to
anotherProcedure.["F", aProcedure.["G", "F", "F"]]▮

The formal syntax of bindings is in the following end note: **15**.

General Message-passing interfaces
Procedure interfaces are a special case of general message-passing interfaces.

A message handler signature consists of a message name followed by argument types delimited by "[" and "]", "↦", and a return type. For example

   Interface Account **with** getBalance[ ]↦Currency,
                               deposit[Currency]↦**Void**,
                               withdraw[Currency]↦**Void**。▮

The formal syntactic definition of named-message sending is in the following end note: **16**

Actors that change, *i.e.*, Actor and ≔
Using the expressions introduced so far, actors do not change. However, some Actors change behaviors over time.

An Actor can be created using "**Actor**" optionally followed by the following:
- constructor name with formal arguments delimited using brackets
- declarations of variables[i] terminated by "。"
- implementations of interface(s).

Message handlers in an Actor execute mutually exclusively while in a region of mutual exclusion which is called "cheese." In this paper assignable variables are colored orange, which by itself has no semantic significance, i.e., printing this article in black and white does not change any meaning. The use of assignments is strictly controlled in order to achieve better structured programs.[17]

---

[i] variable declarations separated by commas

345

ActorScript is referentially transparent in the sense that variable never changes while in a continuous part of the cheese.[18] For example, in the **withdraw** message handler change is accomplished using the following:
 Void afterward myBalance := myBalance+anAmount
which returns **Void** and updates myBalance for the *next* message received.

Variable races are impossible in ActorScript.

Below is a diagram for an Actor, which implements Account:

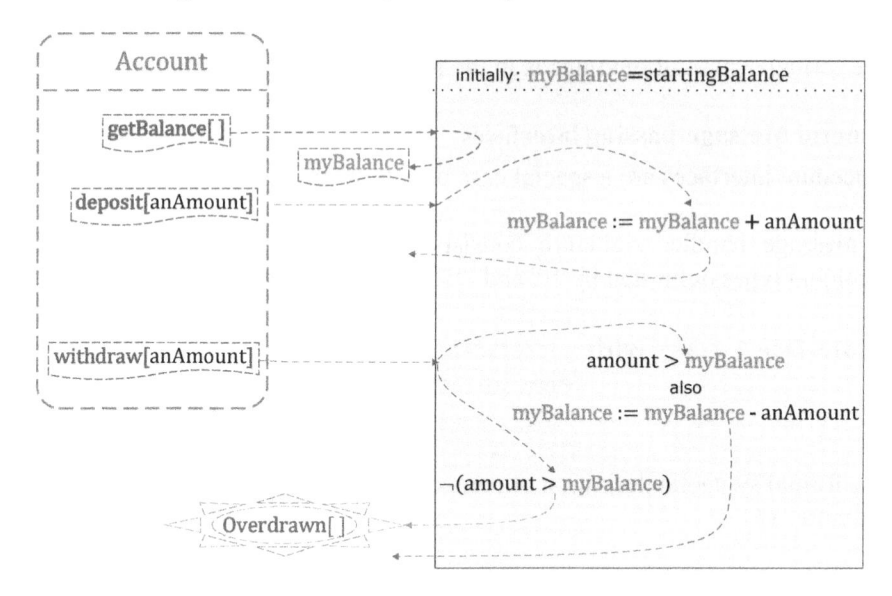

```
      Account                    initially: myBalance=startingBalance
      getBalance[ ]
                      myBalance
      deposit[anAmount]
                                  myBalance := myBalance + anAmount

      withdraw[anAmount]          amount > myBalance
                                        also
                                  myBalance := myBalance - anAmount

                                  ¬(amount > myBalance)
           Overdrawn[ ]
```

346

The implementation of Account above can
be expressed as follows:

> Symbol: assignment
> ≡ → ❖ ⦂ ≔
> ⸘ ¶ § ∎

Actor SimpleAccount[startingBalance:Euro]
 // SimpleAccount has [Euro]↦Account[i]
 myBalance ≔ startingBalance₀
 // myBalance is an assignable variable initialized with startingBalance
 implements Account **using**
  getBalance[ ] → myBalance¶
  deposit[anAmount] →
   Void   // return **Void**
    afterward myBalance ≔ myBalance+anAmount¶
         // the *next* message is processed with
            // myBalance reflecting the deposit
  withdraw[anAmount] →
   (amount > myBalance) ❖
    True ⦂ **Throw** Overdrawn[ ] ☑
    False ⦂ **Void**   // return **Void**
         afterward myBalance ≔ myBalance−anAmount ⸘§∎
         // the *next* message is processed with updated myBalance

The formal syntax of **Actor** expressions is in the following end note: **19.**

Antecedents, Preparations, and Necessary Concurrency, *i.e.,* ◻

Concurrency can be controlled using preparation that is expressed in a continuation using preparatory expressions, "●" and an expression that proceeds only *after* the preparations have been completed.

---

[i] SimpleAccount is a constructor (that can be called as a procedure) with a single argument that is of Euro which returns an Actor of type Account

347

The following expression creates an account anAccount with initial balance €5 and then concurrently withdraws €1 and €2 in preparation for reading the balance:

Let anAccount ← SimpleAccount.[€6]₀ // € is a reserved prefix operator
　anAccount.withdraw[€1],
　anAccount.withdraw[€2]●
　　// proceed only after both of the
　　// withdrawals have been acknowledged
　anAccount.getBalance[ ]₀ ▌

The above expression returns €3.

```
Euro
Symbol
● ← €
 ₀ ▌
```

Operations are quasi-commutative to the extent that it doesn't matter in which order they occur.

Quasi-commutativity can be used to tame indeterminacy while at the same time facilitating implementations that run exponentially faster than those in the parallel lambda calculus.[i]

The formal syntax of compound expressions is in the following end note: **20**

An expression can be annotated for concurrent execution by preceding it with "☐" indicating that the following expression must be considered for concurrent execution if resources are available. For example ☐Factorial.[1000]+☐Fibonacci.[2000]▌ is annotated for concurrent execution of Factorial.[1000] and Fibonacci.[2000] both of which *must* complete execution. This does not require that the executions of Factorial.[1000] and Fibonacci.[2000] actually overlap in time.[21]

The formal syntax of explicit concurrency is in the following end note: **22.**

Implementing multiple interfaces , *i.e.*, ⌈:⌉ and also implements

The above implementation of Account can be extended as follows to provide the ability to revoke some abilities to change an account.[23] For example, AccountSupervisor below implements both the Account and AccountRevoker interfaces as an extension of the implementation SimpleAccount:

---

[i] For example, implementations using Actors of Direct Logic can be exponentially faster than implementations in the parallel lambda calculus.

As illustrated below, a qualified address of an Actor can be expressed using "[:]" followed by the name of the qualifier.[24]

Actor AccountSupervisor [initialBalance:Currency]
   extends SimpleAccount[initialBalance]
     withdrawableIsRevoked := **False**,
     depositableIsRevoked := **False**₀
     implements AccountSupervisor **using**
       getRevoker[ ] → [:]AccountRevoker¶
       getAccount[ ] → [:]Account¶
       withdrawFee[anAmount] →
              Void afterward myBalance := myBalance−anAmount§
              // withdraw fee *even if balance goes negative*[25]
   also partially reimplements exportable Account **using**
     withdraw[anAmount] →
       withdrawableIsRevoked ⬥
         True ⸱ **Throw** Revoked[ ] ▢
         False ⸱ [:]SimpleAccount▪withdraw[anAmount] ▢¶
     deposit[anAmount] →
       depositableIsRevoked ⬥
         True ⸱ **Throw** Revoked[ ] ▢
         False ⸱ [:]SimpleAccount▪deposit[anAmount] ▢§
   also implements exportable AccountRevoker **using**
     revokeDepositable[ ] →
       Void afterward depositableIsRevoked := **True**¶
     revokeWithdrawable[ ] →
       Void afterward withdrawableIsRevoked := **True**§▮

For example, the following expression returns *negative* €3:
   Let anAccountSupervisor ← AccountSupervisor▪[€3]₀
   Let anAccount ← anAccountSupervisor▪getAccount[ ],
      aRevoker ← anAccountSupervisor▪getRevoker[ ]₀
   anAccount▪withdraw[€2]●   // the balance is €1
   aRevoker▪revokeWithdrawable[ ]●
                    // withdrawableIsRevoked in is **True**
   Try anAccount▪withdraw[€5]   // try another withdraw
     catch⬥ _ ⸱ **Void**▢●   // ignore the thrown exception[26]
                    // the balance remains €1
   anAccountSupervisor▪withdrawFee[€4]●
      // €4 is withdrawn *even though* withdrawableIsRevoked
   anAccount▪getBalance[ ]₀ ▮ // the balance is *negative* €3

The formal syntax of the programs below is in the following end note: 27

Swiss cheese

Swiss cheese [Hewitt and Atkinson 1977, 1979; Atkinson 1980][28] is a generalization of mutual exclusion with the following goals:
- *Generality:* Ability to conveniently program any scheduling policy
- *Performance:* Support maximum performance in implementation, e.g., the ability to minimize locking and to avoid repeatedly recalculating a condition for proceeding.
- *Understandability:* Invariants for the variables of a mutable Actor should hold whenever entering or leaving the cheese.
- *Modularity:* Resources requiring scheduling should be encapsulated so that it is impossible to use them incorrectly.

There is a very simple Actor with the following interface that cannot be performed by a nondeterministic Turing Machine (equivalently implemented in the nondeterministic lambda calculus):

Interface Counter **with** go[ ] ↦ **Void**,
 stop[ ] ↦ Integer. ▮

An implementation of the above interface is described below.

By contrast with the nondeterministic lambda calculus, there is an always-halting Actor that when sent a start[ ] message can compute an integer of unbounded size. This is accomplished by creating a Counter with the following variables:
- count initially **0**
- continue initially **True**

and concurrently sending it both a stop[ ] message and a go[ ] message such that:
- When a go[ ] message is received:
    1. if continue is **True**, increment count by 1 and return the result of sending this counter a go[ ] message.
    2. if continue is **False**, return **Void**
- When a stop[ ] message is received, return count and sent continue to **False** for the next message received.

By the Actor Model of Computation [Clinger 1981, Hewitt 2006], the above Actor will eventually receive the stop[ ] message and return an unbounded number.

350

A diagram is shown below for an implementation of Counter. In the diagram, a hole in the cheese is highlighted in grey and variables are shown in orange. The color has no semantic significance.

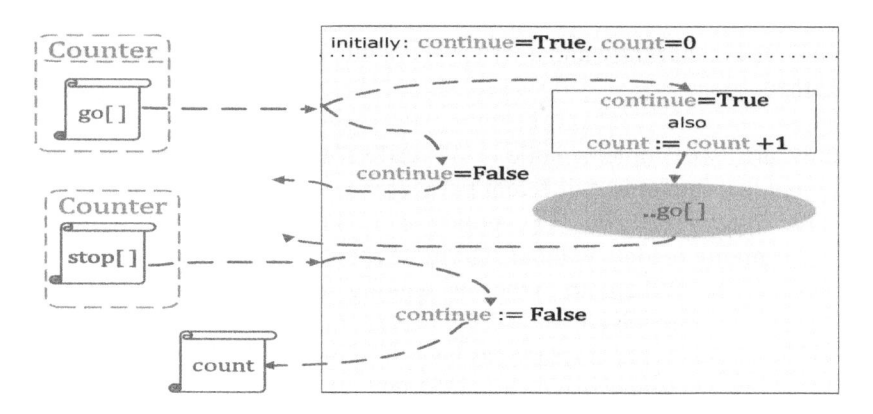

ComputeUnbounded ≡
  Actor implements Unbounded
    start[ ]:Integer →   // a start message is implemented by
      Let aCounter ← SimpleCounter.[ ]∘   // let aCounter be a new Counter
      □aCounter.go[ ],
                      // send aCounter a go message and *concurrently*
      □aCounter.stop[ ]∘ ▮
                      // return the result of sending aCounter a stop message
As a notational convenience, when an Actor receives message then it can send an arbitrary message to itself by prefixing it with "..".

Actor SimpleCounter[ ]
  count := 0,   // the variable count is initially 0
  continue := True∘
  implements Counter **using**
    stop[ ] →
      count   // return count
        afterward continue := False¶
             // continue is updated to False for the next message received
    go[ ] →
      continue ◆
        True ⁊ Hole ..go[ ]   // send go[ ] to this counter after
              after count := count+1☑   // incrementing count
        False ⁊ Void ⸮§▮   // if continue is False, return Void

351

Coordinating Activities

Coordinating activities of readers and writers in a shared resource is a classic problem. The fundamental constraint is that multiple writers are not allowed to operate concurrently and a writer is not allowed operate concurrently with a reader.

Below are two implementations of readers/writer guardians for a shared resource that implement different policies:[29]
1. *ReadingPriority:* The policy is to permit maximum concurrency among readers without starving writers.[30]
    a. When no writer is waiting, all readers start as they are received.
    b. When a writer has been received, no more readers can start.
    c. When a writer completes, all waiting readers start even if there are writers waiting.
2. *WritingPriority:* The policy is that readers get the most recent information available without starving writers.[31]
    a. When no writer is waiting, all readers start as they are received.
    b. When a writer has been received, no more readers can start.
    c. When a writer completes, just one waiting reader is permitted to complete if there are waiting writers.

The interface for the readers/writer guardian is the same as the interface for the shared resource:

Interface ReadersWriter **with** read[Query] $\mapsto$ QueryAnswer, write[Update] $\mapsto$ **Void**₀ ∎

Cheese diagram for ReadersWriter implementations:

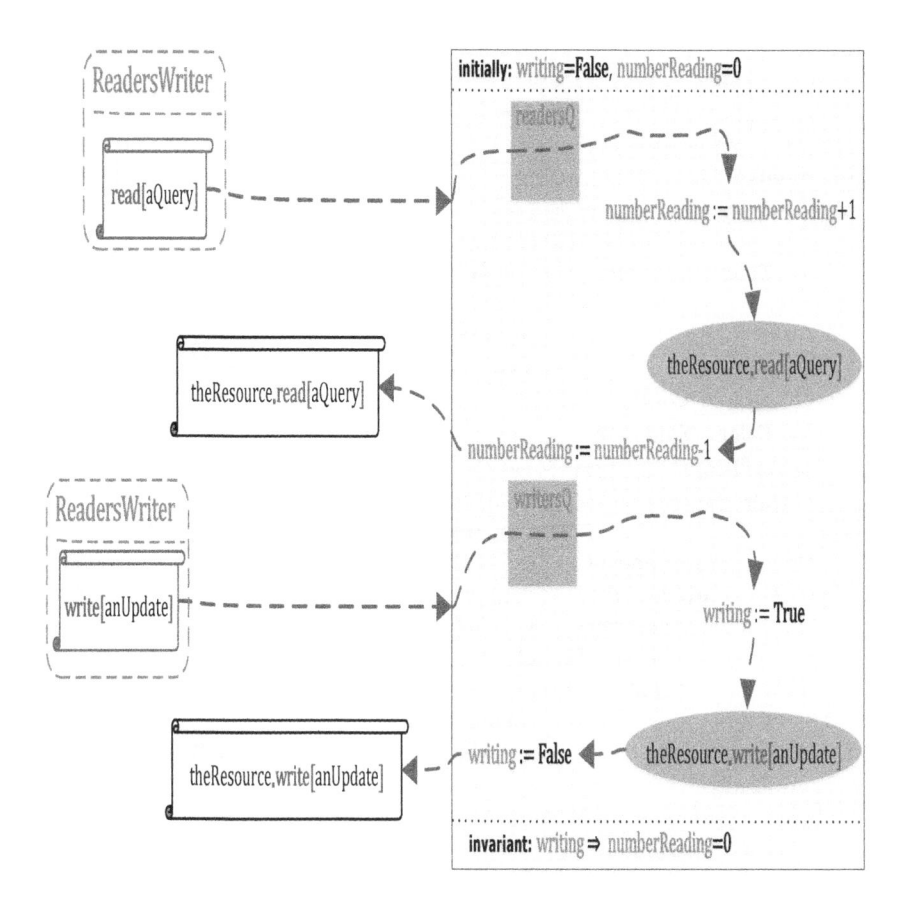

Note:
1. At most one activity is allowed to execute in the cheese.
2. The value of a variable[i] changes only when leaving the cheese.[ii]

The formal syntax of the programs below is in the following end note: **32**

---
[i] A variable is orange in the diagram
[ii] Of course, other external Actors can change.

Actor ReadingPriority[theResource:ReadersWriter]
  invariants writing⇒ numberReading=0。
  queues readersQ, writersQ。   // readersQ and writersQ are initially empty
  writing := False,
  numberReading:PositiveInteger := 0。

Symbols
≡ → ◆ ⸭ ☑ ∧ ∨ ¬
⸭ ¶ § ▮

                // PositiveInteger ≡ Integer thatIs ≧0
  implements ReadersWriter using
   read[query]→
     (writing ∨ ¬IsEmpty writersQ) ◆
        True ⸭ Enqueue readersQ●   // leave cheese while in readersQ
                backout (¬writing ∧ numberReading=0 ∧ IsEmpty readersQ) ◆
                        True ⸭ Void permit writersQ☑
                        False ⸭ Void ⸭
                Void ☑
        False ⸭ Void ⸭●
     Preconditions ¬writing。 [33]
        Hole theResource.read[query]   // leave cheese while
                        // reading after recording that another reader is reading
                after permit readersQ always numberReading++ [34]
                afterward
                  (IsEmpty writersQ) ◆
                        True ⸭ permit readersQ always numberReading-- ☑ [35]
                        False ⸭ numberReading ◆
                                1 ⸭ permit writersQ always numberReading--☑
                                else ⸭ also numberReading-- ⸭ ⸭。¶
   write[update]→
     (numberReading>0 ∨ ¬IsEmpty readersQ ∨ writing ∨ ¬IsEmpty writersQ) ◆
        True ⸭ Enqueue writersQ●   // leave cheese while in writersQ
                backout (IsEmpty writersQ ∧ ¬writing) ◆
                        True ⸭ Void permit readersQ☑
                        False ⸭ Void ⸭
                Void ☑
        False ⸭ Void ⸭●
     Preconditions[36] numberReading=0 ∧¬writing。
        Hole theResource.write[update]   // leave cheese while writing after
                after writing := True   // recording that writing is happening
                afterward (IsEmpty readersQ) ◆
                        True ⸭ permit writersQ always writing := False☑
                        False ⸭ permit readersQ always writing := False⸭。§▮

Illustration of writing-priority:

Actor WritingPriority[theResource:ReadersWriter]
  invariants writing⇨ numberReading=0。
  queues readersQ, writersQ。
  writing ≔ False,
  numberReading:PositiveInteger≔ 0。
  implements ReadersWriter using
   read[query]→
     (writing ∨ ¬Empty writersQ) ◆
       True ⁏ Enqueue readersQ●   // leave cheese while in readersQ
                backout ¬writing ∧ numberReading=0 ∧ IsEmpty readersQ ◆
                    True ⁏ Void permit writersQ☑
                    False ⁏ Void ?
            Void☑
       False ⁏ Void ?●
     Preconditions ¬writing。
       Hole theResource.read[query]
         after IsEmpty writersQ ◆
            True ⁏ Permit readersQ always numberReading++☑
            False ⁏ Also numberReading++?
        afterward
          (IsEmpty writersQ) ◆
            True ⁏ permit readersQ always numberReading--☑
            False ⁏ numberReading ◆
                1 ⁏ permit writersQ always numberReading--☑
                (> 1) ⁏ numberReading--? ?。¶
   write[update]→
     (numberReading>0∨¬IsEmpty readersQ∨writing∨¬IsEmpty writersQ)◆
       True ⁏ Enqueue writersQ●   // leave cheese while in writersQ
                backout (IsEmpty writersQ ∧ ¬writing) ◆
                    True ⁏ Void permit readersQ☑
                    False ⁏ Void ?
            Void ☑
       False ⁏ Void ?●
     Preconditions numberReading=0, ¬writing。
       Hole theResource.write[update]
         after writing ≔ True
         afterward
           (IsEmpty readersQ) ◆
              True ⁏ permit writersQ always writing ≔ False☑
              False ⁏ permit readersQ always writing ≔ False?。§∎

> Symbols
> ≡ → ◆ ⁏ ☑ ∧ ∨ ¬
> ? ¶ § ∎

The formal syntax of queue management in cheese is in the following end note: **37.**

Conclusion

Before long, we will have billions of chips, each with hundreds of hyper-threaded cores executing hundreds of thousands of threads. Consequently, GOFIP (Good Old-Fashioned Imperative Programming) paradigm must be fundamentally extended. ActorScript is intended to be a contribution to this extension.

Acknowledgements

Important contributions to the semantics of Actors have been made by: Gul Agha, Beppe Attardi, Henry Baker, Will Clinger, Irene Greif, Carl Manning, Ian Mason, Ugo Montanari, Maria Simi, Scott Smith, Carolyn Talcott, Prasanna Thati, and Aki Yonezawa.

Important contributions to the implementation of Actors have been made by: Bill Athas, Russ Atkinson, Beppe Attardi, Henry Baker, Gerry Barber, Peter Bishop, Nanette Boden, Jean-Pierre Briot, Bill Dally, Peter de Jong, Jessie Dedecker, Ken Kahn, Henry Lieberman, Carl Manning, Mark S. Miller, Tom Reinhardt, Chuck Seitz, Dale Schumacher, Richard Steiger, Dan Theriault, Mario Tokoro, Darrell Woelk, and Carlos Varela.

Research on the Actor model has been carried out at Caltech Computer Science, Kyoto University Tokoro Laboratory, MCC, MIT Artificial Intelligence Laboratory, SRI, Stanford University, University of Illinois at Urbana-Champaign Open Systems Laboratory, Pierre and Marie Curie University (University of Paris 6), University of Pisa, University of Tokyo Yonezawa Laboratory and elsewhere.

The members of the Silicon Valley Friday AM group made valuable suggestions for improving this paper. Discussions with Blaine Garst were helpful in the development of the implementation of Swiss cheese that doesn't hold a lock as well providing background on the historical development of interfaces. Patrick Beard found bugs and suggested improvements in presentation. Fanya S. Montalvo and Ike Nassi suggested simplifying the syntax. Dale Schumacher found many typos, suggested including a syntax diagram, and suggested improvements to the syntax of collections, binding and assignment. In particular, Dale contributed greatly to the development of the lock-free[i] implementation of cheese in the appendix. Stuart Bailey and Chip Morningstar provided an excellent critique with many useful comments and suggestions.

---

[i] In the sense that the implementation holds a hardware lock.

ActorScript is intended to provide a foundation for information coordination in client-cloud computing that protects citizens sensitive information [Hewitt 2009b].

Bibliography

Hal Abelson and Gerry *Sussman Structure and Interpretation of Computer Programs* 1984.

Paul Abrahams. *A final solution to the Dangling else of ALGOL 60 and related languages* CACM. September 1966.

Sarita Adve and Hans-J. Boehm *Memory Models: A Case for Rethinking Parallel Languages and Hardware* CACM. August 2010.

Mikael Amborn. *Facet-Oriented Program Design.* LiTH-IDA-EX–04/047–SE Linköpings Universitet. 2004.

Joe Armstrong *History of Erlang* HOPL III. 2007.

Joe Armstrong. *Erlang.* CACM. September 2010/

William Athas and Charles Seitz *Multicomputers: message-passing concurrent computers* IEEE Computer August 1988.

William Athas and Nanette Boden *Cantor: An Actor Programming System for Scientific Computing* in Proceedings of the NSF Workshop on Object-Based Concurrent Programming. 1988. Special Issue of SIGPLAN Notices.

Russ Atkinson. *Automatic Verification of Serializers* MIT Doctoral Dissertation. June, 1980.

Henry Baker. *Actor Systems for Real-Time Computation* MIT EECS Doctoral Dissertation. January 1978.

Henry Baker and Carl Hewitt *The Incremental Garbage Collection of Processes* Proceeding of the Symposium on Artificial Intelligence Programming Languages. SIGPLAN Notices 12, August 1977.

Paul Baran. *On Distributed Communications Networks* IEEE Transactions on Communications Systems. March 1964.

Gerry Barber. *Reasoning about Change in Knowledgeable Office Systems* MIT EECS Doctoral Dissertation. August 1981.

Philippe Besnard and Anthony Hunter. *Quasi-classical Logic: Non-trivializable classical reasoning from inconsistent information* Symbolic and Quantitative Approaches to Reasoning and Uncertainty. Springer LNCS. 1995.

Peter Bishop *Very Large Address Space Modularly Extensible Computer Systems* MIT EECS Doctoral Dissertation. June 1977.

Andreas Blass, Yuri Gurevich, Dean Rosenzweig, and Benjamin Rossman (2007a) *Interactive small-step algorithms I: Axiomatization* Logical Methods in Computer Science. 2007.

Andreas Blass, Yuri Gurevich, Dean Rosenzweig, and Benjamin Rossman (2007b*) Interactive small-step algorithms II: Abstract state machines and the characterization theorem.* Logical Methods in Computer Science. 2007.

Per Brinch Hansen *Monitors and Concurrent Pascal: A Personal History* CACM 1996.

Don Box, David Ehnebuske, Gopal Kakivaya, Andrew Layman, Noah Mendelsohn, Henrik Nielsen, Satish Thatte, Dave Winer. *Simple Object Access Protocol (SOAP) 1.1* W3C Note. May 2000.

Jean-Pierre Briot. *Acttalk: A framework for object-oriented concurrent programming-design and experience* 2nd France-Japan workshop. 1999.

Jean-Pierre Briot. *From objects to Actors: Study of a limited symbiosis in Smalltalk-80* Rapport de Recherche 88-58, RXF-LITP. Paris, France. September 1988.

Luca Cardelli, James Donahue, Lucille Glassman, Mick Jordan, Bill Kalsow, Greg Nelson. *Modula-3 report (revised)* DEC Systems Research Center Research Report 52. November 1989.

Luca Cardelli and Andrew Gordon *Mobile Ambients* FoSSaCS'98.

Arnaud Carayol, Daniel Hirschkoff, and Davide Sangiorgi. *On the representation of McCarthy's amb in the π-calculus* "Theoretical Computer Science" February 2005.

Alonzo Church "A Set of postulates for the foundation of logic (1&2)" Annals of Mathematics. Vol. 33, 1932. Vol. 34, 1933.

Alonzo Church *The Calculi of Lambda-Conversion* Princeton University Press. 1941.

Will Clinger. *Foundations of Actor Semantics* MIT Mathematics Doctoral Dissertation. June 1981.

Tyler Close *Web-key: Mashing with Permission* WWW'08.

Eric Crahen. Facet: A pattern for dynamic interfaces. CSE Dept. SUNY at Buffalo. July 22, 2002.

Haskell Curry and Robert Feys. *Combinatory Logic.* North-Holland. 1958.

Ole-Johan Dahl and Kristen Nygaard. "Class and subclass declarations" *IFIP TC2 Conference on Simulation Programming Languages.* 1967.

William Dally and Wills, D. *Universal mechanisms for concurrency* PARLE '89.

William Dally, et al. *The Message-Driven Processor: A Multicomputer Processing Node with Efficient Mechanisms* IEEE Micro. April 1992.

Jack Dennis and Earl Van Horn. *Programming Semantics for Multiprogrammed Computations* CACM. March 1966.

Edsger Dijkstra. *Cooperating sequential processes* Technical Report EWD-123, Technological University, Eindhoven, The Netherlands. 1965.

Edsger Dijkstra. *Go To Statement Considered Harmful* Letter to Editor CACM. March 1968.

Jason Eisner and Nathaniel W. Filardo. *Dyna: Extending Datalog for modern AI.* Datalog Reloaded. Springer. 2011.

Arthur Fine. *The Shaky Game: Einstein Realism and the Quantum Theory* University of Chicago Press, Chicago, 1986.

Frederic Fitch. *Symbolic Logic: an Introduction.* Ronald Press. 1952.

Nissim Francez, Tony Hoare, Daniel Lehmann, and Willem-Paul de Roever. *Semantics of nondeterminism, concurrency, and communication* Journal of Computer and System Sciences. December 1979.

Christopher Fuchs *Quantum mechanics as quantum information (and only a little more)* in A. Khrenikov (ed.) Quantum Theory: Reconstruction of Foundations (Växjo: Växjo University Press, 2002).

Blaine Garst. *Origin of Interfaces* Email to Carl Hewitt on October 2, 2009.

Elihu M. Gerson. *Prematurity and Social Worlds* in Prematurity in Scientific Discovery. University of California Press. 2002.

Andreas Glausch and Wolfgang Reisig. *Distributed Abstract State Machines and Their Expressive Power* Informatik Berichete 196. Humboldt University of Berlin. January 2006.

Brian Goetz *State of the Lambda* Brian Goetz's Oracle Blog. July 6, 2010.

Adele Goldberg and Alan Kay (ed.) *Smalltalk-72 Instruction Manual* SSL 76-6. Xerox PARC. March 1976.

Dina Goldin and Peter Wegner. *The Interactive Nature of Computing: Refuting the Strong Church-Turing Thesis* Minds and Machines March 2008.

Cordell Green. *Application of Theorem Proving to Problem Solving* IJCAI'69.

Irene Greif and Carl Hewitt. *Actor Semantics of PLANNER-73* Conference Record of ACM Symposium on Principles of Programming Languages. January 1975.

Irene Greif. *Semantics of Communicating Parallel Professes* MIT EECS Doctoral Dissertation. August 1975.

William Gropp, et. al. *MPI—The Complete Reference: Volume 2, The MPI-2 Extensions.* MIT Press. 1998

Pat Hayes *Some Problems and Non-Problems in Representation Theory* AISB. Sussex. July, 1974

Werner Heisenberg. *Physics and Beyond: Encounters and Conversations* translated by A. J. Pomerans (Harper & Row, New York, 1971), pp. 63 – 64.

Carl Hewitt. *More Comparative Schematology* MIT AI Memo 207. August 1970.

Carl Hewitt, Peter Bishop and Richard Steiger. *A Universal Modular Actor Formalism for Artificial Intelligence* IJCAI'73.

Carl Hewitt, et al. *Actor Induction and Meta-evaluation* Conference Record of ACM Symposium on Principles of Programming Languages, January 1974.

Carl Hewitt and Henry Lieberman. *Design Issues in Parallel Architecture for Artificial Intelligence* MIT AI memo 750. Nov. 1983.

Carl Hewitt, Tom Reinhardt, Gul Agha, and Giuseppe Attardi *Linguistic Support of Receptionists for Shared Resources* MIT AI Memo 781. Sept. 1984.

Carl Hewitt, *et al. Behavioral Semantics of Nonrecursive Control Structure* Proceedings of *Colloque sur la Programmation*, April 1974.

Carl Hewitt. *How to Use What You Know* IJCAI. September, 1975.

Carl Hewitt. *Viewing Control Structures as Patterns of Passing Messages* AI Memo 410. December 1976. Journal of Artificial Intelligence. June 1977.

Carl Hewitt and Henry Baker *Laws for Communicating Parallel Processes* IFIP-77, August 1977.

Carl Hewitt and Russ Atkinson. *Specification and Proof Techniques for Serializers* IEEE Journal on Software Engineering. January 1979.

Carl Hewitt, Beppe Attardi, and Henry Lieberman. *Delegation in Message Passing* Proceedings of First International Conference on Distributed Systems Huntsville, AL. October 1979.

Carl Hewitt and Gul Agha. *Guarded Horn clause languages: are they deductive and Logical?* in Artificial Intelligence at MIT, Vol. 2. MIT Press 1991.

Carl Hewitt and Jeff Inman. *DAI Betwixt and Between: From "Intelligent Agents" to Open Systems Science* IEEE Transactions on Systems, Man, and Cybernetics. Nov./Dec. 1991.

Carl Hewitt and Peter de Jong. *Analyzing the Roles of Descriptions and Actions in Open Systems* Proceedings of the National Conference on Artificial Intelligence. August 1983.

Carl Hewitt. (2006). "What is Commitment? Physical, Organizational, and Social" *COIN@AAMAS'06*. (Revised version to be published in Springer Verlag Lecture Notes in Artificial Intelligence. Edited by Javier Vázquez-Salceda and Pablo Noriega. 2007) April 2006.

Carl Hewitt (2007a). "Organizational Computing Requires Unstratified Paraconsistency and Reflection" *COIN@AAMAS.* 2007.

Carl Hewitt (2008a) *Norms and Commitment for iOrgs™ Information Systems: Direct Logic™ and Participatory Argument Checking* ArXiv 0906.2756.

Carl Hewitt (2008b) "Large-scale Organizational Computing requires Unstratified Reflection and Strong Paraconsistency" *Coordination, Organizations, Institutions, and Norms in Agent Systems III* Jaime Sichman, Pablo Noriega, Julian Padget and Sascha Ossowski (ed.). Springer-Verlag. http://organizational.carlhewitt.info/

Carl Hewitt (2008e). *ORGs for Scalable, Robust, Privacy-Friendly Client Cloud Computing* IEEE Internet Computing September/October 2008.

Carl Hewitt (2008f) *Common sense for concurrency and inconsistency robustness using Direct Logic™ and the Actor Model* in Inconsistency Robustness. College Publications. 2015.

Carl Hewitt (2009a) *Perfect Disruption: The Paradigm Shift from Mental Agents to ORGs* IEEE Internet Computing. Jan/Feb 2009.

Carl Hewitt (2009b) *A historical perspective on developing foundations for client-cloud computing: iConsult™ & iEntertain™ Apps using iInfo™ Information Integration for iOrgs™ Information Systems* (Revised version of "Development of Logic Programming: What went wrong, What was done about it, and What it might mean for the future" AAAI Workshop on What Went Wrong. AAAI-08.) ArXiv 0901.4934.

Carl Hewitt (2013) *Inconsistency Robustness in Logic Programs* Inconsistency Robustness. College Publications. 2015.

Carl Hewitt (2010a) *Actor Model of Computation* Inconsistency Robustness. College Publications. 2015.

Carl Hewitt (2010b) *iTooling™: Infrastructure for iAdaptive™ Concurrency*

Carl Hewitt (editor). *Inconsistency Robustness 1011* Stanford University. 2011.

Carl Hewitt, Erik Meijer, and Clemens Szyperski "The Actor Model (everything you wanted to know, but were afraid to ask)" http://channel9.msdn.com/Shows/Going+Deep/Hewitt-Meijer-and-Szyperski-The-Actor-Model-everything-you-wanted-to-know-but-were-afraid-to-ask Microsoft Channel 9. April 9, 2012.

Carl Hewitt. *"Health Information Systems Technologies"* http://ee380.stanford.edu/cgi-bin/videologger.php?target=120606-ee380-300.asx Slides for this video: http://HIST.carlhewitt.info Stanford CS Colloquium. June 6, 2012.

Carl Hewitt. *What is computation? Actor Model versus Turing's Model* in "A Computable Universe: Understanding Computation & Exploring Nature as Computation". edited by Hector Zenil. World Scientific Publishing Company. 2012.

Tony Hoare *Quick sort* Computer Journal 5 (1) 1962.

Tony Hoare *Monitors: An Operating System Structuring Concept* CACM. October 1974.

Tony Hoare. *Communicating sequential processes* CACM. August 1978.

Tony Hoare. *Communicating Sequential Processes* Prentice Hall. 1985.

Tony Hoare. *Null References: The Billion Dollar Mistake.* QCon. August 25, 2009.

W. Horwat, Andrew Chien, and William Dally. *Experience with CST: Programming and Implementation* PLDI. 1989.

Anthony Hunter. *Reasoning with Contradictory Information using Quasi-classical Logic* Journal of Logic and Computation. Vol. 10 No. 5. 2000.

M. Jammer *The EPR Problem in Its Historical Development* in Symposium on the Foundations of Modern Physics: 50 years of the Einstein-Podolsky-Rosen

Gedankenexperiment, edited by P. Lahti and P. Mittelstaedt. World Scientific. Singapore. 1985.

Simon Peyton Jones, Andrew Gordon, Sigbjorn Finne. *Concurrent Haskell*, POPL'96.

Ken Kahn. *A Computational Theory of Animation* MIT EECS Doctoral Dissertation. August 1979.

Alan Kay. "Personal Computing" in *Meeting on 20 Years of Computing Science* Instituto di Elaborazione della Informazione, Pisa, Italy. 1975. http://www.mprove.de/diplom/gui/Kay75.pdf

Frederick Knabe *A Distributed Protocol for Channel-Based Communication with Choice* PARLE'92.

Bill Kornfeld and Carl Hewitt. *The Scientific Community Metaphor* IEEE Transactions on Systems, Man, and Cybernetics. January 1981.

Bill Kornfeld. *Parallelism in Problem Solving* MIT EECS Doctoral Dissertation. August 1981.

Robert Kowalski. *A proof procedure using connection graphs* JACM. October 1975.

Robert Kowalski *Algorithm = Logic + Control* CACM. July 1979.

Robert Kowalski. *Response to questionnaire* Special Issue on Knowledge Representation. SIGART Newsletter. February 1980.

Robert Kowalski (1988a) *The Early Years of Logic Programming* CACM. January 1988.

Robert Kowalski (1988b) *Logic-based Open Systems* Representation and Reasoning. Stuttgart Conference Workshop on Discourse Representation, Dialogue tableaux and Logic Programming. 1988.

Edya Ladan-Mozes and Nir Shavit. *An Optimistic Approach to Lock-Free FIFO Queues* Distributed Computing. Sprinter. 2004.

Leslie Lamport *How to make a multiprocessor computer that correctly executes multiprocess programs* IEEE Transactions on Computers. 1979.

Peter Landin. *A Generalization of Jumps and Labels* UNIVAC Systems Programming Research Report. August 1965. (Reprinted in *Higher Order and Symbolic Computation.* 1998)

Peter Landin *A correspondence between ALGOL 60 and Church's lambda notation* CACM. August 1965.

Edward Lee and Stephen Neuendorffer *Classes and Subclasses in Actor-Oriented Design.* Conference on Formal Methods and Models for Codesign (MEMOCODE). June 2004.

Steven Levy *Hackers: Heroes of the Computer Revolution* Doubleday. 1984.

Henry Lieberman. *An Object-Oriented Simulator for the Apiary* Conference of the American Association for Artificial Intelligence, Washington, D. C., August 1983

Henry Lieberman. *Thinking About Lots of Things at Once without Getting Confused: Parallelism in Act 1* MIT AI memo 626. May 1981.

Henry Lieberman. *A Preview of Act 1* MIT AI memo 625. June 1981.

Henry Lieberman and Carl Hewitt. *A real Time Garbage Collector Based on the Lifetimes of Objects* CACM June 1983.

Barbara Liskov and Liuba Shrira *Promises: Linguistic Support for Efficient Asynchronous Procedure Calls* SIGPLAN'88.

Barbara Liskov and Jeannette Wing . *A behavioral notion of subtyping*, TOPLAS, November 1994.

Carl Manning. *Traveler: the Actor observatory* ECOOP 1987. Also appears in Lecture Notes in Computer Science, vol. 276.

Carl Manning. *Acore: The Design of a Core Actor Language and its Compile* Master Thesis. MIT EECS. May 1987.

Satoshi Matsuoka and Aki Yonezawa. *Analysis of Inheritance Anomaly in Object-Oriented Concurrent Programming Languages Research Directions in Concurrent Object-Oriented Programming* MIT Press. 1993.

John McCarthy *Programs with common sense* Symposium on Mechanization of Thought Processes. National Physical Laboratory, UK. Teddington, England. 1958.

John McCarthy. *A Basis for a Mathematical Theory of Computation* Western Joint Computer Conference. 1961.

John McCarthy, Paul Abrahams, Daniel Edwards, Timothy Hart, and Michael Levin. *Lisp 1.5 Programmer's Manual* MIT Computation Center and Research Laboratory of Electronics. 1962.

John McCarthy. *Situations, actions and causal laws* Technical Report Memo 2, Stanford University Artificial Intelligence Laboratory. 1963.

John McCarthy and Patrick Hayes. *Some Philosophical Problems from the Standpoint of Artificial Intelligence* Machine Intelligence 4. Edinburgh University Press. 1969.

Alexandre Miquel. *A strongly normalising Curry-Howard correspondence for IZF set theory* in Computer science Logic Springer. 2003

Giuseppe Milicia and Vladimiro Sassone. *The Inheritance Anomaly: Ten Years After* SAC. Nicosia, Cyprus. March 2004.

Mark S. Miller *Robust Composition: Towards a Unified Approach to Access Control and Concurrency Control* Doctoral Dissertation. John Hopkins. 2006.

Mark S. Miller et. al. *Bringing Object-orientation to Security Programming.* YouTube. November 3, 2011.

George Milne and Robin Milner. "Concurrent processes and their syntax" *JACM*. April, 1979.

Robert Milne and Christopher Strachey. *A Theory of Programming Language Semantics* Chapman and Hall. 1976.

Robin Milner. *Logic for Computable Functions: description of a machine implementation.* Stanford AI Memo 169. May 1972

Robin Milner *Processes: A Mathematical Model of Computing Agents* Proceedings of Bristol Logic Colloquium. 1973.

Robin Milner *Elements of interaction: Turing award lecture* CACM. January 1993.

Marvin Minsky (ed.) *Semantic Information Processing* MIT Press. 1968.

Eugenio Moggi *Computational lambda-calculus and monads* IEEE Symposium on Logic in Computer Science. Asilomar, California, June 1989.

Allen Newell and Herbert Simon. *The Logic Theory Machine: A Complex Information Processing System.* Rand Technical Report P-868. June 15, 1956

Carl Petri. *Kommunikation mit Automate* Ph. D. Thesis. University of Bonn. 1962.

Simon Peyton Jones, Alastair Reid, Fergus Henderson, Tony Hoare, and Simon Marlow. *A semantics for imprecise exceptions* Conference on Programming Language Design and Implementation. 1999.

Paul Philips. *We're Doing It all Wrong* Pacific Northwest Scala 2013.

Gordon Plotkin. *A powerdomain construction* SIAM Journal of Computing. September 1976.

George Polya (1957) *Mathematical Discovery: On Understanding, Learning and Teaching Problem Solving Combined Edition* Wiley. 1981.
Karl Popper (1935, 1963) *Conjectures and Refutations: The Growth of Scientific Knowledge* Routledge. 2002.
John Reppy, Claudio Russo, and Yingqi Xiao *Parallel Concurrent ML* ICFP'09.
John Reynolds. *Definitional interpreters for higher order programming languages* ACM Conference Proceedings. 1972.
Bill Roscoe. *The Theory and Practice of Concurrency* Prentice-Hall. Revised 2005.
Kenneth Ross, Yehoshua Sagiv. *Monotonic aggregation in deductive databases.* Principles of Distributed Systems. June 1992Dana Scott and Christopher Strachey. *Toward a mathematical semantics for computer languages* Oxford Programming Research Group Technical Monograph. PRG-6. 1971
Charles Seitz. *The Cosmic Cube* CACM. Jan. 1985.
Peter Sewell, et. al. *x86-TSO: A Rigorous and Usable Programmer's Model for x86 Microprocessors* CACM. July 2010.
Michael Smyth. *Power domains* Journal of Computer and System Sciences. 1978.
Guy Steele, Jr. *Lambda: The Ultimate Declarative* MIT AI Memo 379. November 1976.
Guy Steele, Jr. *Debunking the 'Expensive Procedure Call' Myth, or, Procedure Call Implementations Considered Harmful, or, Lambda: The Ultimate GOTO.* MIT AI Lab Memo 443. October 1977.
Gunther Stent. *Prematurity and Uniqueness in Scientific Discovery* Scientific American. December, 1972.
Bjarrne Stroustrup *Programming Languages — C++* ISO N2800. October 10, 2008.
Gerry Sussman and Guy Steele *Scheme: An Interpreter for Extended Lambda Calculus* AI Memo 349. December, 1975.
David Taenzer, Murthy Ganti, and Sunil Podar, *Problems in Object-Oriented Software Reuse* ECOOP'89.
Daniel Theriault. *A Primer for the Act-1 Language* MIT AI memo 672. April 1982.
Daniel Theriault. *Issues in the Design and Implementation of Act 2* MIT AI technical report 728. June 1983.
Hayo Thielecke *An Introduction to Landin's "A Generalization of Jumps and Labels"* Higher-Order and Symbolic Computation. 1998.
Dave Thomas and Brian Barry. *Using Active Objects for Structuring Service Oriented Architectures: Anthropomorphic Programming with Actors* Journal of Object Technology. July-August 2004.
Kazunori Ueda *A Pure Meta-Interpreter for Flat GHC, A Concurrent Constraint Language* Computational Logic: Logic Programming and Beyond. Springer. 2002.
Darrell Woelk. *Developing InfoSleuth Agents Using Rosette: An Actor Based Language* Proceedings of the CIKM '95 Workshop on Intelligent Information Agents. 1995.
Akinori Yonezawa, Ed. *ABCL: An Object-Oriented Concurrent System* MIT Press. 1990.
Aki Yonezawa *Specification and Verification Techniques for Parallel Programs Based on Message Passing Semantics* MIT EECS Doctoral Dissertation. December 1977.
Hadasa Zuckerman and Joshua Lederberg. *Postmature Scientific Discovery?* Nature. December, 1986.

Appendix 1. Extreme ActorScript

Parameterized Types, *i.e.,* ◁ , ▷

Parameterized Types are specialized using other types delimited by "◁" and "▷":
   Double◁aType▷ ≡
     Actor implements SingleArgument◁aType, anotherType▷ **using**
      // SingleArgument◁aType, anotherType ▷ ≡ [aType]↦ anotherType
      [x]→ x+x §▮   // addition for aType

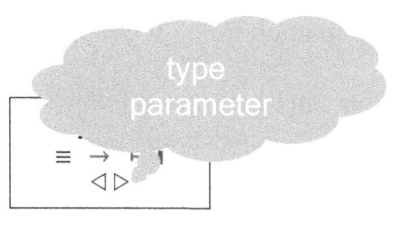

The formal syntax of parameterized types is in the following end note: **38** .

Type Discrimination, *i.e.,* **Discrimination,** ⊘ and ⊖

A discrimination is a type of alternatives differentiated by type using "**Discrimination**" followed by a type name, "**between**", types separated using ",", terminated by "。".

A discriminate can be injected into a discrimination using an expression for the discriminate followed by "⊖" and the discrimination.

A discriminate can be projected as follows:
- In an expression, by using an expression for a discrimination followed by "⊘" and the type to be projected. Also, a discrimination can be tested if it holds a discrimination of a certain type with a expression for the discrimination followed by "⊘?"and the type to be tested.
- In a pattern, by using a pattern followed by "⊘" and the type to be projected

For example, consider the following definition:
   Discrimination IntegerOrFloat **between** Integer, Float。 ▮
Consequently,
- (3⊖IntegerOrFloat)⊘Integer▮ is equivalent to 3▮.
- (3.0⊖IntegerOrFloat) ⊘Integer▮ throws an exception because Integer is not the same as the discriminant Float.
- (3⊖IntegerOrFloat) ⊘?Integer▮ is equivalent to **True▮**.
- The pattern x⊘Float matches 3.0⊖ IntegerOrFloat and binds x to 3.0.
- The expression below is equivalent to 4.0▮:
   3.0⊖IntegerOrFloat ◆ y⊘Integer ⦂ y-1▢
                    x⊘Float ⦂ x+1 ▨▮

A nullable is a discrimination:
   Discrimination Nullable◁aType▷ **between** aType, **Null**◁aType▷。 ∎

A nullable can be created as follows:
   Nullable x:aType ≡ x⊘Nullable◁aType▷

Basic (whose is understood by the pattern matcher) can be defined as follows:
   Discrimination Basic **between** Atomic, Collective。 ∎
   Discrimination Elemental **between**
                  Number, Character, String, Boolean, Nullable◁Basic▷。 ∎
   Discrimination Nonelemental **between**
            List◁Basic▷, Set◁Basic▷, Multiset◁Basic▷, Map◁Basic, Basic▷。 ∎

For example,
- 3⊘Basic∎ is equivalent to 3∎.
- ((3⊘Basic)⊘Elemental)⊘Integer∎ is equivalent to 3∎.
- (3⊘Elemental)⊘Basic∎ is equivalent to 3⊘Basic∎.

The formal syntax of type discrimination is in the following end note: **39.**

Structures, i.e., Structure

A structure can be defined using aa structure identifier by "|", parts separated by ",", and "|".

For example, the structure Leaf can be defined as follows:

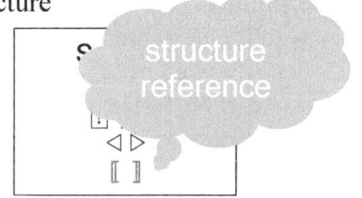

   Structure Leaf◁aType▷[aType]∎   // a terminal must be of type aType
For example,
- The expression **Let** x^i ← 3。 Leaf◁Integer▷[x]∎ is equivalent to Leaf◁Integer▷[3]∎
- The pattern Leaf◁Integer▷[x] matches Leaf◁Integer▷[3] and binds x to 3.

The formal syntax of structures is in the following end note: **40**

Structures with named fields, i.e., 🗐 and :🗐
The structure Fork can be defined as follows:
   Discrimination Tree◁aType▷ **between** Leaf◁aType▷, Fork ◁aType▷。 ∎

---
[i] x is of type Integer

Structure Fork◁aType▷[left⊟ Tree◁aType▷, right⊟ Tree◁aType▷]
　　flip[ ]:Fork◁aType▷ →　　　　　　　　// flip the branches
　　　　Fork◁aType▷[left⊟ right, right⊟ left]▮
For example,
- The expression
  Let x ← 3。 Fork◁Integer▷[left⊟ Leaf◁Integer▷[x],
  　　　　　　　　　　　right⊟ Leaf◁Integer▷[x+1]])▮
  is equivalent to the following:
  Fork◁Integer▷[left⊟ Leaf◁Integer▷[3],
  　　　　　　　right⊟ Leaf◁Integer▷[4]]▮
- The pattern Fork◁Integer▷[left⊟ x, right⊟ y] matches Fork◁Integer▷[Leaf◁Integer▷[6], Leaf◁Integer▷[6]] and binds x to Leaf◁Integer▷[5] and y to Leaf◁Integer▷[6].

The formal syntax structures with named fields is in the following end note: **41.**

Processing Exceptions, *i.e.*, **Try catch**� ⁀ , ⁀ ⁇ *and* **Try cleanup**

It is useful to be able to catch exceptions. The following illustration returns the string "This is a test.":
　　Try Throw Exception["This is a test."] **catch**�
　　　Exception[aString] ⁀ aString ⁇▮

The following illustration performs Reset.[ ] and then rethrows Exception["This is another test."]:
　　Try Throw Exception["This is another test."] **cleanup** Reset.[ ]▮

The formal syntax of processing exceptions is in the following end note: **42.**

Runtime Requirements, *i.e.,* **Preconditions** and **postcondition**
A runtime requirement throws exception an exception if does not hold.
For example, the following expression throws an exception that the requirement x≥0 doesn't hold:
    Let x ← -1 。
      Preconditions x≥0 。
        SquareRoot.[x]▮

Post conditions can be tested using a procedure. For example, the following expression throws an exception that **postcondition** failed because square root of 2 is not less than 1:
    SquareRoot.[2] **postcondition** [y:Float]→ y<1▮

The formal syntax requirements is in the following end note: **43**.

Multiple implementations of a type

For example, Cartesian Actors that implement Complex[i] can be defined as follows:

Actor Cartesian[myReal:Float default 0, myImaginary:Float default 0]
  implements Complex using   // construct a Cartesian of type Complex
    realPart[ ]→ myReal¶
    imaginaryPart[ ]→ myImaginary¶
    magnitude[ ]→
       SquareRoot.[myReal*myReal + myImaginary*myImaginary]¶
    angle[ ]→
     Let theta ← Arcsine.[myImaginary/..magnitude[ ]].
        // ..magnitude[ ] is the result of sending magnitude[ ] to this Actor
      myReal>0 ◆
        True ⸲ theta☑
        False ⸲ myImaginary >0 ◆
            True ⸲180°−theta☑[44]
            False ⸲180°+theta ? ?¶
    plus[argument]→
     Let argumentRealPart ← argument.realPart[ ],
        argumentImaginaryPart ← argument.imaginaryPart[ ].
      Cartesian.[myReal+argumentRealPart,
           myImaginary+argumentImaginaryPart]¶
    times[argument]→
     Let argumentRealPart ← argument.realPart[ ],
        argumentImaginaryPart ← argument.imaginaryPart[ ].
      Cartesian.[myReal*argumentRealPart
          − myImaginary*argumentImaginaryPart,
          myImaginary*argumentRealPart
           + myReal*argumentImaginaryPart]¶
    equivalent[z] →   // test if x is an equivalent complex number
     myReal=z.realPart[ ] ∧ myImaginary=z.imaginaryPart[ ]§∎

---

[i] **Interface** Complex **with** realPart[ ] |··> Float,
                     imaginaryPart[ ] |··> Float,
                     magnitude[ ] |··> Float,
                     angle[ ] |··> Degrees,
                     plus[Complex] |··> Complex,
                     times[Complex] |··> Complex,
                     equivalent[Complex]|··> Boolean. ∎

Consequently,
- Cartesian.[1, 2].realPart[ ]▌ is equivalent to 1▌
- Cartesian.[3, 4].magnitude[ ]▌ is equivalent to 5.0▌
- Cartesian.[0, 1].times[Cartesian.[0, 1]]▌ is equivalent to Cartesian.[-1, 0]▌[45]

Arguments with named fields, *i.e.,* 🗐 **and** :🗐

Polar Actors that implement Complex with named arguments angle and magnitude can be defined as follows:

keyword argument

Symbols
≡ → 🗐
⁇ ¶ § ▌

Actor Polar[angle 🗐 Degrees **default** 0°,
　　　　　　// angle of type Degrees is a named argument of Polar with
　　　　　　// default 0°
　　　　magnitude 🗐 Length]
　implements Complex **using**
　　angle[ ]→ angle¶
　　magnitude[ ]→ magnitude¶
　　realPart[ ]→ magnitude∗Sine.[angle]¶
　　imaginaryPart[ ]→ magnitude∗Cosine.[angle]¶
　　plus[argument]→
　　　Cartesian.[argument.realPart[ ] + ▪▪realPart[ ],
　　　　　　// ▪▪realPart [ ] is the result of sending realPart [ ] to this Actor
　　　　　　　argument.imaginaryPart[ ] + ▪▪imaginaryPart[ ]]¶
　　times[argument]→
　　　Polar.[angle🗐 angle+argument.angle[ ],
　　　　　　magnitude🗐 magnitude∗argument.magnitude[ ]]¶
　　equivalent[z]→
　　　▪▪realPart[ ]=z.realPart[ ] ∧ ▪▪imaginaryPart[ ]=z.imaginaryPart[ ]§▌

Consequently,
- Polar.[theAngle 🗐 0°, theMagnitude 🗐 1].realPart[ ]▌ is equivalent to 1
- (Polar.[theMagnitude 🗐 1]).equivalent[Cartesian.[1, 0]]▌ is equivalent to **True**▌

Lists, *i.e.,* [ ] **using Spread,** *i.e.,* [∨]

A list expression begins with "List" followed by the type of list element[i] and expressions for list elements[ii]. Similarly "Lists" is used for a list of lists. The prefix operator "∨" can be sued to spread the elements of a list. For example
- [1, ∨[2, 3], 4]▮ is equivalent to [1, 2, 3, 4]▮.
- [[1, 2], ∨[3, 4]]▮ is equivalent to [[1, 2], 3, 4]▮
- If y is [5, 6], then [1, 2, y, ∨y]▮ is equivalent [1, 2, [5, 6], 5, 6]▮
- [1, 2] is the list of integers of type Integer with just 1 and 2.

The formal syntax of list expressions is in the following end note: **46.**

Within a list, "∨" is used to match the pattern that follows with the list zero or more elements. For example:
- [[x, 2], ∨y:[Integer*]] is a pattern that matches [[1, 2], 3, 4] and binds x to 1 and y to [3, 4]
- if y:is [3, 4] then [[1, 2], ∨$$y] matches [[1, 2], 3, 4]
- [∨x, ∨y] is an illegal pattern because it can match ambiguously

The formal syntax of patterns is in the following end note: **47.**

---

[i] delimited by ◁ and ▷
[ii] delimited by "[" and "]"

As an example of the use of spread, the following procedure returns every other element of a list beginning with the first:

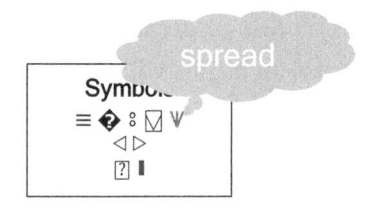

[cloud: spread]

```
Symbol
≡ ❖ ⁞ ☑ V
   ◁ ▷
   ? ▮
```

AlternateElements⊲aType▷∎[aList:[aType*]]:[aType*] ≡
  aList ❖
    [ ] ⁞ [ ] ☑
    [anElement] ⁞ [anElement] ☑
    [firstElement, secondElement] ⁞ [firstElement] ☑
    else ⁞
      [firstElement, secondElement, VremainingElements] ⁞
        [firstElement, VAlternateElements∎[remainingElements]] ?▮

Consequently,
- AlternateElements⊲Integer▷∎[[ ]]▮ is equivalent to [ ]:[Integer*]▮
- AlternateElements⊲Integer▷∎[[3]]▮ is equivalent to [3]▮
- AlternateElements⊲Integer▷∎[[3, 4]]▮ is equivalent to [3]▮
- AlternateElements⊲Integer▷∎[[3, 4, 5]]▮ is equivalent to [3, 5]▮

Sets, *i.e.,* { } **using spreading,** *i.e.,* { V }
A set is an unordered structure with duplicates removed.

The formal syntax of sets is in the following end note: **48.**

Multisets, *i.e.,* {| |} **using spreading,** *i.e.,* {| V |}
A set is an unordered structure with duplicates allowed.

The formal syntax of multisets is in the following end note: **49.**

Maps, *i.e.*, Map{ }
A map is composed of pairs. For example Map{ [3, "a"], ["x", "b"]}▮

Pairs in maps are unordered, *e.g.*, Map{[3, "a"], ["x", "b"]}▮ is equivalent to Map{["x", "b"], [3, "a"]}▮.

However, the expression Map{["y", "b"], ["y", "a"]} throws an exception because a map is univalent. As another example, for the contact records of 1.1 billion people, the following can compute a list of pairs from age to average number of social contacts of US citizens sorted by increasing age:

Age ≡ Integer **thatIs** ≧0≦130▮

AgeToAverageOfNumberOfContactsPairsSortedByAge
  ▪[records:Set◁ContactRecord[i]▷]:[[Age, Float]*] ≡^{50}
  records▪filter[ii][[aRecord:ContactRecord] ⋯>
              aRecord⟦citizenship⟧ ◆
                "US" ⁒ **True** ☑
                else ⁒ **False** ?]
  ▪collect[iii][[aRecord:ContactRecord] ⋯>
      [aRecord⟦yearsOld⟧,
       aRecord⟦numberOfContacts⟧]]
  ▪reduceRange[iv]
      [[aSetOfNumberOfContacts:{Integer*}] ⋯>
       aSetOfNumberOfContacts▪average[v][ ]]
  ▪sort[vi][LessThanOrEqual]▮

---

[i] **Structure** ContactRecord[yearsOld ▭ Age,
                        numberOfContacts ▭ Integer,
                        citizenship ▭ String]▮
[ii] {ContactRecord*} **has** filter[[ContactRecord] ⋯> Boolean]
                        |⋯> {ContactRecord*}。▮
[iii] {ContactRecord*} **has**
    collect [SingleArgumentToPair◁ContactRecord, Age, Integer▷] |⋯>
              Map◁Age, Set◁Integer▷▷。▮
  Interface SingleArgumentToPair◁Type1, Type2, Type3▷ **with**
          [Type1] |⋯> [Type2, Type3]。▮
[iv] Map◁Age, Set◁Integer▷▷ **has**
    reduceRange[FromTo◁{Integer*}, Float ▷] |⋯> Map◁Age, Float▷。▮
  Interface FromTo◁Type1, Type2▷ **with** [Type1] |⋯> Type2。▮
[v] {Number*} **has** average[ ] |⋯> Float。▮
[vi] Map◁Age, Float▷ **has** sort[PairTo◁Age, Age, Boolean▷] |⋯> [[Age, Float]*]。▮
  Interface PairTo◁Type1, Type2, Type3▷ **with** [Type1, Type2] |⋯> Type3。▮

The formal syntax of maps is in the following end note: **51**.

Futures, *i.e.*, **Future** and ↓

A future [Baker and Hewitt 1977] for an expression can be created in ActorScript by using "**Future**" preceding the expression. The operator "↓" can be used to "resolve" a future by returning an Actor computed by the future or throwing an exception. For example, the following expression is equivalent to Factorial.[9999]▮

```
Sym..
← ↓
▮
```
(resolve)

    Let aFuture[i] ←**Future** Factorial.[9999],
    ↓aFuture▮   // do not proceed until Factorial.[9999] has
                     // resolved[ii]

Futures allow execution of expressions to be adaptively executed indefinitely into the future.[52] For example, the following returns a future
    Let aFuture ←**Future** Factorial.[9999],
        g ← ([afuture:Future◁Integer▷]:Integer → 5),
                          // g returns 5 regardless of its argument
        g.[aFuture])▮
            // return 5 regardless of whether Factorial.[9999] has completed[iii]

Note that the following are all equivalent:
- ↓**Future** (4+Factorial.[9999])▮
- 4+↓**Future** Factorial.[9999]▮
- 4+☐Factorial.[9999]▮
- ☐(4+Factorial.[9999])▮

Also ☐Factorial.[9999]+ ☐Fibonacci.[9000]▮ is equivalent to the following:
    Let n[iv] ←☐Factorial.[9999],
          m ←☐Fibonacci.[9000],
          n+m▮ // return Factorial.[9999]+Fibonacci.[9000]

---

[i] f is of type Future◁Integer▷
[ii] i.e. returned or threw an exception
[iii] *i.e.* Factorial.[1000] might not have returned or thrown an exception when 5 is returned. The future f will be garbage collected.
[iv] n is of type Integer

In the following example, Factorial.[9999] might never be executed if readCharacter.[ ] returns the character 'x':
    Let aFuture ← **Future** Factorial.[9999]。
      readCharacter.[ ] ❖
        'x' ⦂ 1☑   // readCharacter.[ ] returned 'x'
        else ⦂ 1+ ↓aFuture ⁇▮
                // readCharacter.[ ] returned something other than 'x'
In the above, program resolution of aFuture is highlighted in yellow.

The procedure Size below can compute the size of a FutureList◁String▷[i] concurrently with its being created:
  Size.[aFutureList:FutureList◁String▷]:Integer ≡
    aFutureList ❖
      [ ] ⦂ 0☑
      [first, ∨rest] ⦂ first.length[ ] + Size.[↓rest] ⁇▮
                // resolving a FutureList resolves only the head

Below is the definition of a procedure that computes a FutureList that is the "fringe" of the leaves of tree.[ii]
  Fringe◁aType▷.[aTree:Tree◁aType▷]:FutureList◁aType▷ ≡
    aTree ❖
      ⊖⊖Leaf◁aType▷[x] ⦂ [x] ☑
      ⊖⊖Fork◁aType▷[tree1, tree2] ⦂
          [∨Fringe.[tree1], ∨**Postpone**^{53} Fringe◁aType▷.[tree2]] ⁇▮

The above procedure can be used to define SameFringe that determines if two lists have the same fringe [Hewitt 1972]:
  SameFringe◁aType▷
        .[aTree:Tree◁aType▷, anotherTree:Tree◁aType▷]:Boolean ≡
                      // test if two trees have the same fringe
  Fringe◁aType▷.[aTree] = Fringe◁aType▷.[anotherTree]▮
    // = resolves futures in the fringes

---

[i] An instance of FutureList◁aType▷ is *either*
    1. the empty list of type FutureList◁aType▷ *or*
    2. a list whose first element is of aType and whose rest is of Future◁FutureList◁aType▷▷.

[ii] See definition of Tree above in this article.

The procedure below given a list of futures returns a FutureList with the same elements resolved:

FutureListOfResolvedElements◁aType▷
  ■[aListOfFutures:[◁Future◁aType▷*]]:FutureList◁aType▷ ≡
aListOfFutures ◆
  [ ] ⸫ [ ] ☑
  [aFirst, ∀aRest] ⸫
    [↓aFirst,
      ∀**Future** FutureListOfResolvedElements◁aType▷■[↓aRest]] ⸮▮

The formal syntax of futures is in the following end note: **54**.

In-line Recursion (*e.g.*, looping) , *i.e.* ■[← , ←] ≜

Inline recursion (often called looping) is accomplished using an initial invocation with identifiers initialized using "←" followed by "≜" and the body.[i]

Below is an illustration of a loop Factorial with two loop identifiers n and accumulation. The loop starts with n equals 9 and value equal 1. The loop is iterated by a call to Factorial with the loop identifiers as arguments.

Factorial■[n ←9, accumulation ←1] ≜
  n ◆ 1 ⸫ accumulation☑
    (> 1) ⸫ Factorial■[n−1, n∗ accumulation] ⸮▮[ii]

The above compiles as a loop because the call to Factorial in the body is a "tail call" [Hewitt 1970, 1976; Steele 1977].

---

[i] This construct takes the place of **while**, **for**, *etc.* loops used in other programming languages.

[ii] equivalent to the following:
  Factorial■[n:Integer ←9, accumulation:Integer ←1]:Integer ≜
    n ◆ 1 ⸫ accumulation☑
      (> 1) ⸫ Factorial■[n−1, n∗ accumulation] ⸮▮

The following expression returns a list of ten times successively calling the parameterless procedure P[i] (of type To◁Integer▷[ii]):
FirstTenSequentially.[n ←10]:[Integer*] ≜
  n ❖ 1 ⁏ [P.[ ]] ▽
    (> 1) ⁏ Let x ← P.[ ]●。
      [x, ∀FirstTenSequentially.[n−1]] ?▮

The following returns one of the results of concurrently calling the procedure P[iii] (which has no arguments and returns Integer) ten times with no arguments:
OneOfTen.[n ←10]:[Integer*] ≜
  n ❖ 1 ⁏ P.[ ] ▽
    (> 1) ⁏ ☐P.[ ] **either** ☐OneOfTen.[n−1]] ?▮

The formal syntax of looping is in the following end note: **55.**

Strings
Strings are Actors that can be expressed using "String", "[", string arguments, and "]". For example,
- String['1', "23", '4']▮ is equivalent to "1234"▮.
- String['1', '2', "34", "56"]▮ is equivalent to "123456"▮.
- String[String['1', '2'], "34"]▮ is equivalent to "1234"▮.
- String[ ]▮ is equivalent to ""▮.

String patterns are delimited by "String", "[" and "]". Within a string pattern, "∀" is used to match the pattern that follows with the list zero or more characters.
For example:
- String[x, '2', ∀y] is a pattern that matches "1234" and binds x to '1' and y to "34".
- String['1', '2', ∀$$y] is a pattern that only matches "1234" if y is "34".
- String[∀x, ∀y] is an illegal pattern because it can match ambiguously.

---

[i] The procedure P may be indeterminate, *i.e.*, return different results on successive calls.
[ii] **Interface** To◁aType▷ **with** [ ]↦ aType。▮
[iii] The procedure P may be indeterminate, *i.e.*, return different results on different calls.

As an example of the use of spread, the following procedure reverses a string:[56]
    Reverse.[aString:String]:String ≡
        aString ◆
            String[ ] ⸳ String[ ] ☑
            String[first, ∀rest] ⸳ String[rest, first] ▯▮

Symbols
≡ ◆ ⸳ ☑ ∀
▯ ¶ § ▮

The formal syntax of string expressions is in the following end note: **57**.

General Messaging, *i.e.,* ⸳ **and** ▯

The syntax for general messaging is to use an expression for the recipient followed by "⸳" and an expression for the message.

For example, if anExpression is of type Expression◁Integer▷ then,
    anExpression.eval[anEnvironment]▮
is equivalent to the following:
    Let aMessage[i] ← eval▯Expression◁Integer▷[anEnvironment]。
    anExpression.aMessage▮

The formal syntax of general messaging is in the following end note: **58**.

---

[i] aMessage:Message◁Expression◁Integer▷▷

Language extension, *i.e.,* 〖 〗

The following is an illustration of language extension that illustrates postponed execution:[59]

〖"**Postpone**" anExpression:Expression ◁aType▷〗:Postpone◁aType▷ ≡
  Actor implements Expression◁Future◁aType▷▷ **using**
    eval[anEnvironment]→
      Future Actor implements aType **using**
              aMessage[i]→   // aMessage received
                Let postponed ← anExpression.eval[anEnvironment]。
                postponed.aMessage
                        // return result of sending aMessage to postponed
                      become postponed§▌
                        // become the Actor postponed for
                        // the next message received[ii]

The formal syntax of language extension is in the following end note: **60**.

---

[i] aMessage:Message◁aType▷
[ii] this is allowed because postponed is of type aType

Atomic Operations, *i.e.* **Atomic compare update updated notUpdated**
For example, the following example implements a lockable that spins to lock:[61]

Actor SpinLock[ ] **nonexclusive**
   locked := **False**.　　　　// initially unlocked
   implements Lockable[i] **using**
     lock[ ]→ Attempt.[ ] ≜　　// perform the loop Attempt as follows
        Atomic locked **compare False update True** ◆
          // attempt to atomically update locked from **False** to **True**
        updated ⁞ **Preconditions** locked=**True**.
          // locked must have contents **True**
            Void☑　　// if updated return **Void**
        notUpdated ⁞ Attempt.[ ] ⁇¶　　// if not updated, try again
   unLock[ ]→
     Preconditions locked =**True**.　　// locked must have contents **True**
     Void afterward locked := **False** §▮　　// reset locked to **False**

The formal syntax of atomic operations is in the following end note: **62**.

Symbols: ≡ → ◆ ☑ ⁞ ⁇ ¶ § ▮

---

[i] **Interface** Lockable **with** lock[ ]↦ **Void,**
                      unLock[ ]↦ **Void**. ▮

Enumerations, *i.e.,* **Enumeration of** using **Qualifiers,** *i.e.,* ▫

An enumeration provides symbolic names for alternatives using "**Enumeration** " followed by the name of the enumeration, "**of**", a list of distinct identifiers terminated by "₀".

For example,

>**Enumeration** DayName of Monday, Tuesday, Wednesday, Thursday, Friday, Saturday, Sunday₀ ▮

From the above definition, an enumerated day is available using a qualifier, *e.g.*, Monday▫DayName. Qualifiers provide structure for namespaces.

The formal syntax of qualifiers is in the following end note: **63**.

The procedure below computes the name of following day of the week given the name of any day of the week:

UsingNamespace DayName▮
FollowingDay▪[aDay:DayName]:DayName ≡
  aDay ◆ Monday ⁸ Tuesday,
       Tuesday ⁸ Wednesday,
       Wednesday ⁸ Thursday,
       Thursday ⁸ Friday,
       Friday ⁸ Saturday,
       Saturday ⁸ Sunday,
       Sunday ⁸ Monday ⁇▮

The formal syntax of enumerations is in the following end note: **64**.

Native types, e.g., JavaScript, JSON, Java, and XML

Object can be used to create JavaScript Objects. Also, **Function** can be used to bind the reserved identifier **This**. For example, consider the following ActorScript for creating a JavaScript object aRectangle (with length 3 and width 4) and then computing its area 12:

    Let aRectangle[i] ← **Object** {"length": 3, "width": 4]},
        aFunction ← **Function** [ ]→ **This**⟦"length"⟧ * **This**⟦"width"⟧。
    Rectangle⟦"area"⟧ ≔ aFunction●
    aRectangle⟦"area"⟧.[ ]。▮

The setTimeout JavaScript object can be invoked with a callback as follows that logs the string "later" after a time out of 1000:

    setTimeout▫JavaScript.[1000,
                  Function [ ]→
                            console▫JavaScript.["log"].["later"]]▮

JSON is a restricted version of **Object** that allows only Booleans, numbers, strings in objects and arrays.[ii]

Native types can also be used from Java. For example (s:String▫Java).substring[3, 5][iii] is the substring of s from the 3rd to the 5th characters inclusive.

Java types can be imported using **Import**, *e.g.*:

Namespace mynamespace▮
Import java.math.BigInteger▮
Import java.lang.Number▮

After the above, BigInteger.new["123"].instanceof[Number]▮ is equivalent to **True**▮.

---

[i] aRectangle is of type Object▫JavaScript
[ii] *i.e.* the following JavaScript types are not included in JSON: Date, Error, Regular Expression, and Function.
[iii] substring is a method of the String class in Java

The following notation is used for XML:[65]
  XML <"PersonName"> <"First">"Ole-Johan" </"First">
                      <"Last"> "Dahl"</"Last"> </"PersonName">
and could print as:
  <PersonName> <First> Ole-Johan </First>
                      <Last> Dahl </Last> </PersonName>

XML Attributes are allowed so that the expression
  XML <"Country" "capital"="Paris"> "France" </"Country">
and could print as:
  <Country capital="Paris"> France </Country>

XML construction can be performed in the following ways using the append operator:
- **XML** <"doc"> 1, 2, ⩔[3] </"doc">]▮ is equivalent to **XML** <"doc">1, 2, 3</"doc">▮
- **XML** <"doc">1, 2, ⩔[3], ⩔[4] </"doc">]▮ is equivalent to **XML** <"doc"> 1, 2, 3, 4 </"doc">▮

One-way messaging, *e.g.*, ⊖, ⇐, and ⇛

One-way messaging is often used in hardware implementations.

Each one-way named-message send consists of an expression followed by "⇐", a message name, and arguments delimited by "[" and "]".

The following is a interface for a customer that is used in request/response message passing for return type aType:[66]

    Interface Customer◁aType▷ **with**
       return[aType] ↦ ⊖,
       throw[anException] ↦ ⊖。▮

one-way message send

For example, if aCustomer is of type Customer◁Integer▷, then 3 can be returned to aCustomer using aCustomer⇐return[3].

The formal syntactic definition of one-way named-message sending is in the end note: **67**

Each one-way message handler implementation consists of a named-message declaration pattern followed by "⇛" and a body for the response which must ultimately be "⊖" which denotes no response.

The formal syntactic definition of one-way named-message implementation is in the following end note: **68**

The following is an implementation of an arithmetic logic unit that implements **jumpGreater** and **addJumpPositive** one-way messages:

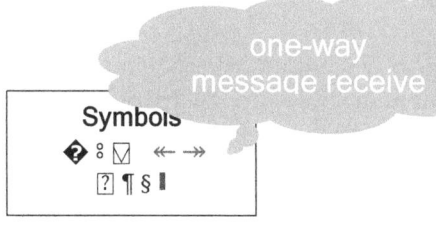

one-way message receive

Symbols
❷ ⁑ ☑ ← →»
❓ ¶ § ▮

Actor ArithmeticLogicUnit◁aType▷[ ]
 implements ALU◁aType▷[i] **using**
  jumpGreater[x:aType, y:aType,
        firstGreaterAddress:Address, elseAddress:Address]→»
    InstructionUnit←Execute[(x>y)] ❷
                True ⁑ firstGreaterAddress☑
                False ⁑ elseAddress ❓]¶
  addJumpPositive[x:aType, y:aType, sumLocation:Location◁aType▷,
        positiveAddress:Address, elseAddress:Address]→»
   Let z ← (x+y)。
    sumLocation ❷
      aVariableLocation:VariableLocation◁aType▷[ii] ⁑
        VariableLocation.store[z]●,
                // continue after acknowledgement of store
          (z >0) ❷ True ⁑ InstructionUnit←execute[positiveAddress] ☑
                 False ⁑ InstructionUnit←execute[elseAddress] ❓☑
      aTemporaryLocation:TemporaryLocation◁aType▷[iii] ⁑
        aTemporaryLocation←write[z],
                // continue concurrently with processing write
          (z >0) ❷ True ⁑ InstructionUnit←execute[positiveAddress] ☑
                 False ⁑ InstructionUnit←execute[elseAddress] ❓ ❓§▮

Arrays
Arrays are lists of locations that can be updated using **swap** messages.

They are included to provide backward compatibility and to support certain kinds of low level optimizations. An array element can be referenced using the array followed by array indices enclosed by "⟦" and "⟧".

---

[i] **Interface** ALU◁aType▷ **with** jumpGreater [aType,] ↦ ⊖,
                addJumpPositive [anException] ↦ ⊖。
[ii] VariableLocation◁aType▷ **has** store[aType]↦ **Void**。
[iii] TemporaryLocation◁aType▷ **has** write[aType] ↦ ⊖。

385

In the in-place implementation of QuickSort[69] (below), left is the index of the leftmost element of the subarray, right is the index of the rightmost element of the subarray (inclusive), and the number of elements in the subarray is right-(left+1).

QuickSort.[anArray:Array◁Number▷, left:Integer, right:Integer]:**Void** ≡
  Preconditions anArray.lower[ ]≦left≦right≦anArray.upper[ ]。
    (left<right) ❖ **True** ⦂   // If the array has 2 or more items
        Let pivotIndex ←
          Partition.[anArray, left, right, left+(right-left)/2]●。
        Preconditions left≦pivotIndex≦right。
        ◻QuickSort.[anArray, left, pivotIndex-1],
          // Recursively sort elements smaller than the pivot
        ◻QuickSort.[anArray, pivotIndex+1, right] ☑
          // Concurrently recursively sort elements at
          // least as big as pivot
    False ⦂ **Void** ⸮∎

                      array reference
                      ⸮ ⫪ ⸱
                      [ ]

Partition.[anArray:Array◁Number▷, left:Integer, right:Integer,
      pivotIndex:Integer]:Integer ≡
Preconditions anArray.lower[ ]≦left≦pivotIndex≦right≦anArray.upper[ ]。
  Let pivot← anArray⟦pivotIndex⟧●。
    anArray.swap[pivotIndex, right]●[70]
    Let finalStoreIndex ←
        Move.[iterationIndex:Integer ← left,
           storeIndex:Integer ←left]:Integer ≜
        Preconditions left≦storeIndex≦iterationIndex≦right。
        iterationIndex<right ❖
        True ⦂
          anArray⟦iterationIndex⟧≦pivotValue ❖
          True ⦂
            anArray.swap[iterationIndex, storeIndex]●
            Move.[iterationIndex+1, storeIndex+1] ☑
          False ⦂ Move.[iterationIndex+1, storeIndex] ⸮☑
        False ⦂ storeIndex ⸮●。
  anArray.swap[finalStoreIndex, right]● // Move Actor to its final place
  finalStoreIndex。∎

For example, consider the following example:
    Let anArray ← Array.[3, 2, 1]。
        QuickSort.[anArray, 0, 1]●
        anArray。∎

The above returns Array[1, 2, 3]▮.

Appendix 2: Meta-circular definition of ActorScript

It might seem that a meta-circular definition is a strange way to define a programming language. However, as shown in the references, concurrent programming languages are not reducible to logic. Consequently, an augmented meta-circular definition may be one of the best alternatives available.

The message eval

John McCarthy is justly famous for Lisp. One of the more remarkable aspects of Lisp was the definition of its interpreter (called Eval) in Lisp itself. The exact meaning of Eval defined in terms of itself has been somewhat mysterious since, on the face of it, the definition is circular.[71]

The basic idea is to send an expression an eval message with an environment to instead of the Lisp approach of send the procedure Eval the expression and environment as arguments.

Each eval message has an environment with the bindings of program identifiers:
  Interface Expression◁aType▷ **with**
      eval[Environment] ↦ aType₀ ▮

The tokens ⦅ and ⦆ are used to delimit program syntax.

⦅anIdentifier:*Identifier*◁aType▷⦆:*Expression* ◁aType▷ ≡
  eval[anEnvironment] → anEnvironment.lookup[anIdentifier]▮

The interface Type

The interface Type is defined as follows:
  Interface Type **with**
      extension?[Type] |··> Boolean
      has?[MethodSignature] |··> Boolean₀ ▮

⦅anotherType:*Type*◁anotherType▷ "⊒" aType:*Type*◁aType▷⦆
              :*Expression*◁Boolean▷ ≡
  eval[anEnvironment]→
    (anotherType.eval[anEnvironment])
      .extension?[aType.eval[anEnvironment]]▮

((anotherType:*Type* ◁anotherType▷ "**has**" aSignature:*Signatture*))
:*Expression* ◁Boolean▷ ≡
eval[anEnvironment]→
  (anotherType▪eval[anEnvironment])
    ▪has?[aSignature▪eval[anEnvironment]]▮

Future, ↓, and □
The interface Future is used for futures:
    Interface Future◁aType▷ **with** resolve[ ]↦ aType。 ▮

("Future" anExpression:*Expression* ◁aType▷)
        :*Expression* ◁Future◁aType▷▷ ≡
Actor implements Expression◁Future◁aType▷▷ **using**
  eval[anEnvironment]→
    Let aFuture:Future◁aType▷ ←
      Future Try anExpression▪eval[anEnvironment]
        catch◆
          anException ⸭
          Actor
            implements Future◁aType▷
              resolve[ ]→**Throw** anException。 [?]
    Actor implements Future◁aType▷**using**
      resolve[ ]→ ↓aFuture §▮

("↓" anExpression:*Expression* ◁Future◁aType▷▷)
        :*Expression* ◁aType▷ ≡
Actor implements Expression◁aType▷ **using**
  eval[anEnvironment]→
    anExpression▪eval[anEnvironment]▪resolve[ ] §▮

("□" anExpression:*Expression* ◁aType▷)
        :*Expression* ◁aType▷ ≡
Actor implements Expression◁aType▷ **using**
  eval[anEnvironment]→
    ↓**Future** anExpression▪eval[anEnvironment] §▮

The message match

Patterns are analogous to expressions, except that they take receive match messages:
    Interface Pattern◁aType▷ **with**
        match[aType, Environment]↦ Nullable◁Environment▷,
        mustMatch[aType, Environment]↦ Environment。▮

⦅anIdentifier:*Identifier* ◁aType▷⦆:*Pattern* ◁aType▷ ≡
    match[anActor:aType, anEnvironment]→
        anEnvironment▪bind[anIdentifier, to ▤ anActor]▮

⦅"_"⦆:*UniversalPattern* ◁aType▷ ≡
    match[anActor:aType, anEnvironment]→ anEnvironment▮

⦅"$$" anExpression:*Expression*◁expressionType▷⦆
                              :*ValuePattern* ◁aType▷ ≡
    match[anActor:aType, anEnvironment]→
    (anActor = anExpression▪eval[anEnvironment]) ◆
      True ⸪ **Nullable** anEnvironment▱
      False ⸪ **Null** ◁Environment▷▯▮

Message sending, *e.g.*, ▪

⦅procedure:*Expression* ◁argumentsType↦returnType▷
    "▪" "[" arguments:*Arguments* ◁argumentsType▷ "]"
      ":" returnType⦆
            :*ProcedureSend* ◁argumentsType, returnType▷ ≡
eval[anEnvironment]→
    (procedure▪eval[anEnvironment])
        ▪[∀(expressions▪eval[anEnvironment])]§▮

⟪(recipient:*Expression* ◁recipient▷ "."
    name:*MessageName* "[" ∀arguments
                            :*Arguments* ◁argumentsType▷ "]"⟫
                    :*NamedMessageSend* ◁expressionType▷ ≡
  eval[anEnvironment]→
    Let aRecipient ← recipient.eval[anEnvironment].
      aRecipient
        .Message[QualifiedName[name recipientType],
              [∀arguments.eval[anEnvironment]]]§∎

⟪(recipient:*Expression* ◁recipientType▷
    "." aMessage:*Message* ◁Message◁recipientType▷▷⟫
                    :*UnnamedMessageSend* ◁expressionType▷ ≡
  eval[anEnvironment]→
    (recipient.eval[anEnvironment])
      .(aMessage.eval[anEnvironment])§∎

List Expressions and Patterns

⟪("[" firstExpression:*Expression*◁aType▷
    "," secondExpression:*Expression* ◁aType▷"]"⟫
                            :*ListExpression* ◁aType▷ ≡
  eval[anEnvironment]→
    Let first ← firstExpression.eval[anEnvironment],
        second ← secondExpression.eval[anEnvironment].
      [first, second]§∎

⟪("[" firstExpression:*Expression*◁aType▷
    "," "∀" restExpression:*Expression* ◁aType▷ "]"⟫
                            :*ListExpression* ◁aType▷ ≡
  eval[anEnvironment]→
    Let first ← firstExpression.eval[anEnvironment],
        rest ← restExpression.eval[anEnvironment].
      [first, ∀rest]§∎

("[" firstPattern:*Pattern* ◁aType▷
                "," "▼" restPattern:*ListPattern* ◁aType▷ "]")
                                        :*ListPattern* ◁aType▷ ≡
  match[anActor:aType, anEnvironment]→
    anActor ◆
      [first, ▼rest] ⸳
        firstPattern.match[first, anEnvironment] ◆
          ⊖⊖**Null** Environment ⸳
              Null ◁Environment▷,
          aNewEnvironment⊖Environment ⸳
              restPattern.match[restValue, aNewEnvironment] [?]▽
      else ⸳ **Null** ◁Environment▷[?]§∎

Exceptions

("**Try**" anExpression:*Expression* ◁aType▷
  "**catch◆**" exceptions:*ExpressionCases* ◁Exception, aType▷ "[?]")
                                        :*TryExpression* ◁aType▷ ≡
  eval[anEnvironment]→
    Try anExpression.eval[anEnvironment] **catch◆**
      anException:Exception ⸳ CasesEval.[anException,
                                        exceptions,
                                        anEnvironment] [?]§∎

("**Try**" anExpression:*Expression* ◁aType▷
        "**cleanup**" aCleanup:*Expression* ◁aType▷)
                                        :*TryExpression* ◁aType▷ ≡
  eval[anEnvironment]→
    Try anExpression.eval[anEnvironment] **catch◆**
      _ ⸳ aCleanup.eval[anEnvironment] ●
          Rethrow[?]§∎

Continuations using perform

A continuations is a generalization of expression for executing in cheese, which receives perform messages:
  Interface Continuation◁aType▷ **with**
        perform [Environment, CheeseQ]↦ aType。∎
  Discrimination Construct◁aType▷ **between**
        Continuation◁aType▷, Expression◁aType▷。∎

```
Execute▪[aConstruct:Construct◁aType▷,
          anEnvironment:Environment,
          aCheeseQ:CheeseQ]:aType ≡
  aConstruct � aContinuation⊗Continuation◁aType▷ ⸰
                 aContinuaton▪perform[anEnvironment,
                                       aCheeseQ] ⍌
             anExpression⊗Expression◁aType▷ ⸰
                 anExpression▪eval[anEnvironment] ⍰▮
```

Atomic compare and update

```
⟬"Atomic" location:Expression◁Location◁anotherType▷,
        "compare" comparison:Expression◁anotherType▷
        "update" update:Expression◁anotherType▷ "�"
        "updated" "⸰"
            compareIdentical:ContinuationList◁aType▷ "⍌"
         "notUpdated" "⸰"
            compareNotIdentical:ContinuationList ◁aType▷⟭
                                                  :Atomic◁aType▷ ≡
  perform[anEnvironment, aCheeseQ]→
    (location▪eval[anEnvironment])
      ▪compareAndConditionallyUpdate[comparison▪eval[anEnvironment],
                                     update▪eval[anEnvironment]] �
        True ⸰ compareIdentifical▪perform[anEnvironment, aCheeseQ] ⍌
        False ⸰
          compareNotIdentifical▪perform[anEnvironment, aCheeseQ] ⍰▮

Actor SimpleLocation◁anotherType▷[initialContents]
  contents ≔ initialContents。
  implements Location◁anotherType▷ using
    compareAndConditionallyUpdate[comparison, update]→
      (contents = comparison) �
          True ⸰ True afterward contents ≔ update⍌
           False ⸰ False ⍰§▮
```

Cases

⦅anExpression:*Expression* ◁anotherType▷ "◆"
　　　　　cases:*ExpressionCases*◁anotherType, aType▷ "⸮"⦆
　　　　　　　　　　　　　　　　:*CasesExpression* ◁ aType▷ ≡
　eval[anEnvironment]→
　　　CasesEval.[anExpression.eval[anEnvironment],
　　　　　　　cases,
　　　　　　　anEnvironment]§∎

CasesEval.[anActor:anotherType,
　　　　cases:[◁ExpressionCase◁anotherType, aType▷*],
　　　　anEnvironment:Environment]:aType ≡
　cases ◆
　　[ ] ⸭ **Throw** NoApplicableCase[ ],
　　[first, ∀rest] ⸭
　　　first ◆ ⦅aPattern:*Pattern* ◁anotherType▷ "⸭"
　　　　　　anExpression:*Expression* ◁aType▷⦆
　　　　　　　　　　　　　　　　:*ExpressionCase*◁aType▷ ⸭
　　　　　aPattern.match[anActor, anEnvironment] ◆
　　　　　　⊘⊘**Null** Environment ⸭
　　　　　　　CasesEval.[anActor, rest, anEnvironment] ☑
　　　　　　newEnvironment⊘Environment ⸭
　　　　　　　anExpression.eval[newEnvironment] ⸮☑
　　　　⦅"**else**" elsePattern:*Pattern* ◁anotherType▷"⸭"
　　　　　　elseExpression:*Expression* ◁aType▷⦆
　　　　　　　　　　　　　　　　:*ExpressionElseCase* ◁aType▷ ⸭
　　　　　elsePattern.match[anActor, anEnvironment] ◆
　　　　　　⊘⊘**Null** Environment ⸭
　　　　　　　Throw ElsePatternMustMatch[ ] ☑
　　　　　　newEnvironment⊘Environment ⸭
　　　　　　　elseExpression.eval[newEnvironment] ⸮☑
　　　　⦅"**else**" "⸭"
　　　　　　elseExpression:*Expression* ◁aType▷⦆
　　　　　　　　　　　　　　　　:*ExpressionElseCase* ◁aType▷ ⸭
　　　　　elseExpression.eval[anEnvironment] ☑
　　　　else ⸭ **Throw** NoApplicableCase[ ] ⸮⸮∎

((anExpression:*Expression* ◁anotherType▷ "◆"
           cases:*ContinuationCases* ◁anotherType, aType▷ "❓")
                        :*CasesContinuation* ◁aType▷ ≡
     perform[anEnvironment, aCheeseQ]→
        CasesPerform.[anExpression.eval[anEnvironment], cases,
                      anEnvironment, aCheeseQ]§∎
CasesPerform.[anActor:anotherType,
              cases:[ContinuationCase◁aType▷*],
              anEnvironment:Environment,
              aCheeseQ:CheeseQ]:aType ≡
  cases ◆
   [ ] � Throw NoApplicableCase[ ],
   [first, ∀rest] ⁚
     first ◆ ((aPattern:*Pattern* ◁anotherType▷ "⁚"
              aContinuation:*Continuation* ◁aType▷)
                           :*ContinuationCase* ◁aType▷ ⁚
        aPattern.match[anActor, anEnvironment] ◆
           ⊖⊖Null Environment ⁚
              CasesPerform.[anActor,
                            rest,
                            anEnvironment,
                            aCheeseQ] ☑
           newEnvironment⊖Environment ⁚
              aContinuation.perform[newEnvironment,
                                    aCheeseQ] ❓☑
     (("else"
        elsePattern:*Pattern*
         ◁anotherType▷ "⁚"
              elseContinuation:*Continuation* ◁aType▷)
                           :*ContinuationElseCase* ◁aType▷ ⁚
        elsePattern.match[anActor, anEnvironment] ◆
           ⊖⊖Null Environment ⁚
              Throw ElsePatternMustMatch[ ] ☑
           newEnvironment⊖Environment ⁚
              elseContinuation.eval[newEnvironment] ❓☑
     (("else" "⁚"
              elseContinuation:*Continuation* ◁aType▷)
                           :*ContinuationElseCase* ◁aType▷ ⁚
        elseContinuation.perform[anEnvironment, aCheeseQ] ☑
     else ⁚ Throw NoApplicableCase[ ] ❓❓∎

Holes in the cheese

⦅anExpression:*Expression* ◁aType▷
  "afterward" someAssignments:*Assignments*".")
                :*Continuation* ◁aType▷ ≡
  perform[anEnvironment, aCheeseQ]→
    Let anActor ← anExpression.eval[anEnvironment]●。
    someAssignments.carryOut[anEnvironment, aCheeseQ]●
    aCheeseQ.leave[ ]●
    anActor。§▮

⦅aVariable:*Variable* ◁aType▷
           ":=" anExpression:*Expression* ◁aType▷⦆:*Assignment* ≡
  carryOut[anEnvironment]→
    anEnvironment.assign[aVariable,
                  to ⊟ anEpression.eval[anEnvironment]]§▮

⦅**"Hole"** anExpression:*Expression* ◁aType▷⦆:*Hole* ◁aType▷ ≡
  perform[anEnvironment, aCheeseQ]→
    aCheeseQ.leave[ ]●
    anExpression.eval[anEnvironment.freeze[ ]]§▮

⦅**"Hole"** anExpression:*Expression* ◁aType▷
  "after"
    aPreparation:*Preparation*⦆:*Continuation*◁aType▷ ≡
  perform[anEnvironment, aCheeseQ]→
    Let frozenEnvironment ← anEnvironment.freeze[ ]●。
      // create frozen environment so that
      // preparation does not affect evaluating anExpression
    aPreparation.carryOut[anEnvironment, aCheeseQ]●
    aCheeseQ.leave[ ]●
    anExpression.eval[frozenEnvironment]。§▮

(("Hole" anExpression:*Expression* ◁anotherType▷
  "afterward" anAfterward:*AfterwardContinuation* ◁aType▷ "[?]")
                                        :*Continuation*◁aType▷ ≡
  perform[anEnvironment, aCheeseQ]→
    Let frozenEnvironment ← anEnvironment.freeze[ ]●。
    aCheeseQ.leave[ ]●
    Try Let anActor ← anExpression.eval[frozenEnvironment]●。
         aCheeseQ.enter[ ]●
         anAfterward.perform[anEnvironment, aCheeseQ]]●
         anActor afterward aCheeseQ.leave[ ]。
    catch◆
       anException:ApplicationException ⋮
         aCheeseQ.enter[ ]●
         anAfterward.perform[anEnvironment, aCheeseQ]●
         throw anException afterward aCheeseQ.leave[ ] [?]。§∎

(("Hole" anExpression:*Expression* ◁anotherType▷
   "returned◆"
       returnedCases:*ContinuationCases* ◁anotherType, aType▷ "[?]"
   "threw◆"
       threwCases:*ContinuationCases* ◁anotherType, aType▷ "[?]")
                              :*Continuation*◁anotherType, aType▷ ≡
  perform[anEnvironment, aCheeseQ]→
    Let frozenEnvironment ← anEnvironment.freeze[ ]●。
    aCheeseQ.leave[ ]●
    Try Let anActor ← anExpression.eval[frozenEnvironment]●。
         aCheeseQ.enter[ ]●
         CasesPerform.[anActor,
                       returnedCases,
                       anEnvironment,
                       aCheeseQ]。
    catch◆ anException:ApplicationException ⋮
                aCheeseQ.enter[ ]●
                CasesPerform.[anException,
                              threwCases,
                              anEnvironment,
                              aCheeseQ] [?]。§∎

⦅"**Enqueue**" anExpression:*QueueExpression* "●"⦆
:*Enqueue*◁aType▷ ≡
  perform[anEnvironment, aCheeseQ]→
    Let anInternalQ ← anExpression.eval[anEnvironment]。
      anInternalQ.enqueueAndLeave[ ] §▮

⦅"**Enqueue**" anExpression:*QueueExpression* "●"
    aContinuation:*Continuation*◁aType▷⦆:*Enqueue*◁aType▷ ≡
  perform[anEnvironment, aCheeseQ]→
    Let anInternalQ ← anExpression.eval[anEnvironment]。
      anInternalQ.enqueueAndLeave[ ]●
      aContinuation.perform[anEnvironment, aCheeseQ]。§▮

A Simple Implementation of Actor

The implementation below does not implement queues, holes, and relaying.

⦅"**Actor**" declarations:*ActorDeclarations*
    "**implements**" *Identifier*◁aType▷
    "**using**" handlers:*Handlers*◁anInterface▷ "§"⦆:*Actor*◁aType▷ ≡
  Actor implements Expression◁anInterface▷ using
    eval[anEnvironment]→
      Initialized.[anInterface.eval[anEnvironment],
                   handlers,
                   declarations.initialize[anEnvironment],
                   SimpleCheeseQ.[ ]]§▮

Initialized.[anInterface:aType,
         handlers:List◁Handler◁aType▷▷,
         anEnvironment:Environment,
         cheeseQ:CheeseQ]:aType ≡
 Actor implements anInterface **using**
  receivedMessage:Message◁aType▷ →
                           // receivedMessage received for anInterface
       aCheeseQ.enter[ ]●
       Let aReturned ← **Try** Select.[receivedMessage,
                           handlers,
                           anEnvironment,
                           aCheeseQ]
                   cleanup aCheeseQ.leave[ ]●。
                           // leave cheese and rethrow exception
       aCheeseQ.leave[ ]●
       aReturned。§▮

Select.[receivedMessage:Message◁aType▷,
       handlers:List◁Handler◁aType▷▷,
       anEnvironment:Environment,
       aCheeseQ:CheeseQ]:aType ≡
  handlers ◆
   [ ] ⸭ **Throw** NotApplicable[ ] ☑
   [((aMessageDeclaration:*MessageDeclaration* ◁aType▷ "→"
      body:*Continuation* ◁aType▷))
                           :*ContinuationHandler*◁aType▷☑
      ∀restHandlers] ⸭
      aMessageDeclaration.match[receivedMessage,
                           anEnvironment] ◆
        ⊖⊖**Null** Environment ⸭ Select.[receivedMessage,
                           restHandlers,
                           anEnvironment,
                           aCheeseQ] ☑
                  // process next handler
        newEnvironment⊖Environment ⸭
          Execute.[body, newEnvironment, aCheeseQ] ⸮⸮▮
                  // execute body with extension of anEnvironment

398

An implementation of cheese that never holds a lock

The following is an implementation of cheese that does not hold a lock:[72]
Actor SimpleCheeseQ[ ] **nonexclusive**
  invariants aTail=Null ⊲Activity⊳ ⇨ previousToTail=Null ⊲Activity⊳ 。
  aHeadHint := **Null** ⊲Activity⊳,   // aHeadHint:Nullable⊲Activity⊳[73]
  aTail := **Null** ⊲Activity⊳ 。   // aTail:Nullable⊲Activity⊳[74]
  implements CheeseQ[75] **using**
    enter[ ] in myActivity →[76]
        Preconditions myActivity⟦previous⟧=Null ⊲Activity⊳,
                      myActivity⟦nextHint⟧=Null ⊲Activity⊳ 。
        attempt▪[ ]:Void ≜
          myActivity⟦previous⟧ := aTail●   // set provisional tail of queue
          Atomic aTail **compare** aTail **update** myActivity ◈
            updated ⸭   // inserted myActivity in cheese queue with previous
                myActivity⟦previous⟧=Null ⊲Activity⊳ ◈
                      True ⸭ Void☑   // successfully entered cheese
                      False ⸭ Suspend [?]☑ // current activity is suspended
            notUpdated ⸭ attempt▪[ ] [?]。¶   // make another attempt
    leave[ ] in myActivity →   // leave message received running myActivity
        Preconditions aTail !=Null ⊲Activity⊳ 。[77]
      Let ahead ← [:]SubCheeseQ▪head[ ]● 。
        Preconditions ahead=myActivity 。
          Atomic aTail **compare** ahead **update** Null ⊲Activity⊳ ◈
            updated ⸭   // last activity has left this cheese queue
              aHeadHint := Null ⊲Activity⊳●
              Void☑
            notUpdated ⸭   // another activity is in this cheese queue
              aHeadHint := ahead⟦nextHint⟧●
              MakeRunnable aHeadHint⊖Activity[?]§
  also implements SubCheeseQ[78] **using**
    head[ ] → **Preconditions** aTail != Null ⊲Activity⊳ 。
      findHead▪[backIterator:Activity ←
              aHeadHint = Null ⊲Activity⊳ ◈
                True ⸭ aTail⊖Activity] ☑
                False ⸭ aHeadHint⊖Activity [?]]:Activity ≜
        backIterator⟦previous⟧ ◈
      ⊖⊖Null Activity ⸭   // backIterator is head of this cheese queue
          aHeadHint := Nullable backIterator●
          backIterator 。☑
        previousBackIterator⊖Activity ⸭
                  // backIterator is not the head of this cheese queue
          previousBackIterator⟦nextHint⟧ := Nullable backIterator●
                      // set nextHint of previous to backIterator
          findHead▪[previousBackIterator] 。[?]§▎

The algorithm used in the implementation of **CheeseQ** above is due to Blaine Garst [private communication] *cf.* [Ladan-Mozes and Shavit 2004].

There is a state diagram for the implementation below:

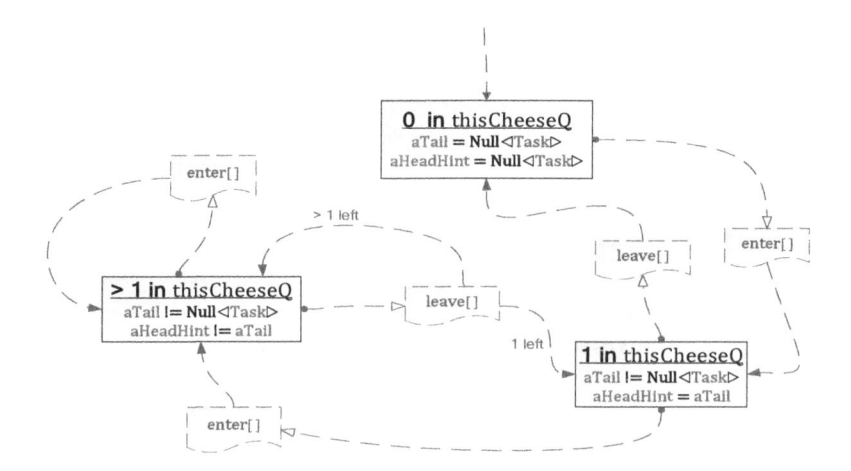

0 in thisCheeseQ
aTail = **Null**<|Task|>
aHeadHint = **Null**<|Task|>

≥ 1 in thisCheeseQ
aTail != **Null**<|Task|>
aHeadHint != aTail

1 in thisCheeseQ
aTail != **Null**<|Task|>
aHeadHint = aTail

Transitions: enter[], > 1 left, leave[], 1 left, enter[]

Actor SimpleInternalQ [aCheeseQ:CheeseQ] **nonexclusive**
  aHead := **Null** ◁Activity▷,   // aHead:Nullable◁Activity▷
  aTail := **Null** ◁Activity▷。
  implements InternalQ[79] **using**
    enqueueAndLeave[ ] in myActivity →
        // enqueueAndLeave message received in myActivity
        [:]SubInternalQ▪remove[myActivity]●

        aCheeseQ▪leave[ ]●   // myActivity is the head of aCheeseQ
        Suspend¶
            // myActivity is suspended and when resumed returns **Void** ¶
    enqueueAndDequeue[anInternalQ] in myActivity →
      Preconditions ¬anInternalQ▪empty?[ ]。
        [:]SubInternalQ▪add[myActivity]●

        ▪▪dequeue[ ]●
        Suspend。¶
    dequeue[ ] in myActivity → **Preconditions** ¬ ▪▪empty?[ ]。
        aCheeseQ▪leave[ ]●   // myActivity is the head of aCheeseQ

        MakeRunnable [:]SubInternalQ▪remove[ ]¶
            // make runnable the removed activity
    empty?[ ] → aTail =**Null** ◁Activity▷§
  also implements SubInternalQ[80] **using**
    add[anActivity] →
      aTail ◆
        ⊖⊖**Null** Activity ⁞
          Void afterward aHead := **Nullable** anActivity,
                          aTail := **Nullable** anActivity。 ☑

        theTail⊖Activity ⁞ **Void afterward** theTail⟦rest⟧ := anActivity [?]¶
    remove[ ] → **Preconditions** ¬ ▪▪empty?[ ]。
      Let theFirst ← aHead⊖Activity●。
        aTail=aHead ◆
          True ⁞ theFirst **afterward** aHead := **Null** ◁Activity▷,
                            aTail := **Null** ◁Activity▷。 ☑

          False ⁞ theFirst **afterward** aHead := (aHead⊖Activity)⟦rest⟧ [?]§∎

Appendix 3. Inconsistency Robust Logic Programs

Logic Programs[81] can logically infer computational steps.

Forward Chaining

Forward chaining is performed using ⊢

("⊢"*Theory* *PropositionExpression*)
  Assert *PropositionExpression* for *Theory*.

("When" "⊢"*Theory* aProposition:*Pattern* "→" *Expression*)
  When aProposition holds for *Theory*, evaluate *Expression*.

Illustration of forward chaining:

⊢$_t$ Human[Socrates]▌

When ⊢$_t$ Human[x] → ⊢$_t$ Mortal[x]▌
will result in asserting Mortal[Socrates] for theory t

Backward Chaining

Backward chaining is performed using ⊩

("⊩"*Theory* aGoal:*Pattern* "→" *Expression*)
Set aGoal for *Theory* and when established evaluate *Expression*.

("⊩"*Theory* aGoal:*Pattern*):*Expression*
Set aGoal for *Theory* and return a list of assertions that satisfy the goal.

("When" "⊩"*Theory* aGoal:*Pattern* "→" *Expression*)
  When there is a goal that matches aGoal for *Theory*, evaluate *Expression*.

Illustration of backward chaining:
     ⊢$_t$ Human[Socrates]▮
     When ⊩$_t$ Mortal[x] → (⊩$_t$ Human[\$\$$x$] → ⊢$_t$ Mortal[x])▮
     ⊩$_t$ Mortal[Socrates]▮
will result in asserting Mortal[Socrates] for theory t.

SubArguments

This section explains how subarguments[i] can be implemented in natural deduction.
     When ⊩$_s$ (*psi* ⊢$_t$ *phi*) →
       Let t' ← extension.[t].
          ⊢$_{t'}$ *psi*,
          ⊩$_{t'}$ *phi* → ⊢$_s$ (*psi* ⊢$_t$ *phi*). ▮

Note that the following hold for t' because it is an extension of t:
- **when** ⊢$_t$ *theta* → ⊢$_{t'}$ *theta*▮
- **when** ⊩$_{t'}$ *theta* → ⊩$_t$ *theta* ▮

---
[i] See appendix on Inconsistency Robust Natural Deduction.

Aggregation using Ground-Complete Predicates

Logic Programs in ActorScript are a further development of Planner. For example, suppose there is a ground-complete predicate[82] Link[*aNode, anotherNode, aCost*] that is true exactly when there is a path from *aNode* to *anotherNode* with *aCost*.

When ⊩ Path[*aNode, aNode, aCost*]→
                 // when a goal is set for a cost between *aNode* and itself
⊢ *aCost*=0▮   // assert that the cost from a node to itself is 0

The following goal-driven Logic Program works forward from *start* to find the cost to *finish*: [83]
When ⊩ Path[*start, finish, aCost*]→
  ⊢ *aCost*=**Minimum** {*nextCost* + *remainingCost*
                 | ⊩ Link[*start, next*≠*start, nextCost*],
                    Path[*next, finish, remainingCost*]}▮
  // a cost from *start* to *finish* is the minimum of the set of the sum of the
  // cost for the next node after *start* and
  // the cost from that node to *finish*

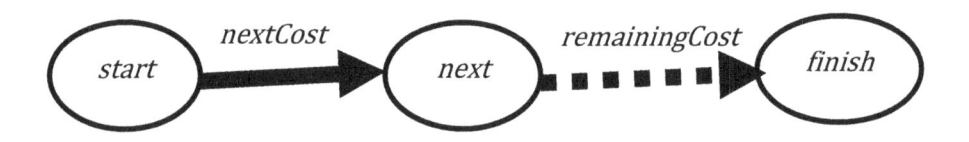

```
           nextCost              remainingCost
  start ─────────────▶   next  ▪ ▪ ▪ ▪ ▪▶  finish
```

The following goal-driven Logic Program works backward from *finish* to find the cost from *start*:
When ⊩ Path[*start, finish, aCost*]→
  ⊢ *aCost*= **Minimum** {*remainingCost* + *previousCost*
                 | ⊩ Link[*previous*≠*finish, finish, previousCost*],
                    Path[*start, previous, remainingCost*]}▮
  // the cost from *start* to *finish* is the minimum of the set of the sum of the
  // cost for the previous node before *finish* and
  // the cost from *start* to that Node

```
        remainingCost                previousCost
  start ▪ ▪ ▪ ▪ ▪▶  previous  ─────────────▶ finish
```

Note that all of the above Logic Programs work together concurrently providing information to each other.

Appendix 4. ActorScript Symbols with Readings. IDE ASCII, and Unicode code points

Symbol	IDE ASCII[i]	Read as	Category	Matching Delimiters	Unicode (hex)
▮	;;	end	top level terminator		32DA
:	:	of specified type	infix		
⸬	[:]	this Actor's aspect	prefix		2360
⊗	(<)	injection	infix		29C0
⊘	(>)	expression/ pattern projection	infix		29C1
↓	\/	resolve	prefix		2139
⊡	[.]	qualified by	infix		22A1
▪	.	is sent	infix		
▪▪	..	delegate to this Actor	prefix		
⊐	|_|	necessarily concurrent	prefix		29B7
↦	|->	message type returns type[84]	infix		21A6
|⋯>	|..>	cacheable message type returns type			
→	-->	message received[85]		¶	2192
←	<--	be[86]	infix		2190
◆	?	cases	separator	?	FFFD
☑	[\/]	alternative case	separator	◆ and ?	29B6
?	[?]	end cases	terminator	◆ and catch◆	2370
¶	\p	another message handler	separator for handlers	→	00B6
§	\s	end handlers	terminator	**implements**	00A7
⁏	(:)	case	separator for case		2982
●	_/	before	separator	Let bindings, Do preparations, Enqueue,	00C4
○	()	end	terminator	Do expressions and ⁏	FF61
≡	===[87]	defined as	infix		2261
≜	=/\=	to be	infix		225C
≔	:=	is assigned	infix		2254
$$	$$	matches value of[88]	prefix		

---

[i] These are only examples. They can be redefined using keyboard macros according to personal preference.

405

=	=	same as?	infix		
▤	[=]	keyword **or** field	infix		2338
:▤	:[=]	assignable field	infix		
◁	<|	begin type parameters	left delimiter	▷ (Unicode hex: 0077)	0076
∀	\\|/	spread[89]	prefix		2A5B
{	{	begin set	left delimiter	}	
|	[	begin list	left delimiter	]	
{|	{|	begin multi-set	left delimiter	]}	2983
⟦	[|	array reference	left delimiter	⟧ (Unicode hex: 27E7)	27E6
(	(	begin grouping	left delimiter	)	
⦅	(|	begin syntax	left delimiter	⦆ (Unicode hex: 2986)	2985
⊖	(-)	nothing[90]	expression		229D
←	<<–	one-way send	infix		219E
↠	–>>	one-way receive	infix	¶	21A0
⊔	|_|	join	infix		2294
⊑	[<=]	constrained by	infix		2291
⊒	[>=]	extends	infix		2292
⇒	==>	logical implication	infix		21E8
⇔	<=>	logical equivalence	infix		21D4
∧	/\	logical conjunction	infix		00D9
∨	\/	logical disjunction	infix		00DA
¬	-|	logical negation	prefix		00D8
⊢	|-	assert	prefix **and** infix		22A2
⊩	||-	goal	prefix **and** infix		22A9
//	//	begin 1-line comment	prefix	EndOfLine	
/*	/*	begin comment	prefix	*/	

Appendix 5. Grammar Precedence

In the diagram below, if there is no precedence relationship, then parentheses *must* be used.

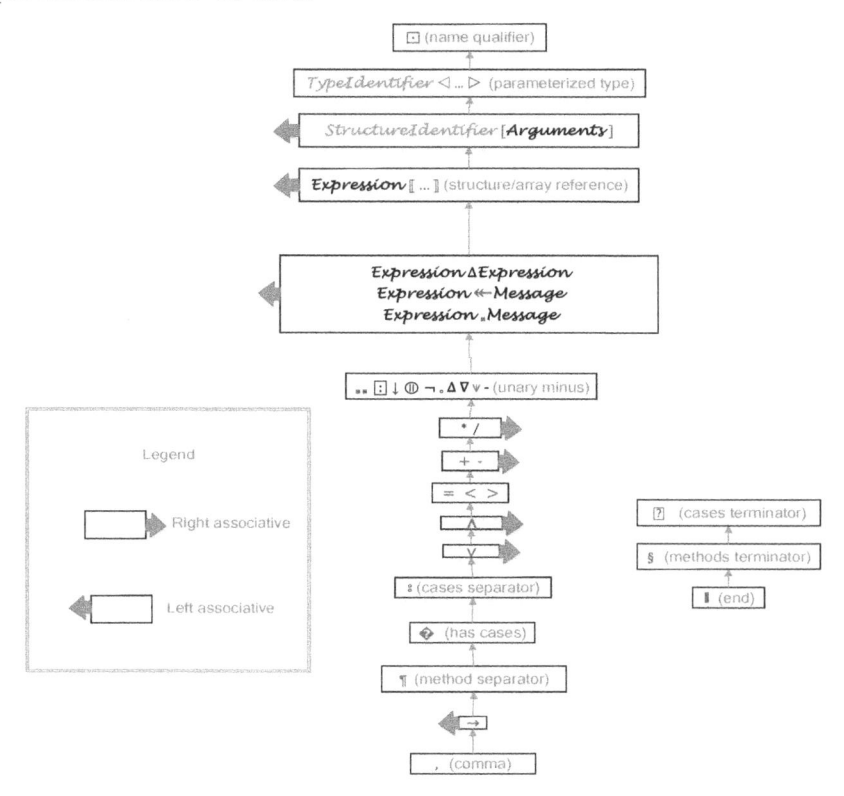

For example, parentheses *must* be used in the following examples:
- (t[p]).m[x]
- (x ❖ p1 ⁏ y1 ⁇) ❖ p2 ⁏ y2 ⁇

407

Type Discrimination, *i.e.*, Discrimination, ⊘ and ⊚

(**"Discrimination"** aDiscrimination **"between"**
  typeExpressions:*Expressions*◁Type▷ "."):*Definition* ≡
Actor implements Definition **using**
  eval[anEnvironment]→
    Let types:List◁Type▷ ←
                    typeExpressions.eval[anEnvironment].
      Let aDiscrimination[aType:Type] ≡
          aType∈types ❖
            True ⦂ DiscriminationInstance.[x, aType] ☑
            False ⦂ **Throw** NotADisciminant[aType] ⁇
        DiscriminationInstance.[x:aType, aType:Type] ≡
          Actor implements aDiscrimination **using**
            discriminate[anotherType]→
              anotherType ❖
                aType ⦂ x ☑
                else ⦂
                  Throw WrongDiscriminant[anotherType] ⁇,
  ((discrimination:*Expression*◁aDiscrimination▷
    "⊘" discriminant:*Expression*◁Type▷))
                        :*Expression*◁discriminant▷ ≡
    Actor implements Expression◁discriminant▷ **using**
      eval[anEnvironment]→
        (discrimination.eval[anEnvironment])
          .discriminate[discrimination
                        .eval[anEnvironment]],
  ((aPattern:*Pattern*◁aType▷
    "⊚" discriminant:*Expression*◁Type▷))
                        :*Pattern*◁aDiscrimination▷ ≡
    Actor implements Pattern◁aDiscrimination▷ **using**
      match[anActor:aType, anEnvironment]→
        apattern.match[anActor
                        ⊘(discriminant
                          .eval[anEnvironment]),
                        anEnvironment].
  Void▮

End Notes

[1] Quotation by the author from late 1960s.

[2] to use a reserved word as an identifier it could prefixed, *e.g.,* _actor

[3] The delimiters ⦅ and ⦆ are used to delimit program syntax with the character " and the character " to delimit tokens. For example, ⦅3 "+" 4⦆ is an expression that can be evaluated to 7. A special font is used for syntactic categories.

For example,
  ⦅x:*Numerical* "+" y:*Numerical*⦆:*Numerical*▮
  Numerical⊑*Expression*▮

Also,
  ⦅*Numerical* "-" *Numerical*⦆:*Numerical*▮
  ⦅"-" *Numerical*⦆:*Numerical*▮
  ⦅*Numerical* "*" *Numerical*⦆:*Numerical*▮
  ⦅*Numerical* "/" *Numerical*⦆:*Numerical*▮
  ⦅"**Remainder**" *Numerical* "/" *Numerical*⦆:remainder:*Numerical*▮
  ⦅"**QuotientRemainder**" *Numerical* "/" *Numerical*⦆
                    :[*Numerical, Numerical*]▮
  ⦅"True" ⊔ "False"⦆:*Expression* ◁Boolean▷▮
  ⦅*Expression*◁Boolean▷ "∧" *Expression*◁Boolean▷⦆
                    :*Expression* ◁Boolean▷▮
  ⦅*Expression* "∨" *Expression*⦆:*Expression* ◁Boolean▷▮
  ⦅"¬" *Expression*◁Boolean▷⦆:*Expression*◁Boolean▷▮
  ⦅"**Throw**" *Expression*⦆:*Expression*▮

[4] See explanation of syntactic categories above. A word must begin with an alphabetic character and may be followed by one or more numbers and alphabetic characters.

  Identifier⊑*Word*⊑*Expression*▮
      // an *Identifier* is a *Word,* which is a subcategory of *Expression*
  ⦅⦅*Expression*⊔*Definition*⊔*Judgment*⦆⦆ "▮"⦆:*Top*▮

[5] *Type*⊑*Expression* ◁Type▷▮
  ⦅ aType:*Type* ⦅ "↦"⊔ "|••>"⦆ anotherType:*Type*⦆:*Type*▮
  ⦅ "[" *Types* "]"⦆:*Type*▮
  ⦅ ⊔ *MoreTypes*⦆:*Types*▮
  ⦅*Type* ⊔ ⦅*Type* "," *MoreTypes*⦆⦆:*MoreTypes*▮

[6] ⦅*Identifier*◁aType▷ ⦅ ⊔ ⦅":" *Type*◁aType▷⦆⦆
      "≡" *Expressions* ◁aType▷⦆:*Definition* ◁Identifier▷▮

(((*Expression* ◁aType▷ (⊔ "₀")))
  ⊔ (*Expression* ("," ⊔ "●") *MoreExpressions* ◁aType▷))
                              :*Expressions* ◁aType▷ ∎

(((*Expression* ◁aType▷ "₀")
  ⊔ (*Expression* ("," ⊔ "●") *MoreExpressions* ◁aType▷))
                              :*MoreExpressions* ◁aType▷ ∎

[7] An overloaded procedure is one that takes different actions depending on the types of its arguments.

[8] Note the Symbols box provided by an Integrated Development Environment (IDE) above to make it easier to construct a program by selecting symbols from a context sensitive picker. Also an IDE can automatically provide syntax completion alternatives Analogous to **ctrl+space** in Eclipse, *etc.*.

[9] ("[" *ArgumentTypes* "]"
     ("↦" ⊔ "|⋯>") returnType: *TypeExpression*): *ProcedureSignature* ∎
ProcedureSignature ⊑ *Expression* ∎
   // signature for a procedure with *ArgumentTypes* and returnType
(⊔ *MoreArgumentTypes*): *ArgumentTypes* ∎
(*TypeExpression*
  ⊔ (*TypeExpression* "," *MoreArgumentTypes*))
                              :*MoreArgumentTypes* ∎
("Interface" *Identifier* ◁Type▷ "with"
    ProcedureSignatures "₀"): *ProcedureInterface* ∎
(⊔ *ProcedureSignature*
    (⊔ *MoreProcedureSignatures*)): *ProcedureSignatures* ∎

[10] ("[" *ArgumentDeclarations* "]" (⊔ (":" *Type* ◁aType▷))
    (⊔ ("**sponsor**" *Identifier* ◁Sponsor▷))
    "→" *Expression* ◁aType▷): *Procedure* ∎
Procedure ⊑ *Expression* ∎
   // Procedure with *ArgumentDeclarations* that returns
       // *Expression* of type returnType.
(⊔ *MoreDeclarations*): *ArgumentDeclarations* ∎
(*SimpleDeclaration* (⊔ ("," *MoreKeywordDeclarations*))
   ⊔ (*SimpleDeclaration* "," *MoreDeclarations*))
                              :*MoreDeclarations* ∎
   // Comma is used to separate declarations.
(((*Identifier*
   ⊔ (*Identifier* ":" *Expression* ◁Type▷))
   (⊔ "default" *Expression*)): *SimpleDeclaration* ∎
(*KeywordArgumentDeclaration*
   ⊔ (*KeywordDeclaration* "," *MoreKeywordDeclarations*))
                              :*MoreKeywordDeclarations* ∎
(*Keyword* "🗏" *SimpleDeclaration*)): *KeywordDeclaration* ∎

Keyword⊑*Word*▮

[11] The symbol ∎ is fancy typography for an ordinary period when it is used to denote message sending.

[12] (Recipient:*Expression* "∎" "[" *Arguments* "]"):*ProcedureSend*▮
ProcedureSend⊑*Expression*▮
   // Recipient is sent a message with *Arguments*
(⊔ *MoreArguments*):*Arguments*▮
(((*Expression* (⊔ ("," *MoreKeywordArguments*))))
      ⊔ (*Expression* "," *MoreArguments*)):*MoreArguments*▮
(*KeywordArgument*
   ⊔ (*KeywordArgument*
      "," *MoreKeywordArguments*)):*MoreKeywordArguments*▮
(*Keyword* "⊟" *Expression*):*KeywordArgument*▮
(*Identifier*◁Procedure▷ "∎" "[" *ArgumentDeclarations* "]"
   (⊔ (":" returntype:*Type* ◁aType▷))
   "="*Expressions*◁aType▷ "▮"):*Definition* ◁Procedure▷▮

[13] ⟨?⟩ takes care of the infamous "dangling else" problem [Abrahams 1966].

[14] (test:*Expression*◁patternType▷ "◆"
   ExpressionCases◁patternType, aType▷ "⟨?⟩"):*Expression* ◁aType▷▮
(*ExpressionCase* ◁patternType, aType▷
   ⊔ *MoreExpressionCases*◁patternType, aType▷)
                        :*ExpressionCases* ◁patternType, aType▷▮
(*ExpressionCase* ◁patternType, aType▷ ⊔
   (*ExpressionCase* ◁patternType, aType▷
                        "▽" *MoreExpressionCases* ◁patternType, aType▷)
   ⊔ *ExpressionElseCases*◁patternType, aType▷)
                        :*MoreExpressionCases* ◁patternType, aType▷▮
(⊔ *ExpressionElseCase* ◁patternType, aType▷
   ⊔ (*ExpressionElseCase* ◁patternType, aType▷
   "▽" *MoreExpressionElseCases*◁patternType, aType▷))
                        :*ExpressionElseCases*◁patternType, aType▷▮
(*ExpressionElseCase* ◁patternType, aType▷
   ⊔ (*ExpressionElseCase* ◁patternType, aType▷
   "▽" *MoreExpressionElseCases* ◁patternType, aType))
                        :*MoreExpressionElseCases* ◁patternType, aType▷▮
((("**else**" "⸱" *Expressions* ◁aType▷)
   ⊔ ("**else**" *Pattern* ◁patternType▷ "⸱" *Expressions* ◁aType▷))
                        :*ExpressionElseCase* ◁patternType, aType▷▮
   // The else case is executed only if the patterns before
      //   the else case do not match the value of test.
(*Pattern* ◁patternType▷ "⸱" *Expressions* ◁aType▷)
                        :*ExpressionCase* ◁aType▷▮

[15] (("**Let**" *MoreLetBindings* ".")
  result:*Expressions*◁aType▷):*Expression*◁aType▷∎
  // Bindings are independent of each other
  ((*LetBinding* ⊔ ((*LetBinding* "," *MoreBindings*)))
                                           :*MoreLetBindings*∎

  ((*LetBinding*
         ⊔ ((*LetBinding* ("," ⊔ "●") *MoreDependentLetBindings*)))
                                           :*MoreDependentLetBindings*∎
  // Each binding before a "●" is completed before its successors
  ((*Pattern* "←" *Expression*):*LetBinding*∎

[16] ((recipient:*Expression*
     "." *MessageName* "[" *Arguments* "]"):*NamedMessageSend*∎
  NamedMessageSend ⊑*Expression*∎
  // Recipient is sent message *MessageName* with *Arguments*
  MessageName⊑*Word*∎
  (("**Interface**" *Identifier*◁Type▷
          (⊔ (("extends" *Identifier*◁anotherType▷))) "with"
  MessageHandlerSignatures "."):*ActorInterface*∎
  ActorInterface ⊑*Definition*∎
  (⊔ *MoreMessageHandlerSignatures*))
                                 :*MessageHandlerSignatures*∎
  ((*MessageHandlerSignature*
        (⊔ *MoreMessageHandlerSignatures*))
                              :*MoreMessageHandlerSignatures*∎
  ((*MessageName* "[" *ArgumentTypes* "]" ("↦"⊔ "|••>")
     returnType:*TypeExpression*):*MessageHandlerSignature*∎
  MessageHandlerSignature ⊑*Expression*∎

[17] Dijkstra[1968] famously blamed the use of the goto as a cause and symptom of poorly structure programs. However, assignments are the source of much more serious problems.

[18] Continuations in ActorScript are related to continuations introduced in [Reynolds 1972] in that they represent a continuation of a computation. The difference is that a continuation of Reynolds is a procedure that takes as an argument the result of the preceding computation. Consequently, a continuation of Reynolds is closer to a customer in the Actor Model of computation.

[19] ("**Actor**" *ConstructorDeclaration ActorBody*):*Expression*▪
    // The above expression creates an Actor with
         // declarations for variables and message handlers
    (⊔ ("extends" *ConstructorList*)))))
    (⊔ "management" *Expression* ◁[aType]↦Manager▷)
    NamedDeclaration
    MessageHandlers
    InterfaceImplementations):*ActorBody*▪
(*Identifier* "[" *ArgumentDeclarations* "]")
                                        :*ConstructorDeclaration*▪
(*Constructor* (⊔ "₀")
    ⊔ (*Constructor* "," *MoreConstructors* "₀")):*ConstructorList*▪
(*Constructor*
    ⊔ (*Constructor* "," *MoreConstructors*)):*MoreConstructors*▪
(*ActorQueues NamesDeclarations*):*NamedDeclaration*▪
(⊔ (*MoreNameDeclarations* "₀")):*NamesDeclarations*▪
(*NameDeclaration*
    ⊔ (*NameDeclaration*
         "," *MoreNamesDeclarations*)):*MoreNameDeclarations*▪
(*Identifier*
    (⊔ (":" *Type* ◁aType▷))
    "←" *Expression* ◁aType▷):*IdentifierDeclaration*▪
IdentifierDeclaration ⊑ *NameDeclaration*▪
(*Variable* (⊔ (":" *Type* ◁aType▷))
    ":=" *Expression* ◁aType▷ *InstanceVariableAQualifications*)
                                        :*VariableDeclaration*▪
VariableDeclaration ⊑ *NameDeclaration*▪
Variable ⊑ *Word*▪
InstanceIVariableQualifications ⊑ *InstanceQualifications*▪
(⊔ *InstanceVariableQualification*
    ⊔ (*InstanceVariableQualification*
         InstanceIVariableQualifications)
                                        :*InstanceIVariableQualifications*▪
"nonpersistent" ⊑ *InstanceVariableQualification* ▪
         // A nonpersistent variable must be of type Nullable◁*aType*▷,
              // and can be nulled out before a message is received
("queues" *QueueNames* "₀") :*ActorQueues*▪
(*QueueName* ⊔ (*QueueName* "," *QueueNames*)):*QueueNames*▪
QueueName ⊑ *Word*▪
QueueName ⊑ *Expression* ◁Queue▷▪
("**Void**"):*Expression*▪

(⟨*InterfaceImplementation*
  (⊔ *MoreInterfaceImplementations*⟩⟩⟩
                                        :*InterfaceImplementations* ∎
(⟨"**also**" *InterfaceImplementation*
  (⊔ *MoreInterfaceImplementations*⟩⟩⟩
                                   :*MoreInterfaceImplementations* ∎
(((⊔ "**partially**")
  (⟨"**implements**" ⊔ "**reimplements**"⟩)
    (⊔ "**exportable**"⟩ *Type* ◁aType▷ "**using**"
      (⟨*MessageHandlers* "§"⟩⊔ *UniversalMessageHandler* ⟩
                         :*InterfaceImplementation* ◁aType▷ ∎
(⟨*MessagePattern*
  (⊔ ⟨":" *Type*⟩⟩⟩
  (⊔ ⟨"**sponsor**" *Identifier* ◁Sponsor▷⟩⟩⟩
  "→" *ExpressionsContinuation* ◁aType▷ ⟩
                         :*UniversalMessageHandler* ◁aType▷ ∎
(⊔ *MoreMessageHandlers* ⟩):*MessageHandlers* ∎
(⟨*MessageHandler*
  ⊔ ⟨*MessageHandler* "¶" *MoreMessageHandlers*⟩⟩⟩
                                   :*MoreMessageHandlers* ∎
    // The message handler separator is ¶.
(⟨*MessageName* "[" *ArgumentDeclarations* "]"
  (⊔ (":" returnType: *Type* ◁aType▷⟩
  (⊔ ⟨"**sponsor**" *Identifier* ◁Sponsor▷⟩⟩⟩
  "→" *ExpressionsContinuation* ◁aType▷⟩):*MessageHandler* ∎
    // For a message with *MessageName* with arguments,
        // the response is *Continuation*
(⟨*Expression* ◁aType▷
  "**afterward**" *Afterward* ⟩):*Continuation* ◁aType▷ ∎
    // Return *Expression* and afterward perform
        // *MoreVariableAssignments*
(⟨*VariableAssignment*
  ⊔ ⟨*VariableAssignment*
    "," *MoreVariableAssignments* "。"⟩⟩⟩
                                        :*VariableAssignments* ∎
(⟨*VariableAssignment*
  ⊔ ⟨*VariableAssignment*
    "," *MoreVariableAssignments*⟩⟩⟩
                                        :*MoreVariableAssignments* ∎
(⟨*Variable* ":=" *Expression* ◁aType▷⟩):*VariableAssignment* ◁aType▷ ∎

[20] ("Do" *MoreExpressions*
　　Continuation◁aType▷ "₀"):*Continuation* ◁aType▷ ▎
　　((Antecedent ⊔ (Antecedent ("," ⊔ "●") *MoreAntecedents*)))
　　　　　　　　　　　　　　　　　　　　　　:*MoreAntecedents* ▎

　　Expression ⊑ *Antecedent* ▎
　　StructureAssignment ⊑ *Antecedent* ▎
　　ArrayAssignment ⊑ *Antecedent* ▎

[21] For example, consider the following:
　Actor SimpleNeedTwo[ ]
　　queues waiting₀
　　hasOne := **False**₀
　　implements NeedTwo **using**
　　　[ ] → hasOne ◆ **True** ⸬ **Void permit** waiting ☑
　　　　　　　　　　　　False ⸬ **Enqueue** waiting
　　　　　　　　　　　　　　　　after hasOne := **True**●
　　　　　　　　　　　　Void[?]§▎

The following expression must return **Void** because of mandatory concurrency:
　Let aNeedTwo ← SimpleNeedTwo.[ ]₀
　　□aNeedTwo.[ ]●,
　　aNeedTwo.[ ]₀▎

However following expression might never return because of optional concurrency:
　Let aNeedTwo ← SimpleNeedTwo.[ ]₀
　　aNeedTwo.[ ]●,
　　aNeedTwo.[ ]₀▎

[22] ("□" anExpression:*Expression* ◁aType▷
　　(⊔ ("**sponsor**" *Expression* ◁Sponsor▷▎)):*Expression* ◁aType▷▎
　// Execute anExpression concurrently and respond with the outcome.
　// In every case, anExpression must complete before execution leaves
　//　the lexical scope in which it appears.

[23] The ability to extend implementation is important because it helps to avoid code duplication.

[24] *cf.* [Crahen 2002, Amborn 2004, Miller, et. al. 2011]

[25] equivalent to the following:
　myBalance▫SimpleAccount := myBalance▫SimpleAccount−anAmount

[26] ignoring exceptions in this way is *not* a good practice

[27] (("Enqueue" *QueueExpression* (⊔ "after" *Preparation*) "●"
  Continuation ⊲aType▷)))):*Continuation* ⊲aType▷∎
  /*
  1. Perform Preparation
  2. Enqueue activity in QueueExpression
  3. Leave the cheese
  4. When the cheese is re-entered perform Continuation . */
(("▪▪" *Message* ⊲aType▷)):*Expression* ⊲aType▷∎
  Delegate message to this Actor.
Cases can be continuations:
((test:*Expression* "◆"
  ContinuationCases ⊲patternType, aType▷ "❓")
                    :*Continuation* ⊲aType▷∎
((*ContinuationCase* ⊲patternType, aType▷
  ⊔ ((*ContinuationCase* ⊲patternType, aType▷
    "☑" *MoreContinuationCases* ⊲patternType, aType▷))
  ContinuationElseCases)
        :*ContinuationCases*⊲patternType, aType▷ ∎
((*ContinuationCase* ⊲patternType, aType▷
  ⊔ ((*ContinuationCase* ⊲patternType, aType▷
    "☑" *MoreContinuationCases* ⊲patternType, aType▷))
        :*MoreContinuationCases* ⊲patternType, aType▷∎
((*Pattern*⊲patternType▷ "₰"
  ExpressionsContinuation⊲patternType, aType▷)
        :*ContinuationCase* ⊲ patternType, aType▷∎
(⊔
  MoreContinuationElseCases ⊲patternType, aType▷)
        :*ContinuationElseCases* ⊲patternType, aType▷∎
((*ContinuationElseCase* ⊲patternType, aType▷
  ⊔ ((*ContinuationElseCase* ⊲patternType, aType▷
    "☑" *MoreContinuationElseCases* ⊲patternType, aType▷))
        :*MoreContinuationElseCases* ⊲patternType, aType▷∎
((("else" "₰" *ExpressionsContinuation*⊲aType▷)
  ⊔ ("else" *Pattern*⊲patternType▷ "₰"
    ExpressionsContinuation⊲patternType, aType▷))
        :*ContinuationElseCase* ⊲patternType, aType▷∎
(((*Continuation* (⊔ "₀"))
  ⊔ (*Expression* ("," ⊔ "●") *MoreExpressionsContinuation*))
        :*ExpressionsContinuation*∎
(((*Continuation* "₀")
  ⊔ (*Expression* "," *MoreExpressionsContinuation*))
        : *MoreExpressionsContinuation*∎
[28] Swiss cheese was called "serializers" in the literature.

[29] ReadersWriterConstraintMonitor defined below monitors a resource and throws an exception if it detects that ReadersWriter constraint is violated, *e.g.*, for a resource r using the above scheduler:
                ReadingPriority[ReadersWriterConstraintMonitor[r]].

Actor ReadersWriterConstraintMonitor[theResource:ReadersWriter]
    writing := **False**,
    numberReading:(Integer **thatIs** ≥0) := 0,
    implements ReadersWriter **using**
      read[query]→
        Preconditions ¬writing。
          Hole theResource.read[query]
            after numberReading++

            afterward numberReading--¶
      write[update]→
        Preconditions numberReading=0, ¬writing。
          Hole theResource.write[update]
            after writing := **True**

            afterward writing := **False** §∎

[30] A downside of this policy is that readers may not get the most recent information.

[31] A downside of this policy is that writing and reading may be delayed because of lack of concurrency among readers.

[32] ("**Enqueue**" *QueueExpression*
    (⊔ "backout" *Expressions*)
    (⊔ "after" *Preparation*) "●"
    Continuation ◁aType▷)))):*Continuation* ◁aType▷∎
  /*
      1. Perform *Preparation*
      2. Enqueue activity in *QueueExpression*
      3. Leave the cheese
      4. When the cheese is re-entered perform *Continuation*. */
("∎∎" *Message* ◁aType▷):*Expression* ◁aType▷∎
// Delegate message to this Actor.
Cases can be continuations:
((test:*Expression*◁patternType▷ "◆"
    ContinuationCases ◁patternType, aType▷ "⁇")
                                  :*Continuation* ◁aType▷∎
((*ContinuationCase* ◁patternType, aType▷
    ⊔ *MoreContinuationCases*◁patternType, aType▷)
                :*ContinuationCases* ◁patternType, aType▷∎

(*ContinuationCase* ◁patternType, aType▷ ⊔
    (*ContinuationCase* ◁patternType, aType▷
            "☒" *MoreContinuationCases* ◁patternType, aType▷)
    ⊔ *ContinuationElseCases*◁patternType, aType▷)
                :*MoreContinuationCases* ◁patternType, aType▷▮
(⊔ *ContinuationElseCase* ◁patternType, aType▷
    ⊔ (*ContinuationElseCase* ◁patternType, aType▷
            "☒" *MoreContinuationElseCases*◁patternType, aType▷))
                :*ContinuationElseCases*◁patternType, aType▷▮
(*ContinuationElseCase* ◁patternType, aType▷
    ⊔ (*ContinuationElseCase* ◁patternType, aType▷
            "☒" *MoreContinuationElseCases* ◁patternType, aType))
                :*MoreContinuationElseCases* ◁patternType, aType▷▮
((("**else**" "⸭" *ContinuationList*◁aType▷)
    ⊔ ("**else**" *Pattern*◁patternType▷
            "⸭"*ExpressionsContinuation*◁aType▷)))
                :*ContinuationElseCase* ◁patternType, aType▷▮
// The else case is executed only if the patterns before
//   the else case do not match the value of test.
(*Pattern* ◁patternType▷ "⸭" *ExpressionsContinuation*◁aType▷)
                :*ContinuationCase* ◁patternType, aType▷▮

[33] Preconditions present for inconsistency robustness.
[34] ++ is postfix increment
[35] -- is postfix decrement
[36] Preconditions present for inconsistency robustness.
[37] The following are allowed in the cheese for a response to message affecting the next message:
    (*Expression* ◁aType▷
        (⊔ ("**permit**" aQueue:*Expression*)))
        (⊔ ("**afterward**" *Afterward*)))):*Continuation* ◁aType▷▮
        /* If there are activities in *aQueue*, then the one of them gets the cheese next and also perform *Afterward*, then leave the cheese and return the value of *Expression*. /*
    The following can be used temporarily leave the cheese:
    ("**Hole**" *Expression*◁aType▷):*Continuation* ◁aType▷▮
        /*
            1. Leave the cheese
            2. The response is the result of evaluating *Expression* */
    ("**Hole**" *Expression*◁aType▷
        (⊔ ("**after**" *Preparation*)))):*Continuation* ◁aType▷▮
        /*
            1. Carry out *Preparation*
            2. Leave the cheese
            3. The result is the result of evaluating *Expression* */

(("Hole" Expression◁aType▷
  (⊔ ("after" Preparation)))
  (⊔ ("afterward" Afterward)):Continuation ◁aType▷∎
  /*
  1. Carry out Preparation
  2. Leave the cheese
  3. Evaluate Expression
  4. When a response is received, reacquire the cheese, carry out Afterward and the result is the result of evaluating Expression */
(("Hole" Expression◁anotherType▷
  (⊔ ("after" Preparation)))
  (⊔ ("returned◆"
    normal:ContinuationCases ◁anotherType, aType▷ "⁇")))
  (⊔ ("threw◆"
    exceptional:ContinuationCases ◁anotherType, aType▷ "⁇")))
                :Continuation ◁aType▷∎
  /*
  1. Carry out Preparation
  2. Leave the cheese
  3. Evaluate Expression
  4. When a response is received, reacquire the cheese
   • If Expression returns, continue using the returned Actor with normal.
   • If Expression throws an exception, continue using the exception with exceptional. */

[38] ((Identifier◁Type▷
  "◁" ParametersDeclarations"▷"
    "≡" Expressions)):ParameterizedDefinition∎
ParameterizedDefinition⊑Definition∎
// Parameterize definition with ParametersDeclarations∎
(⊔ MoreParameterDeclarations)):ParametersDeclarations∎
((ParameterDeclaration
  ⊔ (ParameterDeclaration
    "," MoreParameterDeclarations)))
                :MoreParameterDeclarations∎
((Identifier◁Type▷ (⊔ Qualifier))):ParameterDeclaration∎
(⊔ ("extends" Identifier◁Type▷)):TypeQualifier∎
((Identifier◁Type▷ "◁" Parameters"▷")):TypeExpression∎
((Identifier◁Type▷
  ⊔ (⊔ (Identifier◁Type▷ "," Parameters))):Parameters∎
[39] (("Discrimination" Identifier◁Type▷
  MoreTypeDescriminations"。")):Expression ◁Type▷∎

⦅Identifier◁Type▷
    ⊔ ⦅Identifier◁Type▷ "," MoreTypeDescriminations⦆⦆
                                    :MoreTypeDescriminations∎
⦅Expression ◁aDiscriminationType▷ "⊖" Type ◁aType▷⦆
                                    :Expression ◁aType▷∎
    // Discriminate to have the type Type ◁aType▷ if possible.
    // Otherwise, an exception is thrown.
⦅Pattern ◁aDiscriminationType▷ "⊖" Type ◁aType▷⦆
                                    :Pattern ◁aType▷∎
    // If matching Actor is a discrimination that can be discriminated
    // then Pattern must match the discriminate.
⦅"⊖⊖" Type ◁aType▷⦆:Pattern ◁aType▷∎
    // Matching Actor must be discrimination that can be
    // discriminated as aType

40 ⦅Identifier◁Type▷ "[" Arguments "]"⦆:Expression ◁aType▷∎
⦅Identifier◁Type▷ "[" Patterns "]"⦆:Pattern ◁aType▷∎

41 ⦅"**Structure**" Identifier◁Type▷ "[" FieldDeclarations "]"
    ⦅ ⊔ ⦅ "**extends**" ConstructorList ⦆⦆
    NamedDeclaration
    MessageHandlers
    MoreInterfaceImplementations⦆:Definition∎
    // Structure definition with StructureImplementation
⦅ ⊔ MoreFieldDeclarations ⦆:FieldDeclarations∎
⦅⦅SimpleFieldDeclaration
                    ⦅ ⊔ ⦅ "," MoreNamedFieldDeclarations⦆⦆⦆
        ⊔ ⦅SimpleFieldDeclaration
            "," MoreFieldDeclarations⦆⦆:MoreFieldDeclarations∎
⦅⦅Identifier
    ⊔ ⦅Identifier ":" TypeExpression⦆⦆
        ⦅ ⊔ "default" Expression⦆⦆:SimpleFieldDeclaration∎
⦅NamedFieldDeclaration
    ⊔ ⦅NamedFieldDeclaration
        "," MoreNamedFieldDeclarations⦆⦆
                                    :MoreNamedFieldDeclarations∎
⦅FieldName
    ⦅"▤" ⊔ ":▤"⦆ SimpleFieldDeclaration⦆⦆
                                    :NamedFieldDeclaration∎
FieldName ⊑ QualifiedName∎
    // ":▤" is used for assignable fields.
⦅⦅ ⊔ Identifier⦆ ActorBody⦆:StructureImplementation∎
⦅Expression "⟦" FieldName "⟧" ⦆:FieldSelector∎
    // FieldName of Expression which must be a structure
FieldSelector ⊑ Expression∎

(*StructureName* "[" *FieldExpressions* "]"):*StructureExpression* ▮
StructureExpression ⊑ *Expression* ▮
(⊔ *MoreFieldExpressions*):*FieldExpressions* ▮
(((*SimpleFieldExpression* (⊔ ("," *MoreNamedFieldExpressions*))))
    ⊔ (*SimpleFieldExpression*
        "," *MoreFieldExpressions*))):*MoreFieldExpressions* ▮
(*NamedFieldExpression*
  ⊔ (*NamedFieldExpression*
       "," *MoreNamedFieldExpressions*))
                              :*MoreNamedFieldExpressions* ▮
(*FieldName*
    ("▤" ⊔ ":▤") *SimpleFieldExprression*))
                                      :*NamedFieldExpression* ▮
(*StructureName* "[" *FieldPatterns* "]"):*StructurePattern* ▮
StructurePattern ⊑ *Pattern* ▮
(⊔ *MoreFieldPatterns*):*FieldPatterns* ▮
(((*SimpleFieldPattern* (⊔ ("," *MoreNamedFieldPatterns*))))
  ⊔ (*SimpleFieldPattern* "," *MoreFieldPatterns*))
                                      :*MoreFieldPatterns* ▮
(*NamedFieldPattern*
  ⊔ (*NamedFieldPattern*
       "," *MoreNamedFieldPatterns*))
                                      :*MoreNamedFieldPatterns* ▮
(*FieldName* ("▤" ⊔ ":▤") *SimpleFieldExprression*))
                                       :*NamedFieldPattern* ▮
[42] ("**Try**" anExpression:*Expression* ◁aType▷
    "catch◆" *ExpressionCases* ◁Exception, aType▷ "⌸")
                                  :*Expression* ◁aType▷ ▮
  /*
- If anExpression throws an exception that matches the pattern of a case, then the value of *TryExpression* is the value computed by *ExpressionCases*
- If anExpression doesn't throw an exception, then then the value of *TryExpression* is the value computed by anExpression. /*

(**"Try"** anExpression:*Expression* ◁aType▷
  "catch◆" *ContinuationCases* ◁Exception, aType▷ "[?]")
                              :*Continuation* ◁aType▷ ∎
  /*
  • If anExpression throws an exception that matches the pattern of a case, then the response of *TryContinuation* is the response computed by the expression of the case.
  • If aContinuation doesn't throw an exception, then then the response of *TryExpression* is the response computed by anExpression. */
(**"Try"** anExpression:*Expression* ◁aType▷
  "cleanup" cleanup:*Expression* ◁aType▷):*Expression* ◁aType▷ ∎
  */
  • If anExpression throws an exception, then the value of *TryExpression* is the value computed by cleanup.
  • If anExpression doesn't throw an exception, then then the value of *TryExpression* is the value computed by anExpression. */

[43] (**"Preconditions"** test:*Expressions Expressions*):*Expression* ∎
  // Each of expressions in test must evaluate to **True** or
  //   an exception is thrown
(**"Preconditions"** *Expressions ExpressionsContinuation*)
                              :*Continuation* ∎
  // Each of expressions in *Expressions* must evaluate to **True** or
  //   an exception is thrown
(value:*Expression* ◁aType▷
  "postcondition" pre:*Expression* ◁[aType]↦Boolean▷)
                              :*Expression* ◁aType▷ ∎
  // The expression pre must evaluate to **True** when sent value
  //   or an exception is thrown

[44] ° is a reserved postfix operator for degrees of angle
[45] i.e., i∗i=−1 where i is the imaginary number **Cartesian**[0, 1]
[46] (**"["** *ComponentExpressioons* **"]"**):*Expression* ◁List▷ ∎
  // An ordered list with elements *ComponentExpressions*
(⊔ *MoreComponentExpressioons*):*ComponentExpressioons* ∎
((((⊔ "▼") *Expression*)
  ⊔ (((⊔ "▼") *Expression*
    "," *MoreComponentExpressioons*)))
                              :*MoreComponentExpressioons* ∎
(**"["** *TypeExpressions* **"]"**):*TypeExpression* ∎
(⊔ *MoreTypeExpressions*):*TypeExpressions* ∎
(*TypeExpression* ⊔ (*TypeExpression* "," *MoreTypeExpressions*))
                              :*MoreTypeExpressions* ∎

[47] (**"_"**):*UnderscorePattern* ∎

$UnderscorePattern \sqsubseteq Pattern$ ▮
$Identifier \sqsubseteq Pattern$ ▮
$(Pattern \text{ "suchThat" } Expression):SuchThat$ ▮
$SuchThat \sqsubseteq Pattern$ ▮
$(Pattern \text{ "thatIs" } Expression):ThatIs$ ▮
$ThatIs \sqsubseteq Pattern$ ▮
$(\text{"\$\$"} Expression \triangleleft Type \triangleright):Pattern \triangleleft Type \triangleright$ ▮
$(\text{"["} ComponentPatterns \text{"]"}):Pattern \triangleleft List \triangleright$ ▮
 // A pattern that matches a list whose elements match
   // $ComponentPatterns$
$(\ \sqcup\ MoreComponentPatterns):ComponentPatterns$ ▮
$(Pattern$
  $\sqcup (\text{"\textbackslash"} Pattern\ )$
  $\sqcup (Pattern \text{","} MoreComponentPatterns))$
                               $:MoreComponentPatterns$ ▮

[48] $(\text{"\{"} ComponentExpressioons \text{"\}"}):Expression \triangleleft Set \triangleright$ ▮
  // A set of Actors without duplicates
$(\text{"\{"} ComponentPatterns \text{"\}"}):Pattern \triangleleft Set \triangleright$ ▮

[49] $(\text{"\{|"} ComponentExpressioons \text{"|\}"}):Expression \triangleleft Multiset \triangleright$ ▮
  // A multiset of the Actors with possible duplicates
$(\text{"\{|"} ComponentPatterns \text{"|\}"}):Pattern \triangleleft Multiset \triangleright$ ▮

[50] Optimization of this program is facilitated because:
- The records are cacheable because their type is Set⊲ContactRecord▷
- All of the operators are cacheable
- The operators are annotated as cacheable using "|··>"

[51] $(\text{"Map"} \text{"\{"} ComponentExpressioons \text{"\}"}):Expression \triangleleft Map \triangleright$ ▮

[52] It is possible to define a procedure that will produce a "bottomless" future. For example, $f_\bullet[\ ]$:Future⊲aType▷ $\equiv$ **Future** $f_\bullet[\ ]$ ▮

[53] (**Postpone** $Expression \triangleleft aType \triangleright$ ▮ $):Expression \triangleleft Future \triangleleft aType \triangleright \triangleright$ ▮
  // postpone execution of the expression until the value is needed.

[54] $(\text{"Future"} aValue:Expression \triangleleft aType \triangleright$
   $(\ \sqcup (\text{"sponsor"} Expression \triangleleft Sponsor \triangleright)))$
                               $:Expression \triangleleft Future \triangleleft aType \triangleright \triangleright$ ▮
  // A future for aValue.
$(\text{"↓"} Expression \text{Future} \triangleleft aType \triangleright \triangleright):Expression \triangleleft aType \triangleright \triangleright$ ▮
  // Resolve a future

[55] $(LoopName:Identifier \text{"."} \text{"["} Initializers \text{"]"}$
   $(\ \sqcup\ (\text{":"} ReturnType:aType\ ))$
     $\text{"≜"} Expression \triangleleft aType \triangleright\ ):Expressions \triangleleft aType \triangleright$ ▮
$(\ \sqcup\ MoreInitializers):Initializers$ ▮
$(Initializer \sqcup (Initializer \text{","} MoreInitializers))$
                               $:MoreInitializers$ ▮
$(Identifier (\ \sqcup (\text{":"} TypeExpression))) \text{"←"} Expression):Initializer$ ▮

[56] The implementation below requires careful optimization.

[57] ("String" "[" *ComponentExpressioons* "]"):*Expression* ◁String▷ ▮
   ("String" "[" *ComponentPatterns* "]"):*Pattern* ◁String▷ ▮

[58] (recipient:*Expression* ◁recipientType▷
   "." message:*MessageExpression* ◁recipientType▷):*Expression* ▮
   // Send recipient the message

[59] /* A **Postpone** expression does not begin execution of Expression$_1$ until a request is received. Illustration:
   IntegersBeginningWith.[n:Integer]:◁FutureList◁Integer▷ ≡
      [n, ∀**Postpone** IntegersBeginningWith.[n+1]] ▮
   Note: A **Postpone** expression can limit performance by preventing concurrency */

[60] ("(" *MoreGrammers* ")"):*Grammar* ▮
   ("(" *Grammar* "⊔" *Grammar* ")"):*Grammar* ▮
   (*ReservedWord* (⊔ *StartsWithIdentifier*)):*StartsWithReserved* ▮
   StartsWithReserved ⊑ *MoreGrammers* ▮
   (*Identifier* (⊔ *StartsWithReserved*))):*StartsWithIdentifier* ▮
   StartsWithIdentifier ⊑ *MoreGrammers* ▮
   ("\"" *Word* "\""):*ReservedWord* ▮
   // The use of \ escapes the next character in a string so
   //   that "\"" has just one character that is ".
   (*Grammar* ":" *GrammarIdentifier* "▮"):*Judgment* ▮
   (*Identifier* ◁Grammar▷ "⊑" *Identifier* ◁Grammar▷ "▮"):*Judgment* ▮

[61] The implementation below can be highly inefficient.

[62] (("**Atomic**" aLocation:*Expression*
      "**compare**" comparison:*Expression*
      "**update**" update:*Expression* "◆"
      "**updated**" "⦂"
         compareIdentical:*ExpressionsContinuation*◁aType▷ "☑"
      "**notUpdated**" "⦂"
         compareNotIdenticial:*ExpressionsContinuation*◁aType▷ "❓")
            :*Continuation* ◁aType▷ ▮
   /* Atomically compare the contents of aLocation with the value of comparison. If identical, update the contents of aLocation with the value of update and execute compareIdentical.

[63] (*Identifier* "◌" *Qualifier*):*QualifiedName* ▮
   QualifiedName ⊑ *Expression* ▮
   Identifier ⊑ *QualifiedName* ▮
   (*Identifier* ⊔ (*Identifier* "◌" *Qualifier*)):*Qualifier* ▮

[64] ("**Enumeration**" *Identifier* ◁Type▷
   MoreEnumerationNames "."):*Definition* ▮

⟦*EnumerationName*
   ⊔ ⟦*EnumerationName*
        "," *MoreEnumerationNames*⟧⟧
                                    :*MoreEnumerationNames* ∎
EnumerationName ⊑ *Word* ∎

[65] Declarations provide version number, encoding, schemas, *etc.*
[66] If a customer is sent more than one response (i.e., return or throw message) then it will throw an exception to the sender of the response.
[67] ⟦recipient:*Expression*
   "←" *MessageName* "[" *Arguments* "]"⟧:*Expression* ◁**Void**▷ ∎
   /* recipient is sent one-way message with *MessageName* and *Arguments*. Note that *Expression* ◁⊖▷ cannot be used to produce a value. */
[68] ⟦*MessageName* "[" *ArgumentDeclarations* "]"
        ⟦ ⊔ ⟦"**sponsor**" *Identifier*◁Sponsor▷ ⟧▷⟧⟧
   "↠" *ExpressionsContinuation*◁⊖▷⟧:*MessageHandler* ∎
   /* one-way message handler implementation with *ArgumentDeclarations* that has a one-way continuation that returns nothing */
⟨"⊖" ⟦ ⊔ ⟦"**permit**" aQueue:*Expression*⟧⟧
   ⟦ ⊔ ⟦"**afterward**" *Assignments*⟧⟧⟧:*Continuation* ◁"⊖"▷ ∎

[69] Hoare[1962]. The implementation below is adapted from Wikipedia.
[70] // Move Actor at pivotIndex to end
[71] /* Consider a dialect of Lisp which has a simple conditional expression of the following form:
   ⟦"(" "**if**" test:*Expression* then:*Expression* else:*Expression* ")" ⟧
which returns the value of then if test evaluates to **True** and otherwise returns the value of else.
   The definition of Eval in terms of itself might include something like the following [McCarthy, Abrahams, Edwards, Hart, and Levin 1962]:
   (Eval expression environment) ≡
                       // Eval of expression using environment defined to be
      (if (Numberp expression)   // if expression is a number then
        expression   // return expression else
      (if ((Equal (First expression) (**Quote** if))
                             // if First of expression is "**if**" then
        (if (Eval (First (Rest expression) environment)
                        // if Eval of First of Rest of expression is **True** then
          (Eval (First (Rest (Rest expression)) environment)
                 // return Eval of First of Rest of Rest of expression else
          (Eval (First (Rest (Rest (Rest expression))) environment))
                 // return Eval of First of Rest of Rest of Rest of expression
   ...))

The above definition of Eval is notable in that the definition makes use of the conditional expressions using **if** expressions in defining how to evaluate an **if** expression! */

[72] The implementation CheeseQ uses activities to implement its queue where for type Activity the following holds:
Structure Activity[previous :▤ Nullable◁Activity▷,
// if null then head of queue else,
// pointer to backwards list to head
nextHint :▤ Nullable◁Activity▷]❚
// if non-null then pointer to next
// activity to get cheese after this one

[73] If non-null points to head with current holder of cheese

[74] If non-null, pointer to backwards list ending with head that holds cheese

[75] **Interface** CheeseQ **with** enter[ ] ↦ **Void**,
leave[ ] ↦ **Void**₀ ❚

[76] // enter message received running myActivity

[77] /* this cheese queue is not empty because myActivity is at the head of the queue */

[78] **Interface** SubCheeseQ **with** head[ ] ↦ Activity❚

[79] **Interface** InternalQ **with** enqueueAndLeave[ ] ↦ **Void**,
enqueueAndDequeue[InternalQ] ↦ Activity,
dequeue[ ] ↦ Activity,
empty?[ ] ↦ Boolean₀ ❚

[80] **Interface** SubInternalQ **with** add[Activity] ↦ **Void**,
remove[ ] ↦ Activity₀ ❚

[81] [Church 1932; McCarthy 1963; Hewitt 1969, 1971, 2010; Milner 1972, Hayes 1973; Kowalski 1973]. Note that this definition of Logic Programs does *not* follow the proposal in [Kowalski 1973, 2011] that Logic Programs be restricted only to clause-syntax programs.

[82] A ground-complete predicate is one for which all instances in which the predicate holds are explicitly manifest, *i.e.*, instances can be generated using patterns. See [Ross and Sagiv 1992, Eisner and Filardo 2011].

[83] Execution can proceed differently depending on how sets fit into computer storage units.

[84] Used in type specifications for interfaces.

[85] Used in message handlers.

[86] Used to bind identifiers in **Let**.

[87] Three equal signs because two equal signs have a meaning in Java

[88] Used in patterns.

[89] Used in structures.

[90] Used in one-way message passing.

Part 3

Applications

Some Types of Inconsistency in Legal Reasoning

Anne v.d.L. Gardner, gardner.anne@sbcglobal.net

Abstract. This paper considers three kinds of inconsistency that may be encountered in the course of deciding a legal case: inconsistent findings of fact; inconsistent statutes; and inconsistent judicial opinions. The method is a case study. All the examples are drawn from a case in the United States Supreme Court on which the author worked for several years. The paper responds to Hewitt's call for identifying and exploring the consequences of inconsistencies in robust information systems.

Introduction
Consistency matters in the law. We expect statutes to be consistent with the Constitution; we expect judicial decisions to be consistent with statutes, the Constitution, and judicial precedents. In many matters, we expect the law to be consistent with common sense.

But in a controversial case, it can be very unclear what consistency requires. Legal sources, written in natural language, are open to interpretation. The set of premises for reasoning is open-ended. It may happen that consistency with the authorities seems to require one decision, yet we feel that that decision would be unjust, or absurd, or otherwise wrong. The way out, ideally, is to find previously unarticulated premises – perhaps some overriding principle – that can yield both a satisfying decision and a coherent explanation.

There is a huge literature on these matters. An excellent general introduction is Schauer's *Thinking like a Lawyer* (2009). Some other good entry points are Fuller's *The Morality of Law* (1969) and Posner's *The Problems of Jurisprudence* (1990). Fuller, in his first two chapters, identifies eight requirements for a well-functioning legal system. Two of these concern consistency directly ("Contradictions in the Laws," pp. 65-70, and "Constancy of the Law through Time," pp. 79-81), and several others implicate consistency too. Posner, in his introduction, boils the history of jurisprudence down to fifteen pages, and he titles his first chapter "Law as Logic, Rules, and Science."

This paper will consider three specific kinds of inconsistency that may be encountered in the course of deciding a legal case: inconsistent findings of fact; inconsistent statutes; and inconsistent judicial opinions. The method is a case study. All the examples will be drawn from a case in the United States Supreme Court on which the author worked for several years.

The case in question was *United States v. Alaska,* 521 U.S. 1 (1997). Both the state and the federal government claimed ownership of submerged lands just off Alaska's north coast, in the Beaufort and Chukchi seas. The question mattered because the government that owned the submerged lands would be the one able to decide whether to permit offshore oil drilling and, if so, to issue leases and collect royalties. The suit was initially filed in the Supreme Court, as the Constitution authorizes.[1] The Court, following its usual practice in such cases, appointed a Special Master, who heard the case and reported back to the Court.[2] The Court then heard argument on the parties' exceptions to the Master's report and issued its 1997 decision. The author's work was with the Special Master, Associate Dean J. Keith Mann of the Stanford Law School.

Inconsistent findings of fact: The legal background
There is a general rule, based on statutes, treaties, and cases, that each state owns certain submerged lands. These include lands under the state's navigable inland waters, such as lakes, rivers, and certain coastal features such as tidelands and bays. They also include the submerged lands out to three miles from the state's coastline. But what counts as navigable inland waters, and exactly where does the coastline lie?[3]

This problem arose along one stretch of the coast near Prudhoe Bay, where a string of barrier islands creates a formation known as Stefansson Sound (figure 1). The United States said that each island had its own coastline and its own three-mile belt (figure 2). Alaska said that the coastline was a continuous line along the seaward side of the islands, with straight-line segments between adjacent islands that were no more than ten miles apart. Everything landward of this line would then be inland waters belonging to Alaska, and the state's three-mile belt would be measured seaward from this line.

---

[1] Article III, section 2, clause 2 provides, "In all Cases . . . in which a State shall be Party, the supreme Court shall have original jurisdiction. . . ."
[2] United States v. Alaska, No. 84, Original, Report of the Special Master, March 1996 (565 pages). The report is available in some law libraries or from Anne Gardner.
[3] For an excellent introduction to this area of the law, see Shalowitz 1962. Shalowitz's two-volume work has now been supplemented by a third volume, Reed 2000, which includes an extensive review of the Alaska case. All three volumes are available at http://www.nauticalcharts.noaa.gov/hsd/shalowitz.html.

A similar problem had come up in a 1985 case involving islands along the Gulf Coast in Alabama and Mississippi (figure 3).[4] The Supreme Court there held that Mississippi Sound was inland water. In the opinion, it made a statement of great importance to Alaska: that from at least 1903 to 1961, the United States had a publicly stated "policy of enclosing as inland waters those areas between the mainland and off-lying islands that were so closely grouped that no entrance exceeded 10 geographical miles."[5] For short, let's call this the *ten-mile rule*.

The Master concluded that the Supreme Court's 1985 statement was wrong, and the Supreme Court agreed! How does this work?

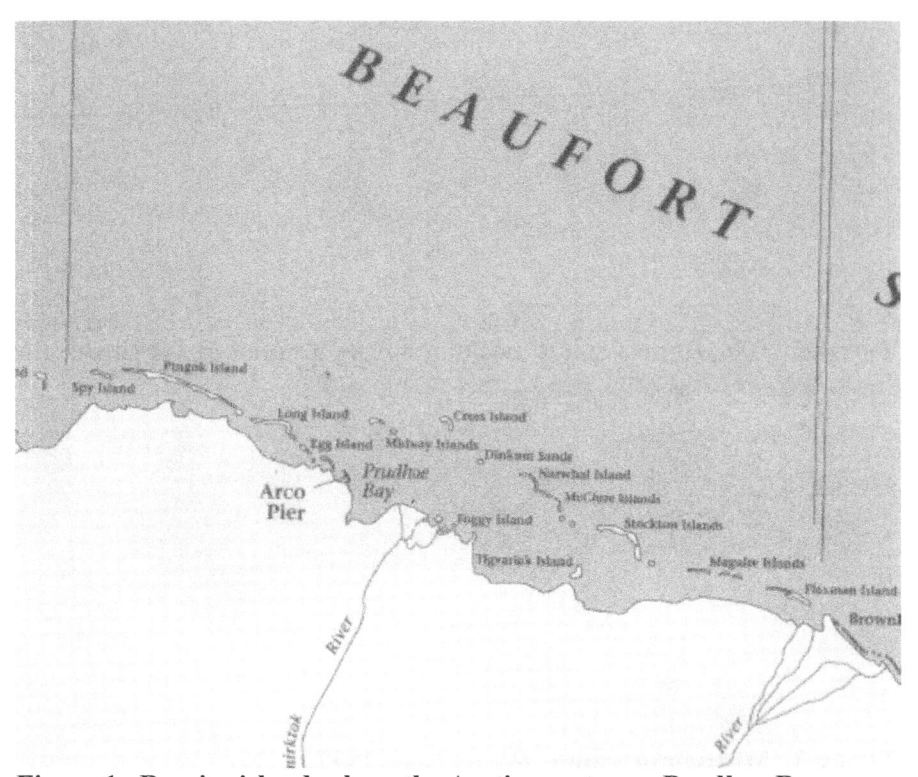

Figure 1. Barrier islands along the Arctic coast near Prudhoe Bay. The stretch of coastline shown is about 100 miles long.

---

[4] United States v. Louisiana (Alabama and Mississippi Boundary Case), 470 U.S. 93 (1985).
[5] 470 U.S. at 106-07.

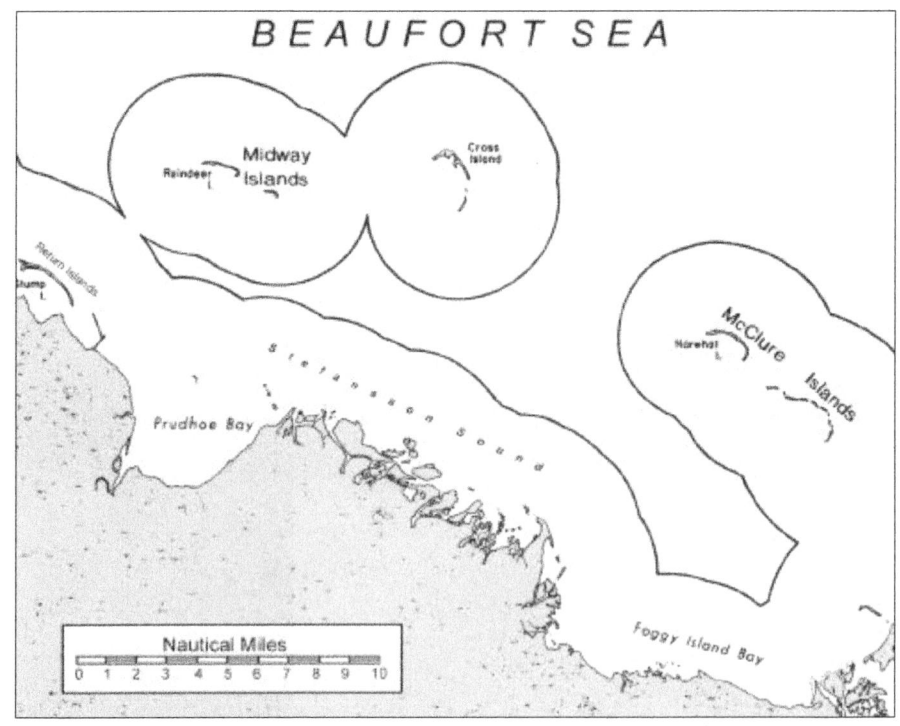

Figure 2. The United States' position on the location of the three-mile limit. (From Reed 2000, p. 332.)

Figure 3. Mississippi Sound. (From Reed 2000, p. 78.)

Handling inconsistent findings
First, there is a basic distinction between findings of fact and conclusions of law. A court's conclusion of law is normally binding on lower courts in future cases. Findings of fact, on the other hand, depend on the evidence in the particular case. They may bind the parties to the lawsuit, but not the world at large. In the Alaska case, both sides agreed that where the United States has historically drawn its coastline is a question of fact, not of law.

If this were the whole story, it would seem to follow that the Court's 1985 statement was simply irrelevant to the new case. But there is a doctrine cutting the other way. Suppose the case of *A v. B* has found P to be a fact. A new case arises, *A v. C*, in which P is again at issue. The doctrine of *collateral estoppel* says that once a court has decided an issue necessary to its judgment, that decision is conclusive in a later suit involving a party to the prior litigation.[6] In our situation, the United States was a party to both the 1985 Gulf Coast decision and the current Alaska case. Hence, Alaska might have been in a position to insist it could use the 1985 statement of the ten-mile rule as a premise in making its own case now. The United States would be estopped from contesting that premise.

But again, there are exceptions. One is that collateral estopped generally cannot be used against the United States. The Court has explained that in some such situations, inconsistent decisions can be a good thing:

> [T]he Government is more likely than any private party to be involved in lawsuits against different parties which nonetheless involve the same legal issues.
>
> A rule allowing nonmutual collateral estoppel against the Government ... would substantially thwart the development of important questions of law by freezing the first final decision rendered on a particular legal issue. Allowing only one final adjudication would deprive this Court of the benefit it receives from permitting several courts of appeals to explore a difficult question before this Court grants certiorari. . . . Indeed, if nonmutual estoppel were routinely applied against the Government, this Court would have to revise its practice of waiting for a conflict to develop before granting the Government's petitions for certiorari. . . .
>
> . . . .
>
> . . . We think that our conclusion will better allow thorough development of legal doctrine by allowing litigation in multiple forums. Indeed, a contrary result might disserve the economy interests in whose name estoppel is advanced by requiring the Government to abandon virtually any exercise of discretion in seeking to review judgments unfavorable to it.[7]

---

[6] United States v. Mendoza, 464 U.S. 154 (1984); Restatement (Second) of Judgments § 27 (1982).
[7] United States v. Mendoza, 464 U.S. at 160, 163.

The explanation just quoted from *United States v. Mendoza* is relevant to the theme of inconsistency robustness. It is not, however, particularly relevant to the Alaska case. In *Alaska,* it was a question of fact that had already been litigated, not a question of law. And there was no potential for conflicting decisions by different Circuit Courts of Appeals. The fact finder in both cases was the Supreme Court itself.

So there were two courses open to Alaska. It could argue that the Court should create an exception to *Mendoza*, or it could set out to prove the ten-mile rule from scratch. Alaska took the second course before the Special Master. When that failed, it argued both alternatives before the Supreme Court.

Why couldn't Alaska re-prove the ten-mile rule? The evidence was mostly documentary and was much the same in both cases. The Special Master in the earlier case had not attempted to give a precise statement of the ten-mile rule. In oral argument before the Supreme Court, counsel for Mississippi and Alabama each offered formulations of the rule. The Court's 1985 opinion used Mississippi's version—while Alabama's version would have been much less favorable to Alaska. The version the Court used turned out not to hold up under a more careful analysis.

Equally important to the outcome was the fact that the ten-mile rule did not have quite the same role in both cases. That is, the states had different theories of their cases. For Mississippi Sound, the states' theory was that the waters were inland because they qualified as a historic bay. Historic bays are a special category, requiring proof that the coastal nation has exercised sovereignty over the area for an extended period of time and has done so with the acquiescence of foreign nations. Thus, there was also a good deal of historical evidence regarding Mississippi Sound, including its use as an intracoastal waterway and the fortification of one of the islands bordering the Sound.

Alaska, in contrast, did not claim to be able to show that Stefansson Sound was a historic bay. There was no evidence that the United States had made any particularized claim to the Sound. Rather, the idea was that the ten-mile rule was so well established at the relevant times as to make inland waters of any body of water that met the rule's requirements.

This difference led to the Court's refusal to hold the United States estopped from challenging the 1985 assertion of the ten-mile rule:

> [W]e see no reason to develop an exception to *Mendoza* here. Even if the doctrine [of collateral estoppel] applied against the Government in an original jurisdiction case, it could only preclude relitigation of issues of fact or law *necessary* to a court's judgment. . . . A careful reading of the *Alabama and Mississippi Boundary Case* makes clear that the Court did not attach controlling significance to any general delimitation formula.[8]

The key idea is that a statement in a judicial opinion is not binding if it was not necessary to the decision. Here, that idea meant that collateral estoppel did not apply and the United States could relitigate the existence of the ten-mile rule. Where the statement is one of law rather than of fact, the idea is phrased in terms of the *holding* or the *ratio decidendi* of a case, which is binding, as opposed to *obiter dictum*, which is not.

Of course, there are plenty of problems about deciding what statements were essential to the decision.[9] Nevertheless, the idea goes a long way toward limiting the set of statements whose consistency we need to worry about.

Inconsistent statutes

In another part of the Alaska case, the interaction between two statutes required interpretation. The Pickett Act (1910) said, roughly, that P is permitted. The Alaska Right of Way Act (1898) said, roughly, that Q Is forbidden.[10] The two statutes appeared to deal with different subject matter, but the facts of the Alaska case were in the extensions of both P and Q.

Such conflicts are often viewed in terms of three maxims: *lex superior* (the higher law prevails), *lex posterior* (the later law prevails), and *lex specialis* (the more specific law prevails).[11]

The first of these is written into the Constitution and is applied every time a statute is held unconstitutional. Article VI provides:

> This Constitution, and the Laws of the United States which shall be made in Pursuance thereof; and all Treaties made, or which shall be made, under the Authority of the United States, shall be the supreme Law of the Land; and the Judges in every State shall

---

[8] 521 U.S. at 13-14.
[9] See, for example, Schauer 2011, pp. 54-57, 180-84; Eisenberg 1988, pp. 50-76, and the essays in Goldstein 1987. An AI approach is reported in Branting 1994, 2000, 2003.
[10] Pickett Act, ch. 421, 36 Stat. 847 (1910); Alaska Right of Way Act, § 2, ch. 299, 30 Stat. 409 (1898).
[11] For example, see Eskridge, Frickey, and Garrett 2006, pp. 281-284.

be bound thereby, any Thing in the Constitution or Laws of any State to the Contrary notwithstanding.

This provision, known as the Supremacy Clause, was no help in the Alaska case. Both the Pickett Act and the Alaska Right of Way Act were acts of Congress.

The other two maxims are better considered as heuristics rather than rules. As applied to our case, they conflicted with each other. The Alaska Right of Way Act, passed in 1898, was quite specific. The Pickett Act, passed in 1910, was very general. The Special Master's report found one way out of the dilemma; the Supreme Court found a different way. Both reached the same conclusion. To explain the two ways of dealing with the inconsistency, it becomes necessary to delve into the legal details. If there is a general lesson from the details, it is that important inconsistencies have to be addressed individually, by going deeply into the particular legal and factual situation of the case.

The conflicting statutes

The general problem was the ownership of submerged lands in the National Petroleum Reserve–Alaska, an area of some 23 million acres in the northwest corner of the state. The Reserve had been created from federally owned lands in 1923, by an executive order of President Warren G. Harding, with the purpose of securing a source of oil for the Navy.[12] As authority for the reservation, including the reservation of submerged lands, the United States relied on the 1910 Pickett Act. It said:

> [T]he President may, at any time in his discretion, temporarily withdraw from settlement, location, sale, or entry any of the public lands of the United States including the District of Alaska and reserve the same for water-power sites, irrigation, classification of lands, or other public purposes to be specified in the orders of withdrawals, and such withdrawals or reservations shall remain in force until revoked by him or by an Act of Congress.[13]

But Alaska said a federal reservation of submerged lands would be inconsistent with the 1898 Right of Way Act. This act extended the homestead laws to Alaska, granted right of way through federal lands for railroads in Alaska, and added that lands under navigable waters should be held in trust for the people of any future state:

---

[12] Exec. Order No. 3797-A (Feb. 27, 1923).
[13] § 1, 36 Stat. 847 (1910).

> [N]othing in this Act contained shall be construed as impairing in any degree the title of any State that may hereafter be erected out of said District, or any part thereof, to tide lands and beds of any of its navigable waters, or the right of such State to regulate the use thereof, nor the right of the United States to resume possession of such lands, *it being declared that all such rights shall continue to be held by the United States in trust for the people of any State or States which may hereafter be erected out of said District.* [Emphasis added.][14]

Resolution through an older rule

After lengthy consideration of the history, the Special Master found that the Pickett Act was intended to authorize reservation of submerged lands, with no special exception for Alaska. As for the Alaska Right of Way Act, the Master noted that the italicized language codified a preexisting nonstatutory principle. The general principle, as stated in a carefully considered Supreme Court case in 1894, was that

> the navigable waters, and the soils under them . . . being chiefly valuable for the public purposes of commerce, navigation and fishery . . . shall not be granted away during the period of territorial government; but, unless in case of some international duty or public exigency, shall be held by the United States in trust for the future States . . . .[15]

The exceptions in the "unless" clause here had not been acknowledged in the Right of Way Act version. Another phrasing of the exceptions, two pages earlier in the 1894 opinion, said the United States could make grants of submerged lands in a territory if necessary to "perform international obligations," to facilitate foreign and interstate commerce, or "to carry out other public purposes appropriate to the objects for which the United States hold the Territory."[16]

The Special Master noted that the exceptions had also been recognized in recent Supreme Court cases; that creating a petroleum reserve was a public purpose, and that Alaska's interpretation would mean the President was not authorized to do anything with Alaska's submerged lands even in response to an "international duty or public exigency."[17] So the general language of

---

[14] § 2, 30 Stat. 409 (1898).
[15] *Shively v. Bowlby,* 152 U.S. 1, 49-50 (1894).
[16] 152 U.S. at 48.
[17] Special Master's report at 414-15.

the later statute prevailed, authorizing the President to establish the Reserve. Further, when Alaska became a state in 1959, the submerged lands remained in federal hands because of a specific provision in the Alaska Statehood Act.[18]

Resolution through a later enactment
The Supreme Court reached the same result on a simpler ground, using only the last provision mentioned and not referring to the Alaska Right of Way Act at all. The Court said that even if Alaska was correct in arguing that the President had no authority to include submerged lands in the Reserve in 1923, the Executive Order made clear the intent to include them. When Congress passed the Alaska Statehood Act in 1958, it was aware of the Order, and it included a special section in the Statehood Act acknowledging the United States' ownership of the Reserve. By this means it ratified the inclusion of submerged lands in the Reserve.[19] Thus, we can view ratification of a previously questionable action as another cure for inconsistency.[20]

Inconsistent options
Sometimes inconsistency lies in the eye of the beholder. The point is illustrated by another part of the Alaska case, this one dealing with the Arctic National Wildlife Refuge (ANWR) (figure 4). The Refuge lies in the northeast corner of Alaska. Like the areas discussed earlier, it has barrier islands along the coast. As with the Petroleum Reserve, the question was what submerged lands were included in the Refuge.

---

[18] Special Master's report at 430-40; Alaska Statehood Act, Pub. L. No. 85-508, § 11(b), 72 Stat. 339, 347 (1958).
[19] United States v. Alaska, 521 U.S. at 43-45.
[20] Compare Fuller 1969, pp. 51-55, on curative laws as a species of retroactive laws.

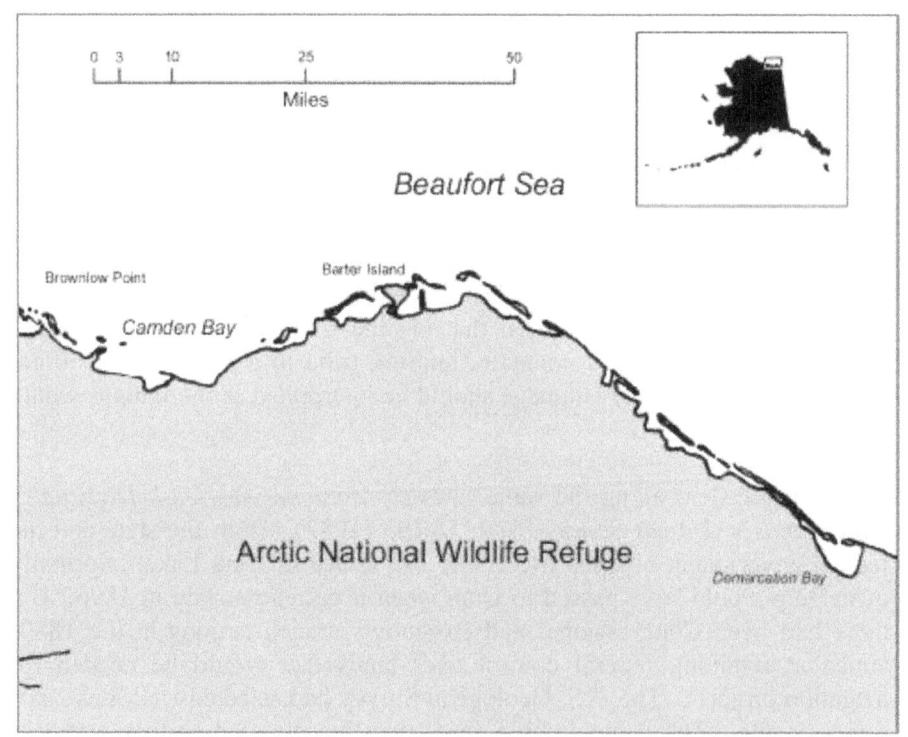

Figure 4. The Arctic National Wildlife Refuge (from Reed 2000, p. 40).

The Special Master found that the northern boundary of the Refuge ran along the seaward side of the islands.[21] Still, it was necessary to consider the principle, mentioned in the last section, that submerged lands normally go to a new State upon its admission to the Union. Two recent Supreme Court decisions had applied that principle. In *Montana v. United States,* 450 U.S. 544 (1981), the dispute concerned ownership of the bed of a river that ran through an Indian reservation. The reservation had been created from federal lands while Montana was still a territory. In holding that the Crow Tribe did not own the bed of the Big Horn River, the Court explained:

> [B]ecause control over the property underlying navigable waters is so strongly identified with the sovereign power of government, it will not be held that the United States has conveyed such land except because of "some international duty or public exigency." A court deciding a question of title to the bed of a navigable water must, therefore, begin with a strong presumption against conveyance by the United States, and must not infer such a conveyance "unless the intention was definitely declared or

---

[21] Special Master's report at 495.

otherwise made plain," or was rendered "in clear and especial words," or "unless the claim confirmed in terms embraces the land under the waters of the stream."[22]

Here, the Court said, the language of the treaty creating the reservation was not strong enough to overcome the presumption against conveyance of the riverbed, and there was no "public exigency" because the Crows "were a nomadic tribe dependent chiefly on buffalo, and fishing was not important to their diet or way of life."[23] The three dissenters (Justices Blackmun, Brennan, and Marshall) objected that (1) the United States was trying to convert the Crow from a nomadic, hunting tribe to a settled, agricultural people and (2) the treaty language should be interpreted as the Indians would have understood it.

Another precedent along the same lines as *Montana* was *Utah Division of State Lands v. United States,* 482 U.S. 193 (1987). Both the state and the federal government claimed ownership of the bed of Utah Lake. Normally ownership would have passed to Utah when it became a state in 1896. But there had been Congressional and Executive Branch actions in the 1880s aimed at retaining federal control over lands that would be needed for irrigation projects. The U.S. Geological Survey had selected Utah Lake as a reservoir site. The Court held, 5 to 4, that the lake bed had nevertheless become Utah's property at statehood. In the majority opinion, Justice O'Connor found that the documents did not show a clear intent to reserve the lake bed or to defeat the future state's claim to the submerged lands. For the dissenters, Justice White wrote that the majority's argument was "singularly unpersuasive" (p. 212) and "quite strange" (p.219), and he complained of the "majority's skewed interpretation of the pertinent statutes and administrative reports" (p. 216).

Given these precedents, the Special Master in *United States v. Alaska* was at some pains to take seriously the state's claim that it owned the beds of the lagoons and rivers inside the boundary of ANWR. It was clear that these areas served the purposes of the wildlife refuge: they were described as providing habitat for polar bears, Arctic foxes, seals, and whales. The problem was one of timing. An application to create an Arctic Wildlife Range was filed with the Secretary of the Interior in 1957, while Alaska was still a territory. Then Congress passed the Alaska Statehood Act in 1958, and a presidential proclamation admitting Alaska to the Union followed in January 1959. The Secretary of the Interior did not approve the application

---

[22] 450 U.S. at 552 (majority opinion by Stewart, J.). Citations omitted.
[23] 450 U.S. at 556.

until nearly two years later, in December 1960.[24] So, the Special Master asked, what would have happened if the Secretary had turned down the application? The dry lands covered by the application would have remained federal property in any case. The submerged lands, assuming the application was sufficient to prevent their passage to Alaska at statehood, would also have remained federal property—for no good reason. If the submerged lands were not going to be part of a wildlife refuge, federal retention would not be justified by a public purpose, much less "some international duty or public exigency."[25] Accordingly, the Master recommended that this issue be decided in favor on Alaska.

This time, the Supreme Court disagreed. Justice O'Connor, again writing for the majority, expressed concern that "the Master's approach arguably calls into question federal ownership of *uplands* as well as submerged lands within the Range."[26] So the Court held that the entire Wildlife Range, both submerged lands and uplands, had remained federal lands after Alaska's statehood.

Justice O'Connor had first raised the issue of the uplands at oral argument, where it came as a surprise to both the parties and the Special Master. The Master's report had said specifically, "The parties agree that the upland parts of the Arctic National Wildlife Range remained in federal ownership after Alaska's statehood."[27] Alaska repeated this position at oral argument and again in a subsequent letter to the Court. (See 521 U.S. at 60.)

Both the Court's reasoning and the Master's reasoning involved an intricate interplay of statutes, regulations, and common law doctrine. Consistency can be sought along various dimensions.

Consistency of approach

One line of analysis would begin with the presumption that federal submerged lands become state property when the state enters the Union. Then we could ask, are the cases consistent in how easy or difficult they make it to overcome the presumption? The verbal tests were generally consistent (although with some variation in phrasing): there must be a clear intention to reserve submerged lands in a territory, the reservation must serve a public purpose, and it must be clear that the reservation was intended

---

[24] The name of the Range was changed to "Arctic National Wildlife Refuge" in 1980. Alaska National Interest Lands Conservation Act, Pub. L. No. 96-487, § 303(2)(A), 94 Stat. 2371, 2390 (1980).
[25] Special Master's report at 459-62.
[26] 521 U.S. at 48.
[27] Special Master's report at 451.

to persist even after the territory becomes a state.[28] The application of the tests is another matter. The majorities in *Utah* and *Montana*, it seems to me, stretched hard to find in favor of the states, and they made no effort to answer the dissenters' objections. In *Alaska*, it seems to me that Justice O'Connor stretched hard to find against the state.

Justice O'Connor reconciled her *Alaska* opinion with *Montana* and *Utah* mainly in terms of the purposes of the reservations:

> In *Montana*, we reasoned that a conveyance of a beneficial interest in submerged lands beneath a river on the Crow Reservation would not have been necessary to achieve the Government's purpose in creating the reservation, because fishing was not important to the Crow Tribe's way of life. . . . Similarly, in *Utah Div. of State Lands*, we concluded that the Federal Government could prevent settlers from claiming lands adjacent to waters suitable for reservoir sites and could control the development of those waters, even if lands beneath the waters in question passed to the State. . . . Here, in contrast, the statement of justification accompanying the 1957 Bureau of Sport Fisheries and Wildlife application demonstrated that waters within the boundaries of the Range were an essential part of the habitats of the species the Range was designed to protect, and that retention of lands underlying those waters was critical to the Government's goal of preserving these aquatic habitats.[29]

The explanation works at a high level, but it assumes that many disputed intermediate conclusions have been accepted.

Consistency of results

Another approach to reconciling the cases might start by asking, what result intuitively seems right in each situation? For *Alaska* the answer is easy. Almost everybody likes polar bears, and there was evidence that polar bears make their dens in the lagoon areas under dispute. So of course the lagoons should be part of the reservation. In *Utah*, recognizing the federal claim to the lake bed was perhaps less appealing because, although the site had been reserved for a reservoir, it had apparently never been used for that purpose. Instead, when the lawsuit began, the federal government was issuing oil and gas leases on the bed of Utah Lake.[30] In *Montana*, the Indians' case was also

---

[28] The third requirement was first stated in *Utah*, 482 U.S. at 502.
[29] 521 U.S. at 52.
[30] See *Utah v. United States*, 780 F.2d 1515, 1516 (10th Cir. 1985), *reversed sub nom. Utah Div. of State Lands v. United States*, 482 U.S. 193 (1987).

less sympathetic than it might have been. Some of the lands on the reservation had been sold by tribe members to non-Indians, and the tribe now wanted to regulate (or prohibit) hunting and fishing by nonmembers of the tribe on the lands it no longer owned. Tribal ownership of the riverbed would have helped toward this end, but it was not the purpose for which the reservation was created initially.

While this approach might account for the results the Court wanted to reach, it does not provide a legitimate justification. If the documents establishing property rights became effective at time t, their proper interpretation depends on the facts at time t and not on things that happened years later. More generally, there are deep problems concerning the relationship between a court's desired outcome and the justification given in its opinion. Traditionally the opinion was assumed to reflect the court's actual reasoning. When it was recognized that extralegal considerations might have a role, one solution was to distinguish between a logic of discovery and a logic of justification. The first permits unconstrained thinking about the right result, while the second requires that opinions conform to legal norms. More radically, judicial opinions may be dismissed as mere rationalizations of results reached on other grounds, and law treated as mere politics. Schauer (2009) provides a good summary (ch. 7) and considers the implications for opinion-writing (ch. 10).

Consistency within an opinion

Finally, we can consider whether an opinion is internally consistent. In *Alaska*, as noted earlier, Justice O'Connor was concerned mainly about ownership of the uplands in ANWR.

The general rule, given in section 5 of the Alaska Statehood Act, said that the United States would retain title to all property it held before Alaska's admission to the Union, while the State of Alaska would acquire title to all property held by the Territory of Alaska or its subdivisions. The Act made several exceptions to this rule. One provided the usual exception that a new state normally becomes the owner of lands under navigable inland waters (section 6(m)). Another dealt specifically with fisheries and wildlife (section 6(e)):

> All real and personal property of the United States situated in the Territory of Alaska which is specifically used for the sole purpose of conservation and protection of the fisheries and wildlife of Alaska, under the provisions of [certain named statutes], shall be transferred and conveyed to the State of Alaska by the appropriate Federal agency . . . . *Provided,* That such

transfer shall not include lands withdrawn or otherwise set apart as refuges or reservations for the protection of wildlife . . . .

If the establishment of ANWR had been completed before statehood, the proviso would have retained it as federal land. The Special Master had found that the application to create ANWR did not bring the lands under the proviso. The application did, by virtue of an Interior Department regulation, "set apart" the lands, but it was not enough to set them apart "as refuges or reservations for the protection of wildlife." Thus the uplands covered by the application would remain federal property under the general rule of section 5, and the submerged lands would go to Alaska under section 6(m).

Justice O'Connor, in contrast, said the application was enough to bring the lands within the proviso.[31] Otherwise, she said, even the uplands would have gone to Alaska:

> Unless all lands—submerged lands and uplands—covered by the application were "set apart" within the meaning of the proviso to § 6(e), they would have passed to Alaska under the main clause of § 6(e).[32]

Thus, she asserted the application caused the lands to be "specifically used for the sole purpose of conservation and protection of the fisheries and wildlife of Alaska" even if it did not "set [them] apart as refuges or reservations for the protection of wildlife." This seems to me to be contradictory.

But contradictions in natural-language reasoning can be hard to pin down. The ontology is not fixed; the background knowledge is not all stated. In the example here, at least three interpretive questions went unaddressed:

    1. What is the relationship between the main clause and the proviso to section 6(e)? The parties and the Special Master assumed they described possibly overlapping sets. Justice O'Connor assumed it was a subset relationship, so that the proviso did not become relevant unless the main clause was satisfied.

    2. What is the role in the main clause of the phrase "under the provisions of [certain named statutes]"? Only one of these statutes, the Alaska Game Law, was conceivably relevant. For Justice O'Connor's argument to hold up, it must be the case that the application to create ANWR

---

[31] 521 U.S. at 59-60.
[32] Id. at 61.

caused the lands to be "specifically used for the sole purpose of conservation and protection of the fisheries and wildlife of Alaska, under the provisions of the Alaska game law of July 1, 1943 (57 Stat. 301; 48 U.S.C., secs. 192-211), as amended." Yet the Alaska Game Law was not mentioned in the application for the wildlife range, the Interior Department order granting the application, or any of the related documents in the record.

   3. What means are there for lands to be "withdrawn or otherwise set apart as refuges or reservations for the protection of wildlife"? Justice O'Connor said the words "otherwise set apart" would be superfluous on the Special Master's interpretation. But that assumes that the ANWR situation is the only possible situation satisfying "otherwise set apart as refuges or reservations for the protection of wildlife." One would need expertise in the terminology and practices of public land law to know whether that is true.

There may have been a cleaner way to achieve the result of protecting the aquatic wildlife in ANWR. Alaska suggested in a brief that, even if the state were held to own the submerged lands, the United States would still have some ability to control their use.[33] The state cited two cases, one upholding a federal prohibition of duck hunting on state waters inside Voyageurs National Park,[34] and the other upholding federal limitations on motorboats and snowmobiles on state waters within the Boundary Waters Canoe Area Wilderness.[35] However, this line of argument was not pursued.

Conclusion

Carl Hewitt complains that large information systems face pervasive inconsistencies and typically try to sweep them under the rug. My conclusion is that the law provides a better source of examples of this phenomenon than it does of solutions. Indeed, the latest order by the Supreme Court (as of July 4, 2014) has a dissenting Justice Sotomayor complaining about inconsistency with a decision rendered three days earlier:

> Those who are bound by our decisions usually believe they can take us at our word. Not so today. After expressly relying on the availability of the religious-nonprofit accommodation to hold that the
> contraceptive coverage requirement [of the Affordable Care Act] violates [the Religious Freedom Restoration Act of 1993], as applied to closely held for-profit corporations, the Court now, as

---

[33] Supplemental Reply Brief before the Special Master, pp. 20-21.
[34] United States v. Brown, 552 F.2d 817 (8th Cir.), cert. denied, 431 U.S. 949 (1970).
[35] Minnesota ex rel. Alexander v. Block, 660 F.2d 1240 (8th Cir.), cert. denied, 455 U.S. 1007 (1982).

the dissent in *Hobby Lobby* feared it might, . . . retreats from that position. That action evinces disregard for even the newest of this Court's precedents and undermines confidence in this institution.[36]

Solid technical reasoning in law is important. How far it is sufficient, when political consensus is lacking, is another question.[37]

References

Branting, L. Karl. 2003. A Reduction-Graph Model of Precedent in Legal Analysis. *Artificial Intelligence* 150, 59-95.

Branting, L. Karl. 2000. *Reasoning with Rules and Precedents: A Computational Model of Legal Analysis.* Dordrecht: Kluwer.

Branting, L. Karl. 1994. A Computational Model of Ratio Decidendi. *Artificial Intelligence and Law* 2, 1-31.

Eisenberg, Melvin Aron. 1988. *The Nature of the Common Law.* Cambridge: Harvard University Press.

Eskridge, William N., Jr., Philip P. Frickey, Elizabeth Garrett. 2006. *Legislation and statutory interpretation.* 2nd ed. New York: Foundation Press.

Fuller, Lon L. 1969. *The Morality of Law.* Rev. ed. New Haven: Yale University Press.

Goldstein, Laurence (ed.). 1987. *Precedent in Law.* Oxford: Clarendon Press.

Posner, Richard A. 1990. *The Problems of Jurisprudence.* Cambridge: Harvard University Press.

Reed, Michael W. 2000. *Shore and Sea Boundaries,* vol. 3. Washington: U.S. Department of Commerce.
http://www.nauticalcharts.noaa.gov/hsd/shalowitz.html.

Schauer, Frederick. 2009. *Thinking like a Lawyer: A New Introduction to Legal Reasoning.* Cambridge: Harvard University Press.

Shalowitz, Aaron L. 1962-64. *Shore and Sea Boundaries.* 2 vols. Washington: U.S. Department of Commerce.
http://www.nauticalcharts.noaa.gov/hsd/shalowitz.html.

---

[36] Wheaton College v. Burwell, 573 U. S. ____ (July 3, 2014).
[37] Cf. Posner 1990, pp. 424-33, on the decline of law as an autonomous discipline.

Rules versus Standards: Competing Notions of Inconsistency Robustness in the Supreme Court and Federal Circuit[#]

Stefania Fusco[‡] and David Olson[†]

Inconsistency robustness in court systems

Inconsistency robustness is a paradigm shift in thinking about information system performance. Inconsistency robustness recognizes that modern, complex information systems must perform notwithstanding persistent and continuous inconsistencies. The focus on inconsistency robustness encourages designers and administrators to recognize the reality of persistent inconsistency when building robust systems that can perform reliably. The focus on inconsistency robustness is a shift from the previous dominant paradigm that sought to solve inconsistencies via inconsistency denial or inconsistency elimination.

Because inconsistency robustness is a new paradigm, the literature about it is only beginning to develop. Thus, we think it is useful to set out our definition of inconsistency robustness at the outset of this position statement. We understand the inconsistency robustness paradigm to situate a system designer so that she operates with a clear-eyed view of the costs and benefits of reducing inconsistencies within the legal system. In other words, we understand the inconsistency robustness paradigm as a "reminder" to a system designer that the ultimate goal is not inconsistency elimination *per se*, but rather a cost efficient inconsistency reduction. This means that the system designer knows that creating an inconsistency-free legal system is a quite unrealistic task, and that, sometimes, even attempting just to reduce inconsistency may not be worth the costs entailed. Consequently, a system designer working within the inconsistency robustness paradigm strives to *manage* inconsistency with a significant appreciation for the costs and benefits of reducing particular inconsistencies, i.e. with a significant appreciation for the value of designing a system so as to be robust in the face of inconsistency that is not able to be reduced, or not worth the cost of reduction.

While inconsistency robustness has great applicability to computing and information systems design and operation, it is also applicable to systems generally. And indeed, many complex systems have been practicing some form of inconsistency robustness for centuries, even if they did not use the terminology. One such complex system that must deal with inconsistency is a legal system. Of course, in this later case one cannot speak in the same precise terms in which one describes inconsistency in mathematical or computing systems. Indeed, the legal "code" is not as precise as computer programming codes, because it is written in prose, which is inherently more nuanced, and therefore more open to multiple interpretations. Also, the application of legal code to the multivariate affairs of humans gives even more complexity to the inconsistency robustness analysis.

Court systems, like complex computer systems, constantly face questions as to what is the state of things, or what is the correctness of a contention. Courts also face legal questions as to which of a number of competing legal rules could apply in a given situation. Often, the policies underlying the competing legal rules are inconsistent with each other and pull the court in different directions. Consequently, courts work in contexts in which significant inconsistency is present, and in which decisions about inconsistency reduction and inconsistency robustness are fundamental to the proper operation of the overall system.

Specifically, it is possible to say that courts must deal both with error correction and with inconsistency. By error correction, we mean the management of *manifest error* that courts make both in terms of the determination of facts and the interpretation and application of law. We identify two main types of inconsistency that courts regularly face. The first type is *horizontal inconsistency*, i.e. discrepancy between courts' decisions at the same level—trial or appellate level (there is only one Supreme Court, and thus no horizontal inconsistency can occur there). The second type is *vertical inconsistency*, i.e. discrepancy between higher and lower courts' decisions, especially when making decisions about the same case.

Moreover, correcting errors, or getting decisions "right," is an important value of any court system; it is a substantial part of what we call *justice*. Thus, to the extent that within a certain court system the presence of factual and legal error is considered an obstacle to achieve *justice*, a system designer has an interest in a correct interpretation of facts and law i.e. has an interest in managing manifest errors. At the same time, being treated equally before the law is also an essential part of what we call *justice*. Consequently, a system designer has an interest in pursuing equality too, i.e. has an interest in managing inconsistency even when it is the result of courts' error management. Indeed, as discussed in the next part, manifest error and inconsistency are sometimes byproducts of the different strategies that courts, and particularly the highest courts, adopt to achieve *justice,* and at times can be "negatively correlated."

Thus to manage errors, the American court system has an intricate scheme of complex rules aimed at providing reliable information to judges and juries and help them achieving a better determination of what are the relevant facts of a particular case. Entire courses in law school are devoted to this system so that attorneys will be trained in their roles and able to aid courts in this task. The American court system also has an intricate scheme for adjudicating legal questions in the form of equally complex rules for construing legal statutes and applying the law to cases. This system is also the subject of numerous courses in law schools.

Notwithstanding this elaborate design, the endless variety of ways in which people get into disputes and the complexities of deciding legal cases combine to result in trial courts getting both factual and legal questions incorrect with regularity. Consequently, the system has federal courts of appeals and the Supreme Court for the purpose of correcting these errors and promoting a proper application of the law by trial courts. Indeed, as previously mentioned, for the rule of law to be just and equitable, citizens should be able to expect consistent, fair, and accurate treatment in the courts.

The higher courts do not seek complete error elimination in lower court decisions, however, especially on factual issues, nor does the system attempt complete equality of treatment across different courts. As one example, it is not uncommon for some courts to develop reputations as venues within which defendants, or plaintiffs, or even patent owners, may have a better chance of success in their cases than other places. Thus, we see that rather than attempting to eliminate all error and inconsistency, the system has developed in a way that shows substantial inconsistency robustness. The court system openly accepts the presence of a certain amount of cost efficient error and inconsistency. This is quite sensible, and is an example of an intuitively inconsistency robust view within the judicial system.

Moreover, if higher courts wanted to attempt correction of all potential factual errors, the higher courts would need to reevaluate the factual issues with the same richness of information available to the trial court—including the ability to observe witness demeanor. Reviewing courts would virtually have to retry the case. This would obviously be very expensive and time consuming. Instead of going to these lengths, appellate courts give deference to trial courts on issues of fact, and only overturn the lower courts when clear error or abuse of discretion has occurred. This allows some inconsistencies to go unresolved, and thus may result in some litigants unfairly having their cases resolved based on mistaken understandings of the facts. But rather than seeking perfectly fair treatment of litigants by attempting perfect error correction, we see once again that the system is designed with knowledge that some error and inconsistency is inefficient to correct. In this way, one might say that the judicial system seeks robustness in the face of known information inconsistencies.

On the other hand, the courts of appeal and Supreme Court strive to reduce a good deal of inconsistency in legal issues. Courts are less concerned about the effect of some factual error and inconsistency on the parties of an individual case than they are about the erroneous and/or inconsistent application of law across numerous cases. For this reason, courts seek to correct more error when it comes to legal questions, and to correct it at a higher level, so that a correct rule can then be applied consistently vertically, down to the trial courts, and horizontally, across numerous trial courts. Thus, we see greater attempts at correcting errors and eliminating inconsistency for legal issues. More specifically, we see that the legal system has made important *determinations* about when to try to decrease error and inconsistency, and when to attempt robust operations in the face of error and inconsistency by weighing the benefits of contemplated error correction or inconsistency reduction against the attendant costs of achieving the desired error or inconsistency reduction.

The judicial system also sometimes adopts inconsistency robustness strategies in one area so as to decrease inconsistency in another area. For example, higher courts sometimes apply the judicial principle of *stare decisis* as a justification for forbearing the correction of a legal standard that is well established. The principle of *stare decisis* does not counsel courts never to overturn well-established legal rules, but instead the principle encourages courts to be hesitant to overturn well-established rules absent compelling reasons. *Stare decisis* is thus very much within the inconsistency robustness paradigm in that it warns against too great a willingness to frequently change the law in an attempt to achieve a "correct" standard, because, among other things, such changes to established legal rules may lead to the risk of creating additional inconsistency in subsequent lower courts decisions as they struggle with the shifting legal standards, or may cause problems for parties who have made business decisions based on the established rule. Thus, *stare decisis* eschews elimination of some manifest error in order to promote robust horizontal and vertical consistency.

The judicial system also seeks horizontal consistency in decision making by courts. Horizontal consistency coherence is an important goal for the American legal system because it is only when people are treated (mostly) consistently under the law that they can truly be said to have equal rights and equal protections. Thus, the federal judicial system is structured so that the courts of appeal are divided into separate geographic circuits each of which pronounces legal decisions that are binding for all of the district courts within the particular circuit court's geographic area. The district courts are bound to apply the decisions of the appellate court in their circuit, and thus a good deal of horizontal coherence is present in each circuit.[1]

The circuit courts also have a rule that a later panel of judges cannot overrule the statement of an earlier panel as to a specific legal rule. This too helps promote horizontal coherence at the district court level because it means that appellate decisions, once made, can only be changed by the circuit court when it meets as a whole ("en banc") to reevaluate an existing rule. Thus, in *Bilski* the Federal Circuit met *en banc* to change the "useful, concrete and tangible result" test for the patentability of processes and substitute it with the "machine-or-transformation" test. More discussion on the *Bislki* decision will follow in the next section.

To achieve even greater horizontal coherence, the Supreme Court is set as the highest court of the land and reviews decisions of the circuit courts. The Supreme Court has discretion as to which cases it will review, but it is more likely to take a case if the circuit courts are split on the interpretation of a particular law. The Supreme Court thus sees part of its mandate as settling disputed interpretations of the law among the circuit courts. Once the Supreme Court has decided an issue, all lower courts—circuit and district courts—are bound to apply the law according to the Supreme Court's interpretation. This obviously results in substantial horizontal consistency (as well as some increased vertical consistency).

The Supreme Court does not value horizontal inconsistency reduction above all else, however. In fact, the Supreme Court is well-known for at times allowing circuit splits to exist for a period of time before deciding the disputed issue so as to have the benefit of the argument among the circuit courts as well as the benefit of seeing how the application of the differing interpretations works within the various circuits. Thus, we see the Supreme Court allowing manifest inconsistency to continue for an indefinite period of time and even attempting to "profit" from its presence.

The second type of inconsistency in the judicial system that we discuss is vertical inconsistency. This is simply the inconsistency that results when higher courts decide cases differently than lower courts. Because higher courts exist to correct errors on the part of lower courts, one should obviously expect that a fair bit of vertical inconsistency will occur, and is indeed expected, in the system. Nevertheless, there are costs of vertical inconsistency. For one thing, litigants will experience a longer period of uncertainty before knowing the ultimate resolution of their disputes if a high level of vertical inconsistency is the norm. In such a vertically inconsistent system, litigants will also tend to spend more money on litigation given that the party that loses below will have more incentive to appeal if the chances of reversal in a higher court are substantial. Thus, the court system has a motive to limit vertical inconsistency, even while not eliminating it. To pursue this objective a number of mechanisms are present in the judicial system that, once again, reflect a robust attitude toward inconsistency reduction. They include, among others, a limited number of possible appeals, a limited number of possible reasons for which an appeal can be pursued and, as previously mentioned, the *discretion* granted the Supreme Court in deciding to hear cases. This *discretion* is based also on the understanding that resources are limited – there is just one Supreme Court – and that only those cases whose decision has the highest potential to benefit society should be taken by this Court. Other cases are "left behind" even if their dispositions could eliminate certain inconsistency present in the legal system. They are just less "worthy" of the limited time that the Supreme

Court has. The inconsistency robustness paradigm is useful in making determinations about error correction and vertical and horizontal inconsistency, and has been applied by courts for a long time, at least intuitively.

Position Statement

Having set out the two types of error and two main forms of inconsistency that exist in the United States federal court system in our introduction, we now focus on one aspect of that system—the interaction of the Supreme Court and the Court of Appeals for the Federal Circuit when it comes to deciding patent cases.[2] Our contention is that the inconsistency robustness paradigm can shed some light on the possible causes of a recurring pattern of disagreement that characterize the Federal Circuit and the Supreme Court's operation in this context. In fact, we believe that this pattern of disagreement is largely driven by the two courts' differing intuitive views as to how to address inconsistencies, and what is the beneficially allowable level of inconsistency in the area of patent law.

This pattern has been present in the past few decades. Indeed, since its creation, the Federal Circuit has increasingly tended towards the refinement of legal rules until they become bright-line rules that can be applied with high levels of predictability and consistency by lower courts. In contrast, the Supreme Court has increasingly overturned Federal Circuit patent decisions that set forth bright-line rules. The Supreme Court has consistently replaced the Federal Circuit's bright-line rules with standards that have the benefit of promoting flexible decision-making, but, simultaneously, allow more inconsistency to persist in the system.

Our contention is, thus, that the Federal Circuit has repeatedly resorted to bright-line rules in an attempt to minimize, if not eliminate, the two types of inconsistency—horizontal inconsistency and vertical inconsistency. More precisely, we observe that the Federal Circuit and Supreme Court may each be focusing on reducing inconsistency—or at least error—in different aspects of the system, and may each be comfortable with inconsistency—or at least error—in other aspects of the system. However, we believe that when it comes to patent cases, the Federal Circuit values horizontal and vertical inconsistency reduction more, while the Supreme Court places greater value on the elimination of manifest error. This means that correspondingly, the Federal Circuit has more tolerance for manifest error that comes from its bright-line rules, while the Supreme Court has more tolerance for horizontal and vertical inconsistency that comes from adopting standards.

A possible explanation for the Federal Circuit's intense focus on horizontal and vertical inconsistency reduction can be found, we believe, in this court's perception that it has a *special* mandate—compared to the other circuit courts—to increase predictability when it comes to the application of patent law. However, as previously mentioned, the Federal Circuit's operation in this context has determined same disagreement with the Supreme Court. The result has been numerous changes in patent law interpretation which, ironically, has led to a widespread feeling that significant uncertainty is present in the patent system requiring reform.

The Federal Circuit's belief that it has a mandate to standardize the application of patent law is unsurprising given the events leading to the court's creation. In the 1960's and 1970's in the United States, there came to be a general perception that the amount of uncertainty about the validity of patents, and the inconsistency with which patent cases were decided in different circuit and district courts (horizontal and vertical inconsistency), was harmful to both innovation and businesses. Accordingly, in 1982, Congress passed the Federal Courts Improvement Act, which merged the Court of Customs and Patent Appeals and the appellate division of the Court of Claims. The Act also mandated that henceforth all appeals of patent cases from any district court would be heard by the Federal Circuit. Prior to the act, patent cases were appealed from the district court in which they had been tried to whichever of the twelve federal appellate courts had geographic jurisdiction over the trial court. The result was that the legal rules governing patents varied from circuit to circuit—horizontal inconsistency. A potential patent defendant had little control over where it might be sued, and thus did not know which of the rules from the circuit courts might be applied to its activities.[3] Likewise, a patent holder faced uncertainty as to the application of patent law because it might be sued by a potential defendant under the declaratory judgment statute in any circuit, or a case that it brought in a circuit of its choosing might be transferred to another venue upon a successful motion by the defendant.[4]

The legislative history makes clear that Congress hoped that the consolidation of all patent appeals in one circuit court would both standardize the law that the district courts are required to apply to patent cases, and allow more expert review of patent appeals by a specialized court with the ability to hire specialized, often scientifically trained, clerks.[5]

In the almost thirty years since the Federal Circuit began hearing cases in 1983, the Court has produced a single body of law to which district courts can look to decide patent cases,[6] i.e. it has significantly reduced horizontal inconsistency. The Supreme Court seems to believe, however, that the Federal Circuit has engaged in a certain amount of suboptimal decision making by choosing to achieve this goal through the adoption of bright-line rules.

Evidence that the Federal Circuit attempted to create consistency in the application of patent laws can be found in numerous patent cases—the most significant of which are discussed below—that involved the creation of bright-line rules in areas such as obviousness (Teaching-Suggestion-Motivation test), prosecution history estoppel (complete bar to doctrine of equivalents in cases of claim amendment during prosecution), the standard for declaratory judgments (reasonable apprehension of suit), and the standard for issuing injunctions (presumptive issuance).[7]

The requirement that a patent be nonobvious was codified in the 1952 Patent Act at 35 U.S.C. § 103. The statute merely says that an invention is not patentable if it "would have been obvious at the time the invention was made," and leaves it to the courts to determine obviousness. Whether an invention is obvious is an inherently difficult question to answer, and one that lends itself to a good deal of inconsistent opinion. The Supreme Court first interpreted the obviousness requirement of the 1952 Patent Act in 1966 in *Graham v. John Deere*. There the Supreme Court set out a complex, contextual, multifactor analysis for determining obviousness. Upon its creation, and for years thereafter, the Federal Circuit struggled with the standard for obviousness, and the inherent unpredictability and uncertainty arising from the Supreme Court's approach. Eventually, the Federal Circuit adopted the "teaching suggestion or motivation" ("TSM") test. Under this test, the Federal Circuit ruled that a patent could not be held invalid unless the district court could point to a particular teaching, suggestion, or motivation in the technical literature that suggested the combination of elements that resulted in the patented invention. There was some debate about whether the teaching, suggestion, or motivation had to be written, but this was at the least greatly preferred.

The benefit of the TSM test was that it gave fairly clear criteria for determining obviousness, and thus decreased horizontal and vertical inconsistency. The detriment of the test was that it allowed patents on a number of inventions that would otherwise have been thought obvious if the patent office could not point to a specific teaching, suggestion, or motivation to combine all of the elements claimed in an invention. Thus, a number of seemingly obvious inventions were patented.

The Supreme Court rejected any rigid, narrow application of the TSM test in 2007 in *KSR v. Teleflex*. The case involved the question of whether a movable gas pedal with an electronic sensor was obvious. Prior automotive pedal designs included movable pedals, and pedals with electronic sensors. The question before the court was whether combining a moveable design with an electronic sensor was obvious. The Federal Circuit had held that it was not, citing the lack of teaching, suggestion, or motivation to combine the two types of pedals. The Supreme Court reversed, finding that such a combination was obvious because it was where the industry was inevitably headed. In its decision, the Court reiterated its contextual approach set out in *Graham v. John Deere*. The Court preferred a more flexible approach that encouraged more nuanced decisions to the bright-line TSM test. Thus we see an example of the Federal Circuit preferring to reduce horizontal and vertical inconsistency while the Supreme Court preferred to reduce manifest error deriving from the application of said bright-line rule. The Supreme Court has the final say, of course, and thus substituted its view of proper inconsistency robustness for that of the Federal Circuit.

A similar pattern can be discerned regarding the law of prosecution history estoppel of infringement claims based on the doctrine of equivalents. Patent law allows a patent owner to exclude others from using both his claimed invention and near equivalents. When a patentee amends his patent during prosecution before the patent office so as to narrow the scope of the claimed invention, the question is whether he may thereafter claim the right to exclude equivalents to his claimed invention. Courts have always been hesitant to allow patentees to narrow their claims during prosecution, only to allow them to broaden the scope later through asserting their rights to exclude equivalents. Thus, the courts adopted the doctrine of prosecution history estoppel to limit the ability of patentees to claim infringement via equivalents if they had narrowed their claims during prosecution.

The question was what the parameters should be for invoking prosecution history estoppel, and what should be the boundaries of the estoppel. The Federal Circuit struggled with these questions and finally settled on a bright-line rule. The Federal Circuit held that if a patentee narrowed his patent claim in any way during prosecution, then he was absolutely barred from invoking the doctrine of equivalents for the narrowed claims. This again promoted great reductions in horizontal and vertical inconsistency.

The Supreme Court reversed in *Festo v. Shoketsu* in 2002. The Supreme Court held that an absolute bar to invoking the doctrine of equivalents was too severe, and that instead, patentees would be estopped from invoking the doctrine only as to equivalents that were foreseeable at the time of patent prosecution. Here again the Supreme Court rejected the Federal Circuit's bright line rule in favor of a more nuanced rule. Interestingly, however, in this case the Supreme Court's rule was also fairly bright. Thus we see an example of the Supreme Court again substituting its preference for a greater reduction of manifest error, but to a lesser degree than in the case of the rule regarding obviousness.

The Federal Circuit's treatment of patentable subject matter also fits within its trend toward bright-line rules, although with some meandering along the way. The Federal Circuit followed a general course of liberalizing the standard for patentable subject matter, including by ruling that business methods are patentable subject matter in the 1999 case of *State Street Bank*. Over the course of the next decade the Federal Circuit struggled with what limits there should be to patentable subject matter, especially for process patents, and eventually settled on a bright-line rule in *In re Bilski*. In Bilski, the Federal Circuit adopted the "machine or transformation" test. Under this test, a process was patentable only if it was tied to a particular machine or caused a transformation of matter. This bright-line rule again decreased horizontal and vertical inconsistency. The Supreme Court, following the pattern, overturned the Federal Circuit's bright-line rule and replaced it with a more amorphous standard. The Supreme Court held that process patent claims are only unpatentable subject matter when they are too "abstract." The Supreme Court left the exact contours of unpatentable abstractness to be developed by courts over time. This is a particularly striking example of the Supreme Court preferring standards over bright-line rule – and, consequently, devaluating horizontal and vertical consistency - to allowing great flexibility in the analysis and development of the law and "cure" previous manifest error.

The pattern emerging from the aforementioned cases is clear. The pattern includes two steps. First the Federal Circuit attempts horizontal and vertical inconsistency reduction via the creation of bright-line rules. Second, the Supreme Court weighs in with a focus on reducing manifest error, and reverses the bright-line rules. Unfortunately, it is also a pattern that, as previously described, has determined idiosyncratic changes in key elements of patent law and, thus, has created possible significant uncertainty for innovators in fields such as the online commerce and the software industry that are of great importance for the US economy.

There is a rich literature on the application of rules versus standards to legal questions. Rules provide predictability and consistency, while standards are less predictable but provide the opportunity for nuanced, contextual decision making. The Federal Circuit's understanding of its mandate as being focused, in part, on creating predictability through horizontal and vertical inconsistency reduction seems to have caused it to move toward bright-line rules and away from contextual standards. The result of the Federal Circuit's rules were that horizontal and vertical consistency were increased (which also increases predictability), but at the "cost" of increased manifest error in the form of more obvious patents being issued, the doctrine of equivalents being made unavailable for amended patent claims, and strict exclusions of some process patent claims.[8] In a series of cases over the last six years, the Supreme Court has reversed each of the Federal Circuit's rules set forth above, and replaced them with more contextual standards intended to decrease manifest error but at the price of some predictability (increased horizontal and vertical inconsistency).

We believe that the reason for this difference in tolerance of error versus inconsistencies can be found in the different role that the Federal Circuit and Supreme Court see themselves as playing. The Federal Circuit's understanding of its mandate to increase predictability in patent law, and its unique situation as the only circuit court hearing patent law cases, encourages the court to attempt nationwide inconsistency reduction by providing bright-line rules to the district courts. The Supreme Court is used to operating within the historic federal court system within which horizontal inconsistency among the circuit courts, and thus correspondingly, the district courts, is the norm. While part of the Supreme Court's mandate is to provide some horizontal and vertical consistency by settling disputed legal questions, it has neither the inclination nor the capacity to drive out anything near all of the horizontal inconsistency in the system. Thus, the Supreme Court has historically been comfortable with a large amount of vertical and horizontal inconsistency and has focused on crafting "correct" decisions as to particularly thorny or disputed legal questions. This difference in focus helps explain why the Supreme Court has repeatedly ruled against Federal Circuit's decisions that the Court considered to be manifest errors.

To make the best decisions on what rules should govern patent litigation issues, and to decrease the likelihood of continued reversals by the Supreme Court, the Federal Circuit should recognize the different way in which the Supreme Court approaches inconsistency robustness in the United States federal court system. Understanding that the Supreme Court is likely to focus more on manifest error than vertical and horizontal inconsistency can help the Federal Circuit predict when the Supreme Court is likely to overturn a legal rule crafted by the Federal Circuit.

At the same time, the Supreme Court would do well to remember that when it reverses patent appeals from the Federal Circuit, it is reversing not just the law in one geographic area of the United States, but rather is reversing the law nationwide. In evaluating the benefit of decreasing manifest error, the Supreme Court should remember that the cost is overturning a high degree of horizontal and vertical consistency that the Federal Circuit has established nationwide. The Supreme Court should contemplate giving some deference to the judgment of the Federal Circuit as to the importance of vertical and horizontal consistency versus error reduction in the realm of patent law. It may be that the Federal Circuit's greater experience day in and day out with patent cases and patent litigants gives the Federal Circuit particular expertise in judging how to balance the elimination and allowance of inconsistencies so as to arrive at the court system that best manages inconsistency robustness in service of the values of the legal system in the unique area of patent law.

Thus, there may be times when a properly nuanced vision of the inconsistency robustness paradigm with respect to the court system would encourage the Supreme Court to consider the costs in terms of inconsistency and predictability of correcting error in Federal Circuit opinions. It may be that at times the Federal Circuit's bright-line rules have greater benefits to society in terms of predictability and consistency of application than nuanced standards that allow for reducing manifest error at the cost of inconsistency and unpredictability.

Endnotes

‡ Lecturer in Law at Santa Clara University School of Law and a Transatlantic Technology Law Forum Research Fellow at Stanford Law School.

† Assistant Professor, Boston College Law School.

[1] The exception to this rule is the Federal Circuit, which has jurisdiction based on subject matter rather than geography. Importantly for purposes of this paper, the Federal Circuit has sole jurisdiction over all appeals of patent cases, no matter what district court tried the patent case.

[2] Note that while this position statement considers only the United States federal court system, much of what is discussed about the interactions between trial and appellate courts has relevance to other court systems.

[3] While horizontal inconsistency among circuits is a common feature of the United States court system, the drafters of the Federal Courts Improvement Act seemed to think that the cost of inconsistency was particularly great when it came to patent law due to the national scope of the production and use of patented goods.

[4] Although in practice declaratory judgment actions and transfers of venue were not common.

[5] There is also evidence that at least some of the proponents of the Act instituting the Federal Circuit hoped that the Court would prove to be more favorably inclined to protecting and enforcing patent rights, especially given that in some circuits prior to the act the rates of invalidation of patents had become quite high.

[6] Many commentators also believe that the Court indeed has been friendlier to patent interests than some of the circuit courts were before 1983.

[7] Although note that the presumption of an injunction remedy in patent cases seems to have been present in patent law for most of United States' history. Nevertheless, the Federal Circuit made the presumption into an explicit rule.

[8] Note, however, that the Federal Circuit has not focused on bright-line rules to minimize vertical inconsistency in all areas. Specifically, in the key patent contexts such as novelty (§102(a) prior art), claim construction, and obviousness, Federal Circuit decisions are characterized by reversal rates of district courts' decision equal to 36%, 33% and 29% respectively. It is beyond the scope of this paper to examine whether this comes from the Federal Circuit balancing the benefit of vertical inconsistency reduction differently in these areas, or whether these areas of patent law simply do not lend themselves to bright-line rules. Whatever the reason, these reversal rates are certainly significant in terms of vertical inconsistency. A recent study has shown that the Federal Circuit's **average** reversal rate across all patent issue is equal to 8-18% and is the same as the reversal rates in regional circuits for private civil actions, particularly complex ones, like Bankruptcy, Securities and Contracts cases. see Ted Sichelman, *Myth Of*

(Un)certainty at The Federal Circuit, (...) 2010. However, the reversal rate of certain **key** patent issues such as novelty (§102(a) prior art), claim construction and obviousness is way above such averages. Sichelman's study seems not to appreciate the relative importance of each of the considered patent issues in concluding that the Federal Circuit is as predictable as other regional circuits i.e. the Federal Circuit is considered less predictable than other regional circuits because the patent issues with very high/above average reversal rates are among those with highest impact on patentability and patent value—not all the patent issues used to calculate the average have the same weight in patent law.

Politics and Pragmatism in Scientific Ontology Construction

Mike Travers, SRI, mt@alum.mit.edu

Ontologies are supposed to define a common representational framework for a domain of knowledge, but in practice achieving "common" is not a simple task. It might seem that achieving mutual agreement about ontology ought to be an inevitable result of the structure of the world, but in practice it is often a laborious and contentious process, filled with argument, negotiations, compromise, power, and politics. Recent debates in the ontology community between "realists" and "conceptualists" hide the true nature of ontology building, and I will examine philosophical pragmatism as an alternate approach. One of the roots of the pragmatic approach is to look at ontologies as a social product, with an attention to how they are constructed, promulgated, and used. I'll look at some examples of the sociology of ontology from my personal work experience building knowledge-based systems for scientists. One of the lessons learned is that ontologies in practice are influenced by a whole variety of factors other than pure logic, such as cost of implementation, the relative status of particular users, and user interface design. The pragmatic view says that rather than bemoan these impurities, or marginalizing them, we should explicitly acknowledge and make use of them.

Ontologies have politics

The process of dividing up the world into well-defined categories is variously referred to as ontology, model building, or simply classification. Socrates in *Phaedrus* characterized this as "carving nature at its joints", implying that the delineation of objects to represent should be as well-defined as carving a chicken. In practice, things are often not well-defined, and the process of defining them is a messy process involving social and political forces.

The defense of "marriage"

Sometimes the politics behind ontological conflict is obvious and explicit – for instance, the current political controversy of what constitutes the proper boundaries of the concept of "marriage" is not only about the formal semantics of the term but also the attendant legal rights, social status, and material benefits. Because of the federal system, different states have different incommensurable definitions of marriage, and to deal with this, there are "meta-level" laws such as the The full faith and credit clause of the US Constitution (which requires states to recognize each other's "public acts and records") and the Defense of Marriage Act (which explictly contradicts this clause). Ultimately this ontological issue will probably be decided by the Supreme Court. It would be hard to find a clearer example of the intersection of ontology with politics and authority.

The representational aspect of this conflict manifests at a more technical level in [1], which examines the issue from the standpoint of a database schema designer. Marriages already have some formal properties that translate directly into computational terms, such as commutativity (if a is married to b, then b is married to a) and exclusivity (assuming that bigamy is just as illegal in the database as it is in real life). There are more complications to representing actual marriages, such as their finite duration, and the fact of serial remarriage. Gay marriage complicates things a bit more:

> So, after removing the "husband and wife" limitation, you would actually have to add in a check constraint or some new application logic to ensure that people didn't marry themselves. It would almost never be called upon but it would have to be in there, somewhere. This minor programming challenge is actually our largest obstacle.

This is largely tounge-in-cheek, but it conveys an important point – that our social institutions are intertwined with our bureaucratic and computational formalisms. A society without bureaucracies, central government, and their attendant databases doesn't have a real problem with defining marriage – marriage is whatever individuals make of it. A society with databases, however, has to fit the messy lives of individuals into a formal structure. Computers are, from this perspective, just the latest technology of bureaucracy.

As computer scientists, our database schemas (or other representations) both reflect and help construct social reality. What if we had databases that, instead of based on rigidly-typed tables, were based on more flexible technologies of representations? Since representation and society have complex and interdependent interactions, the adoption of such technology might go some ways to making society itself more tolerant.

What constitutes a disease?

Other areas in which classification has obvious political and social tensions are in the definitions of psychiatric diseases (which impact eligibility for various government benefits as well as moral culpability for crimes) [75] and the question of what constitutes a person (a pivotal issue for the abortion debate, and of earlier conflicts over slavery) [47].

Post-traumatic stress disorder (PTSD) is a relatively recent diagnostic category, whose adoption involved a political struggle, related to its implications for the Vietnam war and military service in general [66].

> ...not to suggest that this diagnosis [is]..."merely" a social construction, or simply the result of self-interest...the story of

PTSD... help[s] us understand in detail how objective knowledge – and medical scientific knowledge in particular – is produced, secured, and subsequently used...Each new clinical diagnosis of PTSD, each new warrantable medical insurance claim, each new narrative about the disorder reaffirms its reality, its objectivity, its "just thereness". In the story of PTSD we see again how the orderliness of the natural world is to be found in its very accounts of orderliness.

And until quite recently, homosexuality was considered a psychiatric diagnosis, but now it isn't [7], a reclassification born of a political struggle. It may be thought that the cases cited so far are exceptional, since they all involve classifications of humans and their social relationships, and are thus naturally subject to controversy and politics. But I prefer to think of these as just the more obvious cases of a more general phenomenon, and that subtler forms of politics may be found in all representational efforts. In part this is based on Bruno Latour's view of science as a series of "trials of strength" between contending networks of actors [42]. In this view, scientists and their objects of studies are united together to prove a particular point, often against rival theories. There are two very different types of scientific knowledge – settled knowledge, which is relatively uncontroversial, and the products of science-in-process, such as the results of experiments and the representations found in lab notebooks. Such material is always in pursuit of some goal, and because that goal is not necessarily shared by all there is always a quality of contention to be found there, along with situatedness and modal qualifiers.

Contested representations in biology

Even areas that are less obviously fraught with political implications will often involve conflicts of interest or simply divergent but incommensurable viewpoints. Scientific knowledge representation runs into this at many levels. The naive view of science is that it is above politics, and that it, perhaps alone of human activities, should have ontologies that are direct representations of an objective reality. Indeed, objective and disinterested representations are the *aspiration* of science, but the process of achieving them necessarily involves representations that are localized, situated and *interested* in the sense that they are created to favor a particular point of view that is contending for acceptance. Thus designing representations even for things that ought to be value-neutral, such as the component parts of a cellular metabolic process, are often marked with human bias and interests, and thus are not objective in any interesting sense.

Example: mitochondria

Mitochondria are parts of cells (organelles) but have their evolutionary origins as independent organisms that were assimilated symboiotically into ancestral cells. They maintain some of the characteristics of independence to this day, such as their own genomes (mtDNA). A recent article [57] mused that we really should consider mitochondria as separate organisms still, with their own taxonomic codes, evolutionary history, and the other conceptual apparatus that comes with being an organism.

> A wide range of molecular phylogenetic studies has been applied to macromolecules encoded within mitochondrial genomes and all support a bacterial…affiliation for mitochondria. Thus, by the logic of cladistic classification, we have no choice but to accept that mitochondria belong in the domain Bacteria, or to put it plainly, that mitochondria are bacteria.

This is a somewhat atypical example of a biologist consciously toying with ontological issues and their consequences. Are mitochondria separate organisms or parts of another organism? In fact they can easily be seen as both, and this will tend to break ontologies that have a too-rigid distinction between organisms and parts. But this is not merely a terminological question; viewing mitochondria as organisms in their own right puts them front and center for certain types of scientific attention, e.g, it suggests that they can be independent objects of metabolic re-engineering. Pallen also raises issues of *credit*, always an important if unarticulated issue in the process of science:

> If we accept that mitochondria are bacteria, then the record books have to be rewritten. The first bacterial genome sequence was completed not by American *arriviste* Craig Venter and his team in 1995, but instead by a team at the Medical Research Council Laboratories in Cambridge, England, which included double Nobel laureate Fred Sanger, who completed the human mitochondrial genome sequence in 1981!

Pallen mocks his own proposal as "phylogenetic fundamentalism" (that is, his viewpoint involves taking a strict view of biological classification as based solely on the descent relationships of organisms, as opposed to a more functional classification). For our purposes, it suffices to note that this controversy is not really about any facts in the world, since all parties acknowledge the bacterial ancestry of mitochondria. The issue is one of classification, naming, and relationship; and the consequences of such classification, which include intellectual credit, qualifications for funding, different frames of reference being applied to problems, or people from different subfields being drawn in or pushed out of working on a particular problem.

Example: genes and pathways

The definitions of even such basic biological entities such as "gene" or "pathway" pose difficult issues: in the nature of their boundaries; the nomenclature by which they are represented in databases and discourse; and their stability, unity, and reality. Genes by their nature have variant forms within and across species, and even within a single individual (in cancer, e.g., where particular groups of cells become mutated), making it difficult to establish a firm definitional boundary for what constitutes an individual gene. A gene may be an abstract ideal entity, a standard sequence of codons in a reference database, a variant of that standard, or a particular individualized piece of physical DNA in an individual cell. The elastic semantics of "gene" frustrates formalists, but is essential to the everyday discourse of science

A metabolic pathway is a group of functionally related biochemical reactions within a cell, and has been a basic concept of biology from well before the genomic era [49], [65]. The concept of pathways has some of the same fuzzy definitional problems as genes (if indeed they are problems), but in addition suffers from having no obvious well-defined boundaries in the world. Unlike genes or cells, which do have natural boundaries, pathways have no uncontroversial starting and stopping points, but are really just sections of a global reaction graph that have been scissored out of the whole by the informed judgment of scientists.

For instance, the BioPAX standard [25] is an attempt by a coalition of scientists to define a common standard for representing pathways (emphasis added):

> Pathway: Definition: A set or series of interactions, often forming a network, which biologists **have found useful to group together** for organizational, historic, biophysical or other reasons.

The problem with this, of course, is that the utility of a grouping depends upon the context for analysis, which can easily be different for different scientists or projects.

Pathway Tools [] is a long-standing resource for genomic biology, a collection of pathway-genome databases (PGDBs) for over 1000 organisms, and tools to view, edit, and interact with them.

Pathway Tools, due in part to its ontology needs to define pathways as relatively crisp, permanent objects, uses the following definition of pathway:[1]

> Pathway boundaries are defined heuristically, using the judgment of expert curators. Curators consider the following aspects of a pathway when defining its boundaries.
> - What boundaries were defined historically for pathway?
> - When possible, we prefer to define boundaries at the 13 common currency metabolites: D-glucose-6-phosphate pyruvate etc.
> - Coincidence with regulatory units
> - Coincidence with metabolic units that are evolutionarily conserved
>
> The preceding philosophy toward pathway boundary definition contrasts sharply with KEGG maps. KEGG maps are on average 4.2 times larger than BioCyc pathways because KEGG tends to group into a single map multiple biological pathways that converge on a single metabolite.

Note here that (1) there is a specific philosophy of pathway definition, (2) that it depends on the informed judgment of experts, and (3) it is contrasted with the methodology of a rival knowledge base, KEGG [37]. More fundamentally, pathway models necessarily encode a fixed structure of function and explanation, which necessarily excludes pathology (as in the case of pathways disturbed by genetic disease or cancerous mutation) or novelty (in the case of synthetic pathways) [67].

Another interesting ontological issue arises from the fact that ontologies and the software that uses them have histories, and the changing needs of science over the years will cause tensions between established representational usage and new needs. In the case of Pathway Tools, the informations has been organized around separate sets of frames for each organism, so there is a separate knowledge base for each (EcoCyc for *E. coli* [38], Humancyc for *Homo sapiens* [58], plus one special KB called MetaCyc [13] that is essentially the union of all other organisms). The database collection has recently grown to over 1000 separate organisms/knowledge bases.

But now there are new proposed applications for the software that involve things that cross organism boundaries: metabolic engineering, which involves synthesizing new pathways from fragments of multiple microorganisms (for applications like synthesizing fuels and drugs) [35] [17]; the study of metabolic pathways that involve the interaction of a host and symbiote [21]; and metagenomics, which involves sequencing the DNA

---

[1] http://metacyc.org/biocyc-guide.shtml

of large samples without prior knowledge of what organisms they come from [61]. All these applications are possible within the structure of the software, but they put some strain on the existing structures and ontology.

Alignment, social construction, power

It is something of a miracle of human societies that they can accomplish joint ventures of vast complexity despite the conflicting individual goals of the participants. The construction of representations and ontologies is no different; it is a social process and thus subject to social forces like conflict, power, negotiation, signaling, etc. Conflicts over ontologies can take many forms, including disagreements over naming (terminological), over classification (taxonomic), over boundaries of concepts, or any of the other features of representation. In real-world representation construction, these conflicts must be negotiated and the interest groups behind them brought into at least temporary alignment.

The sociology of ontologies

My own experience working on a variety of complex software projects has sparked a fascination with the social processes that underlie the development of ontologies. Building an ontology is a complex social-coordination problem, but ontologies have the added property that their output is something that at least aspires to be a kind of objective, interest-free model of some domain. If this was true – that the structure of ontologies were inevitably determined by the structure of the phenomenon they aim to describe – then anybody could be an ontologist, object models would tend to converge rather than diverge, and the problem of representation would be much simpler than it actually is. In practice, of course this isn't easy at all.

Generally representational projects will have one person occupying a role I like to call the "alpha ontologist" – the one who is the ultimate determiner of the right way to represent something. There are a number of problems with this type of methodology. It's dictatorial, for one thing. Perhaps that's not a real problem, given that some constructed things seem better for having a strong leader (consider Steve Jobs' role at Apple, e.g.). But an ontology is supposed to be universal, and having a universal knowledge schema be the product of a single mind doesn't sit right. More practically, a centralized process like this can't scale up. Broadly, for knowledge representation to succeed, it has to be more accessible and more democratic.

Example: representing cellular space

Here's an example of an ontological negotiation about a relatively trivial matter. This is part of a recent discussion among the developers of Pathway Tools. Underlying Pathway Tools is a frame-based knowledge representation system called Ocelot [16], with a schema that has evolved over fifteen years to capture the important parts of genomic biology as they evolved.

This is part of a longer discussion on how to represent the localization of biological reactions, including transport reactions (which move things from one location to another). The issue is how to solve a problem that has crept into the knowledge base, a confusion about the representation of cellular location (important because some reactions are limited to certain parts of the cell). The issue revolves around the difference between the definitions of *cytoplasm* (the liquid inside the membrane of a cell, excluding the nucleus, but including organelles), and the *cytosol*, which is an almost identical concept except that it excludes the organelles.

The participants include software developers (nl and tq), biologists (sd and pz), and kp the "alpha ontologist". [All emphasis added]

> nl: proposal: An accurate representation of processes inside of a cell needs to take into account... different compartments.. and that the processes and metabolites are partitioned between these compartments... In BioCyc, compartments need to be valid frames in the CCO (Cell Compartment Ontology), which can either be children of CCO-SPACE or CCO-MEMBRANE. The default compartment for metabolites and reactions is assumed to be CCO-CYTOPLASM.
>
> nl: the important function (default-compartment) has been **historically hard-wired** to return CCO-CYTOSOL, but I don't understand why....as we use other locations called periplasm, using cytoplasm would look much more **consistent**. I thus would prefer to use CCO-CYTOPLASM instead.
>
> I don't even see why there should be much of a distinction between CCO-CYTOPLASM and CCO-CYTOSOL anyways. to me, it looks like CCO-CYTOSOL is an unnecessary and not useful concept...after all, we also don't have a perisol either. We only have a periplasm.
>
> sd: While cytosol and cytoplasm are different terms and describe different entities, I think that probably most biologists will be hard pressed to point out the differences without looking it up. So while we **lose some resolution** if we eliminate cytosol, we probably don't lose anything **particularly useful**, and if this serves to eliminate some problems, I vote for the merge.
>
> pz: ...if you decide to remove cytosol and merge it to cytoplasm, there might be problems related to the current ontology. For example, "plastid" is surrounded by "cytosol", and is part of "cytoplasm". If "cytosol" is to be replaced by "cytoplasm", "plastid" will be surrounded by, and is part of "cytoplasm" at the same time. Would that be allowed by the ontology?

nl: I think there is confusion on both counts. What happened in some PGDBs is that for some reactions, sometimes CCO-CYTOPLASM was used instead of the default compartment which was CCO-CYTOSOL. This will **cause needless disconnects** in the reaction network.

pz: By definition, cytoplasm and cytosol **are very different things**. But I agree that people may not distinguish them when using the terms. I am asking opinion from a group at Carnegie who conducts large-scale protein localization experiments.

tq: IMO, if you are going to eliminate either cytoplasm or cytosol, the one to keep is cytosol – that is almost certainly what is intended in nearly all transport reactions... However, I would strongly prefer to keep both, and to **eliminate data inconsistencies** by only allowing reactions to occur between compounds in spaces... Cytoplasm is not classified as a space, it is a super-component, so it should never appear in reactions, and the user should not be given the choice to add it. That way we could keep cytoplasm as a concept (with its correct definition) but **the user would never see it** .

nl: My proposal was that cytoplasm should become the space that will replace the current cytosol. In other words, I don't want the name "cytosol" to show in transport rxn diagrams, but "cytoplasm", for consistency.

tq: You could accomplish that by just **changing the common name** (or whatever name used for reaction display) of CCO-CYTOSOL to "cytoplasm". ... As to whether or not the name change would be misleading or confusing, I'll leave that up to the real biologists. It's possible there could be one answer for bacteria and another answer for eukaryotes, in which case you'd have to decide whether it was worth special case-ing.

The formalist within me recoils in horror at this mess – and I would suppose that any computer scientist would feel the same way at some level – but another part of me says, this is great! It reflects how knowledge representation is done in real-life practice, how human minds come at it through user interfaces, how history and practical considerations blend, how people collectively decide to remold part of one layer of the system to make up for deficiencies in another.

Look at some of the things going on in this discussion: defaults, consistency, history, utility, user confusion, resolution, voting, semantics of part-of vs. surrounded-by, impact on computational processes, user interface, naming vs denotation, status signaling, deference, smileys to deflect possible insult. The proposed solution involves papering over a conceptual fissure by using a different name in the user interface than the internal name. The technical, the social, and domain knowledge are all mixed together in fluid and effortless ways. There is constant effort required to align the interests of the users and the "interests" of formality and inertia, and the builders will use whatever tools are at their disposal – interface tricks, clever defaults, deployment of synonyms or pseudonyms, etc. This sort of thing goes on *all the time* in the course of real-world software development, and there aren't very good tools for describing it, let alone managing it.

Conceptualism, realism, pragmatism

The poverty of realism

The biomedical computing community has tried to grapple with problems of representating its exceedingly complex domain for many years. Recently, a philosophical debate about the nature of ontology has erupted [27] [71] [36] [50] [48] between two schools: "conceptualism", which holds that an ontology is "a formal specification of a conceptualization" [32], versus "realism", a faction led by the philosopher Barry Smith and colleagues at SUNU Buffalo, who insists that terms in an ontology denote real entities in the physical world.

Arguments for realism include: the concept of "concept" is ill-defined; realism is a necessary stance to avoid being sucked into the excesses of idealism and radical constructivism; and that existing conceptual ontologies, because they lack a strong formal grounding in reality, are riddled with incoherence. Conceptual ontologies might be good enough for law, but are inadequate for empirical science:

> The influence of the concept-centered view is a product not merely of the roots of information systems ontology in the field of knowledge representation. It has become entrenched also in virtue of the fact that much work on ontology has been concerned with representations of domains, such as commerce, law, or public administration, where we are dealing with the products of human convention and agreement – and thus with entities which are in some sense merely 'conceptual'. Today, however, we are facing a situation where ontologies are increasingly being developed in close cooperation with those working at the interface between the informatics disciplines and the empirical sciences, and under these conditions the concept-centered view is exerting a damaging influence on the progress of ontology. [70]

This is a very clear statement of the metaphysical basis of Smith's approach to ontology – the physical (empirical) is real, while the social consists of "mere" concepts. This hard boundary between the real and the social is exactly what Latour's approach is attempting to demolish, as I describe in more detail below. However, in the knowledge representation world, the realists seem to be winning in their battle with conceptualists, possibly because nobody in the sciences wants to seen as being against reality.

A realist ontology, the BFO (Basic Formal Ontology) [59] has been adopted by leading biomedical ontology efforts such as OBO [73].

> Realism has chosen wisely in its choice of name. Most scientists believe in reality so, when faced with realism vs conceptualism, their gut feeling is that the former will be right. They believe in a mind-independent reality so, therefore, conceptualism must be wrong.

But realism fails at even quite elementary use cases for scientific knowledge representation. For instance, realists insist that any concept in an ontology has to have a physical instantiation (be "real"). But consider the case of software to support pharmaceutical drug design (here I draw from professional experience as one of the developers of Afferent, a commercial software system to support combinatorial synthetic chemistry [15]). Synthetic chemists, in pharmaceutical research and elsewhere, spend their professional lives imagining molecules that do not exist yet, then figuring out ways to make them exist. Nowadays this is often done with the aid of software that can generate new molecular structures from libraries of parts, along with plans for synthesising them. Are such compounds real-world objects? Are they unreal before synthesis, but real after? These are not questions that are *germane* to a chemist, or to a designer of chemical software. Chemists have no ontological or epistemological distinction between a molecular structure before and after synthesis. Yet realism insists they are different and outlaws talking about the yet-to-exist ones, just as it outlaws talking about unicorns (which you might also want to represent, despite their unreality) and Higgs bosons (which could well be real but have not yet been demonstrated to be so):

> Descriptions and lands do, after all, exist...[but] it would be an error to include in a scientific ontology of drugs terms referring to pharmaceutical products which do not yet (and may never) exist, solely on the basis of plans and descriptions. Rather, such terms should be included precisely at the point where the corresponding instances do indeed exist in reality... [72]

Now, there *is* a clear distinction, which is reflected in software, between an abstract chemical compound (which has properties like structure and molecular weight, but is not a physical object – e.g., **butanol** has a molecular weight but no location) and a physical instance of that compound like **testube-3423** (which has properties like volume, purity, the date it was synthesized, and present location). In Afferent, these are two distinct ontological categories that are linked, called respectively **compound** and **sample**. But this distinction is based on actual practice, not a determination of the reality and metaphysical status of the two concepts.

Genes too were hypothesized abstract entities before their physical basis in DNA was discovered by Watson and Crick, and thus would be problematic to represent if people were doing formal knowledge representation back then – and we can assume that there will be similar problems today and in the future. In practice, advocates of the realist approach may have work-arounds for these problems (such as considering an informational entity to be "real"), but the point is that this is awkward, unnatural, weak, and a distraction from more important issues.

Complexity and barrier to entry

Another common critique of realism is that by forcing representation into a particular framework, the result is useless and forbidding complexity. I think this is one reason that semantic-web style knowledge representation has not had the success, the kind of mass uptake that drove the web to its current universal deployment. The barriers to entry to formal representation are forbiddingly high, and realism makes them worse. For instance, to solve problems like the above (representing an abstract informational entity), the BFO apparently has been patched to handle such cases with an abstraction called "generically dependent continuants" [55]. Here, for example, is the definition of the relationship **is-concretization-of**, which links generically dependent continuants with more "specifically" dependent entities.

> **is-concretization-of** is a relationship between a generically dependent continuant and a specifically dependent continuant. A generically dependent continuant may inhere in more than one entity. It does so by virtue of the fact that there is, for each entity that it inheres, a specifically dependent **concretization** of the generically dependent continuant that is specifically dependent. For instance, consider a story, which is an information artifact that inheres in some number of books. Each book bears some quality that carries the story. The relation between this quality and the generically dependent continuant is that the former is the concretization of the latter.[2]

Whether or not this is a good representation is hard to say, but the point is, very few lay persons not conversant with intricate formal ontology can tell either. In some ways realism is not a natural fit to human cognition (for alternatives that might alleviate this problem, see the section on prototype-based representation below). This may have nothing to do with an ontology's *accuracy*, but will affect its *utility*. There is some question here about what an ontology is for; if it is purely for machines to reason with or also a tool for humans to organize their knowledge. In practice, humans must still be involved at least in the construction of ontologies, if not their

---

[2] http://www.ontobee.org/browser/rdf.php?o=OBI&iri=http://purl.obolibrary.org/obo/OBI_0000294

deployment, so fitting an ontology to the way humans think might be a good idea.

Mental illness and realism

The best illustration of the poverty of the realist approach may be a paper from that school that applies their techniques to the problem of building an ontology for mental disease [14]. The amazing thing about this paper is that, aside from an offhand quotation of Szasz's theory that mental illness does not exist, it makes no mention whatsoever of the controversies about the reality of mental disease, the evolution of the concept over time, the political and social forces involved in its definition, the constant revision of the standard references (DSM-III and its successors) to reflect evolving social standards. In short, *none of the interesting issues* involved in the ontology of mental illness are dealt with. Instead, they are reduced to a single link in a graph:

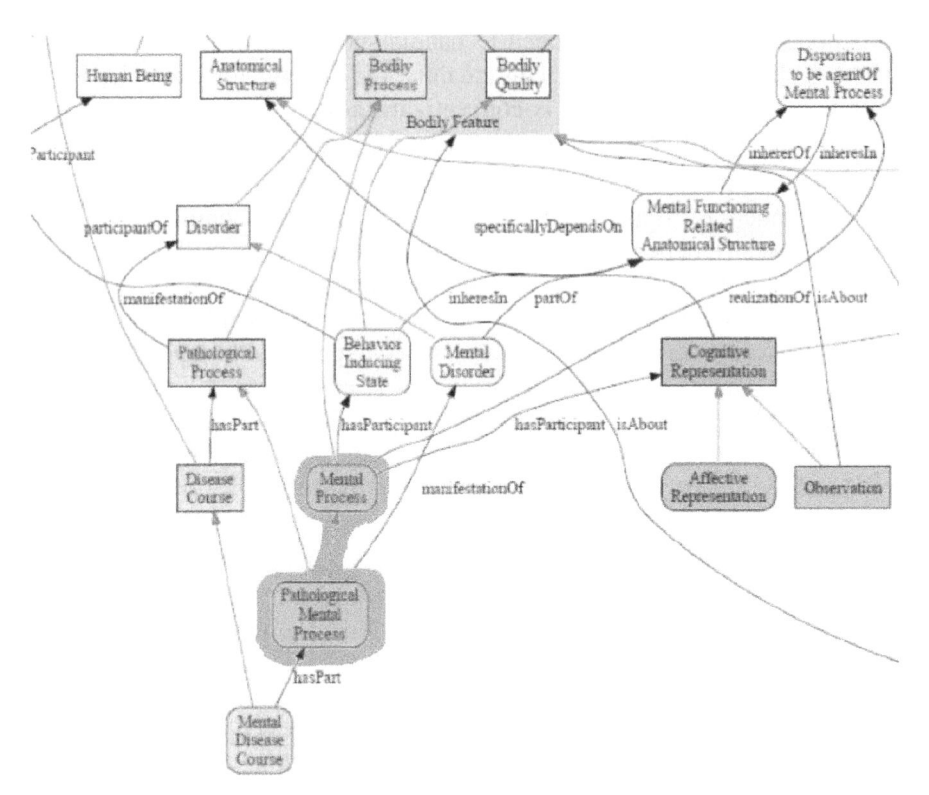

Figure 1: Ontology of mental illness from [14], highlight added

It may be that I'm missing something in realism or otherwise being unfair to it. In *Against Fantology* [60] and in a reply to Merril [71], Smith sets himself against a certain form of logicist representation, implying a willingness and ability to deal with the world's messiness:

> ...we ourselves are interested precisely in really existing scientific theories, and in the associated really existing ontologies, which in normal circumstances are not associated with any claim to completeness. Really existing scientific theories are marked, rather, by messy and inconvenient processes of change and of correction of error, including ontological error, and our formulation of the realist methodology is designed precisely to do justice to this fact.

On the other hand, he doesn't believe conflict is important:

> Where conflicts do arise in the course of scientific development, these are highly localized, and pertain to specific mechanisms, for example of drug action or disease development, which can serve as the targets of conflicting beliefs only because researchers share a huge body of presuppositions.

As best as I can interpret Smith's idea of realism, it is more of an ideal that science and scientific representation should aspire to, rather than a model or tool for science as practiced (despite the first quote above). In that sense, I find no problem with it. But it ignores the need for transient, situated, tentative representations that are the basis of everyday scientific practice, and computing practice as well. As Philip Lord put it, "the choice is between representing reality or representing how we practice science" [48].

Pragmatism

The debate between conceptualism and realism threatens to become as contentious as the so-called "science wars" that took place in the larger scientific and intellectual community in the 1990s [31] [33], and it revolves around some of the same philosophical dichotomies and exaggerations of opposing positions. While I am pretty firmly on the conceptualist side, I find the whole debate somewhat misguided. In general when faced with a hopeless philosophical quarrel, a good tactic is to try to transcend it or find a dimension of the issue that is orthogonal to the debate.

Just like the realist hijacked "realism", I would like to do the same with the "pragmatism", which connotes both a philosophical school (exemplified by William James, John Dewey, and Richard Rorty) and a common desirable attitude. We all want to be pragmatic! Neither biologists nor computer scientists want to get mired in fruitless philosophical debates; we want to model the world and build tools that get used. But sometimes descending into philosophy is necessary if *bad* philosophical assumptions are undermining your efforts at less abstract levels.

Philosophical pragmatism was introduced by William James as a corrective to a roughly similar debate of his own day between materialism and idealism. The essence of pragmatism is to cease looking for the essences of things, but rather to judge them by their consequences, how they are used, how they affect other things. As James put it, "It is astonishing how many philosophical disputes collapse into insignificance the moment that you subject them to this simple test of tracing a concrete consequence." [James, What Pragmatism Means, p27]

> Pragmatism represents a perfectly familiar attitude in philosophy, the empiricist attitude, but... in a more radical and in a less objectionable form than it has ever yet assumed. A pragmatist ... turns away from abstraction and insufficiency....from fixed principles, closed systems, and pretended absolutes and origins. He turns toward concreteness and adequacy, and towards power...It means the open air and the possibilities of nature, as against dogma, artificiality, and the pretense of finality in truth.
>
> ...pragmatism [is] a mediator and reconciler...that 'unstiffens' our theories. ..pragmatism is willing to take anything, to follow either logic or the senses and to count the humblest and most personal experiences.
>
> – William James, [34]

Richard Rorty extended pragmatism into the late 20th century and emphasized its antifoundational character [62], and Paul Feyerabend stretched in even further (perhaps too far) with his notion of "epistemological anarchism" [29], an attitude that all forms of representation and inquiry should be allowable. It is just this tendency of the radical pragmatists to to take things too far that inspires the realist reaction. The motivation for the hard-line realist position of Smith is that anything less than realism risks being pulled into a fuzzy world of uncertainty, conflict, and unanchored reference. Feyeranend, for his part, believed he was defending the practices of scientists from philosophers who wished to impose artificial restrictions on their activity. Is there a happy medium, a path that threads between the dangers of rigidity on one hand and losing the mooring of reality on the other? I maintain that looking at the actual, situated, bottom-up representations of science as actually practiced provides a guide. Carnap is not usually lumped with Feyerabend, but he makes essentially the same point in a more diplomatic way:

> Let us learn from the lessons of history. Let us grant to those who work in any special field of investigation the freedom to use any form of expression which seems useful to them; the work in the field will sooner or later lead to the elimination of those

forms which have no useful function. Let us be cautious in making assertions and critical in examining them, but tolerant in permitting linguistic forms." (Carnap, 1950) (from Merril [51]

Representation from the bottom up

Another inspiration for representational pragmatism is observations of the process of scientists in the laboratory, who regularly invent representational schemes that are deeply embedded in the phenomena they are tracking. The job of a scientist, as described by sociological observers of science, is to turn phenomena into inscriptions ("the transformation of rats and chemicals into paper" – Latour, [43]). The inscriptions of science start out as radically concrete, situated things, in somebody's notebook denoting concrete material entities and observations. But somehow scientists can lever themselves out of their situated perspective into something closer to *objectivity*, where they can issue abstract truths about the world that are deserving of publication. The sheer variety, inventiveness, and richness of the ways in which this happens is a rewarding object of study. Jeff Shrager described some of the realities of lab-notebook based representation, gleaned from his experience training to be a biologist [68]:

> But if you lose your lab notebook, you're hosed, mainly because you'll never figure out what the hell is in the hundreds of obscurely-labeled tubes in the various freezers in the various boxes with the various obscure markings on them. I haven't come upon a perfect scheme for organizing all this yet. The protocols I just put in date order and then I have an index in the front that tells me what date to look at for what protocols. Also, I've given each of the important (or long) protocols a code, for example, Akiko's Gene Inactivation Protocol is called AGN, and if you look on the date/page where it lives, there are various "check points" with labels like "AGN1", "AGN2", and at the end it says "AGNX". These are labels that I'll put on tubes that have reached that stage, so that I know where they are in their chemical careers.

A good ecology of representation needs flexibility. Scientists will invent labeling schemes that they translate into spreadsheets, then into tables in articles. The reality of scientific representation is just as Latour describes, a bottom-up matter of turning reality into inscriptions that are progressively refined. If logically formal representation is here, it comes at the endpoints of the process.

Latour: circulating reference

Bruno Latour is a sociologist of science whose work has generated a good deal of controversy. While he is often taken as an exemplar of the dreaded "social construction of science" and thus an enemy of realism and even of science itself, he vehemently denies this (recently in Pandora's Hope [45], Ch 1, for instance, titled *Do you Believe in Reality?*):

> Who loves the sciences...more than this tiny scientific tribe that has learned to open up facts, machines, and theories with all their roots, blood vessels, networks, rhizomes, and tendrils? Who believes more in the objectivity of science than those who believe it can be turned into an object of inquiry?

Here, we can ignore the metaphysical implications of Latour's viewpoint and concentrate on his picture of science as a process of mobilizing representations. A scientist will examine an object in the field (eg, in Ch 2 of *Pandora's Hope*, the structure of the border of a forest in Brazil), turn that phenomenon into inscriptions in a field notebook, bring those inscriptions back into a laboratory where they will be further condensed, abstracted, computed with, mixed with other representations that strengthen the scientists position. While Latour does not deny truth any more than he denies reality, he focuses not on the truth or veracity of representations but on the ways they circulate between scientists, instruments, laboratories, and publications, and the ways they enable a scientist in a laboratory to make statements that are true of the larger world. Science in this view is not only a social process, but one that unites humans, objects, and representations into seamless networks.

> The same article [on global warming and CFC emissions] mixes together chemical reactions and political reactions. A single thread links the most esoteric sciences and the most sordid politics, the most distant sky and some factory in the Lyon suburbs, dangers on a global scale and the impending local elections or the next board meeting. The horizons, the stakes, the time frames, the actors – none of these is commensurable, yet there they are, caught up in the same story.
>
> – We Have Never Been Modern [44], p1.

Latour views his position as an *enriched* realism, one that considers scientists, representations, social institutions, and politics just as real as rocks and atoms, with the implication that they need to be analyzed together. Now, I maintain that this should be a very *congenial* attitude for computationalists, a much better model of the real than that of the Buffalo ontologists. The essence of computer science is building representations that are at the same time real things, not only encoded in bits in a particular physical location in memory, but also potentially dynamic entities (actants in Latour's vocabulary), participants in a dynamic ecosystem made of software, humans, social relationships and institutions. Furthermore, we do not build representations alone but as part of systems for creating, encoding, and transmitting them. Computational representations are not mere mirrors of nature but parts of networks, of causal systems that connect humans, computers, and the domains of study, and need to be designed as such.

Convergence and objectivity

The goal of scientific representation (or any effort to create an ontology for general use) is *convergence* onto something that accurately represents an underlying reality. Science under construction must pursue divergent and rivalrous paths, but is guided by the faith (which so far seems well-placed) that the paths will ultimately converge on an objective truth. Unlike the more radical epistemologists of science like Feyerabend and Rorty, I believe that the structure of reality does in fact generate this kind of convergence – at least some of the time. Some areas of study are more strongly convergent than others – for instance, it seems likely that mathematical truths are the same for all cultures. However, even in mathematics there are different approaches to truth [22]. The further knowledge gets from mathematics, the more subject it will be to divergent approaches.

The difference between realism and pragmatism as approaches to ontology is that realism thinks that convergence can happen by decree, while pragmatism thinks that it happens more as an endpoint of a bottom-up social process, and that the semantic structures of the endpoint is not knowable in advance. The beautiful book *Objectivity* [23] demonstrates that even the concept of objectivity as an "epistemic virtue" has a history, and the modern idea of objectivity as a mechanical reproduction of nature was a product of a series of revolutions in scientific visualization. To the extent representations are objective, that is an *achievement*, and this applies equally to individuals, scientists, and modelers. Science is a somewhat magical tool for allowing us to escape from our lowly subjective viewpoints and getting a view of the world from above it as objectivity demands. But it's a process, and our tools need to support the process as it happens, not merely its endpoints.

Computational alternatives

> But logic also has its disadvantages... No exceptions are allowed, no matter how closely they match. This approach permits you to use no near misses, no suggestive clues, no compromises, no analogies, and no metaphors. To shackle yourself so inflexibly is to shoot your own mind in the foot—if you know what I mean.
> – Marvin Minsky [53]

My position is that knowledge representation should be a matter of making representations that capture and augment human knowledge and reasoning, rather than attempting to force it into narrow and unproductive channels. Convergence and agreement may be the goals, but the pathway towards it must take into account the divergent representations used in daily life and the ordinary practices of science. This means that representational systems must be fluid, situated, flexible, and social.

A variety of techniques suggest themselves to achieve these goals. These include alternative forms of representation such as prototype-based formalisms, that eliminate class/instance distinctions inherited from formal logic and replace them with structures more attuned to actual human thought. Another class of techniques are those borrowed from the web, open source and agile software communities: versioning, forking, branching, wikis, and explicit technological and institutional support for use cases, unit testing, and refactoring.

A Platform for Knowledge

What would a scalable, non-realist, distributed knowledge representation regime look like? An earlier paper described the concept of a Knowledge Operating System (or KnowOS) [77]. As a traditional operating system provides an abstraction layer between users and applications on one side and computer hardware on the other, a KnowOS provides a knowledge abstraction layer. A common representational framework such as the semantic web is an important aspect of such a service, but just as important are the APIs for programs to interact with knowledge and user interfaces for people to interact with it. Just as an operating system does not dictate what a user or programmer can do with a computer, a knowledge operating system doesn't dictate how a community represents knowledge – it provides a platform. And a truly web-scale knowledge representation scheme has to be a universal platform, not a narrow-minded formalism. How can we, as computationalists, design tools that make it easier for this magic to happen?

Our previous incarnation of the KnowOS concept, BioBike [28], provided a knowledge abstraction in the form of a frame system, along with a web-based framework for collaborative end-user programming by scientists. BioBike serves a number of scientific communities, provided a platform for the development of more complex tools [69] [20], and has been used in education. Later efforts [unpublished] were made to integrate its knowledge representation system with semantic web standards.

Where's the semantic web?

The Semantic Web has ambitions of being a universal framework for knowledge representation, something that would be as successful in the formal representation domain as the non-semantic Web has been for ordinary human communications. It has had at best limited success to date. This is in part due to the objectivist and logicist influences that have resulted in methodologies that are difficult to use, with extremely steep learning curves. This is in contrast to the non-semantic web, where readily understandable and visible standards have resulted in a vast proliferation of content and applications.

The semantic web is in theory a much more distributed effort than a typical knowledge representation, but there too we have seen the emergence of a cadre of alpha ontologists who rove around to various user communities helping them get their concepts in order. There isn't anything wrong with this, but again, it doesn't seem to scale, and may be part of the reason the semantic web has not quite taken off the way successful web efforts do. And it seems also that the semantic web effort has been captured by the realists, with a resultant rigidity and high barrier to entry. This is extremely unfortunate, because the world needs some way to interconnect all its knowledge. A universal standard for sharing formalized knowledge would be a great asset to the world, but only if it's used.

Prototype-based representation

Representation by prototypes rather than classes is an old but currently out-of-favor idea in computation Sketchpad, [46] [78] [74]. It was implicit in early AI work in knowledge representation [52], [9], but has faded in popularity in favor of class-based schemes which are easier to formalize and thus more amenable to algorithmic manipulation. It has several advantages over class-based representation, including:

- Prototypes are a more natural fit with human cognition, at least according to the branch of cognitive science exemplified by Eleanor Rosch [63] and George Lakoff [41];
- Prototype-based systems permit the representation of generalizations, defaults, and exceptions (non-monotonic reasoning), e.g., being able to say that birds fly while permitting exceptions for penguins and ostriches, or that dogs have four legs while permitting an exception for amputees;
- it suggests a different style of computation than strict logical inference, such as reasoning by analogy or by application of concrete cases.

For instance, default reasoning lets us assert that cats are mammals and mammals have hair, except those that don't:

Figure 2: Ripley the exceptional hairless cat

Prototype-based methodologies may be particularly useful for biological representation, since biology is laden with exceptions. Every biological feature started out as an exception (aka mutation) which then became fixated as a new norm. I suggest that our representations should be capable of evolving in a similar fashion. To return to the example we started with: under a prototype-based representational scheme, a marriage would be between a man and a woman, except when it wasn't. This might not make activists completely happy, but it would more accurately match the mind's cognitive structures.

Discourse, argumentation, provenance

Efforts to explictly represent the discourse and argumentation structure of knowledge word are one constructive path towards a more pragmatic model representation. Some examples of this approach include the SWAN ontology for scientific discourse [19], the ScholOnto project [11] for representing scholarly discourse and interpretation, and a large number of projects for representing and visualising argument structure [2], [64], [30], [54]. Perhaps closest in spirit to this paper is the DILIGENT system [18] which explictly supports a role for argumentation in ontology development.

Version control and agile software techniques

The mainstream software engineering community has developed very powerful and widely used tools for allowing divergence and reunification of software, using distributed version control systems (like git or mercurial), and social websites that build upon them (github). These systems positively encourage forking of code into alternate versions. These technologies support a methodology of extreme or agile development [3], which consists of a varied set of techniques whose overarching goal is to make programmers more productive and more connected to their code, to users, and to each other. There have been a few attempts to apply agile software methodologies to knowledge representation problems [39] [5], but ontology creation has its own unique character that makes some techniques difficult to translate (for instance, agile software development relies on unit testing, but it isn't clear how one tests an ontology).

Wikipedia and socially-constructed knowledge bases

Wikipedia is a phenomenally successful collaborative knowledge building effort. Obviously they are not defining a *formalized* knowledge representation, but they are, nonetheless, in effect forming ontologies, with semi-structured data being the norm (there are a variety of variants on Wikipedia that are closer to structured knowledge bases, including DBpedia [4] and Freebase []).

One of the more interesting features of Wikipedia, for the purposes of this paper, is their social structure and their meta-level ontology of problems, bugs, and conflicts about how to write articles. Every article has a corresponding discussion page for these issues to be hashed out, but there is also a semi-formalized ontology of issues, each of which translates into a cleanup template[3] or banner on articles. Typical examples warn of copyright violation, bias, problems with style, or notations such as "This article contains weasel words, vague phrasing that often accompanies biased or unverifiable information. Such statements should be clarified or removed." Wikipedia is an ongoing laboratory for ontology negotiation and policy negotiation as well [8] [12]. The informal nature of Wiki-based knowledge makes this process extremely fluid. The convergence of wikis and more formalized representations [40] suggests that similar processes might be possible for more formalized representations [26].

Conclusion: knowledge systems and open science

Representations of reality that are in some sense objective is what science does best, but objectivity is a destination, an end-goal of science. Scientists in practice use representations that are local, subjective, and subject to the pull of conflicting interest. So, computationalists need to acknowledge the way representations are actually used, by scientists and others, and adjust our tools to enable them to be used *better*. If computational systems are to support the process of science they must take this into account, and in addition to being repositories of finished knowledge, allow tentative and conflicting "pre-knowledge" to be represented, shared, and processed.

Science is almost defined by its values of open publication of results. Science invented open knowledge centuries before the web existed [24], but in this age of the web there is a movement to get science to utilize the tools of the web to share knowledge with greater speed and flexibility than it has been able to do in the past. Such efforts involve any or all of: standard representations for data, public repositories for data (e.g Geo [6]) and workflows [56], open access publications like the Public Library of Science (PLoS), and their convergence in web-scale science [76].

The movement for Open Notebook Science [10] aims to make these representations more public, promising a more collaborative, accelerated, and open form of scientific knowledge management than the traditional publishing models. But such efforts are likely to founder without some kind of shared basis of representation. Between the private, radically situated scribblings in individual lab notebooks and the crystalline, formal, supposedly objective status of realist ontologies lies a vast space of possible representational schemes and practices to be explored.

The fact that ontologies, like anything else, are subject to conflicting social forces should not come as a surprise. Nor should it be something that is swept under the rug. Ontologists are trying to put this process on a sounder footing, but it seems to me they are going about it in the wrong way.

---

[3] http://en.wikipedia.org/wiki/Wikipedia:Template_messages/Cleanup

There is a vast and largely unexplored design space in between pure chaos and rigid formalism.

References

[1] Gay marriage: the database engineering perspective.
[2] Supporting Collaborative Deliberation Using a Large-Scale Argumentation System: The MIT Collaboratorium. pages 1–8, aug 2008.
[3] XP 7, 2006, and Oulu. Extreme programming and agile processes in software engineering, jul 2006.
[4] S Auer, Christian Bizer, G Kobilarov, and J Lehmann. DBpedia: A Nucleus for a Web of Open Data, 4825.
[5] S Auer and H Herre. RapidOWL—An Agile Knowledge Engineering Methodology. *Perspectives of Systems Informatics*, pages 424–430, 2007.
[6] T Barrett, D B Troup, S E Wilhite, P Ledoux, D Rudnev, C Evangelista, I F Kim, A Soboleva, M Tomashevsky, K A Marshall, K H Phillippy, P M Sherman, R N Muertter, and R Edgar. NCBI GEO: archive for high-throughput functional genomic data. *Nucleic Acids Research*, 37(Database):D885–D890, jan 2009.
[7] R Bayer. *Homosexuality and American psychiatry: The politics of diagnosis.* the politics of diagnosis. Princeton Univ Pr, 1987.
[8] I Beschastnikh and T Kriplean. Wikipedian self-governance in action: Motivating the policy lens. *Proc ICWSM 2008*, 2008.
[9] Ronald J Brachman. I Lied About the Trees, Or, Defaults and Definitions in Knowledge Representation. *AI Magazine*, 6:1–14, feb 1985.
[10] Jean-Claude Bradley. Open Notebook Science Using Blogs and Wikis. *Nature Precedings*, (713), jun 2007.
[11] S Buckingham Shum, E Motta, and J Domingue. ScholOnto: an ontology-based digital library server for research documents and discourse. *International Journal on Digital Libraries*, 3(3):237–248, 2000.
[12] Brian Butler, Elisabeth Joyce, and Jacqueline Pike. *Don't look now, but we've created a bureaucracy: the nature and roles of policies and rules in wikipedia.* ACM, apr 2008.
[13] R Caspi, H Foerster, and CA Fulcher. MetaCyc: a multiorganism database of metabolic pathways and enzymes. *Nucleic acids ...*, 2006.
[14] Werner Ceusters and Barry Smith. Foundations for a realist ontology of mental disease. *Journal of Biomedical Semantics*, 1(1):10, sep 2010.
[15] David Chapman, Jeff Shrager, and Mike Travers. Afferent.
[16] VK Chaudhri, A Farquhar, R Fikes, and PD Karp. OKBC: A Programmatic Foundation for Knowledge Base. *aaai.org*.
[17] Ayoun Cho, Hongseok Yun, Jin Hwan Park, Sang Yup Lee, and Sunwon Park. Prediction of novel synthetic pathways for the production of desired chemicals. *BMC Systems Biology*, 4:35, 2010.
[18] Elena Simperl Markus Luczak Rudi Studer H Sofia Pinto Christoph Tempich. Argumentation-Based Ontology Engineering. nov 2007.
[19] T Clark and J Kinoshita. Alzforum and SWAN: the present and future of scientific web communities. *Briefings in Bioinformatics*, 8(3):163–171, may 2007.
[20] R Cornel and RS Amant. Collaboration and modeling support in CogLaborate. 19.

[21] L Cottret, P Milreu, V Acuña, and A Marchetti. Graph-Based Analysis of the Metabolic Exchanges between Two Co-Resident Intracellular Symbionts, Baumannia cicadellinicola and Sulcia muelleri, with .... *PLoS Computational* ..., jan 2010.

[22] Ubiratan d'Ambrosio and Ubiratan d'Ambrosio. Ethnomathematics and Its Place in the History and Pedagogy of Mathematics. 1985.

[23] Lorraine Daston and Peter Galison. *Objectivity*. Zone Books (NY), oct 2010.

[24] PA David. From Keeping "Nature's Secrets" to the Institutionalization of "Open Science". *Code: Collaborative Ownership and the Digital* ..., 2005.

[25] Emek Demir, Michael P Cary, Suzanne Paley, Ken Fukuda, Christian Lemer, Imre Vastrik, Guanming Wu, Peter D'Eustachio, Carl Schaefer, Joanne Luciano, Frank Schacherer, Irma Martinez-Flores, Zhenjun Hu, Veronica Jimenez-Jacinto, Geeta Joshi-Tope, Kumaran Kandasamy, Alejandra C Lopez-Fuentes, Huaiyu Mi, Elgar Pichler, Igor Rodchenkov, Andrea Splendiani, Sasha Tkachev, Jeremy Zucker, Gopal Gopinath, Harsha Rajasimha, Ranjani Ramakrishnan, Imran Shah, Mustafa Syed, Nadia Anwar, Özgün Babur, Michael Blinov, Erik Brauner, Dan Corwin, Sylva Donaldson, Frank Gibbons, Robert Goldberg, Peter Hornbeck, Augustin Luna, Peter Murray-Rust, Eric Neumann, Oliver Reubenacker, Matthias Samwald, Martijn van Iersel, Sarala Wimalaratne, Keith Allen, Burk Braun, Michelle Whirl-Carrillo, Kei-Hoi Cheung, Kam Dahlquist, Andrew Finney, Marc Gillespie, Elizabeth Glass, Li Gong, Robin Haw, Michael Honig, Olivier Hubaut, David Kane, Shiva Krupa, Martina Kutmon, Julie Leonard, Debbie Marks, David Merberg, Victoria Petri, Alex Pico, Dean Ravenscroft, Liya Ren, Nigam Shah, Margot Sunshine, Rebecca Tang, Ryan Whaley, Stan Letovksy, Kenneth H Buetow, Andrey Rzhetsky, Vincent Schachter, Bruno S Sobral, Ugur Dogrusoz, Shannon McWeeney, Mirit Aladjem, Ewan Birney, Julio Collado-Vides, Susumu Goto, Michael Hucka, Nicolas Le Novère, Natalia Maltsev, Akhilesh Pandey, Paul Thomas, Edgar Wingender, Peter D Karp, Chris Sander, and Gary D Bader. The BioPAX community standard for pathway data sharing. *Nature Biotechnology*, 28(9):935–942, sep 2010.

[26] F Dengler, S Lamparter, and M Hefke. Collaborative process development using semantic mediawiki. In *Proceedings of the 5th* ..., 2009.

[27] M Dumontier and R Hoehndorf. Realism for scientific ontologies. *Proceeding of the 2010 conference on Formal Ontology in Information Systems: Proceedings of the Sixth International Conference (FOIS 2010)*, pages 387–399, 2010.

[28] Jeff Elhai, Arnaud Taton, J P Massar, John K Myers, Mike Travers, Johnny Casey, Mark Slupesky, and Jeff Shrager. BioBIKE: a Web-based, programmable, integrated biological knowledge base. *Nucleic Acids Research*, 37(Web Server issue):W28–32, jul 2009.

[29] P Feyerabend. Against method: Outline of an anarchistic theory of knowledge, 1978.

[30] R Glenn and R Chris. Translating Wigmore Diagrams. *Computational models of argument: proceedings of COMMA 2006*, page 171, 2006.

[31] PR Gross and Norman Levitt. *Higher superstition: The academic left and its quarrels with science*. Johns Hopkins University Press, 1994.

[32] TR Gruber. A translation approach to portable ontology specifications. *Knowledge acquisition*, 1993.

[33] Ian Hacking. *The social construction of what?* Harvard Univ Pr, 1999.
[34] W James. What pragmatism means. *Essays in pragmatism*, 1948.
[35] Laura R Jarboe, Xueli Zhang, Xuan Wang, Jonathan C Moore, K T Shanmugam, and Lonnie O Ingram. Metabolic Engineering for Production of Biorenewable Fuels and Chemicals: Contributions of Synthetic Biology. *Journal of Biomedicine and Biotechnology*, 2010:1–19, 2010.
[36] Ingvar Johansson. Bioinformatics and biological reality. *Journal of Biomedical Informatics*, 39(3):274–287, jun 2006.
[37] M Kanehisa. KEGG: Kyoto Encyclopedia of Genes and Genomes. *Nucleic Acids Research*, 2000.
[37.1] P D Karp, S M Paley, M Krummenacker, M Latendresse, J M Dale, T J Lee, P Kaipa, F Gilham, A Spaulding, L Popescu, T Altman, I Paulsen, I M Keseler, and R Caspi. Pathway Tools version 13.0: integrated software for pathway/genome informatics and systems biology. *Briefings in Bioinformatics*, 11(1):40–79, jan 2010.
[38] IM Keseler and C Bonavides-Martínez. EcoCyc: a comprehensive view of Escherichia coli biology. *Nucleic acids ...*, 2009.
[39] H Knublauch. An agile development methodology for knowledge-based systems including a Java framework for knowledge modeling and appropriate tool support. 2002.
[40] M Krötzsch, D Vrandečić, and M Völkel. Semantic mediawiki. *The Semantic Web-ISWC 2006*, pages 935–942, 2006.
[41] George Lakoff. Women, Fire, and Dangerous Things: What Categories Reveal About the Mind. 2010.
[42] B Latour. Science in action, 1987.
[43] B Latour. Drawing things together. In *Representation in Scientific Practice*, 1990.
[44] B Latour. *We have never been modern.* Harvard Univ Pr, 1993.
[45] B Latour. *Pandora's hope.* essays on the reality of science studies. Harvard Univ Pr, 1999.
[46] H Lieberman. Using prototypical objects to implement shared behavior in object-oriented systems. *ACM SIGPLAN Notices*, 21(11):214–223, 1986.
[47] MO Little. HeinOnline. *Rutgers LJ*, 2007.
[48] P Lord and R Stevens. Adding a Little Reality to Building Ontologies for Biology. *PLoS ONE*, 5(9):e12258, 2010.
[49] W Malisoff. What Is a Gene? *Philosophy of Science*, jan 1939.
[50] G Merrill. Realism and reference ontologies: Considerations, reflections and problems. *Applied Ontology*, jan 2010.
[51] GH Merrill. Ontological realism: Methodology or misdirection? *Applied Ontology*, 2010.
[52] Marvin Minsky. A Framework for Representing Knowledge (AI Memo 306), 1974.
[53] Marvin Minsky. Logical Versus Analogical or Symbolic Versus Connectionist or Neat Versus Scruffy. *AI Magazine*, 12(2):1–18, jan 1996.
[54] A Moor and M Aakhus. Argumentation support: from technologies to tools. *Communications of the ACM*, 49(3):98, 2006.
[55] F Neuhaus and P Grenon. A formal theory of substances, qualities, and universals. *... of the 3rd International Conference on ...*, 2004.

[56] D Newman and S Bechhofer. myExperiment: An ontology for e-Research. page 408, 2009.
[57] Mark J Pallen. Time to recognise that mitochondria are bacteria? *Trends in Microbiology*, 19(2):58–64, feb 2011.
[58] Jonathan Wagg Michelle L Green Dale Kaiser Markus Krummenacker Peter D Karp Pedro Romero. Computational prediction of human metabolic pathways from the complete human genome. *Genome Biology*, 6(1):R2, dec 2004.
[59] DM Pisanelli. Biodynamic Ontology: Applying BFO in the Biomedical Domain. *Ontologies in medicine*, page 20, 2004.
[60] ME Reicher and JC Marek. Against Fantology. *Erfahrung und Analyse*, page 153, 2005.
[61] Saul A Kravitz Larry Smarr Paul Gilna Rekha Seshadri and Marvin Frazier. Oceanic Metagenomics: CAMERA: A Community Resource for Metagenomics. *PLoS Biology*, 5(3), mar 2007.
[62] R Rorty. Objectivity, relativism, and truth, 1991.
[63] E Rosch. *Prototype classification and logical classification: The two systems*. an informal discussion of a linguistic myth with Noam Chomsky and other linguists, philosophers, psychologists, and lexicographers. New trends in conceptual representation: challenges to ..., 1985.
[64] Warren Sack. *Design for very Large-scale Conversations*. PhD thesis, sep 2009.
[75] Thomas E Schacht. DSM-III and the politics of truth. *American Psychologist*, 40(5):513–521, 1985.
[65] E Schrödinger. What is life? : the physical aspect of the living cell: with Mind and matter & Autobiographical sketches. Cambridge Univ Pr, 1992.
[66] Wilbur J. Scott. PTSD in DSM-III: A Case in the Politics of Diagnosis and Disease. *Social Problems*, 37:1–18, mar 1990.
[67] J Shrager. The fiction of function. *Bioinformatics*, 19(15):1934–1936, oct 2003.
[68] J Shrager. *Diary of an insane cell mechanic*. Scientific and technological thinking, 2005.
[69] J Shrager, JP Massar, D Billman, and G Convertino. Multistage Collaboration in CACHE: The Bayes Community Model. *Citeseer*.
[70] B Smith. Beyond concepts: ontology as reality representation. *Formal Ontology In Information Systems: Proceedings of the Third International Conference (FOIS-2004)*, pages 73–84, 2004.
[71] B Smith. Ontological realism: A methodology for coordinated evolution of scientific ontologies. *Applied Ontology*, jan 2010.
[72] B Smith, W Kusnierczyk, D Schober, and W Ceusters. Towards a reference terminology for ontology research and development in the biomedical domain. *Proceedings of KR-MED*, 2006:57–65, 2006.
[73] Barry Smith, Michael Ashburner, Cornelius Rosse, Jonathan Bard, William Bug, Werner Ceusters, Louis J Goldberg, Karen Eilbeck, Amelia Ireland, Christopher J Mungall, Neocles Leontis, Philippe Rocca-Serra, Alan Ruttenberg, Susanna-Assunta Sansone, Richard H Scheuermann, Nigam Shah, Patricia L Whetzel, and Suzanna E Lewis. The OBO Foundry: coordinated evolution of ontologies to support biomedical data integration. *Nature Biotechnology*, 25(11):1251–1255, nov 2007.

[74] WR Smith. Using a prototype-based language for user interface: the Newton project's experience. *ACM SIGPLAN Notices*, 30(10):61–72, 1995.

[76] Jay M Tenenbaum. AI Meets Web 2.0: Building the Web of Tomorrow, Today. pages 1–22, dec 2006.

[77] M Travers and JP Massar. KnowOS: The (re) birth of the knowledge operating system. *The International Lisp Conference*, 2005.

[78] D Ungar and RB Smith. Self: The power of simplicity. *Conference proceedings on Object-oriented programming systems, languages and applications*, pages 227–242, 1987.

Sentence Composition in EPGY's Language Arts and Writing Course

Dan Flickinger, Stanford University

Computational linguists who develop grammar implementations often begin with the motivation to encode their hypotheses about the particular structures and the general principles which illuminate the analysis of a given language. Often these hypotheses are tested either on naturally occurring text corpora, or on systematically constructed test suites illustrating the range of linguistic phenomena under study, including both well-formed and ill-formed example sentences. Since many applications that make use of grammar implementations emphasize robustness of analysis over precision, it is nice for the grammarian to encounter an application where precision is demanded.

One such application can be found in online education courses designed to teach basic writing skills, where students are given exercises in which they construct sentences whose grammaticality is then judged by the system. In order to provide accurate and detailed automatic analysis of students' errors in composing sentences, a linguistically informed grammar (and parser) can be useful, and perhaps even essential as the complexity of the sentences increases. Of course, a grammar designed to analyze only well-formed utterances needs to be augmented for this kind of application to include rules or mechanisms that also accommodate certain ill-formed inputs, since students' errors are exactly what present opportunities for learning.

For the present study we draw on two broad-coverage implemented grammars, and show how they can be augmented with an inventory of mal-rules (Schneider and McCoy 1998, Bender et al. 2004) and mal-lexemes which enable precise error analysis of students' sentence composition in language arts and writing courses. Our goal in this work is to provide accurate and detailed instruction to students in response to each sentence that they write while taking these online courses. We are using (and abusing) the fine-grained knowledge of both English and Norwegian encoded in the grammars, together with their mal-rule extensions, to identify characteristic properties of student sentences which we can associate with error types, anchored in the type hierarchies of the lexicon and the syntactic constructions defined in the grammars. One of the central tensions we confront in this teaching application is in balancing the need for a consistent view of grammaticality with a more nuanced approach to good writing style. Since the implemented grammars are designed to be descriptively comprehensive, adapting them to the service of prescriptive instruction is not a straightforward task, though an interesting one. A second continuing challenge is to maintain a good balance between the flexibility of the grammar and high accuracy in disambiguating to choose the one intended analysis for each student sentence, so we can make the right diagnosis of errors as the basis for explanations to the students.

English: Education Program for Gifted Youth

The Education Program for Gifted Youth (EPGY) at Stanford University includes online courses for elementary school students to develop better writing skills. There are currently more than 25,000 elementary school students enrolled in the EPGY Language Arts and Writing online course, Grades 2-6, which includes one large set of exercises asking the students to compose sentences which are automatically evaluated by our software for immediate feedback. Using the existing interface in this writing course, the student sees on the computer screen one or more sentences, followed by a question, which is to be answered with a complete sentence. The student constructs this sentence by using the mouse to click on each word, in order, from lists of words visible on the screen. As each word is clicked, it appears in the box below where the sentence is being constructed. Once the student has composed the sentence for an exercise, the sentence is automatically evaluated, so the student either receives confirmation that the answer is correct, or is given an indication of the nature of the error(s) found. An example of an exercise using this interface is given in Figure 1.

EPGY

3.G.14.01
Sentence Composition

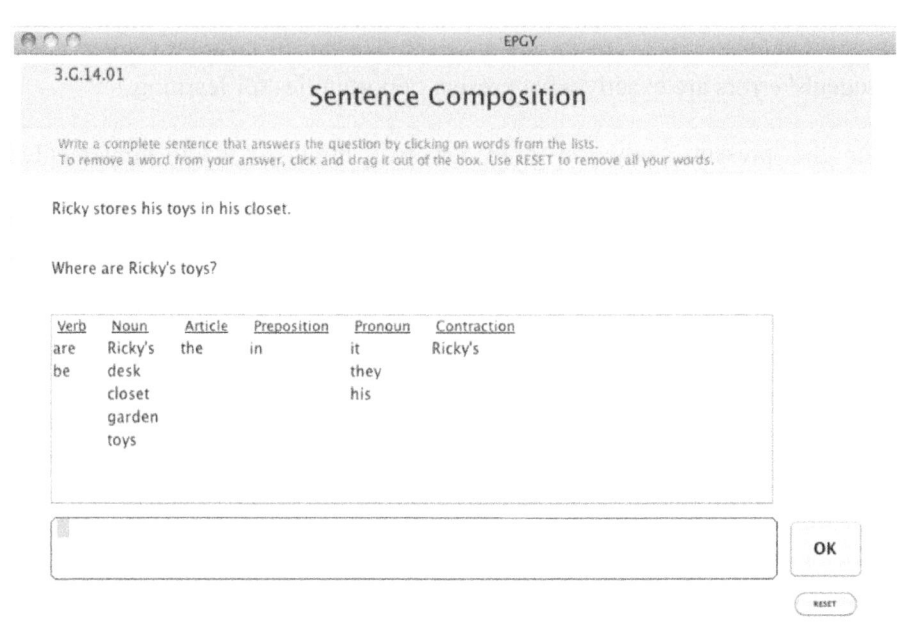

Write a complete sentence that answers the question by clicking on words from the lists.
To remove a word from your answer, click and drag it out of the box. Use RESET to remove all your words.

Ricky stores his toys in his closet.

Where are Ricky's toys?

Verb	Noun	Article	Preposition	Pronoun	Contraction
are	Ricky's	the	in	it	Ricky's
be	desk			they	
	closet			his	
	garden				
	toys				

OK

RESET

Figure 1

Evaluation of student answers

The automatic evaluation of student answers makes use of an efficient parser (Callmeier 2000), and a broad-coverage, precise grammar, the English Resource Grammar (Flickinger 2002) which has been extended to accommodate frequently occurring types of grammatical errors, following Bender et al. (2004). Frequently occurring well-formed and ill-formed answers are manually validated offline and cached to maximize the accuracy of the automatic online evaluation. Presented with the error diagnosis, the student is given the opportunity to correct the sentence and submit it a second time for evaluation. Then, after giving the student feedback on this second attempt, the system moves on to the next exercise.

Adaptation of the ERG has involved both mal-rule extensions and reductions in the grammar's coverage via *masking* to avoid unwanted ambiguity, given the restricted vocabulary made available to the students for each exercise. While the present implementation has focused only on judging syntactic well-formedness, we are also adding support for identifying semantic errors, by testing the equivalence of the semantic representation that the grammar assigns to the student's sentence with that of a set of correct answers supplied for that exercise. To accommodate systematic mismatches in this equivalence due to errors in the student's sentence, we are developing a paraphrase mechanism analogous to the semantic transfer approaches to machine translation.

References

Bender, E. M., D. Flickinger, S. Oepen and A. Walsh (2004). "Arboretum: Using a precision grammar for grammar checking in CALL," in Proceedings of the InSTIL/ICALL Symposium 2004, Venice, Italy.

Callmeier, U. (2002). "Preprocessing and Encoding Techniques in PET," in S. Oepen, D. Flickinger, J. Tsujii and H. Uszkoreit (eds.) Collaborative Language Engineering, Stanford: CSLI Publications.

Flickinger, D. (2002). "On building a more efficient grammar by exploiting types," in S. Oepen, D. Flickinger, J. Tsujii and H. Uszkoreit (eds.) Collaborative Language Engineering, Stanford: CSLI Publications, pp. 1-17.

Schneider, D. and K. McCoy (1998). "Recognizing Syntactic Errors in the Writing of Second Language Learners," in Proceedings of Coling-ACL, pp. 1198-1204. Montreal.

The Singularity is Here

Fanya S. Montalvo

I present aspects of a current crisis in software and argue that business as usual is not going to cut it. I review Kurzweil's Singularity and distinguish two aspects: computers becoming super intelligent, and humans losing control. There are signs that humans are losing control but without computers becoming intelligent enough for us to feel comfortable with them having control. I show how Kurzweil's predictions are measuring the wrong thing and present a possible way to improve our software systems that Kurzweil's Singularity measurements do not take into account, that is, organizational abstraction[1]. To have a chance of succeeding in the current software crisis, we need systems that can embody organizational abstraction. I cover types of organizational abstraction that may help.

Intention
What I would like to do in this paper is convey a feeling for the current crisis in software and demonstrate how business as usual is untenable. I use "the singularity" as a starting point because it is illustrative of our fears that we will, at some point, no longer be in control of our own technology. But could this loss of control already be happening without concurrent increase in the intelligence of our systems?

Kurzweil's singularity
Kurzweil wrote a book in 2006 entitled The Singularity is Near [Kurzweil 2006] in which he details how the exponential growth in technology signals that human-level intelligence by computers will be achieved in or around the year 2048. He considers statistics for exponential growth in all areas of computing: speed, capacity, memory, storage, miniaturization, share of the economy. Moore's law prevails in all areas of computation and technology in general, including penetration of the economy[2]. As the standard argument goes: when computers become smart enough to improve themselves, they won't need humans any longer. The process will run away with itself because humans will not be able to understand how computers are improving themselves, and even if humans could understand at some point in time, computers will be improving at such a rate that it will be impossible for humans to keep up . In other words, humans will no longer be the

---
[1] Although organizational abstraction is a deep computer science issue that is impossible to cover in a footnote, let me just explain it briefly by saying that it is a set of abstractions or categories of structure by which a system is organized.

[2] Hans Moravec and others also popularized this idea in [Moravec 1988] and [Moravec 1998b].

authors of the improvements. This run-away growth is the basis for the exponential in the singularity[3] regarding computers becoming intelligent, which Kurzweil calls "The Singularity" and I will call "Singularity$_{AI}$"; AI because it is about computers becoming artificially intelligent.

But everything that he demonstrates in his long series of exponential graphs is homogeneous: such as number of bits, number of MIPS (millions of instructions per second), cost, comparisons to number of neurons, synapses of neurons, etc.; what I am calling "flat" or homogeneous, easily measurable quantities of simple elements.

One graph in particular (Figure 1), originally created by Hans Moravec [1998a], compares computer MIPS per $1000 to brain power equivalence of biological organism based on their number of neurons, speed of neurons, and number of synapses. There is exponential growth here too. And based on projections, we should be at the computer power equivalent of a lizard by now. But comparison of this graph to the current robotics state of the art clearly illustrates that just by counting MIPS and easy measures of brain power in the biological domain, we don't magically get to the organizational complexity of a lizard. Something else is needed. We certainly aren't at the brain power of a lizard right now with our technology.

What might be the necessary ingredient? What might be the extent to which computer technology is, none-the-less, out of our control? These topics and how they are related will be the topics of this paper.

Organizational complexity

Organizational complexity comes in many forms: hierarchy, fan-out/fan-in of interconnected elements, the system/subsystem relationship, abstraction[4]. Organizations in general take a very long time to evolve--- biological systems, for example: from single cells to mammals; social systems: from tribes to nations; economic systems: from individual trading to multinationals. Intelligence in these organizations does not come for free by accumulating bits or years. It evolves at a different rate than flat substrates[5]. It's easy to scale up numbers of bacterial cells, for example, to create millions of them by reproduction, but for them to organize themselves into multicellular organisms takes a series of serendipitous jumps in organization occurring over millions of years in a very large variety of ecosystems.

---

[3] The term "singularity" can apply to any number of mathematical functions having exponential growth. In this case, however, it is typically used for the exponential growth of computer intelligence.

[4] Abstraction differs from complexity in being a symbolic representation of complexity. An example would be an algorithm being an abstraction of an implementation.

[5] Simple components with little or no organizational complexity.

Organizational jumps are shifts in a level of abstraction: not an easy feat, nor easily measurable using a uniform, simple substrate. Consider biomass. A person weighs as much as a million ants [Hölldobler & Wilson 1994]. How could we measure intelligence in either case in order to tell the difference? Are a million ants as intelligent as one human?

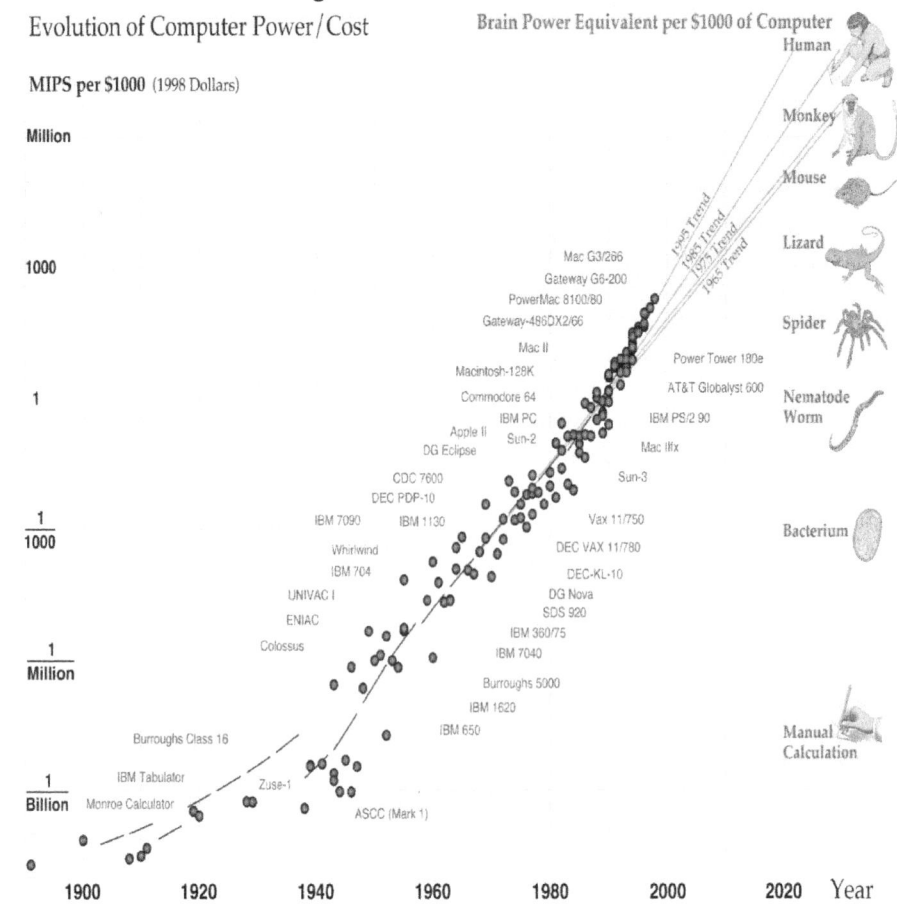

Figure 1. Evolution of Computer Power/Cost [Moravek, 1998a, with permission]

Another kind of singularity

Lately I've been getting the sneaking suspicion that there may be another technological singularity afoot which is much more insidious than Kurzweil's Singularity$_{AI}$, that is, one having to do with control. There are a number of instances where the penetration of computers in everyday life has spelled disaster, or at the very least, poorly understood instabilities.

If you look at any organization these days, you will find computers inextricably involved with people at every level and in every aspect of the work. At this point it's very difficult to tease them apart, so you might as well treat them as similar entities --- either human or computer --- communicating with each other in the larger whole of an organization [Hewitt 2011a]. Hewitt calls these entities participating in a much larger organization "orgs".

Instabilities range from the local, such as, Microsoft's "blue screen of death" where control is wrested out of the hands of users abruptly and without warning, and usually signals destruction of some parts of their environment --- to the annoying, such as the exponential growth of spam, viruses, malware, and protection software's inability to keep up, or the user's inability to keep up with the purchasing and installation cycle. They range from the exasperating, such as, automated telephone answering systems where the caller is unable to ever reach a person that could help them --- to the much more global and destructive example of exotic risk instruments that crashed the world economy. In all these cases there is a marked lack of control by humans and predominant control[6] by computer systems. All of these systems would not be able to exist without computers. It's too late to turn back and get rid of computers entirely. We humans depend on them so extensively now that we cannot reasonably turn back.

This situation I am calling "Singularity$_{ctl}$", the one caused by exponential growth in technology without a corresponding growth in understanding by computers of humans and by humans of computers. I call it Singularity$_{ctl}$ because it is related to loss of human control and understanding of large scale organizations including lots of embedded technology. There is a communications mismatch because understanding requires more than just increased speed, capacity, and bandwidth. It requires a level switch, an abstraction or a set of them because humans communicate using a very different set of abstractions than computers do.

We can look with more detail at some of these financial examples where computers were definitely involved. One example on a small timescale: the stock market Flash Crash of May 6, 2010 [Salmon & Stokes2011]; and the other on a longer scale: the crash of mortgage-backed securities and financial risk instruments [Salmon 2009]. One could argue that these were failures of regulation and politics, but the speed with which instabilities spread was definitely a result of automation. And the failure to unwind these

---

[6] Again, control is a deep issue in computer science. There are mathematical theorems about under which conditions a computer will halt. So the user can wait forever if control is not designed properly. Concurrency addresses the issue of computers never halting but traditional architectures cannot guarantee it.

crashes satisfactorily was at least in large part the opacity[7] of the technology involved.[8]

The upshot being that there is no single person in control of large organizations: not CEO's ---they have boards, shareholders, and bottom lines to respond to. Nor presidents: after being elected Obama seems to have become more responsive to security agencies, the military, and the election cycle than to his constituency.
So people aren't in control, computers aren't entirely in control, large systems are growing exponentially and becoming less and less understandable. But the degree of intelligence of this partnership is not keeping up with its proliferation of unintelligible, large systems. Singularity$_{ctl}$ is here now.

Possible solutions
What can we do about this? There is some hope in message passing systems because they're much more scalable than Turing Machines[9] [Hewitt2011a]. They fit more naturally into the way organizations grow: they are interleaved with humans: every human has at least one computer that they talk to within large organizations. And what's important about these coalitions is the way they communicate with each other, not necessarily what kind of computation they each do. If the bottleneck of communications between human and computer is too narrow, the organizations [Hewitt 2011a] will fail.

The Message Passing (MP) model is not equivalent to the Turing Machine (TM) model of computation [Hewitt 2011a]. MP is inherently concurrent. MP scales better than TM and is a better fit to concurrent systems, the kind that large numbers of humans and computers embody in an organization. What about the intelligence that is so sorely needed in large scale organizations to keep up with exponential technological growth? Well, humans are already intelligent. What is needed is better communication of humans with computers so that each can understand the other and thus achieve shared control. Computers shouldn't run off by themselves without checking in with humans and without explaining[10] what they are doing with

---

[7] No higher level abstractions, complex mathematical algorithms, no reporting between parts of the organizations, lots of proprietary software and algorithms so there could be no reporting between organizations and regulators.

[8] Granted regulators, insurance companies, and banks may have colluded to produce this opacity, but technology certainly aided and abetted to an extent that no set of individuals could be found at fault.

[9] By Turing Machines I mean all classical models of computation which are Turing equivalent, a prime example being the von Neumann architecture.

[10] In order to explain themselves they must have some degree of self-reference. Self-reference is a complex issue but self-documenting code would be a good

humans before they tear off in some unsupervised direction that humans can no longer access or understand. For example, I often click too many times and too quickly in Windows and the operating system freezes. I can no longer communicate with the system. If it were written in a truly concurrent model of software, I would always be able to communicate with it and it would always be able to communicate with me. Message passing would be sustained. A more technical example that illustrates shared control can be found in Hewitt [2011b], in which two processes compute whether the fringe of their respective trees is the same.

We need more transparency on both sides. Humans need a better way of explaining themselves to computers so that computers can incorporate human knowledge in a much more fine grained interaction than present. In order to do this, we need better abstraction tools as an integral part of the communication. MP supplies better tools for representing such abstractions. Detailed knowledge of communication can exist at every level of abstraction in each actor.

Large organizations have always had their instabilities. What's different about the present situation is that our tools --- capacity, speed, bandwidth of computer technology--- are expanding exponentially faster than we can domesticate them[11]. The ways we've used to domesticate computers up to now have not scaled well because of our historical attachment to the Turing Machine model where there is one CPU in control. The Message Passing model scales better with exponential growth because no single entity is globally in charge, but each entity can represent the part of its intelligence relevant to the larger whole and communicate it to necessary partners. In Message Passing systems control can be distributed and can be put where it's needed. An interconnected network's communication scales exponentially whereas top-down or bottom-up communication only logarithmically [Nowak & Highfield 2011].

Conclusion

I will not go into detail of how this integration can be achieved. My main purpose in this presentation is to show how out of the control the current situation is. We have a singularity on our hands, but it's not Kurzweil's Singularity$_{AI}$. It's the Singularity$_{ctl}$ resulting from computers receding from

---

example, but often the documentation, which is given lower-priority, fails to keep up with the code. Unless the consistency of the documentation with the code is self-enforced, it soon goes out of date. A good topic for this conference.

[11] If we think of the domains that computers are applied to as a territory, the territory is growing much faster that our ability to civilize that territory. The construction tools for civilization are just too weak. Of course, this is a metaphor and I'm speaking of organizational tools for software.

human control. Kurzweil's Singularity$_{AI}$ conflates both the degree of intelligence that computers may achieve with the degree to which humans will still be or not be in control of them. I have tried to tease these two aspects apart to show that we can have one, without the other. There are two components to Singularity$_{AI}$: computer superintelligence and loss of control. In its traditional form superintelligence is the cause of the loss of control by humans. But it is possible to lose control for other reasons, such as, disorganization: too rapid growth of lower-order substrates without organizational abstraction that scales. It seems that we could be in this latter form of the singularity: Singularity$_{ctl}$.

Acknowledgements

I'd like to thank Kat Brown, Carl Hewitt, Pete Marks, Martin Perl, Mike Travers, Richard Waldinger, and Jean Wolff for their expert advice and kind encouragement.

Bibliography

[Hewitt 2011a] "Actor model of computation" ArXiv 1008.1459v13.

[Hewitt 2011b] "ActorScript extension of C#, Java, and Objective C, : iAdaptive concurrency for antiCloud privacy and security" ArXiv 1008.2748v14.

[Hölldobler & Wilson 1994] B. Hölldobler & E.O. Wilson. Journey to the Ants. Belknap Press, Cambridge, Massachusetts: 1994.

[Kurzweil 2006] The Singularity is Near, Penguin: 2006.

[Moravec 1988] Mind Children, Cambridge University Press: 1988.

[Moravec 1998a] Hans Moravec, "When will computer hardware match the human brain?" Journal of Evolution and Technology 1, 1998.

[Moravec 1998b] Robot: Mere Machine to Transcendent Mind, Oxford University Press: 1998.

[Nowak & Highfield 2011] Martin Nowak & Roger Highfield. SuperCooperators, Free Press: 2011.

[Salmon 2009] Felix Salmon and Jon Stokes, "Recipe for Disaster: The Formula That Killed Wall Street" Wired 17.03, March 2009.

[Salmon & Stokes 2011] Felix Salmon and Jon Stokes, "Algorithms Take Control of Wall Street" Wired 19.01, January 2011.

Biological responses to chemical exposure: Case studies in how to manage ostensible inconsistencies using the Claim Framework

Catherine Blake

Our daily decisions concerning which foods, drugs and substances to consume have a direct impact on level of exposure to chemicals. At the national level, policies set at by the Food and Drug Administration and the Environmental Protection Agency impact both our direct and indirect exposures. Although the latter is based on the best available scientific evidence, all of these decisions are made against a backdrop of uncertainty. Consider the phrase *median lethal dose (LD_{50})*, which is used in toxicology to capture the dose of a chemical that is required to kill half of the members in a given population. This measure embodies an intrinsic acceptance of inconsistencies in that it removes the need to explain why half the tested population dies at LD_{50} while the other half of the population survives. In addition to individual responses within the same study, differences between studies are inevitable when studying the highly complex and dynamic relationship between biological responses to chemical exposures, for example LD_{50} for acrylamide ranges between 85 and 1148. Our goal is to foreground this uncertainty, which can be hidden when taking only a global view of the biological responses to chemical exposure. To that end, we have developed the Claim Framework that captures how scientists communicate the results of their empirical study. The Claim Framework comprises four information facets (agent, object, change and dimension) that are pieced together to form five different claim types (explicit, implicit, comparison, correlation and observation). This paper provides case studies drawn from toxicology, medicine and epidemiology to illustrate how the level of abstraction provided by the Claim Framework is sufficient to capture experimental results from a variety of different study designs that are used to measure a biological response to chemical exposure.

Introduction

Scientists in medicine, toxicology and epidemiology spend much of their time predicting the biological response(s) that will ensue after chemical exposure. In medicine, the biological responses typically lessen the impact of a disease or injury, while in toxicology the biological response is typically harmful. Despite their differences, both these communities employ controlled experiments to reduce the inherent uncertainty in how an individual will respond to a given chemical; however, the very controls that limit variation within the lab contribute to uncertainty beyond the laboratory where the level and duration of exposure differ from those used in the control group. For example, scientists conducting a clinical trial deliberately select study subjects with the same (typically a single) medical condition, which can be problematic when the treatment is used by the general population who have multiple medical conditions, are of a different age, or have different behavioral factors.

In medicine, Phase Four trials occur after a treatment has been approved by the Federal Drug Administration (FDA). Such trials help to mitigate against the limitations of a laboratory study design by considering how a treatment works in the broader population. This drive to move beyond a laboratory setting is mirrored in toxicology where cumulative risk assessments that consider multiple chemicals are starting to be added to the more than 500+ risk assessments available in the Integrated Risk Information System (IRIS) database (a service provided by the Environmental Protection Agency (EPA)). Cumulative risk assessments can provide insight into the cancelling or synthesis (i.e. much more than additive) effects that multiple chemicals can have on biological responses. However, this change in focus drastically increases the search space of experimental conditions, which can lead to an increase in uncertainty. New ways to conduct experiments in-silica are starting to be explored to bridge this gap, but ultimately the quality of these computational models depends on the quality of the initial parameter settings.

In contrast to the controlled experiments that are employed in the medical and toxicology communities, epidemiologists focus on long term chemical exposures in a naturalistic setting where they can explore chronic health conditions and longer chemical exposure time frames (such as the nurses and teacher's cohort) or opportunistic studies such as exposure during employment. However, observational study designs do not enable the researcher to control the amount of exposure for both ethical and pragmatic reasons and thus the types of claims that can be made from such studies will differ than those made in a controlled experiment.

It is against this backdrop of uncertainty that federal agencies make public policy that impact our direct and indirect exposure to chemicals. The information synthesis processes used in these agencies consider both acute and chronic levels of chemical exposure from a variety of study designs that differ with respect to the underlying population distributions, assumptions, exposures, and time frames and biological responses. Thus the manual processes employed by the FDA and EPA are the gold standard when it comes to biological responses to a chemical, but the effort required to synthesize new scientific findings into public policy can delay the potential health benefits of such findings in the general community. Moreover, many of the decisions about which foods to eat, drugs to take and toxins to consume, are made by individual consumers who do not have access to the resources or expertise in these agencies to synthesize evidence from scientific literature.

Our goal is to enable scientists, decision makers and consumers to better understand the ostensible inconsistencies that surround a biological response to chemical exposure, which ultimately contributes to our health. We believe that understanding discourse in scientific literature holds the key to achieving this goal, as scientific articles provide an underutilized resource in how scientists conduct experiments and reconcile different results. Although scientist operate in a social context [1] which can manifest in biomedical literature as publication bias, articles have been used for centuries to document and extend findings and are thus critical in order to understand not just the current state of the scientific community, but also shed light into the argumentative structures that support a particular result. It is these structures on which the Claim Framework is based [2]. The Claim Framework draws from work in scientific rhetoric and follows a long tradition in sub-languages, which was first introduced by Harris, a linguist who characterized sentence structures used in a set of immunology articles [3]. The Claim Framework captures how scientists communicate the results of an empirical study and comprises four information facets (agent, object, change and dimension) that are pieced together to form five different claim types (explicit, implicit, comparison, correlation and observation). In this paper we draw examples from medicine, toxicology and epidemiology to illustrate how the semantic and quantitative facts captured in the Claim Framework can provide a way to build systems that are robust in the face of the ostensible inconsistencies involved with an individual's biological response to a given chemical.

Related work

Communication patterns used in scientific articles have been studied from several perspectives including computational linguistics, philosophy and have been particularly well-studied with biomedical literature.

Scientific sub-languages

One of the earliest attempts to characterize language used in scientific communication was conducted by Zellig Harris, who analyzed 14 full-text immunology articles that were published between 1935 and 1970 [4]. His manual analysis of each sentence within these articles revealed clear patterns between word classes and sentence constructions and caused to claim that "we have in science language something new: a number of different sentence types distinguished by their word classes, but all having the same operator argument, i.e. subject-verb-object structure" [4]. Fillmore also focused on enumerating argument types for a given set of verbs based on the premise that "The sentence in its basic structure consists of a verb and one or more noun phrases, each associated with the verb in a particular case relation" [5] and subsequent projects such as FrameNet extends this work.

Harris also observed that operators carry 'evidentiality meaning' [4]. The different claim types in the Claim Framework also capture different levels of evidence. Thus you would expect the study design to influence the way in which a scientist describes their results. For example, studies that use a controlled design (such as a randomized clinical trial) would contain more explicit claims, whereas observational studies (such as a longitudinal study) would contain more implicit or comparison claim types.

Scientific rhetoric

Scientific communication has also been explored from a rhetorical standpoint that situates a scientific article is within the research community. In particular the comparison claim type is similar to the Create a Research Space (CARS) model, which includes an 'establishing a niche' phase where an author counter-claims to establish a research gap [6], and the Rhetorical Structure Theory includes a contrast schema and antithesis relation that is used between different nucleus and satellite clauses [7]. Comparisons have been mentioned in these earlier study of physics articles where authors compare their results with previous experimental results (see sections 4.3 and 8.1 in [8]), which is also mirrored in Teufel and Moen's contrast category, which includes the action lexicon, better_solution, comparison and contrast [9]. In contrast to these models, we focus exclusively on the results of an empirical result.

Biomedical text mining

A large body of research has been conducted in biomedical text mining that relates to this work including the Gene Ontology (GO) Consortium (www.geneontology.org), a collaborative effort that provides manual annotations related to cellular components, biological processes and molecular functions of genes. Of the five relationships identified in GO three (regulates, positively_regulates and negatively_regulates) are most similar to the Claim Framework. As with the GO project, the Claim Framework also captures the level of evidence which is done via different claim types. The second area of related biomedical research identifies gene and protein relationships from biomedical literature, which is best summarized in [10]. Another rich resource for existing work is papers written for the Learning Language in Logic (LLL) Challenge, where natural language processing researchers compete for the best method to identify gene protein relationships from MEDLINE abstracts [11].

Automating the claim framework

At this point, we have developed automated methods to identify explicit and comparison claim types. The approach used to populate explicit claims is strongly influenced by Fillmore's emphasis on the implicit and pre-suppositional levels of communication associated with verbs [5]. Specifically, a combination of semantic features related to verbs and syntactic features were used to identify explicit claims (see [2] for details). Verb categories were generated from the full text biomedicine articles from the Genomics Track of the Text Retrieval Conference (TREC) [12]. An important difference between the general verb-argument structures explored by Harris and Fillmore is that explicit must only consider the findings reported in an article.

In addition to semantic features (i.e. the verbs), the system developed to identify explicit claims employs syntactic features which are similar to those used in the RelEx system, which identifies genes and proteins [13] relationships; however, our approach does not apply the apply tight constraints to terminal nodes used by RelEx where a terminal node must be a gene or a protein or in Rosario and Hearst where terminal nodes must be a treatment or disease [14, 15]. Thus, our automated approach is more similar to ARBITER, a computer program that identifies binding relationships from text [16], which was developed as part of the Semantic Knowledge Representation Project [17] and subsequently extended [18].

We have also developed methods to identify comparison claims automatically. In the initial experiment a binary classifier was used with semantic and syntactic features (similar to the explicit claims) to discern a comparison from non-comparison sentence [19]. Our subsequent work focuses on identifying the specific agent, object and dimension of change from a given sentence [20]. As with the earlier work semantic and syntactic features are employed, but rather than discerning a comparison from a non-comparison sentence, the system classifies noun phrases as an agent, object or dimension of change.

At this point we have not developed automated methods to identify implicit, observations and correlations. The current implementations do not contain domain specific terms, but experimental results thus far have focused on biomedical texts, with limited work on social science literature[21].

Case studies

The best way to explain how the how biological responses to chemicals are captured using the Claim Framework is to provide real examples from actual papers in toxicology, medicine and epidemiology. The case studies below illustrate how scientists describe grapple with uncertainty and why a representational language that reflects that uncertainty must include semantic and quantitative components.

Toxicology

The toxicology phrase *median lethal dose (LD_{50})*, which describes the dose of a chemical at which half of a tested population dies. An article may provide the dose-response curve (usually as a graphic), and the time-frame in which death occurred, but LD_{50} alone enables a toxicologist to convey to a colleague that a chemical is acutely toxic. This term, which appears in nearly ten thousand MEDLINE sentences, is an interesting example of the toxicology sublanguage because the term does not appear in our general vernacular and because it embodies the inherent uncertainty associated with a biological response to a chemical. Specifically the acceptance that although half of a population will die, the other half will survive and that science is not able to provide the biological responses for an individual (usually mice or rats), but rather can only provide a summary for the overall population.

At first glance LD_{50} values can appear to be inconsistent. Consider acrylamide, which is used in a range of products such as paper and dyes and water treatment plans and is produced naturally when cooking at high temperatures. Acrylamide levels are currently regulated in the US under the Safe Drinking Water Act, which requires that water treatment plants not exceed 0.05 percent dosed at 1mg/L [1] and reported under California's Proposition 65, which doesn't limit chemical exposure per se, but provides consumers with a list about chemicals that have been deemed carcinogenic (acrylamide was added in 1990) or cause reproductive toxicity (acrylamide was added in 2011). Other exposures to acrylamide, such as the levels in foods are not currently regulated in the US.

Table 1. Ranges of LD_{50} Reported from Acrylamide Exposures (see [22])

Species (route)	LD_{50} in mg/kg bw	References
Rat (oral)	107 – 251	IPCS (3), EU (5), NTP (54)
Rat (dermal)	400	IPCS (3), NTP (54)
Rat (i.p.)	90 – 120	IPCS (3), NTP (54)
Mouse (oral)	107 – 170	IPCS (3), NTP (54)
Guinea pig (oral)	150 – 180	IPCS (3), EU (5)
Rabbit (dermal)	1,148	EU (5)
Cat (i.v.)	85	IPCS (3)

Table 1 shows LD_{50} values for acrylamide ranges, which between 85 and 1,148. More acrylamide is required to induce toxicity in rats through their skin (dermal) than by ingesting the chemical (oral) and toxicity also depends on the species, where rabbits require a concentration that is almost 3 times higher than the rate reported for rats given the same delivery mechanism (dermal). Note also that LD$_{50}$ is reported as a rate (in this case mg/kg) to control for members of a population who are of a different size. Some might argue that identifying factors that influence LD$_{50}$ is a core mission of toxicology research.

So how might an information system capture the data reflected in Table 1? One strategy is to encode the known factors into Resource Description Framework (RDF) triples, which have become a staple for representing knowledge in the semantic web. The RDF triple shown in (1) is problematic because acrylamide only caused some of the population to die. A better RDF triple would employ the toxicology sublanguage of LD$_{50}$ as a predicate and the chemical and amount as arguments (see 2 and 3).

> causes (Acrylamide, death) (1)
> General form: LD$_{50}$ (Chemical, Amount mg/kg body weight) (2)
> For this instance: LD$_{50}$ (Acrylamide, 85) (3)

Additional RDF triples could be added to capture the species and method of delivery from Table 1 that influence LD$_{50}$, however trying to define all the factors apriori would be perpetually incomplete as factors continue to unfold as new experiments are conducted. For example, sentence (4) below reveals a temporal component to LD$_{50}$ that is not reflected in Table 1.

> The LD$_{50}$ (and 95% CI) were estimated to be 251 mg/kg (203-300 mg/kg) of acrylamide at 24hr post-dosing and 175 mg/kg at 168 hr post dosing. PMID=452021 (4)

Rather than trying to identify every feature that influences LD$_{50}$, the claim framework focuses on how a scientist, in any discipline, describes the result of their study. For example the results from sentence 4 would be captured as the two separate observational claims:

> Claim 1: Claim Type: Observation
> Object: LD$_{50}$
> Object$_{Modifier}$: acrylamide, 251 mg/kg, 203-300
> Change$_{Modifier}$: 24 hr postdosing
> Source: PMID=452021, section= Results

> Claim 2: Claim Type: Observation
> Object: LD$_{50}$
> Object$_{Modifier}$: acrylamide,175 mg/kg, 159-191
> Change$_{Modifier}$: 168 hr postdosing
> Source: PMID=452021, section= Results

The claim framework is not the first (and we daresay not the last) effort to annotate rhetoric from scientific articles. The difference is that the claim framework focuses on how scientists communicate results rather than an array of rhetoric types [9, 23] which is critical when working with full-text articles. Several other efforts have taken a Message Understanding Conference approach were the system first identifies entities, which are then used to identify relationships [24-26]. We propose an approach that focuses on the general sentence structures and leaves the unification of noun phrases to subsequent processing steps. From a public policy standpoint, the most important gap in the RDF triples in 1-3 is that the results are de-coupled from the article, which is a sharp contrast to how scientific results are currently used to inform public policy where a direct connection between the claim and the original source document is critical to maintain transparency (see the right hand column of Table 1). A knowledge representation that does not include this link is unlikely to be adopted by agencies who conduct risk assessments in toxicology.

Medicine

Biomedicine has a long history of honing study designs that mitigate against bias, such as the triple-blind randomized cross-over design where the patient, principal investigator and statistician are all blinded to the treatment and where patients change treatments within the study. Several study designs have become so formulaic that the data that a scientist should report has been operationalized, such as in the CONSORT[2] group who created a 25 point checklist of information that should be reported when publishing a randomized clinical trial [27], and CARE for case reports [28].

Despite agreement on study design and formalization of the data that should be reported, the lack of head-to-head drug comparisons has recently received attention to the point where editors of several leading medical journals developed a set of recommendations for Comparative Effectiveness Research (CER) who collectively stated that a key challenges was that "CER should directly compare tests or active treatments - so called head-to-head comparisons - of viable clinical alternatives within the current stand or practice (which in some cases may be no intervention)" [29]. Their argument was based in part on an analysis of rheumatoid arthritis articles, where only 5 of 91 trials included a head to head comparison [30]. They go on to say that "Under the current incentives for drug development, we have more medicines and more choices, but we often lack the scientific evidence to make choices among them. The use of "placebo-only practice" reduces risk for the pharmaceutical industry, but clearly it does not translate into good medicine or good public policy." [31]. This discussion underscores the limitations of using science articles that mirrors observations made in the social sciences[1].

The call to action by journal editors underscores the importance of direct comparisons between different drugs, but we have observed that scientists often report their results by comparing subjects who were given a particular drug with a placebo or control group. The claim framework includes a comparison claim type that includes at the two entities being compared and the way in which the entities were compared, which we call the basis of the comparison. Comparison sentences can be further decomposed into gradable comparatives, which enable us to order the entities, for example in sentence (10) tamoxifen (TAM) is less than the control animals with respect to uterine weights. In addition to the entities (depicted with bold and underline), comparison sentences must provide a comparison basis. In sentence (10) and (11) the basis of the comparison is uterine weights (depicted with an underline). Gradable comparative sentences also include a change term (depicted as italic and underline) and may include a set of change modifiers (depicted in italics).

> In the present study, uterine weights of intact animals treated with **TAM**[Agent] was *decreased* as compared with **controls**, although *not significantly*. PMID=12189200 (10)

Non-gradable comparison sentences do not provide the information necessary to order entities with respect to the comparison basis. For example, sentence (11) is a non-gradable comparison because we cannot rank tamoxifen and 4-hydroxytamoxifen with respect to uterine weight. Non-gradable sentences can be further characterized as similar and different, where sentence (11) is a similar non-gradable comparison.

> Since **tamoxifen**[Agent] and **4-hydroxytamoxifen**[Object] had *nearly identical* [Basis Modifier] effects on uterine weight[Comparison Basis], ... PMID=10190564 (11)

> ... rats treated with **tamoxifen**[Agent] and 4-hydroxytamoxifen, the uterine weights[Comparison Basis], were *decreased*[Change] by *25% (P < 0.05)* [ChangeModifier] compared with the **solvent control group**[Object]. PMID=10190564 (12, claim 1)

> ... rats treated with tamoxifen and **4-hydroxytamoxifen**[Agent], the uterine weights[Comparison Basis], were *decreased*[Change] by *25% (P < 0.05)* [ChangeModifier] compared with the **solvent control group**[Object]. PMID=10190564 (12, claim 2)

> **E2 treatment** *increased*[Change] the uterine weight[Comparison Basis], compared with **control animals**[Object] *(P < 0.001)* [ChangeModifier], whereas raloxifene did not significantly affect the uterine weight. PMID=12639932 (13)

One reason that comparisons are not considered is because from a natural language processing perspective comparative structures have earned a reputation of being "notorious for its syntactic complexity" [32] and as a "very difficult structure to process by computer" [33]. However, despite that difficulty from a processing perspective recent efforts have been successful in identifying comparison sentences [19, 34] and our own work is extending these methods to identify the specific agent, object and basis of change [20].

Preliminary results suggest that the basis of the comparison can be a powerful way to summarize research results. For example, sentences 10-13 describe the difference between breast cancer treatments and their effect on uterine weight, which is measured because the uterus is very sensitive to estrogen, and some of the most prescribed breast cancer treatments operate by blocking estrogen. Using these automated methods would enable help to explain the inconsistent results in treatments by providing users with a detailed summary of the specific items that were measured during the controlled study, for example breast cancer drugs may be similar with respect to their impact on reducing the uterine weight, but very different with respect to actually treating cancer.

Epidemiology

Epidemiologists employ both descriptive and analytical methods to "study of the distribution and determinants of disease frequency" [35]. In contrast to typical study designs used in medicine and toxicology that allow the researcher to control the amount and duration of chemical exposure, most epidemiologists employ opportunistic strategies to collect data. The field has also developed a sub-language to communicate key findings, such as reporting odds ratios for case-controlled study designs and relative risk or standardized mortality rates for cohort study designs [36] and such data is beginning to be formalized such as in the STROBE standard [37] and meta-analysis [38] for cohort studies.

An observational study design better captures the naturalistic setting in which chemical exposure occurs and can thus be used to mitigate against the limited number of randomized head to head trials [31] and the tight constraints that are imposed during subject selection in controlled trials. However, because the researcher does not specifically control the amount or duration of chemical exposure, nor do they control the range of factors that influence exposure, identifying the characteristics that will be studied apriori is even more unrealistic than in a medical setting. Consider the following results of a study that used a population of men who were exposed to styrene (STY) and butadiene (BD) as part of their employment at a styrene-butadiene rubber plant [39].

> During 1943-1991, the cohort had a total of 386172 and an average of 25 person-years of follow-up, with **3976 deaths observed**[Agent] compared to **4553 deaths expected**[Object] based on *general population mortality rates* [Comparison Basis] *(standardized mortality ratio (SMR) = 87, 95% confidence interval (CI) = 85-90 Basis Modifier])* PMID= 8901897   (14)

> *More*[ChangeDirection] than **expected**[Agent] *leukemia deaths*[Comparison Basis] occurred in the **overall cohort**[Object] (**48**[Agent] **observed/37**[Agent/Object] **expected**[Object], *SMR = 131*[ChangeMod], *CI = 97-174*[ChangeMod]) and among ever hourly subjects (45/32, SMR = 143, CI = 104-191). PMID= 8901897   (15, claim 1)

> *More*[ChangeDirection] than **expected**[Agent] *leukemia deaths*[Basis of Comparison] occurred in the overall cohort (48 observed/37 expected, SMR = 131 CI = 97-174[ChangeMod]) and among **ever hourly subjects**[Object] (**45/32**[Agent/Object], *SMR = 143*[ChangeMod], *CI = 104-191*[ChangeMod],). PMID= 8901897   (15, claim 2)

Authors use the standardized mortality rates to report their findings such as SMR=87 (see sentence 14), which means that the number of deaths was lower than the expected. One factor that appears to play a role is where the study subject worked which would influence the amount of chemical exposure, however the researchers had no control over how and when people transitioned between different jobs or how the work environment changed. The highest SMR value of 431 was reported for men who had worked in the laboratories, had worked at the plant for more than 10 years and who were hired more than 20 years ago (sentence not shown).

From a claim framework perspective the claims in sentences 14 and 15 are captured in the claim framework as comparison claim type, but we also see claims in this article reported as an as observations and as an implicit claims where factors such as age of subjects, role at the rubber plant, race, time worked are typically used as agents, the disease is the object and the SMR values including the confidence intervals are captured as change modifiers. Interestingly the results of the study (see 16 and 17) use the explicit claim type:

> ... **mortality patterns**[Object] by **race, years worked and process group within the SBR industry**[Agent] did *not* indicate a *causal association*[Change] with occupational exposures. PMID= 8901897
> (16)
>
> These results indicate that exposures in the **SBR industry**[Agent] *cause*[Change] **leukemia**[Object]. (17)

Observational studies are particularly prone to publication bias that occurs when the results when an article that finds a relationship between the disease and potential factors are more likely to be published than studies that do not detect a relationship. Negation, which is captured as a modifier in the claim framework could play a critical role in mitigating against this type of publication bias, as would considering the main body of a full text article. For example the rubber plant study reported the 22 different SMR values but only 7 of those appear in the abstract. Prior work shows that fewer than 8% of the claims appear in the abstract [2], and more importantly that there are systematic differences in information that is reported in the abstract and the full text [40].

Closing comments

Biological responses to chemical exposure play an important role in human health. Government agencies such as the FDA and EPA use the results reported in scientific literature to determine if there is an association between individual chemicals and harmful responses and if such an association exists, they work with law-makers to establish limits to protect human health. In addition, our daily decisions about foods, drugs and substances to consume also has a direct impact on our chemical exposure.

We have developed a bottom-up approach to identifying claims from scientific articles that assumes that there exists a sub-language that scientists use to convey their experimental results. The Claim Framework employs four information facets (agent, object, change and dimension) that are pieced together to form five different claim types (explicit, implicit, comparison, correlation and observation) to capture results. In contrast to systems that first identify entities and then try to find relationships that include those entities, we focus first on the claim type, and leave noun phrase unification to latter steps of the process. This late binding approach is well suited for scientific literature where new factors are established with each new experiment. Moreover, maintaining fidelity to the original terms used from an article (or at the very least mapping back to the original terms) is a critical component of this approach, in much the same way that risk assessment in toxicology and meta-analyses in medicine must cite the exact text and maintain the link back to the original source document.

The case studies from toxicology, medicine, and epidemiology presented in this paper illustrate how the claim framework can accurately reflect the information necessary to remove ostensible inconsistencies when working with biological responses to chemical exposure. There is still much work to be done with respect to unifying noun phrases (in particular new kinds of anaphoric references), but systems that employ the claim framework will be able to foreground the factors that influence biological responses to chemical exposure. More importantly, such as system could identify areas where inconsistencies are not explained. These edges of scientific knowledge are precisely the areas in which both scientists and policy makers should focus.

References

[1] B. Latour, *Science in action : how to follow scientists and engineers through society*. Cambridge, Mass.: Harvard University Press, 1987.

[2] C. Blake, "Beyond genes, proteins, and abstracts: Identifying scientific claims from full-text biomedical articles," *Journal of Biomedical Informatics,* vol. 43, pp. 173-189, 2010.

[3] Z. S. Harris, *Mathematical structures of language*: Wiley, 1968.

[4] Z. S. Harris, M. Gottfried, T. Ryckman, P. Mattick, A. Daladier, T. N. Harris*, et al.*, *The Form of information in science : analysis of an immunology sublanguage*. Dordrecht Netherlands ; Boston: Kluwer Academic Publishers, 1989.

[5] C. J. Fillmore, "The case for case," in *Universals in Linguistic Theory*, E. Bach and R. T. Harms, Eds., ed New York: Holt, Rinehart and Winston Inc, 1968, pp. 1-90.

[6] J. Swales, *Genre Analysis: English in Academic and Research Settings*: Cambridge Applied Linguistics, 1990.

[7] W. C. Mann and S. A. Thompson, "Rhetorical Structure Theory: Toward a Functional Theory of Text Organization," *Text,* vol. 8, pp. 243-281, 1988.

[8] J. G. Kircz, "Rhetorical structure of scientific articles: the case for argumentational analysis in information retrieval.," *Journal of Documentation,* vol. 47, pp. 354-372, 1991.

[9] S. Teufel and M. Moens, "Summarizing Scientific Articles -- Experiments with Relevance and Rhetorical Status," *Computational Linguistics,* vol. 28, pp. 409-445, December 2002 2002.

[10] D. Zhou and Y. He, "Extracting interactions between proteins from the literature," *Journal of Biomedical Informatics,* vol. 41, pp. 393-407, 2008.

[11] J. Cussens and C. Nédellec. Learning Language in Logic Workshop (LLL05) at the *22nd International Conference on Machine Learning,* Bonn, Germany, 2005.

[12] W. Hersh, A. Cohen, L. Ruslen, and P. Roberts, "Genomics track overview," in *TREC 2007 Working Notes,* 2007.

[13] K. Fundel, R. Kuffner, and R. Zimmer, "RelEx - Relation extreaction using dependency parse trees," *Bioinformatics,* vol. 23, pp. 365-371, 2007.

[14] B. Rosario and M. A. Hearst, "Classifying Semantic Relations in Bioscience Texts," in *Proceedings of the 42nd Annual Meeting on Association for Computational Linguistics,* Barcelona, Spain, 2004, pp. 430-8.

[15] B. Rosario and M. Hearst, "Multi-way relation classification: application to protein-protein interaction," in *Proceedings of the conference on Human Language Technology and Empirical Methods in Natural Language Processing* Vancouver, British Columbia, Canada 2005, pp. 732-9.

[16] T. Rindflesch, C., J. V. Rajan, and L. Hunter, "Extracting Molecular Binding Relationships from Biomedical Text," in *Proceedings of the 6th Applied Natural Language Processing Conference,* 2000, pp. 188-95.

[17] T. C. Rindflesch, M. Fiszman, H. Kilicoglu, and B. Libbus, "Semantic Knowledge Representation Project," Lister Hill National Center for Biomedical Communications, National Library of Medicine, National Institutes of Health, Department of Health and Human Services, September 25, 2003.

[18] M. Fiszman, T. C. Rindflesch, and H. Kilicoglu, "Summarizing Drug Information in Medline Citations," in *AMIA Annu Symp Proc,* 2006, pp. 254-8

[19] D. Hoon Park and C. Blake, "Identifying comparative sentences in full-text scientific articles," presented at the Workshop on Detecting Structure in Scholarly Discourse at Association of Computational Linguistics, Jeju, South Korea., 2012.

[20] A. Lucic and C. Blake, "Automatically Summarizing Medical Literature," presented at the GSLIS Research Showcase, University of Illinois, 2014.

[21] S. Ahmed, C. Blake, K. Williams, N. Lenstra, and Q. Liu, "Identifying Claims In Social Science Literature," in *iConference*, Fort Worth TX, 2013.

[22] "NTP-CERHR Monograph on the Potential Human Reproductive and Developmental Effects of Acrylamide," Center for the Evaluation and Risks to Human Reproduction, National Toxicology Program, Ed., ed: NIH Publication No 05-4472, 2005.

[23] A. de Waard and J. Kircz, "Modeling Scientific Research Articles - shifting perspectives and persistent issues," in *Conference on Electronic Publishing*, Toronto, Canada, 2008.

[24] T. C. Rindflesch and M. Fiszman, "The interaction of domain knowledge and linguistic structure in natural language processing: interpreting hypernymic propositions in biomedical text," *Journal of Biomedical Informatics,* vol. 36, pp. 462-77, December 2003 2003.

[25] J.-D. Kim, T. Ohta, Y. Teteisi, and J. i. Tsujii., "GENIA corpus - a semantically annotated corpus for bio-textmining," *Bioinformatics,* vol. 19, pp. i180-i182, 2003.

[26] S. Van Landeghem, J. Bjorne, C. H. Wei, K. Hakala, S. Pyysalo, S. Ananiadou, *et al.*, "Large-scale event extraction from literature with multi-level gene normalization," *PLoS One,* vol. 8, p. e55814, 2013.

[27] D. Moher, K. F. Schulz, and D. G. Altman, "The CONSORT Statement : Revised Recommendations for Improving the Quality of Reports of parallel-group randomized trials," *Journal of the American Medical Association,* vol. 285, pp. 1987-91, 2001.

[28] J. J. Gagnier, G. Kienle, D. G. Altman, D. Moher, H. Sox, D. Riley, *et al.*, "The CARE guidelines: consensus-based clinical case report guideline development," *J Clin Epidemiol,* vol. 67, pp. 46-51, Jan 2014.

[29] H. C. Sox, M. Helfand, J. Grimshaw, K. Dickersin, P. L. M. Editors, D. Tovey, *et al.*, "Comparative effectiveness research: challenges for medical journals," *PLoS Med,* vol. 7, p. e1000269, Apr 2010.

[30] C. Estellat and P. Ravaud, "Lack of head-to-head trials and fair control arms: randomized controlled trials of biologic treatment for rheumatoid arthritis," *Arch Intern Med,* vol. 172, pp. 237-44, Feb 13 2012.

[31] S. Malozowski, "Comparative efficacy: what we know, what we need to know, and how we can get there," *Ann Intern Med,* vol. 148, pp. 702-3, May 6 2008.

[32] J. W. Bresnan, "Syntax of the Comparative Clause Construction in English," *Linguistic Inquiry,* vol. 4, pp. 275-343, 1973.

[33] C. Friedman, "A General Computational Treatment Of The Comparative," presented at the Association of Computational Linguistics, Stoudsburg, PA, 1989.

[34] M. Fiszman, D. Demner-Fushman, F. M. Lang, P. Goetz, and T. C. Rindflesch, " Interpreting Comparative Constructons in Biomedical Text," in *Proc. 2007 Workshop on Biomedical Natural Language Processing (BioNL'07)*, Prague, Czech Republic., 2007, pp. 37-144.

[35] B. MacMahon and T. F. Pugh, *Epidemiology; principles and methods*, 1st ed. Boston,: Little, 1970.

[36] C. H. Hennekens, J. E. Buring, and S. L. Mayrent, *Epidemiology in medicine*, 1st ed. Boston: Little, Brown, 1987.

[37] J. Poorolajal, Z. Cheraghi, A. D. Irani, and S. Rezaeian, "Quality of Cohort Studies Reporting Post the Strengthening the Reporting of Observational Studies in Epidemiology (STROBE) Statement," *Epidemiol Health,* vol. 33, p. e2011005, 2011.

[38] D. F. Stroup, J. A. Berlin, S. C. Morton, I. Olkin, G. D. Williamson, D. Rennie*, et al.*, "Meta-analyses of Observational Studies in Epidemiology," *Journal of the American Medical Association,* vol. 283, pp. 2008-12, 2000.

[39] E. Delzell, N. Sathiakumar, M. Hovinga, M. Macaluso, J. Julian, R. Larson*, et al.*, "A follow-up study of synthetic rubber workers," *Toxicology,* vol. 113, pp. 182-9, Oct 28 1996.

[40] C. Blake, "Using Secondary Information to inform Public Policy," presented at the Internet, Politics, Policy 2012, Oxford Internet Institute, University of Oxford, 2012.

---

[1] See http://www.epa.gov/safewater/consumer/pdf/mcl.pdf
[2] See http://www.consort-statement.org/home/

From Inter-Annotation to Intra-Publication Inconsistency

Alaa Abi Haidar (Université Pierre et Marie Curie Paris 6)
Mihnea Tufiș (Université Pierre et Marie Curie Paris 6)
Jean-Gabriel Ganascia (Université Pierre et Marie Curie Paris 6)

What are effective ways to help people with chronic illness, e.g. diabetes and heart disease?
Computational linguistics relies on human-annotated data to train machine learners. Inconsistency among the human annotators must be carefully managed (otherwise, the annotations are useless in computation). How can this annotation process be made scalable?

Abstract
Curing chronic illnesses and diseases requires the huge effort of collecting all available information on this matter and piecing it together with the aids of mathematical and computer modeling. Both phases of information collection and piecing together are prone to error. Errors may result from human annotation inconsistency, machine learning and parameterization when using supervised learning. On a different scale, published results that need to be collected may suffer from another kind of disagreement either due to varying experimental methodologies or assumptions. Here, we discuss these inconsistencies and disagreements in scientific literature and we investigate those of the inter-annotation of named entities in bioliterature from empirical perspectives.

Introduction
Mathematical modeling and simulation help us understand the underlying mechanisms behind complex and barely understood systems, such as immune systems in order to advance biomedical and drug studies and cure diseases [10]. However, mathematical modeling requires huge amounts of parametric data, usually published in experimental and theoretical manuscripts and dispersed in the scientific literature. Pubmed comprises more than 19 million scientific articles [9] and this amount is growing at astounding rates. The manual extraction of valuable information and their classification into predefined labels, such as parametric values, units and species names, is very costly and inefficient. Hence, we use text mining, and more specifically, named entity recognition [8], in order to automatically and accurately extract and classify numerical and textual entities, that can later be plugged into mathematical models and simulated.

Nevertheless, a significant number of parametric values describing experimental results in the bio-literature are inconsistent due to variations in experimental approaches or imperfection in the experiments [19]. For example, the amount of T cells that mature from the thymus through the process of negative selection[1] remains a huge debate [1-7] and may vary between "less than 5%" to "10%". Our study focuses on analysing all reported rates for such processes in biological and other complex systems in order to study their statistical variations while identifying average values and outliers.

Background

Most techniques for named entity recognition rely on supervised machine learning that require human-annotated training data. Studies have shown that there is at least 25% human inter-annotation disagreement (inconsistency) when annotating biological named entities [24]. According to the G-theory [20], sources of inconsistency might be of external influences like alterations in the tools used for annotations, increasing time pressure, removal or adding of rewards, or changes in the annotation scheme. A study reports 55% and 82% F1 scores for exact and relaxed[2] inter-annotation agreement respectively when the task was to extract interactions between enzymes and marine drugs in over 230 full-text articles [11]. In another study, the relaxed inter-annotator agreement showed that 94% of the time curators were precisely extracting GO[3] annotation from the literature and 72% of the time curators recalled all possible valid GO terms from the text [14]. Yet another study reports an inter-annotator agreement rate of over 60% for triggers and of over 80% for arguments using an exact match constraint [16]. More recently, a study reported inter-annotator agreement (IAA) F-measures for medication names and medication types, 94.2% and 88.2% respectively [13]. However, the rates of inter-annotation agreement vary not only from study to study but also from domain to domain. For instance, Wiebe et al. report 82.0 F1 score of human annotation agreement for opinion expression [12].

Consequently, the human inter-annotation inconsistency creates a gray area of uncertainty that the machine learner depends on to create fine-tuned rules and exceptions. Furthermore, human annotation is often used as the gold standard for evaluating machine learning methods [15] and therefore it is very important to have as few disagreements as possible. Nevertheless, the human

---

[1] T cells that recognize self antigens are eliminated in the thymus through a process known as negative selection so that they do not bind to self and cause auto-immune diseases

[2] Unlike exact matches, relaxed matches may span over less or more words to describe the same concept.

[3] The Gene Ontology, or GO, is a bioinformatics attempt to unify the representation of genes and gene product attributes across various species

inter-annotation disagreement can be reduced by using strictly agreed-upon annotations, the reasonings of a single annotator, majority rules or by identifying mislabeled annotations [17, 18].

Results and discussion

Here, we attempt to quantify human annotation inconsistency based on a biological article annotated by several annotators. More specifically, we study the annotation inconsistency of a biomedical article [24] that is annotated by three experts for 9 categories of named entities. The following table lists the number of annotated entities for each of the 9 categories by each of the three annotators:

almeida_annotation_Al.tag	almeida_annotation_Veronique.tag	almeida_annotation_Florence.tag
17 UNIT	17 UNIT	28 LOCATION
22 LOCATION	20 LOCATION	30 UNIT
34 NUM	65 NUM	38 INDIVIDUAL
63 INDIVIDUAL	74 INDIVIDUAL	58 NUM
227 METHOD	226 METHOD	161 METHOD
255 COFACTOR	231 COFACTOR	356 COFACTOR
344 PROCESS	360 PROCESS	454 PROCESS
950 POPULATION	907 POPULATION	904 POPULATION
8140 O	8152 O	8014 O

Table 1. The number of annotated entities in a biomedical article [24] for each of the 9 categories by each of the three annotators

The categories describe biological concepts. In the following example "The T cell proliferation is 0.4 cells/hr" can be annotated as follows: "T cell proliferation" describes a PROCESS, "0.4" a NUM (numerical value) and "cells/hr" a UNIT. More complex entities are harder to classify into concepts which may create annotation inconsistencies between several annotators.

For the example at hand, we identify inconsistencies varying from 1.5% to 8.3% out of a total of 10052 terms as shown in table 2. Our average values are below those reported by [24]. However, that might be due to the fact of working on a different dataset and with different entities.

	Al	Ver	Flo
Al	0%	1.5%	7.8%
Ver		0%	8.3%
Flo			0%

Table 2. Inter-annotator inconsistencies varying from 1.5% to 8.3% out of a total of 10052 terms

Next, we study to what extent inter-annotation inconsistency in training data can influence the robustness of machine learning and the predicted results. We hypothesize that factors such as the size of annotated training data, the number of annotators, the number of class labels, and the over-fitness of supervised machine learners play major roles in the robustness of the learning and the classification results. We attempt to answer these questions using empirical approaches inspired by [21] a study of robustness when classifying noisy land rover data from satellite images.

Evaluating inter annotator agreement

Determining inter annotator agreement (IAA) can be a daunting task for reasons such as proper choice of agreement coefficients and lack of consensus on the interpretation of such coefficients [26].

Taking into account the recommendations of Artstein and Poesio [26 - 590] considering the better quality measure given by chance corrected coefficients as compared to simple percentage agreement, we have performed the reliability testing over the annotations performed over our corpus of text. Given that we are in a scenario of multi-annotators (namely, three) using a nominal variable, we will discuss the results we've obtained for the computation of the adapted versions of Cohen's κ and Fleiss' multi-π as well as for Krippendorff's α.

As a reminder, the first 2 coefficients above are based on the basic coefficients used in 2-annotators scenarios: Scott's π (1955), Cohen's κ (1960).
where A_o is the observed agreement and A_e is the expected agreement. [26 - 559]

$$\pi, k = \frac{A_o - A_e}{1 - A_e}$$

As explained in [26 - 560], the difference between π and κ lies in the assumptions made to compute the probability for a coder (annotator) to categorize an utterance in a certain category.

The indices we used are the generalizations of Scott's π and Cohen's κ made by Fleiss (1971) and Davies and Fleiss (1982) respectively.

To generalize, Fleiss' multi-π uses a different interpretation of the observed

annotation A_o, namely the pairwise agreement, which is the number of pairs agreeing on an utterance out of the total number of pairs of coders.
Equally, multi- κ involves the computation of the expected agreement A_e based on individual coder marginals.

Finally, Krippendorff's α. is a versatile coefficient which addresses the limitations of (multi-) κ and (multi-) π regarding the equal treatment of all

$$\alpha = 1 - \frac{D_o}{D_e}$$

disagreements [26 - 564]
where D_o is the observed disagreement and D_e is the expected disagreement. [26 - 565, 566]
We computed the coefficients in the following 2 situations [27, 28]:

1. Full annotations, taking into account the large number of utterances classified as *O(ther)* by all annotators (Coders = 3, Utterances = 10043).

Average Pairwise Agreement [%]	Pairwise (1-2) Agreement	Pairwise (1-3) Agreement	Pairwise (2-3) Agreement
94.162%	98.457%	92.283%	91.745%

Table 3a. Average Pairwise Agreement [%]

Avg. Pairwise CK	Pairwise (1-2) CK	Pairwise (1-3) CK	Pairwise (2-3) CK
0.828	0.953	0.774	0.758

Table 3b. Average Pairwise Multi-κ (based on Cohen's κ)

multi-□	Ao	Ae
0.827	0.942	0.662

Table 3c. multi- π (based on Scott's π)

Krippendorff's □	No. of decisions
0.827	30129

Table 3d. Krippendorff's α

Looking at the "classical" agreement reporting, the average pairwise percentage agreement is at 94.2%, with the best agreement rate being between coder 1 and coder 2 at 98.5%.

As expected, the values for multi-π and average pairwise multi-κ are approximately equal and since all disagreements are treated equally, Krippendorff's α is also nearly equal to the two before. The approximate value of 0.82 for multi-κ, classifies the annotation process as "perfect" according to the strength scale given by Landis and Koch (1977) [26 - 576].

2. Altered annotations, discarding the utterances classified as *O(ther)* by all annotators (Coders = 3, Utterances = 2349).

Average Pairwise Agreement [%]	Pairwise (1-2) Agreement	Pairwise (1-3) Agreement	Pairwise (2-3) Agreement
75.039%	93.401%	67.007%	64.708%

Table 4a. Average Pairwise Agreement [%]

Avg. Pairwise CK	Pairwise (1-2) CK	Pairwise (1-3) CK	Pairwise (2-3) CK
0.675	0.914	0.569	0.543

Table 4b. Average Pairwise Multi-κ (based on Cohen's κ)

multi-□	Ao	Ae
0.674	0.75	0.233

Table 4c. multi-π (based on Scott's π)

Krippendorff's □	No. of decisions
0.674	7047

Table 4d. Krippendorff's α

In this case, almost 8000 utterances which have been all annotated as *Other* by all three coders were completely discarded from the reliability study.

The classic pairwise percentage agreement thus records a drop of the average value (75%); however, it is interesting to notice that the agreement between coders 1 and 2 stays as high as in the original situation (93.4%) which indicates a very high agreement for their annotations on the "main" classes (excepting the all-*O(ther)*) as well.

As before, the values of the three coefficients are (not surprisingly) almost equal, but are dropping this time, somewhere around 0.67, which on the strength scale of Landis and Koch (1977) [26 - 576] indicates only a "substantial" agreement in the annotation process, making the annotation suitable for "tentative conclusions". Interesting enough, this is exactly the value which was set as the original threshold by Krippendorff (although he referred to it as "highly tentative and cautious") before he reviewed it and later set it at 0.8.

Conclusion

In this manuscript, we identify and discuss two forms of inconsistencies, one in published parametric results that we are studying in collaboration with immunologists[4], and another in manually human annotated data for machine learning. Both forms of inconsistencies influence the accuracy of biomedical research to a significant extent that we are interested in quantifying in our research. We expect our study to shed a light on both forms of inconsistencies, ones resulting from human inter-annotation and those published in biological literature.

Acknowledgements

"This work has been done within the LABEX OBVIL project, and received financial state aid managed by the Agence Nationale de la Recherche, as part of the programme "Investissements d'avenir" under the reference ANR-11-IDEX-0004-02". We thank the expertise and effort of Veronique THOMAS-VASLIN and Florence GIESEN for the help with the annotation and valuable discussions.

Bibliography

1. Faro, J. & Velasco, S. González-Fernández, Á., & Bandeira, A. (2004). *The Journal of Immunology, 172*(4), 2247-2255.
2. Starr, T. K., Jameson, S. C., & Hogquist, K. A. (2003). *Annual review of immunology, 21*(1), 139-176.
3. Egerton, M., Scollay, R. & Shortman, K. (1990) Proc. ntnl. Acad. Sci., U.S.A. 87, 2579–2582.
4. Huesmann, M., Scott, B., Kisielow, P. & von Boehmer, H. (1991) Cell 66, 533–540.
5. Scollay, R. & Godfrey, D.I. (1995) Immun. Today 16, 268–273.
6. Surh, C.D. & Sprent, J. (1994) Nature 372, 100–103.
7. Bevan, M.J. (1977) Nature 269, 417–418.
8. Nadeau, D., & Sekine, S. (2007). *Lingvisticae Investigationes, 30*(1), 3-26.
9. Eliot, T. S. (2011).. *Evidence-Based Public Health*, 158.
10. Kitano, H. (2002). *Science, 295*(5560), 1662-1664.

---

[4] The team of Integrative Immunology (I2) is based at the Pitié Salpêtrière. 83, Bld de l'hôpital. 75013 Paris, France

11. Rafal Rak, Andrew Rowley, William Black, Sophia Ananiadou (2012). Database (Oxford) . doi: 10.1093/database/bas010
12. J. Wiebe and T. Wilson and C. Cardie (2005).. In Language Resources and Evaluation, volume 39, issue 2-3.
13. Zhai, H., Lingren, T., Deleger, L., Li, Q., Kaiser, M., Stoutenborough, L., & Solti, I. (2013). *Journal of medical Internet research*, *15*(4).
14. Camon, E. B., Barrell, D. G., Dimmer, E. C., Lee, V., Magrane, M., Maslen, J., ... & Apweiler, R. (2005). *BMC bioinformatics*, *6*(Suppl 1), S17.
15. Gaudan S, Jimeno Yepes A, Lee V, Rebholz-Schuhmann D (2008). EURASIP journal on bioinformatics & systems biology.
16. Mihaila, C., Ohta, T., Pyysalo, S., & Ananiadou, S. (2013). *BMC bioinformatics*, *14*(1), 2.
17. Brodley, C. E., & Friedl, M. A. (2011). *arXiv preprint arXiv:1106.0219*.
18. Guan, D., Yuan, W., Lee, Y. K., & Lee, S. (2011).. *Applied Intelligence*, *35*(3), 345-358.
19. Furey TS, Cristianini N, Duffy N, Bednarski DW, Schummer M, et al. (2000). *Bioinformatics* 16: 906–914
20. Bayerl, P. S., & Paul, K. I. (2007). *Computational Linguistics*, *33*(1), 3-8.
21. DeFries, R. S., & Chan, J. C. W. (2000). *Remote Sensing of Environment*, *74*(3), 503-515.
22. Valiant, L. G. (1984).. *Communications of the ACM*, *27*(11), 1134-1142.
23. Kearns, M. J., & Vazirani, U. V. (1994). The MIT Press.
24. Van Mulligen, Erik M., et al. *Journal of biomedical informatics* 45.5 (2012): 879-884.
25. Almeida, Afonso RM, et al. *Frontiers in immunology* 3 (2012).
26. Artstein, R., & Poesio, M.(2008). *Computational Linguistics*, 34(4), 555-596.
27. Freelon, D. *ReCal3: Reliability for 3+ Coders*. [Online] Available: http://dfreelon.org/utils/recalfront/recal3/ [2013, March 6]
28. Freelon, D. (2010) *International Journal of Internet Science*, 5(1), 20-33

Index

--, 354
◆, 343, 344, 394, 406
◆ ... ?, 393
☑, 407
⦅, 407
⟦, 372, 381, 384, 399, 401, 407
!=, 399
●, 347, 364, 406, 407
∘, 406
$$, 388, 403, 406
{, 371, 407
(, 407, *See* Expressions
/*, 407
//, 407
:, 388, 406
:⊟, 407
[, 341, 342, 345, 375, 376, 390, 407
␣ 388
{, 407
++, 354
⊖, 383, 407
▫, 377, 378, 380, 406, *See* Qualifiers
=, 368, 369, 379, 382, 399, 406
⊘, 364, 399, 401, 406
⊘, 364
⊘⊘, 364, 374, 406
⁌, 342, 377, 389, 406
⁌⁌, 351, 367, 369, 401, 406
□, 347, 351, 385, 387, 406
∨, 221, 370, 371, 374, 375, 376, 389, 390, 407
≔, 347, 384, 395, 399, 401, 406
≜, 375, 376, 379, 385, 399, 406
≡, 340, 406, *See* ActorScript definitions
⊑, 266, 267, 349, 407
⊒, 386
⊔, 407

⊢, 287, 289, 329, 404, 407
⊩, 287, 289, 329, 404, 407
⊟, 369, 406
▫, 348, 399, 401, 406
?, 343, 396, 406
❙, 340, 406, *See* Expressions
→, 342, 347, 354, 355, 406
↠, 383, 407
↦, 341, 345, 406
⇒, 407
↓, 373, 374, 387, 406
←, 375, 406, *See* Binding locals
↞, 383, 407
↢, 341
⇔, 407
§, 342, 345, 406
¶, 342, 345, 406
⁊, 343, 406
1984, lviii
abandonment, 178
Abi Haidar, A., xlviii, lxv, 512
absolute inconsistency, 188
abstraction, xxvii, 491
ACLU, lvii
Actor, 27, 28
  address, 205, 207, 209, 222, 237, 241, 265
  customer, 209, 262
  delegation, 265Erlang, 259
  Fog Cutter, 257, *See* Fog Cutter
  Future, 373
  interface, 215
  InternalQ, 401
  JavaScript, 224, 262
  locality, 209
  multi-level security, 265
  Orleans, 224, 259
  promise, 231, 261, 262
  revocation, 265
  security, 209

Swiss cheese, 219, 350
π-Calculus, 256
Actor, 303, 345, 351, 397
  enqueueAndLeave, 401
  enqueueAndDequeue, 401
  dequeue, 401
Actor Message
  Virtual Procedure, 247
Actor Model, xxxiv, 5, 206
  capability system, 264
  Message passing, 336
  Object Capability Model, 265
  types, 336
Actors
  Squeak, 259
  uncountably many, 217
Actorscript, 302
  Actor, 342, 345, 347, 354, 364, 397
  afterward, 346 379
  ASCII, 406
  Atomic, 379
  Atomic ... compare ... update ... then ... else ..., 392
  become, 378
  between, 364
  cases, 343
  Continuation, 391
  Customer, 383, 384
  default, 369
  definitions, 340
  Discrimination, 364
  Enqueue, 396
  Enumeration, 380
  eval, 386
  Expression, 340
  extends, 349
  Future, 387
  Future, 387
  general messaging, 377
  Grammar Precedence, 408
  has, 345, 350
  having, 386
  Hole, 395
  Hole ... after, 395
  Hole ... returned ... **threw**, 396
  implements, 342, 364
  in, 399
  Integrated Development Environment, 340
  isExtension, 386
  Let, 344, 345
  MakeRunnable, 399
  match, 387
  Message, 378
  mustMatch, 387
  Null, 364
  Null, 364
  patterns, 343
  perform, 391
  Precondition, 367
  postcondition, 367
  Postpone, 378
  procedure, 342
  procedure interface, 341
  resolve future, 373
  return, 383 384
  String, 376
  Structure, 365
  Suspend, 399
  Symbols, 406
  throw, 383, 384
  Try ... catch❖, 391
  Try ... cleanup, 391
  Type, 340
  Type, 386
  variable, 345, 353
  Void, 347
  XML, 382
  Unicode, 406
Adams, J., 265
addiction, xlix
address
  Actor, 205, 207, 209, 222, 237, 241, 265
adjunction, 193
after, 28, 303, 351, 354

afterward, 28, 303, 347, 351, 379, 401
Agha, G., xxxv, 246, 257, 301, 356
agile software techniques, 480
Ahmad, K., lii
Allison, D., lxv, 224
Alterovitz, G., lxvi, lxvii
ambiguation, 168
ambiguation strategy, 168, 183
Ambiguation Strategy, xxxii
Anderson, A., 174
Anderson, C., 14
annotations, 512
Any, 367
Apple, lvii
argument, 460
argumentation, xxiii, 12, 480
Armstrong, J., xxxv, 259
Arrays, 384
Athas, W., 250, 356
Atkinson, R., 251, 356
Atomic, 379, 399
Atomic ... compare ... update ... then ... else ..., 392
Attardi, G., 356
auditing against backdoors, lx
authentication services, lii
backdoor, lv, lx
  mandatory, lx
backout, 354, 355
Bagehot, W., l
Baker, H., 30, 209, 218, 243, 356
Bamford, J., li
Bankston, K., lv
Baran, P., 206
Barber, G., 356
Barker-Plummer, D., 35, 107
Barwise, J., 35, 107, 138
Bashar, N., 182
Basic, 365
Baumgart, B., 292
Beall, JC, 179
Beard, P., 356

become, 378
belief revision, xxiii, 9
Belnap, N. Jr., 174
Bench-Capon, T., lxvi, 315
Bender, E., lxvi
Berenji, H., xxix
Bernstein, P., 224, 259
Berry's Paradox, 145
Berto, F., lxvi
Bertossi, L., 9, 181
Besnard, P. 183, 195
between, 364
Bėziau, J., 9
Bilski decision, 450
Bishop, P., 25, 206, 241, 250, 291, 356
Blake, C., xlvii, 497
Bledsoe, W., 284
Boden, N., 250, 356
Boethius, 172, 173
Bohr's model, 184
Boland, R., lxvii
Boley, H., 225, 315
Boole, G., 18
Boolos, G., 158
bounded nondeterminism, 33
Bourbaki, 39
Bowker, G., lxvi, 298
Bracha, G., lxvi
Brady, R., 174
Brandom, 193
Bright line rule, 455
Brinch Hansen, P., 251
Briot, J., 250, 356
Brouwer, L. E. J., xxix
Brown, 194
Brown, K., 496
Bruynooghe, M., 294
Bundy, A., lxvi, lxvii, 315
Burton, R., lviii
Bush, liii
Bykov, S., 224, 259
Caesar, J., xxvii
CALEA, lxi

Callon, M., 298
capability, 206, 207, 221, 242,
    See Actor address
    Actor Model, xxxiii
capability system
    Actor Model, 264
Cardelli, L., 256
Carnap, 180
    nihilism:, 192
Carnap, R., 166, 167
Carnielli, W., 9
Carnielli, W., 175
Carroll, L., 22
Cartesian, 367
Cartwright, N., lxvii
catch◆, 366
Catch-22, 10
categoricity
    integers, 80
    natural numbers, 133
    over sets of reals, 134
    real numbers, 81
    reals, 133
    sets over natural numbers, 81
Cerf, V., lvii
Chang, H., xxiii, 123
Charniak, E., 287
cheese, xxxvii, 220, 308, 353
    hole, xxxvii, 220, 308, 351, 354, 355
CheeseQ, 399
Cheney, D., liii
chronic illnesses, 512
Church, A., xxxviii, 3, 17, 34, 40, 83, 104, 117, 143, 205, 236, 280
Church, F., liii
Church'S Paradox, 143
Claim Framework, 497
Classical Direct Logic, xxi, xxii, xxv, xxxii, 286, 311
    ex falso, 189
    Hewitt, C., 188
    Notation, 129
    Proposition, 129
    Sentence, 131
    Term, 130
Classical Logic
    Natural Deduction, 148
    Soundness, 3
Classical Proof by Contradiction, 173, 189, 201
cleanup, 366
Clinger, W., 30, 252, 303, 356
Comey, J., lv, lxi
commerce agent, lix
completeness
    logical, 36
Complex, 367, 369
compromise, 460
computational linguistics, 487, 512
Computational Representation Theorem, 31
concurrency, 5
Coniglio, M., 175
Conniver, 290
consistency
    preservation, 185
Consistency of Mathematics, 34
Continuation, 391
continuous authentication, lii
contradiction, xxviii, xix, 12, 206
    ameliorate, lxviii
    circumvent, lxviii
    defer, lxviii
    ignore, lxviii
Contrapositive for Implication, 3
Cook, S., 171
Cook, T., lvii
Copeland, J., lxvi
correlations, 14
Cosmic Cube, 251
CSP, 252
Cumberbatch, B., lviii
Curry, H., 85, 144

Customer, 383, 384
Cusumano, M., 7
CyberLocalism, lix
cyberspace, li
CyberTotalism, lviii
cyberwar, lv
da Costa, N., 175
Dahl, O., 26, 239, 247, 336
Dally, W., 256, 356
D'Angelo, A., 21
DataCenterism, lviii
Davies, J., 293
Davies, N., lviii
Dawes, A., lxv
Dawson, J., 121
de Bruijin, N., 79
de Jong, P., 356
Decker, H., 284
Dedecker, J., 356
Dedekind, R., 82
delegation
   Actor, 265
Dennis, J., 206, 264
Deutsch, P., 254
dialetheism, 188
Diamond, C., 17
Dijkstra, E., 243, 251
Direct Argumentation, 3
Direct Inference, 3
Direct Logic, 4, 17, 158, 187
   bounded nondeterminism, 33
   Classical Direct Logic, xxi, 4
   Expression, 130
   Inconsistency Robust Direct
     Logic, xxi, 4
   Type, 129
discourse, 480
Discrimination, 364
disease, 461
DL. *See* Direct Logic
Do, 351, 385
Do ... ●, 347, 381, 384, 399
Dolin, R., lxvi
Döpfner, M., lvi

Dunn, M., 12
Dyson, F., 120
Easterbrook, S., xx, lxviii, 182
Easterbrook, S., 8
economics, xlix
Edinburgh Logic for
   Computable Functions, 292
Edwards, P., lxvi
Einstein, A., 24
either, 113, 376
Eliot, T. S., 83
Ellsberg, D., lii
Elster, 186
Elster, J., 185
empirically discernible, 187
encryption, lii
   RAM, lii
endpoint security, lii
Enqueue, 354, 355, 396
Enumeration, 380
epidemiology, 506
Erlang
   Actor, 259
Etchemendy, J., 35, 107
Euler formula, 108
eval, 386
every-word-tagged
   architecture, lii, lxi
ex falso quodlibet, 170, 185,
   188, See IGOR
   IGOR, xxii, xxxii
exception, 366
Excluded Middle, 201
Expression
   Direct Logic, 130
extends, 349
Facebook, liv
Fahlman, S., 315
Federal Circuit, 447
Feferman, S., xxi, 4, 42
Feyerabend, P., 298
Feynman, R., 213
First-Order Thesis, 138

fixed points on untyped
    sentences, 141
Flash Crash, 493
Flickinger, D., xlvi, lxv, lxvi, 487
Fog Cutter
    Actor, 257
    event loop, xxxv
    mailbox, xxxv, 257
    thread, xxxv, 257
Ford, D., lxv
Fork, 250, 307, 365, 374
forward chaining, 85
Franzén, T., xxvii, 23
Frege, G., 82, 121
FriAM, 356
Fuller, 429
Function (JavaScript), 381
Funder, A., lviii
Fusco, S., xliii, lxvi, 447
future, 209, 218, 220, 249, 256, 261
Future, 221, 373, 374, 375, 387
FutureList, 375
fuzzy logic, xxiii, 9
Gabbay D. and Woods, J.
    Agenda Relevance, 171
Gabbay, D., 9, 171, 175, 182
Galbraith, J. K., 146
Galileo, 184
Gallagher, R., l
Ganascia, J., lxvi, 512
Ganascia, Jean-G., xlviii
Gardner, A., xliii, lxv, lxvi, lxvii, 429
Garst, B., lxv, lxvii, 224, 356, 400
Gedeck, M., lviii
Geller, A., 259
genes and pathways, 464
Genesereth, M., 42, 197, 201
Gerson, E. M., lxvi, lxvii, 298
Glennon, M., liii
Gödel, K., xxvi, xxxi, lxv, 25, 135
    validity of incompleteness arguments, 110, 189

Goldberg, A., 254
Google, lvi, lvii
Gordon, A., 256
Gordon, M., 292
Gore, A., lvi
Green, C., 284
Greenwald, G., l, liii
Greif, I., 243, 356
Griffin, M., 176
Guenthner, F., 175
Hack Attack: The Inside Story of How the Truth Caught Up with Rupert Murdoch, lviii
hairy control structure
    J operator, 290
    Planner, 290
Hardy, G., 106
Harris, S., l, liv
Hattem, J., lv
having, 386
Hayes, P., 243, 290, 292, 297, 315
Hayes, T., 224
Heller, J., 10
Hewitt, C., xix, xx, xxv, xxxiii, xxxv, xxxviii, xli, lxii, lxiii, lxiv, lxv, lxvi, lxvii, lxviii, 25, 158, 164, 167, 170, 187, 188, 189, 190, 197, 201, 206, 243, 251, 258, 429, 445, 493, 494, 496
Hibbert, C., 224
Hilbert, D., xxix, 36
Hoare, CAR, 209, 251, 253
Hobbes, T., v
Hoehndorf, R., lxvi
Hole, 28, 303, 351, 354, 395
Hole ... after, 395
Hole ... returned ... threw, 396
Hoofnagle, C., lvi
Hopwood, D., 224
House, C., lxvii
Huhns, M., lxvi, lxvii, 224
Hunter, A., 9, 181, 182, 195
Hurt, J., lviii

Icard, T. F. III, lxvi
IGOR, xxii, xxxii
   ex falso quodlibit, xxii, 168, 170, 174, 177, 179, 189, 191
   Inconsistency in Garbage Out Redux, 16
   Jaśkowski, S., 4
   Lewis-Langford proof, 173, 174, 176, 188
   paraconsistency, 174, 188
IGOR
   Inconsistency in Garbage Out Redux, 282
implements, 364
Import, 381
in, 399, 401
inconsistencies
   ameliorate, 8
   defer, 8
   ignore, 8
   circumvent, 8
   bugs, 7
inconsistencies in scientific literature, 512
inconsistency, 159
   abandonment, 169, 179
   absolute, 159, 191
   ameliorate, 182
   belief-management systems, 184
   circumvent, 182
   clarification-stipulation spectrum, 165 166
   conceptual field, 165, 167
   conceptual innovation, 167
   conceptual map, 167, 178
   conceptual space, 165
   consistency-stabilization, 171
   containment, 169, 170, 178
   damage control, 169
   defer, 182
   denial, xix, 206
   diagnosis, 164, 169
   dialethic, 178
   Disjunctive Syllogism, 159
   economic impacts, 159
   elimination, xix, 206
   empirical considerations, 184
   environmental impacts, 159
   erasure, 171
   expulsion, 170, 173, 179, 188
   fact-finding, 166, 167
   fact-making, 167
   globalization, 169
   globalization effect, 160, 161 169, 180
   hostile Containment, 173
   human memory, 185
   human preferences, 185
   hyperinconsistency-robustness, 191
   ignore, 181
   in human brain, l
   inconsistency management, 171
   inconsistency-management sensibility, 173
   intractability problem, 171
   invention space, 165
   irrealism, 167
   K unrecognizable logics, 166
   liar sentences, 176
   operating manual, 165
   invention space, 165
   management, 164, 175
   maxim of minimum mutilation, 170
   metaphysical footprint, 169
   monster-barring, 164
   Most Difficult Problem, 164
   negation, 159, 160, 164, 168, 169, 181, 188, 190
   nihilism, 167
   norms of rationality, 186
   pervasive, 7
   plans of consumption, 185
   pluralism, 166, 178

preclusion, 170 172, 178 188
premissory inertia, 185
Principle of Tolerance, 166
probabilities, 13
probabilistic reasoning, 186
prognosis, 164 169
Putter of Things Right, 171
quasi-realism, 167
rational performability, 191
realism, 167
recognizability space, 165, 167, 173
reconcilation strategy, 168
self-cancellation, 172, 173
self-cancelling, 178
Seer of Trouble Coming, 171
semantic self-extinction, 172
stipulationism, 166, 167
stipulative conceptual innovation, 173
symptoms, 164
system-relative, 167
system-relativity, 179, 180
tolerance, 173 181
tolerant containment, 180
treatment, 164 169
treatment manual, 165
treatment space, 165
triage, 169
unrecognizability as a truth value, 178
welcoming containment, 180
Inconsistency Robust Direct Logic, xxi, xxii, xxxii, 3, 158, 187, 191, 195, 286, 311
adaptive logics, 194
Boolean Inconsistency Robust Direct Logic, 195
discussive logics, 188, 193
Disjunctive Syllogism rule, 194
ex falso, 189, 193
explosiveness, 197
inconsistency container, 188
non-adjunctive, 193
opt-out rule, 167, 190
paraconsistency, 193
preservationism, 193
re-motivate rule, 168, 190
relevant logicians, 173, 174
Inconsistency Robust Proof by Contradiction, xxii, 3
inconsistency robustness, xxxii
clarification, 162
clarification-stipulation spectrum, 163
conceptual improvement, 162
explication, 162
idea, 191
nominal definition, 162
rational reconstruction, 162
stipulation, 162
Inconsistency Robustness, xx, xxii, 10, 158, 187, 188, 189, 447, 457
Applications, xlii
desired feature, 158
future prospects, 191
Hewitt, C., 189
Illustrative Issues, xlviii
inconsistency denial, 158
inconsistency elimination, 158
mathematical foundations, xx
observed phenomenon, 158
program committee members, lxv
software foundations, xxxiii
videos, xix
Inconsistency Robustness 2014, lxv
Panel Discussions, l
Inconsistency Robustness in Cyberspace Security and Privacy, l

Inconsistency Robustness in Foundations of Mathematics, lxiv
Inconsistency Robustness in Medical Informatics, lxii
Inconsistency-preclusion, 171
Inconsistency-robust Natural Deduction, 3
Inconsistency Robustness, 191
inconsistent, xix, 206
  findings of fact, 429
  judicial opinions, 429
  Post, 160
  statutes, 429
Inconsistent findings of fact, 430
Inconsistent statutes, 435
inconsitency
  Russell's paradox, 177
indeterminacies, 14
indeterminacy, 209
information
  circular, 15
  Direct Logic, 6
information coordination, 37
  concurrency, 37
  lossless, 37
  persistence, 37
  quasi-commutativity, 37
  pluralism, 37
  provenance, 37
  scalable, 38
  sponsorship, 37
Ingalls, D., 254, 259
  Smalltalk-72, 240
innovation, xlix
interaction, 5
interdependencies, 14
interface
  Actor, 215
Internet, li
Internet of Things, lix
Internet Security Commission, lx

invariance, 39
Ioannidis, J., lxii, lxiii
IoT. *See* Internet of Things
IR. *See* Inconsistency Robustness
IRDL. *See* Inconsistency Robust Direct Logic, *See* Inconsistency Robust Direct Logic
iRobust, xix, lxviii
  board, lxvii
iRobust Scientific Society, lxvii
isExtension, 386
Israel, D., lxvi, 42
J operator, 247
Japanese 5th Generation Project (ICOT), 306
Japanese Fifth Generation Project, 33
Jaśkowski, S., v, 3, 4, 104, 107, 148, 172, 193, 280, 287
  IGOR, 4
  Natural Deduction, 35
JavaScript, 381
  Actor, 224, 262
Jewler, S., lvi
J–Machine, 256
JSON, 381
Kaehler, t., 254
Kaehler, T., 259
Kahn, K., lxv, 224, 250, 315, 356
Kant, I., 161
Kantian
  analysis, 161
  synthesis, 161
Kao, E., lxv, lxvi, 17, 75, 195, 197, 284, 315
Karmani, R., xxxv, 257
Karp, A., lxvi, 224, 315
Kay, A., xxxiii, 39, 206, 254, 259, 291
  Smalltalk-71, 240
  Smalltalk-72, 240
Kepler's laws, 184

Kline, M., xxix
Kliot, G., 224, 259
Knabe, F., 253, 256
Knies, 141
Konica-Minolta, 201
Kornfeld, W., 298
Kowalski, R., xl, 33, 292, 293, 295, 297, 300, 310, 312, 315
Kuhn, T., xxiv, 146, 314
Kuipers, B., 42
Kurzweil, R., 490
Lakatos, I., 19, 108
lambda calculus, 4, 205
Lambda calculus, 236
Landin, P., 247, 290
  J operator, 247
Langford, 159, 173
Langley, P., 42
Larus, J., 259
Latour, B., 22, 298, 462, 475
law enforcement, liii
Law, J., lxvii, 7, 42, 298
Leaf, 250, 307, 365, 374
Lehmann, J., lxvi
Leslie, W., 224
Let, 344, 345, 348, 351, 365, 367, 373, 377, 378, 381, 384, 385, 403
Let, 373
Let ... ●, 385, 399, 401
Levitt, K., lxii
Levy, H., 265
Lewis, 159, 173
Lewis, C., 168
Lieberman, H., lxvi, 250, 251, 356
Lifschitz, V., 42
Lighthill, J., 293
Liskov, B., 218
Lisp, 206, 286
LISP, xxxviii
List, 221, 370, 374
Lists, 370
Löb, M., 85, 142, 144

locality
  Actor, 209
logic
  adaptive, 174, 175
  classical, 10
  completeness, 36
  conceptual field, 161
  conceptual recognizability, 163
  conceptually adequate, 163
  dialethic, 176
  dialethic negation, 177
  dialethism, 177
  discussive, 174, 175
  mathematical virtuosity, 163
  non-adjunctive, 174, 175
  paraconsistent, 175, 176
  preservationism, 174
  preservationist, 175
  relevant, 174, 175
  three-value logic, 177
  trivalence, 176
Logic
  Classical, xxiii, 16, 215, 282
Logic of Paradox, 176, 177
Logic Program, xxxviii, 310, 312
  backward chaining, 402
  definition, xxxix
  forward chaining, 402
  subarguments, 403
Logic Programming, 312
  according to Kowalski, xl
  programming using Logic Programs, xl, 312
Logic Programs, 85
LP. *See* Logic of Paradox, *See* Logic of Paradox
Lustig, R., lxii, lxiii
machine or transformation test, 455
Mackay, C., 110
MakeRunnable, 401
Mallery, J., lxii, lxv, lxvi
Malone, D., v, 5, 41, 120

Manning, C., 356
Manor, 193
Map, 372
Marcos, J., 175
Marks, P., 496
Mashey, J., lxv, lxvi
Mason, C., lxvi
Mason, I., 356
mass surveillance, lii
match, 387
Matsuoka, S., 250
McCarthy, J., 3, 42, 237, 240,
    243, 286, 287
McDermott, D., 248
    hairy control structure, 290
McGinnis, N., lxvi
median lethal dose, 497
Meijer, E., xix, xxxv, lxvi, lxviii,
    258
Meisser, E. Jr., lxv
Meltzer, B., 294
mental illness, 472
Mercier, H., lxvi
Mermin, N. D., 13
Merry, D., 254
Message, 377, 378
message passing, 494
Meyer, J. J., lxiii, lxiv, lxv, lxvii
Meyer, J.J., lxvi
Meyer, R., 174
Michie, D., 293
Microsoft, liv
Miller, M. S., 224, 265, 356
Milner, R., 255, 256, 292
Minsky, M., xxiii, lxvii, 3, 11,
    240, 287
mitochondria, 463
Miya, E., 224
Model Checking, 32
Mol, A., lxvi, lxvii, 15, 31, 213
Monk, R., 110
Montalvo, F. S., xxvii, xlvii, lxv,
    lxvi, 42, 356, 490
Montalvo, F.S., lxvii

Montanari, U., 356
Moravek, H., 492
Morningstar, C., 356
Mühe, U., lviii
multi-level security
    Actor, 265
Murdoch, R., lviii
Musen, M., lxiii, lxiv, lxvi, lxvii
mustMatch, 387
Nakashima, H., lxvi
Napier, J., lii
Nassi, I., lxvi, lxvii, 356
Natural Deduction, 35., 86
    Classical Logic, 148
    Jaśkowski, S., 35
negotiations, 460
Nekham, A., 159
Neumann, P., lxii, lxv, lxvi, lxvii,
    42
Newell, A., 287
Newton-Leibniz calculus, 184
Nielsen, 131
nihilism
    Carnap, 192
nonexclusive, 399, 401
NSA, liii, lvi, lvii
Null, 364, 399
Nullable, 364, 387, 399
Nuseibeh, B., xx, lxviii
Nuseibeh, B., 8
Nygaard, K., xxxv, 26, 238, 239,
    247, 257, 336
Obama, B., xlix, liii, lx
Object, 381
    versus Actor, 247
Object (JavaScript), 381
Object Capability Model
    Actor Model, 265
Object-oriented
    versus Actor Model, 247
Olson, D., xliii, lxvi, 447
One-way messaging, 383
ontologies, 460
open science, 481

operating manual, 165
Organick, E., 265
organizational complexity, 491
Orleans
    Actor, 224, 259
Orwell, G., lviii
packet switching, xxxiii, 206
Pandya, R,, 259
Papert, S., 240, 291, 293
parameterized
    type, 364
Park, D., 256
parsing, xxvii
Pathway Tools, 466
patterns of passing messages, 291
Peleg, M., lxiii, lxiv, lxvi
Pereira, L., 294
perform, 391
Perl, M., 496
Perlis, A., 24
Perlroth, N, liv
permit, 354, 355
Perrault, R., 42
pervasive inconsistencies, 7
    code, 7
    documentation, 7
    use cases, 7
pervasive inconsistency, 5, 187
Peters, S., lxvii
Petri Nets, xxxiii, 206
philosophical pragmatism, 460
Planck, M., xxiv, 314
Planner, xxxviii, 240, 280, 286
Plotkin, G., 27, 243
Plumwood, V., 174
Poincaré, H., 76
Poitras, L., l
Polar, 369
politics, 460
Polya, G., 287, 296
Popper, K., 7, 287, 298
Posner, 429
postcondition, 367

Postpone, 113, 250, 307, 374, 378
power, 460
pragmatism, 473
Pratt, V., 224
Precondition, 355, 367
Priest, G., 174, 175, 176, 177, 194
Principia Mathematica, xxxi
privacy, lvi
probabilities
    inconsistent, 13
probability, xxiii, 9
Procedural Embedding, 286
program control structure, 247, 290
Prolog (**PRO**grammation en **LOG**ique), 295
promise
    Actor, 231, 261, 262
Proposition
    Classical Direct Logic, 129
propositions, xxvii
prototype-based
    representation, 479
Provability Logic, 141
provenance, 480
public key cryptography, lii
Pythagoreans, xxviii, 104
Qualifiers, 380
Quasi-classical system, 195
quasi-commutative, 209
queues, 354, 355
Quine, W. , 163, 170
    dialethic negation, 163
    Mathematical Logic, 169
Rajunas, S., 265
RAM-processor encryption, lxi
Read, S., 159
realism, 469, 471, 472
reality, 5
Reasoning by disjunctive cases, 3

reception order indeterminacy, 29
recognizability space, 165
Reductio ad absurdum, 173
regulation, xlix
Reinhardt, T., 356
Relational Physics, 6
representation, 475
Resche, 193
Rescher, 193
resolution, 284
resolution theorem proving, xxxviii
Restall, G., lxvi, lxvii, 167, 179, 200
return, 383, 384
revocation
  Actor, 265
Reynolds, J., 247
Ripley, D., lxvi
Risen, J., liii, lv
Roark, D., l
Robinson, A., xxiv
Robinson, J., 284
Roderigues, O., 171
Rogers, M., lxi
Rosental, C., xxviii
Routley, R., xxiv, 174, 176
Rovelli, C., lxvii, 6, 21, 213
Rubens, N., lxvi
Rubin, D., lxiii, lxiv
Rules versus Standards, 447
Rulifson, J., lxvi, lxvii
Russell, B., 82, 111, 161, 170, 176
  Mathematical Logic, 170
  Principles of Mathematics, 161
Russell, M., lxvi, lxvii
Russell's paradox, xxxi
Russo, A., xx, lxviii, 181, 182
Russo, A., 8
Saki, 10
scalability, 512

Schaub, T., 9, 181
Schauer, 429
Scheme, 248
Schmidt, E., liv, lvi
Schmidt, L., lxiii, lxiv
Schotch, 194
Schumacher, D., 224, 356
scientific credit, 463
Scott, D., lxiv, 205
security, lii
  aaw enforcement, liii
  Actor:, 209
  authentication services, lii
  continuous authentication, lii
  endpoint, lii
  every-word-tagged architecture, lii
  public key cryptography, lii
Seitz, C., 251, 356
Selby, R., 7
self-referential propositions, xxxi, 110, 111, 112, 120, 121, 136, 141, 142, 143, 144
  Gödel, 110
Semantic Web, 478
Sen, A., 186
Sentence
  Classical Direct Logic, 131
sentences, xxvii
Set, 372
Shankar, N., 42
Shapiro, J., 265
Sherman, M., liii
SHRDLU, 293
Siekmann, J., 294
Simi, M., 356
Simon, H., 287
Simula, 238
Simula 67, xxxiii, 206, 240, 291
singularity, 490
Singularity$_{AI}$, 496
Singularity$_{ctl}$, 493
Smalltalk-72, xxxiii, 206, 240, 254, 291

Smalltalk-80, 254
Smith, B., liv
Smith, S., 356
Snowden, E., l, li, lvii
sociology of ontologies, 466
Soghoian, C., lvii
Sorrell, M., lvii
Soundness
 classical, 3
Squeak, 259
Stanford CSLI, lxv
Stanford Education Program for Gifted Youth (EPGY), 488
Stanford Logic Group, 201
Stanford Media X, lxv, 201
Star, S., 298
stare decisis, 450
Stasi, lviii
Stasiland, lviii
Staten, J., liv
statistical reasoning, 15
Steele, G., 247
Steiger, R., 25, 206, 241, 291, 356
Stickel, M., 42
Strauss, A., 298
strict implication, 168, 173, 175
String, 372, 376
Structure, 365, 372
Suchman, L., 298
suchThat, 343
Sun, Y., lxiii, lxiv
supervised machine learning, 513
Suppes, P., lxvii, 224
Supreme Court, 447
Surden, H., lxvi
surveillance, lii
 massive, lviii
Suspend, 401
Sussman, G., 247, 248, 287, 293
 hairy control structure, 290
swap message. *See* Arrays
Swire, P., lii

Swiss cheese, 350
 Actor:, 219
Szyperski, C., xix, xxxv, lxviii, 258
Talcott, C., 356
Tanaka, K., 174
Tarski, A., 67, 143, 323
Tarskian Set Models, 143
teaching, xlix
Term
 Classical Direct Logic, 130
Terminator, 141
Thati, P., 356
thatIs, 344, 354
The Last Enemy, lviii
The Lives of Others, lviii
Thelin, J., 259
Theriault, D., 250, 356
This (JavaScript), 381
throw, 383, 384
Throw, 347, 366
Toffler, A., 13
Tokoro, M., lxv, lxvii, 356
tolerance, 167
Toulmin, S., 315
toxicology, 502
Travers, M., xlv, lxv, 460, 496
Traxler, J., lxv
Tree, 250, 307, 365, 374
triage, 164
trials of strength, 462
Try, 366
Try ... catch�, 391
Try ... cleanup, 391
Tufiş, M., xlviii, 512
Turing Machine, 494
Turing, A., v, 4, 9, 17, 24, 34, 83, 117, 236
type, 386
 Basic, 365
 Direct Logic, 129
 paramaterized, 364
uncertainty, xxiii, 9
undecidability

computational, 34
inferential, 36
Ungar, D., lxv
uniform proof procedure, 284
United States v. Alaska, 430
unpatentable abstractness, 456
using, 342
UsingNamespace, 380
van Emden, M., 294, 315
van Horn, E., 206, 264
Varela, C., 356
variable
   ActorScript, 345
videos
   Inconsistency Robustness, xix
Virtual Procedure
   Actor Message, 247
Void, 346
von Neumann architecture, 494
Waldinger, R., lxv, 42, 284, 315, 496
Wallace, S., 254
Wang, H., 169, 170
Wasow, T., lxv
Weber, Z., 174

Weil, A., 39
When, 287, 289, 329, 404
whistleblowers, liii
Williams, M., lxv, lxvii
Wing, J., 218
Winograd, T., 287
Winsberg, E., lxv
Wittgenstein, L., v, xxxi, lxv, 3, 5, 9, 104, 110, 172
Woelk, D., 250, 356
Wolff, J., 496
Woodruff, J., 265
Woods, C., lxv
Woods, J., xix, xxxi, lxv, lxvii, 171, 175, 206, 315
   Paradox and Paraconsistency, 168, 171
Wos, L., 284
XML, 382
Yanofsky, N., 158, 169
Yee, KP, 265
Yonezawa, A., 250, 356
Zermelo, E., 104, 131, 134, 137
Zuckerberg, M., liv
π-Calculus, 255

Lightning Source UK Ltd.
Milton Keynes UK
UKOW06f1917221215

265277UK00008B/236/P